THE FRESH & SALT WATER
FISHES
OF THE WORLD

THE FRESH & SALT WATER
FISHES
OF THE WORLD

by EDWARD C. MIGDALSKI

and GEORGE S. FICHTER

Illustrations by Norman Weaver

ALFRED A. KNOPF
NEW YORK   1976

THIS IS A BORZOI BOOK
PUBLISHED BY ALFRED A. KNOPF, INC.

Designed and produced by Vineyard Books, Inc.,
New York, New York

Library of Congress Cataloging in Publication Data

Migdalski, Edward C
  The fresh and salt water fishes of the world.

  1. Fishes. I. Fichter, George S., joint author.
II. Weaver, Norman. III. Title.
QL615.M49   597   76-13704
ISBN 0-394-49239-0

Manufactured in Hong Kong

First Edition

CONTENTS

AUTHORS' NOTES

INTRODUCTION

THE WORLD OF FISHES

Technicalities   12

Fishes from Past to Present   18

The Fish's Body and Its Functions   21

Commercial and Sport Fishes   37

THE FISHES

The Jawless Fishes   39

The Cartilaginous Fishes   43

The Bony Fishes   85

SELECTED BIBLIOGRAPHY   299

FRESH- AND SALTWATER RECORDS   300

INDEX   302

AUTHORS' NOTES

In presenting a comprehensive view of the fishes of the world, two major problems immediately become apparent. The first is to select or establish a system or format to follow. Then, how many species should be included, and to what extent should each be treated without being burdensome to the nonscientist?

Any attempt to classify technically, describe in form, and investigate in detail the habits of approximately 20,000 species of living fishes of the world would be a monumental undertaking. That sort of task would involve volumes produced by the intensive labors of ichthyologists, fisheries biologists, anatomists, physiologists, taxonomists, and other scientists over a period of many years. Nor is it a simple matter to gather, analyze, and coordinate published or other known facts and to interject personal experiences and observations into a cohesive manuscript that would in essence summarize the massive subject. Although the material here, geared primarily for popular consumption, must not contain ichthyological jargon, it has to be correct in fact and accurate in statement, so that the intellectual armchair critic will not be offended.

It is abundantly clear that it is impossible to involve in this book in complete detail all the world's fishes. Nevertheless, by treating the generally accepted orders and families, by the inclusion of important facts concerning family characteristics, by an analysis of the more common or better-known species, and as a supplement to Norman Weaver's extremely well-portrayed fishes in color, we can indicate some of the grandeur of the fishes of the world—their great profusion and diversity of form and habitat, their beauty, and their tremendous importance to the human race.

The contents of this book have been gathered from many published sources. However, as the senior author, I have contributed to the text sprinklings of observations obtained from extensive sport-fishing experiences as well as from participating in over twenty scientific expeditions throughout the world as an ichthyologist for the Bingham Oceanographic Laboratory and the Peabody Museum of Yale University.

EDWARD C. MIGDALSKI
Yale University, New Haven, Connecticut

For more than half a century, and in varying degrees of intensity, I have been involved with the world of fishes—as a fisherman, biologist, writer, editor, and observer. Over these years I have played a role in numerous projects, but of them all, this volume evolved into the most exciting because of its broad scope. To explain the immensity of the undertaking and the difficulty of maintaining proper levels of accuracy in such an undertaking would only add echoes to the words of the senior author. We have been gratified and awed by Norman Weaver's stunning renditions—brushwork that masterfully delineates detail while duplicating the colors and form of nature with remarkable fidelity. All of us recognize that this has become a once-in-a-lifetime opportunity—ours the privilege of being able to make such a presentation and yours to enjoy and to use the result.

GEORGE S. FICHTER
Homestead, Florida

INTRODUCTION

Everyone knows what fishes are, but few people really know anything about them. Millions of people eat them, catch them for sport, and keep them as pets; and if you ask someone what lives in water, nine times out of ten the answer will be "fish." Along with this familiarity, however, goes a surprising amount of ignorance. Take some of our everyday expressions, for example. We may understand what we mean when we say that something is fishy or appears to be neither fish, flesh nor fowl, or when we tell someone to fish or cut bait or not to fish in troubled waters. No special knowledge is necessary to appreciate these common phrases. On the other hand, we say that we feel like a fish out of water without the slightest idea what a fish *does* feel, whether in water or out; and although too many of us may know people who drink like a fish, only the experts among us realize that some fishes drink copiously while others seldom swallow any water at all. Our acquaintance with fishes, extensive though it may be, is superficial indeed. Of all the well-recognized forms of life, fishes are undoubtedly the most mysterious and misunderstood.

Although we ought to know more about fishes than we do, the reason for our lack of knowledge is not difficult to understand. It is, in fact, so obvious that it is often overlooked. The simple truth is that fishes are aquatic and inhabit water, while people are terrestrial and live on land.

Our planet is called Earth, but seven-tenths of its surface is covered by water, and what makes Earth unique in the entire solar system is not its rocks and soil but its abundant water supply. Earth has about 330 million cubic miles of water—an immensity that for most of our history has been as impenetrable and unknown as the interior of the planet itself. Since time immemorial, except for a handful of hardy divers, to sink beneath the water's surface was to drown, not to explore another environment. "One world" may be a political or philosophical ideal, but physically there always will be a separate world right here on Earth: the world of water, which still is to us an uninhabitable, fearful, and wondrous place.

Fishes are the masters of that world. For more than 360 million years they have inhabited it. Compared with them, the whales, for example, are only upstarts that can claim a mere 55 million years' residence. There are more different kinds of fishes—and in bulk they total more—than all other moderate-sized aquatic animals put together. There are few places that do not support at least a small number of fishes, since members of the finny tribe have adapted themselves to seemingly uninhabitable environments such as the deepest parts of the ocean, the waters under the earth, ponds with brine four times saltier than the sea, and temporary pools that contain no water at all for months at a time.

For centuries knowledge of life in the water world was limited to an examination of what we could catch out of it and could then learn from studying, say, a fish's anatomy, the different stages in its life history, and what it had eaten. Later, as our sampling methods improved and became more systematic, we could determine the exact depth from which it came, how it changed throughout the seasons, and even how fast it grew and how long it lived. Direct observation, however, was almost unheard of. (Even the simple practice of catching fishes alive and putting them into aquariums for study is less than two hundred years old.) The idea of being able to stay under water to watch what was going on was only a dream in the fertile minds of such men as Leonardo da Vinci and Jules Verne. Diving equipment was at first scarcely practicable and then too dangerous, cumbersome, or expensive to be used to satisfy scientific curiosity. Only the promise of ample financial rewards lured people under water—in helmets with pressurized suits, in caissons, or in submarines. Not until the invention of SCUBA (self-contained underwater breathing apparatus) in the early 1940s did fish-watching become a practical pursuit. This breathing apparatus enabled the diver to carry a supply of air and swim freely through the water—not unlike the fish being observed. Today's students of ichthyology learn to dive with SCUBA just as they learn to use a microscope or operate a calculator.

Modern technology did not stop with SCUBA, however. Ichthyologists now have at their disposal an entire battery of modern devices: submersibles to carry them deep beneath the surface, underwater habitats that make it possible literally to live with the fishes, and remote-controlled cameras and television monitors that can record observations in the most inaccessible spots. Add to these the new and improved ways of capturing fishes alive and keeping and rearing them in captivity and it does not seem too optimistic to predict that we are on the threshold of ichthyological accomplishments such as we have never even imagined.

These advancements will not come a bit too soon. Remote as the world of water may seem in our minds, in reality our connection with it is intimate and our dependence on it absolute. Human impact on lakes and streams has always tended to be detrimental, and we can now claim the dubious honor of having completely destroyed many of them—that is, ruined them as habitats for other animals and as a source of water and food. Today, even the mighty oceans show signs of becoming polluted. One indication of this is the accumulation of toxic substances like PCB (polychlorinated biphenyls) or mercury in certain food fishes to the point that they are no longer fit to eat. The remarkable sensitivity of aquatic animals and plants to poisons in their environment is generally not appreciated. Fishes and aquatic invertebrates live much more closely with the water surrounding them than do terrestrial creatures with the air. For example, it takes only a drop or two of some insecticides dissolved in thousands of gallons of water to kill fishes in a couple of days. Another serious problem is the depletion and even the disappearance of food fishes as a result of overfishing. With millions of people on the verge of starvation, maritime governments must come to realize that the sea cannot be regarded as a great cornucopia. Scientifically established regulations are required to ensure a maximum yield year after year.

No matter how well we learn to regulate our fisheries or control aquatic pollution, there will still be a great deal that we do not know about fishes. The world's great lakes, rivers, and oceans are vast, and there are thousands upon thousands of smaller bodies of water. The fishes of only a few of these are at all well known. After more than two centuries of study by ichthyologists, amazing facts about the life history, behavior, and physiology of fishes are continually being brought to light. Nearly a hundred new species of fishes are discovered every year. But above and beyond all the new discoveries, the romance of ichthyology will prevail.

As this book will show you, fishes are the diverse, beautiful, marvelous, and awesome inhabitants of a wonderful but alien world into which human beings can only temporarily intrude. And what could be more romantic that that?

DR. JAMES W. ATZ
Curator, Department of Ichthyology
The American Museum of Natural History
New York

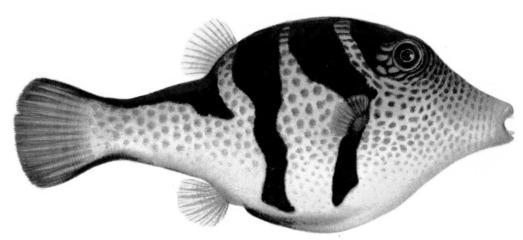

THE WORLD
OF FISHES

TECHNICALITIES

Choice of Format

To present the fishes of the world in an organized manner, several formats or methods of classification can be considered. The fishes can be treated in geographical groups by hemispheres, by continents, by oceans or divisions of oceans. They can be placed in regional groups—Arctic, north temperate, tropical, south temperate, and Antarctic. They can be treated by environmental separation—that is, by the various types of natural surroundings in which they live. For example, freshwater fishes can be differentiated by lakes, ponds, rivers, streams, brooks, bogs, and marshes. In salt water, the divisions may be inshore and offshore species; or the sections may include the bottom dwellers, open-ocean swimmers, coastal and inshore groups, reef inhabitants, dwellers of the ocean depths, and so on. Interesting groupings can be developed by sectioning fishes into their water-temperature tolerances, or by their method of propagation, or by their dentition and how and what they eat.

All of the above examples of segregation systems are interesting; some are practical, others are not. Approaches such as treating the fishes by regional latitude, geographical areas or environmental confinement are workable, but many species occupy more than one niche. Consequently, it is practically impossible, by using such criteria, to classify fishes into clear-cut divisions. Artificially arranged compartments, as well as arbitrary decisions and educated guesses in categorical placement of species, are accepted reluctantly by professionals. The general classification of fishes employed by scientists is based on morphological relationships—that is, on the comparison of form and anatomy, one group to another, as applied to evolutionary progression, from the most primitive to the most highly advanced. This is the format used in this volume.

Criteria for Classification

In constructing various systems of fish classification, renowned investigators, since the earliest days of fisheries research, have relied heavily on the skeleton, the only organ system available for detailed comparison with fossil fishes. Today, even though the full informational context of skeletal and other morphological aspects are far from exhausted, progressive taxonomists feel strongly that researches on the nervous, digestive, muscular, and vascular systems are greatly needed to enlighten further the mysteries of the evolutionary process in fishes. Therefore, it is not surprising that professionals interested in the taxonomy of fishes do not agree on many points involving the proper alignment of groups of fishes and, in many cases, on the placement of individual species within a group. Modern fisheries workers freely admit that some of the most generally recognized teleostean orders (groups of fishes with true backbones) are simply catchalls for separate lineages that have acquired similar stages of specialization or conformity. The possibility of acquiring a stable classification of fishes in the near future is further diminished because the discovery of new species and genera is not a rarity; and new forms, especially deepsea types and fossils that have an evolutionary bearing on the relationships of fishes, are still being found. Consequently, fisheries academicians agree that the available classifications produced by respected scientists are far from perfect.

Past and Present Systems of Classification

The history of fish classification records that the first scientific attempt to produce a classification of recent fishes was made by Johannes Müller (Berlin, 1844). Subsequently, scientists from various countries published their opinions on the subject. Some of the major contributions were made by L. Agassiz (1857), G. A. Boulenger (1904), E. S. Goodrich (1909), C. T. Regan (1909), D. S. Jordan (1923), and A. S. Woodward (1932). In 1940 Leo S. Berg, an eminent ichthyologist at the Academy Museum in Leningrad and a member of the Russian Academy of Science, authored the highly respected *Classification of Fishes, Both Recent and Fossil*. Shortly thereafter (1941), Carl L. Hubbs and Karl F. Lagler, two well-known American ichthyologists, conceived a plan to publish Berg's work in the United States. Consequently, Lagler received permission from Berg to reproduce the book. It contains both Russian and English text.

In 1945 Alfred S. Romer, in his book *Vertebrate Paleontology* (Second Edition), produced a comprehensive classification of vertebrates that includes fishes. In recent years Berg's has been the most widely accepted general classification of bony fishes. Romer's work is also used widely, and fisheries scientists today are not criticized by their peers if they basically employ either Berg's or Romer's systems.

The present-day attitude of fisheries scientists concerning classification can best be exemplified by a statement made by Daniel M. Cohen, editor-in-chief of Part Six of *Fishes of the Western North Atlantic*, published in 1973 by the Sears Foundation of Marine Research, Yale University. We quote from his Introduction:

> *Secure in the wisdom of hindsight we must also call attention to a statement in the Introduction to Part One, which notes that a widely accepted general outline of classification will be followed. Although such may have existed in 1948, a decade of research by a number of ichthyologists studying both recent and fossil fishes has demonstrated that there does not presently exist any easy way to chart the family tree of fishes. Although the overall study of fish phylogeny is not an active field, the end point, an adequately documented and widely accepted classification, is not yet available.*

The most recent, meaningful contribution to the general taxonomy of fishes is a work by four outstanding investigators: P. Humphrey Greenwood of the British Museum of Natural History; Donn E. Rosen, American Museum of Natural History; Stanley H. Weitzman, Smithsonian Institution; and George S. Myers, Stanford University. Their "Phyletic Studies of Teleostean Fishes, with a Provisional Classification of Living Forms" appeared in 1966 as a bulletin of the American Museum of Natural History. This classification is based on an analysis the authors consider to be the predominant evolutionary trends in the largest and most advanced group of bony fishes. They recognize the families and their placement according to Berg's system, but they make emendations based on manuscripts published subsequently and also on unpublished facts contributed by many investigators.

The arrangement of orders and families of the jawless fishes (Agnatha) and the cartilaginous fishes (Chondrichthyes) in this volume generally follows the latest list of fishes from the United States and Canada produced by the American Fisheries Society. The organization of the bony fishes (Osteichthyes) follows that of Greenwood, Rosen, Weitzman, and Myers.

COMMON AND REPRESENTATIVE FAMILIES
OF LIVING FISHES

CLASS AGNATHA: JAWLESS FISHES

ORDER MYXINIFORMES
  Family Myxinidae—*hagfishes*
ORDER PETROMYZONTIFORMES
  Family Petromyzontidae—*lampreys*

CLASS CHONDRICHTHYES:
  CARTILAGINOUS FISHES

ORDER CHLAMYDOSELACHIFORMES
  Family Chlamydoselachidae—*frill sharks*
ORDER HEXANCHIFORMES
  Family Hexanchidae—*cow sharks*
ORDER HETERODONTIFORMES
  Family Heterodontidae—*bullhead sharks*
ORDER SQUALIFORMES
  Family Orectolobidae—*nurse sharks*
    Rhincodontidae—*whale shark*
    Odontaspidae—*sand tigers*
    Scapanorhynchidae—*goblin sharks*
    Alopiidae—*thresher sharks*
    Lamnidae—*mackerel sharks*
    Scyliorhinidae—*cat sharks*
    Carcharhinidae—*requiem sharks*
    Sphyrnidae—*hammerhead sharks*
    Pristeophoridae—*saw sharks*
    Squalidae—*dogfish sharks*
    Squatinidae—*angel sharks*
ORDER RAJIFORMES
  Family Pristidae—*sawfishes*
    Rhinobatidae—*guitarfishes*
    Torpedinidae—*electric rays*
    Rajidae—*skates*
    Dasyatidae—*stingrays*
    Myliobatidae—*eagle rays*
    Mobulidae—*mantas*
ORDER CHIMAERIFORMES
  Family Chimaeridae—*chimaeras*

CLASS OSTEICHTHYES: BONY FISHES

ORDER COELACANTHIFORMES
  Family Coelacanthidae—*coelacanths*
ORDER DIPTERIFORMES
  Family Ceradontidae—*Australian lungfishes*
    Lepidosirenidae—*South American and African lungfishes*

ORDER POLYPTERIFORMES
  Family Polypteridae—*bichirs*
ORDER ACIPENSERIFORMES
  Family Acipenseridae—*sturgeons*
    Polyodontidae—*paddlefishes*
ORDER SEMIONOTIFORMES
  Family Lepisosteidae—*gars*
ORDER AMIIFORMES
  Family Amiidae—*bowfins*
ORDER ELOPIFORMES
  Family Elopidae—*tarpons*
    Albulidae—*bonefish*
ORDER ANGUILLIFORMES
  Family Anguillidae—*freshwater eels*
    Muraenidae—*morays*
    Congridae—*conger eels*
    Ophichthidae—*snake eels*
    Saccopharingidae—*swallowers*
    Eurypharyngidae—*gulpers*
ORDER CLUPEIFORMES
  Family Clupeidae—*herrings*
    Engraulidae—*anchovies*
    Chirocentridae—*wolf herrings*
ORDER OSTEOGLOSSIFORMES
  Family Osteoglossidae—*arapaimas and arawanas*
    Pantodontidae—*freshwater butterflyfish*
    Hiodontidae—*mooneyes*
    Notopteridae—*featherbacks*
ORDER MORMYRIFORMES
  Family Mormyridae—*mormyrids*
ORDER SALMONIFORMES
  Family Salmonidae—*salmons, trouts, graylings, and whitefishes*
    Plecoglossidae—*sweetfish*
    Osmeridae—*smelts*
    Argentinidae—*argentines*
    Bathylagidae—*deepsea smelts*
    Opisthoproctidae—*spookfishes*
    Galaxiidae—*galaxiids*
    Esocidae—*pikes*
    Umbridae—*mudminnows*
    Gonostomatidae—*deepsea bristlemouths*
    Sternoptychidae—*deepsea hatchetfishes*
    Chauliodontidae—*deepsea viperfishes*
    Stomiatidae—*deepsea scaly dragonfishes*
    Alepocephalidae—*deepsea slickheads*

ORDER MYCTOPHIFORMES
Family Synodontidae—*lizardfishes*
Alepisauridae—*lancetfishes*
Scopelarchidae—*pearleyes*
Myctophidae—*lanternfishes*
ORDER CETOMIMIFORMES
Family Giganturidae—*deepsea giganturids*
ORDER GONORYNCHIFORMES
Family Chanidae—*milkfish*
ORDER CYPRINIFORMES
Family Characidae—*characins*
Gasteropelecidae—*hatchetfishes*
Gymnotidae—*electric eels and knifefishes*
Cyprinidae—*minnows and carps*
Gyrinocheilidae—*gyrinocheilids*
Catostomidae—*suckers*
Homalopteridae—*hillstream fishes*
Cobitidae—*loaches*
ORDER SILURIFORMES
Family Ictaluridae—*North American freshwater catfishes*
Bagridae—*bagrid catfishes*
Siluridae—*Eurasian catfishes*
Schilbeidae—*shilbeid catfishes*
Clariidae—*labyrinthic catfishes*
Malapteruridae—*electric catfishes*
Mochokidae—*upside-down catfishes*
Ariidae—*sea catfishes*
Doradidae—*doradid armored catfishes*
Aspredinidae—*banjo catfishes*
Plotosidae—*plotosid sea catfishes*
Pimelodidae—*pimelodid catfishes*
Trichomycteridae—*parasitic catfishes*
Callichthyidae—*callichthyid armored catfishes*
Loricariidae—*loricariid armored catfishes*
ORDER PERCOPSIFORMES
Family Amblyopsidae—*cavefishes*
Aphredoderidae—*pirate perch*
Percopsidae—*trout-perches*
ORDER BATRACHOIDIFORMES
Family Batrachoididae—*toadfishes*
ORDER GOBIESOCIFORMES
Family Gobiesocidae—*clingfishes*
ORDER LOPHIIFORMES
Family Lophiidae—*goosefishes*
Antennariidae—*frogfishes*
Ogcocephalidae—*batfishes*
Melanocetidae—*black devils*
Ceratiidae—*sea devils*

ORDER GADIFORMES
Family Gadidae—*codfishes*
Ophidiidae—*cusk-eels and brotulas*
Carapidae—*pearlfishes*
Zoarcidae—*eelpouts*
Macrouridae—*grenadiers*
ORDER ATHERINIFORMES
Family Exocoetidae—*flying fishes and halfbeaks*
Belonidae—*needlefishes*
Scomberesocidae—*sauries*
Cyprinodontidae—*killifishes*
Anablepidae—*foureye fishes*
Poeciliidae—*livebearers*
Atherinidae—*silversides*
ORDER BERYCIFORMES
Family Polymixiidae—*beardfishes*
Anomalopidae—*lanterneye fishes*
Holocentridae—*squirrelfishes*
ORDER ZEIFORMES
Family Zeidae—*dories*
Caproidae—*boarfishes*
ORDER LAMPRIDIFORMES
Family Lampridae—*opahs*
Lophotidae—*crestfishes*
Trachipteridae—*ribbonfishes*
Regalecidae—*oarfishes*
ORDER GASTEROSTEIFORMES
Family Gasterosteidae—*sticklebacks*
Aulostomidae—*trumpetfishes*
Fistulariidae—*cornetfishes*
Centriscidae—*shrimpfishes and snipefishes*
Sygnathidae—*pipefishes and seahorses*
ORDER CHANNIFORMES
Family Channidae—*snakeheads*
ORDER SYNBRANCHIFORMES
Family Synbranchidae—*swamp eels*
ORDER SCORPAENIFORMES
Family Scorpaenidae—*scorpionfishes and rockfishes*
Triglidae—*sea robins*
Hexagrammidae—*greenlings*
Anoplopomatidae—*sablefishes*
Cottidae—*sculpins*
Agonidae—*poachers*
Cyclopteridae—*lumpfishes and snailfishes*
ORDER DACTYLOPTERIFORMES
Family Dactylopteridae—*flying gurnards*
ORDER PEGASIFORMES
Family Pegasidae—*seamoths*

ORDER PERCIFORMES

Family Centropomidae—*snooks*
Serranidae—*sea basses*
Grammistidae—*soapfishes*
Teraponidae—*tigerfishes*
Kuhliidae—*aholeholes*
Centrarchidae—*sunfishes*
Priacanthidae—*bigeyes*
Apogonidae—*cardinalfishes*
Percidae—*perches*
Branchiostegidae—*tilefishes*
Pomatomidae—*bluefish*
Rachicentridae—*cobia*
Echeneidae—*remoras*
Carangidae—*jacks and pompanos*
Coryphaenidae—*dolphins*
Leiognathidae—*slipmouths*
Lutjanidae—*snappers*
Lobotidae—*tripletails*
Gerridae—*mojarras*
Pomadasyidae—*grunts*
Sparidae—*porgies*
Sciaenidae—*drums*
Mullidae—*goatfishes*
Monodactylidae—*fingerfishes*
Bathyclupeidae—*deepsea herrings*
Toxotidae—*archerfishes*
Kyphosidae—*sea chubs*
Ephippidae—*spadefishes*
Scatophagidae—*scats or argus fishes*
Chaetodontidae—*butterflyfishes*
Nandidae—*leaffishes*
Embiotocidae—*surfperches*
Cichlidae—*cichlids*
Pomacentridae—*damselfishes*
Cirrhitidae—*hawkfishes*
Mugilidae—*mullets*
Sphyraenidae—*barracudas*

Polynemidae—*threadfins*
Labridae—*wrasses*
Scaridae—*parrotfishes*
Trichondontidae—*sandfishes*
Opisthognathidae—*jawfishes*
Dactyloscopidae—*sand stargazers*
Uranoscopidae—*stargazers*
Blenniidae—*combtooth blennies*
Anarhichadidae—*wolffishes*
Clinidae—*clinids*
Stichaeidae—*pricklebacks*
Pholidae—*gunnels*
Callionymidae—*dragonets*
Gobiidae—*gobies*
Acanthuridae—*surgeonfishes*
Siganidae—*rabbitfishes*
Gempylidae—*snake mackerels*
Trichiuridae—*cutlassfishes*
Scombridae—*mackerels and tunas*
Xiphiidae—*swordfishes*
Luvaridae—*louvar*
Istiophoridae—*billfishes*
Stromateidae—*butterfishes*
Anabantidae—*climbing perches*
Belontiidae—*labyrinthfishes*
Icosteidae—*ragfishes*
Mastacembelidae—*spiny eels*

ORDER PLEURONECTIFORMES

Family Bothidae—*lefteye flounders*
Pleuronectidae—*righteye flounders*
Soleidae—*soles*
Cynoglossidae—*tonguefishes*

ORDER TETRADONTIFORMES

Family Balistidae—*triggerfishes and filefishes*
Ostraciidae—*boxfishes*
Tetraodontidae—*puffers*
Diodontidae—*porcupinefishes*
Molidae—*molas*

Method of Animal Classification

In order to portray clearly the relationship of fishes to the rest of the animal world, the following is a brief review of the basic organization used by zoologists the world over.

The animal kingsom is divided into two major divisions: vertebrates and invertebrates. Five sections comprise the vertebrate assemblage: fishes, amphibians, birds, reptiles, and mammals. The fishes are separated into three major divisions or classes: jawless fishes, technically referred to as Agnatha; cartilaginous fishes, Chondrichthyes; and bony fishes, Osteichthyes. Within these differentiations the fishes of similar major anatomical characteristics are grouped in orders (-formes endings). Closely related fishes within each order are segregated into individual families (-idae endings). Then a scientific name in two parts (genus and species) is applied to each kind. For example, the largemouth bass, in a textbook procedure, is classified as follows: class—Osteichthyes; order—Perciformes; family—Centrarchidae; genus—Micropterus; species—salmoides.

The attachment of a person's name (the authority) to the scientific name, as used in many publications, may seem curious to the nonscientist. Actually, the inclusion of such names is not necessary in popular publications because it is meaningful only to professionals. In line with the International Rules of Zoological Nomenclature, the author's name(s) follows the specific name directly and without punctuation if it retains the original genus; if the species was described in another genus, the author's name(s) appears in parenthesis. For example, the brook trout was originally named Salmo fontinalis by Mitchell; the genus was changed and is presently Salvelinus fontinalis (Mitchell).

The Scientific Name

The first letter of the genus or generic name is always capitalized. The species or specific name does not have its first letter capitalized. The scientific name is important because many species of fishes have assorted common names, usually varied with the locality where the fish is taken. For example, the red drum, Sciaenops ocellata, is also commonly known as channel bass and redfish. The striped bass, Morone saxatilis, in its southern range is also known as rockfish; and the popular western cutthroat trout, Salmo clarki, has been known

by 70 common or vernacular names. At times the lay person may be perplexed on seeing different scientific names applied to one species in different books or listings. Occasionally a researcher finds new evidence, anatomical or historical, and through publication proposes a change, usually in the specific name. Thus the striped bass in 50 years has changed from Roccus lineatus to Ruccus saxatilis to Morone saxatilis. An additional complexity enters the picture when other specialists do not agree on the name change. The nonscientist should recognize these facts but should not be concerned.

The common and scientific names within this volume have been secured from many sources. The most valued single reference, which we followed closely, is A List of Common and Scientific Names of Fishes from the United States and Canada, published by the American Fisheries Society (Third Edition, 1970).

Number of Fishes

The futility of attempting to compile a complete list of fishes of the world is graphically portrayed by the fact that in recent ichthyological literature there has been confusion as to the total number of living fishes of the world. For example, from 1948 through 1965, six scientists individually declared, in various publications, the following estimates of the number of fishes on earth today: 15,000 to 17,000; 20,000; 25,000; 32,000; 33,000; 40,000. One wonders how trained researchers could differ so widely in offering estimates. The difference between 15,000 and 40,000 is not a small divergence.

Daniel M. Cohen, associated with the Bureau of Commercial Fisheries, Washington, D.C., decided that an attempt at producing a rational estimate of the total number of fish species (rather than guesses) should be made. Consequently, over a seven-year period of gathering information, with the cooperation of about 50 specialists, he authored a manuscript in 1970 that appeared in the Proceedings of the California Academy of Sciences. His paper, titled "How Many Fishes Are There?" gave the following figures (the estimates are intended to be the actual number of living species rather than the number that have been described): jawless fishes, about 50; cartilaginous fishes, 515 to 555; bony fishes, 19,135 to 20,980—for a total estimate of 19,700 to 21,585. Cohen's percentages of species living in various habitats indicates that of the total number of fishes, about 40 percent are freshwater inhabitants and 60 percent are marine.

FISHES FROM PAST TO PRESENT

Ostracoderms

Fishes are the most ancient group of vertebrates. Fossil records indicate that they first appeared in the Ordovician period, more than 400 million years ago. The earliest types were covered with several kinds of armor, from which the name "ostracoderms," or shellskinned, is derived. The oldest positive remains were found in rocks from Colorado and other western states. The nature of the sediments involved suggested that the ostracoderms lived in inland waters, supporting the theory that vertebrates were of freshwater origin. Recent analyses of the habitats of early fossils by paleontologists, however, have led to the conclusion that, as a group, the vertebrates were originally marine. Ostracoderms are now extinct. Their living relatives are the Agnatha, or Cyclostomes (hagfishes and lampreys), the most primitive of the present-day fishes. Generally eel-like in shape, cyclostomes lack a well-defined head and have no scales, jaws, or paired fins; totally, there are about 50 species. Although outwardly, in bodily outlines and in the presence of hard skeletal parts, the ostracoderms appear to be remote from the cyclostomes, they, like the living cyclostomes, are characterized by the absence of jaws and by the absence or weak development of paired fins. Other resemblances in many structural features also exist within the two groups.

Placoderms

In the Devonian period of the geologic time scale, often called the "Age of Fishes," the placoderms, or plate-skinned fishes, were the most abundant forms. This group of fishes, peculiar in structure, consists of several types, now long extinct. The various fossil groups have been assigned to many different positions in the classification system, and presently there is no complete agreement about their arrangement. Anyone with an academic interest in this subject should read *Palaeozoic Fishes* by J.A. Moy-Thomas and R.S. Miles (1971).

Chondrichthyes

After the ostracoderms and placoderms we have the sharks and their relatives reaching the evolutionary level of modern types of jawed fishes. In such forms, the jaws are highly developed, and the fins and general body structure resemble a more familiar design. These types of higher fish forms are easily divided into two

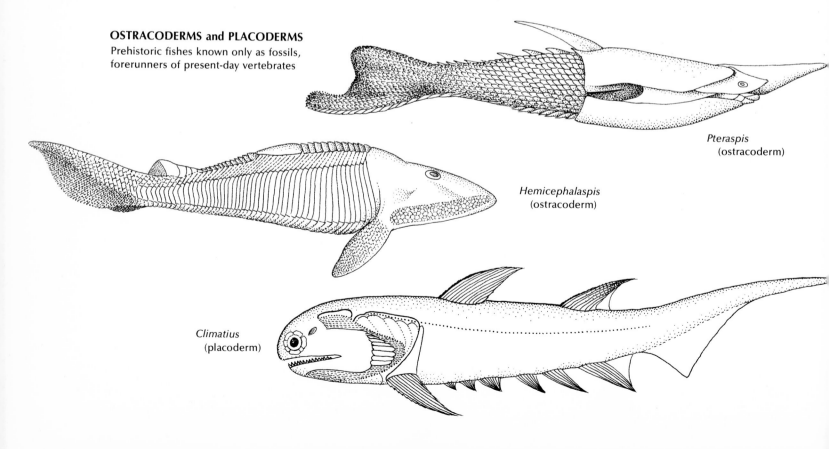

OSTRACODERMS and PLACODERMS
Prehistoric fishes known only as fossils, forerunners of present-day vertebrates

Pteraspis
(ostracoderm)

Hemicephalaspis
(ostracoderm)

Climatius
(placoderm)

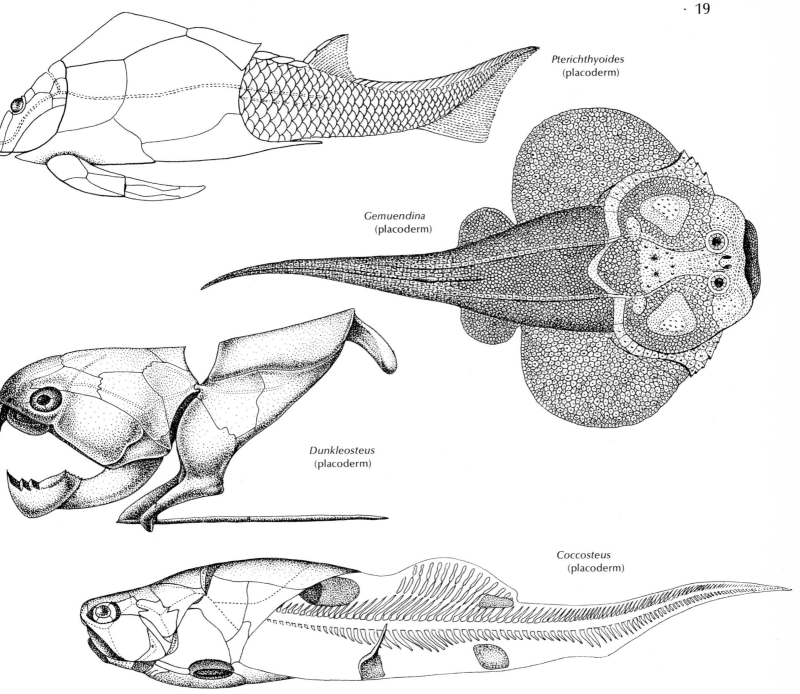

Pterichthyoides
(placoderm)

Gemuendina
(placoderm)

Dunkleosteus
(placoderm)

Coccosteus
(placoderm)

definite groups that may have evolved in a separate but parallel fashion from placoderm ancestors. They are the Chondrichthyes: cartilaginous, jawed fishes (sharks, skates, and rays); and the Osteichthyes, or higher bony fishes.

In the Chondrichthyes, bone is completely absent; the internal skeleton is entirely cartilaginous. Their principal advancements over earlier types are their scales, paired fins, and well-developed jaws on a definite head. Some of their chief or distinguishing characteristics are five to seven pairs of gill clefts, all opening separately to exterior; dorsal fin or fins, and fin spines, if present, rigid, not erectile; spiracles present or absent; skin covered with many placoid scales, or "dermal denticles"; teeth numerous. In bottom-dwelling types of skates and rays, where the mouth is on the underside, water enters through a pair of spiracles on the top of the head and is expelled through the gill clefts, located on the underside of the head. In males, the pelvic fins bear projecting claspers that aid in internal fertilization. Development is oviparous (eggs laid before hatching), ovoviviparous (eggs hatching and embryos developing within the mother but without placental attachment), or viviparous (born alive, embryos attached to the uterine wall of the mother by a yolk-sac placenta).

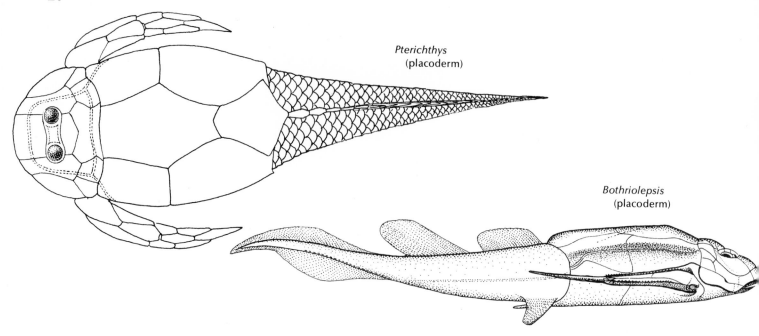

Pterichthys
(placoderm)

Bothriolepsis
(placoderm)

Osteichthyes

The archaic fishes preceding the bony fishes in the evolutionary scale were prominent in the older geologic periods, but in later times they diminished in numbers. In contrast, the Osteichthyes, or the higher bony fishes, became more abundant and more important as they eventually dominated the lakes and streams. This group, at present, includes all freshwater fishes and the great majority of marine types.

The prominent characteristics of the bony fishes are skeletons of bone; a single gill cover or operculum over the cavity containing the gills; fins strengthened by spines or soft rays; scales partially or completely covering the body or absent entirely. Today the bony fishes far outnumber the cartilaginous fishes. The most reliable estimates indicate Osteichthyes to include about 20,000 species, in contrast to approximately 550 species for the Chondrichthyes.

Human Involvement

Human interest in fishes predates recorded history. First, fishes were caught for food, probably by hand or by traps in shallow pools. Later they were taken with spears and with nets. Finally, and with no precise record of how or when it came about, the human learned how to make hooks and to catch fishes with baits.

Fishes continue to be important as food, with many billions of pounds harvested annually. Added to the traditional nets, hooks, and lines are various tools of modern technology—aircraft, sonar, depth-finders and similar kinds of equipment—to help with the harvest and to get the catches to market quickly. Some kinds of fishes have suffered greatly from overfishing and from the destruction of their habitats. Others are still available in great abundance, though it may be necessary in the future to utilize kinds that have in the past been regarded only as trash fish or to begin "farming" areas of the sea to increase production of desirable kinds. Some types can be processed into tasteless and odorless high-protein concentrates that provide essential nutrients. Today huge quantities of fishes are processed into fertilizer and other commercial compounds.

Fishes are of extreme importance to human beings, not only commercially but in other ways as well. In sport fishing they provide countless hours of fun and relaxation so necessary in relieving the pressures of present-day living. And sport fishing puts billions of dollars into our economy in the production and sale of fishing tackle, boats and motors and through associated necessities such as gasoline, food, and accommodations in traveling. Not to be discounted is the ever-increasing number of books, magazines, and other literature published annually that offer untold hours of reading pleasure. Observing fishes in their natural habitat by SCUBA (self-contained underwater breathing apparatus) and snorkeling (face mask and plastic breathing tube) offers as much recreation to aquatic enthusiasts as bird watching does to many bird followers on land. A surprising number of people in all walks of life derive great pleasure in nurturing, as a hobby, the strikingly colorful tropical aquarium fishes.

THE FISH'S BODY
AND ITS FUNCTIONS

Size

Fishes range widely in size, from tiny Philippine gobies less than half an inch long, the smallest of all animals with backbones, to giant whale sharks 65 to 70 feet long. Despite their diminutive size—it takes literally thousands of them to weigh a pound—the little gobies are harvested commercially for use in many foods. Equally surprising, the behemoth whale sharks that may weigh as much as 25 tons are so docile they even allow inquisitive men to pull alongside them with boats and then climb aboard them to prod and poke as they give the big plankton-eaters a close examination. Between these extremes are seemingly limitless shapes and sizes among the estimated 20,000 species, exceeding the combined numbers of all other vertebrate animals—the amphibians, reptiles, birds, and mammals.

Among the other giants of the sea is the mola, or ocean sunfish, which goes also by the name of headfish because its fins are set far to the rear on its broad, almost tailless body. Molas, which have the unusual habit of basking at the surface, lying on their side as though dead, may weigh nearly a ton. In salt water the bluefin tuna, swordfish, and certain sharks and marlins reach weights of more than a thousand pounds.

The white sturgeon, among the largest of the freshwater fishes, formerly reached weights of well over a thousand pounds in the Columbia and Fraser rivers, but it is uncommon now for catches to exceed 400 pounds. In the 1800s monstrous sturgeons of over 2,000 pounds were reported, but fishery workers have not been able to verify such legends. European sturgeons, especially along the Siberian coast from the Volga River, also attained tremendous proportions but no longer do so. Some of the Asian catfishes may weigh 100 pounds or more. The arapaima, found in Peru, Brazil, and British Guiana, will reach about 200 pounds. The prehistoric-looking alligator gar of the southeastern United States may attain a weight of 300 pounds.

Fish size is of special interest to sport fishermen. The International Game Fish Association, with headquarters in Fort Lauderdale, Florida, registers the records for saltwater catches; *Field and Stream* magazine keeps the official freshwater records. Each has special regulations that must be met to assure the acceptance of bona fide weights and measurements.

These records are only for the maximum sizes caught on rod and reel. In many cases fishes are known to grow much larger. The record tarpon taken on rod and reel, for example, weighed 283 pounds, admittedly sizable but still much smaller than the 350-pounders that have been caught in nets. The rod-and-reel record catches, however, greatly exceed the average size of most species. As one illustration, most brook trouts taken by sport fishermen weigh less than half a pound, but the record for the species caught on rod and reel weighed 14 pounds 8 ounces.

A fish does not have to be gigantic to provide fun, however. In this regard, tackle plays an important role. Fishermen, using ultra-light tackle in ponds and lakes, find it challenging to catch quarter-pound bluegills, rarely if ever hooking one that approaches a pound in weight (the record for the species is 4 pounds 12 ounces). The International Game Fish Association long ago recognized that the kind of tackle used deserved recognition as well as the size of the catch, and so they set up special divisions for the various weights of tackle for each species. This also gives a measure of credit to the angler for his fishing skill.

Form

The typical fish, such as the yellow perch, largemouth bass, striped bass, and groupers, has a compressed body, flattened from side to side. In others the body is depressed from top to bottom, as in flounders, rays, and other bottom-hugging types. Still others are spindle-shaped or streamlined, like mackerels, tunas, and trouts, and some, such as eels, have an elongated or snakelike body. All fishes fit into one of these four categories, but each form in turn may differ with various adaptations in certain portions of its anatomy. These

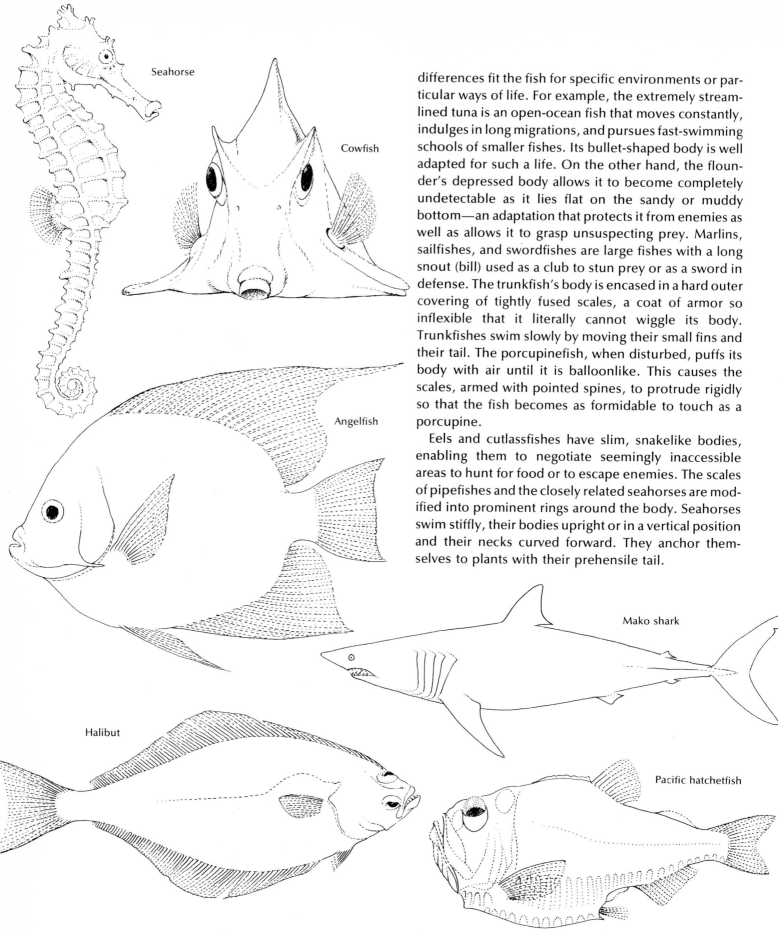

differences fit the fish for specific environments or particular ways of life. For example, the extremely streamlined tuna is an open-ocean fish that moves constantly, indulges in long migrations, and pursues fast-swimming schools of smaller fishes. Its bullet-shaped body is well adapted for such a life. On the other hand, the flounder's depressed body allows it to become completely undetectable as it lies flat on the sandy or muddy bottom—an adaptation that protects it from enemies as well as allows it to grasp unsuspecting prey. Marlins, sailfishes, and swordfishes are large fishes with a long snout (bill) used as a club to stun prey or as a sword in defense. The trunkfish's body is encased in a hard outer covering of tightly fused scales, a coat of armor so inflexible that it literally cannot wiggle its body. Trunkfishes swim slowly by moving their small fins and their tail. The porcupinefish, when disturbed, puffs its body with air until it is balloonlike. This causes the scales, armed with pointed spines, to protrude rigidly so that the fish becomes as formidable to touch as a porcupine.

Eels and cutlassfishes have slim, snakelike bodies, enabling them to negotiate seemingly inaccessible areas to hunt for food or to escape enemies. The scales of pipefishes and the closely related seahorses are modified into prominent rings around the body. Seahorses swim stiffly, their bodies upright or in a vertical position and their necks curved forward. They anchor themselves to plants with their prehensile tail.

Seahorse

Cowfish

Angelfish

Mako shark

Halibut

Pacific hatchetfish

The shape of its body reveals much about a fish's way of life. Streamlined for swiftness in open water, flat for hugging the bottom, large eyes to see in the darkness of the ocean depths, a shell-like covering, spines, or camouflage for protection—the diversity is great, adapting fishes for every watery niche.

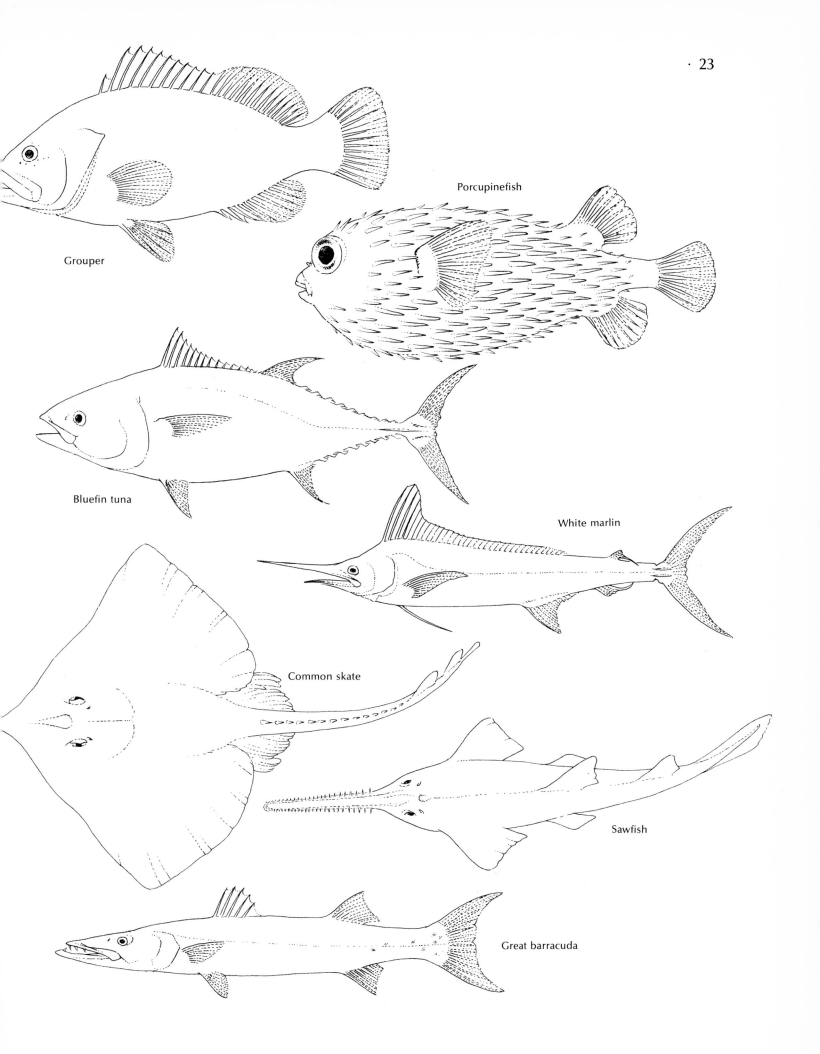

Grouper

Porcupinefish

Bluefin tuna

White marlin

Common skate

Sawfish

Great barracuda

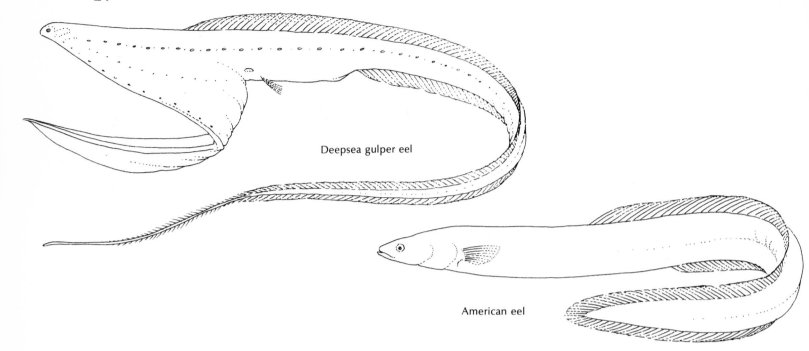

Deepsea gulper eel

American eel

Among the most unusual fishes in shape are those that live in the deep sea. Many have luminous spots or stripes along their body, and fins may be reduced to slim filaments, some bearing bulbous and luminous tips. Many have long barbels around the mouth, with lighted tips that serve as lures for attracting smaller prey within reach of their strong jaws. In some, the tail is long and snakelike. Most have extremely large mouths and an array of long, dagger-sharp teeth that help in holding their catches. The mouth is generally stretchable, as is the stomach. When the fish has the good fortune to capture a meal in the dark depths where food, as a rule, is scarce, it attempts to devour the prey regardless of size.

The most extreme body shape in fishes is that of the males of some ceratioid anglerfishes that attach themselves to a female and live the remainder of their lives as parasites. The male's body degenerates until nothing is left but a tumorlike mass of reproductive tissue that is fed by the female's body.

Scales

A typical fish's body is covered with thin scales that overlap each other like the shingles of a roof. They are prominent outgrowths of skin, or epidermis, in which there are numerous glands that secrete a protective coating of slime. The slime is a barrier to the entry of parasites, fungi, and disease organisms that might infest the fish, and it seals in the fish's body fluids so that they are not diluted by the watery surroundings. The slime also reduces friction so that the fish slides through the water with a minimum of resistance; and it makes the fish slippery when predators, including man, try to grab hold. Some fishes, such as lampreys and hagfishes, give off copious amounts of slime.

As a fish grows, its scales increase in size but not in number. Lost scales may be replaced, however. The ridges and spaces on some types of scales become records of age and growth rate. These can be read or counted like the annual rings in the trunk of a tree to determine a fish's age—the fish's growth slowing or stopping during winter when food is scarce and becoming much more rapid during the warm months when food is plentiful. Experts in reading scales can tell when a fish first spawned and each spawning period thereafter. They can determine times of migration, periods of food scarcity, illness, and similar facts about the fish's life. The number of scales in a row along the lateral line may be used to identify closely related species, particularly the young. Growth rings occur also in the vertebrae and in other bones of the body, but to study these requires killing the fish. A few scales can be removed without harm to the fish.

Most bony fishes have tough, shinglelike scales—with a comblike or serrated edge (ctenoid) along their rear margin, or with smooth rear margins (cycloid). The scales of garfishes are hard and almost bony, fitting one against the other like the bricks on a wall. These are called ganoid scales. Sturgeons also have ganoid scales, some of which form ridges of armor along portions of their sides and back.

Sharks have placoid scales, the most primitive type. They are toothlike, each with a central spine coated on the outside with enamel and with an intermediate layer of dentine over a central pulp cavity. The skin of sharks,

Ctenoid scales

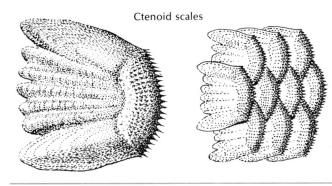

Cycloid scales

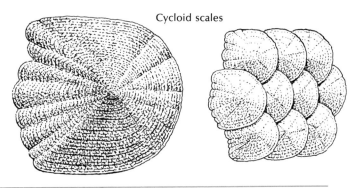

Ganoid scales

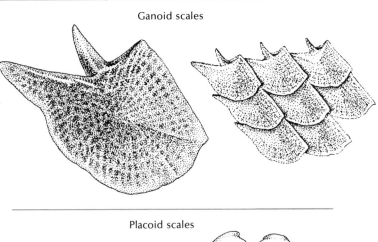

with the scales still attached, is the shagreen of commerce, widely used in the past and still used today in primitive areas as an abrasive, like sandpaper, or to make nonslipping handles for knives and tools.

The scales may be variously modified on different species. Some fishes do not have scales at all. Most species of catfishes, for example, are "naked" or smooth-skinned. Their skin is very slippery, however, and some of the rays in their fins are modified as sharp spines. Paddlefishes and sculpins have only a few scales. The scales of mackerels are minute. Trouts also have tiny scales. Those of eels are widely separated and buried deep in the skin.

Coloration

The beautiful coloration of fishes can be appreciated only when observing them alive, for at death the brilliance and intensity of color begin to fade immediately. Unquestionably, many fishes equal or surpass in appearance the most spectacularly colored bird or butterfly, and some of the blends and contrasts of body color are impossible to describe with justice.

The color in fishes is primarily produced by skin pigments, and basic or background color is due to underlying tissues and body fluids. Iridescent colors are present in body scales, eyes, and abdominal linings of some fishes. The rainbowlike reflecting hues of certain kinds of fishes are caused by skin pigmentation fragmenting through the irregular ridges of transparent or translucent scales.

All fishes are not highly colored, however; the range extends widely from fishes with gay colors to species that are uniformly drab in brown, gray, and even pitch-black. In nearly all species, the shades and acuteness of color is adapted to the particular environment a fish inhabits.

In oceanic fishes, basic color may be separated into three kinds: silvery in the upper-water zone, reddish in the middle depths, and violet or black in the great depths. Those that swim primarily in the upper layers of ocean water are typically dark blue or greenish blue on

Placoid scales

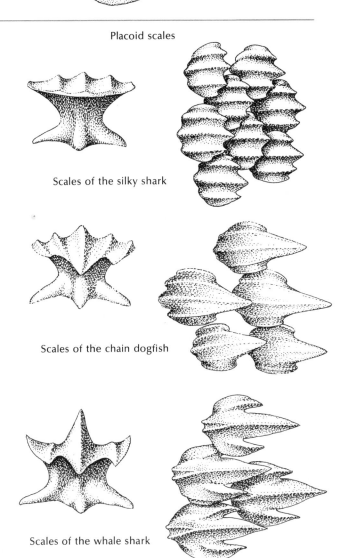

Scales of the silky shark

Scales of the chain dogfish

Scales of the whale shark

the dorsal portions, grading to silvery sides and white belly. Fishes that live on the bottom, especially those living close to rocks, reefs, and weed beds, may be busily mottled or striped. The degree of color concentration also varies depending on the character of the fish's surroundings. For example, a striped bass caught from a sandy area will be lighter in general coloration than one captured from deeper water or from around dark rocks.

The same natural rules apply to freshwater fishes. A northern pike, pickerel, or musky is patterned in mottled greens because its habitat is primarily lily pads and weed beds where it is well camouflaged in alternating light and dark shadows. The bottom-dwelling, dark-backed catfishes are almost impossible to detect against the muddy background.

Many anglers are bewildered by the color variances in trouts. Often the same species taken from different types of localities in the same stream may differ in coloration to a startling degree. For example, a trout taken from shallow, swiftly running water over sand and pebbles will be bright and silvery in comparison to his relative that lives under a log in a deep, quiet pool. The steelhead, a sea-run rainbow trout, is another good example of color change. When it leaves the ocean to enter our western rivers it is brilliantly silver; but as it remains in fresh water, the characteristic coloration of the rainbow trout develops: dark, greenish blue back; crimson lateral band; and profuse black spots over most of the body.

Regardless of the confusing differences under varying conditions, anglers who know the basic color patterns can easily identify any trout. Each species has recognizable characteristics that do not change. The brook trout, *Salvelinus fontinalis,* for example, always has reticulated or wormlike markings on its back, while the under edge of the tail fin and the forward edges of the pectoral, ventral, and anal fins are white.

Most types of fishes change color during the spawning season; this is especially noticeable among the trout and salmon tribes. As spawning time approaches, the general coloration becomes darker and more intense. Some examples are surprising, especially in the salmons of the U.S. Northwest. All five species are silvery in the ocean, but as they travel upstream to their spawning grounds they gradually alter to deep reds, browns, and greens—the final colors so drastically different that it seems hardly possible the fishes were metallic bright only a short time earlier. Each type of salmon, however, retains its own color characteristics during the amazing transition.

In some types of fishes, the coloration intensifies perceptibly when the fish is excited by prey or by predators. Dolphins, a blue-water angler's delight, appear to be almost completely vivid blue when seen from above in a darting school in calm waters. When a dolphin is brought aboard, the unbelievably brilliant golden yellows, blues, and greens undulate and flow magically along the dolphin's body as it thrashes madly about. These changes in shade and degree of color also take place when the dolphin is in varying stages of excitement in the water.

A billfish, such as a striped marlin or blue marlin, following a surface-trolled bait is a wondrous spectacle to observe. As it eyes its quarry from side to side, while maneuvering into position to attack, the deep, cobalt-blue dorsal surface and bronze-silver sides are at their zenith. This electrifying display of color is lost almost immediately when the fish is boated.

Fins and Locomotion

Fishes are propelled through the water by fins, body movement, or both. In general, the main moving force is the caudal fin, or tail, and the area immediately adjacent to it known as the caudal peduncle. In swimming, the fins are put into action by muscles attached to the base of the fin spines and rays. Fishes with a fairly rigid body, such as the filefish, trunkfish, triggerfish, manta, and skate, depend mostly on fin action for propulsion. Eels, in contrast, rely on extreme, serpentlike body undulations to swim, with fin movement assisting to a minor extent. Sailfishes, marlins, and other big-game fishes fold their fins into grooves (lessening water resistance) and rely mainly on their large, rigid tails to go forward. Trouts, salmons, catfishes and others are well adapted for sudden turns and short, fast moves. If water is expelled from the gills suddenly in breathing, it acts like a jet stream and aids in a fast start forward.

A fish can swim even if its fins are removed, though it generally has difficulty with direction and balance. In some kinds, however, the fins are highly important in swimming. For example, the pectoral fins of a ray are broad "wings" with which the fish sweeps through the water almost as gracefully as a swallow does in the air. The sharks, close relatives of the rays, swim swiftly in a straight line but have great difficulty in stopping or turning because their fins have restricted movement.

Flying fishes glide above the surface of the water with their winglike pectoral fins extended. Sometimes they get additional surges of power by dipping their tails into the water and vibrating them vigorously. This may enable them to remain airborne for distances as great as a quarter of a mile. Needlefishes and halfbeaks skitter over the surface for long distances, the front half of their bodies held stiffly out of the water while their still-submerged tails wag rapidly. An African catfish often swims upside down, and seahorses swim in a "standing up" position.

Many kinds of fishes jump regularly. Those that take to the air when hooked give fishermen their greatest thrills. Often, however, there is no easy explanation for why a fish jumps, other than the possibility that it derives pleasure from these momentary escapes from its watery world. The jump is made to dislodge a hook or to escape a predator in close pursuit; or the fish may try to shake its body free of plaguing parasites. Some species make their jumps by surging at high speed from deep water. Others swim rapidly close to the surface, then suddenly turn their noses skyward and give a powerful thrust with their tails as they take to the air. Sailfishes and other high jumpers may leap several feet into the air when hooked, often leaping as many as twenty times before being brought to gaff.

A fish's air bladder, which may serve in some species as a supplementary breathing organ and in others as an amplifier of sounds, also assists the fish in swimming. By varying the amount of gas in the bladder, the fish is able to adjust its body weight so that it equals the weight of water that its body has displaced. This makes the fish become virtually weightless so that it can remain suspended at whatever depth it elects and can then utilize all its energy in a driving force for swimming. Sharks, flatfishes, catfishes, and others that have no air bladders can dive to the bottom quickly when necessary.

Skeleton and Muscles

A fish's skeleton is composed of cartilage or bone. Basically, the skeleton provides a foundation for the body and fins, encases and protects the brain and spinal cord, and serves as an attachment for muscles. It contains three principal segments: skull, vertebral column, and fin skeleton.

The meat or flesh covering the fish's muscular system is quite simple. All vertebrates, including fishes, have three major types of muscles: smooth (involuntary), cardiac (heart), and striated (skeletal). Functionally, there are two kinds: voluntary and involuntary.

In fishes, the smooth muscles are present in the digestive tract, air bladder, reproductive and excretory ducts, eyes, and other organs. The striated muscles run in irregular vertical bands; and various patterns are found in different types of fishes. These muscles compose the bulk of the body and are functional in swimming by producing body undulations that propel the fish forward. The muscle segments, called myomeres, are divided into an upper and lower half by a groove running along the mid-body of the fish. The myomeres can be easily seen if the skin is carefully removed from the body or scraped away with a knife after cooking. These broad muscles are the part of the fish that we eat. Striated muscles are also attached to the base of the fin spines and rays and maneuver the fins in swimming.

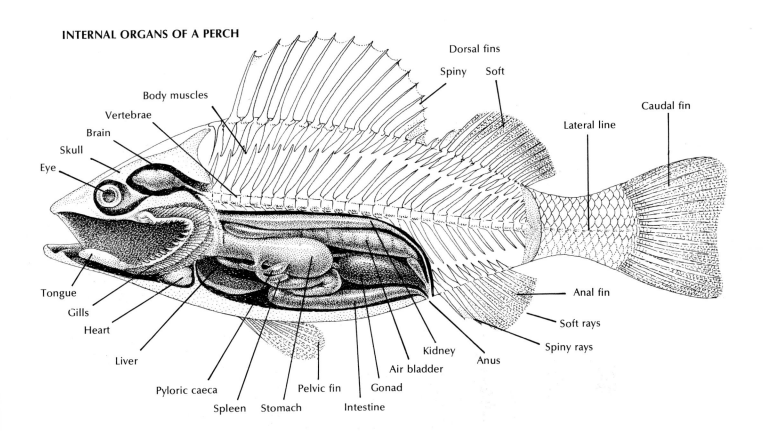

INTERNAL ORGANS OF A PERCH

Dorsal fins — Spiny, Soft · Caudal fin · Lateral line · Body muscles · Vertebrae · Brain · Skull · Eye · Tongue · Gills · Heart · Liver · Pyloric caeca · Spleen · Stomach · Pelvic fin · Intestine · Gonad · Air bladder · Kidney · Anus · Spiny rays · Soft rays · Anal fin

Teeth, Food, and Digestion

A tremendous diversity exists in the form and size of fish teeth. The character of the dentition is a clue to the fish's feeding habits and the kind of food it consumes. Of all the fishes, some sharks display the most awesome array of teeth: profuse and well structured for grasping, tearing, and cutting. The barracuda's teeth are different from any shark's, but they also draw attention because of their ferocious appearance. They are flat, triangular, closely set, and extremely sharp. Such teeth are ideally adapted for capturing live fishes, the barracuda's main diet. Small victims are usually swallowed whole; the larger ones may be cut in two and each piece swallowed separately. The bluefish, well known for its ability to "chop up" a school of bait fish, has teeth of a similar nature but smaller in size.

Some fishes possess sharp, conical teeth (called canine, or dog, teeth); pike, pickerel, and musky are good examples. Such teeth cannot cut but do a good job of grasping and piercing. Fishes fortified with canine teeth generally hold a bait fish until its struggles diminish before swallowing it—a fact taken into consideration by fishermen before setting the hook. Anglers must exercise extreme caution when removing hooks from sharks, bluefishes, barracudas, the pikelike fishes, and other fishes with dangerous dentition.

The yellow perch, sea bass, catfish, and other species have multiple rows of numerous short and closely packed teeth that resemble the tips of a stiff brush. Such an arrangement meets the needs of grasping a variety of food off the bottom or holding prey in a sandpaperlike grip until ready to be eaten.

Some kinds of fishes have sharp-edged cutting teeth called incisors located in the forward part of the mouth; some are saw-edged, others resemble human teeth, and still others are variously fused into parrotlike beaks. Parrotfishes, for example, have such teeth and thrive on small organisms nibbled from corals, rocks, and reefs. Some bottom-dwelling fishes, such as skates, rays, and drums, have molarlike teeth that are well adapted for crunching crustaceans, mollusks, and other organisms.

Many fishes, including some of the more common types such as carps, minnows, and suckers, have teeth in their throats. These pharyngeal teeth are sharp in some species, molariform in others, and still others have only remnants. There are fishes that have teeth on the roof of the mouth (vomerine and palatine) and on the tongue. Pike, pickerel, and musky, for example, have vomerine teeth that are profuse and closely packed, whereas other fishes, such as certain trouts, have comparatively few teeth on these areas. One of the distinguishing features between a true trout and a char (rainbow trout versus brook trout, for example) is the presence or absence of vomerine teeth. The vomerine bone in the center of the char's mouth has a few teeth only, located on its forward end; whereas the vomer of a true trout is much longer and has teeth all along it. Some fishes have teeth on the very edges of their mouths (premaxillary and/or maxillary). And many planktonic feeders, such as the menhaden, have no teeth at all; instead, their long gill rakers help in retaining the microscopic organisms they take into their mouths.

Fishes are a tremendously diversified group of animals that feed on an extensive variety of foods. Some, when mature, feed exclusively on fishes; others feed entirely on plants. The sea lamprey, a parasitic, highly unattractive eel-like fish, uses its funnel-shaped mouth, lined with radiating rows of sharp teeth, to attach itself to the body of a live fish; then, using its toothed tongue, it rasps a hole in its prey and sucks out blood and body fluids.

In general, the food plan of a fish's life is to eat and be eaten. Such a scheme involves a food chain. Nutrients in the water nourish various types of free-flowing aquatic plants (phytoplankton) that are eaten by a variety of microscopic animals (zooplankton). A tiny fish feeds on zooplankton, and the bigger fish feeds on the smaller fish. There are many steps in this food chain, as larger fishes eat smaller ones until the chain may end with, for example, a bluefin tuna. The tuna eventually expires and sinks to the bottom, where it is eaten by worms, crabs, and other bottom dwellers. Lastly, bacteria return the nutrients to the water in a soluble inorganic form, which the phytoplankton again utilize. The food chain is then complete.

Insects, worms, snails, mussels, squids, and crabs are some of the important larger invertebrates that provide food for fishes. Amphibians, reptiles, birds, and mammals, as well as other fishes, are also included in the diet of fishes. Largemouth bass and muskies, for example, commonly eats frogs and occasionally small turtles or snakes. Gars have been caught that contained bird remains in their stomachs. And goosefishes—bottom dwellers with huge mouths—will capture such unusual prey as a diving duck.

Fishes also differ in the way they feed. "Predators" entrap or cut their prey by use of their well-developed teeth. Those that feed on the bottom may be called "grazers" or "browsers." Fishes that feed on tiny organisms sifted from the water by use of their long gill rakers may be classifiied as "strainers." Suckers and sturgeons have fleshy, distensible lips well suited to suck food off the bottom; they are known as "suckers."

Some lampreys depend on the blood and fluids of other fishes to live; they are categorized as "parasites."

Here are a few examples of the structural adaptations of fishes that assist them in feeding: catfishes and sturgeons have whiskerlike feelers for touching and tasting food before accepting it; sailfishes, marlins, and swordfishes may stun their prey with their clublike bills before devouring them. The paddlefish employs its long, sensitive, paddlelike snout to stir up the bottom organisms on which it feeds. Gars have elongated snouts filled with needlelike teeth that make a formidable trap for capturing prey. The goosefish, also known as the angler, has a long, slim appendage with a piece of skin at its tip, located on the forward part of its upper snout; it can be wiggled like a worm and acts as a lure to entice fish on which it preys.

Generally, fishes that live in a temperate zone, where seasons are well defined, will eat much more during the warm months than they will during the cold months. In this zone a fish's metabolism slows down greatly during winter. The body temperature of most fishes changes with the surrounding environment, and it is not constant as it is in mammals and birds.

The digestive system of fishes, as in all other vertebrates, dissolves food, thereby facilitating absorption or assimilation. This system, or metabolic process, is capable of removing some of the toxic properties that may be present in foods on which fishes feed.

The basic plan of the digestive tract in a typical fish differs in some respects from that of other vertebrate animals. The tongue cannot move as it does in higher vertebrates, and it does not possess striated muscles. The esophagus, or gullet (between the throat and stomach), is highly distensible and usually can accept any type or size food that the fish can fit into its mouth. Rarely does a fish choke to death because of food taken into its mouth.

Fish stomachs differ in shape from group to group. The predators have elongated stomachs. Those that are omnivorous generally have saclike stomachs. Sturgeons, gizzard shad, and mullets, among others, have stomachs with heavily muscled walls used for grinding food, just as the gizzard of a chicken does. Some of the bizarre deepsea fishes possess stomachs capable of huge distention, thereby enabling them to hold relatively huge prey. On the other hand, some fishes have no stomachs; instead, they have accessory adaptations such as grinding teeth that crush the food finely so that it is easily absorbed.

Intestinal structure also differs in fishes. The predators have shortened intestines; meaty foods are more easily digested than plant foods. In contrast, herbivores, or plant eaters, have long intestines, sometimes

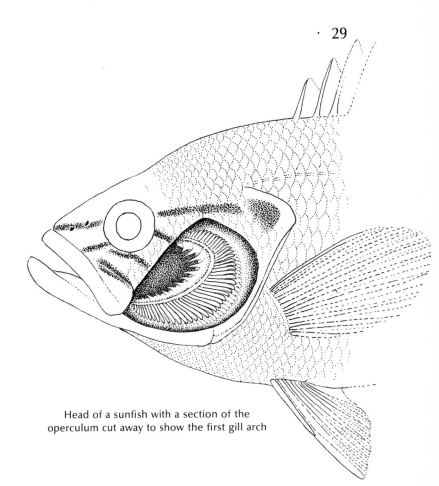

Head of a sunfish with a section of the operculum cut away to show the first gill arch

consisting of many folds. Sharks and a few other fishes have intestines that incorporate a spiral or coiled valve that aids in digestion. Lampreys and hagfishes have no jaws and do not have a well-defined stomach or curvature of the intestine. Lampreys need a simple digestive system because they are parasites that subsist on the blood and juices they suck from other fishes. During the long migration from the sea upriver to spawn, the various species of salmon never feed. Their digestive tracts shrink amazingly, allowing the reproductive organs to fill up the abdomen.

Gills and Respiration

Like all other living things, fishes need oxygen to survive. Most kinds utilize the oxygen dissolved in the water, absorbing it into their blood through the gills.

Water is taken in through the mouth and then forced out over the gills. This rhythmic process can be observed in many aquarium fishes: the mouth opens and the gill cover remain closed; then the mouth closes and the gills covers open. In some kinds of fishes, the floor of the mouth cavity is lowered as the water is drawn in; in others, the cheeks puff out. Some fishes depend on their movement through the water to cause the current of water to flow over the gills; they will die if they cannot continue to swim.

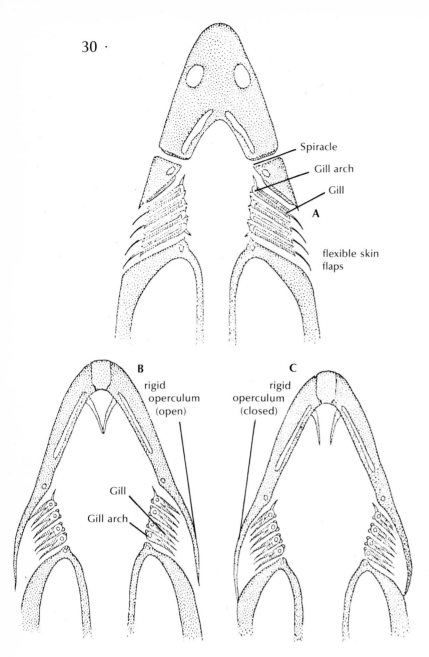

DIAGRAMS OF HORIZONTAL SECTIONS OF HEADS OF A SHARK (A) AND A BONY FISH (B) AND (C)

Skin flaps covering shark gills (A) passively prevent reverse water flow through the gills, whereas the rigid structure of the operculum, or gill covers, in bony fishes (B and C) permits the passage of water through the mouth and gills by opening and closing.

A fish's gills are much-divided, thin-walled filaments where capillaries lie close to the surface. In a living fish, the gills are bright red. In the gills, carbon dioxide, a waste gas from the cells, is released; at the same time, the dissolved oxygen is taken into the blood for transport to the body cells. This happens quickly and is remarkably efficient—about 75 percent of the oxygen contained in each gulp of water is removed in the brief exposure.

Different kinds of fishes vary in their oxygen demands. Trouts and salmons require large amounts of oxygen. The cold water in which they live can hold a greater amount of dissolved oxygen than can warm water. Further, many live in fast-flowing streams in which new supplies of oxygen are churned into the water constantly. Most of the catfishes are near the opposite extreme; their oxygen demands are so low that they thrive in sluggish warm-water streams and also in ponds and lakes where the oxygen supply is low. A catfish can, in fact, remain alive for a long time out of water if the fish is kept cool and moist. Like the carp and similar kinds of fish, catfishes can be shipped for long distances and arrive at markets alive.

A few fishes, such as the various walking catfishes, climbing perches, bowfins, gars, gouramis, and others, can breathe air. Air breathers utilize only about 5 percent of the oxygen available to them with each breath of air. The best-known air breathers are the lungfishes that live in tropical Africa. Their "lung" is an air bladder connected to the lungfish's mouth by a duct, its walls richly supplied with blood vessels. A lungfish gets new supplies of oxygen by rising to the surface and taking in gulps of air. It will drown if kept under the water. When the stagnant pool in which it lives dries up, which happens seasonally, the lungfish burrows into the soft mud at the bottom and secretes a slimy coating over its body. It continues to breathe air through a small hole that connects to the surface through the mud casing. When the rains come again and the pool fills, the lungfish wriggles out of its cocoon and resumes its usual living habits.

Blood Circulation

The circulatory system of a fish, which consists of the heart, blood, and blood vessels, carries to every living cell in the body the oxygen and nourishment required for living; it carries away from the cells carbon dioxide and other excretory products.

In function, the fish's muscular heart is similar to that of other vertebrates, acting as a pump to force the blood through the system of blood vessels. It differs from the human heart in having only two rather than four compartments—one auricle and one ventricle. The fish's heart is located close behind the fish's mouth. Blood vessels are largest close to the heart and become progressively smaller, terminating in a network of extremely fine capillaries that meander through the body tissues. The blood of a fish, like blood in all vertebrates, is composed of plasma (fluid) and blood cells (solid).

A fish's circulatory system is much simpler than that of humans. In humans, the blood is pumped from the heart into the lungs, where it is oxygenated; it then returns to the heart and receives a good thrust to travel

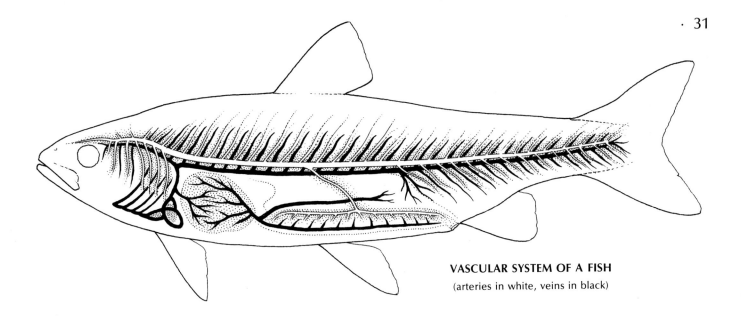

VASCULAR SYSTEM OF A FISH
(arteries in white, veins in black)

throughout the body. In contrast, fish blood passes from the heart to the gills for purification and then travels directly to all other parts of the body.

Fishes are often referred to as "cold-blooded" creatures, but this is not entirely true. Some are "warm-blooded," although they cannot sustain a constant body temperature as humans do. Instead, the fish's body temperature approximates that of its surrounding medium—water. Fish blood is thicker than human blood and has low pressure because it is pumped by a heart with only two chambers. Consequently, the flow of blood through a fish's body is slow. Because the blood flows slowly through the gills where it takes on oxygen, and because water contains less oxygen than air, fish blood is not as rich in oxygen as is human blood. Also, because of the slow flow of blood through the gills, the blood cools and approaches the temperature of the water surrounding the fish.

Senses and Nerves

A fish's eyes are adapted or modified for underwater vision, but they are not very different from human eyes. Fishes do not have true eyelids. Human eyelids prevent the eyes from becoming dry and also protect against dirt. A fish's eyes are always covered by water; therefore, they require no lids.

The metallic-looking ring, called the iris, encircling the dark center, or lens, of the fish's eye cannot move as it does in the human eye. The human iris can expand or contract depending upon light conditions. Because light never attains great intensity underwater, a fish needs no such adaptation. The big difference between a human eye and the eye of a fish occurs in the lens. In humans it is fairly flat, or dishlike; in fishes, spherical or globular. Human eyes are capable of changing the curvature of the lens to focus at varying distances—flatter for long-range focusing and more curved for shorter range. Although the eye of a fish has a rigid lens and its curvature is incapable of change, it can be moved toward or away from the retina (like the focusing action of a camera). Scientists note one outstanding similarity between the eye of a human and the fish's eye. In both, six muscles move the eyeball. They are the same six muscles controlled by the same six nerves and act the same way to provide eye movement.

Although fishes have no eyelids, they do sleep. Schooling fishes commonly separate periodically to rest. Then they become active again, and the schools reassemble. Some fishes lie on their sides when they rest; others lean against rocks or slip into crevices. Some kinds wriggle their way into the soft ooze at the bottom to take a nap, and some of the parrotfishes secrete a blanket of slime over the body at night. The preparation of this "bed" may take as long as an hour.

Important to fishermen is the fact that a fish can distinguish colors. Experimenters have found, for example, that largemouth basses and trouts quickly learn to tell red from other colors when red is associated with food. They can also distinguish green, blue, and yellow. There are indications that some kinds of fishes prefer one color to another and also that water conditions may make one color more easily distinguished than others. Although lure action is most important, fishermen can increase their chances of taking a fish by presenting lures of the proper color.

Many kinds of fishes have excellent vision at close range. This is made especially clear by the archerfish that feeds on insects. By squirting drops of water forcefully from its mouth into the air, it may shoot down a hovering fly or one resting on grass or weeds. As an archerfish prepares to make its shot, it approaches carefully to make certain of its aim and range. An archerfish is accurate at distances up to about three feet and is sometimes successful with even longer shots.

The foureyed fish, one of the oddities of the fish world, lives in shallow, muddy streams in Central America. On the top of its head are bulbous eyes that are half in and half out of the water as the fish swims along near the surface. These eyes function as four eyes because of their internal structure—the lens is egg-shaped rather than spherical. When the fish looks at objects under the water, light passes through the full length of the lens, and the foureyed fish is as nearsighted as any other fish. When it looks into the air, the light rays pass through the shorter width of the lens, giving the fish good distance vision.

Fishes that live in the dusky or dimly lit regions of the sea commonly have eyes that are comparatively larger than the eyes of any other animal with backbones. Fishes that live in the perpetual darkness of caves or other subterranean waters usually have no eyes, but those that inhabit the deep sea, far below the depth to which light rays can penetrate, may or may not have eyes. The reason that most deepsea fishes have well-developed eyes is the prevalence of bioluminescense. Deepsea squid, shrimp and other creatures, as well as fishes, are equipped with light-producing organs. The light they produce is used to recognize enemies or to capture prey.

Many fishes with poor vision have well-developed senses of smell, taste, and touch. Improbable as it may seem, fishes do possess nostrils. Four nostrils are located close to the top of the snout, one pair on each side. Each pair opens into a small blind sac immediately below the skin. Water carrying odors passes through the sacs, which are lined with the receptors of smell. Some fishes, including the sharks, possess an extremely acute sense of smell.

Fishes generally have taste organs located in the skin of the snout, lips, mouth, and throat. A fish's tongue, unlike the human tongue, is flat, rigid, and cartilaginous and moves only when the base below it moves; nevertheless, it does possess taste buds that indicate to the fish whether to accept or to reject anything taken into its mouth.

There is a close relationship between the senses of smell and taste in fishes, just as in humans. Many types of fishes are first drawn to food by its odor. For example,

catfishes and sturgeons, first attracted by food odor, will feel and taste the food with their chin barbels before taking it. These whiskerlike appendages contain taste buds. Some catfishes have taste buds all over their bodies; certain kinds can actually taste with their tails.

Although it is obvious that fishes do not possess outer ears as humans do, they are capable of hearing. The human ear is composed of an outer, middle, and inner ear; each part interacts with the other for both hearing and maintaining equilibrium. Fishes possess only an inner ear, which is found in the bones of the skull. Outer and middle ears are not necessary in fishes because water is a much better conductor of sound than air. In many fishes, these ear bones are connected to the air bladder. Vibrations are transmitted to the ear from the air bladder, which acts as a sounding board.

The lateral-line system, a series of sensory cells usually running the length of both sides of the fish's body, performs an important function in receiving low-frequency vibrations. Actually, it resembles a "hearing organ" of greater sensitivity than human ears. The typical lateral line is a mucous-filled tube or canal under the skin; it has contact with the outside world through pores in the skin or through scales along the line or in between them. A nerve is situated alongside the canal and at intervals sends out branches to it. In some cases the lateral line extends over the fish's tail, and in many fishes it continues onto the head and spreads into several branches along the outer bones of the fish's skull, where it is not outwardly visible. The fish utilizes its lateral line to determine the direction of currents of water and the presence of nearby objects as well as to sense vibrations. The lateral line helps the fish to determine water temperature and to find its way through murky waters or when traveling at night. It also assists schooling fishes in keeping together and may help a fish to escape enemies.

Many fishes are noisy creatures. They make rasping, squeaking, grunting, and squealing noises. This came as a great surprise to military forces during World War II when their sound-detecting devices, designed to pick up the noises of submarines, instead were literally "jammed" by fish noises. Some fishes produce sounds by rubbing together special extensions of the bones of their vertebrae. Others make noises by vibrating muscles that are connected to their air bladders, which amplify the sounds. Still other fishes grind their teeth, their mouth cavities serving as sound boxes to amplify the noises. Many fishes make sounds when they are caught. Grunts and croakers got their names from this habit.

Some fishes are capable of generating electricity. To our present knowledge, no other animal possesses organs that can perform such a function. The electric eel can produce an electric current of shocking power. In a properly constructed aquarium it can be demonstrated that electricity expelled by an electric eel can operate light bulbs. The current also stuns enemies and prey and acts as a sort of radar system. Sensory pits located on the fish's head receive the reflections of these electrical currents from objects close by. The electric ray and electric catfish are also capable of producing electrical currents strong enough to stun prey. South African gymnotids and African mormyrids are among other kinds of fishes that produce electric shocks of lesser strength. The electrical field set up around them serves as a warning device to any intruding prey or predator.

Since fishes have a nervous system and sense organs, it would appear that they could feel pain. The fish's brain is not highly developed, however. There is no cerebral cortex (the part of the brain that stores impressions in higher animals), and so the fish has little or no memory. It is not uncommon, for example, for an angler to hook the same fish twice within a short time. Many fishes are caught with lures or hooks imbedded in their jaws. Fishes are essentially creatures of reflex rather than action produced or developed by use of the brain. In all probability, physical pain in fishes is not very acute, and if any impression of pain is made in the brain, it is quickly lost.

Reproduction

The fish, like most animals, begins life as an egg, and, as in all other vertebrates, the single-cell egg cannot develop unless it is fertilized by a sperm produced by the male. Fish sperm is most commonly referred to as milt.

Eggs may be fertilized either externally or internally. External fertilization takes place when the egg is penetrated by the sperm after the egg leaves the female's body. The vast majority of fishes are reproduced by this system. Internal fertilization is accomplished when the male introduces the sperm into the female's body, where it makes contact with and fertilizes the egg. Some sharks and the live-bearing toothed carps (popular aquarium fishes) are ovoviviparous—that is, the egg is fertilized internally and held within the female without attachment to her until it is ready to be extruded alive. In other species—such as some of the sharks and sculpins, a few catfishes, and the skates—the egg is penetrated by the sperm inside the female's body, but it does not hatch until some time after being released from the female.

Reproduction and associated activities in fishes are generally referred to as spawning. The spawning season, or breeding period, is that time when the eggs of the female and the milt, or sperm, of the male are ripe. This period may last only a few days, as in some warm-water species such as the largemouth bass. Or it may extend into weeks and even months in cold-water species such as the whitefish and the Arctic char. Fishes that live in tropical waters of fairly constant temperature may spawn year round.

Depending on the species, spawning may take place in a variety of environments. But, regardless of where the spawning occurs, all fertilized eggs require special conditions for successful development. Sunlight, oxygen, water agitation, salt and chemicals, water temperature, and other factors have an influence on egg development. In the marine environment, spawning may take place in the open ocean or close to shore. In fresh water, spawning may occur in rapidly moving rivers and streams where the parents leave the eggs, or in quiet waters where the fish makes a nest and then protects it. Some fishes leave the salt water to travel up rivers and streams to spawn. Eels leave salt water to enter fresh water but return to the sea to spawn.

Fishes such as mackerels, which travel in the open ocean in large schools, take part en masse in external fertilization. They form huge groups and release their reproductive cells indiscriminately into the water. No attempt is made at pairing. The fertilized eggs are at the mercy of temperature, winds, currents, water clarity, salinity, and other factors. In this open-sea type of spawning, the eggs of most species float freely. In other species, the fertilized eggs sink to the bottom, where they are greedily fed upon by bottom fishes. In either system, the parents show no concern for the eggs.

The striped bass, a popular sport fish, is an example of a fish that leaves the salt water to spawn in rivers and streams. Its eggs are fertilized more or less freely, and a single female may be attended by as many as fifty males. The non-adhesive eggs are slightly heavier than water and are rolled along the bottom by the current. The parents protect neither eggs nor young.

Six species of salmons, one on the North American East Coast and five along the Pacific, enter freshwater rivers to spawn. Often they travel hundreds of miles before reaching the spawning site. Unlike the striped bass, they pair off and build a type of nest. These nests, called redds, are built in clear water that is well oxygenated and runs over pebbly areas. The eggs sink in between the pebbles of the nest, where they are safe from predators. The parents, however, do not protect eggs or young. If the nest gets covered by silt, the eggs suffocate.

Trouts and basses, among the most popular of sport

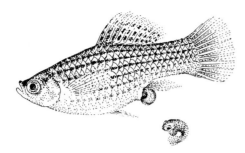

Female guppy delivering her young

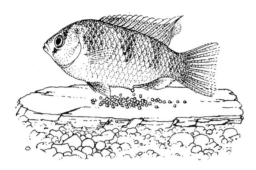

Female pelmatochromis laying eggs

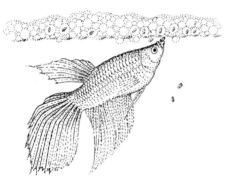

Male betta placing fertilized eggs
in its foamy mucous nest

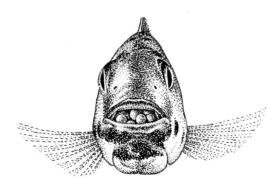

Male tilapia incubating eggs
in its mouth

fishes, have contrasting spawning habits. Basses usually select quiet, sheltered spawning areas, in water about 2 to 6 feet deep. The male excavates a depression in the sand or gravel bottom or among the roots of vegetation. The nest averages 2 to 3 feet in width and 6 inches in depth. It is constructed by the male fanning the spot with his tail and transporting the small pebbles away in his mouth. Depending on her size, a female largemouth bass usually carries from 2,000 to 26,000 eggs. There are cases on record of a female carrying as many as 40,000 eggs! The pugnacious male guards the nest, eggs, and young until the school scatters.

In contrast, the female brook trout usually digs her nest in riffles or at the tail end of pools. She turns on her side and with rapid movements of her tail pushes around the gravel, pebbles, and other bottom materials. When the nest, or egg pit, is of proper size and depth, both male and female assume a parallel position over the area; when ready, the eggs and milt are extruded at the same time. Young females may carry 200 to 500 eggs, while larger ones may carry over 2,500.

As soon as the spawning procedure is completed, the female brook trout hollows out another nest a short distance upstream from the first nest. The disturbed pebbles from the second excavation travel downstream, thereby covering the eggs of the first nest with a layer of gravel. Several nests may be required before the female has shed all her eggs.

Time requirements for incubation of eggs depend on the species of fish and the water temperature. For example, largemouth bass eggs hatch in about 5 days in water of about 66 degrees F. The incubation period for brook trout is about 44 days at 50 degrees F. and about 28 days at 59 degrees F. A sudden ten-degree drop in temperature during the breeding season is usually enough to kill bass eggs or the newly hatched fry.

Attached to the typical newly hatched young fish, called a larva, is an undigested portion of the yolk. This is usually enough food to last until the little fish has time to adjust to its aquatic world before it must begin hunting food for itself. Some kinds of fishes start to resemble their parents soon after coming from the egg and may themselves spawn within the year. Others require years of development before they mature.

Young flounders and other members of the flatfish family start life in an upright position, looking like any other little fish; but during the course of development, the skull twists and one eye migrates to the other side of the head until finally both eyes are on the upper side of the fish. Another startling example of differences in appearance between young and adult occurs in the prolific American eel (large specimens deposit 15 to 20 million eggs). The adult eels leave lakes, ponds, and streams to spawn in midwinter in the Sargasso Sea southwest of Bermuda and off the east coast of Florida. In its larval stage the American eel is thin, ribbonlike, and transparent. Its head is small and pointed; its mouth contains large teeth, although at this stage it apparently takes no food. The larval form lasts about a year. Then it metamorphoses to the elver, at which time the length and depth of the body shrinks but increases in thickness to a cylindrical form resembling the adult eel. The large, larval teeth disappear, and the head also changes shape. The elver, however, does not take on the adult color, and it does not begin to feed until it reaches North American shores. Averaging 2 to 3½ inches in length, the elvers appear in spring.

Carps and sturgeons are two of the big egg producers among freshwater fishes. When a female sturgeon is full of roe, the eggs may account for as much as 25 percent of her weight. The salted and processed eggs of sturgeons are prized as caviar, as is the roe of salmons, herrings, whitefishes, codfishes, and other fishes.

Bullheads and many tropical fishes lay their eggs in burrows scooped out of the soft mud at the bottom. Gouramis make a bubble nest, the males blowing bubbles that rise to the surface, stick together, and form a floating raft. After the nest is built, the female lays her eggs; the male then blows each egg up into the bubbles, where it remains until it hatches. The male stands guard under the raft to chase away intruders.

Male seahorses carry their eggs and also their young in a belly pouch. A female South American catfish carries her eggs attached to a spongy disc on her belly. Sea catfish males use their mouths as brooding pouches for their eggs; once the young are born, the pouches serve as a place of refuge until the young are large enough to fend for themselves.

Many species of fishes make nests. Some nests are elaborate, much like those made by birds. The male stickleback, for example, makes a neat nest of twigs and debris and defends it with his life. Other fishes simply sweep away the silt and debris where the eggs are to be laid and then continue to keep the nest clean and the water aerated until the eggs hatch.

During the spawning season, the sex of most fishes is easily discernible. Because of the huge quantity of eggs she carries, the female is usually potbellied compared to the male. As the reproductive apparatus becomes ripe, a slight press on the belly will cause the whitish milt of the male or the eggs of the female to be seen in the vent. When the milt and eggs are in advanced stages of ripeness, they can be forced out by massaging the belly firmly from the head toward the vent. Hatcheries force out the reproductive products in this manner. The eggs are exuded into a pan, and then the milt is forced over them. Milt and eggs are gently mixed, and fertilization takes place. Except in spawning conditions, the sex of many fishes cannot be determined unless the belly is dissected and the immature eggs or milt sac found.

As spawning time approaches, some kinds of fishes develop outward signs that make the sexes easily distinguishable. Male trouts and salmons acquire hook jaws. Smelts, suckers, and most species of minnows have on their head and snout small horny tubercles that disappear shortly after spawning has finished. Males of many species possess larger fins or extensions on the fins. And color is often different in the sexes. The male may sport much brighter and more intense coloration than the female. Some fishes have permanent differences in their anatomy; for example, the male bull dolphin has an extended or square forehead, whereas the female's forehead is rounded. Males of many species develop large fins or extensions on some of the fins. Male sharks, skates, and rays have tubelike extensions of the pelvic fins that function in mating.

Age and Growth

Although birds and mammals cease to grow after becoming fully mature, fishes continue to grow until they die, provided food is abundant. Growth is fastest during the first few years of life and continues at a decreasing rate. It accelerates during warm-weather months when food is abundant. During the cold months, fishes do not feed much; their metabolism slows down, and growth is retarded.

Proper determination of age and growth in fishes is important in order to regulate the harvest. In both sport and commercial fishes, the age and growth rate must be known in order to reap the crop wisely. Fisheries are controlled by rules and regulations based on facts in the life history of the fishes.

Generally, fishes in warm climates reach sexual maturity and grow faster than their cousins farther north, because the growing seasons are longer and the food supply is not shortened by cold weather. For example, the Florida largemouth bass may spawn after one year; in Wisconsin the same species does not spawn until the third year, and in Canada the largemouth bass may not reach maturity until the fourth or fifth year. Under average conditions, the largemouth bass may attain 3 inches in length in the first five months, 5 to 6 inches in one year, 8 to 10 inches in two years. By the third year, they may be 12 or more inches.

A fish's growth rate is also influenced by its environment. A pond or lake can support only a limited poundage of fishes, just as a piece of farm land produces only a limited harvest of vegetables or other crops. In some bodies of water fishes never attain natural size because there are too many of them for the available food supply. Yellow perches are found "stunted" because only a few, if any, predators, such as basses and pickerels, are present to feed on them. Stunting may also take place because not enough fish are caught or perhaps because anglers throw back all the small ones.

The age of fishes that live in temperate climates can be determined fairly accurately from various bony portions of their anatomy, because definite changes in seasons cause annual marks to appear in the bone. These year zones of growth are produced by the slowing down of metabolism in the winter and its rapid increase in the spring. In some species the annual ridges, called annuli, are especially pronounced and easy to read in the scales and cheekbones. In fishes with tiny scales these annuli are difficult to see, even with the aid of a microscope; spines, vertebrae, jawbones, and earbones have to be studied to determine the fish's age. In cross-section, these various bones may show annual rings that appear similar to the rings in the cross-section of a tree trunk.

In tropical areas with seasonal rainfall, the age of freshwater fishes can be denoted from seasonal growth marks that are caused by dry and wet seasons. In uniformally warm waters, such as the equatorial currents, fishes demonstrate little, if any, seasonal fluctuation in growth, and age determination is difficult.

Migration

Migration is the mass movement of fishes (or any other animals) along a route from one area to another at about the same time annually. This "group travel" is induced basically by factors of food and spawning. At times, mass movement may take place for other reasons, but such travel should not be confused with migration. Sudden adverse conditions, such as pollution, excessive sedimentation, or water discoloration caused by unusually severe storms, may force large groups of fishes to leave the affected area.

Some fishes, called "tide-runners," move with the tide to shore and then out again while searching for food. This movement is simply a daily feeding habit and is not considered to be a migration. Some fishes, such as the largemouth bass, remain in deep water during the day and move to shore at night for feeding.

In some lakes the entire population of a certain species may move at times from warming shallows to deeper, cooler waters to survive. The lake trout and the walleye are good examples of sport fishes that make such seasonal movements of this sort.

The bluefin tuna, one of the largest of the oceanic fishes, migrates about the same time each year between the coasts of southern Florida and the Bahamas, where it spawns, to waters off Nova Scotia, Prince Edward Island, and Newfoundland. On reaching these far northern waters, the bluefin will find and follow huge schools of herring, sardines, mackerel, or squid in the same localities, year after year. If temperature rises higher than usual, or other water changes take place, the bait schools will depart from their customary haunts, and the bluefin will follow.

Inshore fishes such as the shad and the striped bass may travel varying distances along the coast before arriving in freshwater rivers or brackish stretches that meet the requirements for their spawning activities. Some species do not travel along a coast or migrate north and south; instead, they move offshore into deeper water in cold weather and inshore during warm weather. Others combine a north-south movement with an inshore-offshore migration.

The California grunion, a small, silvery fish, is an example of a unique and precisely timed migration. It spawns at the turn of high tide and as far up the beach as the largest waves travel. This action takes place during that period when the water reaches farthest up shore. The grunion deposits eggs and sperm in pockets in the wet sand. Two weeks or a month later, at the time of the next highest tide, when the water reaches the nests and stirs up the sand, the young are hatched and scramble out to sea before the tide recedes and prevents them from escaping.

Members of the salmon family participate in what may be termed classical migration. All have the same general life pattern. The eggs are hatched in shallow streams; the young spend their early life in fresh water, grow to maturity in the ocean, and then return to the stream of their birth to spawn. The length of time spent in freshwater and saltwater habitats varies among the species and among populations of the same species. All five species of northwestern Pacific salmons die after their first spawning. The Atlantic salmon drops back to salt water; those fishes that survive the hazards of the sea return to spawn again. Salmons migrate varying distances to reach their spawning sites. The chum and the pink salmon usually spawn a few miles from salt water and often within reach of the tides. The chinook, largest of the salmon family, may cover thousands of miles and surmount many obstacles before reaching its ancestral spawning grounds. And after spending from one to about four years far out to sea, each invididual returns to spawn in the river where it was born.

Silver badger

COMMERCIAL
AND SPORT FISHES

Wilkinson

Humans are engaged in many activities associated with fishes, all of which contribute to human enrichment. The two most important involvements concern commercial fishes and sport fishes. Commercial, or food, fishes are those that are caught to be sold. The fishes that are important commercially number about 350 to 400 species, mostly marine bony fishes, which constitute 85 percent of the total commercial catch. About half the total of market fishes is consumed fresh; the other half is frozen, canned, cured, or rendered into fish meal, fertilizer, or oil. The scales and abdominal linings of some kinds are used in the processing of paints and other products.

Methods of harvesting commercial fishes vary with the type of fish and the area of fishing. The ocean fishery is usually conducted from large boats employing drift nets, purse seines, trawl nets, and long lines (hook and line). Trap, weirs, and nets, set close to shore, also produce significant quantities of fishes for market.

The most important food fishes brought to the markets of the United States are anchovies, barracudas, bluefishes, bonitos, butterfishes, codfishes, croakers, cusks, drums, eels, flatfishes or flounders, groupers, haddocks, hakes, halibuts, herrings, lingcods, mackerels, mullets, Pacific yellowtails, pollocks, pompanos, porgies, rockfishes, rosefishes, sablefishes, salmons, sardines, sea basses, sea trouts, shad, sharks, smelts, snappers, soles, swordfishes, and tunas.

In the United States, marlins and sailfishes are consumed only when smoked and are generally rejected as table fishes; in Ecuador, Peru, Chile, and elsewhere, every part of these billfishes is welcomed by the coastal people. The Japanese annually harvest huge numbers of marlins by long-line methods; they are marketed and prepared in various ways, including fishcakes and fish sausages. The giant bluefin tuna is another example of a fish refused as table fare in the United States but commanding a high price on the Japanese market.

The freshwater commercial fishing industry in the United States is small in comparison to the saltwater fishery; nevertheless, it is important. The bulk of the freshwater catch comes from the Great Lakes and the Mississippi River and its tributaries. At one time as many as 5,000 fishermen and 2,000 boats were involved annually in the Great Lakes fishing industry. Some of the formerly important market species, such as sturgeons and ciscos, have been reduced to insignificant numbers primarily because of pollution. Old reliables—lake trouts, whitefishes, pikes, and perches—are no longer abundant. The lake trout, for many years the most valuable Great Lakes fishery resource, was reduced almost to extinction by the sea lamprey, an ugly, primitive, eel-like fish that attaches itself to the trout's body by its suctorial, disk-shaped mouth and then proceeds to suck out its victim's blood and juices. Fishery scientists have done some great work in controlling the lamprey in recent years. Young lampreys are killed by the use of toxic chemicals applied in the spawning streams.

The importance and type of freshwater fishes used for market varies from one area to another. Within the United States, for example, catfishes, pickerels, northern pikes, carps, and suckers are considered a delicacy in some localities and ignored as table fishes in others. In the southeastern part of the United States, the catfishes are considered fine food fishes, while mullet are used strictly as bait fish in angling; but in British Guiana catfishes are considered inferior to mullet because mullet have scales and catfishes do not. Some South Americans will not eat a catfish because of this prejudice against scaleless fishes. In Central European countries, carp and northern pike are especially appreciated as gourmet dishes. In the United States, the eel is accepted as a table fish by an insignificant part of the population, while in Japan and some parts of Europe it is considered a delicacy.

Freshwater fishes are usually sold fresh, but lake herrings, ciscos, whitefishes, and salmons are among those especially esteemed when smoked. The best-known freshwater commercial fishes in the United States are carps, catfishes (including bullheads), chubs, ciscos, eels, lake herrings, northern pikes, pickerels, saugers, sheepsheads, smelts, sturgeons, suckers, trouts (grown in commercial hatcheries and now a common item in markets), walleyes (blue pike, yellow pike), white basses, whitefishes, and yellow perches.

The greatest numbers of the fishes listed above are harvested commercially only on the Great Lakes and on large rivers. Freshwater fishes are much more valuable in our economy as sport fishes, and state laws restrict their capture only to rod and reel or hand line. Also, the angler must purchase a state license and abide by seasons, sizes, and bag limits.

THE FISHES

THE JAWLESS FISHES
(Class Agnatha)

ORDER MIXINIFORMES

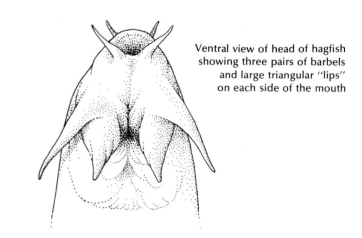

Ventral view of head of hagfish showing three pairs of barbels and large triangular "lips" on each side of the mouth

Opinions differ as to whether the jawless fishes should be considered as a distinct class or as a subclass of the true fishes. They are fishes or fishlike vertebrates, eel-like in form, with a cartilaginous or fibrous skeleton that has no bones; they have no paired limbs and no definitively developed jaws or bony teeth. Their extremely slimy skin lacks scales.

The jawless fishes are considered the most primitive true vertebrates. Structurally, they are the simplest. Their peculiar jawless mouth, single nostril, and very elementary cranium make them easily distinguishable from all the higher fishes. The Agnatha consist of two groups or orders—the hags, or hagfishes, and the lampreys.

Hagfish obtaining leverage while tearing the flesh from its victim

Family Mixinidae
hagfishes

The repulsive-looking hags are the most primitive of all living fishes. They resemble outsize, slimy worms. Hags are exclusively marine, and only one family, Myxinidae, is known. The hag has the ability to discharge slime from its mucous sacs far out of proportion to its size.

Their habit of feeding primarily on dead or disabled fishes makes hagfishes doubly unattractive. Fishermen consider them a great nuisance because they penetrate the bodies of hooked or gill-netted fishes, eating out first the intestines and then the meat, leaving nothing but skin and bones. The hagfish bores into the cavity of its victim by means of a rasplike tongue. Contrary to some beliefs, the hagfish is not a parasite; that it ever attacks living uninjured fishes is unsubstantiated.

The commercially valuable fishes most often destroyed by hags in American waters are haddocks and hakes; they are the species fished for over the type of bottom the hag prefers. Other fishes of value devastated by this loathsome scavenger are cods, herrings, and mackerels. The hag's eyes are not visible externally, and they are considered blind. Food is apparently detected by scent, and large numbers of hags can often be taken in deep-set eel pots baited with dead fish.

The hag can be differentiated from its close relative, the lamprey, by the following characteristics: the hag has prominent barbels on its snout, no separate dorsal fin, eyes not visible externally, nasal opening at tip of snout, mouth not funnel-shaped or disklike. The largest specimens of hags reach 2 feet or more in length.

Body coloration of hags may correspond more or less

Atlantic hagfish (Myxine glutinosa)
2½ ft (75 cm)

with the local color of the sea bottom. Dorsal surfaces may be reddish brown either plain or mottled with dark or light gray, brown, or bluish. The undersides are usually whitish or pale gray.

The hag was considered a functional hermaphrodite with its single unpaired sex organ developing sperm only in the posterial portion, then eggs later in the anterior portion. Further investigation, however, showed that this was not the case. Either the male portion of the common sex organ matures in each individual, with the female portion remaining rudimentary, or vice versa. The eggs are large, horny-shelled, and few in number, no more than 30 having been counted in a single female. The eggs are deposited on the ocean bottom and adhere in clusters to some fixed object by their filaments and strings of slime. There is no evidence that the newly hatched hag passes through a larval stage. The smallest hag found—about 2½ inches in length and probably not long out of the egg—resembled the adult. Spawning takes place throughout the hag's range and throughout the year. Females nearing ripeness, and others nearly spent, have been recorded in spring and fall as well as summer and winter. Hags are found mostly, if not always, in soft mud or clay bottom areas. From studies of aquarium specimens, it has been noted that hags spend most of their time imbedded in the soft bottom, with only the tip of the snout and nasal barbels projecting. They are most active after dark and are capable of determined action when disturbed or when stimulated by the presence of food in the vicinity.

Hags range the cold, deep waters of high salinity and low temperature. They have been taken from the continental shelves and slopes of the North Atlantic in north temperate and subarctic latitudes, including the Mediterranean, and off the coasts of California, southern Argentina, Chile, Japan, South Africa, and in the Gulf of Panama at a depth of 1,335 meters.

Four species inhabit waters off the coasts of North America. Of the three that occur in the Pacific, the black hagfish, *Eptatretus deani*, and the Pacific hagfish, *E. stouti,* are common; the whiteface hagfish, *Mixine circifrons*, is uncommon. The Atlantic hagfish, *Myxine glutinosa*, is the only Atlantic inhabitant.

ORDER PETROMIZONTIFORMES

Family Petromyzontidae
lampreys

The jawless, eel-like lampreys are just as ugly as their hagfish cousins in form and feeding habits; they differ in other respects, however. Hags are strictly marine, while lampreys are either totally freshwater inhabitants or, if they live in the sea, they return to freshwater rivers to spawn. Like the hags, the lampreys have no paired fins. Lampreys possess one or more dorsal fins separate from the caudal, or tail, fin. The hags have no separate dorsal fins. Lampreys have no prominent barbels on their snout; their eyes are well developed in the adult and visible externally; there are seven external gill openings on each side; the nasal opening is on the upper part of the head; the mouth opens as a funnel or disk and is armed with circular rows of horny teeth.

Hags and lampreys differ in another major respect: hags scavenge dead or dying fishes and secure their nourishment by entering the body cavities of their victims, literally consuming them from inside outward; lampreys are usually parasitic. The lamprey attaches itself to the side of a live fish by using its suctorial mouth; then, by means of its horny teeth, it rasps through the victim's skin and scales and sucks the blood and body juices. The lamprey's mouth glands produce anticoagulating secretions, thereby assisting the flow of blood. After exhausting the blood supply of its weakened or dying host, the lamprey seeks another fish to attack.

Not all lampreys are parasitic, however. In the Great

Sea lamprey *(Petromyzon marinus)*
1 to 3 ft (30 to 90 cm)

Lakes region, for example, three species—silver, chestnut, and sea lampreys—prey on fishes. Two are nonparasitic—the northern brook lamprey and the American brook lamprey. In these species the digestive tract of the adult degenerates; the metamorphosed individual does not feed but merely lives until the next spawning season, when it reproduces and expires. The nonparasitic lampreys do not grow after metamorphosis. Most parasitic types gain a length of about 12 inches. The marine species are the largest. The Pacific lamprey's maximum length is about 27 inches; the sea lamprey of the Atlantic may reach a length of 36 inches.

Lampreys spawn in the spring. They ascend streams where the bottom is stony or pebbly and build shallow depressions by moving stones with the aid of their suctorial mouths. Usually, the male and female cooperate in constructing the nest. When ready to spawn, the pair stir up the sand with vigorous body movements as the milt and eggs are deposited at the same time. The eggs stick to particles of sand and sink to the bottom of the nest. The pair then separate and begin another nest directly above the first, thereby loosening more sand and pebbles which flow down with the current and cover the eggs. The procedure is repeated at short intervals until spawning is completed. The adults die after spawning. After a period of several days, depending on the species and water temperature, the young appear and drift downstream until they are deposited in a quiet stretch of water where they settle down and burrow into the bottom to spend several years as larvae (called *ammocetes*). In this stage they feed on materials that they strain from the bottom ooze. When they reach a few inches in length (it varies with the species), the ammocetes transform during late summer or fall into adultlike lampreys, complete with sucking disk and circular rows of horny teeth.

The sea lamprey, *Petromyzon marinus*, is the most notorious as a despoiler of valued sport and commercial fishes. It ranges the North Atlantic from Iceland and northern Europe (including the North Sea and the Baltic, western Mediterranean, and Adriatic seas) to northwestern Africa and from southern Greenland, Gulf of St. Lawrence, and Newfoundland south to Florida. It breeds exclusively in fresh water and is landlocked in certain American lakes.

A dwarf landlocked race of the sea lamprey is abundant in Lake Ontario and the waters tributary to it in northern New York State, where it is extremely destructive to other fishes. At one time it was prevented from entering the upper Great Lakes by Niagara Falls. When the Welland Canal was constructed, however, a passage was created, and by 1921 this lamprey had reached Lake Erie; by 1936 the infestation reached Lake Michigan and continued to spread. The valued commercial and sport fisheries on the Great Lakes were on the verge of extinction because of the lamprey and water pollution. Fortunately, fishing is being revived here because the waters are slowly being cleared, and the lamprey has been brought under control by biologists who developed chemicals that specifically kill off the larvae when applied to the streams where the lampreys spawn.

Young specimens, when in salt water or en route to salt water, are white underneath and blackish blue, silvery, or lead-colored above. Large specimens approaching maturity are usually mottled brown or dressed in different shades of yellow-brown and various hues of green, red, or blue. Sometimes they appear black when the dark patches grade with each other. The ventral surface may be white, grayish, or a lighter shade of the ground color of the dorsal surface. Colors intensify during the breeding season.

Mature sea lampreys are from 2 to 2½ feet long. The maximum recorded length is about 3 feet. A specimen of that size would weigh about 2¼ pounds. Reproductive activity is the same as in other lampreys. A single female may contain 236,000 small and spherical eggs.

Little is known of lamprey habits in the sea, except that they are extremely aggressive in their attacks on other fishes and are capable of swift travel by body undulations similar to that of an eel. Lampreys never take the fisherman's hook, but they are often seen by trout anglers in shallow water. Although lampreys are usually close to land during their stay in the sea, they sometimes stray far offshore to water hundreds of fathoms deep. The sea lamprey is tolerant of a wide range of temperatures and water salinities, ranging from fresh water to that of full oceanic saltness.

Sea lampreys were considered a delicacy in Europe during the Middle Ages. Also, at one time, large numbers were caught for human consumption in New England, especially in the Connecticut and Merrimack rivers. Today a few are eaten as table fishes, but in general the only value the lamprey has is in its larval form as bait for fishermen. Lampreys also have been used as study specimens in schools. Commercial biological houses supply preserved specimens prepared for dissection. The larval lamprey is considered a likely prototype of the vertebrates.

Commonly, but erroneously, the lamprey is known as "lamprey eel." It is not a true eel of the family Anguillidae. For easy differentiation, eels possess jaws and pectoral fins; these are lacking in the lamprey.

The lamprey family consists of about 24 species distributed in the temperate portions of both hemispheres, with 14 species inhabiting the waters of the United States and Canada.

THE CARTILAGINOUS FISHES

(Class Chondrichthyes)

The class Chondrichthyes includes sharks, skates, and rays, usually called *elasmobranchs*, and chimaerids, or chimaeras. The most notable characteristics of these fishlike vertebrates are well-developed lower jaws; bony teeth; cartilaginous skeletons, more or less calcified but lacking true bone; scales mostly toothlike in structure (placoid); two nostrils, not opening into mouth; and no swim bladder.

In relation to other classes of fishes, the Chondrichthyes are separated from the Agnatha, or jawless fishes, mainly by their well-developed jaws and bony teeth and by having paired limbs. They are distinguished from the so-called true, or higher, fishes by the lack of true bone in the skeleton. Sharks, skates, and rays are characterized most obviously by having from five to seven pairs of gill clefts, all opening to the exterior but not covered by an opercular fold of skin (operculum); a dorsal fin or fins with fin spines, if present, rigid and not erectile; numerous teeth in several series; and skin with numerous placoid scales.

Chimaeras are easily distinguishable from sharks, skates, and rays by their soft heads, which are rounded or conical in front and lack an extended beak or hoe-shaped appendage. The lower part of the head shows a conspicuous groove running from one side to the other, close in front of the nostrils. The second dorsal fin is much longer and lower than the first and is separated from the first only a short distance by skin minus rays.

The cartilaginous fishes are here separated into three groups or orders, one to include all living sharks, another to contain the skates and rays, and the third the chimaeras.

Sharks

Although this group of ancient fishes appears to be as numerous and as varied as ever, there are many fewer species of sharks than of bony fishes. In all, there are about 225 to 250 species of sharks. Sharks are predominantly marine, but a few species run far upstream into brackish or even into fresh water in large rivers such as the Ganges, the Tigris, and the Zambezi. One land-locked species of shark is known in Lake Nicaragua. Many sharks roam the open ocean, far from shore; others spend most of their time on the ocean bottom or close to it. Most species dwell in comparatively shallow water, but a few prefer the continental slopes at depths of hundreds of fathoms; the greatest depth at which a shark was captured was about 1,500 fathoms. Sharks are

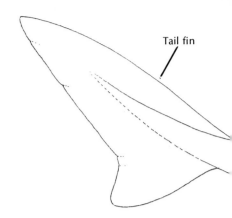

Tail fin

INTERNAL ORGANS OF A SHARK

cosmopolitan in distribution, but the great majority inhabit the tropical-subtropical belt; they are fewer in numbers in temperate zones, and only one genus, *Zomniosus*, is a year-round resident of polar waters.

Many skeletal differences separate sharks from skates and rays, but they can be easily distinguished by the location of the gill openings and the attachment of the edges of the pectoral fins. The gill openings of sharks are at least partly lateral; in skates and rays they are restricted ventrally. The edges of a shark's pectoral fins are not attached to the sides of its head in front of the gill openings; in skates and rays the edges are ahead of the gill openings.

Sharks are typically subcylindrical in form. Some, such as the so-called mackerel sharks, are handsomely streamlined. At the other extreme are a few species that are so flattened dorso-ventrally and expanded laterally that they resemble skates and rays more than they do sharks. Swimming abilities also vary among the various types. Mackerel sharks, for example, are swift, powerful, and highly active. Others, such as the Greenland and Portuguese sharks, are extremely sluggish and seem hardly to move. Sharks also vary greatly in size. The whale shark, largest of all fishes, reaches a length of 50 to 60 feet; yet certain scyliorhinids and triakids mature when less than 1½ feet long.

Generally, whenever sharks are mentioned, one immediately visualizes awesome dentition. The large, fiercely predacious species do possess extremely efficient and shockingly brutal-looking teeth; many smaller sharks have teeth more adapted to crushing than to tearing and cutting. The number of series of teeth in use at any one time varies from one to five in the different species of sharks and varies also in the different parts of the jaw of a particular individual. One or more additional series of teeth lie in reserve also, and as

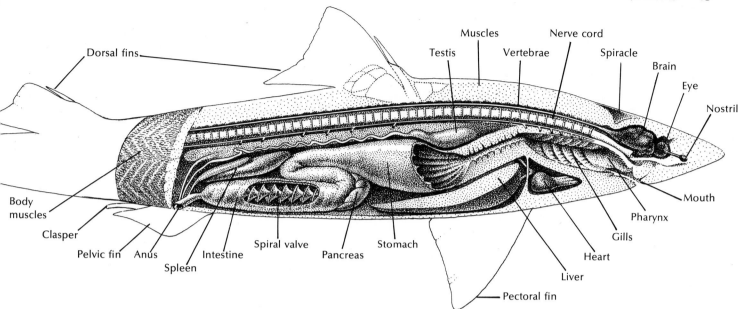

functional teeth are lost, by accident or by natural movement to the outer anterior edge of the jaw, the next younger series moves forward to replace them. This process of tooth replacement continues throughout a shark's life. As the shark grows, its teeth increase in size. Among the majority of sharks, teeth are lost and replaced individually by the younger teeth.

Compared to most of the bony fishes, sharks generally are drab-colored creatures, usually with dorsal surfaces of varying shades of grays and browns. There are exceptions, however. The mako shark, an especially fine sport fish, is dark blue with silvery sides. When a mako first comes out of the water it is truly a handsome fish. The tiger shark, particularly younger specimens 5 or 6 feet long, are prominently marked on the dorsal surface with brown spots over a background of gray or grayish brown. Some of the smaller species may be variously marked with spots and bars. The spiny shark, which averages 3 feet in length, may have reflections of violet, silver, gold, or coppery yellow over a dull-colored background. The huge whale sharks vary in color, the back and sides ranging from gray to shades of reddish or greenish brown and marked profusely with round white or yellow spots. Some sharks are actually luminiscent; that is, the skin may be strongly sprinkled with luminescent points.

Reproduction in sharks takes place through internal fertilization of the female's eggs. Males are equipped with a pair of copulatory organs called claspers that are located on the inner edges of the pelvic fins. When copulating, the claspers are inserted into the cloaca of the female. In some species, only one clasper is inserted at a time, and coitus may last about 20 minutes. In most sharks, development is ovoviviparous; in some, oviparous; in others, viviparous. Compared to many bony fishes, the number of young is small.

Sharks have extremely low intelligence, and they seem to have no sense of pain. There have been many cases reported of a disemboweled shark feeding on its own viscera. It is also not uncommon for severely mutilated sharks to continue grabbing a bait. Their sense of smell, however, is particularly well developed; many fishermen can attest to that fact. Often, a shark will cross the path of a fisherman's trolled bait, such as a

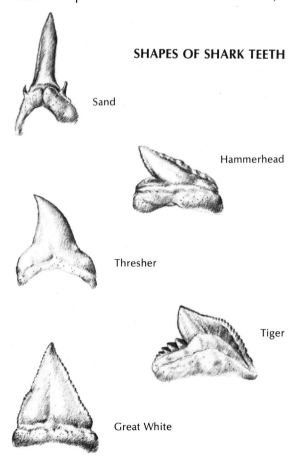

SHAPES OF SHARK TEETH

Sand

Hammerhead

Thresher

Tiger

Great White

mackerel, and take pursuit. The shark will soon pinpoint the bait even though the boat may have changed course. The shark's keen sense of smell and rather poor eyesight is apparent when it cruises the vicinity where a cut-bait is suspended from a line close to the water's surface. The shark will become active when it smells the bait and proceed to circle or crisscross the area. When the shark finds the odor becoming concentrated, it will make a beeline spurt for the bait.

It is a well-established fact that the shark's auditory nerves, as well as the nerves of its lateral-line system, are sensitive to water vibrations. Therefore, some questions arise. Is the shark that follows a bait influenced first by the vibrations of the boat propellors rather than the trolled bait? Often, far out in the open ocean, sharks will follow a steamship and wait to feed on the garbage thrown overboard. In well-established shipping lanes sharks conceivably may establish cruising patterns influenced by the gigantic steamship propellors whose vibrations must carry long distances.

Sharks, without exception, are carnivorous; the seaweed sometimes found in their stomachs is taken with the animals on which they were preying. Some smaller species of sharks have crushing teeth and feed mostly on hard-shell crustaceans or on mollusks; the great majority, however, prey primarily on fishes smaller than themselves. Yet the gigantic whale shark and the basking shark live entirely on tiny planktonic forms, chiefly crustaceans, and on small schooling fishes. Some species make a regular diet of sea turtles and seals. Some of the more fiercely predacious sharks may attack other fishes, including sharks, as large or larger than themselves—especially if the prey indicates distress. For example, it is common in some warm-water areas for sharks to attack and tear out huge chunks of a hooked giant bluefin tuna as it is tiring and acting unnaturally while resisting the fisherman's rod and reel. In warm waters, sharks will not only mutilate large game such as marlins, sailfishes and tunas but may bite off half or more of any small species being played by the angler.

Sharks, as a group, cannot be classified as harmless, although the danger of attack to an ordinary bather is small, except in special localities under special circumstances. Most species of sharks live at too great a depth or are too small or too sluggish to be of any danger to humans. Some larger sharks with highly armed dentition are not dangerous to man because they habitually feed on small prey. Nevertheless, shark attacks on humans have occurred in many parts of the world. The white shark, the tiger shark, the lemon shark, and the larger hammerheads are the most notorious among the dangerous species. The white shark, also known as the man-eater, is undoubtedly the most dangerous. Fortunately they are not common anywhere. Sharks discover and converge on their food mostly by scent, but because humans are not the habitual prey of any sharks, their scent is not especially attractive. A person with a bleeding wound, of course, is in grave danger of attack in shark-frequented waters. Fishermen, trailing behind them fish on a stringer in shallow water, are also susceptible to attack. Spear fishermen who carry their catch in a net receptacle also invite a shark assault because the speared fishes ooze blood and juices that will attract a shark.

Many instances of shark attacks on humans are well verified by hospital records. As can be expected, these attacks are much more frequent in warm-water zones than in colder areas. About 50 percent of shark attacks are fatal. Any shark bite is extremely dangerous because of the nature of the wound. The ragged lacerations are followed by rapid bleeding, and the victim quickly falls into shock. Australian waters are especially known for shark harassment of humans; in some areas, extensive precautions must be taken to protect popular bathing beaches. The areas are constantly patrolled, and some beaches provide added protection by the erection of wire screens or netting.

Although shark attacks have been recorded in many places around the world, the incidence of attacks is very irregular. It is especially interesting to note that although sharks are plentiful along the beaches of Florida, where many thousands of persons bathe throughout the year, very few assaults on humans have occurred. In continental waters in temperate and boreal latitudes, the chances of a swimmer being attacked are possible but so highly improbable that the risk is almost nonexistent.

Sharks are of minor commercial importance. In the warmer parts of the world they have been captured in quantity largely for their liver oil, which is high in vitamin content; for their fins, which are used in soups; and to a lesser extent for their flesh and hides. Sharks with firm meat are better food fishes than is generally appreciated. In Chile, for example, more than 2 million pounds of sharks may be landed to be consumed locally. In recent years the larger sharks have become more marketable along the coasts of the United States. The value of mako shark as a food is being increasingly recognized by American anglers. Properly prepared, mako is difficult to separate in quality from the highly touted swordfish. For best results, the shark should be skinned and stored in a cooler for a few days so that the ammonia odor, caused by the high content of urea in the meat, may be allowed to evaporate.

Shark scrap, like other fish scrap, is also processed into feed for poultry and other livestock.

The International Game Fish Association (IGFA) recognizes seven sharks as worthy of pursuit by rod and reel and lists them in *World Record Marine Fishes*.

The white shark attracts great attention because of its tremendous size and reputation as a man-eater. The mako, now called shortfin mako, is considered the best sport-fishing shark because it is the most active when hooked, often clearing the water's surface by several feet while displaying violent resistance to being reeled in. The porbeagle shark resembles the mako in appearance but does not put up much resistance when hooked; it does not jump in attempting to escape as the mako does. The blue shark is one of the most common open-sea sharks. It takes a bait readily, and many blue sharks are caught by sport fishermen. The tiger shark is always dangerous when hooked; specimens of over 1,000 pounds are not rare. The thresher shark draws attention because of the unusually long upper lobe of its tail fin swaying above the water, from side to side, as it pursues its prey; it is a good sport fish, with specimens over 500 pounds not uncommon. The hammerhead is an active shark that appears grotesque with its eyes located on the outer ends of its flattened and widely expanded head. This shark was added to the list of sport-fishing sharks by the IGFA only recently (1974). Because of the uncertainty among scientists regarding species of hammerheads, the IGFA simply lists this shark under its family name, Sphyrnidae.

Rules and regulations concerning world-record catches on rod and reel may be obtained from IGFA headquarters, 3000 East Las Olas Boulevard, Fort Lauderdale, Florida 33316.

The IGFA list also includes the name of the person who caught the fish and the place where it was taken.

ORDER CHLAMYDOSELACHIFORMES

Family Chlamydoselachidae
frill sharks

The single species in this family is a primitive shark that resembles fossil sharks more than any of the modern sharks. The frill shark, *Chlamydoselachus anguineus*, has six gill openings, the first one on each side continuing across the throat and joining the slit from the opposite side. Both the single dorsal and anal fins are very small and are set far back on the body. The frill shark may be as much as 6 feet long but is usually less. Its tail has only a suggestion of an upper lobe, adding to the shark's snakelike appearance. This is further emphasized by a flat head, large mouth, and numerous sharp teeth. The frill shark lives in deep water, feeding mainly on squid. Individuals have been caught off the coasts of Asia, Europe, and North America, but the extent of the shark's distribution is not known. Development is ovoviviparous.

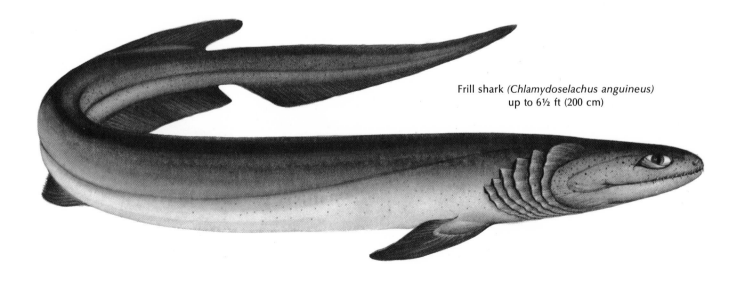

Frill shark *(Chlamydoselachus anguineus)*
up to 6½ ft (200 cm)

ORDER HEXANCHIFORMES

Family Hexanchidae
cow sharks

Among the most primitive of all the sharks, cow sharks have only one dorsal fin, their most obvious external identification feature, and six or seven gill slits on each side. The teeth in the upper jaw are completely different in shape and size from those in the lower jaw. Development is ovoviviparous.

The sixgill shark, *Hexanchus griseus*, named for its six gill slits, is also known as cow shark, gray shark, and mud shark. A sluggish shark, it is cosmopolitan in distribution, though more abundant in some regions than in others. It is, for example, especially prevalent in the Mediterranean. This shark commonly reaches a length of 15½ feet, rarely as long as 25 feet (if reported correctly), and it may weigh 1,000 to 1,300 pounds. Its head is flattened above, and the snout is broadly rounded and short. The body is a dark brownish gray, with a pale streak along the lateral line in some specimens. The lower surface is light brown or whitish. The sixgill shark normally is a deepwater species that has been recorded from depths as great as 800 to 1,875 meters off Portugal. However, specimens have been taken from the North

Sea in depths no greater than 15 fathoms. Litters are large, with as many as 108 embryos reported.

The sevengill shark, *Notorynchus maculatus*, looks much like the sixgill shark except for its seven gill slits. Predominantly gray with dark spotting on the back, fins, and jaws, it grows to a length of about 8½ feet. This shark is a Pacific species, common in California bays and distributed in the waters of Japan, China, and Australia.

Some authors recognize another sevengill shark, *Heptranchias perlo*, as a distinct species ranging the Atlantic, west and east, including the Mediterranean; the Cape of Good Hope; and off Japan in the north Pacific. It may be represented in Australian waters by a close relative, *H. dakini*, considered by some to be the same as *perlo*.

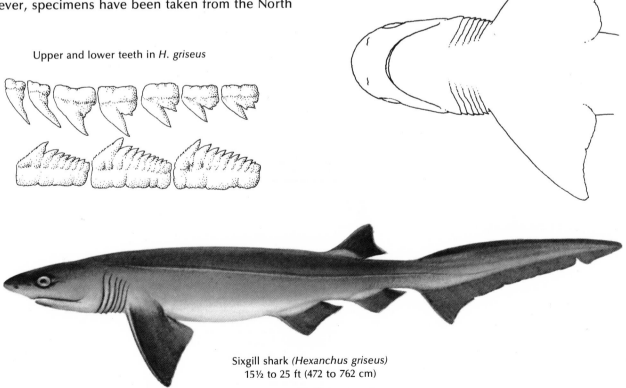

Underside of head of *H. griseus*

Upper and lower teeth in *H. griseus*

Sixgill shark (*Hexanchus griseus*)
15½ to 25 ft (472 to 762 cm)

ORDER HETERODONTIFORMES

Family Heterodontidae
bullhead sharks

Fewer than ten species comprise this family of primitive sharks that shows close linkage to the sharks of ancient seas. The single genus, *Heterodontus*, has no representatives in the Atlantic or Mediterranean, but species of horned sharks are found in all other seas. These sharks have two dorsal fins, each with a hornlike spike on its leading edge. The teeth in both jaws are divided into two types: those in front are small and pointed for grasping, and those at the rear are large and flat-surfaced for crushing. Development is oviparous; eggs cases are horny with spiral flanges but without tendrils.

The horned shark, *H. francisci*, about 4 feet long, is common in shallow to deep water off southern California, from Point Conception southward. Like other members of the family, the horned shark feeds mainly on shellfish, which it picks up from the bottom and crushes with its broad, flat teeth. Because of this feeding habit, the Port Jackson shark, *H. portusjacksoni*, of Australian waters, is also known as oyster crusher.

Port Jackson shark *(Heterodontus portusjacksoni)*
7 to 10 ft (213 to 305 cm)

ORDER SQUALIFORMES

Family Orectolobidae
carpet sharks

In this family of sharks, the first and second dorsal fins are both located far back on the body—behind the pelvis—and both fins are large. There are five gill slits, the fourth and fifth so close together they appear to be one. Two barbels are located on the anterior margin of each nostril, near the tip of the snout. The lower lobe of the tail is greatly reduced in size or is absent in these bottom-dwellers, and the long upper lobe is low in profile—no higher than the line of the body. Development is ovoviviparous.

Atlantic nurse shark *(Ginglymostoma cirratum)*
5 to 14 ft (152 to 427 cm)

Underside view of mouth
in *G. cirratum*

The Atlantic nurse shark, *Ginglymostoma cirratum*, is the only member of this family inhabiting the Atlantic. Sometimes it strays as far north as New York but is most abundant in the warmer waters from North Carolina to Brazil and also off the warm tropical coast of Africa. Its average length is 5 feet, but it is not uncommon to see an 8-footer or, rarely, one even larger—to 14 feet. This brownish shark, found close to shore, is normally sluggish and considered harmless, but it will bite quickly in self-defense if molested.

All other members of this family live in Indo-Pacific waters. These include the bottom-dwelling zebra shark, *Stegostoma fasciatum*, about 9 feet long and one of the most colorful of all sharks, its dark back crossed with white stripes and spots. Most unusual is the banded wobbegong, or Australian carpet shark, *Orectolobus ornatus*, which in addition to a mottling of lighter colors on its brownish black back wears a fringe of fleshy barbels around its broad snout. The mottling is a perfect camouflage against the bottom on which these sharks rest. The spotted wobbegong, *O. maculatus*, is similar but has numerous "eyespots" on its brownish body. These species are similar in size to the zebra shark. There are several smaller species in the same genus.

Family Rhincodontidae
whale shark

The single member of this family, the whale shark, *Rhincodon typus*, is the largest shark, one of the mammoths of the sea. It is known to reach a length of 50 feet, though 20 to 30 feet is average. This sluggish giant roams the tropical seas of the world, and, like the big basking shark, it feeds primarily on plankton that it collects on a sievelike mesh over its gills. It also feeds on crustaceans, squids, and small fishes such as anchovies and sardines. Unlike many sharks, it has no snout protruding beyond its mouth. Its gray back is sometimes

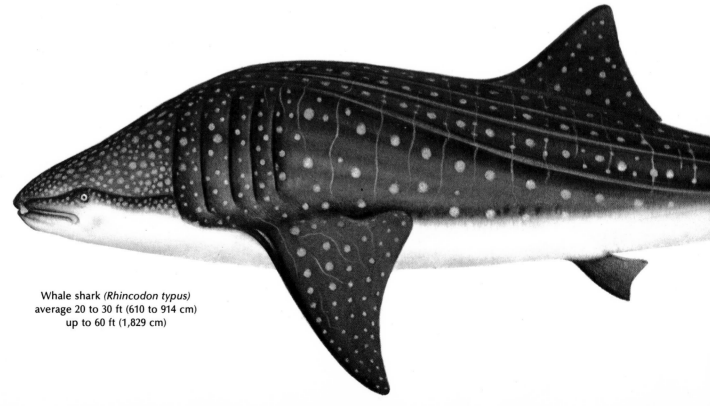

Whale shark *(Rhincodon typus)*
average 20 to 30 ft (610 to 914 cm)
up to 60 ft (1,829 cm)

tinged with green or red, and yellowish spots and transverse stripes are scattered over its body. There are three prominent ridges down its back. Sixteen eggs have been counted in a specimen from Ceylon. Whether or not these hatch before birth is not definitely known.

These huge sharks are so docile that swimmers have moved around them examining their bodies, probing and prodding, without disturbing the sharks greatly. Some people have even climbed on the back of whale sharks basking on the surface and walked over them. Because of its tremendous size, the whale shark is well known, but it is not abundant.

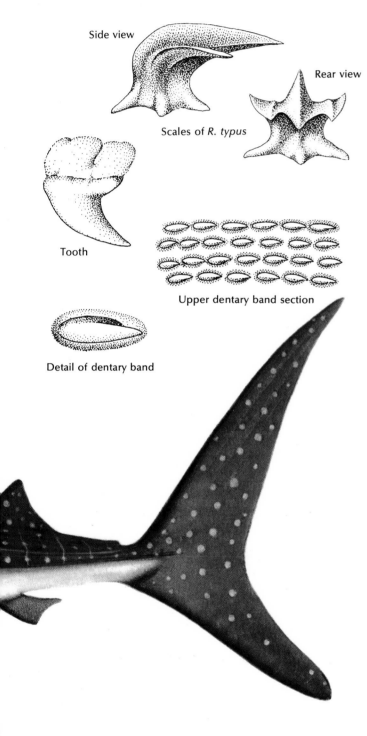

Side view

Rear view

Scales of *R. typus*

Tooth

Upper dentary band section

Detail of dentary band

Family Odontaspididae
sand sharks or sand tigers

Members of this family have gill openings that are all in front of the pectoral fins, with the two dorsal fins and anal fin almost identical in shape and size. Teeth are large, awl-shaped, with or without lateral denticles, and not very numerous. Only one genus, *Odontaspis*, is known. The Commission on Zoological Nomenclature recently changed the family name from Carchariidae to Odontaspididae.

The gray nurse shark, *O. arenarius*, usually more brownish than gray, roams the warm seas but is most abundant off the coasts of Australia and southern Africa. In both areas it appears to be responsible for a major share of attacks on humans in the shallows along beaches, in estuaries, and even far up rivers. Since it grows to a length of 15 feet and its mouth is filled with large, curved teeth, it is indeed fearsome, capable of shearing off an arm or a leg in one slashing attack.

The sand tiger *O. taurus*, found in the warm, temperate Atlantic waters off European and North American coasts, is a smaller shark—it grows to about 9 feet. It is the most common shark seen along the beaches. Generally it cruises slowly, but when stimulated it can put forth an astonishing burst of speed. The sand tiger is of little commercial importance. It is of interest to sport fishermen because many are caught, usually by surfcasters fishing for other fish. When hooked, however, sand tigers are sluggish and do not offer much resistance to rod and reel. There is no record of attack on humans in North American waters, although bathers often come close to sand tigers. In East Indian waters they have a bad reputation.

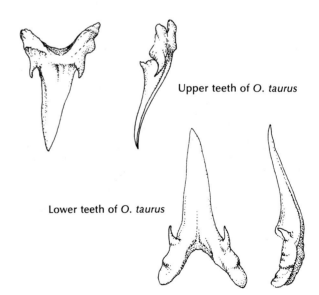

Upper teeth of *O. taurus*

Lower teeth of *O. taurus*

Sand tiger *(Odontaspis taurus)*
9 ft (275 cm)

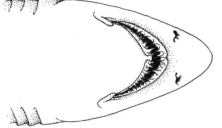

Underside of head of *O. taurus*

Some biologists believe that the gray nurse shark and the sand tiger represent a single species. Others divide the group still further, into four more species: One type lives in the Indian Ocean, another is found off the coasts of Japan, another off Argentina, and still another inhabits the eastern Atlantic and Mediterranean. The rugged-tooth shark, *Odontaspis ferox*, is a rare species found off the coast of California and southward.

Family Scapanorhynchidae
goblin sharks

The goblin shark, *Scapanorhynchus owstoni*, a rare shark that lives in deep waters, is distinguished by its unusually long, thin snout, very long tail, greatly protruding jaws, and eyes set over the corners of the mouth. It grows to at least 11 feet in length in Japanese waters. The goblin shark's nearest relatives were a group of sharks that became extinct millions of years ago, making this "living fossil" especially interesting to scientists.

Family Alopiidae
thresher sharks

The thresher shark, *Alopias vulpinus*, draws interest because of its exceptionally long upper tail lobe. In younger sharks, this lobe may actually be longer than the remainder of the body. Threshers commonly exceed 14 feet in length and are known to reach lengths of

20 feet. The rod-and-reel record is 729 pounds, taken off Mayor Island, New Zealand; but thresher sharks may weigh as much as 1,000 pounds. These spectacular sharks are found in warm seas throughout the world, sometimes straying northward in summer. They travel in small schools and are said to work cooperatively in heading schooling fish into shallows or into more compact groups to make it easier to capture them.

The bigeye thresher, *Alopias superciliosus*, also found in warm seas, is rare.

Family Lamnidae
mackerel sharks

Members of this family are the swiftest and most voracious of all the sharks. They have a torpedo-shaped body; a large tail fin with the two lobes of near-equal size in most species; a high dorsal fin situated in the middle of the back; small second dorsal and anal fins; and a long, narrow caudal peduncle with keels along each side. The pectoral fins are sickle-shaped, and the spiracles are lacking or minute. Like most pelagic fishes, mackerel sharks are typically ocean-blue above and white below.

The white shark, or man-eater, *Carcharodon carcharias*, roams all warm and temperate seas but appears most abundantly in waters off Australia. It is not common anywhere. The white shark averages 12 feet in length, but there is a record of a giant 36½-foot white shark caught off Australia. This fish was not weighed, but to get a notion of what it might have weighed, a 15-foot shark weighed slightly more than 2,500 pounds and a 21-foot shark 7,100 pounds! The liver of the 21-footer weighed 1,005 pounds. The largest specimen taken by an angler off Australia weighed 2,664 pounds. Smaller individuals can be distinguished from related species by their greatly reduced second dorsal fin and by the equally small anal fin. Tips of the pectoral fins are black; also, they may or may not have a dark spot just behind each pectoral fin. The broad triangular teeth are serrated on both edges. In color, specimens up to 12 to 15 feet in length may be a slate brown, dull slate blue, leaden gray, or almost black above, shading to dirty white below.

This giant shark vies with the killer whale as being the most ferocious animal in the sea. It may attack without provocation and is credited with the majority of the shark attacks on humans. Normally it prowls the open sea, but on occasion it comes into the shallows, its high dorsal fin cutting the surface like a knife.

The shortfin mako, *Isurus oxyrhinchus*, also known as mako, bonito shark, and sharpnose mackerel shark, averages 6 to 8 feet in length but is known to reach a length of more than 12 feet and to weigh more than 1,000 pounds. The largest caught on rod and reel weighed 1,061 pounds; it was taken off Mayor Island,

New Zealand. The mako is distributed worldwide in warm and temperate seas. Known as the fastest shark in the sea, it makes spectacular leaps and resists strongly when hooked, thereby making it sought by sport fishermen. Makos normally use their speed in pursuit of prey such as mackerels, bonitos, and other swift-swimming fishes that also live in the open sea. Makos are often seen basking, their large dorsal fin visible above the water's surface. Their dorsal coloration of blue is more vivid than most other pelagic sharks, and the sides are almost silvery in live specimens. The belly is white, snout sharply pointed.

The porbeagle, blue, or mackerel shark, *Lamna nasus*, of Atlantic waters, and the salmon shark, *L. ditropis*, found in the Pacific, are swift, rather stout-bodied sharks averaging 5 to 6 feet in length, with records of a few measuring 10 feet or more. The largest taken by sport fishing weighed 369 pounds. These sharks live in temperate seas, occupying in these cooler waters the

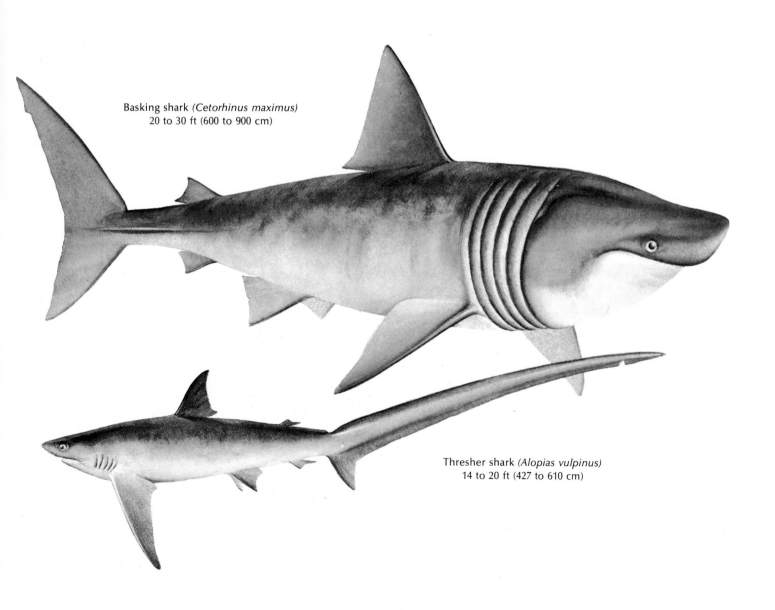

Basking shark *(Cetorhinus maximus)*
20 to 30 ft (600 to 900 cm)

Thresher shark *(Alopias vulpinus)*
14 to 20 ft (427 to 610 cm)

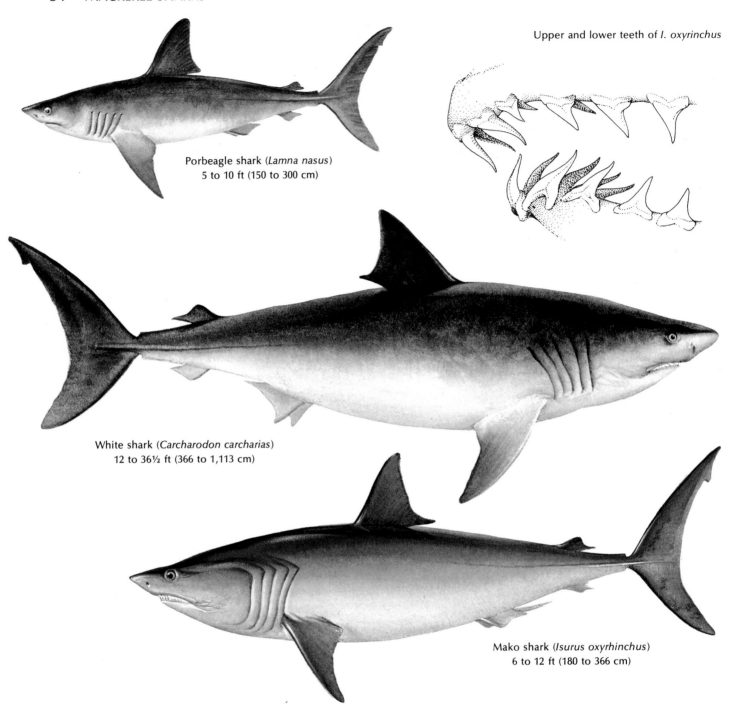

Upper and lower teeth of *I. oxyrinchus*

Porbeagle shark (*Lamna nasus*)
5 to 10 ft (150 to 300 cm)

White shark (*Carcharodon carcharias*)
12 to 36½ ft (366 to 1,113 cm)

Mako shark (*Isurus oxyrhinchus*)
6 to 12 ft (180 to 366 cm)

same niche as the mako and bonito sharks in warm and tropical seas. Like them, they feed on mackerels and other fast fishes that inhabit the open sea.

The basking shark, *Cetorhinus maximus*, is placed in a separate family, Cetorhinidae, by some authorities. The largest shark of temperate seas, it averages 20 to 30 feet in length, with occasional individuals attaining a length of 40 feet or more and weighing as much as 5 tons. This shark has a large mouth, minute teeth, long gill rakers on the gill arches, and exceptionally long gill slits, al-

most joining on the throat. Found in temperate to cool seas around the world, the basking shark is named for its habit of basking at the surface with parts of its back protruding above the water. It feeds wholly on small planktonic organisms which it sifts out of the water by means of its gill rakers.

In previous years the livers of basking sharks were valued for their oil for use in lamps. Medium or large basking sharks have livers that may yield from 80 to 200 gallons of oil. The basking shark is harmless.

Family Scyliorhinidae
cat sharks

The cat shark group includes numerous species of small sharks in tropical and temperate latitudes, from both deep and shallow waters. They are the most spectacularly marked of all sharks. Spotted dogfishes, two of the most common and best-known European sharks, are members of this family, but as to genera and species the cat sharks are most abundant in the western Pacific, Australasian region, and Indian Ocean to South Africa. In the western North Atlantic there are only a few little-known deepwater species.

Facts concerning their life histories are sparsely recorded; neither the eggs nor the embryos of most cat sharks have been seen. And much confusion exists regarding technicalities and classification within this family. Opinions continue to differ widely as to the number of genera deserving recognition; one extreme lists 11, the other a single genus encompassing the 10 South African representatives.

The following cat sharks are generally recognized to inhabit the coasts of the United States and Canada: brown cat shark, *Apisturus brunneus*, Pacific; swell shark, *Cephaloscyllium ventriosum*, Pacific; filetail cat shark, *Parmaturus xaniurus*, Pacific; longnose cat shark, *Apisturus kampae*, Pacific; false cat shark, *Pseudotriakis microdon*, Atlantic; chain dogfish, *Scyliorhinus retifer*, Atlantic. *Scyliorhinus boa* is a rare cat shark known only in Brazilian and Cuban waters and from Barbados. The length of its claspers suggests that this species becomes mature at about 2 feet.

The lesser spotted dogfish, *Scyliorhinus caniculus*, and the large spotted dogfish, *S. stellarius*, are two common species inhabiting deeper waters (250–750 feet) of the Atlantic off Europe. The chain dogfish, *S. retifer*, its body marked with a chainlike pattern of dark stripes, is found also at this depth in the Atlantic off North America.

The unusual swell sharks fill their stomachs with air when they are removed from the water; when they are returned to the water, they float belly-up for hours, like blown-up balloons. The Australian swell shark, *Cephaloscyllium laticeps*, is reportedly able to live out of water for more than a day, presumably obtaining the oxygen needed for its survival from the supply taken in when it inflates its stomach. The swell shark, *C. ventriosum*, lives in shallow-water kelp beds from Monterey Bay, California, southward into Mexican waters. Its brownish-yellow body is marked with black and white spots and broad black bars.

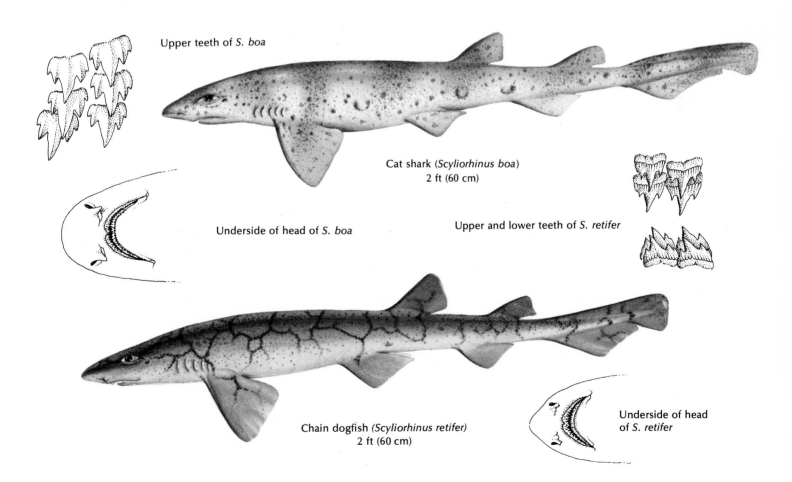

Upper teeth of *S. boa*

Cat shark (*Scyliorhinus boa*)
2 ft (60 cm)

Underside of head of *S. boa*

Upper and lower teeth of *S. retifer*

Chain dogfish (*Scyliorhinus retifer*)
2 ft (60 cm)

Underside of head of *S. retifer*

The skaamong, or shy eye shark, *Holohalaelurus regani*, one of several South African species in its genus, is another handsomely marked cat shark, its body decorated with a delicate pattern of fine black lines. It has the unusual habit of curling its tail over its eyes and concealing them when it is taken from the water.

The largest of the cat sharks—sometimes placed in a separate family, Pseudotriakidae—are the so-called false cat sharks, *Pseudotriakis microdon* of the Atlantic and *P. acrages* of Japanese waters, both attaining a length of nearly 10 feet. They are distinguished from other cat sharks in having a long, low first dorsal fin. These rare sharks inhabit water to as deep as 5,000 feet; hence, they prowl over a wide range of the ocean at depths where the temperature of the water is comfortable for them. Development is ovoviviparous.

Family Carcharhinidae
requiem sharks

In appearance, these are the "typical" sharks. They comprise the largest family of sharks inhabiting tropical and temperate seas throughout the world. In requiem sharks, the first dorsal fin is much larger than the second and is located far in front of the pelvic fins. The small second dorsal fin is located directly above the anal fin, and the two are of the same size. The upper, sickle-shaped lobe of the caudal fin is two or three times larger than the lower lobe, and the spiracles are either much reduced in size or are lacking. The teeth are triangular and razor sharp. The majority of the species are harmless, but a few types are dangerous to bathers. Development is ovoviviparous, or viviparous.

The genus *Carcharhinus* includes a much larger number of species than any group of modern sharks and many of the most familiar larger sharks that inhabit tropical seas. Many of the species resemble one another so closely that they are difficult to distinguish unless attention is paid to precise characteristics. Members of this genus are universally distributed in the Atlantic, Pacific, and Indian oceans. Their coloration is generally drab, being brownish or grayish above and whitish below. The first dorsal is much larger than the second and located well forward. The second dorsal is small and situated above the anal. *Carcharhinus* involves many species inhabiting tropical and temperate waters of all oceans, and a number of the specific types are not well known, especially those from the Indo-Pacific. It is obvious that some species, widespread in distribution, are recognized by two or more names. There is a great need for comparing similar species from different regions to enlighten the issue.

The blacknose shark, *C. acronotus*, is a small shark, seldom exceeding a length of 5 to 6 feet. It has a relatively long snout, and its upper teeth are noticeably asymmetrical with deeply notched outer edges. This is another species that is not well known, ranging in western tropical and subtropical Atlantic including the Gulf of Mexico. It strays to North Carolina.

Another little-known species, the bignose shark, *C. altimus*, is a deepwater shark apparently common in the western North Atlantic. It grows to about 10 feet in length and is distinguished by having 15 upper teeth on each side and a long, rounded snout tip.

The silky shark, *C. falciformis*, is one of the larger members of the genus, reaching a length of 8 to 10 feet. Little is known of this Atlantic species except that off Salerno, Florida, it is usually captured where lines are set at a depth of 100 feet or more. The silky shark probably occurs generally throughout the tropical belt of the western Atlantic. It derives its name from the small size of its dermal denticles.

The bull shark, *C. leucas*, also known as cub shark, was previously considered a different species from the Lake Nicaragua shark, *C. nicaraguensis*. Most scientists today consider them one and the same. This fairly large shark, commonly 6 to 8 feet long and reaching a maximum length of about 10 feet and a weight of 144 pounds, is distributed worldwide in warmer seas. It always cruises close to shore and may travel far up rivers on its food-hunting prowls. Its reputation as an extremely dangerous shark has conflictions, with records of attacks on bathers in Lake Nicaragua but practically no reports of such assaults in Florida and the West Indies, where it is one of the more common of the larger coastal sharks.

The river shark, *C. zambezensis*, of South African coastal waters, is another species that travels up rivers regularly. The small Atlantic sharpnose shark, *Rhizoprionodon terraenovae*; the Pacific sharpnose shark, *R. longurio*; and *R. walbeehimi* of the Indian Ocean are other coastal species that sometimes stray into fresh water.

The oceanic whitetip shark, *C. longimanus*, is an active, dangerous shark of tropical and subtropical seas that occasionally strays into the temperate areas of the Atlantic; it has been reported from the Pacific and Indian oceans. It grows at least 11½ feet in length.

The smalltail shark, *C. porosus*, differs from its close cousins in that the second dorsal originates about over the midpoint of the base of the anal. Also, the terminal section of the caudal is smaller. This shark attains a length slightly over 4 feet, and it ranges the tropical Atlantic. Not much is known concerning the smalltail shark; technical literature concerning it is confusing.

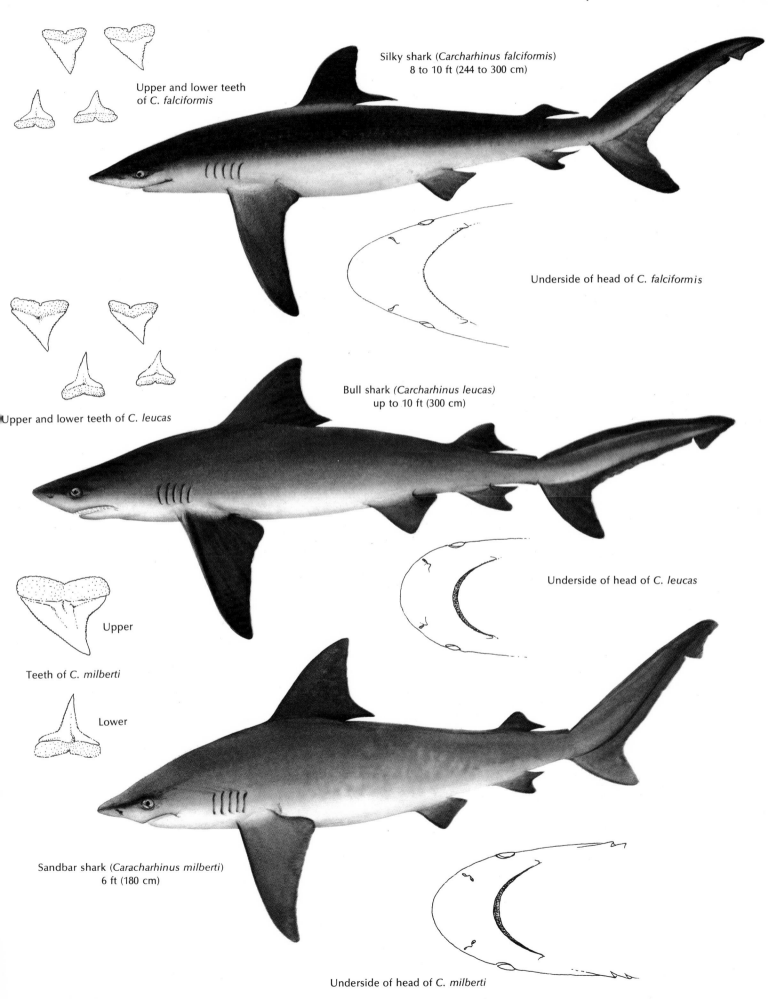

Upper and lower teeth
of *C. falciformis*

Silky shark (*Carcharhinus falciformis*)
8 to 10 ft (244 to 300 cm)

Underside of head of C. *falciformis*

Upper and lower teeth of *C. leucas*

Bull shark *(Carcharhinus leucas)*
up to 10 ft (300 cm)

Underside of head of *C. leucas*

Upper

Teeth of *C. milberti*

Lower

Sandbar shark (*Caracharhinus milberti*)
6 ft (180 cm)

Underside of head of *C. milberti*

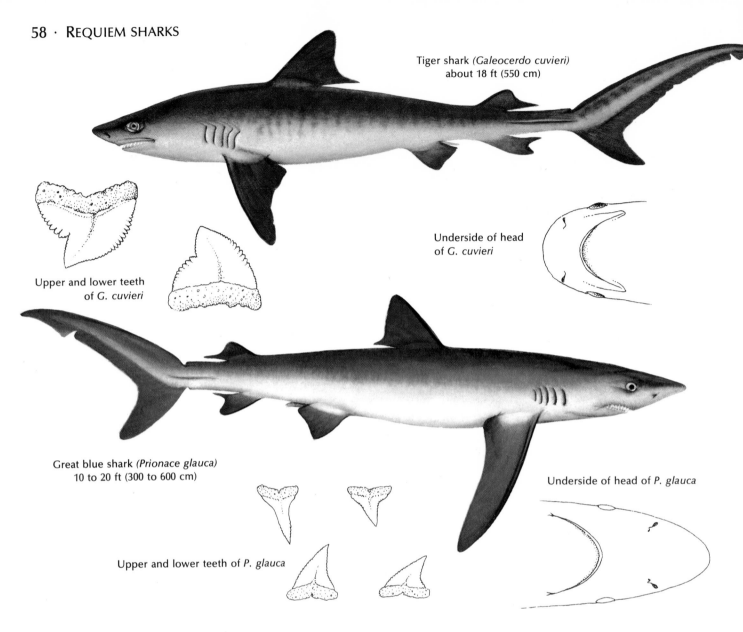

Tiger shark *(Galeocerdo cuvieri)*
about 18 ft (550 cm)

Underside of head
of *G. cuvieri*

Upper and lower teeth
of *G. cuvieri*

Great blue shark *(Prionace glauca)*
10 to 20 ft (300 to 600 cm)

Underside of head of *P. glauca*

Upper and lower teeth of *P. glauca*

The sandbar shark, *C. milberti*, is probably the most common shark seen along the Atlantic coasts of North America, South America, Europe, and Africa. It appears also in the Mediterranean. The sandbar shark's average length is about 6 feet, some individuals attaining a length of 10 feet or more. Its distinctive characteristics are large first dorsal fin positioned far forward and wide spacing of the dermal denticles, whose free edges are without definite teeth. Dorsal color varies from slate gray to brownish gray or brown. Development is presumably viviparous. In feeding habits, the sandbar shark is both a predator and a scavenger.

The dusky shark, *C. obscurus*, resembles the sandbar shark; it is worldwide in distribution in tropical and subtropical waters. It is slimmer than the sandbar shark, however, and may be as much as 14 feet long; its back and sides are a bluish gray rather than brown.

Another Atlantic species, most abundant in the subtropics and the tropics, is the 6- to 8-foot blacktip shark,

C. limbatus, which commonly travels in schools and is generally found only far at sea. It has a habit of leaping from the water and then somersaulting in midair before falling back. Like most pelagic species, it is dark blue on the back and sides. Often a tinge of bronze can be seen. Below the lateral line and on the belly, it is white or yellowish white. The fins are black-tipped.

The spinner shark, *C. maculipinnis*, closely resembling the blacktip shark and inhabiting the same waters, also has black-tipped fins but can be distinguished from the blacktip shark by such details as the position of the dorsal fin, which begins farther to the rear on the body, and by the teeth, which are smooth in the spinner and finely serrated in the blacktip. When the two sharks can be compared side by side, the spinner shark has proportionately smaller eyes and longer gill slits. This is another species that seems to delight in somersaulting out of the water.

The narrowtooth shark, *C. remotus*, closely resem-

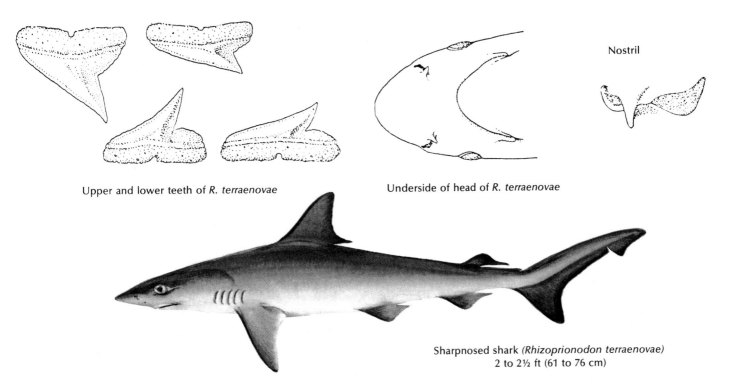

Upper and lower teeth of *R. terraenovae*

Underside of head of *R. terraenovae*

Nostril

Sharpnosed shark *(Rhizoprionodon terraenovae)*
2 to 2½ ft (61 to 76 cm)

bles the blacktip and spinner sharks, but it has shorter gill openings. It ranges worldwide in warm seas, grows to about 6 feet, but is rather rare and not much is known of its habits. Similarly, the reef shark, also known as springer's shark, *C. springeri*, is not well known and is difficult to distinguish from close cousins. It is recorded as being "not uncommon" in the Caribbean.

Other members of the genus *Carcharhinus* include the black whaler, *C. macrurus*; the South Australian whaler, *C. grevi*; and the bronze whaler, *C. ahenea*. These are among the most dangerous sharks in Australian waters.

The sharp-nosed shark, *Rhizoprionodon terraenovae*, of warm Atlantic and Gulf waters prowls the coasts but may also stray far up rivers into fresh water, as do its relatives—*S. longurio* of the Pacific and *S. walbeehmi* of the Indian Ocean.

The lemon shark, *Negaprion brevirostris*, averaging 6 to 8 feet in length but occasionally exceeding 10 feet, is found in warm seas. It is especially abundant in the Caribbean. The two dorsal fins are about equal in size. Its color is yellowish brown on the back and sides, grading into yellowish white below. Strictly an inshore species, common around docks, in saltwater creeks, and in enclosed sounds, it feeds mostly on fish.

The blue shark, *Prionace glauca*, is a pelagic species, cosmopolitan in tropical, subtropical, and warm-temperature seas. It is found far out at sea and in continental waters and is often seen at the surface, swimming slowly with its first dorsal fin and the tip of its tail out of water. It is primarily a fish-eater. The blue shark has a long, slim, pointed snout and extremely long pectoral fins. The first dorsal is located about midway on the body—far back compared to other members of the family. This shark is also distinguished by its brilliant blue upper parts. A length of 10 feet is not uncommon, with reports of some measuring as much as 20 feet.

Perhaps the best known of the requiem sharks is the tiger shark, *Galeocerdo cuvieri*; specimens 18 feet long are not uncommon. The tiger shark lives in warm and tropical seas around the world. Small specimens up to about 5 or 6 feet long have tigerlike stripes and blotches on their sides and back, even on the high dorsal fin and the lunate upper lobe of the tail fin. In older sharks these markings become faint. The tiger shark's snout is blunt, appearing almost sawed off. Development is ovoviviparous. Broods are very large, containing as many as 30 to 50 embryos.

A voracious feeder and one of the most dangerous sharks, the tiger shark will attack almost anything that moves. It is also a scavenger. Stomachs of these sharks have revealed an astonishing variety of items, from cans and boots to bags of coal and parts of human bodies. The tiger shark is obviously so indiscriminate in its diet that it gobbles indigestibles as readily as it does edibles. Until recent years, the tiger shark was harvested in large numbers commercially both for its hide, which is made into leather, and for the oil from its liver.

The soupfin shark, *Galeorhinus zyopterus*, grows to a length of about 6½ feet. It is dark gray above, white

Smooth dogfish *(Mustelus canis)*
up to 5 ft (150 cm)

Underside of head of *M. canis*

below, and black on forward edges of dorsal and pectoral fins. In previous years it was heavily harvested for its valuable oil, rich in vitamin A. The catch reached its peak during World War II when the shark was probably known best as the oil shark. Common along the California coast, it has long been prized by Orientals for its fins. These are skinned, defleshed, and sun-cured to preserve the translucent cartilage. The fins are then used in cooking to prepare the broth in the high-priced gourmet dish, sharkfin soup.

In Australian waters, the school shark, *G. australis*, is similar in appearance, habits, and usefulness to the soupfin shark. Some authorities believe it is actually the same species.

The finetooth shark, *Aprionodon isodon*, is easily recognized among the Carcharhinidae by its slender, symmetrical smooth-edged teeth and very long gill openings. It ranges widely on both sides of the Atlantic. This shark is primarily a tropical species that strays north in the summer.

The distinctive characteristics of the moderately large night shark, *Hypoprion signatus*, are a very long, pointed snout, smooth-cusped teeth with the uppers strongly serrated at the base, and a low mid-dorsal ridge. This shark is an Atlantic form, best known off the coast of Cuba, where it is caught well off shore at depths greater than 150 fathoms and only at night. It strays northward in warm weather.

The smooth dogfishes form a group so distinctive from the other requiem sharks that they are often placed in a separate family, Triakidae. In the smooth dogfishes, the second dorsal fin is smaller than the first, as in other requiem sharks, but it is distinctly larger than the anal fin. Members of the genus *Mustelus* are separated from others of this family by their low, rounded teeth, arranged in mosaic. All of the more than two dozen species are rather small, none exceeding a length of 5 feet. They occur in warm and warm-temperate seas.

The smooth dogfish, *Mustelus canis*, is common along the mid-Atlantic coast, with stragglers southward to Uruguay. It is gray or brown and has the ability to change its color slowly to achieve a better match with its background. Rarely is this species found in water more than 50 feet deep, and it may stray into brackish waters of rivers and estuaries. The teeth of the smooth dogfish and its relatives are adapted for crushing mollusks and crustaceans, their principal food. Similar to all other sharks, they find their food mainly by its odor.

The Florida smoothhound, *M. norrisi*, lives in the shallow waters off the Florida peninsula. The spotted shark, *M. punctulatus*, about 5 feet in length, occurs from the Mediterranean southward along the African coast. Three species occur off the Pacific coast of North America—the gray smoothhound, *M. californicus*, which attains a length of no more than 3 feet; the slightly larger (to about 5 feet) sicklefin smoothhound, *M. lunulatus*; and the brown smoothhound, *M. henlei*. The brown smoothhound is probably the most abundant shark along the California coast; it rarely exceeds a length of 3 feet.

The slightly larger leopard shark, *Triakis semifasciatus*, heavily marked with black crossbars and blotches, is found in the same range as the Pacific smoothhound. A similar species, with less pronounced bars, *T. scyllia*, is found off the coasts of Asia and Japan.

The whitetip shark, *Triaenodon obseus*, of the Pacific and Indian oceans and also found in the Red Sea, has distinctly white-tipped dorsal and caudal fins.

Family Sphyrnidae
hammerhead sharks

Hammerheads are clearly distinguished from all other sharks by their flattened heads, extended in the typical species into hammerlike lobes on each side. At its tip, each lobe bears an eye. In other features, the hammerheads resemble requiem sharks. Hammerheads are swift swimmers, commonly being the first to follow a trace of blood to its source. Hammerheads are considered dangerous; several attacks on humans are documented. They prowl shallow warm seas, sometimes wandering into cooler regions when the water is warmed in summer; but they return quickly to subtropical and tropical haunts during cold months. Confusion exists at present about the number of species of hammerheads. Apparently the whole group stands in need of critical revision. Five species are recognized from the waters off North America.

The smooth hammerhead, *Sphyrna zygaena*, is cosmopolitan in subtropical and tropical seas. Along the East Coast of North America, it sometimes roams as far north as Cape Cod in summer but is not generally found north of Cape Hatteras. Off the California coast, it occurs south of Point Conception. Gray to brownish, the smooth hammerhead averages about 9 feet in length, occasionally attaining a length of 12 feet or more.

The great hammerhead, *S. mokarran*, inhabiting the same waters as the smooth hammerhead, commonly reaches a length of 15 feet. Both species seem to have a special fondness for stingrays, but they will literally eat anything that moves and can be caught.

The scalloped hammerhead, *S. lewini*, averaging about 6 feet in length, occurs in the warm Atlantic; it is especially common off the coast of Florida. The mallets are much less distinct than in either the smooth hammerhead or the great hammerhead, and their edges are scalloped.

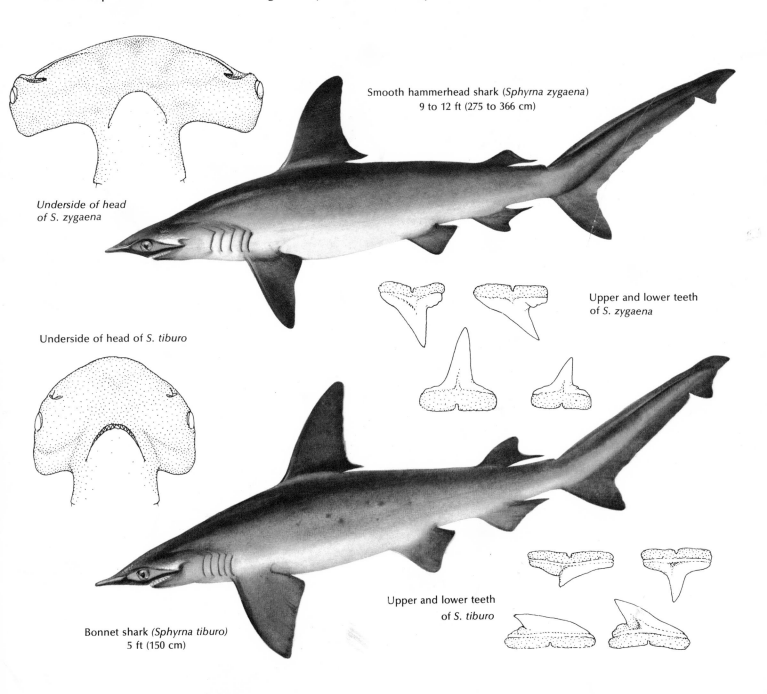

Underside of head
of S. zygaena

Smooth hammerhead shark (Sphyrna zygaena)
9 to 12 ft (275 to 366 cm)

Upper and lower teeth
of S. zygaena

Underside of head of S. tiburo

Upper and lower teeth
of S. tiburo

Bonnet shark (Sphyrna tiburo)
5 ft (150 cm)

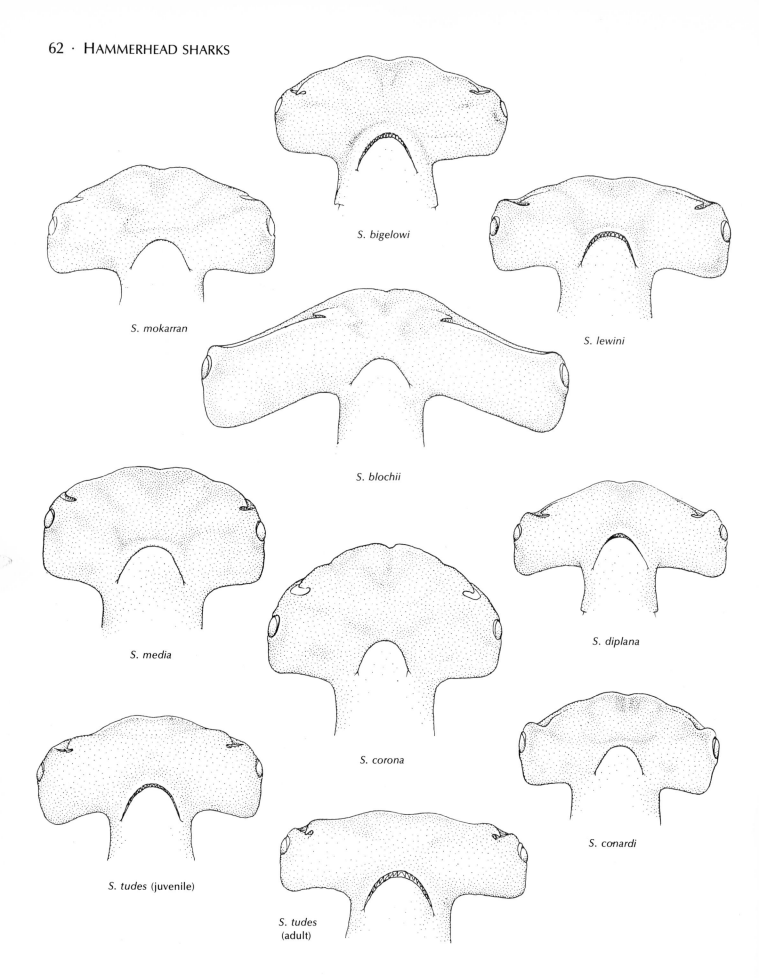

S. bigelowi

S. mokarran

S. lewini

S. blochii

S. media

S. corona

S. diplana

S. tudes (juvenile)

S. tudes
(adult)

S. conardi

HEADS SHAPES OF THE FAMILY SPHYRNIDAE

The bonnet shark, *S. tiburo*, about 5 feet long, has still less prominent lobes; the front of its head is more rounded and shovellike. The bonnet shark is found more regularly in shallow waters than are the more typical hammerheads.

The smalleye hammerhead, *S. tudes,* was recorded as appearing in the Gulf of Mexico.

Family Pristiophoridae
saw sharks

The members of this small family of sharks are found off the coasts of Australia, Japan, and South Africa. Like the sawfishes, which are rays, saw sharks have an extended snout that is toothed along each side. But in saw sharks—and only four species are known—the pectoral fins are small, with the gill openings located just in front of them; in sawfishes, the pectoral fins are large, and the gills are on the underside. Saw sharks also have two long barbels, or whiskers, on the underside of the saw, and the teeth along the edges of the saw are of two sizes—large and small, alternating.

The common species off the coast of Australia is *Pristiophorus cirratus*, attaining a length of 4 feet. It is often caught commercially, for its flesh is of excellent quality. Species off the coast of Africa are generally large, to 10 feet or more.

Family Squalidae
dogfish sharks

Dogfish sharks are widely distributed in the Atlantic, Pacific, and Indian oceans, in tropical to subarctic and subantarctic latitudes. Some of the many species live in relatively shallow water close to shore; others inhabit the deep sea. They vary in length from an average of 2 to 3 feet to a maximum of about 21 feet. One of their chief anatomical characteristics is the lack of an anal fin. Development is usually ovoviviparous but is probably oviparous in some cases. There is much confusion and disagreement among scientists concerning the dogfish sharks; some "lump" them into one family, others split the group into several families. The American Fisheries Society recognizes eight species inhabiting North American waters—five from the Atlantic, two from the Pacific, and another that ranges in both oceans.

The spiny dogfish, *Squalus acanthias*, is one of the most widely distributed members of the clan inhabiting the cool temperate waters of the Atlantic and Pacific in the coastal waters of North America, Asia, and Europe. Along the North American coasts, it seldom strays south of Point Conception, California, or south of Cape Hatteras on the Atlantic coast. The spiny dogfish averages 2 to 3 feet in length; occasionally, however, specimens 5 feet long are caught. Females grow larger than males. In color, most of them are dark gray or brownish gray with whitish or whitish yellow spots along the sides.

The spiny dogfish is considered a great nuisance by both commercial and sport fishermen. In large schools they invade fishing grounds regularly and mutilate fishes caught in nets or by hooks. The harvest loss and the damage to fishing gear amounts to millions of dollars annually. In many fishing areas, such as off the coasts of Maine and Nova Scotia, sport fishermen especially despise the spiny dogfish because these small sharks can appear in great profusion. They take the baited hook as soon as it comes close to the bottom, thereby making it impossible to catch such desirable fishes as cods, pollocks, and flounders.

Attempting to eradicate the marauding dogfish, bounty programs have been established but have had little or no effect on the total population of this pest. Europeans have perhaps the happiest solution: the dogfish is harvested commercially and millions of pounds are sold annually as food. They are usually sold

Saw shark *(Pristiophorus cirratus)*
4 to 10 ft (122 to 305 cm)

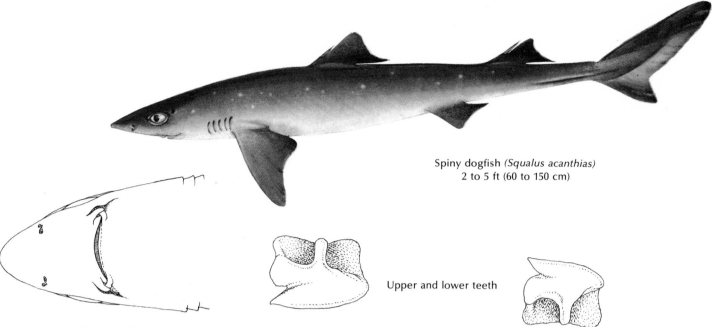

Spiny dogfish *(Squalus acanthias)*
2 to 5 ft (60 to 150 cm)

Upper and lower teeth

Underside of head of *S. acanthias*

in markets as "grayfish." Like other species in this family, the spiny dogfish is a squirming creature when caught in a net or on a hook and is often successful at stabbing with its spines. The wounds are slow to heal, partly because of the mild toxin that flows into the wound from the spine and also because of secondary infections.

The Cuban dogfish, *S. cubensis*, is closely related to the spiny dogfish but inhabits Caribbean waters, usually staying in rather deep, cool water. Some biologists do not recognize it as a separate species, simply as a variation to the spiny dogfish.

The piked dogfish, *S. megalops*, is an Australian species that is caught commercially and sold in markets. It, too, may be a variation of the widely distributed spiny dogfish.

Dogfish sharks of the genus *Etmopterus* have their dorsal spines largely exposed. They live in deep waters, and most of them, perhaps all, possess luminous organs. Supposedly, there are about a dozen species of these small, deeply pigmented sharks, but they resemble one another so closely that some may be one and the same fish.

Among the better known, the blackbelly dogfish, *E.*

Portuguese shark *(Centroscymnus coelolepis)*
3 ft (90 cm)

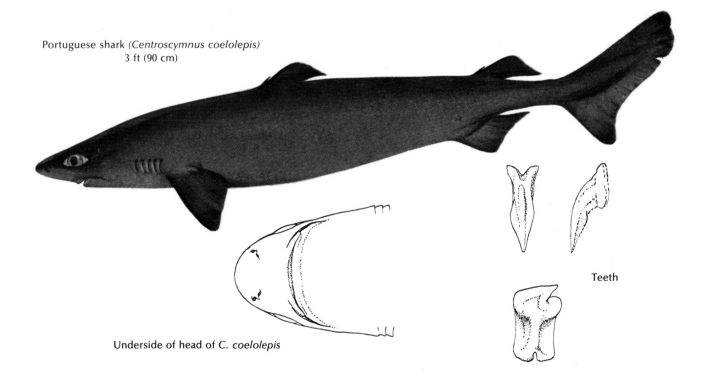

Teeth

Underside of head of *C. coelolepis*

hillianus, one of the smallest sharks, reaches a length of about 12 inches. It is found in the deep waters of the Atlantic and Caribbean, from Maryland and Virginia southward through the West Indies. A similar species, *E. spinax*, inhabits the eastern Atlantic from the Mediterranean to South Africa.

Within this group there is another foot-long species, the green dogfish, *E. virens*, found in the northern Gulf of Mexico. Its belly is marked with iridescent green, and it has light bluish gray stripes along its sides and back.

The Portuguese shark, *Centroscymnus coelolepis*, is a dark chocolate brown below as well as above. It grows to about 3 feet long and has been taken in the Atlantic at depths of more than 8,000 feet. It also comes into shallower water and was fished for commercially off the coast of Portugal, which explains its name. The black dogfish, *C. fabricii*, is similar in size and inhabits the same waters as the Portuguese shark.

The prickly dogfish, *Oxynotus bruniensis*, found off Australia and New Zealand, is an uncommon 2-foot species that is easily identified by its high, saillike first dorsal fin and by its extremely rough skin.

Members of the genus *Somniosus* are here placed in the family Squalidae; some scientists, however, prefer to consider them in a separate family, Dalatiidae. This group is known collectively as sleeper sharks or spineless dogfish. Their first and second dorsal fins are smaller than are those of other dogfishes, and there is no spine in front of the second dorsal or, in most species, in front of the first dorsal. The gill slits are extremely short, and the teeth in the upper and lower jaws are distinctly different in size and shape. Some of the species inhabit deep water and have luminous spots on their body. All are sluggish.

The kitefin shark, *Dalatias licha*, also placed in the family Dalatiidae by some investigators, reaches a size of about 5 feet. It is rare in the western Atlantic, but it is well distributed in the eastern Atlantic and is common off the Mediterranean coasts of France and Portugal and off western Ireland. In waters off South Africa, in the New Zealand–Australian region, and in Japanese waters it is represented by allies so close that they appear to be identical with the Atlantic form.

The Greenland shark, *Somniosus microcephalus*, lives in the Arctic waters of the Atlantic, rarely straying southward. This harmless shark is so large that it cannot be confused with any other dogfish shark in the Atlantic. An average length is 10 feet, but there are numerous records of Greenland sharks 16 to 18 feet long. The largest recorded is 21 feet. Presumably this shark spends much of its time lying on or near the bottom, rising only to feed. It makes its meals of just about anything available: various crustaceans, cods, halibuts, salmons, capelins, herrings, skates, and even an occasional seal, which is truly astonishing because the shark moves so slowly. The Greenland shark also feeds on dead animals. This shark has been utilized chiefly for its liver oil. In Greenland the flesh is also dried for dog food, and in Iceland small amounts have been consumed for human food in the past. The flesh produces

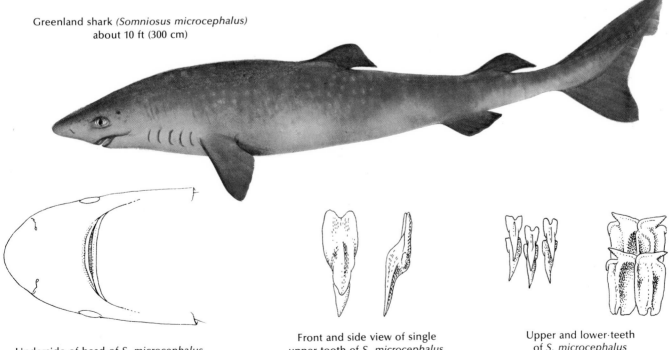

Greenland shark *(Somniosus microcephalus)*
about 10 ft (300 cm)

Underside of head of *S. microcephalus*

Front and side view of single
upper tooth of *S. microcephalus*

Upper and lower teeth
of *S. microcephalus*

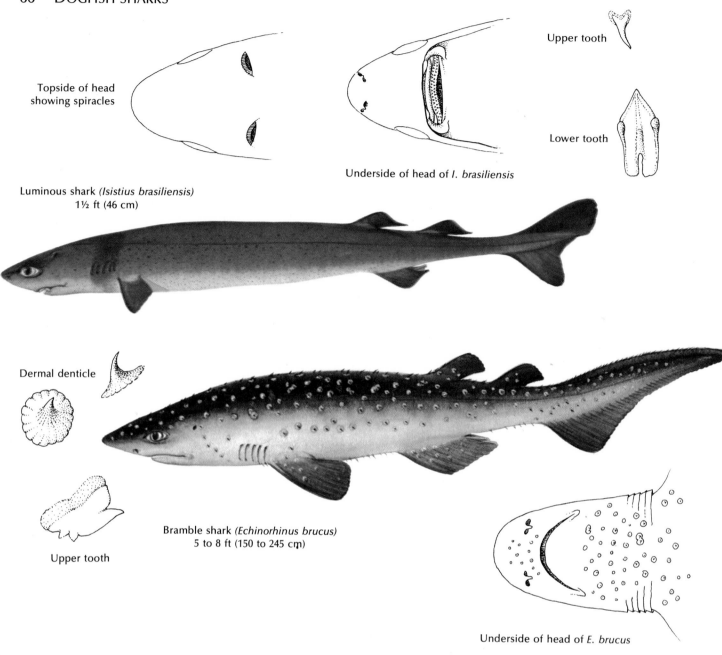

Topside of head
showing spiracles

Upper tooth

Lower tooth

Underside of head of *I. brasiliensis*

Luminous shark *(Isistius brasiliensis)*
1½ ft (46 cm)

Dermal denticle

Bramble shark *(Echinorhinus brucus)*
5 to 8 ft (150 to 245 cm)

Upper tooth

Underside of head of *E. brucus*

"a sort of intoxicant poisoning" if eaten fresh; but if boiled several times, the water from each cooking discarded, and the flesh then dried, it is safe to eat. The Eskimos prefer it when the dried flesh is allowed to season awhile.

The Pacific sleeper shark, *S. pacificus*, closely related to the Greenland shark, is found in northern Pacific waters. The Mediterranean sleeper shark, *S. rostratus*, occurs only in the Mediterranean. Another species, the Antarctic sleeper shark, *S. antarcticus*, has been identified from only one specimen.

The luminous shark, *Isistius brasiliensis*, is also in the sleeper-shark group. This 1½-foot pelagic species is of special interest because of the bright green lumines-

cence given off from the underside of its body. It is cosmopolitan in the tropical and subtropical belts of all three oceans.

The bramble or alligator shark, *Echinorhinus brucus*, is another spiny dogfish that is sometimes placed in a separate family, Echinorhinidae. Its hide is covered with dermal denticles in the form of flat shields, varying in diameter and each with one and sometimes two sharp-pointed spines in the center. It is dark gray or brown above with reflections of violet, silver, gold or coppery yellow. The dorsal fins lack spines, and there is no anal fin. Averaging 5 to 8 feet in length but known to reach a length of 10 feet occasionally, the bramble shark is rare off the North American Pacific and Atlantic coasts. It is seen more regularly along the eastern Atlantic, including the Mediterranean, and also in the Indo-Pacific waters.

A close relative of the bramble shark, the prickly shark, *E. cookei*, ranges from Peru to Moss Landing, California. It has been recorded as reaching a length of 13 feet.

Family Squatinidae
angel sharks

Angel sharks, also commonly called monkfish, are flat-bodied, like rays, but other features identify them clearly as sharks. Their gill slits, for example, are on the sides of the neck region, curving onto the underside, and their pectoral fins are free rather than being attached to the head as in rays. Like rays, their two dorsal fins are small and are located far back on the body. They have a row of spines down the middle of the back and a large spiracle behind each eye. They have no anal fin.

Angel sharks swim by using their bodies and tails, as typical sharks do; rays, in contrast, are propelled forward by undulating their pectoral fins. Angel sharks live on or close to the bottom, often burying themselves partially in the sand or mud. Development is ovoviviparous. Only one genus is known.

Angel sharks are not common anywhere; thus they attract considerable attention when caught. The Atlantic angel shark, *Squatina dumerili*, ranges along the East Coast of the United States from New England to southern Florida and the Gulf of Mexico; it is also reported from Jamaica. It can reach a length of about 5 feet but is usually shorter.

The European angel shark, *S. squatina*, occurring in the Atlantic off Europe, attains a length of as much as 8 feet. The Pacific angel shark, *S. californica*, reaching a length of about 5 feet, is found from Alaska to Chile. The orange angel shark, *S. tergocellata*, of Australian waters, is yellowish orange with large brown rings and small blue spots over its body. An estimated half dozen other species of angel sharks occur in Indo-Pacific waters.

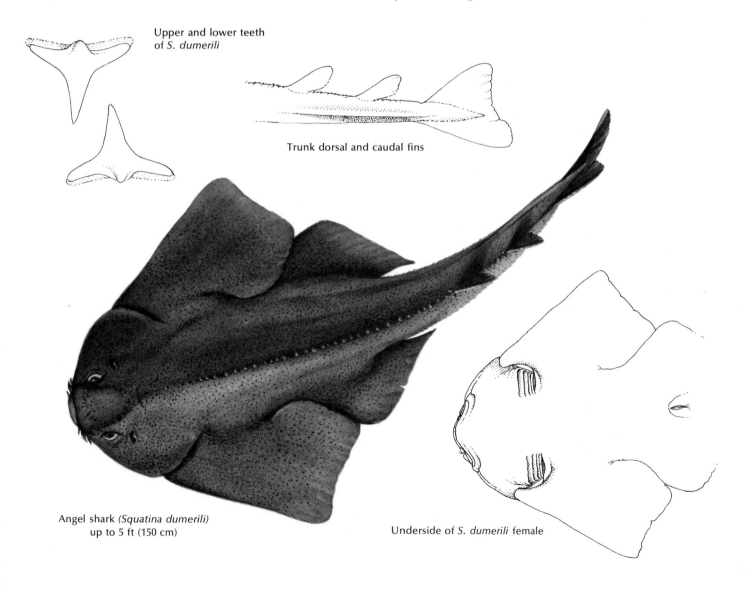

Upper and lower teeth
of *S. dumerili*

Trunk dorsal and caudal fins

Angel shark *(Squatina dumerili)*
up to 5 ft (150 cm)

Underside of *S. dumerili* female

ORDER RAJIFORMES

Skates and Rays

Although the Rajiformes are generally referred to as skates and rays, the order includes sawfishes, guitar fishes, electric rays, skates, stingrays, eagle rays, and mantas. Some of the dominant distinguishing features of this group are gill openings wholly on the ventral surface and forward edges of the pectoral fins connected with the sides of the head and situated forward, past the five pairs of gill openings; eyeballs not free from the upper edges of the orbits, as they are in sharks; no anal fin.

Most Rajiformes are easily recognized by their form. Their bodies are flattened dorso-ventrally, and the pectoral fins extend widely and seem to be part of the body. The tail section is more or less defined from the body, the eyes and spiracles are on the top side, and the mouth and entire lengths of the gill openings are situated on the bottom side. The sawfishes, however, are sharklike in general appearance. They are classified among the order Rajiformes on skeletal considerations as well as for the relationship of pectorals to the gills and because of the absence of upper eyelids. The shape of the majority of guitarfishes resembles a cross between sharklike and skatelike forms.

Some members of this order have no dorsal fin, others have one or two. Some possess a distinct caudal (tail) fin, others do not. The spiracles are larger than those of most sharks and are always located on top of the head. The majority have well-developed eyes. In a few species, however, the eyes are degenerate. Without exception, the order Rajiformes has five pairs of gill openings. Some have smooth skins; others are covered with thorny or prickly protrusions; and some have tails armed with dangerous, saw-edged spines. The shape of the teeth varies. Teeth may resemble thorns, knobs or plates or be sharply pointed. They may be in bands, transverse rows, or mosaic patterns. None has luminescent organs, but some members of this group have electric organs.

In those Rajiformes that lie on the bottom or bury themselves in the sand, the spiracles are important in the process of respiration. Water taken in through these passages passes over the gills and out through the gill openings. Skates, however, may hold their heads slightly above the bottom when resting and take in some water through the mouth. Mantas swim more freely and inhale water mostly or completely through the mouth; they have proportionately smaller spiracles.

The members of this clan range in size from only a few inches to giant mantas with a breadth of about 23 feet and a weight of over 3,000 pounds. The spectacularly armed sawfishes reach a length of over 20 feet.

The mode of locomotion varies within the group. Skates and stingrays are propelled forward smoothly along the bottom by undulating the pectoral fins from front to rear. Guitarfishes use their tails chiefly in swimming, with an assist from the pectorals. Mantas and eagle rays, with their more pointedly shaped pectoral fins, swim with a flapping motion of the fins or "wings," more or less resembling bird flight. In the process of swift motion, some eagle rays and mantas hurl themselves into the air, often doing a complete somersault, one of the most spectacular sights of the sea. Sawfishes swim chiefly by lateral undulations of the posterior portion of their trunk, aided by the caudal fin or tail and to a lesser degree by the pectorals.

All members of this order effect fertilization internally; the act is facilitated by a pair of claspers developed along the inner edges of the male's pelvic fins, in the same manner as it is in sharks. The inner edges have deep grooves, with the edges more or less overlapping, thereby aiding the transportation of the sperm into the female.

Development in the skate family is oviparous. The eggs encased in horny capsules are commonly seen washed up on sandy beaches. As far as is known, however, all other members of this order are ovoviviparous—that is, embryos develop inside the oviducts of the female until ready for extrusion. In this type of development there is no placental attachment between mother and young.

Most Rajiformes live on the bottom or close to it and are comparatively sluggish. Some of them lie buried in the sand or mud most of the time and are poor swimmers. The skates are capable of swift propulsion when necessary, although they usually swim slowly and close to the bottom. Sawfishes also spend a good part of the time along the bottom, but rise to pursue fish at mid-depths or higher. The eagle rays are quite active and often swim close to the surface, although they feed on the bottom. In opposition to its close cousins, the mantas seem to have abandoned bottom living and spend most of their lives swimming near the surface or not too far beneath it.

Skates and rays subsist on a variety of animal food, including all available invertebrates that inhabit sandy or muddy bottoms. The eagle rays, as a group, prefer hard-shelled mollusks, while the sawfishes occasionally will leave their bottom foraging to crash into a school of closely packed fish. The electric rays are strictly fish-eaters, sometimes taking surprisingly large prey in comparison to their size. The mantas, including the giants of the group, feed on tiny plankton, small crustaceans, and small fishes. It is interesting to note that their mode of feeding is similar to that of the huge whale sharks and basking sharks. Food is carried into the mouth by the intake of water and sifted by the so-called prebranchial apparatus, as the water passes over the gills and out through the gill openings.

Commercially, skates and rays are not of much value. Small quantities are used from time to time as fertilizer and as bait for lobster traps along the New England coast. When caught along the Atlantic coasts of the United States and Canada, the great majority are thrown back. There is a greater demand for skates in northern Europe, where thousands of pounds are taken annually. Rays in considerable variety are available in fish markets in various tropical areas of the world, but the quantity used is small. These bottom dwellers can be a great nuisance to fishermen because they take baited hooks meant for other fishes. Also, they are capable of inflicting a painful wound with their serrated spines when stepped on or handled incautiously.

Rajiformes are widely distributed in latitude and depth in the Atlantic, Pacific, and Indian oceans, including adjacent seas. They also cover a broad thermal range, from cold polar waters to warm tropical seas. The most numerous group, the skates, are found primarily in the temperate belts of the two hemispheres, while their cousins are found predominantly in tropical and subtropical waters. The electric rays may be grouped as occupying an intermediate geographical position.

As an order, Rajiformes constitutes a saltwater group, but several species of stingrays have colonized in fresh water in the lower portions of South American rivers draining into the Atlantic. They may be found far up the rivers—a couple of hundred miles from the sea up the Ruppununi River in British Guiana, for example. Sawfishes also are often found in fresh water.

The basic grouping and general position in classification of the order Rajiformes is today fairly stable, although over the last fifty years opinions by scientists have differed widely as to the number of subdivisions recognized and names employed for these groups.

Family Pristidae
sawfishes

These sharklike rays have a long snout that is formidably armored with sharp teeth along each side. Typical rays, sawfishes are bottom dwellers, but they will rise toward the surface to slash their way through a school of mullets or other fishes, turning to pick up any that have been stunned or wounded. Sometimes they succeed in impaling several fishes on the toothed snout; these are then scraped off on the bottom and eaten. The long snout is also used to probe into sand or mud to dig up shellfish. If molested, a sawfish turns this food-getting snout into a powerful weapon of defense and may inflict serious injury, but there is no evidence of an unprovoked attack by sawfishes on bathers anywhere in the world. Like rays, the sawfishes have gill slits on the underside of the body on each side just behind the mouth, and the large pectoral fins are joined broadly to the head. The body is long and slim, more like that of a shark, however. The several species of sawfishes are cosmopolitan in distribution in warm to tropical seas, inhabiting shallow waters and straying into brackish or even fresh water. A sizable population has become landlocked in Lake Nicaragua.

The smalltooth sawfish, *Pristis pectinata*, is commonly 15 feet long, sometimes reaching a length of 20 feet. It may weigh as much as 800 pounds. This species is common throughout warm Atlantic waters, from the Mediterranean southward to Africa and from Cape Hatteras to Brazil. The largetooth sawfish, *P. perotteti*, also an Atlantic species, is similar to the smalltooth but slightly larger, most notably its teeth in proportion to its body.

Species that live in Indo-Pacific waters, however, are the giants of the clan. Huge specimens of *P. microdon* and *P. cuspidatus* are found in Thailand rivers. In rivers along the African coast, *P. pristis* is caught regularly, often many miles from the sea. An Australian species, *P.*

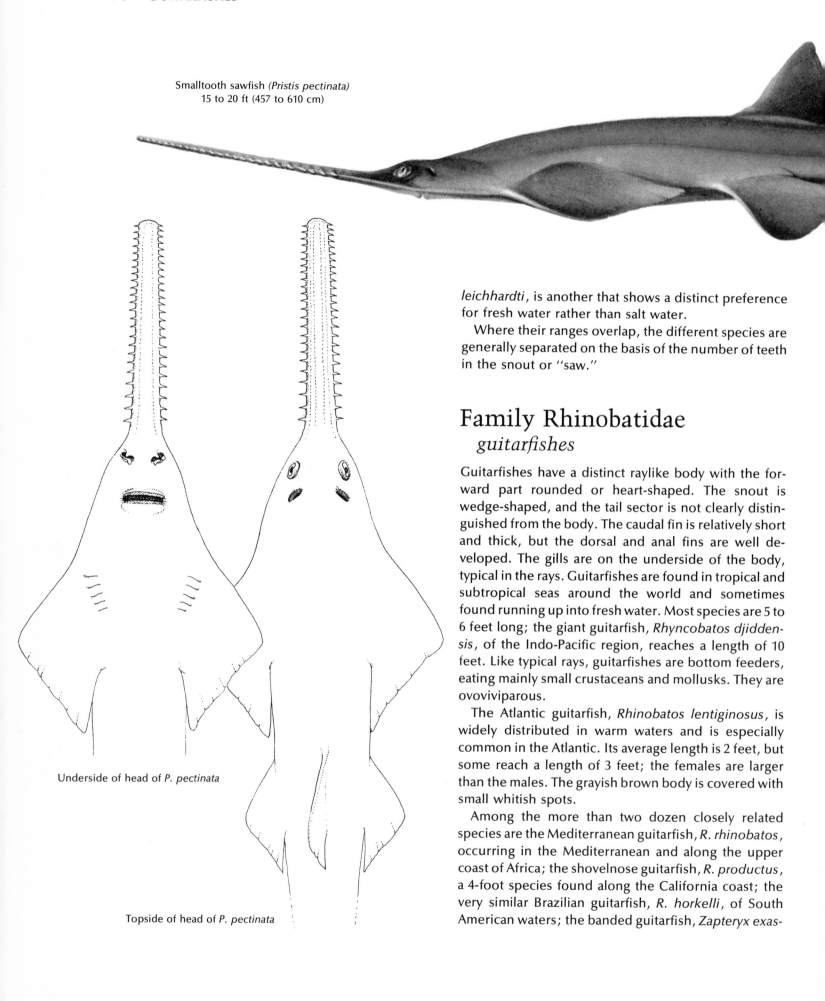

Smalltooth sawfish *(Pristis pectinata)*
15 to 20 ft (457 to 610 cm)

Underside of head of *P. pectinata*

Topside of head of *P. pectinata*

leichhardti, is another that shows a distinct preference for fresh water rather than salt water.

Where their ranges overlap, the different species are generally separated on the basis of the number of teeth in the snout or "saw."

Family Rhinobatidae
guitarfishes

Guitarfishes have a distinct raylike body with the forward part rounded or heart-shaped. The snout is wedge-shaped, and the tail sector is not clearly distinguished from the body. The caudal fin is relatively short and thick, but the dorsal and anal fins are well developed. The gills are on the underside of the body, typical in the rays. Guitarfishes are found in tropical and subtropical seas around the world and sometimes found running up into fresh water. Most species are 5 to 6 feet long; the giant guitarfish, *Rhyncobatos djiddensis*, of the Indo-Pacific region, reaches a length of 10 feet. Like typical rays, guitarfishes are bottom feeders, eating mainly small crustaceans and mollusks. They are ovoviviparous.

The Atlantic guitarfish, *Rhinobatos lentiginosus*, is widely distributed in warm waters and is especially common in the Atlantic. Its average length is 2 feet, but some reach a length of 3 feet; the females are larger than the males. The grayish brown body is covered with small whitish spots.

Among the more than two dozen closely related species are the Mediterranean guitarfish, *R. rhinobatos*, occurring in the Mediterranean and along the upper coast of Africa; the shovelnose guitarfish, *R. productus*, a 4-foot species found along the California coast; the very similar Brazilian guitarfish, *R. horkelli*, of South American waters; the banded guitarfish, *Zapteryx exas-*

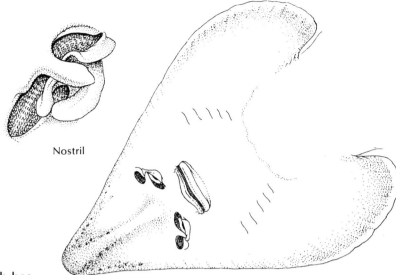

Nostril

Underside of head of *R. lentiginosus*

perata, from Panama into California waters, which has dark bands on its body and a distinctly heart-shaped body disk; and the thornback, *Platyrhinoidis triseriata*, common off southern and Baja California and ranging to San Francisco.

Family Torpedinidae
electric rays

More than 30 species of electric rays inhabit seas throughout the world. Some live at great depths, others in shallow inshore waters. Some are large—as much as 6 feet long and weighing 200 pounds; others are less than a foot long. Eyes are small and functional in most

Side view of tail of the guitarfish

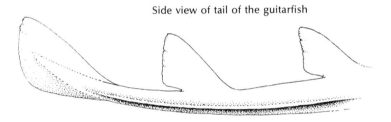

Atlantic guitarfish *(Rhinobatos lentiginosus)*
2 to 3 ft (60 to 90 cm)

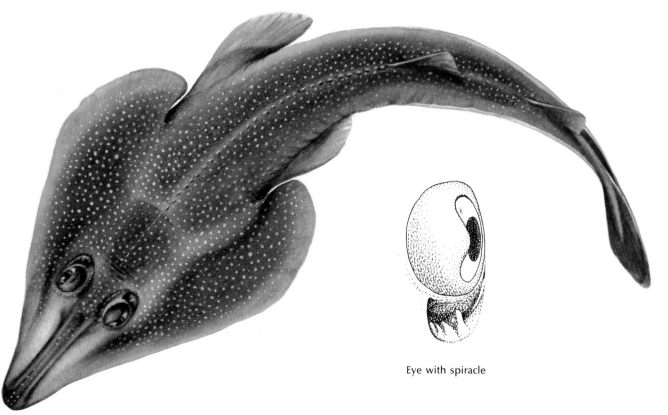

Eye with spiracle

species but rudimentary or obsolete in a few deepwater forms. No electric rays are good swimmers; they spend most of their time partly buried in the sand or mud on the bottom and move only sluggishly. Their bodies are soft and flabby compared to skates and the other rays, and the skin of most species is soft and marked. All share the unusual feature of being able to generate jolting charges of electricity. Development is ovoviviparous.

In all animals, muscles are capable of generating electricity, usually in small, almost immeasurable amounts. Much research has been done on this subject with electric rays, resulting in an extensive literature. The special electric organs in nearly all fishes are derived from muscle tissue. In electric rays, these organs are located in the front half of the body, one on each side. They account for about one-sixth of the fish's total weight. Visible as clear gelatinous masses, easily distinguished from the darker surrounding muscles, they consist of fibrous-walled, hexagonal columns, like a honeycomb, filled with a jellylike matrix. They are partitioned crosswise by connective tissue into numerous units, each of which is connected to a nerve served directly from the brain.

Each unit acts as a battery, or generator, the lower side of the plate negative and the top side positive. On stimulation, all the units discharge simultaneously in one powerful pulse. A large electric ray may have as many as a million generating units in the two organs and can give an initial shock of more than 200 volts. If the shocks are repeated immediately, they become successively weaker as the "battery" literally loses strength. An exhausted ray must rest for a while before it can produce electricity again.

Fishermen, swimmers, divers—many people who have come close to or have tried to handle an electric ray—know the power of these shocks, which apparently serve the rays as protection from would-be predators and as stunning blows to capture prey that would otherwise be too fleet for these slow-moving fishes. Ordinarily, however, these rays eat crustaceans, worms, and similar small animals that can be captured without the need for discharging electricity. Because this is so, it has been suggested, though not clearly established either by observation or research, that these fishes may use electrical signals as a means of species or even sex recognition by small, repeated discharges or as a radarlike means of navigation in murky waters.

Literature on the electric ray includes innumerable references, from classic times onward, to the electrical shocks received by persons contacting these rays. Interestingly, the Greek word for electric ray was *narke*,

from which our word *narcotic* stemmed. The Greeks attributed to the torpedo, or numbfish, many mystical and medicinal powers because they had no understanding of the electrical shocks produced by the fish.

The Atlantic torpedo, *Torpedo nobiliana*, which ranges both sides of the Atlantic as well as into the Mediterranean and southward along the coast of Africa, is the giant of the clan: it averages about 30 pounds in weight, with reports of individuals as much as 6 feet long and weighing 200 pounds. Despite its name, this fish is anything but speedy or torpedolike in our usual interpretation of the word. Like other members of the family, it is *torpid*, its name coming from the Latin word for sluggish. A related 1½-foot species, *T. marmorata*, lives in the Mediterranean and along the Atlantic coast of Europe. The Pacific electric ray, *T. californica*, is similar to the Atlantic species but smaller.

Among the other smaller species are the lesser electric ray, *Narcine brasiliensis*, which is rarely more than a foot long and is found primarily in warmer American waters from North Carolina southward and also in the Gulf of Mexico. It is distinguished from the larger Atlantic torpedo by the numerous dark spots over its body. Each spot has a lighter center.

Other electric rays are: Australian numbfish, *N. tasmaniensis*, of southern Pacific waters; Australian crampfish, *Hypnos monopterygium*; the blind torpedo ray, *Typhlonarke aysoni*, inhabiting waters off New Zealand, which has no functional eyes and "stumps" along the bottom on its thick, leglike ventral fins; and *Diplobatus pictus*, found off the northern coast of South America, an unusual electric ray with a body much like a guitarfish.

Family Rajidae
skates

In skates, the dorsal and anal fins are greatly reduced in size, and the pelvic fins are deeply notched so that they appear as four fins rather than two. The pectoral fins are large and winglike, joined at the front of the head to form a shelflike snout. The tail is moderately slender. Males have long, prominent claspers used in mating.

Skates produce unusual leathery egg cases called sea purses or sailor's purses. At each of the four corners of the case is a thin projection that helps to anchor the case to objects on the sea bottom. These egg cases are nevertheless commonly washed ashore and are among the curios picked up by beach wanderers.

Skates can dart swiftly, when necessary, using their pectoral fins in undulating motions for graceful under-

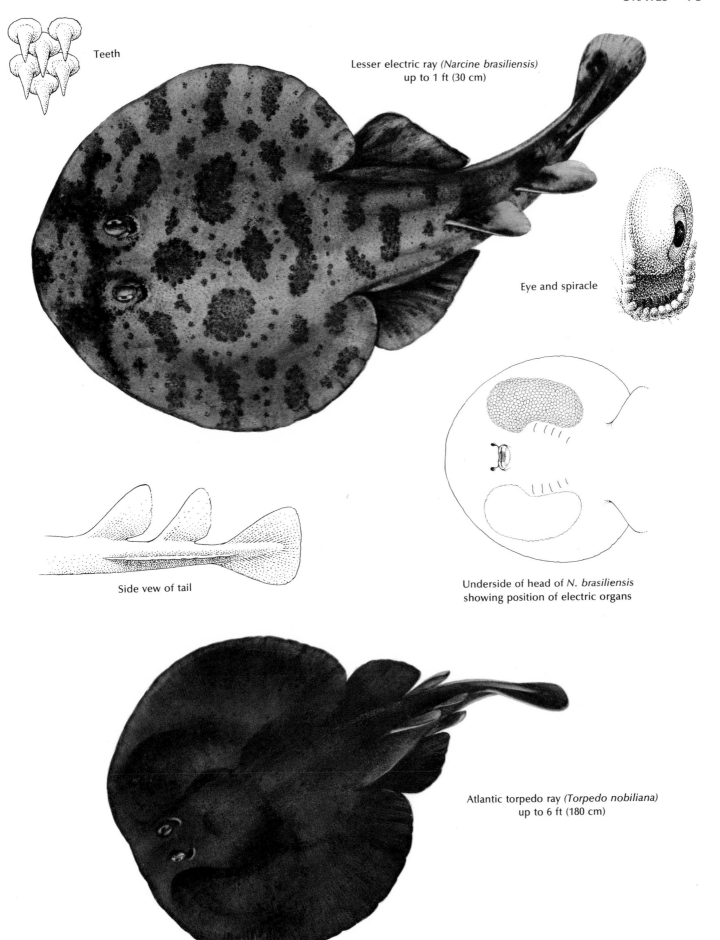

Teeth

Lesser electric ray *(Narcine brasiliensis)*
up to 1 ft (30 cm)

Eye and spiracle

Side vew of tail

Underside of head of *N. brasiliensis*
showing position of electric organs

Atlantic torpedo ray *(Torpedo nobiliana)*
up to 6 ft (180 cm)

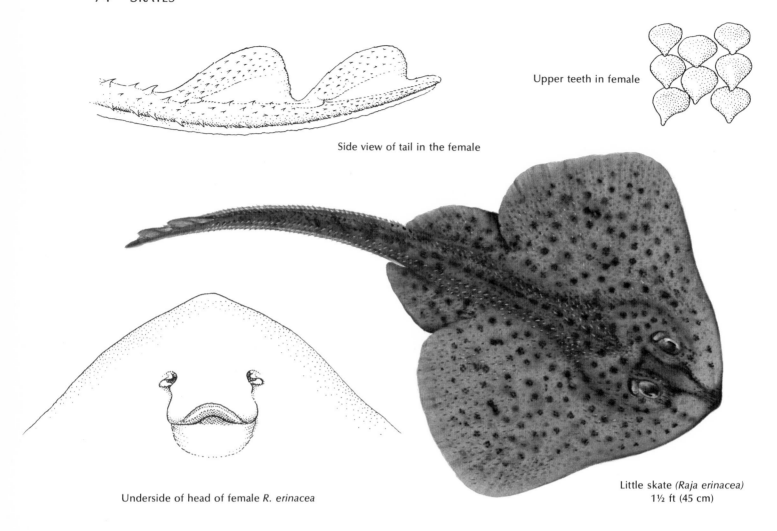

Side view of tail in the female

Upper teeth in female

Underside of head of female *R. erinacea*

Little skate *(Raja erinacea)*
1½ ft (45 cm)

Common skate *(Raja batis)*
1 to 1½ ft (30 to 45 cm)

water propulsion. But they are essentially bottom dwellers, usually lying quietly half buried in the sand or mud during the daylight hours and stirring to feed at night, although they also take the fisherman's bait during daytime. Skates are brown or grayish, commonly mottled, blending well with the bottom. When they rest, they usually fan the sand or soft sediment as they settle so that only their eyes and spiracles are above the surface. By forming a suction with their body, they can cling to the bottom so tightly that they are difficult to dislodge. If forced out of hiding, they squirm and twist, frequently managing to impale a victim with their tail spine. A few species can deliver a mild shock, their electric organs located in the tail and connected to spinal nerves.

Skates sometimes eat fishes, making their catches by darting up quickly from the bottom and then holding the fishes down with their bodies until they can grab them with the mouth, which is on the underside of the skate's body. Mostly, however, skates feed on shellfish and crustaceans which they secure by grubbing them from the bottom. Skates have flat, pavementlike teeth for crushing the shells. In many countries, skates are caught commercially and are prized as food.

Most skates live in rather shallow water and close to shore, but there are also some deepwater species. The largest genus is *Raja*, containing more than a hundred species that are found in cool to temperate waters throughout the world. The Pacific abyssal skate, *R. bathyphila*, is one of the deepwater species; it has been taken at depths greater than 7,000 feet. Other species have been hauled up from depths as great as 20,000 feet.

The little skate, *R. erinacea*, is the most common species along the Atlantic coast of North America. About 1½ feet long and weighing only about a pound, it has a row of spines along its back, from just behind the eyes to the end of the tail fin. This has earned it the common name of hedgehog skate.

The big skate, *R. binoculata*, reaches a length of 8 feet. It is found along the Pacific coast from Alaska to Point Conception off the California coast.

Much more abundant in California waters than the big skate is the California skate, *R. inornata*, averaging only about 2 feet in length and with four to five rows of prickly spines on its tail.

Also notably thorny is the clearnose skate, *R. eglanteria*, with spines on its back as well as on its tail. This species is common along the middle and northeastern Atlantic coast in summer but retreats to warmer waters off Florida and in the Caribbean in winter. It gets its name from the translucent areas on each side of its snout.

The barndoor skate, *R. laevis*, one of the most aggressive of all skates, grows to a length of about 5 feet. It is common from Newfoundland to Cape Hatteras and is often caught on baited hooks. The barndoor skate's counterpart off the coast of Europe is the common skate, *R. batis*, which is harvested commercially.

The longnose skate, *R. rhina*, found from southern California to Alaska, is distinguished by its long, tapered snout. It may reach a length of 5 feet, which is large for a skate.

The winter, or eyed, skate, *R. ocellata*, about 2½ feet long, is an Atlantic species that is marked with numerous eyelike spots on its upper surface. The roundel skate, *R. texana*, from the Gulf of Mexico, has one eyespot on the upper surface of each "wing."

The European longnosed skate, *R. oxyrinchus*, which grows to 4 feet long, is brownish and mottled, its most distinctive feature being its long, pointed snout. It occurs off the coasts of Africa and Europe.

Two other species, principally European but found also along the northern coast of Africa, are the thornback skate, *R. clavata*, and the European skate, *R. miraletus*. About 22 species of skates are generally accepted to inhabit the waters off the United States and Canada; 10 are in the Pacific and 12 in the Atlantic.

Family Dasyatidae
stingrays

Stingrays are best known for their long, slim, whiplike tails that are armed with one to several spines near the base. When caught or stepped on, a stingray lashes its tail and invariably manages to impale a spine in its molester. Poison from glands along the grooves on each side of the spine flows into the wound, adding additional and excruciating pain to the injury. The venom should be flushed from the wound as soon as possible, and it is best to see a doctor for treatment and antibiotics. Deaths have resulted from untreated stingray wounds, particularly when they have been inflicted in the trunk area rather than on the limbs.

Stingrays generally lie on the bottom, almost completely buried in the sand or soft sediment. Camouflaged also by their grayish brown, often mottled coloration, they are almost impossible to see, even when a large school has settled in an area and literally paved the bottom.

Nearly a hundred species of stingrays are distributed in warm, shallow waters around the world. Eleven species frequent American waters—three in the Pacific, seven in the Atlantic, and one found in both oceans. A few stray into brackish or even into fresh water. They range in size from species that measure only a foot across their wings to others that have spans as great as 7 feet. In nearly all species, the body disk, including the winglike pectoral fins, is nearly round. Although stingrays feed on worms, the main items of diet are crustaceans and mollusks, which they crush between their flat-topped teeth. A few stingrays are active and aggressive enough to catch fish.

One of the most common stingrays along the Atlantic coast of North America is the bluntnose stingray, *Dasyatis sayi*, which measures about 3 feet across its pectorals. It ranges from Brazil to Cape Hatteras, sometimes straying into cooler waters during the warmer months of the year.

The Atlantic stingray, or stingaree, *D. sabina*, measures only slightly more than a foot across its wings, which are very rounded. The snout is pointed and is larger than in most stingrays. There is a dark band down the middle of the back, which also bears numerous

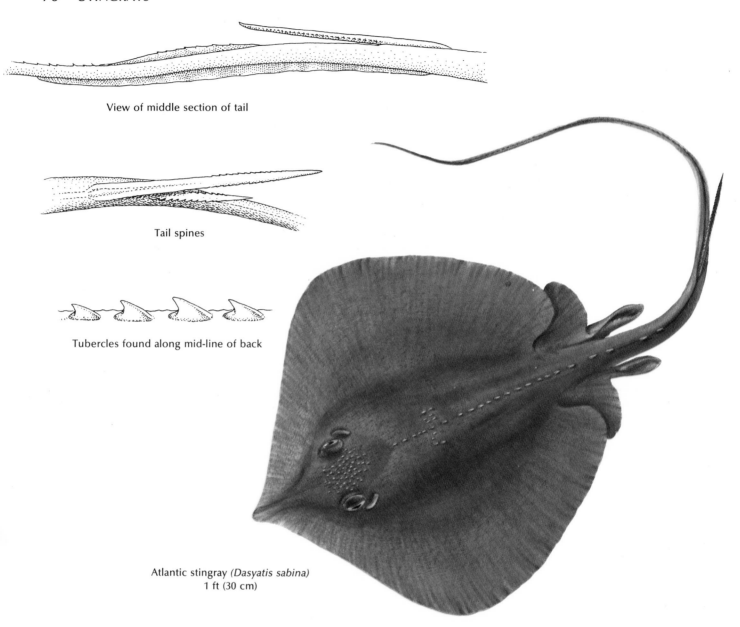

View of middle section of tail

Tail spines

Tubercles found along mid-line of back

Atlantic stingray (Dasyatis sabina)
1 ft (30 cm)

small, prickly spines. Otherwise the body color is almost uniformly yellowish brown. The Atlantic stingray is found in the Gulf of Mexico and the Caribbean, ranging northward along the Atlantic coast to Cape Hatteras and, rarely, even farther north.

More common than the Atlantic stingray and in the same general area is the southern stingray, *D. americana*, which averages about 3 feet wide. On the underside of its tail, just behind the spine, are finlike folds; and above them, the tail is keeled.

North of Cape Hatteras is the still larger roughtail stingray, *D. centroura*, averaging 5 feet across its pectorals and sometimes larger. The tail of one giant specimen that was 7 feet in length was broken, but it was estimated to be about 14 feet long! Except for size, the roughtail stingray is almost identical to the southern stingray. The young are born alive.

The Australian smooth stingray, *D. brevirostris*, is another giant of the clan, equaling the roughtail stingray in size. Almost as large is the diamond stingray, *D. dipterura*, found from northern South America to southern California.

The pelagic stingray, *D. violacea*, inhabits the open sea rather than inshore waters; and two Thailand species, *D. sephen* and *D. bleekeri*, frequent freshwater streams and lakes in Thailand. *D. sephen*, which is found in tropical seas throughout the Indo-Pacific, has an exceptionally long tail—as much as twice the length of the body disk, which may be 4 feet across.

Stingrays of one group live so exclusively in fresh water that they are usually placed in a separate family, Potamotrygonidae, and are referred to as river rays. They are abundant in some coastal rivers of southeastern Asia, Africa, South America, and Central America.

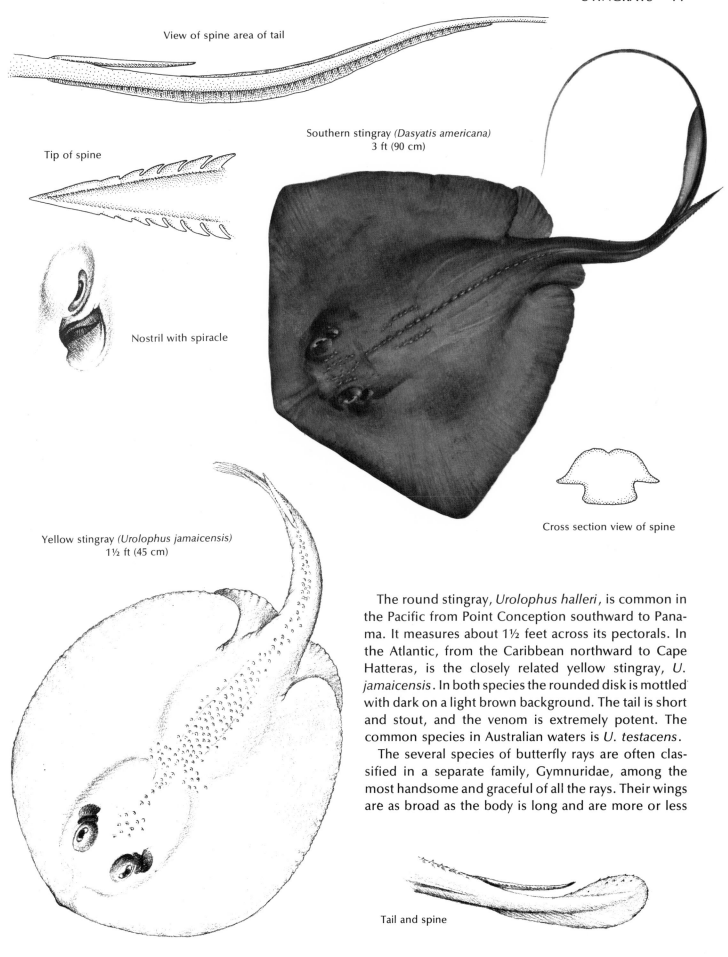

View of spine area of tail

Tip of spine

Nostril with spiracle

Southern stingray *(Dasyatis americana)*
3 ft (90 cm)

Cross section view of spine

Yellow stingray *(Urolophus jamaicensis)*
1½ ft (45 cm)

Tail and spine

The round stingray, *Urolophus halleri*, is common in the Pacific from Point Conception southward to Panama. It measures about 1½ feet across its pectorals. In the Atlantic, from the Caribbean northward to Cape Hatteras, is the closely related yellow stingray, *U. jamaicensis*. In both species the rounded disk is mottled with dark on a light brown background. The tail is short and stout, and the venom is extremely potent. The common species in Australian waters is *U. testacens*.

The several species of butterfly rays are often classified in a separate family, Gymnuridae, among the most handsome and graceful of all the rays. Their wings are as broad as the body is long and are more or less

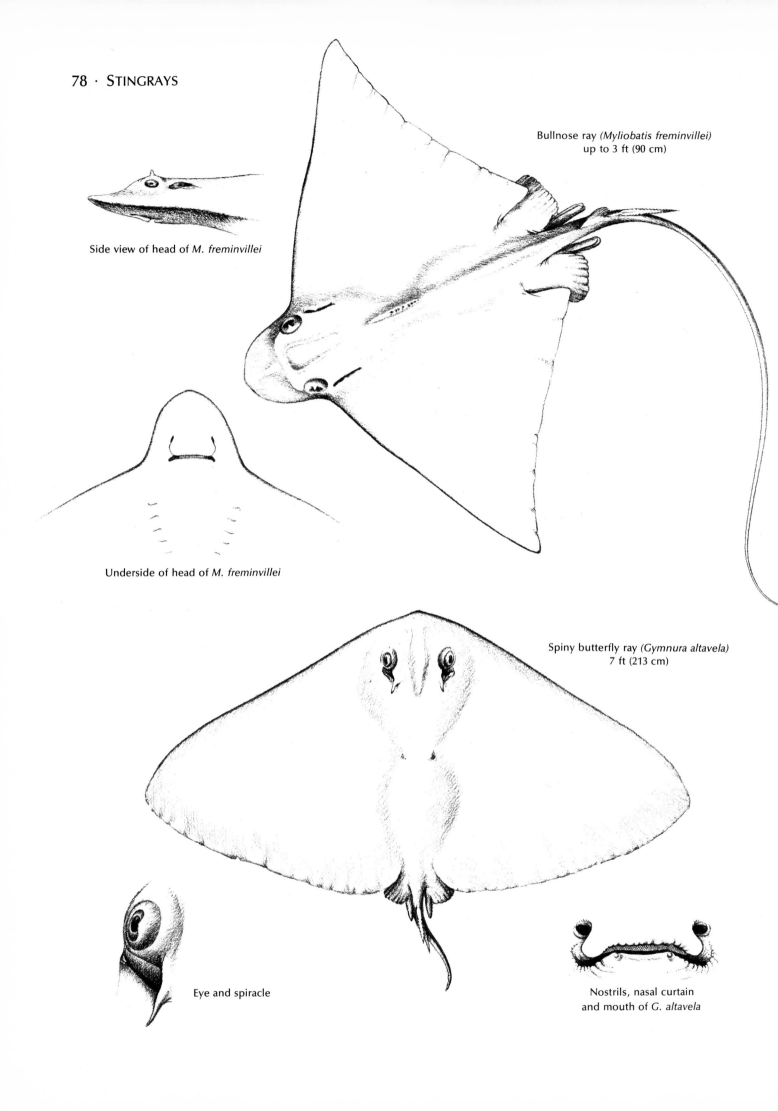

Side view of head of *M. freminvillei*

Underside of head of *M. freminvillei*

Bullnose ray *(Myliobatis freminvillei)*
up to 3 ft (90 cm)

Spiny butterfly ray *(Gymnura altavela)*
7 ft (213 cm)

Eye and spiracle

Nostrils, nasal curtain
and mouth of *G. altavela*

pointed at their tips. The tail is very short. The basic body color is brownish gray and is attractively inscribed with purple, green, or dark brown lines. These rays can also vary their coloration from light to dark to achieve a closer match with their background. Compared to the typical stingrays, the butterfly rays are more active, spending less of their time at rest on the bottom.

The common Atlantic species is the smooth butterfly ray, *Gymnura micrura*, averaging about 2 feet across its pectoral fins, though sometimes 4 feet or more. It occurs from Cape Cod southward to Brazil but is most common in the warmer waters of this range. The smooth butterfly ray does not have a stinging spine in its tail.

Found in the same range is the spiny butterfly ray, *G. altavela*, distinguished by its larger size (to 7 feet across its "wings") and also by the several small spines at the base of its tail. When taken from the water, it makes loud grunting noises, as do several other species of rays.

Nearly as large is the California butterfly ray, *G. marmorata*, found from Point Conception to southern Mexico. It also has a small spine at the base of its tail. *G. japonica* occurs off the coasts of northern Asia and Japan.

Butterfly rays found off South Africa and in Indo-Pacific waters belong to the genus *Aetoplatea*, differing from *Gymnura* species mainly in having small dorsal fins.

Family Myliobatidae
eagle rays

As a group, these are among the most pelagic of the rays, though not as completely so as the mantas. They still seek their food mainly from the bottom, however, probing for shellfishes and crustaceans, which they crush with their powerful flat teeth to get at the soft insides. At other times, they swim almost swallowlike through the water. Now and then an eagle ray will burst into the air in a brief, spectacular "flight."

Unlike the typical bottom-dwelling rays, the members of this group have a distinct head region, with the eyes and spiracles located on each side rather than on top. A distinctive fleshy lobe, or crown, caps the front of

Spotted eagle ray *(Aetobatus narinari)*
7 ft (213 cm)

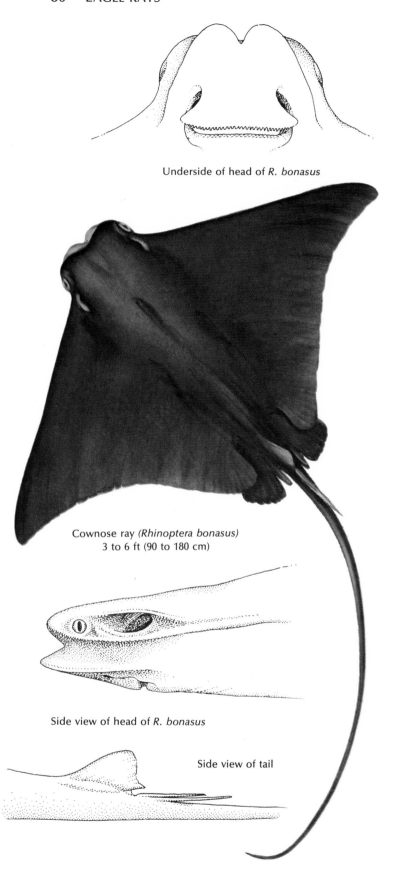

Underside of head of *R. bonasus*

Cownose ray *(Rhinoptera bonasus)*
3 to 6 ft (90 to 180 cm)

Side view of head of *R. bonasus*

Side view of tail

the head. Most species have one or more poisonous spines at the base of the tail, but the spines are so short and so close to the body that they cannot be used very effectively even in defense. Eagle rays occur in all warm and tropical seas.

The spotted eagle ray, *Aetobatus narinari*, is cosmopolitan in warm seas. One of the giants of its clan, it may measure more than 7 feet across its "wings" and reaches weights of about 400–500 pounds. Its tail carries more than one spine—frequently as many as five. Because its snout resembles a duck's bill, this species is known also as the spotted duckbilled ray. Its wings and body are heavily spotted, earning it also the name of leopard ray.

The bullnose ray, *Myliobatus freminvillei*, inhabits the same waters as the spotted eagle ray but lacks spots and is considerably smaller, measuring only about 3 feet across. A close relative, the southern eagle ray, ranges in the Atlantic from South Carolina southward along the coast of South America. Like other rays, the range is extended as the weather and the water warm, but subtropical waters are home for this species.

Closely related is the bat ray, *M. californica*, occurring in the Pacific off the California coast and sometimes straying as far north as Oregon. Like other eagle rays, it has a special fondness for shellfishes and becomes a destructive pest where oysters and clams are being harvested commercially. Often the rays appear in large schools and settle over the shellfish beds, destroying in a single night a crop that is almost ready for harvest. To prevent or at least discourage the rays from settling onto the beds, sharp-pointed stakes are driven into the bottom only six inches or a foot apart so that the rays cannot settle without impaling themselves.

Cownose rays possess a peculiar extension of the lower surface of the head. Called a subrostral fin, it is deeply incised in the midline, thereby forming two distinct lobes but connected at the base. It looks like the split upper lip of a bovine. Because of this feature, these rays are sometimes placed in a separate family, Rhinopteridae.

The Atlantic cownose ray, *Rhinoptera bonasus*, averages about 3 feet in width, with occasional individuals as large as 6 feet across their wings. This is perhaps the most common of all the eagle rays living in warm to cool waters around the world. It is less common in tropical waters than are other eagle rays.

A similar species, *R. brasiliensis*, is found only in waters along the western coast of South America; another, *R. marginata*, lives in the Mediterranean; and *R. javanica* is abundant in the western Pacific.

The cownose genus has a poison spine and has been observed jumping quite far out of the water..

Atlantic manta *(Manta birostris)*
up to 20 ft (611 cm) wing span

Family Mobulidae
mantas

The mantas, also called devil rays, comprise a small family that spans a wide spectrum of size from ocean giants to species that measure only a few feet across the pectoral fins. Mantas are easily distinguished by two flexible head protrusions, called cephalic fins, that form narrow lobes, one on each side of the head. These appendages are used chiefly to facilitate the entrance of small pelagic food organisms into the wide mouth. The cephalic fins, separated widely and extending forward from the head, resemble "horns," from which the name devil ray originates.

Mantas lack a caudal fin. Their skin, aside from tail spines, is naked or covered with small tubercles or prickles. The minute teeth are in both jaws or in only one, in series and forming a band. The Atlantic manta and the Pacific manta have a terminal mouth—that is, the mouth is at the end of the snout rather than directed downward as in their close cousins, the mobulas. Development is ovoviviparous. They range in tropical to warm-temperate belts of all oceans.

Tales of mantas grasping swimmers, divers, and towing boats by engaging anchor lines with their "horns" have never been substantiated. Actually, the giant mantas are generally harmless; they are only dangerous when harpooned because of their tremendous size and power. The reason for their spectacular habit of leaping into the air, sometimes in a somersault, may be to rid themselves of parasites, to crash down to stun small fish, or simply to enjoy jumping. On a calm day the sound of a big manta hitting the water can be heard a long distance.

Although many accounts in the literature state that the mantas travel alone (and they may at certain times), the senior author, in searching for them in the Pacific and Indian oceans, has observed that the giants travel in groups of from two to six. During these hunts a manta, basking on the surface at a distance, was easily mistaken for a marlin or a shark because the only visible parts were the curled-up tips of the huge wings, resembling dorsal and tail fins protruding above the water surface.

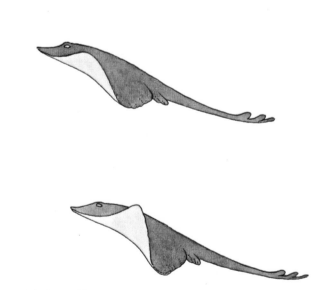

Devil ray *(Mobula hypostoma)*
4 ft (120 cm)

Atlantic manta
(Manta birostris)
up to 20 ft (611 cm)

Skates use their winglike pectoral fins in graceful undulating motions for underwater propulsion. Mantas and rays are known for their spectacular leaps out of the water.

The Atlantic manta, *Manta birostris*, and the Pacific manta, *Manta hamiltoni*, largest of the mantas, can have wing spans of over 20 feet and weigh well over 3,000 pounds. One specimen collected by a Yale expedition off Cabo Blanco, Peru, had a spread 18 feet 6 inches; it was weighed in chunks for a total weight of 3,200 pounds. It was cut up and weighed after it had been on the beach for two days while a plaster mold was made of its entire ventral surface for museum purposes. It may be assumed that this manta had lost about 250 pounds when weighed due to dehydration and loss of blood and body fluids.

The dorsal color of these mantas is dull, with variations from dark olive brown to black. There may be a lighter patch on each shoulder and various blotches and indistinct markings. The superficial areas of coloration may be natural in some and accidental in others because the dark pigmentation is easily rubbed off. The underside of the body is white or creamy white.

The European manta, *Mobula mobular*, belongs to a genus of mantas that have teeth in both jaws and that have the mouth on the underside of the head. Measuring about 4 feet across its wings, the European manta is further distinguished by its possession of a spine, or sometimes two, at the base of the tail, as in other types of rays. This species occurs from Iceland southward to West Africa but is most abundant in the Mediterranean region.

On the western side of the Atlantic, the devil ray, or little devilfish, *M. hypostoma*, is about the same size as the European manta and has a long tail, lacking a spine. The devil ray is extremely active in its feeding habits, commonly forcing schools of small fishes into the shallows as several mantas rush into the milling fishes to scoop up a mouthful. This manta also easily and regularly leaps clear of water, while the giant Atlantic manta, because of its size, has difficulty in getting completely into the air. The devil ray usually travels in small schools.

In the Pacific, the small Australian mobula, *M. diabola*, measures only about 2 feet across its wings. It does not have a spine at the base of its tail.

A spine is also lacking in the smoothtail mobula, *M. lucasana*, found from southern California to northern South America. This species may measure about 4 feet across its wings. The spinetail mobula, *M. japonica*, found in temperate waters of the Pacific to Japan and California, is similar in size but does have a spine at the base of its tail.

Other members of the manta family include the Jamaican ray, *Ceratobatis robertsi*, which has teeth only in its upper jaw; and a species in the genus *!ndomanta*, occurring only off the coast of India and distinguished by teeth in both jaws.

ORDER CHIMAERIFORMES

Family Chimaeridae
chimaeras

Chimaeras, awkwardly shaped fishes that live mostly in the deep sea, have features that make them appear to be links between cartilaginous and bony fishes. They are believed, however, to have descended directly from shark ancestors. Another common name for the group is ratfishes because most of the species have a long, pointed, rodentlike tail.

All modern chimaerids have bodies that are more or less compressed laterally, tapering toward the rear to a slender tail. The snout is either rounded-conical, or resembles an extended pointed beak, or possesses a queer-looking hoe shape. The first of the two dorsal fins contains a sharp spine positioned anteriorly.

The big eyes are located on the sides of the head. Nostrils, close in front of the mouth, are unusually large for a fish. In breathing, the chimaerids inhale water chiefly through the nostrils rather than directly into the mouth as do other fishes. The water is conveyed

Ratfish *(Hydrolagus colliei)*
3 ft (90 cm)

through a deep groove leading from the nostril to the corner of the mouth. The groove is roofed over by a lateral lobe of the upper lip, thereby forming a complete channel. Tooth structure is two pairs of dental plates in the upper jaw and one pair in the lower jaw. As do all modern elasmobranchs, males have pelvic claspers, intromittent organs for facilitating internal fertilization.

Chimaerids are poor swimmers, using mostly undulations of the posterior part of the body for propulsion. They are also delicate, struggling feebly and expiring soon after being removed from the water. They eat whatever small invertebrates and small fishes are available. Those inhabiting shallow water take a bait readily.

As a group, chimaerids range extensively in the Atlantic, Pacific, and Indian oceans and in the Mediterranean. Their depth range is also wide, from close to the surface down to about 1,400 fathoms or deeper.

Commercially, the chimaerids are not of significant importance. Chimaerid liver, however, is rich in oil and makes an excellent lubricant. In the Scandinavian countries this liver oil has also been used for medicinal purposes. Thousands of pounds of chimaerids are marketed for food in New Zealand, and they are a common market fish on the coast of mid-China.

As far as individual species of chimaerids are concerned, confusion exists in the literature. Not enough specimens have been studied for comparative purposes. The American Fisheries Society lists only one chimaerid, the ratfish, *Hydrolagus colliei*, as occurring in waters of the United States and Canada. Some authors prefer to separate this group into three families—Chimaeridae, Rhinochimaeridae, and Callorhinchidae. Actually, little is known about the habits and life history of any of the chimaeras.

The ratfish, *Hydrolagus colliei*, one of the most common species, lives in relatively shallow waters from southern California northward to Alaska.

In the Atlantic, the common species off the coast of Europe is *Chimaera montrosa*. The very similar deepwater chimaera, *C. affinis*, occurs off the Atlantic coast of North America. *C. phantasma* is found off the coasts of Asia and Japan.

The longnose chimaera, *Harriotta raleighana*, found in deep water (2,000 to 8,000 feet) along the Atlantic coast of North America, is one of a group of chimaeras that have exceptionally long snouts; and in males the claspers are united to form a single rod. Other species of chimaeras are found off the coasts of Japan and Africa, but because of the depth at which they live, they are seldom seen.

Still more unusual are the plownosed, or elephant, chimaeras, *Callorhinchus*, which have a thick, tubular snout that hangs down like an elephant's trunk. The fewer than half a dozen species in this group are known only from cool, deep waters of the Southern Hemisphere, where they are sometimes caught commercially.

THE BONY FISHES

(Class Osteichthyes)

The class Osteichthyes, or the true bony fishes, incorporates the vast majority of living fishes, both freshwater and marine. The presence of bone in their anatomy is the major factor in classifying or distinguishing them from the jawless fishes, class Agnatha, and the cartilaginous fishes, class Chondrichthyes.

The bony fishes may be separated into four major divisions:

1. The lobefins. These are highly important in the evolutionary scale as the predecessors of the tetrapods, or land animals.

2. The lungfishes of Australia, Africa, and South America. Lungfishes were considered the most primitive of the bony fishes before the discovery of the coelacanth.

3. The bichirs. In some respects these show a resemblance to the lobefins or coelacanths, especially in head structure.

4. The rayfinned fishes. These are fishes whose fins are supported by soft rays or by spiny rays.

In the general classification of the bony fishes, the number of orders and families varies, depending on the taxonomist producing the list.

ORDER COELACANTHIFORMES

Family Coelacanthidae
coelacanths

A sensational zoological discovery was made in the 1930s when a coelacanth, *Latimeria chalumnae*, was netted up from the depths off the Comoro Islands along the coast of South Africa. Before then, coelacanths were known only from fossil records from the Devonian period, considered to be more than 300 million years ago. These fishes, ancestors of present-day vertebrates, were believed to have become extinct many millions of years ago. The first specimen captured was sent to a taxidermist, who saved only the skin. Understandably, the loss of the internal organs was considered a disaster

by scientists. Since then, through a reward program to commercial fishermen in the area, other specimens have been made available to scientists and studied in detail. Although the capture of a living representative of the coelacanths is considered extremely important in the field of natural history, their habits remain a mystery, as are the causes for their survival over the ages and their peculiar restriction to the north of the Mozambique channel between Madagascar and Africa.

All the coelacanths have been taken in deep water at depths from 75 to 200 fathoms at rocky areas with steep

Coelacanth (*Latimeria chalumnae*)
4 ft (120 cm)

gradients. Undoubtedly they are to be found in deeper water, but they are bottom fish and cannot be taken easily because the ragged rocks prevent the fishermen's nets from reaching them.

The largest specimens taken weigh about 160 pounds. They are not handsome fish, being bulky in form and with grotesque mouths. Their color is a deep metallic blue with shades of brown toward the belly. The scales are large, and the fish is well marked with irregularly shaped whitish or creamy splotches. They are predacious creatures, feeding exclusively on other-fishes. The fin structure is the coelacanth's most unusual external feature. The second dorsal, pectorals, and pelvics are supported by a stalklike arrangement or lobes, thus the name lobefins, or lobefin fishes. The fins are supported

by their own skeleton and are fortified by an elaborate system of muscles, enabling the coelacanths to move in a wide range of positions.

Basically, the value of living coelacanths is their great antiquity; they are by far the oldest vertebrates alive today. Their unchanging form throughout the ages, while dominating animals suchs as the dinosaurs disappeared from the earth, is an incredible fact proved by the imprints in geological strata and by the reconstructions of these fossils by paleontologists before the first coelacanth was taken alive. Another important fact is that coelancanths are the only survivors of the large group of crossopterygians, the focal group from which evolved the entire lineage of air-breathing vertebrates up to man.

ORDER DIPTERIFORMES

Until the discovery of the coelacanth, lungfishes were the most ancient of all living fishes. They are still among the most unusual, though their distinction of being able to breathe air is shared with some other groups. The ancestry of lungfishes relates them directly to similar species that lived in swamps and brackish waters more than 300 million years ago. Their uniqueness is the re-

placement or development of the air bladder into a highly vascularized lunglike structure that enables the fish to breathe air. If kept moist, lungfishes can live out of water just as any air breathers do.

Only half a dozen species of lungfishes are known today, inhabiting the rivers and streams of tropical Africa, Australia, and South America.

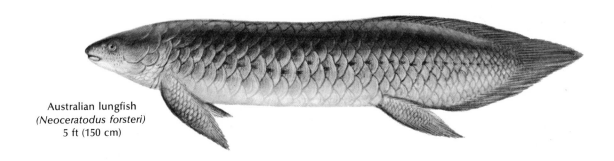

Australian lungfish
(*Neoceratodus forsteri*)
5 ft (150 cm)

Family Ceratodontidae
Australian lungfishes

The most primitive lungfish is the Australian lungfish, *Neoceratodus forsteri*. This species has only one lung and has functional gills. It can survive in water as well as on land; and because the waters in which it lives do not dry up for a portion of the year, it has no occasion to form a "cocoon" sanctuary of the sort other species use

when the rains stop. This species uses its lung only when the water becomes fouled or stagnant. The Australian lungfish grows to a length of 5 feet and may weigh more than 20 pounds. It has large scales, and its fins are not reduced as they sometimes are in the other lungfishes.

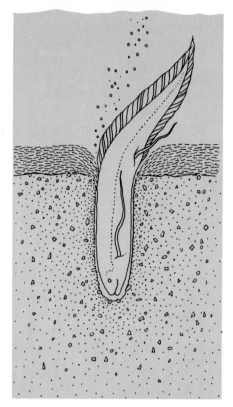
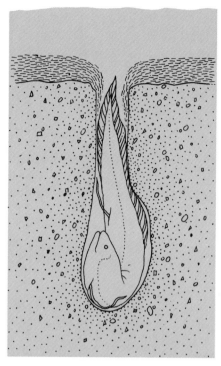
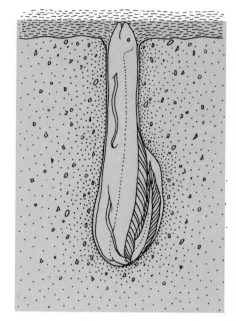

Protopterus preparing for estivation, making the burrow, retreating as the water table falls, and becoming torpid inside the cocoon it has secreted.

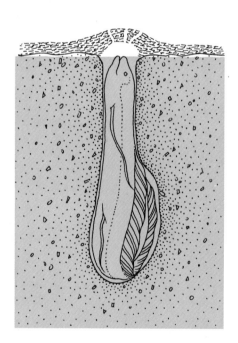
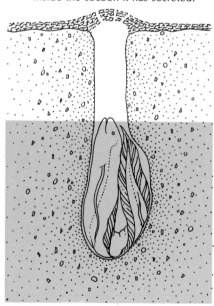
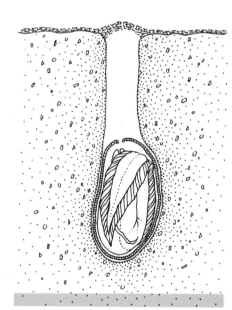

Family Lepidosirenidae
South American and African lungfishes

The 4-foot, eel-like South American lungfish, *Lepidosiren paradoxa*, lives in marshy regions along the Amazon River and its tributaries. It squirms through very shallow water, often with much of its body exposed, and breathes almost wholly with its "lung." In this species

the gills are greatly reduced in size and apparently do not function well even as auxiliary breathing devices. If the fish is kept underwater, it drowns. During the dry season, when the marshes lose their water, the fish burrows into the soft muck and becomes dormant. It subsists on the fat stored in its body during the months when it fed voraciously on the abundance of living creatures in the marsh. While it is dormant, it breathes the oxygen that is trapped in the burrow and continues to filter in though the mud.

South American lungfishes hatch from eggs that are laid in a nest at the bottom of a mud tunnel. Until the eggs hatch, they are guarded by a male that remains in the underwater burrow with them even when the rains come. During this period the male develops gill-like outgrowths from the pelvic fins. The young fishes, which resemble tadpoles, have gills on their head.

The most famous lungfishes are four African species of the genus *Protopterus*. The mucous-lined cocoons in which they spend the dry months become baked so hard that the fishes can be dug up and shipped in these encasements without disturbing them. The fishes breathe through tubelike vents connected to the surface. When the clay is softened with water (by rain in natural conditions), the dormant fishes inside come alive again. These fishes have been kept in their cocoons for several years. During a long period of dormancy, a fish may lose as much as half its weight. In the African lungfishes, the fins are cordlike filaments.

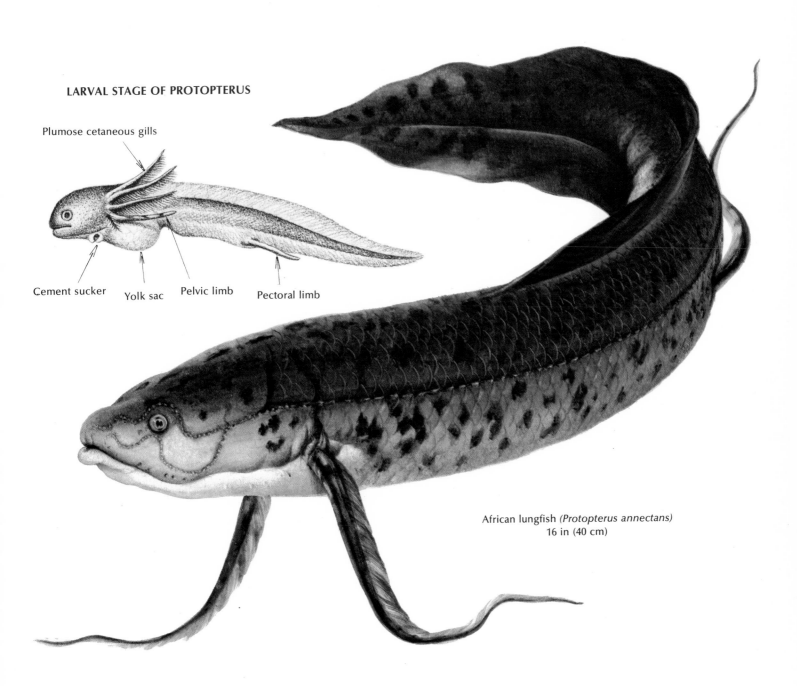

LARVAL STAGE OF PROTOPTERUS

Plumose cetaneous gills

Cement sucker   Yolk sac   Pelvic limb   Pectoral limb

African lungfish *(Protopterus annectans)*
16 in (40 cm)

Bichir *(Polypterus weeksi)*
up to 3 ft (90 cm)

ORDER POLYPTERIFORMES

Family Polypteridae
bichirs

Bichirs, also known as reedfishes, are ranked among the most primitive bony fishes. Much of the skeleton consists of cartilage, and they have a breathing spiracle similar to that in sharks and rays. The scales are large, rhomboidal, and composed of ganoin, as in gars. The rays in the fins are soft. Most unusual is the long dorsal fin, consisting of 15–20 finlets that can be raised or lowered. *Polypterus*, the generic name for the bichirs, literally means "many fins."

Nearly a dozen species of bottom-dwelling bichirs are found in Africa, where they live in the shallow floodwa-ter areas of tropical rivers and feed on the abundance of aquatic insects, worms, and other small animals in these waters. The air bladder of these fishes serves as an auxiliary lung, but it is not heavily enough vascularized to permit the bichirs to survive long out of water. None exceeds 3 feet in length, and most are much smaller.

The only other genus in this family contains a single species, the reedfish, *Calamoichthys calabaricus*, a slim, eel-like fish that has only one ray attached to each finlet spine rather than several, as is common in bichirs. It lives in rivers and swamps of tropical Africa.

ORDER ACIPENSERIFORMES

Family Acipenseridae
sturgeons

Like paddlefishes, sturgeons are "living fossils," the two dozen or so species alive today representing a group that was much more abundant in the geologic past. Sturgeons are not abundant, but they are widely distributed in cool waters of the Northern Hemisphere. Among them are the largest fish that live in fresh water. Some spend much of their lives in brackish or salt waters, moving into rivers to spawn in spring. Those dwellers in lakes travel up feeder streams at spawning time.

Sturgeons are long-lived, some estimated to exceed 150 years of age. Like that of paddlefishes, the skeleton of sturgeons is mainly cartilage. Several rows of bony plates extend down along the body. The snout is long, blunt-ended in some and pointed in others but generally shovel-shaped; its underside holds four sensory barbels that are used to detect morsels of food on the bottom. The food is then picked up by the protrusible, tubelike mouth located behind the barbels. The single dorsal fin is far back on the body, directly above the anal fin.

Sturgeons have long been prized as food fishes. The roe commands an especially high price, though when sturgeons were very common in America, the roe was a giveaway food to attract customers to saloons. Because of the scarcity of the fish, commercial fishing for sturgeons is now limited. A few species are still sought by sport fishermen, however, because of the brutish battle they give when taken on light tackle.

The white sturgeon, *Acipenser transmontanus*, is the largest freshwater fish in North America. Among those taken during the 1800s were three reported to weigh more than 1,500 pounds; many weigh over 1,000 pounds. The largest authenticated catch weighed 1,285 pounds and was taken by gill net in the Columbia River near Vancouver. All the giant-size catches come from Oregon, Washington, and British Columbia, principally from the Columbia and Fraser rivers. The species ranges from Alaska southward to middle California.

As the name implies, the white sturgeons are light in color—mostly grayish brown but with variations due to

differences in the water in which they live and also with the age of the particular fish. Younger specimens are lighter than older ones. The belly is white. Specimens 8 or 9 feet in length are about 50 years old.

Female sturgeons carry prodigious amounts of eggs. A female 10 feet long, for example, may contain more than 3 million eggs that have a total weight of as much as 250 pounds. Biologists are anxious to give these spawners an opportunity to lay their eggs and thus perpetuate the species. Much remains to be learned about the spawning habits of the fish. Meanwhile, protective legislation now generally limits the allowable number and size of the sturgeons that can be harvested. In most states, large fishes are especially protected because they are usually egg-producing females.

Inhabiting the same waters is the smaller green sturgeon, *A. medirostris*, which reaches a maximum length of about 7 feet and a weight of about 350 pounds. It is distinguished from the white sturgeon by its definite greenish color as well as by such anatomical differences as the location of the barbels near the mouth (they are closer to the tip of the snout in the white sturgeon), a

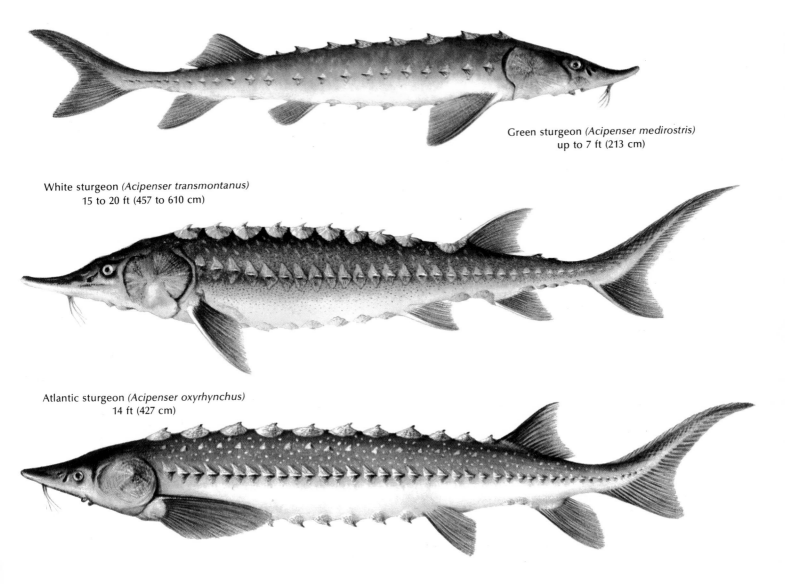

Green sturgeon *(Acipenser medirostris)*
up to 7 ft (213 cm)

White sturgeon *(Acipenser transmontanus)*
15 to 20 ft (457 to 610 cm)

Atlantic sturgeon *(Acipenser oxyrhynchus)*
14 ft (427 cm)

Lake sturgeon *(Acipenser fulvescens)*
up to 4 ft (120 cm)

narrower snout and flatter head, and fewer bony plates in the five rows down the back. Unlike the white sturgeon, this species rarely enters fresh water, though it does congregate at the mouths of rivers. This species is caught also in Japanese waters.

Along the Atlantic coast of North America, the largest fish taken in fresh water is again a sturgeon—the Atlantic sturgeon, *A. oxyrhynchus*, with an authenticated record of a 14-foot specimen that weighed 811 pounds. Most of those caught today weigh less than 200 pounds, but there are reports now and then of 300-pounders. The Atlantic sturgeon is olive brown above, often tinged with red; the belly is white. The centers of the horny scutes, or shields, along the back and sides are light—almost white—which makes them stand out in sharp contrast to the darker color around them. The shields are set very close together, the bases of most of them overlapping. Like Pacific sturgeons, this species is becoming rare because of pollution and dams in the streams in which it formerly spawned in abundance in spring. It has also been overfished in many areas, especially for its roe. Originally, the Atlantic sturgeon was common from South Carolina northward to the St. Lawrence River. It feeds on a variety of plants and animals, both living and dead, that are picked up from the bottom with the suctionlike mouth. It is not uncommon for the Atlantic sturgeon to leap from the water, presumably to shake off bothersome parasites.

The European sturgeon, *A. sturio*, is considered by some biologists to be the same species as the Atlantic sturgeon but inhabiting the eastern Atlantic. It reaches the same size; story-told behemoths cannot be disputed or verified.

Inhabiting the same waters as the Atlantic sturgeon but ranging southward to Florida is the shortnose sturgeon, *A. brevirostrum*, a small species that rarely exceeds a length of 3 feet and generally weighs less than 10 pounds. It also differs from the Atlantic sturgeon in that the plates in the rows down the back and sides are clearly separated from each other. The snout is proportionately much shorter than the Atlantic sturgeon's.

The lake sturgeon, *A. fulvescens*, known also as the rock sturgeon and red sturgeon, lives in lakes and rivers from the St. Lawrence westward through the Great Lakes and into the Mississippi River and its tributaries. Only rarely does it move into brackish or salt water. Older fish often acquire a reddish or greenish cast. Valid records show fish of this species more than 6 feet long and weighing over 200 pounds, but most lake sturgeons caught today are less than 4 feet long and weigh less than 50 pounds. In color and general appearance the lake sturgeon resembles the Atlantic sturgeon, but it has only a single row (rarely two) of bony plates on its underside between the anal fin and the vent; the Atlantic sturgeon has two to four rows.

Lake sturgeons spawn in spring or early summer, the females swimming into tributary streams to lay their eggs. A female 3 feet long may lay more than half a million eggs that will weigh in mass about 10 pounds. The eggs hatch in about a week, but the growth of a young fish is slow. The fish does not mature until it is about 20 years old, and spawning occurs only every two or three years. The lake sturgeon, like its cousins, feeds on a great variety of plants and animals that are sucked up from the bottom. Because of their gizzardlike stomachs, they are able even to crush the shells of clams or snails. Both the flesh and the roe are highly prized—and priced accordingly—but the population of these sturgeons has suffered greatly as a result of man's alteration and destruction of their natural habitat.

The shovelnose or hackleback sturgeon, *Scaphirhynchus platorynchus*, lives in much the same range as the lake sturgeon, but it is not found in the Great Lakes. It prefers swift, large streams. As its name implies, this

Shovelnose sturgeon *(Scaphirhynchus platorynchus)*
up to 3 ft (90 cm)

species has a very flat, shovel-shaped snout, and its caudal peduncle is armored with bony plates. The shovelnose sturgeon has a threadlike extension on the upper lobe of its caudal fin, but this may be worn off in older individuals. This is a small species, seldom reaching a length of 3 feet or exceeding 6 pounds in weight. The reason for its decline, in addition to its being caught commercially, is obvious: it inhabits the nation's most polluted streams.

The pallid sturgeon, *S. albus*, is closely related to the shovelnose but is limited in distribution to the upper Mississippi River and its tributaries. The two species can be differentiated only by examination of anatomical features. The pallid sturgeon has 37–43 rays in its dorsal fin; the shovelnose, fewer (30–36). The pallid has 24–28 rays in its anal fin; the shovelnose, 18–23. The pallid sturgeon has no horny scutes on its belly, its snout is more pointed, and its head is larger than the shovelnose's. The inner pair of barbels is distinctly shorter than the outer pair. The pallid sturgeon reaches a length of about 6 feet and a weight of more than 30 pounds.

The giant of the sturgeon clan is the beluga, *Huso huso*, which lives in the Black and Caspian seas and in the Volga River, where it spawns. No evidence has been found for the often quoted record catch of nearly 1½ tons and 28 feet long.

Family Polyodontidae
paddlefishes

The paddlefish, also known as spoonbill, may be found in some lakes, but it is primarily a fish of large, silty rivers. The common name is derived from the long, flat paddlelike projection in which the snout terminates. This extension, reaching far beyond the mouth, is used to stir up the mud where the tiny organisms and small crustaceans, worms, and leeches on which the fish feeds are found. The food is strained from the muddy waters as it passes over the gill rakers before exiting through the gill openings.

If the snout extension is cut off, the paddlefish may superficially resemble a shark. The mouth of the paddlefish is wide and large, the eyes are small, and gill covers long and flabby. Young paddlefishes have numerous fine teeth on the jaws and palate; but as a fish grows to maturity, its jaws become large, feeble, and toothless. The snout and parts of the head and gill covers are dotted with small porelike depressions which may be sensory terminations. The smooth skin is without scales and resembles that of a catfish. The skeleton is largely cartilaginous. Paddlefish coloration varies—slate gray, bluish gray, or purplish dark blue.

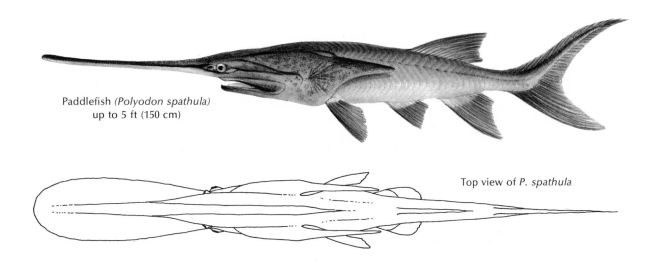

Paddlefish *(Polyodon spathula)*
up to 5 ft (150 cm)

Top view of *P. spathula*

The single American species, *Polyodon spathula*, is found throughout the Mississippi system, from the Missouri River in eastern Montana southward. The literature contains old reports of paddlefishes weighing over 200 pounds, but authenticated records in recent years show a 63-pounder for Ford Randall Reservoir, South Dakota, and a 72-pound fish taken in Lake Cumberland, Kentucky, as being close to maximum weight. Records from Ford Peck Reservoir, Montana, list specimens weighing over 90 pounds.

A second species, *Psephurus gladius*, inhabits two great rivers of China, the Yangtze and the Hoang Ho. It resembles the American species but has a narrower snout and fewer gill rakers.

Although greatly reduced in numbers in North America in recent years, the paddlefish seems to be increasing in a few localities, and it is still numerous enough in certain areas to be considered a good commercial fish.

Between the years 1900 and 1925, the paddlefish supported a valuable commercial fishery in the Mississippi Valley. The fish commanded good prices, and the roe was considered excellent as caviar. The paddlefish is captured in nets, and anglers snag them with large treble hooks pulled through the water with fairly heavy tackle. Although a paddlefish resembles a catfish and sometimes is called a spoonbill cat, it is not related to any catfish group.

ORDER SEMIONOTIFORMES

Family Lepisosteidae
gars

Another family of primitive fishes, the gars were once abundant and widely distributed. The few species in existence today are found mainly in eastern North America, ranging as far south as Central America and Cuba. They live in shallow, weedy fresh water. Like the bowfins, the gars have a highly vascularized air bladder that serves as an auxiliary lung, enabling these fishes to take in air at the surface and thus survive in water that has become too fouled for most fishes to tolerate. Much of the gar's time is spent resting quietly near the bottom or basking at the surface, but it can swim swiftly for short distances to catch its prey.

A gar is cigar-shaped, its tooth-filled snout broad and flat in some species and slender in others. The single dorsal fin is located far back on the body, directly above the anal fin. The vertebrae resemble those of amphibians—that is, convex in front and concave at the rear so that they fit together like ball-and-socket joints. In most fishes, the vertebrae are concave at both ends. The ganoid-type scales of the gar fit one against the other like the bricks in a wall and are composed of ganoin, an extremely hard compound. Indians used the scales of large gars for arrowheads, and pioneer farmers covered their wooden plowshares with gar hides. Today

the tough hides are sometimes processed to make luggage or novelties.

The longnose gar, *Lepisosteus osseus*, is the most widely distributed member of the family, ranging from the St. Lawrence River westward through the Great Lakes and southward to Florida and Texas. It occurs most abundantly in the Mississippi River drainage system, usually living in shallow, weedy, quiet waters in the warmer parts of its range but seeming to prefer clearer streams and lakes the farther north it goes. The longnose gar averages 2 to 3 feet in length but occasionally reaches a length of 5 feet. Its most distinguishing feature is its long, very slim snout. Round dark spots are scattered over its fins and body but are lacking on its head. Its body is olive gray above and light below, the coloration typical of all gars. In spring, gravid females swim into shallow waters, each usually followed by two or more males that fertilize the eggs. A 3-foot female will lay more than 35,000 eggs. In some parts of its range, the longnose gar is netted and sold in markets as a food fish, but it gets limited attention from sport fishermen.

The shortnose gar, *L. platostomus*, occurs only in weedy, silted streams of the Mississippi River drainage system. It has a short, broad snout and no spots on its head, though there is a scattering of spots on its dorsal, anal, and caudal fins. This is the smallest of the gars, rarely exceeding 2½ feet in length.

Sometimes found in the same habitat with the shortnose gar but ranging farther north and west, the spotted gar, *L. oculatus*, exceeds 2½ feet in length regularly but is rarely more than 3 feet long. Like the shortnose gar, it has a short, broad snout, but it is distinguished from other gars by the large dark spots on its head and snout.

In peninsular Florida, the spotted gar is replaced by the slightly smaller Florida gar, *L. platyrhincus*, which may be seen by the thousands in canals, ditches, and weedy ponds and lakes. Its snout is slightly broader than the spotted gar's, and the spots on its body sometimes run together to form stripes.

The giant of the gar clan in North America is the alligator gar, *L. spatula*, which lives only in the large

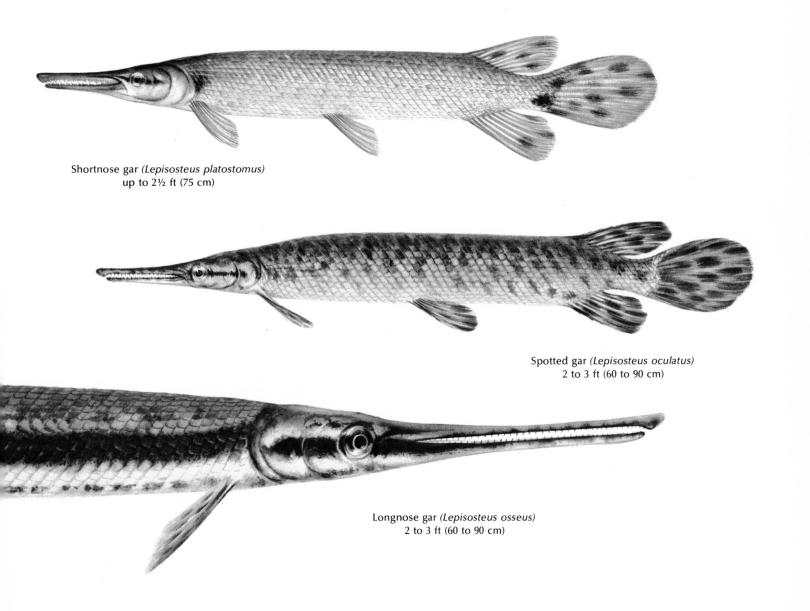

Shortnose gar *(Lepisosteus platostomus)*
up to 2½ ft (75 cm)

Spotted gar *(Lepisosteus oculatus)*
2 to 3 ft (60 to 90 cm)

Longnose gar *(Lepisosteus osseus)*
2 to 3 ft (60 to 90 cm)

tributaries of the Gulf of Mexico. Sometimes, though rarely, it strays far up the Mississippi. The alligator gar has two rows of teeth on each side of its upper jaw; other gars have only one. The beak or snout of the alligator gar is short and broad. No other gars in North America are as large—to 10 feet long and weighing as much as 300 pounds, though unauthenticated reports of alligator gars are twice as large. Nowadays a 6- or 7-foot fish is considered large. Like other gars, this giant is a voracious feeder that will take dead as well as living animals. Though gars are feared, and many tales are told about their attacks on humans, none has so far been authenticated. The fish does deserve great respect, however, for it is capable of being dangerous and is certainly not discriminating. A few fisherman specialize in catching these giant armored fish, mainly because of the challenge of tangling with such a stubborn big fish and one that others make a special effort to avoid. A few gars are caught commercially, their flesh smoked and sold in the markets.

The giant gar, *L. tristoechius*, of Cuban, Central American, and Mexican waters is a close relative that rivals the alligator gar in size. It is also caught commercially.

ORDER AMIIFORMES

Family Amiidae
bowfins

The bowfin, *Amia calva*, is the only living representative of its family. During the geologic past, the family contained a number of species, especially in Europe, but the single species alive today is found only in quiet, near-stagnant waters from the St. Lawrence River southward to Florida and westward through the Great Lakes on the north and to Texas on the south. It is a sluggish fish, averaging about 3 pounds, with a maximum of 7 or 8 pounds. Statements that this fish reaches a weight of 20 pounds are without substantiation. The bowfin rests near the bottom or swims along slowly. When alarmed or in pursuit of prey, it can move with great speed. It has long, sharp teeth and is a voracious predator. The single, spineless, and ribbonlike dorsal fin stretches over more than half of the fish's back. Just in front of the rounded tail fin a large black spot is conspicuous; in males it is circled with bright orange-red. A large gular plate is situated under the chin. The bowfin's olive-green body is covered with small, rounded overlapping scales. Bowfins can survive in water that is too foul for other kinds of fishes because their air bladders are highly vascularized and serve as lungs. They rise to the surface from time to time to gulp air.

In spring, the male bowfin makes a circular nest by clearing away debris, fanning the area with its fins, and chewing off plants. One or more females are lured to the nest to lay their eggs, which the male fertilizes. The male then stands guard over the nest, aggressively driving away any intruders. The eggs hatch in about ten days, but the male continues his vigil. He accompanies the young fishes as they swim, keeping them in a tight, milling school until they are 3 or 4 inches long. One male may be the guardian of as many as 1,000 young fish.

Because of its predatory habits and because its flesh is not particularly tasty, the bowfin is not held in high esteem. It does provide a stubborn battle when hooked and will accept most baits and lures. On light tackle, bowfin fishing can be real sport. Other common names for the bowfin are mudfish, dogfish, and grindle or spottail grindle.

Bowfin *(Amia calva)*
2 ft (60 cm)

ORDER ELOPIFORMES

Family Elopidae
tarpons

Tarpons and their relatives comprise a small family that is sometimes divided into two separate families based on minor differences. Tarpons have soft rays in their fins, and the pelvic fins are located far back on the body. The tail fin is forked. These are primitive bony fishes that resemble closely the ancestral type from which all other bony fishes developed.

The tarpon, *Megalops atlantica,* is the giant of the group, averaging 5 feet in length with a weight of 25 to 50 pounds. It is known to reach a length of 8 feet and weigh as much as 300 pounds. Sport fishermen often refer to the tarpon as the "silver king," for its scales, the size of silver dollars, reflect light like polished metal. The last ray in the dorsal fin is extended into a long filament that

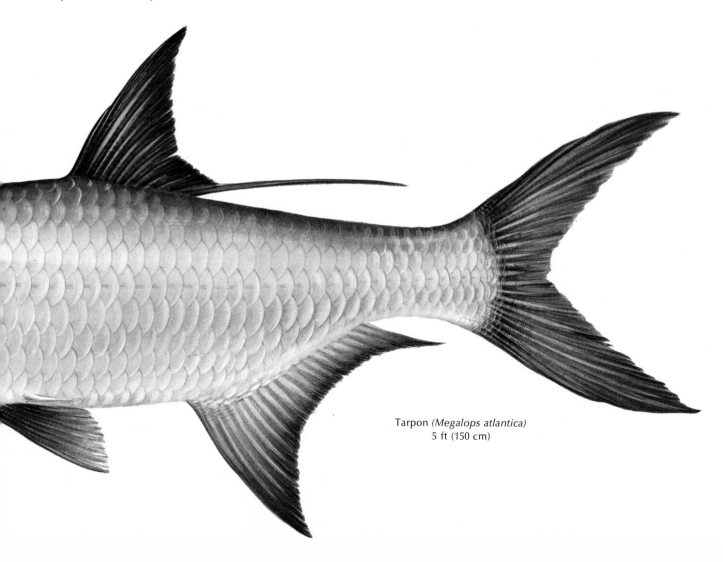

Tarpon *(Megalops atlantica)*
5 ft (150 cm)

may be worn off in older fishes. This much sought-after game fish occasionally strays as far north as Cape Cod and is found southward to Brazil and Argentina as a stray along the western Atlantic coast. It is also known off the northwestern coast of Africa, but the nucleus of its range is the Atlantic and Gulf coasts of Florida and throughout the Caribbean. It has invaded the west coast of Central America through the Panama Canal. Often it wanders as far as 100 miles up rivers.

The tarpon is a delight for many anglers because it is found close to shore, often being caught from bridges and jetties or from skiffs and always giving a spectacular and memorable fight. Almost the instant the hook is set, the tarpon takes to the air in turning, twisting leaps as it tries to throw the hook—and often succeeds in so doing. The principal means of taking tarpon today is by spinning tackle, although conquering one by fly rod and fly is considered an angling feat. Many weighing more than 125 pounds have been caught. The record is a 283-pounder taken in Lake Maracaibo in Venezuela.

Tarpons are not considered edible, and so most catches are released to provide sport for more anglers. In Florida waters the tarpons begin to appear in numbers during late winter and reach their peak in spring and summer. Shallow estuaries are the nursery grounds for the young, and the draining and polluting of these areas is the greatest danger to the tarpon population.

A closely related species, the Pacific tarpon, *T. cyprinoides,* occurs in Indo-Pacific waters. It is much smaller, seldom exceeding a weight of 40 pounds.

In another genus and sometimes placed in a separate family are two species in the genus *Elops*: the ladyfish or ten-pounder, *E. saurus*, and the machete, *E. affinis*. Sometimes referred to as the tarpon's little cousin, the ladyfish resembles the tarpon but is much smaller, averaging less than 5 pounds and only rarely reaching a weight of 15 pounds and a length of 3 feet. The scales are proportionately much smaller than the tarpon's, and the ladyfish lacks the filament on the last ray of the dorsal fin.

The ladyfish is most abundant in Florida and Caribbean waters, but it sometimes strays as far north as Massachusetts. Because of its small size, it inhabits shallow water, where it prowls in small schools or singly in search of food—mainly crustaceans and small fishes. It also wanders up streams in fresh water. To the delight of the light-tackle angler, the ladyfish takes baits and lures readily; as soon as the fish feels the hook, it takes to the air in repeated jumps that send it skittering and tail-walking across the surface. The little fish's performances are active and exciting. Like the tarpon, this species is bony and its flesh is oily; hence it is not edible and often released.

The machete occurs in the Pacific from southern California to Peru. It may be the same species as the ladyfish. Other species (or perhaps the same species) occur off the coast of Africa, in Hawaiian waters, and throughout much of the South Pacific.

Family Albulidae
bonefish

The single species in this family—the bonefish, *Albula vulpes*—is found in warm seas throughout the world. In North American waters it is most abundant in the warm shallows of the Florida Keys, where it is much sought after by sport fishermen. In some other areas, along the Pacific Coast, for example, it is oddly ignored. Considered one of the most wary of all fishes (a literal translation of its scientific name is "white fox"), the bonefish, when hooked, takes extremely long and powerful runs. Though its average size is 2 to 5 pounds, the bonefish is known to exceed a weight of 15 pounds. The world-record catch taken in Zululand, South Africa, in 1962 weighed 19 pounds.

Fishermen sometimes refer to these slim, silvery fishes as "ghosts of the flats." Bonefishes travel in loose schools, rooting in the sand and mud with their turned-down, piglike snouts as they grub for shrimps,

Ladyfish (*Elops saurus*)
3 ft (90 cm)

Bonefish (*Albula vulpes*)
up to 3 ft (90 cm)

shellfishes, crabs, small fishes, and other animals on which they feed. Often they search for food in water so shallow that the tail and dorsal fin stick above the surface. Fishermen stalk these feeding fishes, wading the shallows or poling flat-bottomed skiffs over the mudflats searching for signs of the feeding fishes. They cast their baits or lures directly into the paths of the shadowy fish, which scares easily and streaks away at great speed. But when a fish does take a bait or lure, the reel hums as the line flies off the spool. On light tackle, the bonefish is a superb sport fish.

Young bonefishes resemble larval eels in having a small head and a transparent body. During early development the body shrinks in length and gradually changes form to resemble an adult bonefish. After hatching, the young move offshore with the currents, where they spend their early lives as open-ocean planktonic forms, and then return to shallow waters as juveniles.

Not much is known concerning the deepsea bonefish of the family Pterothrissidae that inhabits the Pacific and eastern Atlantic. It has a long dorsal fin.

ORDER ANGUILLIFORMES

More than 20 families form a large group, or order, of fishes called eels, sharing a number of features that make them unique in the fish world. All have spineless fins and long, slim snakelike bodies that lack ventral fins. In most, the dorsal, caudal, and anal fins are joined to form one continuous fin over the rear of the body. Except in a few species there are no visible scales, though microscopic examination will reveal numerous very tiny scales—a hundred or more to the square inch. All the different families of eels are marine except the family Anguillidae.

Family Anguillidae
freshwater eels

Such better-known species as the American eel, *Anguilla rostrata*; European eel, *A. anguilla*; Japanese eel, *A. japonica*; Indian eel, *Phisodnopsis boro*; and about a dozen other species that live in the Indo-Pacific region are members of this family. Freshwater eels are curiously absent from the eastern Pacific and South Atlantic, presumably due to the more saline water conditions.

These eels have been prized as food since ancient times and have been caught in eel traps or pots, in nets, or on hook and line. But little was known about their life history until the late 1800s. All sorts of stories were told about how eels came into being, including a persistent tale that they came from horsehairs that fell into the water and somehow came to life. A Danish scientist finally unraveled the true story, which is indeed a strange one.

The American eel and European eel both spawn in the same area of the Atlantic Ocean—in deep water at the north edge of the Sargasso Sea. There each female lays as many as 10 to 20 million eggs, which the males fertilize. The adults then die. The eggs float slowly upward to the surface and soon hatch into slim, transparent leptocephali, or larvae, commonly called glass fish.

The baby eels begin drifting and swimming in the ocean currents. They swim to keep themselves directed toward their ultimate home waters. Baby American eels travel toward North America, while baby European eels swim toward Europe. How they know which way to go when neither has ever seen its "home" is an unanswered question. For the American eels, the trip is about 1,000 miles; the journey requires about a year. European eels travel 3,000 miles or more, their trip taking nearly three years. Equally astonishing is the fact that the growth rates of the two eels differ so that each has developed to about the same size by the time they reach their destination. By this time they have metamorphosed from the leaflike leptocephalus stage and have become thick-bodied little eels, or elvers.

Male eels stay near the mouths of rivers, but the more venturesome females continue to swim upstream into the headwaters. Or sometimes they slither through dewy grass to get from one body of water to another. Eventually they find a place that apparently suits their needs and settle there to feed and grow. The female may reach a length of 3 feet; males rarely grow more than a foot long. After several years, the females lose their greenish color, becoming almost black. They begin their downstream journey to the sea, where they are joined by the mature males, who swim with them to the spawning area. Eels that have established themselves in ponds or lakes without tributary streams do not move out even after maturing. They remain landlocked, living in these waters for 50 years or longer and never spawning.

The adult American eel and the adult European eel are so similar in appearance that they can be distinguished only by counting their vertebrae. An American eel has 103–111 vertebrae; the European, 110–119. Both have sharp snouts and numerous teeth. Some scientists believe the two are really one and the same species.

In Europe the eel ranks as a delicacy, as it does in Japan. In America it is less favored even though it makes a delicious dish fried, grilled, or pickled. In sport fishing, eel skins and whole eels are used as bait for striped bass and other fishes, but artificial eels are now more commonly used than the real ones.

Family Muraenidae
morays

Morays are the most infamous group within the order Anguilliformes. They constitute a family of more than 80 species occurring in greatest abundance in tropical and subtropical waters but with a few species straying into waters of temperate regions during warm months. Primarily, the morays live in coral reefs or in similar rocky areas. The typical moray's body is flattened from side to side, pectoral fins are lacking, and the scaleless skin is thick and leathery. The dorsal and anal fins are low, sometimes almost hidden by the wrinkled skin around them. The gill opening is small and round, and the teeth are large. Most morays are large, reaching a length of 5 to 6 feet. Some are as much as 10 feet long; a few are less than 6 inches long.

A moray will anchor the rear half of its body in coral and rocks, allowing the front of its body to sway with the current. In this position, with its mouth gaped, it is ready to grasp any prey that comes close. Morays have vicious tempers, as divers will attest, and it is unwise to torment them. Their bites are not poisonous, as many believe, but a large moray can make multiple deep wounds that not uncommonly become infected and are slow to heal. Deaths have resulted from encounters with morays. Normally morays are nocturnal, but they never miss an opportunity to appear from their rocky lairs when a meal is in the offing. Morays themselves are captured and eaten in many parts of the world.

Many morays are attractively colored. The green moray, *Gymnothorax funebris*, which lives in tropical and subtropical waters of both North and South America, is an unusual brownish green, a color produced by a combination of yellow slime over the eel's blue body.

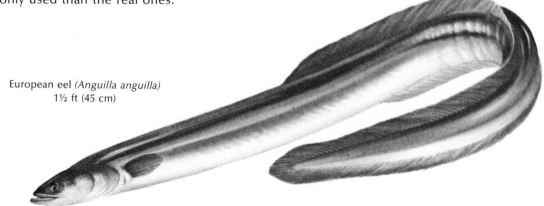

European eel *(Anguilla anguilla)*
1½ ft (45 cm)

Though most green morays are less than 5 feet long, there are occasional reports of 10-footers. The green moray inhabits coral reefs, sometimes going into deep water to prowl for food.

The spotted moray, *G. moringa*, occurs in the same range as the green moray. Smaller, almost never exceeding 3 feet in length, it has prominent dark spots or a chainlike pattern of dark lines on its usually yellowish body. The basic body color commonly matches the eel's surroundings, however, and may vary from white to dark brown.

Off the Pacific Coast, the California moray, *G. mordax*, is similar in appearance and habits to the spotted moray; it grows to a length of 5 feet. The blackedge moray, *G. nigromarginatus*, prevalent in the subtropical Atlantic, the Caribbean, and the Gulf of Mexico, is of similar size, but the black pattern is more pronounced, with black margins on the dorsal and anal fins.

The puhi-paka, *G. flavimarginatus*, which grows to 4 feet long, is common in Hawaiian waters and elsewhere in the western Pacific. Its fins are bordered with bright green. Also prevalent in the same area is *G. eurostus*, growing to 2 feet long.

Morays of the genus *Echidna,* most abundant in Indo-Pacific waters, are among the most striking eels in bright colors and patterns. The zebra moray, *E. zebra*, is marked with vertical bands or rings of white the full length of its dark, brownish yellow body. The chain moray, *E. catenata*, found in the warm Atlantic from Florida to South America, is marked with a black chainlike pattern over a yellowish background. Many of the Indo-Pacific morays of this genus have flattened molars for crushing the shells of mollusks and the hard outer skeletons of sea urchins, crabs, and other sea creatures.

The dragon moray, *Muraena pardalis*, of the western Pacific is one of several attractive species in its genus, distinguished by its curiously elongated, tubelike nostrils, the posterior pair of which is located far back on the head, just in front of the eyes. In some species, the nostrils are large and leaflike. The dragon moray has irregularly shaped red-and-white spots on a dark background.

Among the smallest of the morays are species of *Anarchis*, including the pygmy moray, *A. yoshiae*, of the Atlantic coast of North America, all measuring less than 8 inches long.

Another widely distributed species in the Indo-Pacific region is the 1½-foot *Lycodontis petelli*, marked with alternating broad light and dark bands.

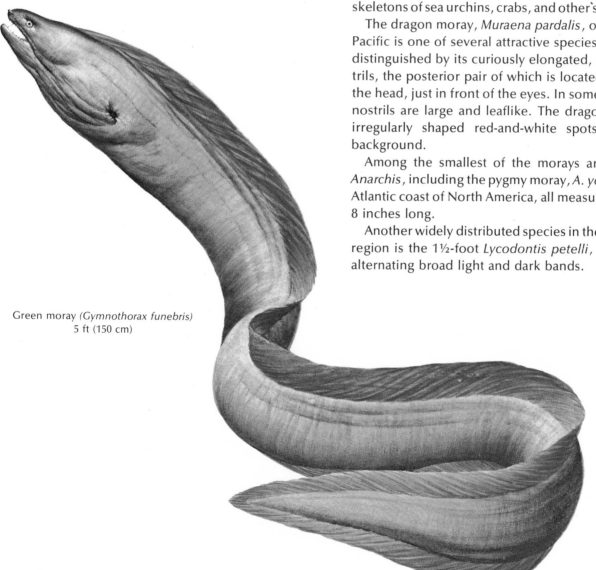

Green moray *(Gymnothorax funebris)*
5 ft (150 cm)

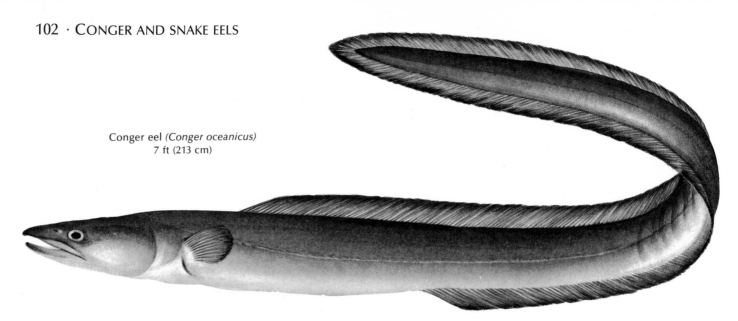

Conger eel *(Conger oceanicus)*
7 ft (213 cm)

Family Congridae
conger eels

Conger eels are a small family of marine eels distinguished from the morays by having pectoral fins and by the black margin on the dorsal and anal fins. Conger eels are found in temperate as well as tropical seas and sometimes in shallow inshore waters, where they may be mistaken for the American eel. Conger eels are scaleless, however, and the dorsal fin originates over the tips of pectorals. Some conger eels live only in deep water. Nine species are found off the North American coasts, eight in the Atlantic and one in the Pacific.

The best-known species is the conger eel, *Conger oceanicus*, widely distributed in European waters, the Mediterranean, the Baltic Sea, off the Atlantic coast of Africa, and North and South America. It reaches a length of about 7 feet and weighs about 22 pounds.

The most common species in Japanese waters is *Astroconger myriaster*. It is caught on hook and line.

Family Ophichthidae
snake eels

Like crayfishes, snake eels move most effectively backward. The tail is stiff and sharp rather than broad and flat as in morays. It is used like an awl to burrow tail first into sand or mud. The nostrils are located in two short, stout barbels on top of the nose, which the eels use to probe into crevices and cavities as they search for food. Compared to morays and most other eels, snake eels are docile creatures, commonly seen crawling about over the bottom like snakes.

In most snake eels the dorsal fin extends almost the full length of the body, beginning just behind the head but stopping short of the tip of the tail. The anal fin is only about half as long, also stopping before the tip of the tail. Pectoral fins are lacking or very small. Only a few of the profuse species reach a length exceeding 3 feet; most of them are less than a foot long. They are typically brightly colored and generally marked strik-

Snake eel *(Ophichthus macrorhynchus,*
2 to 4 ft (60 to 120 cm)

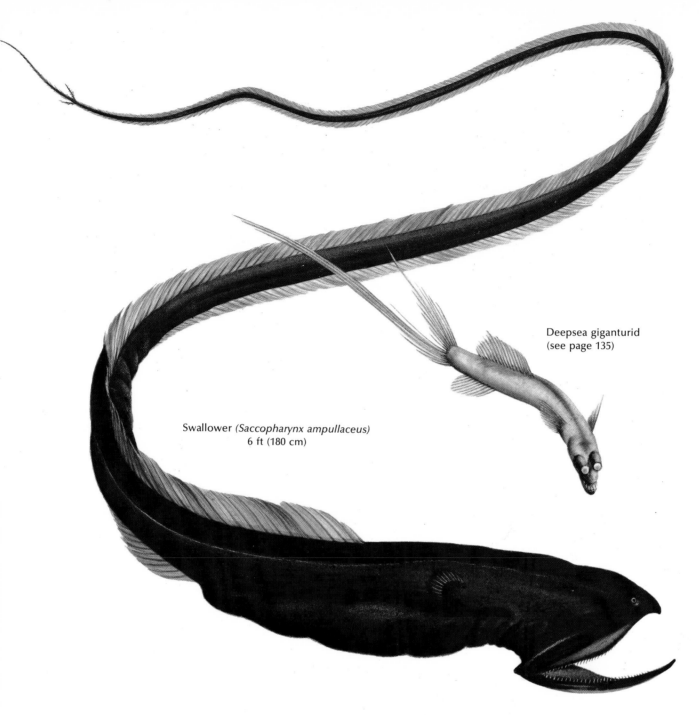

Deepsea giganturid
(see page 135)

Swallower *(Saccopharynx ampullaceus)*
6 ft (180 cm)

ingly with bands, spots, or both. Snake eels are found throughout the world in subtropical and tropical seas, a few ranging into temperate waters.

One of the several dozen species in the Atlantic and the Caribbean is the spotted snake eel, *Ophichthus ophis*, averaging 2 feet in length and occasionally growing to 4 feet. Its yellowish body is covered with large brown spots. The yellow snake eel, *O. zophochir*, is a similar species that lives in the Pacific.

Another genus represented by numerous species is *Myrichthys*, which includes the sharptail eel, *M. acuminatus*, in the Atlantic and the tiger snake eel, *M. tigrinus*, in the Pacific. In Indo-Pacific waters, *M. maculosus* is marked attractively with dark bands between which are round dark spots.

Family Saccopharyngidae
swallowers

The few species in this family, closely related to the gulpers, have large mouths and numerous sharp teeth. A swallower's stomach can be distended to unbelievable size.

The black swallower, *Chiasmodus niger*, measures only about 5 inches long but may swallow fish up to 10 inches long. Swallowers inhabit waters at about the same depth as the gulpers, but the swallowers are larger fishes. *Saccopharynx ampullaceus*, for example, attains a length of 6 feet; *S. harrisoni* may exceed 4 feet. These fishes have whiplike tails with a light at the tip, which they are believed to wrap around victims to hold them.

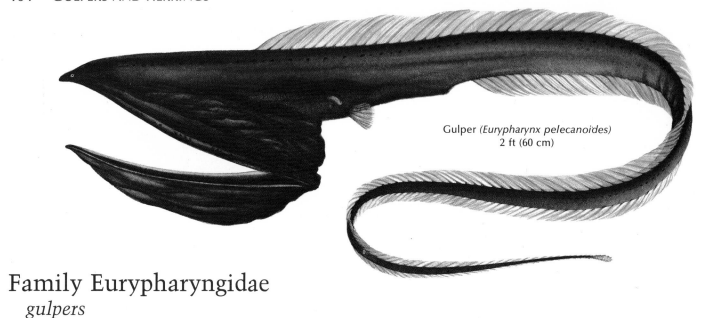

Gulper (*Eurypharynx pelecanoides*)
2 ft (60 cm)

Family Eurypharyngidae
gulpers

The few species in this and two closely related families are known for their especially large mouths. The lower jaw is joined loosely to the upper so that the mouth can be stretched to accommodate astonishingly large prey when compared to the fish's size. At the depths where gulpers live—from about 5,000 to 9,000 feet—food is seldom abundant, and the inhabitants have adapted to utilizing all they can when it is available. Compared to other deepsea fishes, the gulpers are surprisingly long. One of the most common species, *Eurypharynx pelecanoides*, reaches a length of 2 feet. A long, whip-like tail accounts for much of this length. The tail ends in a reddish light that attracts fish. *Eurypharynx* does not eat large animals; it feeds mainly on plankton.

ORDER CLUPEIFORMES

This is a large family of small, silvery fish; only a few species exceed 10 pounds in weight, and most of them weigh a pound or less. Herrings are among the most important of all commercial fishes; some countries in the past depended totally on the herring fishery for their economic well-being. Wars have been waged over the rights to particularly productive fishing grounds for herring, which are found in all seas except the very cold waters of the Arctic and the Antarctic. Large herrings may be eaten fresh, but most of the herrings harvested are first processed by pickling, smoking, or salting them. Smaller herrings are generally canned and sold as sardines.

Most members of the herring family are strictly marine. Some spawn in fresh water, and a few species never go to sea. Typically, herrings travel in gigantic schools that may extend for miles. This makes it possible to harvest them in great quantities. In the sea the herrings serve as a basic food for many other kinds of fishes, plus gulls, seals, whales, and other carnivorous animals. The herrings themselves are plankton feeders, screening their food from the sea on the numerous gill rakers that make a comblike mesh over which water taken into the mouth must pass as it travels out through the gill openings. With few exceptions, the tail is deeply forked, and no lateral line is visible.

Family Clupeidae
herrings

The Atlantic herring, *Clupea harengus harengus*, generally less than a foot long, is the most abundant pelagic fish in the cool waters of the North Atlantic off both the North American and European coasts. In recent years, however, herring stocks have been seriously depleted through overfishing. Schools of herrings contain uncountable billions of individuals. The scales on the midline of the belly form a sharp-edged ridge, which is typical of herrings. Teeth on the roof of the mouth distinguish the Atlantic herring from alewives, which are otherwise similar. Usually in the fall, but sometimes in spring and summer, the herrings move into shallow water to spawn. Each female lays from 25,000 to 40,000 eggs, which are heavy and sink to the bottom. The eggs are coated with sticky mucus so that they stick to any object they contact. Though the time required for the eggs to hatch varies with the depth and temperature of the water, it is generally less than two weeks. The young herrings are nearly 5 inches long by the end of their first year. It may require two more years before they have doubled this length, and typically they do not spawn until they are in their fourth year. The small herrings of this or other species are commercially called sardines. By the time they are 10 inches long, they are known in the commercial trade as "fats" because they have begun to store enough fat in their bodies to make them valuable as a source of oil. Also taken from European waters is the sprat or brisling, *C. sprattus*, which is about half the size of the Atlantic herring.

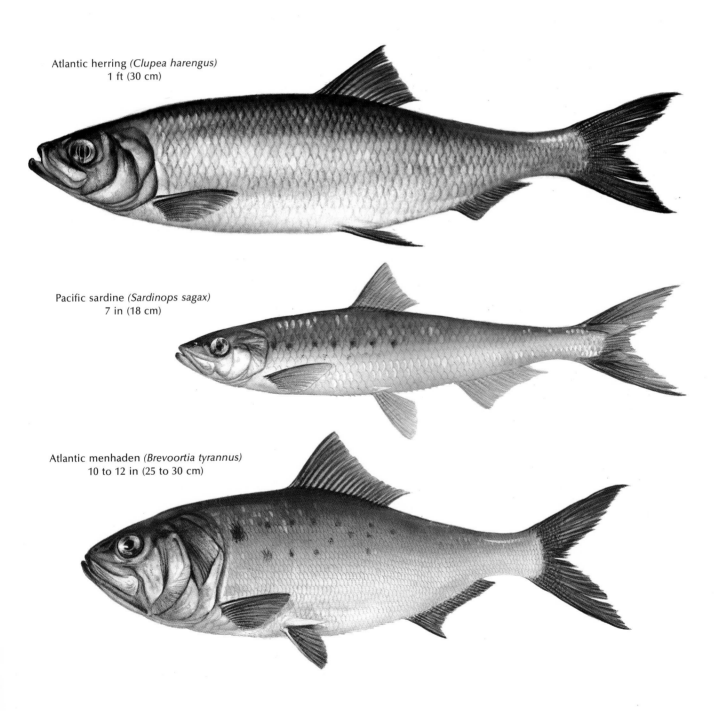

Atlantic herring *(Clupea harengus)*
1 ft (30 cm)

Pacific sardine *(Sardinops sagax)*
7 in (18 cm)

Atlantic menhaden *(Brevoortia tyrannus)*
10 to 12 in (25 to 30 cm)

The Pacific herring, *C. harengus pallasi*, occurs throughout the North Pacific southward to San Diego along the North American coast and also off the coasts of Japan and northern Asia. Because of its greater abundance, it may be more important commercially than the Atlantic herring. It is the principal food of salmons.

The Pacific sardine, *Sardinops sagax*, was one of the most important commercial fishes along the Pacific Coast until pollution and overfishing drastically reduced its numbers in recent years. This species and several others in its genus found along the Pacific coast of South America and in Australia, New Zealand, and Japanese waters is a true sardine, differing from the typical herrings in not having a sharp ridge of scales down the midline of the belly, as herrings do, and in having vertical ridges on its gill covers, which herrings do not. Unlike herrings, Pacific sardines produce eggs that float. Most of the commercial catch is canned or is processed to make fish meal, fertilizer, or oil.

In the Atlantic, the Spanish sardine, *Sardinella anchovia*, is another member of the true sardine group. It is abundant and prolific but never reaches large size. At least another half dozen species of the sardine group roam North American waters, but it takes an expert to identify them.

Among the others in this large family of very similar fishes is the Atlantic menhaden, or mossbunker, or bunker, *Brevoortia tyrannus*, which is the most abundant fish in mid-Atlantic coastal waters off North America. Compared to other herrings, the menhaden is deep-bodied, with a large head, toothed rear margins on its scales, and a large black spot just above and behind the gill covers. Menhadens typically weigh less than a pound. Too oily to be eaten, they are netted in large numbers and processed to make fertilizer, fish meal, and oil. Menhadens were one of the fishes that the Indians used for fertilizer, and they taught the colonists to plant a fish with each seed put into the ground. In this way the menhadens contributed greatly to the bountiful autumn harvests now celebrated by Thanksgiving. In the early days the fishes were used whole and raw, as many as 10,000 per acre spread over the fields. Now they are processed first to get the oil, which is as valuable as the fertilizer. When schools of menhadens move near the surface, they make the water swirl. Sometimes virtually all the fishes in a school will leap from the water simultaneously. Commercial fishermen find the schools by watching flocks of seabirds that hover over the menhadens or they use airplanes or helicopters to help them find the schools.

The bunker is extremely important to the coastal sport fishery where bluefishes and striped basses feed voraciously on the densely packed schools. Highly efficient commercial netters and trawlers came in close to share and wipe out the bunkers. Such action has brought violent reactions from sportsmen.

Three other menhadens that inhabit the Atlantic waters of North America are finescale menhaden, *B. gunteri*; Gulf menhaden, *B. patronus*; and yellowfin menhaden, *B. smithi*.

The menhaden is replaced in southern waters of the Atlantic and also in the Carribbean by the Atlantic thread herring, *Opisthonema oglinum*, distinguished by the long, threadlike last ray in its dorsal fin. The similar middling thread herring, *O. medirastre*, of the Pacific occurs from southern California to the Galapágos Islands. Neither is of great importance commercially except as a bait fish. Like other small species in this family, they contribute significantly to the food of larger fishes that inhabit the same waters.

The American shad, *Alosa sapidissima*, averages more than 3 pounds and may weigh as much as 12 pounds, ranking it as the largest herring. A native of the Atlantic coast from the St. Lawrence River southward to Florida, it makes spawning runs up tributary rivers in the spring. In the late 1800s, the American shad was introduced to the Pacific Coast and is now found from Alaska southward to central California. In some areas its numbers are now greatly diminished as a result of pollution and overfishing. Fresh shad is a delicacy, the roe highly prized. Shad is also canned and frozen.

In the spawning runs, males are the first to appear; females, or "roe shad," come later. Each female carries a tremendous number of eggs—an average of about 30,000 but with exceptionally large females producing four or five times as many. These are spread widely in the water. They are heavy, sinking quickly and sticking to the bottom or to objects along the way. The young shad spend some time in the stream in which the eggs were laid before heading out to sea. The majority of males mature and return to spawn in their fifth year. Females are as much as six or seven years old before they make their first spawning run.

The American shad resembles the alewife, *A. pseudoharengus*, but the adult is toothless, has a distinct indentation in the front of the upper jaw and has deeper cheeks. The sides are silvery, and the back is a metallic green. On the shoulder, just behind each gill cover, is a round black spot followed by several smaller spots, each less distinct than the one in front.

Though long harvested as a commercial fish, the American shad became widely recognized as a sport fish only after World War II. It can be caught on a wide variety of artificial lures. On light tackle, it provides

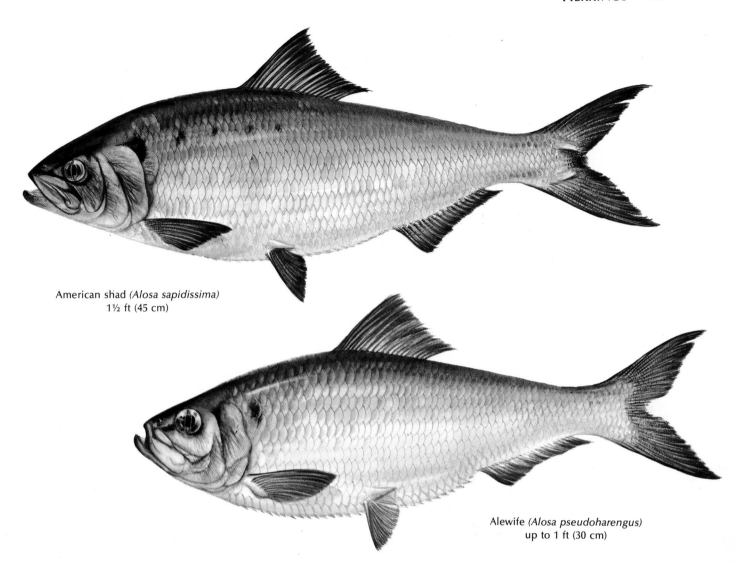

American shad *(Alosa sapidissima)*
1½ ft (45 cm)

Alewife *(Alosa pseudoharengus)*
up to 1 ft (30 cm)

great sport and may leap occasionally in an exciting display of flashing, silvery sides. A hooked fish must be played carefully, for the mouth is tender and tears easily. Shad are generally caught only on their upstream runs to spawning sites. On their return they are too spent to be interested in baits and lures; they utilize all their energy in getting back to the sea, where they recuperate and are ready to spawn again the following spring.

Several other species in the genus *Alosa* also live in the Atlantic coastal waters and in tributary streams. The Ohio shad is harvested in limited numbers commercially, principally for use as bait. The Alabama shad, *A. alabamae*, is another small shad that is most abundant in river systems tributary to the Gulf of Mexico, which it also enters. Compared to other shad, it has a much chunkier body, and its upper jaw is slimmer and more pointed. The Ohio shad and the Alabama shad are now considered one and the same species, and the "Ohio"

has been dropped. Several species of *Alosa* are harvested in European waters.

The hickory shad, *A. mediocris*, averages about 2 pounds in weight, but occasional individuals weigh twice as much. Though it ranges from Nova Scotia to Florida, it is most abundant in the mid-Atlantic region. While most herrings are plankton feeders, consuming perhaps more plants than animals, the hickory shad feeds primarily on animals—small fishes and a wide variety of invertebrates. It can be distinguished from other shad by its projecting lower jaw; also it has 19 to 21 gill rakers, while other shad have 30 or more. Like the American shad, this species is great sport on light tackle. It enters freshwater rivers to spawn.

Skipjack herring, *A. chrysochloris*, also called river herring, are found in the same waters as the Alabama shad but move into the Gulf of Mexico, ranging along the coast from Florida to Texas. Like the hickory shad, this species prefers small fishes or other animals rather

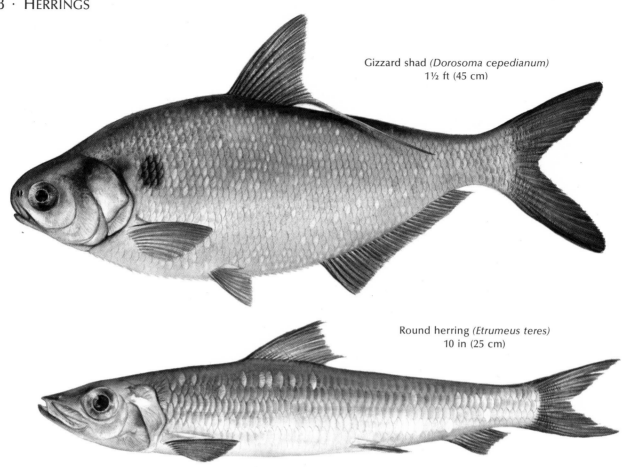

Gizzard shad *(Dorosoma cepedianum)*
1½ ft (45 cm)

Round herring *(Etrumeus teres)*
10 in (25 cm)

than plant food. It has a projecting lower jaw, but the posterior end of the upper jaw extends beyond the middle of the eye (it does not in the hickory shad). About half the eye is covered with a thick, fatty eyelid. Skipjacks generally weigh less than a pound. The maximum recorded was 3½ pounds.

The alewife, *A. pseudoharengus*, is a small Atlantic Coast species that spawns in freshwater streams. It rarely exceeds a foot in length. Those that have been landlocked average about half the size of those that live in the sea. In addition, the American shad has two winglike, or alar, scales on each side at the base of the tail; the alewife has none. The blueback herring, *A. aestivalis*, is found in the same range, but the lining of its body cavity is bluish black, while in other shad it is whitish.

Gizzard shad, *Dorosoma cepedianum*, are primarily freshwater fish, though they may stray into brackish waters. Like other herrings, gizzard shad travel in large schools, but they do not make special spawning runs as the others do. They feed on tiny plants and animals, both living and dead, grubbed from the mud and silt on the bottom of lakes and streams. The adults lack teeth, but they grind up food in their muscular stomach, which

is much like a bird's gizzard. The young have teeth, but these are lost by the time the fish is past the fingerling stage. Gizzard shad are an important forage fish for predators in the waters where they live, and they have been introduced into many lakes out of their native range precisely for this purpose. Rarely more than a foot long, the gizzard shad is distinguished from other herrings by the long, threadlike last ray of its dorsal fin as well as by its gizzardlike stomach. Because of those distinctive features, it is sometimes placed in a separate family, along with about half a dozen other species found in the Indo-Pacific region. The other species are all mainly marine.

The threadfin shad, *Dorosoma petenense*, closely resembles the gizzard shad, but it inhabits the Gulf of Mexico and enters streams from Florida into Mexico. It has been introduced into California freshwater lakes.

Round herrings, often classified in a separate family, differ from typical herrings in that the scales along the midline of the belly do not form a knifelike ridge. As the name implies, the body is more rounded in cross-section. The largest members of the group appear worldwide in warmer seas and belong to the genus *Eutrumeus*, which includes the round herring, *E. teres*,

European anchovy (*Engraulis encrasicolus*)
5 to 6 in (12 to 15 cm)

worldwide in warmer seas, and several other species of tropical waters. Slimmer than typical herrings and seldom exceeding a foot in length, they are not abundant enough to be important in commercial harvests but are occasionally used as bait. Approximately a dozen other species, all small, are abundant in warm waters, sometimes seen in swarming masses. In some tropical countries these little fishes are netted and made into fish pastes to be eaten with rice.

Family Engraulidae
anchovies

Anchovies are small, weak, silvery fishes that resemble miniature herrings. They have a long snout that projects beyond the lower jaw. The mouth is very large and the maxillary extremely long. All of the more than 100 species are very similar in appearance, and few of them measure more than 4 inches in length. They feed on tiny organisms, travel in large schools near shore, and are rarely found at depths greater than 200 feet. Anchovies are worldwide in distribution but are most abundant in subtropical and tropical waters, where they are an important forage fish for a wide variety of predator fishes. They are also netted commercially for human food, generally filleted and salted or made into a paste.

The northern anchovy, *Engraulis mordax*, reaches a length of 9 inches, an exceptional size for an anchovy. It ranges from British Columbia to southern California. Along the western coast of North America, it is one of the most important bait fishes, with a lesser percentage of the harvest processed for human food. As in other species of anchovies, the eggs are elliptical or oval, and they float near the surface. They hatch within a few days after being released, and the young do not mature for three or four years. The closely related European anchovy, *E. encrasicolus*, is harvested in large quantities from the Mediterranean northward to the Scandinavian countries and is the principal anchovy used for human food.

Other species of anchovies occurring off the Pacific coast of North America include the deepbody anchovy, *Anchoa compressa*; the slough anchovy, *A. delicatissima*; the slim anchovy, *Anchoviella miarcha*; and the anchoveta, *Cetengraulis mysticetus*. All are used mainly as bait fishes. The anchoveta, which is most abundant in Central American waters, is especially popular as a bait for tunas.

There are also many kinds of anchovies in Atlantic waters. The striped anchovy, *Anchoa hepsetus*, is particularly abundant in Florida and Caribbean waters. The average length is less than 4 inches. The bay anchovy, *A. mitchili*, was reported from permanent fresh water in the St. Johns River, Florida.

There is confusion regarding the anchovies; common and scientific names continue to be changed by taxonomists.

Family Chirocentridae
wolf herrings

While herrings typically feed on plankton and are small, the slim, intensely silvery wolf herring, *Chirocentrus dorab*, is a voracious predator that averages 5 feet in length and may reach a length of 10 feet. It has almost no gill rakers but does have large fanglike teeth for holding its prey. Internally, the wolf herring has a spiral valve in its intestine, a feature it shares with sharks, rays, and only a few other bony fishes. None of the other herrings has a spiral valve. The wolf herring does look like a herring, however, and the rows of scales down the midline of the belly form a knifelike ridge. It is widely distributed in Indo-Pacific waters.

Wolf herring (*Chirocentrus dorab*)
5 to 10 ft (150 to 300 cm)

ORDER OSTEOGLOSSIFORMES

Family Osteoglossidae
arapaimas and arawanas

These large-scaled, big-eyed fishes, with heads protected by hard bone, live in freshwater streams of South America, Africa, southeastern Asia, and northern Australia. Their enlongated dorsal and anal fins are located so far back on the body that they are scarcely separated from the tail fin, and their heavily vascularized air bladder opens directly to the pharynx, thus functioning as a lung. The family contains only five species.

The arapaima, *Arapaima gigas*, also called pirarucu or paiche, lives in northern South America, chiefly in the Amazon drainage of Brazil and Peru. Reaching a length of about 8 feet and a weight of about 200 pounds, the arapaima is the largest fish that lives wholly in fresh water. Its average length is about 6 feet. The young of these giants are commonly exhibited in public aquariums, but their life in captivity is short. In their native range they are fished for commercially and have gained popularity with sport fishermen.

The arapaima lays its eggs in a nest fanned clear of debris on a sandy bottom. The nest area is generally about 2 feet in diameter. A closely related African species of the genus *Clupisudis* is less than half as long as the arapaima but builds a nest that is twice as large, lining the outside with a ridge of plants and debris removed from the center.

The arawana, *Osteoglossum bicirrhosum*, lives in the same waters as the arapaima. Usually less than 2 feet long, it has on its lower jaw two fleshy barbels that are presumably sensory in function. The lower jaw slants upward sharply, a distinctive and identifying feature. The arawana is believed to carry its eggs in its mouth, as do related species, also with barbels, of southeastern Asia and Australia. A fine sport fish, it jumps like a salmon when hooked and is excellent on the table. The arawana is seldom still and swims in a slow circular pattern in captivity. It is thought to be a mouth breeder.

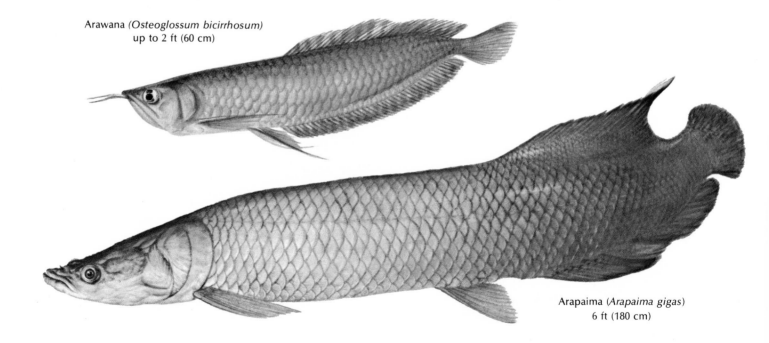

Arawana *(Osteoglossum bicirrhosum)*
up to 2 ft (60 cm)

Arapaima *(Arapaima gigas)*
6 ft (180 cm)

Family Pantodontidae
freshwater butterflyfish

A single species, with unique pelvic fins, the freshwater butterflyfish or chisel-jaw, *Pantodon buchholzi*, comprises this family. It lives in freshwater streams of western Africa, swimming just beneath the surface and sometimes making leaps that span a distance of 5 feet or more. The broad pectoral fins are attached to the body by a flap of skin and resemble the wings of a butterfly, accounting for the fish's name; they presumably aid the fish in gliding for short distances. Even more unusual are the pelvic fins, which consist of long, bristly filaments that do not have a connecting membrane between them. The dorsal fin is located far to the rear, directly over the anal fin. This fish is sometimes kept in aquariums, but a large amount of space is needed.

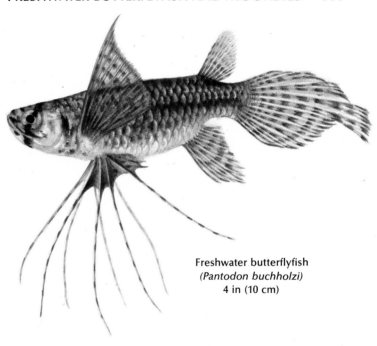

Freshwater butterflyfish
(Pantodon buchholzi)
4 in (10 cm)

Family Hiodontidae
mooneyes

Mooneyes are freshwater fishes of eastern North America. They resemble herrings but lack the sharp ridge of scales down the middle of the belly. Their eyes are large, and they have small teeth, accounting for the name toothed herrings that is often used for the family.

The family's largest member is the mooneye, *Hiodon tergisus*, which commonly reaches a weight of 2 pounds. Found from Hudson Bay westward through the Mississippi River and its tributaries and southward to Alabama and Arkansas, the mooneye lives mainly in large rivers and lakes but may travel into smaller streams to spawn. Though it is rarely fished for specifically, it is a fairly common catch, taking flies and other small artificials and giving a game fight.

The goldeye, *H. alosoides*, occurs in much the same range as the mooneye but does not inhabit the Great Lakes. Slightly smaller than the mooneye, it averages less than a pound in weight, though occasional individuals weigh twice as much. The two species are superficially identical, but they can be distinguished by the color of the iris (gold in the goldeye, silver in the mooneye), by the 9–10 dorsal fin rays in the goldeye as opposed to 11–12 in the mooneye, and by the position of the dorsal fin (anterior margin begins behind the front of the anal fin in the goldeye and in front of the anal fin in the mooneye). Like the mooneye, this species is caught on light tackle and provides the angler with considerable fight. In Canada it is netted commercially, then smoked and sold as a delicacy. When smoked in willow wood, the flesh becomes pinkish red; since this was the way smoked goldeyes were first marketed, red coloring is used to tint the flesh even if the fish are smoked in some other wood.

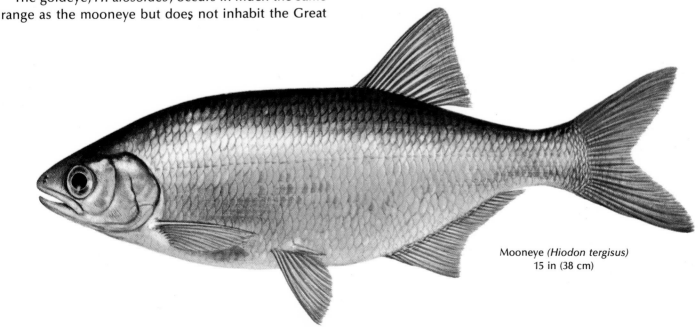

Mooneye *(Hiodon tergisus)*
15 in (38 cm)

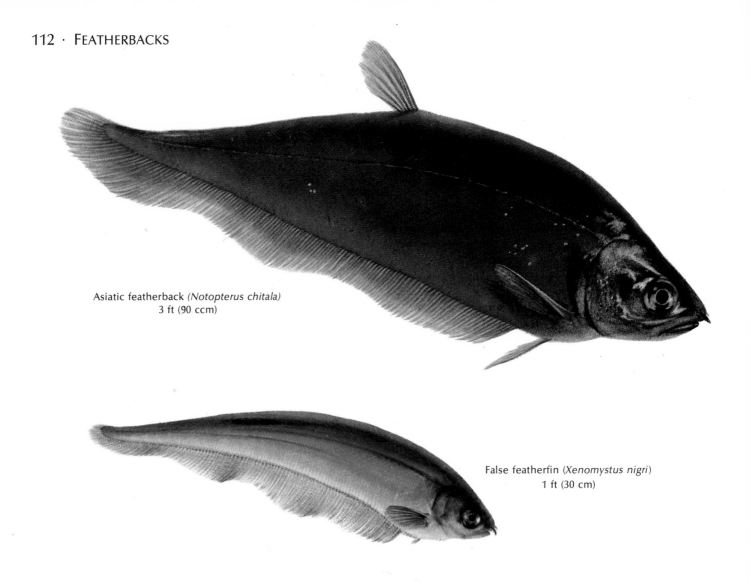

Asiatic featherback (Notopterus chitala)
3 ft (90 ccm)

False featherfin (Xenomystus nigri)
1 ft (30 cm)

Family Notopteridae
featherbacks

The featherbacks, or knifefishes, are members of a small family of elongated freshwater fishes confined to tropical Africa and Southeast Asia. They are easily identified by their exceptionally long anal fin. The fin starts near the head or just under the pectoral fins and extends all the way to the tail, where it joins with the caudal fin, which is not separate or identifiable from it. The feathery fin moves with a rippling motion to propel the fish through the water. A featherback can move backward or forward with gliding grace. The scales are small. The mouth is large and contains numerous teeth.

The banded knifefish, Notopterus chitala, found in Australian and Indian waters, is the largest member of the family, occasionally attaining a length of 3 feet. It is much esteemed as a food fish, and local governments have established programs to help increase the success-ful spawning of the species. A small species, N. notop-terus, occurs in the same range and is valued as a food.

The African knifefish, N. afer, may reach a length of 2 feet. When young, it is brownish, mottled, or reticulated with black; as it grows older these markings disappear, and the entire fish becomes darker. Like other members of the family, it inhabits slow-moving streams or quiet pools in which there is a dense growth of plants. It spawns in marshy shallows. All the species of Notopterus tend to be quarrelsome in aquariums and cannot be kept with other fishes.

The false featherfin, Xenomystus nigri, also found in tropical African waters, is not vicious and can be kept sucessfully with other fishes. Unlike other members of the family, it lacks a dorsal fin. It reaches a length of about a foot.

ORDER MORMYRIFORMES

Family Mormyridae
mormyrids

More than a hundred species comprise this family of unusual freshwater fishes that are found only in tropical African waters. All are distinguished by a peculiar mouth, projected like an elephant's trunk. This long, flexible snout is used to probe in the mud for food. The mouth is small and contains only a few teeth. Still another distinctive feature is that all mormyrids are capable of producing mild electrical shocks from modified muscles located on each side of the caudal peduncle. The electricity is used as a sort of radar in locating food rather than as a shocking mechanism to kill or stun prey. The many-rayed dorsal fin is located far to the rear, directly over the anal fin.

Many species of mormyrids are small—no longer than 6 inches—but there are also species that reach a length of 4 or 5 feet. As oddities, the mormyrids are sometimes displayed in aquariums, but they are generally too quarrelsome for most hobbyists. They are typically active only at night, preferring to keep hidden and out of the light during the day.

The tapir fish, *Mormyrus kanumae*, rarely exceeding a length of 1½ feet, is a Nile River species that is commonly exhibited in public aquariums, as is the elephant-nosed mormyrid, *Gnathonemus numenius*. The snout of *G. curvirostris* is unusal in that it curves downward sharply.

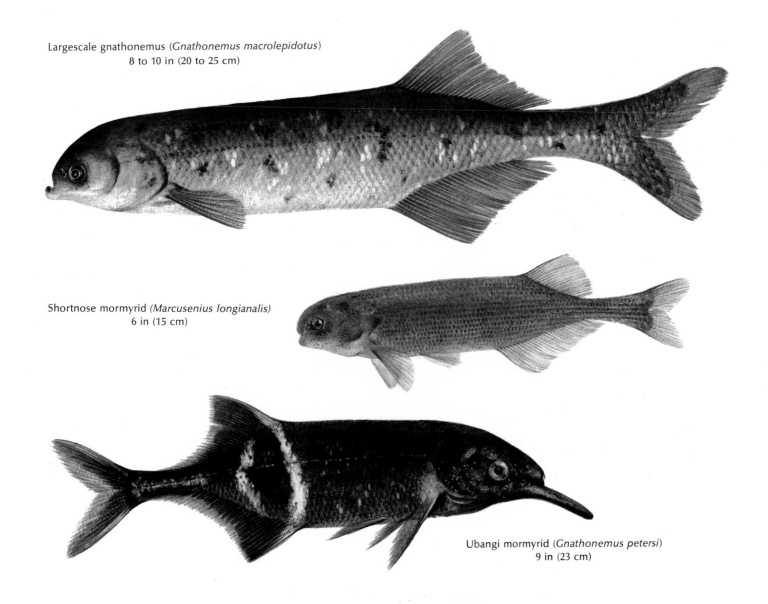

Largescale gnathonemus (*Gnathonemus macrolepidotus*)
8 to 10 in (20 to 25 cm)

Shortnose mormyrid (*Marcusenius longianalis*)
6 in (15 cm)

Ubangi mormyrid (*Gnathonemus petersi*)
9 in (23 cm)

The Ubangi mormyrid, *G. petersi*, is one of several species in its genus in which only the lower jaw is extended. Measuring only about 9 inches long, this species is one of the most desirable for a small aquarium. In another species, *G. macrolepidotus*, the extension of the lower jaw is small and rounded.

The eel-like *G. niloticus* reaches a length of 5 feet. It lacks tail, anal, and pelvic fins but has an unusually long dorsal fin, which extends the full length of its body.

Members of the genus *Marcusenius* diverge completely from the family by not having long snouts. Their mouths, normal in size, are directed downward, toward the bottom where the fishes get their food. All are less than 6 inches long, and several species of this genus are kept in aquariums. Like other mormyrids, they can generate small amounts of electricity.

ORDER SALMONIFORMES

Family Salmonidae
trouts, salmons, whitefishes, and graylings

These are among the best known and most important of all fishes, sought after both commercially and by sport fishermen. Distributed throughout the temperate and cool regions of the Northern Hemisphere, many species have been introduced to the Southern Hemisphere as well as to other suitable waters in the Northern Hemisphere.

Biologically, salmons and their relatives are primitive fishes, with fossil relatives dating to more than 100 million years ago. Evidence indicates that many of the more advanced or specialized families of modern-day bony fishes have ancestral stock closely resembling these primitive fishes.

The most clearly evident primitive feature of the group is the lack of spines in the fins. Most of the soft rays in the fins are branched. The pelvic fins are situated far back on the body—in the "hip" region, where the legs of amphibians articulate with the body. This is in contrast to the position of the pelvic fins in a largemouth bass, a member of a more advanced family, which are so far forward they are almost directly beneath the pectoral fins. Internally, members of the family Salmonidae have a primitive type of air bladder, again revealing the antiquity of the group. Salmons and trouts are further identified by the possession of a small to medium-size adipose fin, which is located on the dorsal surface of the body directly above the anal fin.

To most people, salmons and trouts signify cold, often rushing streams. Essentially this is true. Their demands for oxygen are high. Many of the species are also closely tied to the sea, spending at least a portion of their lives there. All members of the family spawn in fresh water, however, and most of them require running water. Members of some of the sea-running species have become landlocked, living and reproducing successfully without ever taking a journey to sea.

Atlantic salmon *(Salmo salar)*
3 ft (90 cm)

The Atlantic salmon, *Salmo salar*, has attracted man both as a sport fish and a food fish since recorded history. Though much has been known about its life in fresh water, where it spawns and where some species are landlocked, surprisingly little was known about the life of the Atlantic salmon in the sea until recent years. Not until the mid-1960s was a general feeding ground for Atlantic salmon off Greenland discovered and an exploitation of this sea sanctuary begun, largely by Danish commercial fishermen. Another feeding ground was later located off Norway. Unlike the Pacific salmon, which makes its spawning runs to the headwaters of streams and then dies, the Atlantic salmon spawns, returns to the sea, and then comes back the next season to spawn again. Some individuals make these annual treks three or four times during their lifetime. These spawning runs occur along the northern coasts of both North America and Europe—from Greenland southward to Maine and from Sweden and Norway to as far south as Spain. In bygone days heavy runs entered the Connecticut River; today, only an occasional stray reaches it. Projects to restore the Atlantic salmon in the Connecticut River are in process. Salmons have found their pathways to spawning areas blocked by dams. This is often of little relevance because the streams are so polluted that the salmons find it unlivable.

Whether the Atlantic salmon will survive or will go the way of other creatures exterminated by the avarice of humans is yet in the balance. Needed is international legislation that will not only control harvests but also insist on the return of the fish's freshwater and saltwater environments to what they were originally.

Compared to the size of its body, a mature Atlantic salmon has a small head. Its body is long and slim; and in adults, the caudal or tail fin is nearly square. Salmons that return to spawn prematurely are mostly males; they have a slightly forked tail. While in the sea, the Atlantic salmon is dark blue on the top of its head and back; its sides are shiny silvery, and the belly is white. The fins are dark, and there are numerous black marks in the shape of an *X* on its head and along its body above the lateral line. When the fish enters fresh water to spawn, it gradually loses its metallic shine and becomes dull brown or yellowish. Many, particularly males, are splotched with red or have large black patches on the body. At spawning time the males are further distinguished by their greatly elongated, hooked jaws that meet only at the tips; the fins become thicker, and a heavy coat of slime covers the body.

Young salmons—4 to 8 inches long—that migrate to sea are called smolts. In the ocean, they eat voraciously and grow rapidly. Some of the males reach a weight of 2

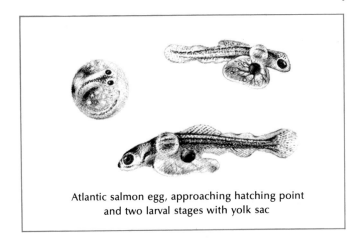

Atlantic salmon egg, approaching hatching point and two larval stages with yolk sac

to 5 pounds after a year of sea life and may participate in the spawning runs. These are called grilse. Salmons returning to the rivers after two or more years in the sea average about 10 to 12 pounds, depending on which river is involved. Occasionally, a salmon weighing as much as 40 pounds is caught, but such fishes are becoming increasingly scarce. An official hook-and-line record weighed 79 pounds 2 ounces and was caught in the Tana River off Norway. There are unofficial but reasonably reliable records of fishes weighing as much as 100 pounds.

Spawning runs occur in autumn, the exact time varying with the river as does also the distance the fishes travel upstream. In some places, the spawning areas are actually close to the sea, not far above the high-tide level. In other streams, the spawners may travel a hundred miles or more to find the proper conditions. The early spawners begin to appear in streams during the spring months. These fish have the firmest flesh and are most sought after. They are followed soon by the grilse and then by more mature fish, the runs slacking off during the hot summer months but increasing again in early autumn. Early-run fish do not move upstream rapidly; their gonads are not yet well enough developed for the actual spawning act. Sometimes the late arrivals catch up with them, and they reach their destination at the same time. Spawning takes place from October through December.

The female salmon digs a nest, or redd, in the gravel at the spawning site, fanning the spot with her tail and letting the current wash away the silt and fine particles. The nest is generally large—about 10 feet long and 3 to 4 feet wide. As soon as the nest is completed, the female deposits her eggs in it, and one or more males spread milt over them. Meanwhile, the female has moved immediately upstream, where she begins making another nest. As she digs into the gravel there, she automatically covers the fertilized eggs in the nest behind her. A large female will deposit more than 800 eggs per pound of fish during the spawning period.

Salmon eggs that are laid in autumn hatch the following spring. The tiny fry, about an inch long, still have an egg sac attached to them, and they survive on this "lunch bag" for a month or longer before they begin to hunt food for themselves. When the fingerlings begin to grow, the young, brownish fishes, now called parrs, are covered with spots and show several bars or parr marks on their sides. Some parrs remain in fresh water for as long as six years before traveling downstream to the sea, but a stay of two or three years is average. The males may even become sexually mature before their journey to the sea. Like trouts, they feed mainly on aquatic insects, both the immature and adult stages. As the little salmons move toward the sea, their parr marks gradually disappear, and by the time they leave fresh water they are silvery smolts.

Salmons that remain in the sea for two years or longer before making their first spawning run become the largest, heaviest fishes. Those that mature early, returning for the first time as grilse, are not large. Some may make a spawning run only once or twice during their lifetime of about eight years; others will spawn three or four times, returning in consecutive years to the same spawning grounds.

On its spawning run, the Atlantic salmon does not feed, though it can be caught on skillfully presented artificial flies. It is a prime conquest of the fly fishermen. In clear water where the fish can be seen, it is not uncommon for a fisherman to present his lure with literally dozens of accurate casts before the fish's interest is sufficiently sparked to move to the offering.

Lake populations of the Atlantic salmon are variously known as ouananiche, lake Atlantic salmon, landlocked salmon, and Sebago salmon. They are fishes that live in deep, cold lakes of New York, New England, and southeastern Canada and are not distinguishable from those that go to sea except by their smaller size. The average size is less than 5 pounds. The record caught on rod and reel weighed 22½ pounds, and commercial fishermen reportedly netted one that weighed 35 pounds. Fishing for landlocked salmons is best in early spring immediately after the ice goes out. The salmons then move into the shallows, where they feed actively. At this time they can be caught on natural baits or flies. As the water warms, the salmons move into the depths where it is still cold enough for their comfort.

The five species of Pacific salmons are native to both northern Pacific coasts, from Monterey Bay in California and from northern Japan on the Atlantic coast northward beyond the Bering Strait between Alaska and the Soviet Union. An additional species is found in northern Japan.

All Pacific salmons belong to the genus *Oncorhynchus*. Of these the Chinook, or king salmon, *O. tshawytscha*, is the largest. Most of those caught on rod and reel weigh less than 40 pounds and are generally in the 10-pound category. The record rod-and-reel catch weighed 83 pounds, however; and a salmon weighing 126½ pounds was netted. They are usually caught as they travel up rivers to spawn. This is a wide-ranging species—from California to Alaska and then southward in the western Pacific to China.

The Chinook salmon begins moving into rivers to spawn as early as March and continues to appear through spring. There is a reduction in its numbers during the summer, and then the runs begin again in late summer or early autumn. For some individuals the trips are short, as in the case of the Atlantic salmon, but many travel hundreds of miles to the headwaters of streams. The longest spawning trip known is from the

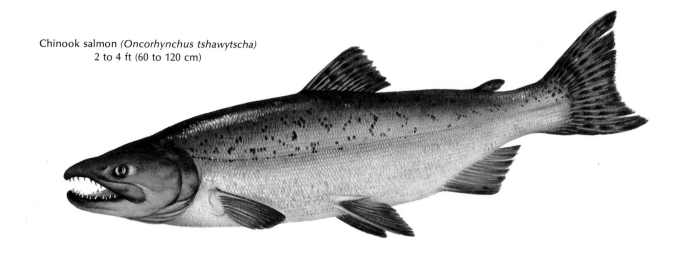

Chinook salmon *(Oncorhynchus tshawytscha)*
2 to 4 ft (60 to 120 cm)

Bering Sea up Alaska's Yukon River to Lake Teslin in Canada, a total distance exceeding 2,400 miles. The journey requires two months of traveling 40 miles a day, and the climb is from sea level to an altitude of 2,200 feet. Over most of the Chinook salmon's range, dams and pollution as well as heavy fishing have been damaging to the population.

The fishes that enter the streams early in the season are younger and much more brightly colored than those arriving later. All salmons turn darker as spawning time approaches in the rivers. Each species has a characteristic change in coloration that varies from greens and browns to lavender and dark red. They all lose the bright bluish green upper parts and silvery sides that they have in the sea. The jaws of the males become elongated and hooked at their tips. They can no longer close their mouths completely; and they develop long, fierce-looking canine teeth. In both sexes, the eyes are set deep in their sockets, and their fins are frayed. A salmon at spawning time has lost its attractive appearance.

When a female salmon of the Pacific reaches the spawning site, she prepares a nest, or redd, in the gravel, as the Atlantic salmon does, and lays her eggs there. They are immediately fertilized by males. The female covers the eggs lightly with gravel as she prepares another nest immediately above the first, sometimes making several such nests before she has exhausted her supply of eggs. A total of 5,000 eggs may be produced by a large female during a single spawning season. After their long trip and the spawning act, both males and females are completely "spent." They struggle feebly back into the current of the stream and try to find refuge in deeper pools; but within a few days all are dead, their bodies washing onto the shore.

The eggs usually hatch in about two months, the fry staying in the protective gravel until the yolk sac is completely absorbed. Then they squirm free and move out into the stream. Young salmons feed on immature and adult aquatic insects. Some return to the sea while they are still fingerlings; others may stay in the streams for more than a year. As in other young salmons, the Chinook fingerlings have dark parr markings on their sides. The Chinook salmon stay in the sea for two to eight years before returning to the same stream to spawn.

In the Pacific, the coho, or silver salmon, *O. kisutch*, a favorite of sport fishermen, is found from California to Alaska. This species has also been introduced successfully into the Great Lakes as a replacement for the lake trout. A hooked coho salmon generally fights near the surface and may make several spectacular leaps into the air, much to the delight of the angler. Most coho salmons caught on rod and reel weigh 5 to 10 pounds; the

Chum salmon (*Oncorhynchus keta*)
up to 3½ ft (105 cm)

largest recorded weighed 31 pounds. The coho salmon can be distinguished from the Chinook salmon by two features: (1) the coho's gums are white, the Chinook's black; and (2) the coho has black spots on only the upper portion of its tail, while the Chinook has black spots over its entire tail.

Coho salmons spawn in streams, some remaining close to the sea and others traveling far upstream to the headwaters. Spawning occurs from November through February, the eggs hatching in spring or early summer. Some of the fry migrate to the sea immediately, but most of the fingerling coho salmons remain in fresh water until the following spring. Their growth becomes rapid as soon as they enter the ocean, some of them maturing by the end of their second year but most maturing in their third year. Both sport and commercial fishing become active as the fishes move back to the streams in which they hatched.

The sockeye salmon, *O. nerka*, is an important commerical fish, but since it seldom takes baits or lures, sport fishermen have little interest in this species. Other common names are blueback salmon and red salmon. Unlike other members of the Pacific salmon group, the

Coho salmon *(Oncorhynchus kisutch)*
1½ to 3 ft (45 to 90 cm)

sockeye has very small black spots on its back. Males undergo tremendous changes in body form at spawning time, becoming distinctly "humped." Their sides turn a bright red, the head greenish. As in other salmons, the jaws elongate and become hooked at the tip. Most of the sockeye salmons returning to streams to spawn are four years old, and they weigh 4 to 6 pounds. There are

Male

Sockeye salmon (*Oncorhynchus nerka*)
up to 3 ft (90 cm)

Female

The pink salmon, *O. gorbuscha*, is the smallest Pacific salmon and highly important commercially. Because it responds to baits and lures, it is sought after by sport fishermen as well. Males develop a very pronounced hump just behind their head at spawning time, hence the species goes also by the name of humpback salmon. Though it ranges from California to Alaska, it occurs in greater abundance farther south than do other species. In the pink salmon, maturity always comes at two years of age, at which time a fish will weigh an average of 3 pounds; occasionally individuals weigh as much as 10 pounds. Pink salmons rarely migrate far inland to spawn, most of their spawning taking place just above the high-tide level. Unlike other salmons, the fry lack parr marks.

Pink salmon (*Oncorhynchus gorbuscha*)
up to 2½ ft (75 cm)

records of a five-year-old fish weighing 15 pounds. Sockeye salmons range from Oregon northward to Alaska. The kokanee is a landlocked form of the sockeye found in some lakes of British Columbia, Washington, Idaho, and Oregon; it has been introduced into California, Connecticut, and elsewhere. It is a smaller fish, weighing only about a pound; the record is 5 pounds. This fish provides great sport for anglers. With the large rainbow trout, the kokanee has helped make Lake Pend Oreille in Idaho a mecca for sport fishermen.

The chum salmon, *O. keta*, also called dog salmon, is mainly a commercial species but provides good sport on rod and reel. It has only a very light sprinkling of dark spots on its back, scarcely noticeable at all in a fish in salt water. Otherwise it resembles the chinook salmon. At spawning time, males are mottled with lavender-red and green on their sides, and their back is black. The spawners generally enter streams when they are four years old, weighing 5 to 10 pounds. The record was a 35-pounder taken in a net. The chum salmon ranges from San Francisco to Alaska, with the greatest abundance in Alaska. It occurs also off the coast of Japan.

Trouts rank highly as popular sport fishes. They thrive in cold, unpolluted waters. Some species spend a portion of their lives in the sea. Most species cannot tolerate water that is consistently warmer than 70 degrees F., but there are a few exceptions. For most species, it is the need for oxygen as much as the temperature of the water. Warm water can hold less oxygen than cool or cold water. In addition, warm waters are generally slow-moving while cold streams are fast-flowing and constantly churning in a fresh supply of oxygen from the air. Many species of trouts have been introduced into areas where they are not native but where the waters are suitable.

The rainbow trout, *Salmo gairdneri*, one of the most popular sport fishes of western North America, has been introduced to many other parts of the world. Those that migrate to sea and return to fresh water to spawn are called steelheads. A special race found in British Columbia and in northwestern United States, most notably in Idaho's Lake Pend Oreille, is called the kamloops trout. The color is variable—so much so that, based on color, the species was once divided into more

Rainbow trout *(Salmo gairdneri)*
1 to 1½ ft (30 to 45 cm)

Cutthroat trout *(Salmo clarki)*
8 to 14 in (20 to 36 cm)

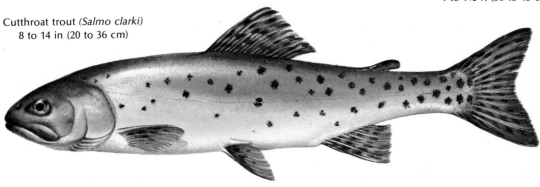

than a dozen different species. The young are spotted and have pronounced parr marks along the sides of the body. In adults the spots are subdued in lake environments but are usually heavy in rivers and streams. Typically, a pink stripe extends from gill covers to tail. There is no pink or red on the underside of the jaw, as in cutthroat trout, however. Steelheads lack the pink lateral band when in the sea but acquire it after a period of time in fresh water. Rainbows do not have teeth behind the tongue; cutthroats do. Although the presence of these hyoid teeth is one of the most reliable characteristics for distinguishing cutthroats from rainbows, some cutthroats do not have them.

Rainbow trouts normally spawn in the spring, some in the fall. Less commonly, these trouts will spawn twice a year—both spring and fall. Those living in lakes move into streams, where the females make a nest in which they lay their eggs. The male immediately fertilizes them, and the female then covers the nest loosely with gravel as she constructs another nest immediately above the first. The eggs hatch in about two months, and the fry may move back to the lake immediately or may remain in the stream for as long as three years.

Steelheads travel to sea, where they live for several years before returning to freshwater streams to spawn.

They become generally larger than those remaining in fresh water, averaging about 8 pounds and not uncommonly weighing more than 20 pounds. There are authenticated records of both groups weighing considerably more (a 42-pound steelhead was caught on rod and reel in Alaskan waters in 1970), but these are rare. As with the salmons, the construction of power dams on spawning streams threatens the survival of these fishes, either by blocking their travel or by polluting the waters. Both salmons and trouts are highly sensitive to changes in natural water conditions. Excesses of nitrogen in spawning streams have been most damaging.

Similar to the rainbow trout is the gila trout, *S. gilae*, which is found only in the Gila and San Francisco rivers of New Mexico. It is heavily spotted, like the cutthroat, but lacks teeth on the back of the tongue. Because of its limited distribution and the ease with which it crosses with other species, the gila trout could easily disappear as a distinct species.

The cutthroat trout, *S. clarki*, inhabits the same general area as the rainbow trout and is popular with sport fishermen. The cutthroat has many local common names, but most of them refer in some manner to the blood-red slash on each side of the lower jaw. Those that have just returned from the sea are bluish green

Brook trout (*Salvelinus fontinalis*)
½ to 2 ft (15 to 60 cm)

and only lightly spotted, but in fresh water they are heavily spotted over most of the body, the spots extending onto the tail fin. As indicated earlier, the cutthroat is further distinguished from the rainbow by the prominent teeth on the back of its tongue. Cutthroats returning from the sea average only about a pound in weight. Individuals weighing 4 pounds are not uncommon, and there are numerous records of fish in the 15- to 20-pound category. The largest ever recorded was a 41-pounder caught on rod and reel in Pyramid Lake in Nevada in 1925.

Still another of the western aristocrats is the golden trout, *S. aguabonita*, found originally only in a few high, cold mountain streams and lakes of the California Sierras. It has since been more widely distributed in the Sierras and in other mountain areas. This handsome trout derives its name from its gold or yellowish sides. The dorsal fin is tipped with gold, the ventral and anal fins with white. Its belly is white, a red stripe extends from its head to its tail, and its head and back are olive. The cheeks and gill covers are pink. In a typical specimen, there are parr marks along the sides and black spots on the head and body above the lateral line. The entire caudal peduncle is spotted with black. As with most fishes, there is considerable color variation from one body of water to another. Golden trout average less than a pound; a record catch weighed 11 pounds.

The brown trout, *S. trutta*, can survive in warmer waters than other trouts. Brown trouts from several different parts of Europe, mainly from Germany and Scotland (the latter called loch levens), were introduced to North America years ago, and this hardy species has also been taken to other parts of the world. In the United States, the different races have become so mixed that their original slight differences are no longer distinguishable. Brown trouts are one of the most challenging trouts to catch, and for this reason they have generally increased in numbers where native trouts have suffered from heavy fishing. Further, because of

their aggressive and predatory habits, they are highly competitive with native species, making it unwise to stock brown trouts in waters where it is desirable to maintain native populations. To the angler's delight, the brown trout takes flies readily.

Brown trouts have brownish backs, grading into yellowish on the sides. There are dark brown or black spots on the head, back, and sides, and in some there is also a scattering of bright red or orange spots. In most individuals, the black spots occur also on the dorsal and adipose fins and on the upper half of the tail fin. The caudal or tail fin is distinctly square, and there are well-developed teeth on the roof of the mouth.

In Europe and also in northeastern United States, there are sea-run populations of brown trouts. These fishes resemble the Atlantic salmon and are difficult to distinguish by the layman. Brown trouts generally weigh less than a pound, but 5-pounders are not unusual. The record, caught in Scotland, weighed 39½ pounds. Brown trouts are fall spawners. The average number of eggs deposited by a female varies with the size of the fish, anywhere between 200 and 6,000 per female.

In Europe, a species closely related to the brown trout is found only in one lake in Italy. Because of the limited distribution of this species, *S. carpio*, its survival is in doubt, resembling in this respect the gila trout of the western United States.

The brook trout, *Salvelinus fontinalis*, is the most widespread of the group called chars. All members of the genus *Salvelinus*, the chars have smaller scales, rounder bodies, and fewer teeth on the roof of the mouth than do trouts of the genus *Salmo*. The brook trout was originally found in streams of northeastern United States and southern Canada and as far west as the feeder streams of the upper Mississippi. It has since been introduced to streams throughout North America as well as to other countries. The brook trout is easily identified by the light wormlike markings on its back and sides and by the white forward edges, sharply out-

Brown trout *(Salmo trutta)*
10 to 18 in (25 to 46 cm)

Lake trout *(Salvelinus namaycush)*
1 to 3 ft (30 to 90 cm)

lined with black, on the pectoral, pelvic, and anal fins. Most individuals have numerous yellowish spots and fewer reddish spots that are outlined with blue. The tail is square. The brook trout has a strong affinity for cool waters and commonly spawns in feeder springs of streams or lakes. Splakes are hybrids of brook trouts and lake trouts.

Because they take baits and lures eagerly and provide a hard, exciting fight, brook trouts are extremely popular with anglers. The average size is less than half a pound, but fishes weighing 2 to 3 pounds are common enough to keep anglers' appetites whetted. A record rod-and-reel catch weighed 14½ pounds.

The lake trout, *S. namaycush,* once supported a large commercial fishery in the Great Lakes, the harvest annually in the millions of pounds because of the abundance of these large trouts in the deep, cold waters. Siltation and pollution, combined with the decimation of the population by parasitic sea lampreys, totally destroyed this fishery.

Lake trouts are caught by sport fishermen, too. During the spring months, when the fishes move into the shallows to feed, they can be caught on surface or shallow-running lures and baits; in winter, they are fished for through the ice. Most of the year, however, they can be taken only by trolling, using wire lines to work depths as great as 100 feet where these fishes move to find water at a temperature at which they are comfortable—50 degrees F. or less. The average size of the lake trout is less than 10 pounds, but there are records of individuals weighing as much as 100 pounds. These large fish are known to be 35–40 years old.

The lake trout has a deeply forked caudal or tail fin. The general body color is greenish, grayish, brownish, and sometimes almost black with numerous pinkish or yellowish spots on the back and sides, even below the lateral line and extending also onto the dorsal and caudal fins. The teeth on the roof of the mouth are prominent. Females do not make a definite nest in which to deposit their eggs. At spawning time, in October or November, several females and males gather, preferably near shore. The males spread milt over the eggs as soon as the females deposit them.

The Arctic char, *S. alpinus,* is circumpolar in distribution in the Arctic. One race, called the Alpine trout, is found only in the high mountain streams and lakes of mid-Europe. Because it is found in such distant areas, few sport fishermen are fortunate enough to catch this species, but it is an important food for people living in Labrador and other northern areas. The Arctic char has a forked tail, though less prominently so than the lake trout, and pink spots along its sides. Like the lake trout, it has strong teeth on its tongue. In most individuals the back and sides are olive green, the belly white. Most Arctic chars weigh a pound or less, but 3-pounders are not uncommon; and among the sea-runners, 5- and 10-pounders are not unusual. There are records of some individuals weighing 25 pounds.

The Sunapee trout, found only in deep, cold lakes in Maine and New Hampshire, is considered by some

Arctic char (*Salvelinus alpinus*)
1½ ft (45 cm)

Arctic grayling *(Thymallus arcticus)*
1½ ft (45 cm)

biologists to be a race of the Arctic char. Others give it a separate species rank, *S. aureolus*. Similarly, the blueback trout and the Quebec red trout are regarded by some authors as being distinct from the Arctic char.

The Dolly Varden trout, *S. malma*, lives primarily in streams, but there are also sea-running populations. This species occurs in western North America from northern California to Alaska and then southward along the coast of Asia to Korea. The back is greenish, becoming lighter on the sides and white on the belly. The back and sides are sprinkled with yellowish white spots. On some individuals the leading edges of the pectoral, pelvic, and anal fins have a light border, though not as pronounced as in the brook trout. Dolly Varden trouts average about 1 to 2 pounds in weight, with a record catch of 32 pounds. Some taxonomists consider the Dolly Varden to be identical with, or a subspecies of, the Arctic char, along with several other subspecies that are found in eastern waters. Because of its predatory habits, this species is looked upon with disfavor in salmon-fishing waters.

The Arctic grayling, *Thymallus arcticus*, a species intermediate between trouts and whitefishes, is some-

times placed in a separate family, Thymallidae. The adipose fin is very small; and in males, the dorsal fin is large, rounded, and sail-like. The tail is forked, and the mouth is small. The scales on the body are large. This species was once found as far south as Montana, but its range has been steadily diminished except in far northern waters. It occurs also in the extreme northern sections of Europe and Asia. Arctic graylings are excellent sport fishes and take artificial flies with consistency. They seldom weigh as much as 5 pounds. Graylings spawn in the spring from March to about the middle of June, depending on the locality.

The inconnu, or sheefish, *Stenodus leucichthys*, closely related to the whitefish, is circumpolar in Arctic waters, inhabiting streams and also brackish waters. Fishermen catch it mainly by still fishing with natural baits or by casting or trolling metal spoons. The silvery inconnu is long-jawed and, unlike other whitefishes, has numerous bristlelike teeth. The tail is forked. The average weight is about 5 or 6 pounds, but fish weighing as much as 30 pounds are not uncommon.

Whitefishes and ciscos, sometimes placed in a separate family, Coregonidae, are similar to salmons and

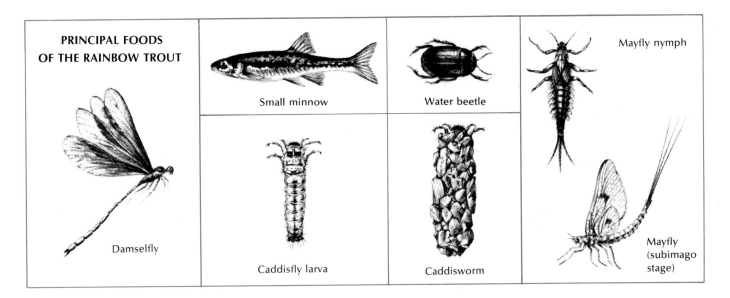

PRINCIPAL FOODS
OF THE RAINBOW TROUT

Damselfly

Small minnow

Water beetle

Mayfly nymph

Caddisfly larva

Caddisworm

Mayfly
(subimago
stage)

trouts in some respects; they prefer cold northern waters and also have an adipose fin. They differ in having large scales and small mouths. All are silvery white, none displaying the flashes of color that make salmons and trouts so spectacular. All have forked tails. Most species live in deep, cold lakes; they spawn in the fall in shallow waters. A few, such as the European whitefish, *Coregonus oxyrhynchus*, live in salt water but return to fresh water to spawn.

Largest of the group is the lake whitefish, *C. clupeaformis*. Ice fishermen catch large numbers of lake whitefishes, generally "chumming" the fishing spot for several days before dropping hooks baited with minnows or grain, but they are caught mainly by commercial fishermen using traps or gill nets. Lake whitefishes range in size from an average of less than 2 pounds up to 15 or 20 pounds; but large specimens are now rare. They are found in deep lakes from New England and New

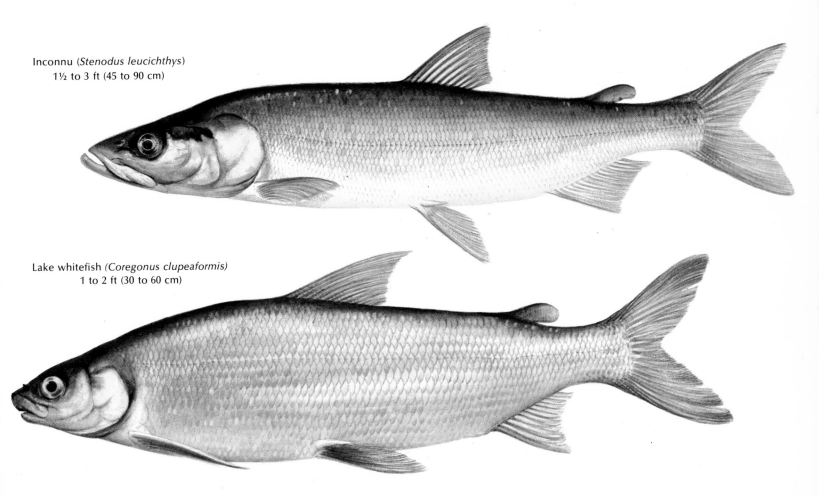

Inconnu (*Stenodus leucichthys*)
1½ to 3 ft (45 to 90 cm)

Lake whitefish (*Coregonus clupeaformis*)
1 to 2 ft (30 to 60 cm)

Cisco *(Coregonus artedii)*
10 to 15 in (25 to 41 cm)

York westward to British Columbia and then northward throughout Canada and Alaska. They are also found in brackish and salt water. In this broad range, they vary considerably in such features as the number of rays in their fins, the scale count along the lateral line, and other details that are noted by the taxonomists. Compared to other species in the group, they have a huskier body build; a significant feature is their blunt nose, the upper lip overhanging the lower.

Lake herrings, or ciscos, *C. artedii*, inhabit the same waters as the lake whitefish but live in shallower areas of the lakes. They are never found at depths greater than 150 feet, usually much less. Lake herrings are much smaller than the lake whitefish. The average size is about half a pound, and only a few exceeding a weight of 2 pounds have ever been recorded. The snout is pointed rather than blunt. This is an important commercial species and is also popular with sport fishermen because of its willingness to take baits and light lures readily, even rising to surface lures like trouts.

Another species in the group is the longjaw cisco, *C. alpenae*, which lives in exceptionally deep water (400–600 feet) in the Great Lakes and, where it still survives, is caught commercially. The small kiyi, *C. kiyi*, also inhabits very deep water in the same lakes. The shortjaw cisco, or chub, *C. zenithicus*, lives in water no deeper than 200 feet, usually shallower, in the Great Lakes and westward throughout Canada; it is also an important commercial species. Half a dozen other small species of ciscos live in the cold lakes and streams of the North Temperate region.

In still another genus, the round whitefish, *Prosopium cylindraceum*; the mountain whitefish, *P. williamsoni*; and several other species differ from species of *Coregonus* in having only a single flap rather than two in the nostrils. The round whitefish is widely distributed, from New England and British Columbia north-

ward throughout Canada and Alaska, including the Arctic Ocean. A subspecies inhabits Siberia. This is also an important commercial species that is usually taken in water less than 30 feet deep.

The mountain whitefish, similar in size, is less widely distributed, living in lakes and streams from the Rocky Mountains through the Pacific Northwest. Sport fishermen especially enjoy catching the mountain whitefish because it take lures and baits eagerly and gives a reasonable fight. Where it inhabits the same waters as trouts, it competes and generally crowds out the trouts, putting the mountain whitefish in disfavor.

Family Plecoglossidae
sweetfish

The sweetfish, or ayu, *Plecoglossus altivelis*, is sometimes classified in the same family with the salmons and trouts or in the family with smelts. Averaging about a foot long, the much-esteemed sweetfish is abundant in freshwater streams of Taiwan and Japan. The method used to catch these fishes in years gone by was unique. Cormorants were fitted with leather collars at the base of their necks. These birds were then turned loose and allowed to catch one or several sweetfish, which could be swallowed but could not go past the collar around the bird's neck. The birds, attached to lines or leather tethers, were then retrieved by the fisherman, and the fish were stripped from their throats. When the fisherman had all the sweetfishes he wanted or when no more seemed available, some of the catch was shared with the birds. Interestingly, it was necessary to put the collar around a bird's neck above the fish it swallowed to prevent it from regurgitating its food. This style of fishing has given way to modern methods, but the art is preserved in some regions as a tourist attraction.

Family Osmeridae
smelts

Smelts are small, silvery fishes that live primarily in the sea but make spawning runs into freshwater streams, as salmons do. A few smelts are strictly marine; others live only in large freshwater lakes and spawn in the tributary brooks and streams. They inhabit the cool waters of the Northern Hemisphere, and most of the dozen or so species are harvested commercially. Like salmons and trouts, smelts have a stubby adipose fin just in front of the tail. The lower jaw projects slightly beyond the tip of the snout. A lateral line is prominent, and there are no scales on the head.

The European smelt, *Osmerus eperlanus*, is harvested in large numbers in northern European waters. In quantity, freshly caught smelts have an odor more nearly like cucumbers than fishes. The average size is only about 8 inches, the weight about 8 ounces.

Rainbow smelts, *O. mordax*, also known as American smelts, are similar in size and habits to the European variety; they range from Nova Scotia southward to Virginia along the coast and occur also in inland lakes. In the early 1900s the rainbow smelt was introduced to the Great Lakes and other large, cold bodies of water to serve as forage fish. In nearly all instances, the smelts prospered. In spring, rainbow smelts make spawning runs up tributary streams, usually moving in greatest numbers at night. Typically they return to the lake or to the ocean by morning; but in overcast weather, they may stay all day. Each female produces thousands of small eggs that stick to the gravel on the bottom. The eggs hatch in about a week, and the young fishes quickly make their way downstream to the lake or to the ocean from which their parents came.

Smelts provide great sport for fishermen who stand along the streams during the spawning runs and use dipnets to make their catches. In winter, they catch them on hook and line by fishing through the ice. Fly fishermen sometimes take smelts on artificial flies in summer, though the fishes generally stay in deep, cool water. No matter how or when they are caught, smelts are among the tastiest of all fish for the platter.

The capelin, *Mallotus villosus*, which is circumpolar in Arctic seas but sometimes strays southward along the coast—to Maine along the Atlantic coast and to southern British Columbia along the Pacific coast in North America—is small-scaled and slender, seldom more than 7 inches long. The capelin spawns in shallow saltwater areas. It is caught commercially and, like other smelts, is a popular table fish.

The smelt family is more generously represented in Pacific waters than Atlantic. All of the more than half a dozen species are so similar in appearance that they are difficult to distinguish. One of the largest is the eluachon, *Thaleichthys pacificus*, which may attain a length of 12 inches. Found throughout northern Pacific waters, the eulachon is an extremely oily fish. Indians dried the fish, ran wicks through its body, and then let it burn like a candle, earning the fish the name candlefish. As with other smelts, they are important in the diets of other fish and are also caught commercially and for sport.

Among the other smelt species are the surf smelt, *Hypomesus pretiosus*, which, as its name suggests, spends most of its life in the surf. It also spawns there. The closely related pond smelt, *H. olidus*, lives wholly

Sweetfish *(Plecoglossus altivelis)*
1 ft (30 cm)

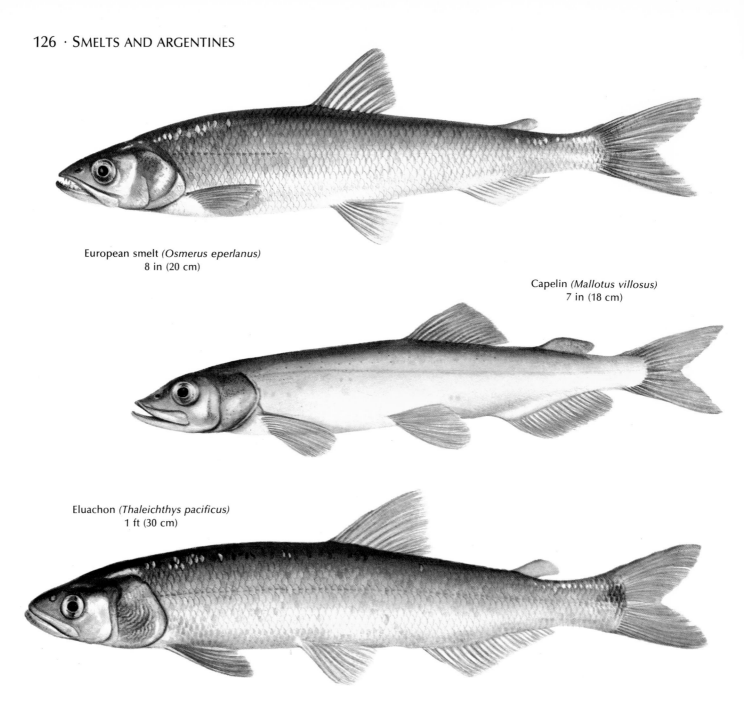

European smelt *(Osmerus eperlanus)*
8 in (20 cm)

Capelin *(Mallotus villosus)*
7 in (18 cm)

Eluachon *(Thaleichthys pacificus)*
1 ft (30 cm)

in freshwater ponds along the west coast of North America, apparently having become landlocked in the geologic past. The same species occurs also in Japan, where it is marine but goes into freshwater streams to spawn. The delta smelt, *H. transpacificus*, is a species from Japan and the Sacramento–San Joaquin River, California, where it lives in fresh and brackish water. The whitebait smelt, *Allosmerus elongatus*, sometimes as long as 9 inches but generally shorter, and the smaller night smelt, *Spirinchus starksi*, are two other Pacific Coast species that are fished for commercially to a limited extent and are used also as bait. A smaller species in the genus *Spirinchus*, the longfin smelt, *S. thaleichthys*, may be included in the net hauls for bait smelts.

Family Argentinidae
argentines

This is a small family of silvery, smeltlike fishes that live in deeper water and do not travel into fresh water to spawn. Several of the species are netted commercially, particularly in northern Europe and in Japan. The Atlantic argentine, *Argentina silus*, is abundant in cold North Sea waters but is only seldomly netted off the coast of North America. The Pacific argentine, *A. sialis*, is uncommon along the coasts of California and Oregon. Another species, *A. sphyraena*, is found along the coasts of southern Europe and northern Africa and also in the Mediterranean. Species that occur in the Pacific include *A. sialis* and *A. semifasciatus*.

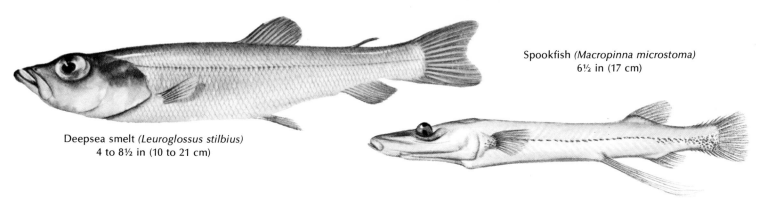

Spookfish *(Macropinna microstoma)*
6½ in (17 cm)

Deepsea smelt *(Leuroglossus stilbius)*
4 to 8½ in (10 to 21 cm)

Family Bathylagidae
deepsea smelts

Most deepsea smelts are bathypelagic; few enter water less than 200 meters deep. They are small fishes reaching a length of about 4 to 8½ inches. They have large eyes, a single dorsal fin, and a long anal fin; an adipose fin is present and the tail is more or less forked. Most deepsea smelts are brownish, but some are uniformly black to blackish brown, and others have silvery sides. Five uncommon species are found off the California coast, but only one, the California smoothtongue, *Leuroglossus stilbius*, is abundant in offshore waters, although it is rarely taken.

Family Opisthoproctidae
spookfishes

The spookfishes, also known as barreleyes, are small, dark brown fishes. The Pacific barreleye, *Macropinna microstoma*, is about 6½ inches long and frequents waters from 324 to 2,940 feet deep. Their eyes are situated atop barrel-like cylinders that are directed upward. The long pelvic fins are attached high on the sides of the body.

Family Galaxiidae
galaxiids

Galaxiids are freshwater fish found only in the Southern Hemisphere—extreme South America, Australia, New Zealand, and South Africa. Slim and scaleless, they occupy the same ecological niche as salmons and trouts in the Northern Hemisphere. Most galaxiids are small, however, averaging less than 6 inches long. One New Zealand species, *Galaxiias alepidotus*, may attain a length of 2 feet, though usually they are about half this size. Slim and pikelike, it rarely weighs more than 3 pounds.

The brown mudfish, *Neochanna apoda*, burrows in the soft mud at the bottom of pools and makes a cocoonlike chamber in which it estivates during dry periods and waits for the rains to come again, a habit it shares with the lungfishes of Africa and South America. *Saxilaga anguilliformis*, an eel-like species that lives in Tasmania, also burrows in the mud.

Several smaller species are attractively marked with bright bands of color, and some spend a portion of their lives in salt water off Australia, New Zealand, and some of the smaller islands. Presumably they have become widely distributed as a result of their journeys through the ocean.

Argentine *(Argentina silus)*
1½ ft (45 cm)

Galaxiid *(Galaxiias attenuatus)*
2 ft (60 cm)

Family Esocidae
pikes

All pikes, pickerels, and the muskellunge share in having the dorsal and anal fins located far to the rear, just in front of the forked caudal fin. The rays in the fins are soft. The front of the head is flattened into a ducklike snout, and the large mouth contains numerous sharp teeth. All have slim bodies.

Pikes, pickerels, and the muskellunge are solitary, aggressive predators. They do not build nests. In spring, the female scatters or broadcasts her eggs in shallow water where the males fertilize them. A large muskellunge or northern pike may lay 200,000 or more eggs every year. The young are given no parental attention.

Where their ranges overlap, the species hybridize, making the identification of some individuals extremely difficult.

Five species of this family live in North America. One—the blackspotted or Amur River pike, *Esox reicherti*—is found in eastern Siberia. The northern pike, *E. lucius*, and the muskellunge, *E. masquinongy*, are among the most prized of all freshwater fishes. Even the smaller species, particularly the chain pickerel, *E. niger*, provide sport if fished for with light tackle. The redfin pickerel, *E. americanus*, and the grass pickerel, *E. americanus vermiculatus*, are generally caught only by

Ventral view showing the position of sensory pores on the jaws of the musky

Side view showing the scaled areas on the cheek of the musky

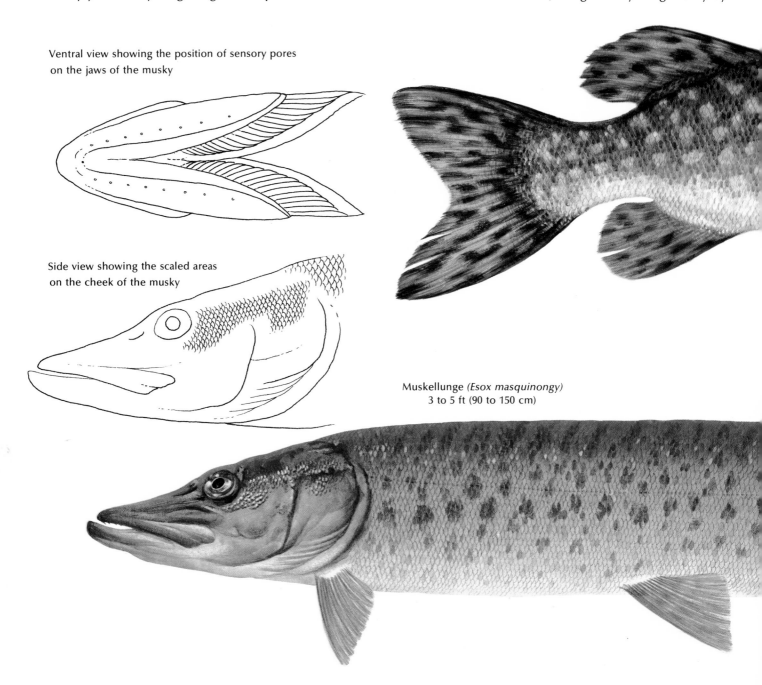

Muskellunge (*Esox masquinongy*)
3 to 5 ft (90 to 150 cm)

accident. The northern pike is the most widely distributed of the species, ranging over northern Asia and Europe as well as North America.

The largest and most famous member of the family is the muskellunge, or musky. The record catch had a length of more than 5 feet and weighed nearly 70 pounds. Fishes weighing more than a hundred pounds have been reported. Muskies live in eastern and central Canada southward through the Great Lakes region, the upper Mississippi and Ohio river valleys. They prefer clear, weedy waters of large streams and lakes, often retiring to deep water in summer. Because of their large size and voracious appetites, muskies make their meals of other large fishes or, reportedly, muskrats, ducks, and other animals that live in or near the water.

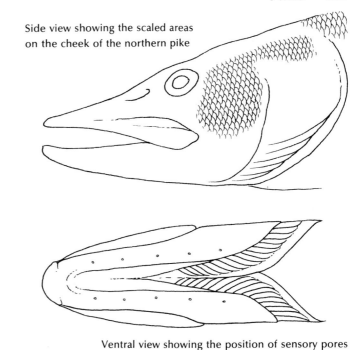

Side view showing the scaled areas on the cheek of the northern pike

Ventral view showing the position of sensory pores on the jaws of the northern pike

Northern pike (*Esox lucius*)
1½ ft (45 cm)

Fishermen who set out to catch muskies bait their hooks with suckers 10 to 12 inches long, or they use specially designed and equally large spoons or plugs. As with other large predators, muskies are not numerous. A body of water can support only a limited number of giant-size musky, and so a fisherman may work for days before finding his quarry. Trolling makes it possible to cover more fishing territory in less time, but trolling for muskies is prohibited by law in some regions. Like other predators, the musky is moody and wholly unpredictable. On some days it ignores the most tempting morsel literally dragged under its snout; on others, it prowls actively. A hooked musky is a spectacular fighter, leaving the water in turning, twisting jumps time after time.

The northern pike does not reach as large a size as the musky, though 50-pounders have been recorded. The average is about 5 pounds, with individuals weighing up to 10 pounds not uncommon. In the musky, only the upper half of the cheek and gill cover bear scales; in the northern pike, the entire cheek and upper half of the gill cover are scaled. The light, oval spots along the sides of

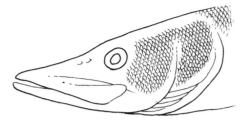

Side view showing the scaled areas
on the cheek of the redfin pickerel

Ventral view showing the position of sensory pores
on the jaws of the redfin pickerel

the dark-greenish body tend to form rows in the northern pike. The spots on the musky are dark and scattered, definitely not in rows. Because of its generally smaller size, the northern pike is found in smaller streams and lakes than the musky, but like all members of the family, it shows a distinct preference for clear, weedy waters.

Northern pikes are caught on both natural and artificial baits of a much smaller size than those used for the musky. Like the musky, the northern pike gives the fisherman moments of incomparable excitement as the lunging fish bursts through the surface in leap after leap or makes racing dashes for weeds or brush where a line can be hopelessly tangled or broken.

Fishing for the northern pike is best in spring and fall. In summer natural foods are abundant, and the fish may also move into deep water where it is cool. Some northern pikes are caught in winter by fishing through the ice. As with other members of the family, the northern pike can easily cut through nylon line; it is wise to use wire leaders.

The chain pickerel lives in shallow, weedy water from central Canada southward to Texas and Florida, but it is most abundant by far in the eastern United States. In addition to its smaller size—averaging less than 2 pounds, with only an occasional individual weighing as much as 6 pounds—the chain pickerel is distinguished from both the northern pike and the musky by its fully scaled cheeks and gill covers. Also, there are no markings on the fins, while the other two species have spots on their fins. The light markings on the sides are interlaced or chainlike.

In some areas the chain pickerel is ignored by sport fishermen; in others it is popular both as a food and sport fish. Where it is legal, many chain pickerels are caught by fishing through the ice.

The redfin pickerel and its subspecies, the grass pickerel, are both small fishes, rarely more than 10 inches long. Like the chain pickerel, they have fully scaled cheeks and gill covers, but the snout is much shorter than in other members of the family. The redfin pickerel's snout is usually convex; the grass pickerel's, concave. The redfin pickerel occurs from the St. Lawrence southward along the Atlantic coast to Florida and inland to Georgia and the Appalachians. The grass pickerel lives west of Georgia and the mountains to Texas and Wisconsin. In both species, the sides are marked with numerous dark, wavy bars.

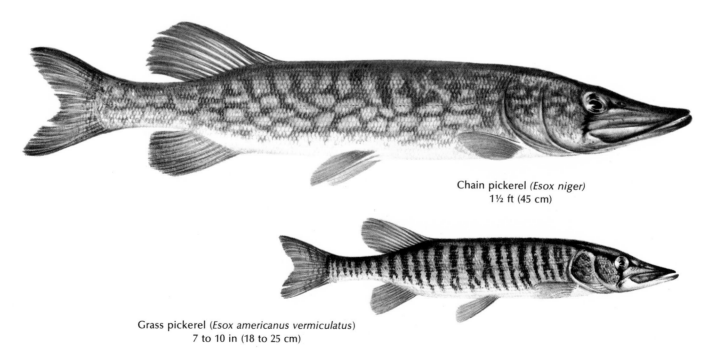

Chain pickerel (Esox niger)
1½ ft (45 cm)

Grass pickerel (Esox americanus vermiculatus)
7 to 10 in (18 to 25 cm)

Blackfish *(Dallia pectoralis)*
5 in (13 cm)

Eastern mudminnow *(Umbra pygmaea)*
3 in (8 cm)

Family Umbridae
mudminnows

Of the fewer than half a dozen species that comprise this family, all are small. Only one—the central mudminnow, *Umbra limi*—attains a length of 6 inches (it averages only 3 inches). The eastern mudminnow, *U. pygmaea*, is typical of the family. About 3 inches long, it lives in weedy ponds and streams along the Atlantic coast from New York to Florida, sometimes squirming into soft mud to a depth of 8 or 10 inches to hide. It can apparently survive for a number of days without water as long as its surroundings are moist. This species and others in the family are commonly used as bait because they are so remarkably tenacious both in the bait bucket and on the hook.

All the mudminnows resemble members of the pike family in having their dorsal and anal fins located far back on the body. The tail fin is rounded, with a dark bar on each side at its base. Males typically develop brighter colors during the mating season.

The European mudminnow, *U. krameri*, is similar in appearance and habits to the eastern variety. The olympic mudminnow, *Novumbra hubbsi*, inhabits the Pacific Northwest; and the Alaskan blackfish, *Dallia pectoralis*, is a common bait minnow of Alaskan waters.

Family Gonostomatidae
deepsea bristlemouths

Herrings are the most abundant pelagic fishes, but investigations into the deep sea in recent years have disclosed that several species of bristlemouths, so named because of their small, bristlelike teeth, are far more abundant than herrings both in numbers and in total weight. Many authorities are convinced that these fishes, particularly species of the genus *Cyclothone*, will eventually contribute greatly to feeding the world. Because they are small, about 2½ inches long, they will be utilized mainly in pastes or processed to make high-protein concentrates. Bristlemouths are also called lightfishes, because they possess self-luminous cells called photophores.

Family Sternoptychidae
deepsea hatchetfishes

Hatchetfishes are among the more commonly illustrated mid-depth inhabitants of the sea. Their bodies are extremely flattened from side to side. None of the dozen or so species is more than 4 inches long; most are smaller. Like other deepsea fishes, their mouths are

Deepsea bristlemouth *(Cyclothone pallida)*
2½ in (6 cm)

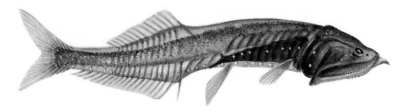

huge. Their eyes are large and bulging, and their scaleless bodies are silvery. Most hatchetfishes have a scattering of luminous organs over their body. Members of the genus *Argyropelecus* have telescopic eyes, which are directed upward.

Family Chauliodontidae
deepsea viperfishes

Of all the fishes of the deep sea, the three species in this family are among the most commonly illustrated. Though they average less than 12 inches long, the viperfishes of the genus *Chauliodus* are among the most fearsome predators of the depths. By day they stay in the dark waters at 5,000 to 8,000 feet. At night they move upward to about 1,500 feet, where food is more plentiful. Some viperfishes have luminous organs inside their mouths as well as over their bodies. The second ray of the dorsal fin also bears a luminous organ, which can be swung in front of the mouth as a special additional lure

to attract prey. Small fishes that make the mistake of swimming inside a viperfish's mouth are caught in a formidable and inescapable trap when the predacious fish shuts its mouth. Sometimes prey are impaled on the teeth of the upper jaw, for these teeth project straight forward, like needlelike spears, when the viperfish's mouth is open.

Many other deepsea fishes similar to the ones included here are known, but there is confusion regarding classification.

Family Stomiatidae
deepsea scaly dragonfishes

A small family containing fewer than ten species, scaled dragonfishes live at about the same depth as viperfishes. The most abundant and most typical members of the family belong to the genus *Stomias*. They have large heads and slim, tapered bodies; the dorsal fin is about the same size as the anal fin and is located directly above it near the tail. The pectoral fins are thin, almost filamentlike. Similar to viperfishes, the scaly dragonfish has a huge mouth, powerful jaws, and an imposing set of fangs. As with most deepsea predators, its mouth can be opened so wide that it will accommodate a fish as large as itself. Presumably, the scaly dragonfish can never close its mouth completely.

Deepsea hatchetfish (*Argyropelecus hemygenus*)
up to 4 in (10 cm)

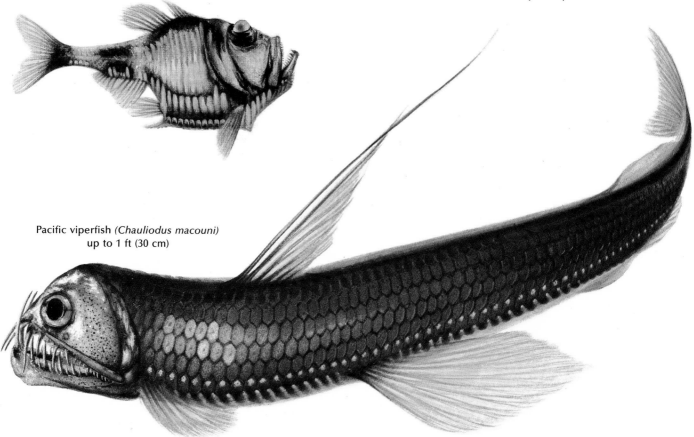

Pacific viperfish *(Chauliodus macouni)*
up to 1 ft (30 cm)

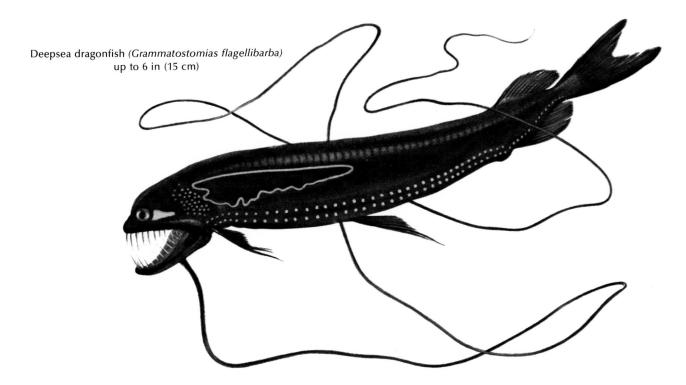

Deepsea dragonfish *(Grammatostomias flagellibarba)*
up to 6 in (15 cm)

Nearly all dragonfishes have a long barbel attached to the chin. In some, this "whisker" is more than five times longer than the fish itself. The barbel may taper to the tip, or it may be branched. It may end in a bulbous knob or may have numerous swellings toward the end. These represent the location of luminous organs. The barbel is evidently used to attract prey to the rapacious jaws, but exactly how this is done is not clear. It may also function as a sensory organ or to attract mates. All dragonfishes are small, averaging less than 6 inches long. Most are black or dark brown, often with an iridescence.

The species in a larger, closely related family, Melastomiatidae, lack scales, and their fins are set so high on the sides of the body that they look misplaced. In still another family, Idiacanthidae, the distinctive feature is the peculiar larval stage in which the eyes are located on long stalks at the sides of the head. The eyes can be pivoted so that the fish is able to look in different directions.

Family Alepocephalidae
deepsea slickheads

Deepsea slickheads comprise a large family of fishes that live at depths of 2,000 feet or more. They are seen only by those few investigators who work in the sea's depths or in their collections of deepsea fishes in museums and laboratories. Relatives of herrings, salmons, and trouts, the deepsea slickheads are among the few soft-rayed fishes inhabiting great depths. They are herringlike in general appearance but have a proportionately larger head, which is typically darker than the body. Their anal and dorsal fins are set far back on the body, and they lack an adipose fin. Also, they do not have an air bladder. Some species have light organs along the sides of the body. One bizarre member of the family has long, slim filaments on its pectoral fins; they are as long as the fish's body. The large telescopic eyes are elongated vertically. The largest of the deepsea slickheads measures only about 12 inches long, and most members of the family are much smaller.

California slickhead *(Alepocephalus tenebrosus)*
up to 1 ft (30 cm)

ORDER MYCTOPHIFORMES

Family Synodontidae
lizardfishes

Lizardfishes are reptilian in appearance, their head particularly lizardlike. Most of them live on sandy bottoms, their blotched, sand-colored bodies giving them perfect camouflage. They spend a good deal of their time sitting on the bottom, propped up on their ventral fins. When a fish or a shrimp swims close, they dart out so quickly that their movement is almost too fast to follow. Lizardfishes have exceptionally large mouths and can usually swallow their prey whole. To propel themselves in these dashes, they use their tail fin; their pectoral fins act as planing "wings." Normally, however, lizardfishes do not swim. They crawl along the bottom, using their pelvic fins like legs.

The family contains about three dozen species that live in warm, shallow seas throughout the world. Most of them are less than 12 inches long. An Indo-Pacific species, *Saurida undosquamis*, commonly exceeds 18 inches in length. Other members of this genus occur in tropical Atlantic waters. These include the largescale lizardfish, *S. brasiliensis*; the shortjaw lizardfish, *S. normani*; and the smallscale lizardfish, *S. caribbaea*.

The inshore lizardfish, *Synodus foetens*, which lives in the Atlantic from Cape Cod southward to Brazil, is one of the common members of the family. Related species with overlapping ranges include the sand diver, *S. intermedius*; the offshore lizardfish, *S. poeyi*; and the red lizardfish, *S. synodus*, of shallow tropical Atlantic waters of both hemispheres.

The snakefish, or offshore lizardfish, *Trachinocephalus myops*, so called because its body is nearly round in cross-section, is most abundant in the West Indies but ranges northward along the Atlantic coast of North America to South Carolina; it occurs also in the Gulf of Mexico and is found southward to Brazil. It reappears in the subtropical waters of the Pacific and as far north as Japan.

The California lizardfish, *S. lucioceps*, ranges from Guaymas, Mexico, to San Francisco. It grows to a length of about 25 inches.

Family Alepisauridae
lancetfishes

Lancetfishes are distributed worldwide in warmer seas. The longnose lancetfish, *Alepisaurus ferox*, has a range in the eastern Pacific from Chile to Dutch Harbor, Unalaska Island, Alaska. It grows to about 6 feet and is uniformly blackish with silvery and brassy reflections. The longnose lancetfish, *A. ferox*, is found in both the Atlantic and Pacific.

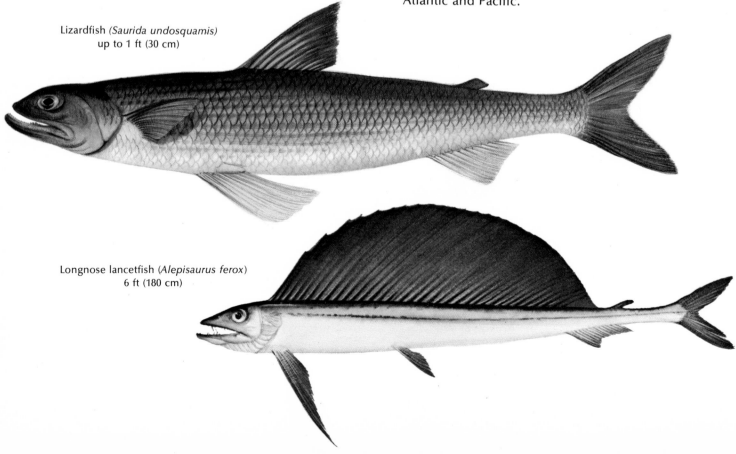

Lizardfish *(Saurida undosquamis)*
up to 1 ft (30 cm)

Longnose lancetfish *(Alepisaurus ferox)*
6 ft (180 cm)

Pearleye
(*Benthabella dentata*)
7 in (18 cm)

Family Scopelarchidae
pearleyes

These are small, slender deepsea forms. The northern pearleye, *Benthabella dentata*, ranges the eastern Pacific from California into the Gulf of Alaska. It is about 7 inches long and distinguished by a bright, silvery area along the outer margin of the eye.

Lanternfish (*Myctophum affine*)
5 in (15 cm)

Family Myctophidae
lanternfishes

Lanternfishes live in the middle depths of the sea but make daily vertical migrations to the surface, ascending at night and returning to the darkness below at day-break. Some authorities speculate that these fishes may spend as much as half their lives in these trips. Fewer lanternfishes are at the surface on moonlight nights than on dark nights.

This family contains 150 or more species, all of them more or less conventional in general appearance with the exception of their larger-than-average eyes and the light-producing organs on their head and body, extending also onto the tail. Species of the genus *Diaphus* have especially large, bright headlights; members of the genus *Neoscopelus* have their brightest lights on the underside of their body. The number and placement of the lights is distinctive with each species. Those on the head and body generally function independently of those on the tail, which in most species are the brightest. In most kinds the lights are greenish, but some are yellowish or reddish.

Lanternfishes average less than 6 inches in length. Unlike the permanent residents of the deep sea, these fishes are generally attractively colored—gray, brown, silvery white, or even bluish. Many are iridescent. Lanternfishes appear in all seas, from the Arctic to the Antarctic. They are among the most common deepsea fishes. Species of the genus *Myctophum* have been studied in considerable detail.

ORDER CETOMINIFORMES

Family Giganturidae
deepsea giganturids

Only four known species comprise this family of small, predatory deepsea fishes. They have been netted in both the Atlantic and Indian oceans. Giganturids, or giant tails, belong to the genus *Gigantura*. They have exceptionally long tail fins, with the lower lobe greatly extended. They lack scales, and their eyes, which protrude from the sides of the head, are telescopic. Pelvic fins are lacking, the dorsal and anal fins are located far to the rear, and the pectoral fins are large. Their colors are metallic. Like other deepsea fishes, giganturids have very large mouths, enabling them to swallow prey that is literally larger than themselves.

Deepsea giganturid (*Bathyleptus lisae*)
2 to 4 in (5 to 10 cm)

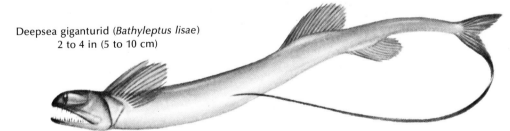

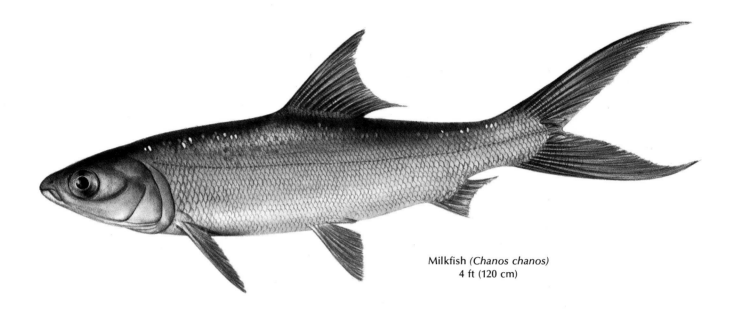

Milkfish *(Chanos chanos)*
4 ft (120 cm)

ORDER GONORYNCHIFORMES

Family Chanidae
milkfish

The milkfish, *Chanos chanos*, the only representative in its family, has big eyes, a toothless mouth, and—similar to herringlike fishes—only one dorsal fin. The tail is deeply forked, and the scales are large and silvery. The fish's color shades from greenish on the back to white on the belly. The fins have a yellowish cast. The milkfish attains a length of 4 feet and may weigh as much as 30 pounds.

The milkfish is found in the Pacific along northern South America and may stray into lower California. It occurs abundantly in the western Pacific and in the Indian Ocean. In the Philippines and in tropical Asiatic countries, the milkfish is an important food. Many are netted in coastal waters, but the largest harvests now come from "fish farms." Milkfishes grow rapidly and do not need expensive feeding programs. They will tolerate crowding without becoming cannibalistic. These are important features in the selection of a species suitable for "farming" operations.

In nature, the milkfish spawns in coastal shallows. Each female releases several million eggs, which are fertilized by the males. The tiny fry feed on microscopic plants. Fish farmers net these little fish and stock them in inland ponds or diked areas. Wise farmers sort through their catch to get rid of potential predators, stocking their impoundments with as pure a population of milkfishes as possible. If food is plentiful—and this varies with the sophistication of the farming method, which can be primitive in some regions and advanced in others—the milkfish grows rapidly, reaching a weight of as much as a pound within six months. At this stage they are ready to harvest.

Some farmers specialize in producing or handling only the fingerlings. These may be held in overcrowded ponds where the food is inadequate and the fish become stunted. When these are sold to farmers ready to stock a pond, they grow much more rapidly than do fingerlings in normal growth stages. Well-managed farms will yield at least two crops every year. Customarily, after a harvest the ponds are drained and allowed to dry. Then they are refilled with water and lush, matted growths of algae, called lab-lab in the Philippines, are permitted to grow before a new stock of fish is introduced. Steps are taken to ensure a greater control over predators and parasites and also to supply the stocked fish with an abundance of food immediately.

ORDER CYPRINIFORMES

Family Characidae
characins

A family of about 500 species of mostly small fishes, all living in fresh water, characins are restricted in distribution to the tropics and subtropics of Africa, South America, and Central America. Though wide variation occurs in size and shape, they resemble generally minnows (Cyprinidae), differing from them in possessing teeth (and lacking pharyngeal teeth) and, in most, having a small adipose fin. Most characins live in schools, as minnows do. They inhabit all types of waters, from quiet and weedy to clear, rushing streams. Similarly, the family includes some species that are strictly plant eaters and others that are predators. Many are brightly colored. Among them are some of the most popular aquarium fish.

The best known of the characins are the South American piranhas of the genus *Serrasalmus*. Of the more than a dozen species, all of them deep-bodied or sunfish-shaped, the most commonly seen in aquariums is *S. nattereri*, attaining a length of about 12 inches. The largest, reaching a length of two feet, is *S. piraya*. Both species, plus several close relatives, live in northern South America, particularly in the Amazon River basin. Laws now prohibit the importation and sale of piranhas for aquarium hobbists without special permits, though the fish are exhibited in public aquariums. It is generally feared that escaped or released fish might breed in the wild, particularly in the warm waters of southern regions, and their population might run rampant. This often happens with exotics.

Piranhas are voracious predators, dangerous even to humans. They are not the proper fishes for home aquariums, as they will bite anything that moves and have no respect for the hand that feeds them. Aquarium

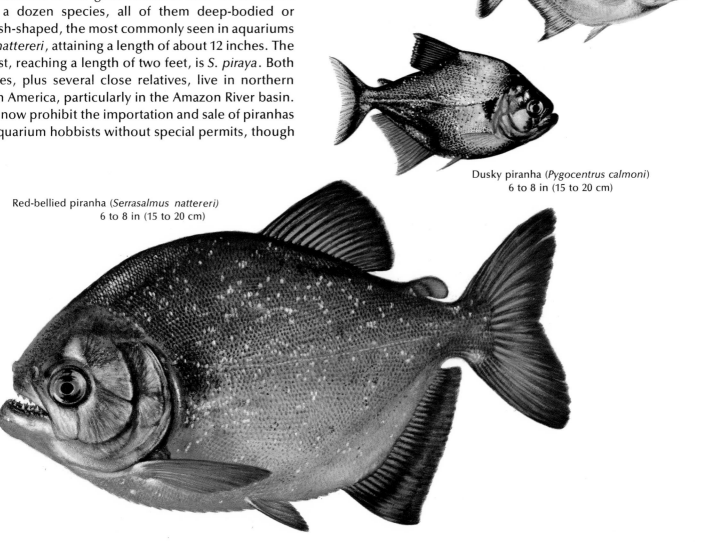

White piranha (*Serrasalmus rhombeus*)
up to 1 ft (30 cm)

Dusky piranha (*Pygocentrus calmoni*)
6 to 8 in (15 to 20 cm)

Red-bellied piranha (*Serrasalmus nattereri)*
6 to 8 in (15 to 20 cm)

specimens, however, do not display the same vicious-ness as do the fishes in nature because they are fed regularly.

In the wild, prowling schools of hungry piranhas quickly appear whenever a commotion in the water signals the possible location of a meal. Traces of blood in the water send them into a frenzied search for the source. Size of the victim is never a discouragement. Each fish makes lightning dashes to slice off bites of flesh with its razor-sharp teeth. Within minutes, a large school of piranhas can cut a hog-sized animal into un-identifiable pieces in a swirling pool of blood. In the process, many piranhas become victims themselves, for these fish are not at all averse to eating their own kind. Ordinarily, of course, piranhas feed on other small fishes. The taking of larger animals is completely by accident. Larger piranhas are first-rate sport fishes. When taken on rod and reel, they strike lures avidly and are strong fighters. Piranhas are also excellent on the table; their flesh is white and firm.

The tigerfish, *Hydrocyanus goliath*, which lives in streams of the Congo region in Africa, is the largest characin, attaining a length of 5 feet and weighing more than 100 pounds. Salmonlike in shape, the tigerfish has numerous daggerlike teeth. The tigerfish is another so-called exotic sport fish. It leaps when hooked and commands respect from anglers.

Another of the family's giants is the pike characin, *Boulengerella lucius*, so called because of its slim, pikelike snout and body. About 2 feet long, it seizes smaller fish and devours them. It is not known to be dangerous to humans. Attempts to keep the pike chara-cin in aquariums have been generally unsuccessful. It needs a large tank and cannot be kept with other fish because of its predatory habits.

Tetras—*Hyphessobrycon* and other genera—are among the attractively colored small South American characins that are popular with aquarium hobbyists. In most species the body is long and slim, but the throat and belly tend to be plumped or arched forward. The anal fin is exceptionally long, and in some species the dorsal fin is high. There are no scales on the caudal peduncle. Fish culturists have worked intensively to produce new varieties with qualities that are especially appealing to hobbyists. The jewel tetra, *H. callistus*, is typical of the genus. Its basic body color is red. The upper three-fourths of the dorsal fin is black, and the anal fin is edged with black. A conspicuous black spot appears on the shoulder. Jewel tetras thrive on compan-ionship of their kind in aquariums. Varieties are availa-ble with bluish fins, with no black shoulder spots, with high or flaglike dorsal fins, or with other deviations from the basic type.

Other popular species are the neon tetra, *H. innesi*, which has a striking luminous green-blue stripe running from its eye to its red caudal peduncle; the flame tetra, *H. flammeus*, colored with a full range of rainbow hues—greenish blue or violet toward the front and bright red at the rear, with several black stripes on the shoulder. Other popular tetras are rosy, *Hyphessobry-con rosaceus*; false vineyi, *H. heterohabdus*; bleeding heart, *H. rubrostigma*; black neon, *H. herbertaxelrodi*; lemon, *H. pulchripinnis*; croaking, *Mimagoniates in-equalis*; spotted leporinus, *Leporinus maculatus*; half-striped leporinus, *L. agissiz*; cardinal, *Cheirodon axel-rodi*; and splash, *Copeina arnoldi*.

Among the most unusual of the characins is the blind cave fish, *Anoptichthys jordani*, the only member of its genus. It lives in cave waters in the San Luis Potosi region of Mexico. Typical of cave inhabitants, its body lacks pigment, and its eyes are reduced to pinhead-size nodules. This species is commonly kept in aquariums by hobbyists who marvel at the ability of the blind fishes to move through a tank without bumping into objects or into one another. The blind cave fish presumably evolved in recent times from a Mexican species of the genus *Astyanax*, which inhabits nearby waters outside caves. Except for the loss of pigment and eyes, the two species resemble each other closely. The so-called Mex-ican tetra, *A. mexicanus*, the only characin with a range extending into the southern United States, is probably this species. Other members of the genus live in South and Central America.

Included among the many South American characins kept as aquarium fishes is the more conventional splash tetra, *Copeina arnoldi*, which has an unusual behavior in courtship. The male chases the female of his choice until she indicates that the time has come for her to lay eggs. Then he leads her to the place he has selected—a rock, branch, or leaf an inch or so above the surface. Each makes several trial jumps and clings to the spawn-ing site. Then the female begins laying eggs there each time she jumps, the male fertilizing them. More than a dozen leaps may be made and over 200 eggs laid. After her eggs are laid, the female departs and does not re-turn. The male comes back every half hour or hour and splashes water on the eggs with his tail. He continues until the eggs hatch, which can take as long as three days. As they hatch, the fry either fall directly into the water or are washed in by the male's splashing. Because of this unusual habit, splash tetras are among the most interesting characins for the home aquarium. They must be provided with a surface on which to spawn (usually a rough-surfaced piece of glass). Because they are jum-pers, as are most characins, the aquarium must be kept covered.

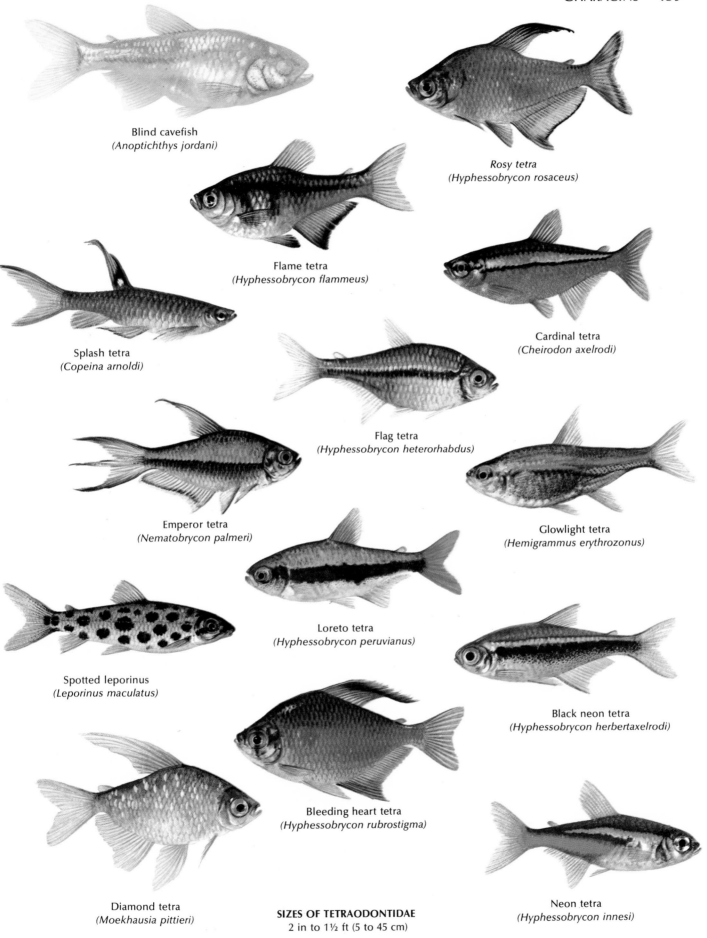

Blind cavefish
(*Anoptichthys jordani*)

Rosy tetra
(*Hyphessobrycon rosaceus*)

Flame tetra
(*Hyphessobrycon flammeus*)

Splash tetra
(*Copeina arnoldi*)

Cardinal tetra
(*Cheirodon axelrodi*)

Flag tetra
(*Hyphessobrycon heterorhabdus*)

Emperor tetra
(*Nematobrycon palmeri*)

Glowlight tetra
(*Hemigrammus erythrozonus*)

Loreto tetra
(*Hyphessobrycon peruvianus*)

Spotted leporinus
(*Leporinus maculatus*)

Black neon tetra
(*Hyphessobrycon herbertaxelrodi*)

Bleeding heart tetra
(*Hyphessobrycon rubrostigma*)

Diamond tetra
(*Moekhausia pittieri*)

SIZES OF TETRAODONTIDAE
2 in to 1½ ft (5 to 45 cm)

Neon tetra
(*Hyphessobrycon innesi*)

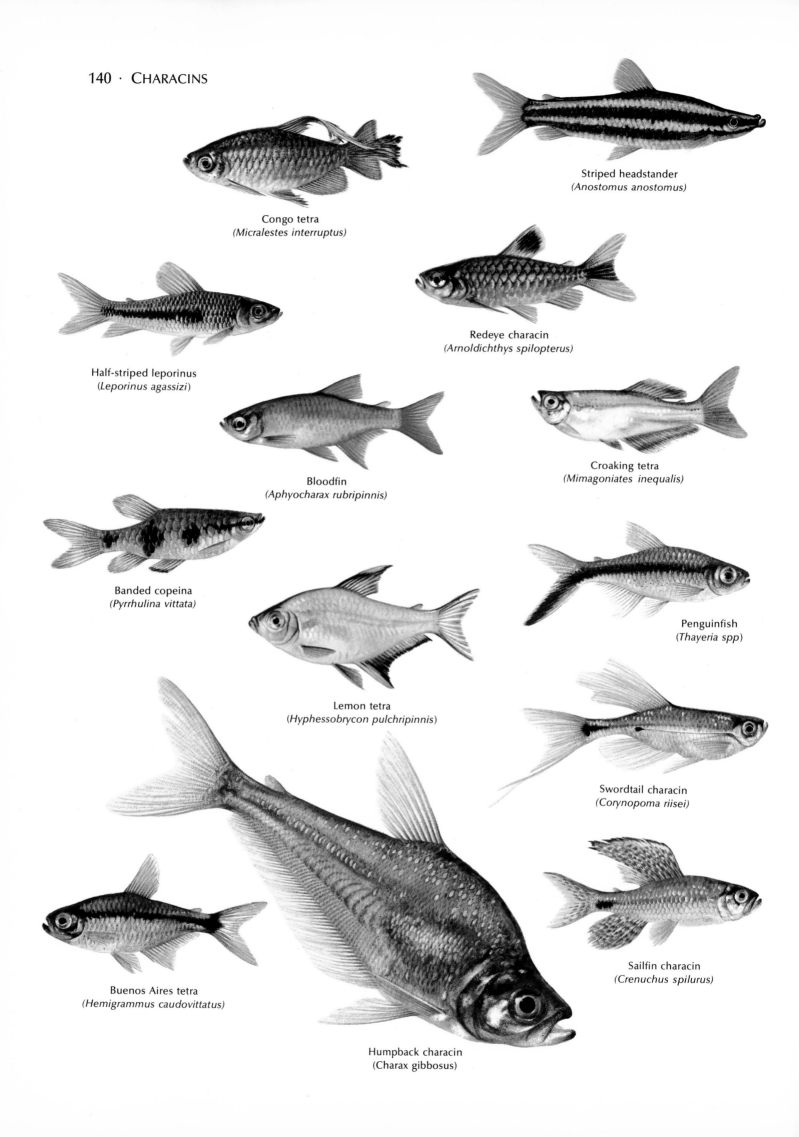

Striped headstander
(*Anostomus anostomus*)

Congo tetra
(*Micralestes interruptus*)

Redeye characin
(*Arnoldichthys spilopterus*)

Half-striped leporinus
(*Leporinus agassizi*)

Croaking tetra
(*Mimagoniates inequalis*)

Bloodfin
(*Aphyocharax rubripinnis*)

Banded copeina
(*Pyrrhulina vittata*)

Penguinfish
(*Thayeria spp*)

Lemon tetra
(*Hyphessobrycon pulchripinnis*)

Swordtail characin
(*Corynopoma riisei*)

Buenos Aires tetra
(*Hemigrammus caudovittatus*)

Sailfin characin
(*Crenuchus spilurus*)

Humpback characin
(*Charax gibbosus*)

The swordtail characin, *Corynopoma riisei*, is a slim fish with almost no arch in its back. Males have spoon-shaped extensions on their gill covers. These are lifted during courtship. Males also have larger fins than females, and the long lower lobe of the tail fin, particularly in older males, is drawn into threadlike filaments.

The humpbacked characin, *Charax gibbosus*, is a contrast in shape to the swordtail characin. Its back is highly arched, sloping abruptly to the forehead. The forehead thus appears to be indented. The mouth of the humpbacked characin slants upward.

The sailfin characin, *Crenuchus spilurus*, another of the numerous South American characins kept by hobbyists, is distinguished by the male's large sail-like dorsal and anal fins.

Among the most interesting of the characins are the several species of pencilfish, also native to north South America. These are very slim fish with pointed heads. Members of the genus *Nanostomus* swim in characteristic short spurts, coming to rest with their heads higher than their tails. The penguinfish, *Thayeria spp.*, has a deeply forked tail fin, the lower lobe much longer than the upper. They also swim and rest with their heads higher than their tails. Headstanders, of the genera *Abramites*, *Chilotus*, and *Anostomus*, swim with their heads down as they search for food on the bottom.

Metynnis, or silver dollars, are sunfish-shaped characins, the scales along the midline of the belly forming a sharp keel. They resemble piranhas, their close relatives, but lack the sharp teeth. Metynnis eat plants. One of the most popular species with aquarists is the spotted metynnis, *Metynnis maculatus*.

Family Gasteropelecidae
hatchetfishes

Gasteropelecids, closely related to the characins, have a distinctive body shape: the back almost in a straight line with the head; the ventral surface extremely bowed, particularly at the front, as though the fish's stomach were stuffed with lead shot. The pectoral fins are long and winglike and are used in gliding "flights" along or just above the surface of the water. In aquariums, which must be kept covered, these fishes need adequate surface area to allow for this unusual habit.

The species lives in freshwater streams in northern South America or in Central America. Several are popular with tropical-fish hobbyists. These include the silver hatchetfish, *Gasteropelecus sternicla*; the marbled hatchetfish, *Carnegiella strigata*; and the winged disc, *Pterodiscus levis*. Of these, the marbled hatchetfish is the most successful in aquariums.

Family Gymnotidae
electric eels and knifefishes

The fifty or so species in this South American family are distinguished by their slim, knifelike or eel-like shape. The body is either naked or covered with very small scales. All members of the family have tiny eyes and a small head and mouth. Peculiarly, the anus is located far forward—in the region of the chin in some species. Both dorsal and ventral fins are lacking, but the anal fin is exceptionally long, extending from the pointed, whiplike tail the full length of the underside of the body—almost to the anus. This giant fin is the principal force used by this unusual fish in its gliding movements through the water. It can move backward, forward, or up and down with equal grace. In some species, the long threadlike tail serves as a sort of "feeler" for the fish when it is moving backward. Because all its vital organs are located far forward, about three-fourths of a fish can be lopped off by a predator without causing death. Remarkably, the wounded fish heals rapidly and regenerates the lost portions. Nearly all species can generate electricity.

The best-known gymnotid, sometimes placed in a separate family, Electrophoridae, is the electric eel, *Electrophorus electricus*, an eel-like species that may attain a length of nearly 8 feet. The vital organs are in the front 20 percent of the body, but the long tail contains the specialized muscles that can generate electric shocks measured at more than 600 volts per discharge, the releases in a series of short, pulsing emissions. The electric eel uses its electricity as a navigational aid, much like radar, and also as a means of stunning prey or discouraging attackers. The electricity is of low voltage and comes from a different set of muscle "batteries"

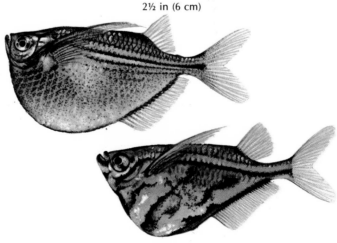

Silver hatchetfish (*Gasteropelecus sternicla*)
2½ in (6 cm)

Marbled hatchetfish (*Carnegiella strigata*)
2½ in (6 cm)

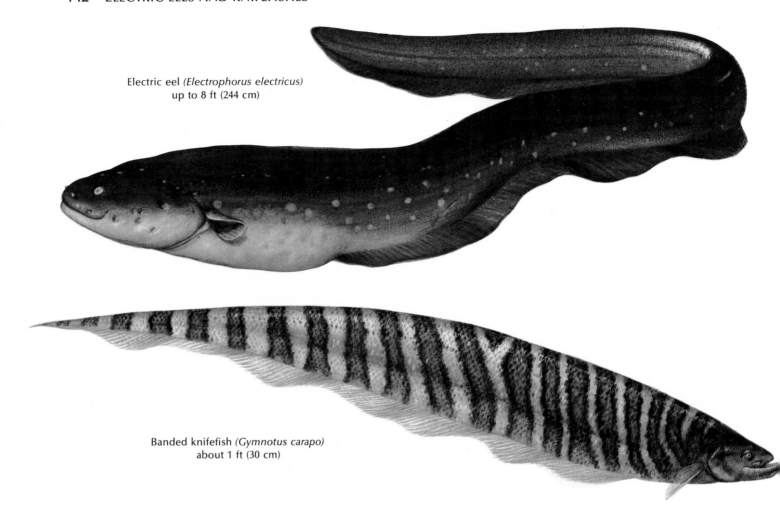

Electric eel *(Electrophorus electricus)*
up to 8 ft (244 cm)

Banded knifefish *(Gymnotus carapo)*
about 1 ft (30 cm)

than the main charge. The bounced-back impulses are received by special receptors in the head.

When young, the electric eel has functional eyes, but these become increasingly useless as the fish becomes older. Reliance on electricity increases with age. Interestingly, young fishes produce almost total voltage, but as they become older the shocks have a greater amount of amperage. The electric eel is commonly exhibited in public aquariums but is obviously not a species for the hobbyist. Electric eels have gills modified to serve as "lungs" for breathing air and they must come to the surface from time to time to get air.

Several relatives of the electric eel are also kept in aquariums. Among these is the spotted (striped or banded) knifefish, *Gymnotus carapo*. It averages less than 12 inches in length, but some specimens may be as much as 24 inches long. They have alternating light and dark bands or stripes, slanted forward, along the sides of the body. Like the electric eel, this species produces electric shocks. They are of low voltage and are useful

primarily as a navigational mechanism in the murky waters of the fish's natural habitat in the streams of tropical South America.

The family also contains several species that are harvested locally for food. One of these is *Rhamphichthys rostratus*, which may be nearly 5 feet long.

Family Cyprinidae
minnows and carps

This large family of freshwater fishes, more than 1,500 species, is abundantly represented in Europe, North America, and Asia but has no native species in Australia and South America. Cyprinids lack teeth, though many have pharyngeal teeth for masticating plant material. Feeding habits vary; in many species the mouth is somewhat protractile, or suckerlike, for feeding on the bottom, and many have sensory barbels on the chin or lips. Typically, the rays in the fins are soft, but in some (carps and goldfishes) the first ray is spinelike. Most cyprinids are small—6 inches or less in length—but they are highly important ecologically as food for larger fish. Many of the smaller fishes are used as bait. The few larger species provide sport for fishermen or are harvested as food fish.

The largest of the minnow family is the carp, *Cyprinus carpio*. In its native Asia the carp once graced the private fish ponds of emperors, to be harvested only on festive occasions. It was one of the first species of fish to be "farmed" to control and increase its production. European explorers transported the carp to their continent where the big minnow continued to be choice fare on royal menus; it is highly rated even today. In England, Izaak Walton, the patron saint of sport fishermen, selected the carp as a favorite fish. "The carp is the queen of rivers: a stately, good and very subtle fish," he wrote in his classic *Compleat Angler*. "And my first direction is," he continued, "that if you fish for carp, you must put on a very large measure of patience."

Carp fishing still demands that "large measure of patience," not because of the scarcity of the fish but because of its cunning and caution. Many fishermen in Europe rank the carp among the most difficult to catch of all freshwater fishes. Carps are powerful fishes that can tear up tackle and leave a fisherman muttering to himself, but the challenge is to get them on the hook. In Europe the sport is engaged in with craftsman's care. Careful account is taken of the weather. The bait is not touched with the bare hands, which often are scented with oil of anise or a similar aromatic to destroy the carp-spooking human odor. Thick-soled shoes are worn to soften the vibrations caused by walking along the bank, and the face is daubed with mud or hidden behind a bee veil. When a school of fishes is sighted, the fisherman creeps along on all fours to stalk the wary carps until they begin to feed.

Carps average less than 5 pounds in weight. A 10-pounder is ranked as big. In England, a carp that weighs more than 20 pounds is considered a once-in-a-lifetime catch, worthy of taking to a taxidermist. It is said that the man who caught the biggest carp ever landed in England "looked as if he had been in heaven and hell and had nothing more to hope for from life." The world record for a hook-and-line-caught carp is 55 pounds 5 ounces, taken from Clearwater Lake, Minnesota. Carps weighing more than 80 pounds have been netted.

In the United States the carp is generally more cussed than caught. Their importation in the 1880s was much heralded. States and cities waited anxiously for their quota to come from the progeny of the several hundred carps brought into the country by the federal government. On the grand day of the carp's arrival, bands played and parades celebrated the arrival. But enthusiasm soon soured. Carps made themselves so much at home that they began to crowd out native species. Like the rabbits of Australia, carps spread unhindered, with no natural enemies to keep them in control. Biologists are less accusing, for they point out that this adaptable fish inhabits waters that have become undesirable as habitats for native species. Carps can prosper

Carp *(Cyprinus carpio)*
1½ to 2 ft (45 to 60 cm)

even in mud and pollution. In clean streams and lakes where they must compete directly with already established species, carps do not fare as well.

Carps feed on tiny plants and animals obtained by rooting in the mud. They draw in this rich organic ooze with their suckerlike mouths. Wallowing in the mud like hogs, they roil the water and may cause stifling clouds of silt to settle over the nests and spawn of basses and other game fishes if there are no more suitable places for these fishes to make their nests. Carps may also accidentally suck in the eggs or newly hatched young of these fishes.

At the same time, carps themselves mate and bring forth bumper crops of their own in these muddy backwaters. A large female broadcasts her eggs over a wide area of shallows as she swims along, laying more than a million eggs in a season. The males fertilize the eggs by releasing clouds of milt in the areas where the eggs are laid. Neither the eggs nor the young get attention from the parents, but the carp population spirals upward because of the quantity of eggs and young produced.

There are three varieties of carps: the common and abundant scaled type, a scaleless variety called the leather carp, and a variety with only a few oversize scales that is known as the mirror carp. Some of those cultivated in the Orient have gold-tinged scales, showing the close relationship of this species to the goldfish.

Carps take artificial baits only occasionally or by accident. They are fished for mostly with worms or doughballs. Cheese mixed with cotton makes a good smelly bait that sticks to the hook; boiled potatoes, fresh corn, marshmallows—the variety of baits possible is great. A hooked carp resists strongly. If a fisherman is using heavy tackle, he can horse in his catch quickly; but if he is out for sport and is using light tackle, he learns that he has a powerful fish at the end of his line. Bow-and-arrow fishermen have fine sport seeking the carp in shallow waters.

Many fishermen in the United States turn their backs on the carp as a food fish because they are convinced

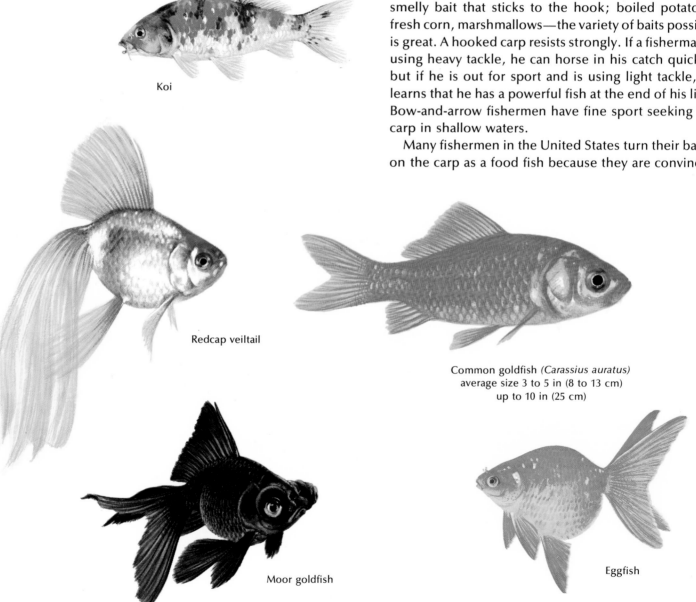

Koi

Redcap veiltail

Moor goldfish

Common goldfish *(Carassius auratus)*
average size 3 to 5 in (8 to 13 cm)
up to 10 in (25 cm)

Eggfish

that its flesh is tainted by the polluted waters in which it lives. In some situations this may be true, but generally the flavor is not greatly affected. To eliminate whatever "muddiness" they may have acquired, carps can be put in clear, clean ponds or springs and kept there for several weeks before they are eaten. This also helps firm the flesh. Carps can be fried, boiled, broiled, baked, smoked, pickled, frozen, canned—prepared and served in whatever manner is most appealing. Put up in cottonseed oil, they taste like chicken or tuna; in tomato sauce, like beef; in mustard sauce, like sardines.

Carps are sometimes reared in flooded paddies. In this way protein and starch are produced simultaneously on the same acres, a technique that holds great promise as a means of producing food for overpopulated, protein-poor countries. In the United States the carp is sometimes on the restaurant menu under various disguises, but in Europe the carp is often featured. It is so popular that it may be difficult to get at the market. For a Christmas holiday feast, for example, orders must be placed in summer to assure delivery. Often, carps

Shubunkin

Lionhead

Celestial goldfish

Pearlscale goldfish

Wild goldfish

Comet goldfish

Bristol shubunkin

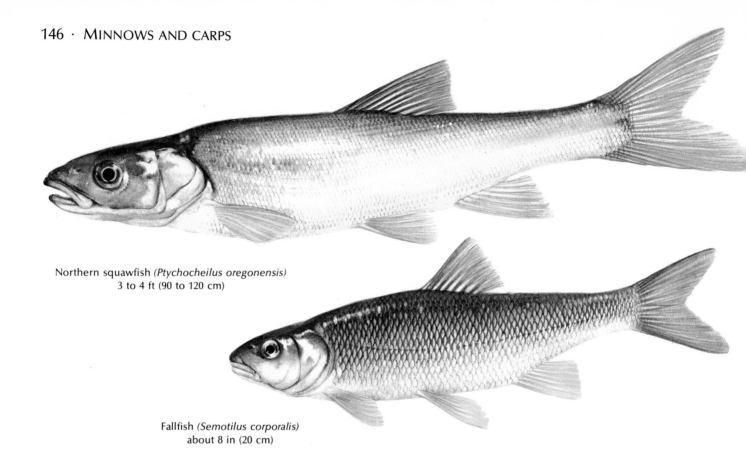

Northern squawfish *(Ptychocheilus oregonensis)*
3 to 4 ft (90 to 120 cm)

Fallfish *(Semotilus corporalis)*
about 8 in (20 cm)

are kept in special fattening pens before they are sent to market; they can be shipped alive because they are hardy and will survive long periods out of water as long as they are kept cool and moist. Carps are commonly used to make gefilte fish, a great favorite with Jewish people.

The white amur, or grass carp, *Ctenopharyngodon idellus,* an Asian fish related to the carp, was introduced into the inland waters of the United States in recent years. It is one more example of why the importation of exotic species must be given serious study. The white amur was released in Arkansas waters and subsequently escaped into the Mississippi Basin, where it continues to spread. This hardy fish feeds primarily on aquatic plants and was brought in to clean up vegetation-choked lakes and ponds. The size and habits of the white amur, however, result in its squeezing out other fishes, including desirable food and game species. Time will tell whether this controversial carp will benefit American fisheries or turn into another disastrous introduction.

The goldfish, *Carassius auratus*, vies with the carp in fame and for the length of time it has been associated with man. The goldfish has been kept in ponds and aquariums in the Orient for many centuries. Goldfishes in the wild resemble carps in shape and sometimes in color, but they lack barbels under the chin, which carps have. Those goldfishes that escape captivity or that live in large outdoor ponds revert in only a few generations to their original natural colors—greenish or black. They also attain large size, weighing two pounds or more. For aquariums, they have been bred to produce a variety of shapes and colors, including rich black, red, yellow, and spotted as well as the conventional gold. Some have bulging or "telescope" eyes; others have tremendously enlarged fins.

Goldfishes are extremely hardy, accounting for their ability to survive in small fish bowls and in poorly tended aquariums. Given proper space, a goldfish 2 inches long should have a minimum of 2 gallons of water, or roughly about a gallon of water for each inch of fish. It may not die if kept in a container with less water, but its growth will be stunted and its life shortened. Well cared for, a goldfish should live for more than ten years.

The goldfish is a good beginner fish, stimulating an interest in aquariums as a hobby. As the hobby assumes more serious dimensions, other species will be turned to, including a number of the more delicate tropicals that also belong to the minnow family.

Ecologists caution against the release of goldfishes, intentionally or by accident. Though they will not breed in small aquariums, they will spawn and produce prodigious numbers in the wild. They can soon become so abundant that they crowd out native species. Because of this threat, laws prohibit the sale of goldfishes for bait, and people are warned not to release unwanted goldfishes from bowls or aquariums into streams or ponds.

Among the giants of the minnow family are the squawfishes that inhabit streams of western United States and southern Canada. These include the northern squawfish, *Ptychocheilus oregonensis*; Sacramento squawfish, *P. grandis*; Umpqua squawfish, *P. umpouae*; and Colorado squawfish, *P. lucius*. The largest sizes recorded in recent years were occasional individuals measuring 3 to 4 feet in length. Older literature mentions that the Colorado squawfish once reached a length of 5 feet and weighed as much as 80 pounds. Salmon and trout fishermen sometimes shift their attention to squawfishes, which put up a respectable fight on light tackle and are also good to eat.

The hardhead, *Mylopharodon conocephalus*, found in California streams, reaches a length of 1½ feet, approaching the squawfish in size. Its pharyngeal teeth are flat, like molars, while those of the squawfish are slender and curved. Another large species of western waters is the foot-long splittail, *Pogonichthys macrolepidotus*, so named because of its deeply forked tail.

The largest of the minnow family in eastern North America is the fallfish, *Semotilus corporalis*, occurring from southern Canada southward to Virginia and westward to the Appalachians. Also called silver chub, or dace, it sometimes reaches a length of 1½ feet but is generally smaller. It builds unusually large nests—as much as 6 feet across. On light tackle, the fallfish puts up an exciting battle for sport fishermen. Its flesh is sweet, but the fallfish is generally too bony to make good eating.

Close relative of the fallfish is the creek chub, *S. atromaculatus*, its range west of the fallfish's to the Great Plains. It averages about 8 inches long, rarely larger, and is popular as a bait for large fishes as well as providing sport itself when fished for with light tackle.

Another member of the same genus is the pearl dace, *S. margarita*, also robust but never more than about 4 inches long. It occurs in the same range as the fallfish but prefers smaller streams. During the breeding season, the males develop a bright red stripe down the sides of their body just below the lateral line.

A number of minnows are called "shiners" because of their shimmering silvery sides which flash as the little fishes turn in the water. The largest group of "shiners" form the genus *Notropis*, which includes more than a hundred species in North America. All are slender fish, their fins relatively large as compared to the size of their body.

Typical of the group is the common shiner, *N. cornutus*, which is olive-green above and silvery on its sides and belly. At spawning time in spring, the male's body takes on a pinkish tinge, and the tail and fins become bright orange or red, particularly at their bases. Hard bumps, or tubercles, develop on the top of the head and on the front portion of the body. Males are larger than females, sometimes attaining a length of 8 inches, although they are usually sold for bait when they are half this size. The common shiner is widely distributed, inhabiting small streams from southern Canada southward over much of the United States east of the Rockies.

Another widely distributed minnow of this group is the emerald shiner, *N. atherinoides*, which often is

Common shiner *(Notropis cornutus)*
up to 8 in (20 cm)

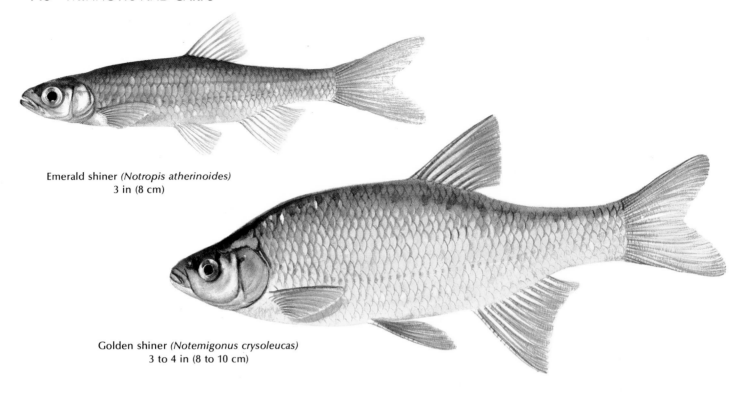

Emerald shiner *(Notropis atherinoides)*
3 in (8 cm)

Golden shiner *(Notemigonus crysoleucas)*
3 to 4 in (8 to 10 cm)

found in tremendously large schools. It is smaller than the common shiner, rarely exceeding 3 inches in length, and has a proportionately shorter snout.

Some of the more attractive and hardy species of *Notropis* are kept in aquariums. Among these is the sailfin shiner, *N. hypselopterus*, which has exceptionally high fins that are streaked handsomely with red in males during the spawning season.

The golden shiner, *Notemigonus crysoleucas*, rates as one of the best bait minnows and is commonly reared in ponds specifically for this market. Unlike most members of the minnow family, the golden shiner has a sharp keel on the midline of its belly, from the pelvic fins to the end of the body. The lateral line bows sharply downward, and the mouth angles upward. While young, these minnows are silvery; as adults, they be-

come a bright metallic or brassy gold. The average size is 3 to 4 inches, but in some large lakes the golden shiner attains a length of 10 inches or more. Found throughout eastern Canada and in the United States east of the Rockies, the golden shiner is adaptable to a wide range of water conditions and temperatures, from cool and swift-flowing, which they cohabit with trouts, to warm and weedy sluggish streams and ponds of the South.

About 16 species of minnows comprise the genus *Hybopsis* in North America. The flathead chub, *H. gracilis*, representative of the group, occurs west of the Mississippi, including many of its tributaries, from Oklahoma northward and westward to the Rockies. A slim fish, it averages only about 5 inches in length but is occasionally larger. At each corner of its large mouth is a small barbel. In addition to being good bait for larger

Hornyhead chub *(Nocomis biguttatus)*
6 to 8 in (15 to 20 cm)

fishes, the flathead chub may itself be caught on small hooks and thread line.

Another common and closely related species is the hornyhead chub, *Nocomis biguttatus*, a 6- to 8-inch, thick-bodied minnow found in streams of the eastern United States and westward to Arkansas and North Dakota. Its name is derived from the numerous sharp tubercles that appear on the male's head at spawning time.

Southern redbelly dace *(Phoxinus erythrogaster)*
4 in (10 cm)

Dace, *Phenacobius* and *Rhinichthys*, are slim minnows, most of them about 3 inches long, that show a preference for cool waters, often swift-flowing streams. Because of their hardiness, they are among the popular bait minnows. The northern redbelly dace, *Phoxinus eos*, is a favorite bait for brook trouts, as are also the southern redbelly dace, *P. erythrogaster*, blacknose dace, *Rhinichthys atratulus*, and the longnose dace, *R. cataractae*.

The fathead minnow, *Pimephales promelas*, and the bluntnose minnow, *P. notatus*, are, in contrast, rather deep-bodied minnows that prefer ponds and sluggish streams. Because they demand oxygen, these minnows can tolerate considerable crowding in a bait bucket.

Popular as a bait minnow, the cutlips minnow, *Exoglossum maxillingua*, is found from the St. Lawrence southward along the Atlantic coast to Virginia in streams of mostly small size. Its name is derived from its three-lobed lower lip.

In western North America, the roundtail chub or bonytail, *Gila robusta*, commonly exceeds 12 inches in length. Compared to other members of its genus, it has a deeply forked tail and a slender caudal peduncle. Among its relatives are the thicktail chub, *G. crassicauda*; the Rio Grande chub, *G. nigrescens*; the Utah chub, *G. atraria*; and others—all provide respectable sport on light tackle. In some areas these large minnows compete with trouts for food and living space.

The stoneroller, *Campostoma anomalum*, is a stream-dweller that gets its name from its habit of grubbing in rocky riffles for its food—the algae it scrapes from the surfaces of rocks. In this process, the stoneroller literally does move small rocks in the stream. Males do so even more industriously when they make a nest just above a riffle, rolling the rocks out of the way to create a depression in which the female lays her eggs. Typical of many members of the minnow family, the males develop tubercles and also become much more colorful—brassy with dark bars on the fins—at spawning time. The stoneroller's most unusual feature is its long intestine, which makes a dozen or more coils around the swim bladder.

Cyprinids are well represented in Europe and Asia, where some members of the family are among those sought after by fishermen. One of these is the tench, *Tinca tinca*, which has also been introduced to parts of North America. A fat-bodied fish weighing 6 to 8 pounds but occasionally twice as large, the tench is greenish to coppery, often with an orangish belly that has earned it the name of golden tench. The body is covered with a thick coating of slime, but this does not come off so easily that the fish is objectionable to handle. British fishermen derive great sport from catching tenches, which are strong fighters—their battling consisting mainly of long runs as they try to bore deeper into the water. They are not aerialists. Tenches prefer the weedy waters of sluggish streams and apparently spend their winters buried in the mud.

Stoneroller *(Campostoma anomalum)*
4 in (10 cm)

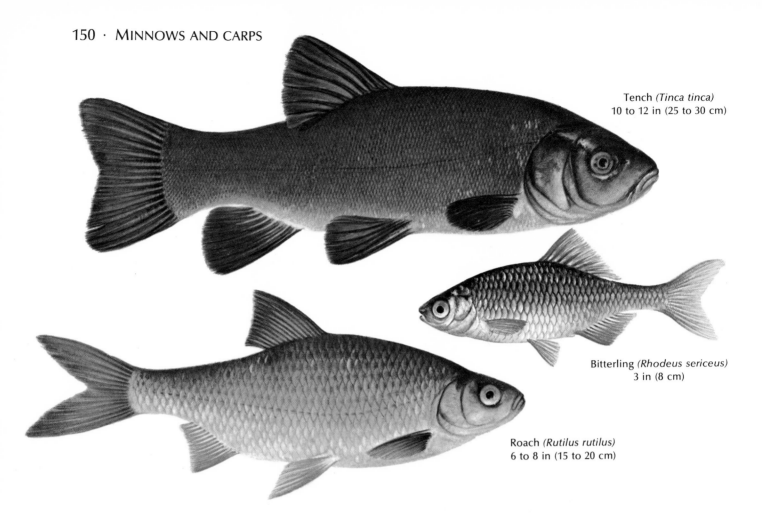

Tench *(Tinca tinca)*
10 to 12 in (25 to 30 cm)

Bitterling *(Rhodeus sericeus)*
3 in (8 cm)

Roach *(Rutilus rutilus)*
6 to 8 in (15 to 20 cm)

The roach, *Rutilus rutilus*, is another minnow commonly caught by sport fishermen in Europe. It is not difficult to catch and is also abundant. Weighing as much as 4 pounds, the roach also inhabits sluggish waters. It sometimes wanders into brackish coastal waters too, rare for a cyprinid.

The female bitterling, *Rhodeus sericeus*, about 3 inches long, develops a 2-inch yellowish or red ovipositor with which she deposits her eggs surreptitiously inside the mantle cavity of a clam or mussel. The male, decked in red, spreads milt that is drawn into the shell chamber and fertilizes the eggs. In this protective enclosure the eggs develop and hatch, and the fry spend their first few days here. Bitterlings are kept by aquarium hobbyists because of this interesting and unusual breeding habit.

European cyprinids also include the bottom-feeding bream, *Abramis*, which may exceed 10 pounds in weight and is fished for by anglers. Its resistance to being caught is a broad-size pull against the line rather than an energetic fight.

An equally unspectacular fighter but common enough to provide great amounts of sport is the rudd, *Scardinius*, which sometimes weighs as much as 4 pounds but more commonly less than a pound.

Also there are numerous smaller minnows, such as various species of *Phoxinius, Leucisus, Gardonus,* and

Bitterling female investigating
freshwater mussel

Female with ovipositor fully inserted
into the mussel's siphon

Male shedding his milt over the siphon
to be drawn in by the mussel's respiration

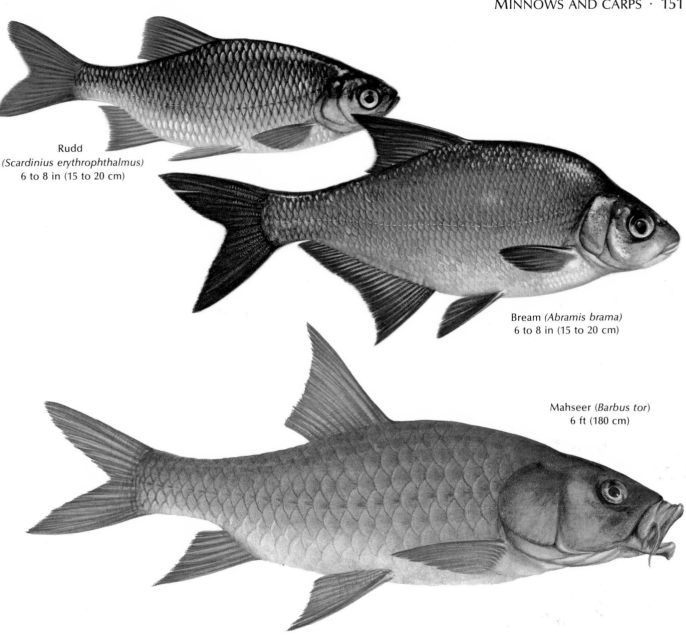

Rudd
(*Scardinius erythrophthalmus*)
6 to 8 in (15 to 20 cm)

Bream (*Abramis brama*)
6 to 8 in (15 to 20 cm)

Mahseer (*Barbus tor*)
6 ft (180 cm)

others inhabiting streams, lakes, and ponds, that are sometimes kept in aquariums.

The behemoths of the minnow clan live in southeastern Asia. These include the mahseer, *Barbus tor*, which may exceed 8 feet in length and weigh well over 100 pounds. A famous sport fish in India, it inhabits huge, sluggish streams in southern regions as well as clear, sparkling streams of the Himalayas. The rod-and-reel record was a mahseer taken in Mysore that weighed 128 pounds. Other giants are the rohu, *Labeo rohita*, and the catla, *Catla catla*, both of which may exceed 5 feet in length and attain weights of 50 pounds or more. Unusual Asiatic cyprinids include the silver carp, *Hypophthalmichthys*.

Among the hundreds of species of attractive small cyprinids inhabiting fresh waters of the tropics and sub-

tropics are dozens of species that are kept in aquariums. Compared to many tropicals, they are as a group more hardy. Barbs, *Barbus*, are widely distributed in Africa, Asia, and southern Europe. Like typical cyprinids, the barbs are schooling fishes that generally prefer sunny water, hence well-lighted aquariums. Typically, the female scatters her adhesive eggs over a wide area; a few species take special care to stick them to leaves or stems. The male fertilizes the eggs by spreading milt over them.

In aquariums, the adults must be separated immediately from the eggs, or they will eat them. Despite their name, some members of this genus lack barbs; others have a single pair, still others two pairs. Of the several dozen species of barbs kept in aquariums, among the favorites are the tinfoil, *B. schwanenfeldi*, to

12 inches long; tiger, *B. tetrazona;* cherry, *Capoeta titteya;* checkerboard, *C. oligolepis;* half-banded, *C. semifasciolatus;* two-spot, *Puntius ticto;* and black-spot, *P. filamentosus.* The Katanga lampeye, *Aplocheillichthys katangae,* is another small cyprinodont popular with hobbyists.

Also popular are the rasboras, *Rasbora,* large-scaled, barbless tropicals from southeastern Asia. Some rasboras like to feed on flying insects that skim along just above the surface, and they will jump out of an aquarium if it is not kept covered. Of about two dozen species that have been imported for sale to hobbyists,

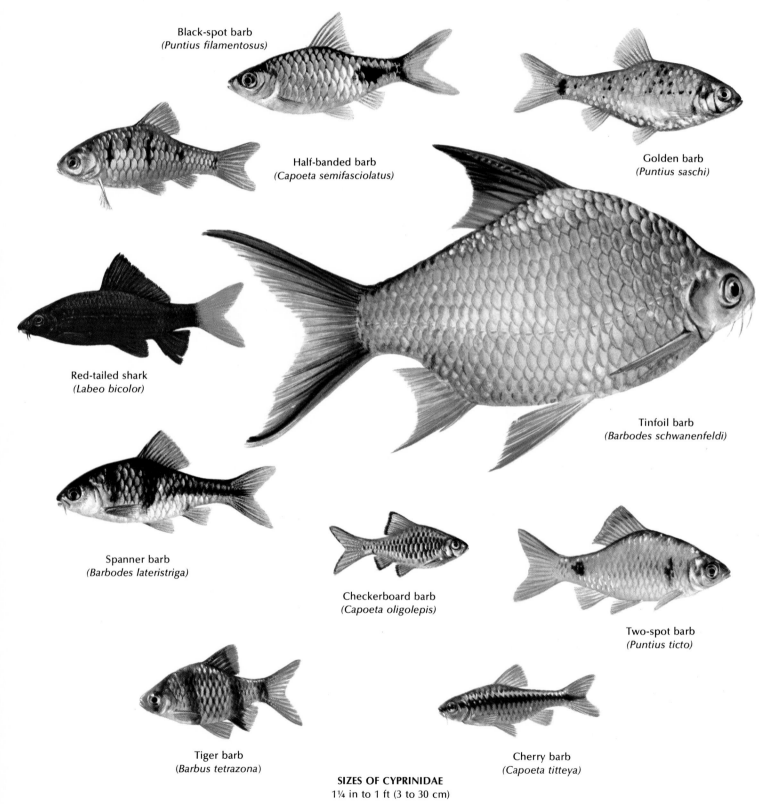

Black-spot barb
(*Puntius filamentosus*)

Half-banded barb
(*Capoeta semifasciolatus*)

Golden barb
(*Puntius saschi*)

Red-tailed shark
(*Labeo bicolor*)

Tinfoil barb
(*Barbodes schwanenfeldi*)

Spanner barb
(*Barbodes lateristriga*)

Checkerboard barb
(*Capoeta oligolepis*)

Two-spot barb
(*Puntius ticto*)

Tiger barb
(*Barbus tetrazona*)

Cherry barb
(*Capoeta titteya*)

SIZES OF CYPRINIDAE
1¼ in to 1 ft (3 to 30 cm)

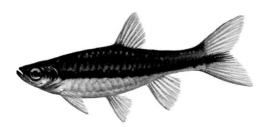

Brilliant rasbora
(*Rasbora einthoveni*)

Scissor-tailed rasbora
(*Rasbora trilineata*)

Exclamation-point rasbora
(*Rasbora urophthalma*)

among the favorites are the harlequin rasbora, *R. heteromorpha*; brilliant rasbora, *R. einthoveni*; Ceylonese fire barb, *R. vaterifloris*; Scissortail rasbora, *R. trilineata*; and exclamation-point rasbora, *R. urophthalma*.

Danios, *Danio*, are another group of Asiatic cyprinids popular with tropical-fish hobbyists. Similar and closely related are the leopard danio, *Brachydanio frankei*, and the spotted danio, *B. nigrofasciatus*.

The rare trunk barb, or flying fox, *Epalzeorhynchus kallopterus*, is distinguished by a long snout used to probe in the bottom oozes for mud. In contrast, the

Ceylonese fire barb
(*Rasbora vaterifloris*)

Harlequin rasbora
(*Rasbora heteromorpha*)

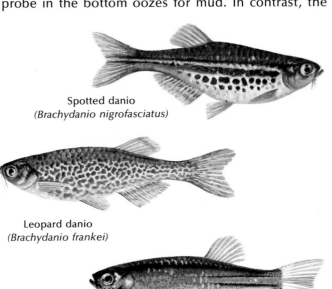

Spotted danio
(*Brachydanio nigrofasciatus*)

Flying fox
(*Epalzeorhynchus kallopterus*)

Leopard danio
(*Brachydanio frankei*)

Pearl danio
(*Brachydanio albolineatus*)

flying barbs, *Esomus danrica*, feed at the surface. To accommodate this habit, their mouths are slanted upward. More than a dozen species comprise this genus. All of them leap from the water, making a cover for the aquarium essential.

The red-tailed shark, *Labeo bicolor*, its velvety black body sharply contrasting with its scarlet tail and fins, is one of several "shark" cyprinids, so called because of the sharklike shape of their body. Several species, including the 6-foot, 100-pound rohu, *L. rohita*, attain large size and are harvested for food.

Family Gyrinocheilidae
gyrinocheilids

This small family consists of only a few species, all belonging to the genus *Gyrinocheilus*, native to fresh waters of southeastern Asia. They have been classified with catfishes and also with loaches, showing similarities to both. The thick, fleshy lips form a sucking disk used by the fish to hold itself on the bottom in swift-flowing streams and also to remove algae, its principal food, from the surfaces of rocks. The mouth cannot be used for taking in water for breathing as in other fishes, but the gill chambers are divided into an upper compartment that "inhales" water and a lower compartment that "exhales" water. Water apparently also enters through a slit at the base of the lips.

The species most commonly kept in aquariums is *G. aymonieri*, which is imported from Thailand. It grows to a length of 8 inches. In aquariums it performs a valuable service by scraping the growths of algae from the glass, but it is sometimes quarrelsome.

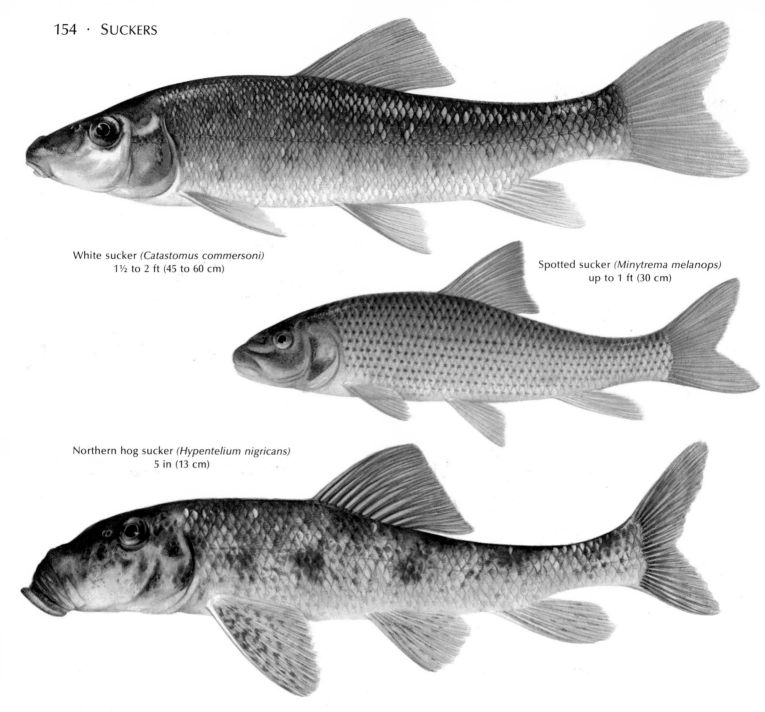

White sucker *(Catastomus commersoni)*
1½ to 2 ft (45 to 60 cm)

Spotted sucker *(Minytrema melanops)*
up to 1 ft (30 cm)

Northern hog sucker *(Hypentelium nigricans)*
5 in (13 cm)

Family Catostomidae
suckers

Most of the nearly a hundred species of suckers live in North America, although some occur in northern Asia. They resemble minnows but have a distinctly protrusible mouth for sucking in bottom oozes from which they get their food. Another and more precise distinction is the distance from the anal fin to the tail fin: more than 2½ times in suckers, less than 2½ times in minnows. Typically, a sucker's body is round in cross-section, and the scales are large. Suckers spawn in spring, usually in the gravel of riffles in streams.

The white sucker, *Catostomus commersoni*, found in streams and some lakes from the Rockies eastward throughout Canada and the United States, is one of the most abundant and widely distributed freshwater fishes in North America. During the winter, schools of these suckers retire to deep water. They begin their upstream spawning migrations in early spring, generally with the first floods. They travel mainly at night. A female measuring 1½ feet long may lay as many as 50,000 eggs, which hatch in about a week. The fry are indistinguishable at a glance from many minnows that are similar in size.

Like other members of the family, the white sucker uses its sucker mouth to draw in bottom oozes, sifting out the solid food matter in the mesh of its gill rakers. It has pharyngeal teeth that can crush the shells of small mollusks or the hard outer skeletons of crayfish or other arthropods. While young, these suckers serve importantly as food for trouts and other game fishes. Those that reach large size are considered serious competitors with these fishes.

In lakes, the white sucker may attain a length of 2 feet and weigh from 6 to 8 pounds. About half this size is large for stream-dwellers. The color is olive-green above and whitish on sides and belly; the fins and sometimes the belly are tinged with yellow. At spawning time, the males develop a prominent dark stripe on their sides. Black circles the snout at the front of the body. In some males, the sides may become blushed with pink and the whole upper half of the body becomes dark, which has earned the fishes their contrasting common name of black sucker.

Spring-caught suckers are firm-fleshed and sweet, though bony. At this time of the year, many are caught by fishermen. Worms are the most popular and most productive baits, but some suckers are caught on wet flies or other small artificials. Tackle for sucker fishing need not be elaborate. Cane poles are commonly used. Late in the season, as the water warms, the flesh of suckers becomes soft and undesirable.

More than a dozen other species of suckers comprise the genus *Catostomus*. Most of them are smaller and have limited distributions, but all are similar in habits and general appearance to the white sucker.

Another large genus of suckers is *Moxostoma*. The northern redhorse, *M. macrolepidotum*, is representative of the group. It ranges from the Hudson River westward through the Great Lakes to Montana and then northward to the Mackenzie River and its tributaries. All the members of this group, called redhorses, are distinguished by their red fins, particularly the tail fin; this color is most pronounced in older fish. Because it lives in cool waters, the northern redhorse is firm-fleshed and quite desirable for eating, despite its bones. Rarely, it attains a length of 1½ feet and weighs as much as 2 pounds; more commonly it is half this size or less. It is fished for with natural baits, mainly worms. There are more than a dozen other species of redhorses with limited distributions.

The spotted sucker, *Minytrema melanops*, of eastern United States, is a small sucker, rarely exceeding 12 inches in length. It can be identified by the black spot on each of its scales.

The northern hog sucker, *Hypentelium nigricans*, found in streams of central and eastern Canada and the United States, is also a small sucker, seldom weighing as much as a pound. It inhabits the rapids of streams, darting from the protective lee side of one rock to

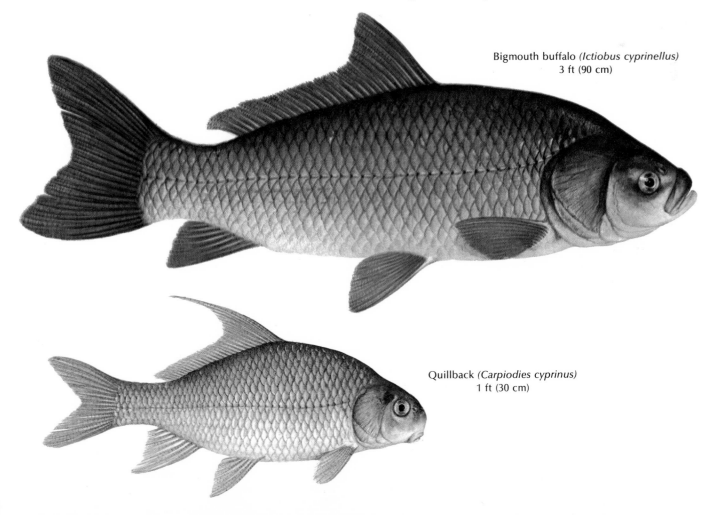

Bigmouth buffalo *(Ictiobus cyprinellus)*
3 ft (90 cm)

Quillback *(Carpiodies cyprinus)*
1 ft (30 cm)

another to avoid being swept away by the current. It gets its food by rolling stones or small rocks and sucking up the small animals or other organic matter dislodged. The northern hog sucker and its several close relatives are little valued for sport and are much too bony to be desirable as food.

The largest of the sucker family is the bigmouth buffalo, *Ictiobus cyprinellus*, found in lakes and streams from Alabama to Texas and northward into southern Canada. Superficially, it resembles the carp but has no spines on its dorsal fin. Its mouth slants upward and is terminal rather than subterminal and protrusible as in other suckers. Gray-blue above and coppery below, the bigmouth buffalo may be more than 3 feet long and weigh as much as 80 pounds, though generally it weighs less than 50 pounds. A large female broadcasts as many as 300,000 eggs during spawning. The bigmouth buffalo is caught only occasionally on hook and line, but it is an important commercial species, taken mainly in nets and to a lesser degree on trotlines.

The quillback, *Carpiodes cyprinus*, is another carp-shaped sucker, distinguished by its dorsal fin—exceptionally high in front. Smaller, seldom more than 12 inches long, this silvery species is found in the same range as the buffalos.

Family Homalopteridae
hillstream fishes

This family of fishes, containing fewer than 50 species, seems to be intermediate between the cyprinids and the loaches. Native to southeastern Asia, the species are bottom-feeders, their mouths subterminal and surrounded by barbels. Their large, rounded pectoral and pelvic fins are joined to the body at the sides, permitting the fishes to hug the bottom closely and also preventing them from sinking into soft oozes. In those that live in swift streams, the bases of the fins form a disk that

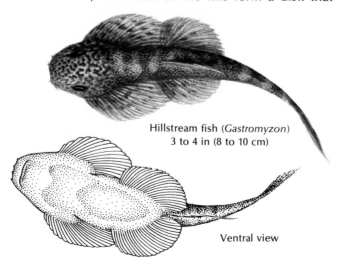

Hillstream fish (*Gastromyzon*)
3 to 4 in (8 to 10 cm)

Ventral view

becomes a suction device for holding on in currents. Hillstream fishes adapt to aquarium life but are not colorful enough to be popular. Further, their rooting in the bottom is not appreciated, as it roils the water and spoils the decor.

Family Cobitidae
loaches

A small family of Old World fishes with representatives in Africa, Asia and Europe, loaches are typically slim, some of them almost eel-like. Their tiny scales are covered by thick mucus. Loaches lack teeth in their jaws, but most species do have pharyngeal teeth. The thick-lipped protrusible mouth bears three to six pairs of barbels.

Loaches use their highly vascularized intestine as a supplementary breathing organ. When the oxygen supply in a body of water they inhabit begins to be deficient, they rise to the surface to take in gulps of air. Oxygen is removed from the air and enters the blood as it passes through the digestive tract. This enables loaches to survive in water that is too stagnant to support other fishes.

Loaches have small fins, and their eyes are commonly covered with a protective transparent lid. Just in front of or below the eyes is a pronged spine that may be used for probing or possibly as a weapon. These fishes are typically nocturnal, their sensory barbels aiding them in finding food. Several of the tropical species are kept in aquariums, but they must be provided with a place where they can hide during the day.

Many loaches are well known for their sensitivity to changes in atomospheric pressure. Among these is the European weatherfish, *Misgurnus fossilis*, which becomes much more active as the barometer drops—a signal of approaching stormy weather. The changes in pressure are apparently registered in the fish's two-compartmented air bladder, the front portion of which is incased in a bony capsule. Weatherfish may grow to a length of 18 inches but usually are less than 8 inches long. They are frequently kept in aquariums and are watched with interest to see if their variations in activity are reliable prognostications of weather changes. The oriental weatherfish, *M. anguillicaudatus*, is a similar Asiatic species that now occurs as an escaped species in North American fresh waters.

Popular with aquarium hobbyists is the coolie loach, *Acanthopthalmus kuhli*, because it is a scavenger and cleans up food and other organic debris. The half-banded loach, *A. semicinctus*, is similar in habits and general appearance.

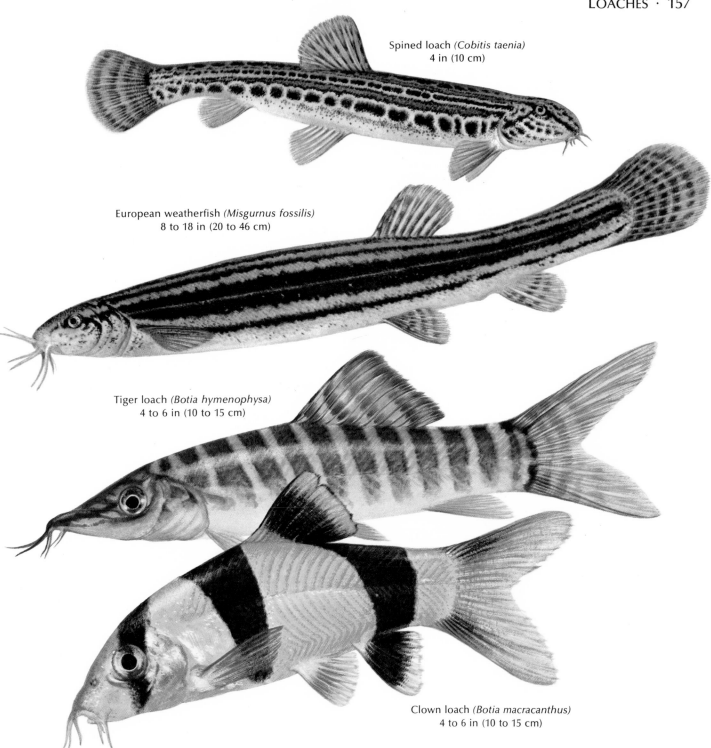

Spined loach *(Cobitis taenia)*
4 in (10 cm)

European weatherfish *(Misgurnus fossilis)*
8 to 18 in (20 to 46 cm)

Tiger loach *(Botia hymenophysa)*
4 to 6 in (10 to 15 cm)

Clown loach *(Botia macracanthus)*
4 to 6 in (10 to 15 cm)

The spined loach, *Cobitis taenia*, found in freshwater ponds and lakes throughout the temperate regions in Europe and Asia, is another species that reacts to weather changes. In some areas it is called the spotted weatherfish. Rarely more than 4 inches long and with three pairs of barbels, the spined loach remains buried in the sand or mud during the day and comes out at night to feed. Those kept in aquariums must be provided with suitable gravel or sand in which to hide. The two-pronged spine under each eye can be lifted at will.

Also popular with hobbyists are several species and varieties of kuhli loaches, *Acanthophthalmus*, which have small heads and long, wormlike bodies that are unusually marked with bands of dark and light colors. The stiff spines under each tiny eye are used to help in rooting in the sand.

Members of the genus *Botia*, in contrast, have plump bodies compared to other loaches. The caudal peduncle is almost as thick as the body, and the pointed snout bears as many as four pairs of barbels on the upper lip.

Coolie loach
(*Acanthophthalmus kuhlii*)
4 in (10 cm)

Sucker loach (*Gyrinocheilus aymonieri*)
4 in (10 cm)

The eyes are high on the head, and the two-pronged spine beneath each eye is directed backward. These are schooling fishes in aquariums; they do best if they are kept with several others of their kind.

Among the common species of *Botia*, all 4 to 6 inches long, are the clown loach, *B. macracanthus*, a bright gold-orange or yellowish red with red fins and three broad, black vertical bands across the body; blue (orange-finned) loach, *B. modesta*, the body greenish blue but the fins orange; tiger (striped) loach, *B. hymenophysa*, the blue-green body marked with thin brownish bands; and skunk loach, *B. horae*, the body an evenly colored greenish but with a black stripe down the middle of the back, broadening and vertical around the caudal peduncle. When young, the skunk loach may have narrow black stripes along the sides of its body.

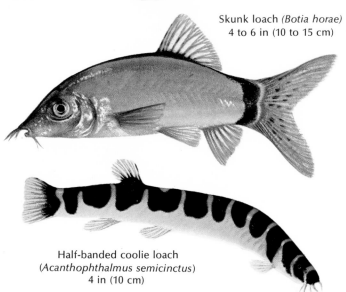

Skunk loach *(Botia horae)*
4 to 6 in (10 to 15 cm)

Half-banded coolie loach
(*Acanthophthalmus semicinctus*)
4 in (10 cm)

ORDER SILURIFORMES

Catfishes constitute a large group of chiefly freshwater fishes distributed around the world. South America is especially rich in quantity and species of catfishes. Some catfishes are armored with heavy scales; the majority, however, are scaleless. They vary in size from tiny types that are popular as aquarium fishes to huge specimens that may weigh hundreds of pounds. Most catfishes prefer the sluggish localities of lakes and rivers; some do best in fairly swift waters. Tenacious of life, they can stay alive out of water for a considerable time, especially if kept moist. They are characterized by having a single dorsal and an adipose fin; strong, sharply pointed spines in dorsal and pectoral fins; and whiskerlike sensory barbels on the upper and lower jaws. The head and mouth are broad, the eyes small. They are important commercially and are considered fine sport

fishes. As with other orders of fishes, the families and other taxonomic factors are not clearly defined; classification listings differ in various publications. This order may be separated into from 15 to over 25 families, depending on whose classification is followed.

Family Ictaluridae
North American freshwater catfishes

The North American freshwater family of catfishes, distributed from Canada to Guatemala, contains about 50 species. The American Fisheries Society lists 37 kinds inhabiting Canada and the United States. These bottom-loving fishes are important commercially; mill-

Yellow bullhead catfish *(Ictalurus natalis)*
8 to 10 in (20 to 25 cm)

ions are harvested annually. Thousands of anglers fish for them. A wide variety of methods is employed in catching catfishes, and all species obtained from fairly clear waters are delicious on the table. Many fish farms specialize in raising and marketing catfishes. All members of this group are naked-skinned and have a stiff, sharp spine at the leading edge of the dorsal fin and pectoral fins. Just in front of the tail, on the dorsal surface, is a fleshy adipose fin. Their eight barbels are sensory structures helping them to locate their food. Nearly all North American catfishes live in sluggish streams or in the quiet waters of lakes and ponds. They are bottom-feeders, taking both live and dead foods. They are typically active at night, on dark, cloudy days, or in roiled, murky water. Catfishes spawn in spring and early summer, fanning a nest area in the sand or mud. One or both parents stand guard until the eggs hatch and then shepherd the young until they are large enough to fend for themselves.

Perhaps the most abundant and best-known members of the clan of about a dozen species of the genus *Ictalurus* are the three principal species of bullheads—the brown bullhead, *I. nebulosus*; black bullhead, *I. melas*; and yellow bullhead, *I. natalis*.

Bullheads abound in fresh waters from coast to coast in North America. In some regions they have been introduced by man—either accidentally when a bait bucket containing a few baby bullheads was emptied or intentionally when a bullhead fisherman longed for the kind of fishing he knew "back home" and had bullheads stocked in his private pond. Settlers from the East carried bullheads over the Rockies to stock the waters with their familiar favorite. Until then, bullheads were not found west of the Rockies. Nature's way of moving bullheads into new habitats is more unique. The bullheads travel on the feet of wading birds that unknowingly carry the adhesive eggs with them from pond to pond. The eggs wash off as the birds wade, and in this

way a new population of bullheads becomes established. These catfishes can survive in water that is so low in oxygen that the bullheads must come to the surface from time to time to gulp air. In these emergency conditions, the air bladder acts as an auxiliary lung.

In the confinement of a pond in which conditions are initially favorable, bullheads may soon multiply beyond the food capacity. The result is an overpopulation of stunted, freakish fishes—weird-looking creatures with oversize heads and shrunken bodies. A few years ago biologists in Wisconsin poisoned a nine-acre pond that seemed crowded with bullheads. It contained nearly 250,000 bullheads. The pond was supporting about 1,500 pounds of fish per acre, but not one bullhead was big enough to grace a skillet.

East of the Rockies, all three species are in abundance. Most common—and the species that has been introduced most widely—is the brown bullhead. In their original distribution the black bullhead was the most widely distributed. In habits and flavor, the three species are scarcely distinguishable.

The brown bullhead has dark mottlings over its brown to olive body, and its anal fin contains 21–24 rays. The spines in the pectoral fins are stiff and sharp, and the tail fin in squared. A popular name for this species in the East is horned pout. Its maximum weight is 3 pounds; length, 1½ feet. Those most commonly caught are much smaller, weighing less than a pound and only 8 or 10 inches long.

The black bullhead is, on the average, smaller than the brown bullhead, and its body is only rarely mottled. The sides are a dark color; the membranes in the fins are black, making the rays stand out distinctly. The caudal fin is slightly indented at the middle, and there are 17–21 rays in the anal fin. The barbels are black, and a light or whitish vertical bar circles the caudal peduncle just in front of the caudal fin or tail.

The yellow bullhead, a light yellowish brown, has a

Channel catfish *(Ictalurus punctatus)*
up to 4 ft (120 cm)

rounded caudal fin, white barbels, and 24–27 rays in its anal fin. In size, it is more nearly like the brown bullhead.

Also commercially important in some areas are the channel catfish, *I. punctatus*; blue catfish, *I. furcatus*; white catfish, *I. catus*; and flathead catfish, *Pylodictus olivaris*. The largest is the blue catfish, which may tip the scales at more than 150 pounds. The record caught on rod and reel weighed 97 pounds and was 57 inches long. A 25-pound catch is considered large, however. Slate blue above and white below, this big catfish ranges throughout the large streams of the Mississippi River system but is most abundant by far in the deep, warm waters of the South. Small-size blue catfish are most easily confused with channel catfish. Both have forked tails, though the blue cat's is less forked than the channel cat's. The blue catfish has 30–36 rays in its anal fin, which is straight along its free edge; the channel catfish has only 24–30 rays in its anal fin, and the free edge is rounded.

A channel catfish's maximum weight is about 30 pounds, but the average is less than 5 pounds. A young channel catfish has black spots over its bluish body, and its fins are also margined with black. The black becomes subdued or is absent in older fish. Of all the catfishes, the channel cat shows the greatest preference for clear, flowing waters, but it does equally well in lakes and ponds. Because of its strong fight at the end of a rod and line, many rate it as a top sport fish. It is stocked regularly in farm ponds to provide fishing fun as well as food and is the principal fish stocked in "pay as you fish" ponds. The channel catfish is also the species most commonly used in "farming" enterprises that now represent a burgeoning business in the South.

The white catfish lives primarily in streams feeding into the Atlantic, ranging southward from New England to Florida. Until the introduction of the channel catfish, it was the largest catfish inhabiting these waters. It reaches a maximum size of about 15 pounds, but the average is less than 3 pounds. The tail is only slightly forked, and there are 18–24 rays in the anal fin. There are no spots on the light bluish-gray body.

The flathead catfish has a broad, flat head, and the lower jaw projects beyond the upper, the opposite of the species of *Ictalurus*. The anal fin, with 12–16 rays, is very short, and the caudal fin is straight with only a suggestion of an indentation. Found in the Mississippi River system, the flathead catfish is known to reach a weight of 100 pounds. The average size caught weighs less than 3 pounds, though 20-pounders are not especially rare.

Ictalurids are not finicky about what they eat. They will accept almost anything offered for bait—from a hotdog to a bare, shiny hook. Biologists have found strange collections of debris in the stomachs of catfishes—and quite an array of fishermen's lures and hooks. But catfishermen rate as superior the so-called stink baits—and the stinkier the better for luring catfishes. Most catfishes, in fact, have taste glands located over much of their body, though they are concentrated in their long, sensory whiskers. Among the favorite stink baits are "soured" clams, "ripened" chicken entrails, coagulated blood, and a variety of cheese and doughball mixtures, allowed to "cure" until they acquire a more potent odor. A good catfish bait will attract catfishes from a long distance.

Finally, the North American catfish family includes the madtoms, with about two dozen species in the genus *Noturus*. All are small, most of them less than 5 inches long. Their adipose fin is long but is either continuous with the caudal fin or separated from it by only a notch. In some, the caudal fin is abruptly squared, as though trimmed with scissors; in others, it is rounded. The anal fin is short. Venom glands at the bases of the spines cause stab wounds to swell and become very painful. Some madtoms live in the fast waters of streams, living in the rapids or riffles; others prefer slow-moving streams or the still waters of ponds and lakes, much like other members of the catfish family.

The stonecat, *N. flavus*, is one of the largest of the genus, sometimes attaining a length of 12 inches though usually less than half this size. It is found in the fast water of streams over most of the United States and southern Canada—from the St. Lawrence River system southward to Florida, westward to Oklahoma and across the northern tier of states to Wyoming and north to Manitoba. The tadpole madtom, *N. gyrinus*, seldom more than 3 inches long, occurs in much the same range but prefers sluggish waters.

The freckled madtom, *N. nocturnus*, also small, has numerous black specks over its body. It is sometimes found in swift waters but may as frequently inhabit weedy, quiet waters.

fishes commonly come out of the water and move about on land, like the walking catfish. The air bladder serves as a "lung" during these sojourns on land.

The African spotted catfish, a voracious predator, is found in the rivers of equatorial West Africa. In aquaria, it prefers sandy bottoms and secluded spots. It reaches a length of about 8 inches.

Glass catfish *(Kryptopterus bicirrhus)*
4 in (10 cm)

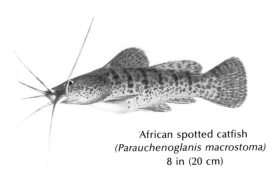

'African spotted catfish
(Parauchenoglanis macrostoma)
8 in (20 cm)

Family Bagridae
bagrid catfishes

These Old World counterparts of the pimelodid catfish provide hobbyists with some of the most interesting and attractive catfishes. The bumblebee catfish, *Leiocassis siamensis*, from Thailand, is dark brown with broad white or light yellowish bands across its body, which is high-arched or rounded. Like many other catfishes, it makes grunting or croaking noises when taken from the water. A carnivorous catfish, it has no hesitancy about attacking other fishes kept in the same aquarium with it.

The striped Indian catfish, *Mystus vittata*, from Thailand and India, may exceed 8 inches in length. It is one of the most handsome catfishes, three or four broad bluish stripes extending from head to tail over the yellowish body. There are four pairs of long barbels, those of one pair attached to the upper jaw almost as long as the fish's body. In their natural environment, these

Family Siluridae
Eurasian catfishes

One of the largest of all freshwater fishes belongs to this Old World family of catfishes: the wels, *Siluris glanis*, which is said to exceed 12 feet in length and weigh hundreds of pounds. The wels lives in freshwater streams and lakes from central Europe through western Asia. Typical of the family, its body is scaleless, the anal fin is long, and there are only two pairs of barbels—one on the upper jaw and one on the lower. (Another catfish that is known for its huge size, in the hundreds of pounds, is the lau-lau, *Brachyplatystoma jilamentosum*, of South America. The "hundreds of pounds," often quoted, has not been substantiated.)

Fish hobbyists know this family best for the glass catfish, *Kryptopterus bicirrhus*, a 4-inch species native to southeastern Asia. The body is so "glassy" that it reflects light in glittering rainbow hues and is transparent enough so that, particularly in young fishes, the internal organs are visible. The dorsal fin consists of a single small ray, but the exceptionally long anal fin may contain as many as 60 rays. Unlike many catfishes, this species thrives on the companionship of others of its kind. In nature, it lives in small schools.

Several closely related species, including *K. macrocephalus*, are similar to the glass catfish but are not as popular with hobbyists. Species of *Ompok* are sometimes imported from the same region but grow to larger size—up to 1½ feet—and thus are not generally desirable for the small aquarium. The namazu, *Parasilurus asotus*, weakly distributed in China, Korea, and Japan, reaches a length of 1½ feet and is caught for food, its flesh firm when the fish comes from cool water.

Three-striped glass catfish *(Etropiellus debauwi)*
up to 4 in (10 cm)

Family Schilbeidae
shilbeid catfishes

One of the largest catfishes, *Pangasianodon gigas*, belongs to this family. A native of southeastern Asia, this giant is said to weigh more than 250 pounds and exceed 7 feet in length. Typical of the family, it has a deeply forked tail, a small adipose fin, a very long anal fin, a short but high dorsal fin, and a bristling of barbels (two or three pairs) around its mouth.

Aquarium hobbyists know the family best for the several 3- to 4-inch glass catfish, of which *Physailia pellucida* is one of the most common. It lacks a dorsal fin. In contrast, the 3-inch *Etropiellus debauwi*, also from Africa, has a high, flaglike dorsal fin.

Family Clariidae
labyrinthic catfishes

Clarid catfishes are unique in possessing an expanded, lunglike cavity in front of the gills and extending along each side of the spine as a much-branched or labyrinthic structure that is well supplied with blood vessels. As a result, these catfishes can breathe air, enabling them to remain out of water for long periods if their bodies stay moist. Typically they inhabit fouled or stagnant water that no other fish can tolerate. This auxiliary breathing apparatus makes the front of the body thick; the tail portion is thin, flat, and, in some species, almost ribbonlike. Both the dorsal and anal fins are long and spineless, and most species do not have an adipose fin. The body is naked, but the skin is thick and covered with mucus, an additional feature that makes possible their long exposure to the air.

The famed walking catfish, *Clarias batrachus*, is a member of this family. A native of southeastern Asia, it was imported to the United States as an oddity for fish hobbyists. Some were either set free or escaped captivity in southern Florida, where the fish now poses a serious threat to native species in many bodies of water. With snakelike movements and by using their pectoral fins as "legs," these catfishes literally walk on land. When attempts were made to poison bodies of water to kill them, the walking catfish simply moved out of the undesirable water and traveled overland to a new home, leaving the native species to die.

Similarly, when ponds dry up during the dry season or in periods of drought, walking catfishes keep moving to find pools with water. As a last resort, they bury themselves in the mud at the bottom of a pool of water where, like lungfishes, they manage to survive until rains come again. Aggressive, reaching a length of about 8 inches, they do not hesitate to attack fishes larger than themselves and soon become the dominant fish in whatever waters they inhabit. Ecologists are justifiably concerned about the long-range effects of this now well-established species. Many states prohibit the importation or possession of walking catfishes, of which there are, in addition to *Clarias batrachus*, about half a dozen other species—some from Africa, others from Asia.

Other genera in the family include *Gymnallabes*, containing a single eel-shaped, 10-inch species that is native to West Africa. It is unusual in that the dorsal, caudal, and anal fins are connected, forming a single ribbon around the rear of the body that is not much larger than a lead pencil in diameter.

Also eel-shaped but with less exaggeration are the several species of the genus *Heterobranchus*, of India and Ceylon. The wide, thick-lipped mouth bears four pairs of barbels. An adipose fin is present in this genus, and the pectoral fins have sharp spines that can inflict slow-to-heal wounds. Like many catfishes, they often make grunting noises as they cruise through the water or when they are picked up.

Electric catfish *(Malapterurus electricus)*
8 in to 4 ft (20 to 120 cm)

Family Malapteruridae
electric catfishes

A single species, *Malapterurus electricus*, comprises this family. Oddly shaped, with a thick head, large lips, and a fat, stubby body, the electric catfish does not have a dorsal fin. The adipose fin, however, is prominent and is located just in front of the caudal peduncle. The eyes are tiny; they reflect light at night, literally shining like pinpoint-sized cat's eyes. The electric catfish is an aggressive fish, sometimes exceeding 3 feet in length and weighing as much as 50 pounds. It is fearless, attacking and feeding on other fishes.

A large electric catfish can deliver a shocking 100 volts—enough to kill small fishes or stun large ones. The initial jolt is generally followed by a series of smaller ones. In addition to serving as a weapon of defense or as a means of overcoming prey, the electrical impulses may act as a sort of sonar for navigation in the murky tropical African waters where the electric catfish lives.

The electric organs are located just under the skin along the full length of the body and tail. They are derived from glandular cells in the epidermis rather than from muscle tissue as in other fishes capable of generating electricity. In polarity, the electric catfish is negative toward the head and positive toward the tail—the reverse of the electric eel, for example.

Upside-down catfish (*Synodontis nigriventris*)
3 in (8 cm)

Family Mochokidae
upside-down catfishes

Favorites for aquariums, these unusual catfishes have branched or "feathery" barbels and an extraordinarily long adipose fin. The most important genus is *Synodontis*, containing a number of species exported from tropical Africa for fish hobbyists. All have large fins, and the tail is deeply forked in most species. Most of them are strikingly marked with blocks or bands of a dark color.

The African polka-dot catfish, *S. angelicus*, which grows to 7 inches long, is one of the most popular species. Most unusual is the 3-inch backswimmer, or upside-down catfish, *S. nigriventris*, which can swim on its back for long periods of time. An indication that the habit has a long evolutionary history is revealed by the fish's reversed color pattern: dark on the belly and light on the back. The very young fishes swim with their bellies down, but as they mature they spend increasing amounts of time on their backs. All members of this genus are hardy and live peaceably with other fishes in an aquarium.

Family Ariidae
sea catfishes

Sea catfishes are best known for the remarkable way they incubate their eggs. The male picks up the eggs as the female lays them and holds them in his mouth until they hatch. This can indeed be a mouthful—50 or more pea-size eggs. More astonishing, when the eggs hatch, the male continues to serve the needs of his progeny by permitting them to use his mouth as a place of refuge. Up to a month may pass before the swarming mass of black baby catfishes set off on their own. By this time, six or eight weeks have passed since the male has had a meal. Once his appetite is triggered, he does not hesitate to gobble up even his own offspring if they foolishly swim too close.

Sea catfishes are found in tropical and subtropical seas throughout the world, sometimes straying into temperate waters that are warmed in summer. Compared to their cousins of fresh water, they are much more active than most, though they are essentially bottom-feeders. They have a sharp spine at the front edge of the dorsal fin and another in each of the pectoral fins. The stab wounds are slow to heal. While sea catfishes do not rate as sport fishes, they are commonly caught, mostly by accident and to the annoyance of the fishermen. Most are thrown back into the water as quickly as they are unhooked, which is seldom gently. In some countries, they are harvested as food.

The sea catfish common in the Gulf of Mexico and along the southern Atlantic coast of the United States is *Arius felis*. About 12 inches long and rarely weighing as much as 2 pounds, the sea catfish has two barbels in its upper jaw and four on the lower. The tail is deeply forked. It is generally abundant, traveling in schools of a hundred or more. In some areas it enters fresh water.

The gafftopsail catfish, *Bagre marinus*, occurs in much the same range as the sea catfish but is more abundant southward through the Caribbean and off northern South America. Twice as large, attaining a length of 2 feet and a weight of 4 pounds, the gafftopsail has only two barbels on the lower jaw rather than four as in the sea catfish. In color, the gafftopsail is bluish above and silvery white below, while the sea catfish tends to be more greenish. The gafftopsail's most distinguishing feature is its high dorsal fin, the first ray drawn into a long, slim filament. The pectoral fins also end in long filaments. As in the sea catfish, the male carries the eggs, which may be as much as an inch in diameter, in his mouth until they hatch.

In the West Indies and to a lesser degree in Florida, the cleaned, dried, and bleached skulls of the gafftop-

Sea catfish *(Arius felis)*
3 ft (90 cm)

sail are sold as curios. From below, the bone structure has the shape of a cross, and with a bit of imagination a figure can be seen—the head bowed and the arms outstretched.

Other members of the sea catfish family, consisting of about 40 species in all, occur in warm seas throughout the world, but the family is notably absent from European waters. The Kanduli catfish, *Arius dispar*, found off southeastern Asia, is similar in size to the gafftopsail. The salmon catfish, *Netuma thalassima*, to 3 feet long, occurs along the coast and in estuaries of Australia. More common in the same waters is the smaller, to 1½ feet long, blue catfish, *Neoarius australis*.

Family Doradidae
doradid armored catfishes

These are fat-bodied South American catfishes, their armor consisting of a row of thick, overlapping spiny plates along each side of the body. The dorsal and pectoral fins bear spines that can inflict painful, slow-to-heal stabs. They have two or three pairs of chin barbels.

The best-known member of the family is the talking catfish, *Acanthodoras spinosissimus*, so named be-

cause of the croaking sounds the fish makes, particularly when caught. These noisy grunts are produced by the air bladder, possibly by changes in pressure that force air in and out as the pectoral fins are pumped. The talking catfish may reach a length of 8 inches.

The helmeted catfish, *Astrodoras asterifrons*, about 4 inches long, is a similar species that also comes from the Amazon region. Another species similar in size and from the same region is the spiny catfish, *Amblydoras hancocki*, its brownish body attractively marked with black patches outlined with white. It also makes grunting noises.

Family Aspredinidae
banjo catfishes

Fewer than a dozen species comprise this family of South American catfishes. All lack armor, and their naked bodies are much flattened, especially in the head region—which gives them their banjo shape. Like most other catfishes, they are nocturnal. In an aquarium they must be provided with places to hide during daylight hours; they come out at night to scavenge for food.

Most common of the several species kept by hobbyists is *Bunocephalus coracoideus*, which has wartlike

Spiny catfish *(Amblydoras hancocki)*
4 in (10 cm)

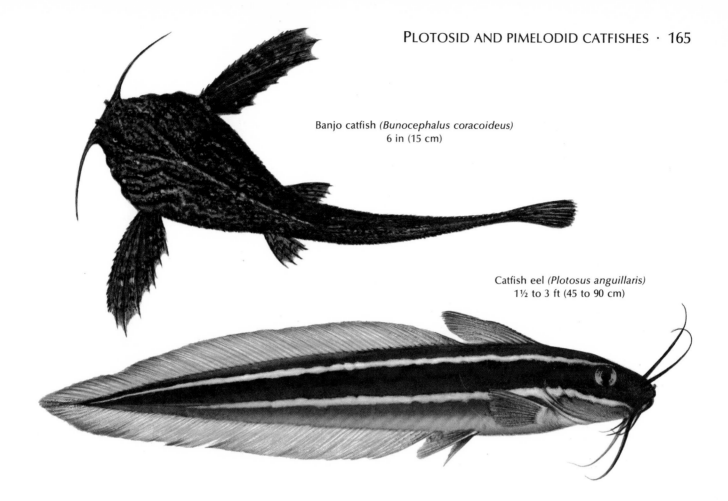

Banjo catfish *(Bunocephalus coracoideus)*
6 in (15 cm)

Catfish eel *(Plotosus anguillaris)*
1½ to 3 ft (45 to 90 cm)

bumps on its head and sides. In addition to liking to hide under objects, this species also likes to bury itself in the soft bottom. An aquarium cannot support both these catfishes and an attractive growth of rooted plants. This species reaches a length of about 6 inches; others in the genus are larger. Species of this genus have spawned successfully in captivity, the females laying their eggs in depressions in the sand made by fanning their fins. The female of a species of *Aspredinichthys* carries her eggs with her until they hatch.

Family Plotosidae
plotosid sea catfishes

The few species comprising this family are confined largely to tropical waters of the Indo-Pacific, occasionally straying as far north as Japan. They are primarily reef fishes. The spines in their dorsal and pectoral fins are connected to venom glands that release poison into the stab wounds. The pain is excruciating, and deaths have been reported. Compared to other marine catfishes, these are colorful, which is not unusual for venomous animals. Some are striped with bright yellow. The most commonly seen species is the 3-foot catfish eel, or gonzui, *Plotosus anguillaris*, occurring from South Africa throughout the tropical seas of the Indo-Pacific region.

It sometimes attains a length of 3 feet but more commonly less than 1½ feet long. Its second dorsal fin is joined to the caudal and anal fins, the three making one continuous, rippling unit. It often occurs in large schools. Abundant in the same region but only half as large is *P. arab*. Both species travel in schools consisting of several hundred fishes.

Family Pimelodidae
pimelodid catfishes

Ranging from Mexico southward through South America except for the cold southern regions, this is the largest family of freshwater catfishes in South America. They are distinguished from other catfishes mainly by their very large adipose fins. All have naked skins. The caudal fin is forked, and the medium-size, spined dorsal fin is high and located far forward on the body. The pectoral fins are also spineless. Typically there are three pairs of long barbels that stretch back halfway or more along the body. Some of the numerous species in the more than 20 genera in the family are favorites with fish hobbyists.

The pintado, or polka-dot catfish, *Pimelodus clarias*, is strikingly marked with large bluish-gray spots when young; these generally fade and then disappear as the fish becomes older. The eyes are very large, the head flattened, and the barbels on the upper jaw exceptionally long—stretching backward almost the full length of the body. In nature this species may attain a length of 10 inches or more, a potential size that precludes it from most home aquariums.

The mandi, or slender catfish, *Pimelodella gracillis*, is smaller than the pintado—about 6 inches long. The young are striped with bands of dark grayish green, but the colors fade as the fish becomes older. In shape and other features, this species resembles the polka-dot catfish. Both are handsome, graceful creatures. They are strictly nocturnal in habits and seem to derive great pleasure from rooting up plants or turning over objects on the bottom of the aquarium. A blind cave catfish, *Typhlobagrus kronei*, that inhabits cave waters near Sao Paulo, Brazil, is believed to have evolved from the slender catfish, which lives in the lighted waters above.

Most other pimelodids are too large for keeping in home aquariums. Occasionally a hobbyist is lured into acquiring a shovelnose catfish, *Sorubium lima*, but success in an aquarium requires a tank of about 40 gallons to accommodate the fish when it is full grown. It attains a length of 1½ feet or longer. The shovelnose catfish is so named because its flat head is projected into a ducklike snout. The mouth projects down under the snout, conveniently located for picking up food rooted from the bottom. Tiger catfishes, members of the genus *Pseudoplatystoma*, are similarly long-snouted.

Family Trichomycteridae
parasitic catfishes

Among the smallest of all catfishes, the few members comprising this family have a fearsome reputation. The species most responsible is the candiru, or carnero, *Vandellia cirrhosa*. Only about 2 inches long, this little catfish may swim into the urogenital openings of waders or bathers, where it erects its spines and lodges itself inside. The pain is agonizing, and the fish can be removed only by surgery. It is not truly parasitic, however; when disturbed from its natural hiding place, it seeks any orifice or protective situation.

Parasitic catfishes are natives of South America. The dorsal fin is soft-rayed and lacks a spine, and there is no

Parasitic catfish, juvenile (*Vandellia cirrhosa*)
2 in (5 cm)

adipose fin. The gill covers are equipped with curved spines, however, and the little fishes need only lift these covers to engage their hooks and hold themselves in place while they make their meals of the victim's blood or tissues. Members of the genus *Stegophilus* swim into the gill chambers of larger fishes and chew on the gill filaments to receive the blood.

Family Callichthyidae
callichthyid armored catfishes

The armor of these South American catfishes consists of two rows of spineless plates along each side of the body, one above and one below the lateral line. Typical of most catfishes, the dorsal and pectoral fins bear spines. In many members of this family the adipose fin also has a spine. Most species have a single pair of short barbels on the upper jaw and two or more on the chin. The air bladder, enclosed in a bony casing, is divided into two compartments.

These catfishes live in waters that are low in oxygen, and they supplement their needs by coming to the surface from time to time to gulp air. Oxygen is removed from the air as it passes through the intestine, which is richly supplied with blood vessels and thus serves as an auxiliary breathing organ. Some members of the family can survive for long periods out of water if kept moist.

Several species of callichthyid catfishes are popular with aquarium hobbyists. Most notable among these are members of the genus *Corydoras*, in which the distinctly arched back is totally lacking in armor. Because all the species are small, averaging about 3 inches long, and because they are hardy and undemanding and derive their nourishment from both live foods and organic wastes picked up from the bottom, these catfishes present few problems for hobbyists. In fact, these catfishes generally earn their keep by helping to keep the aquarium clean.

Among the more than a dozen *Corydoras* species kept in aquariums, some of the most common are the bronze or aeneus catfish, *C. aeneus*, so called because of the shiny, metallic hue of its scales; the streamlined or skunk cat, *C. arcuatus*, distinguished by the black band extending from its snout through the eye to the tail on each side; the spotted corydoras, *C. melanistius*, its body speckled with small black dots; the leopard catfish, *C. punctatus*, in which the black spots on the body are large and leopardlike, extending also onto the fins; the peppered catfish, *C. paleatus*, mottled and dotted with black, less strikingly than the leopard catfish but much more strongly than in the spotted catfish; the dwarf catfish, *C. hastatus*, so called because

Aeneus catfish *(Corydoras aeneus)*
3 in (8 cm)

it rarely exceeds a length of 1½ inches; and rabaut's catfish, *C. rabauti*, resembling the streamlined or skunk catfish but with the stripe starting just in front of the dorsal fin and stopping at the caudal peduncle.

Members of the smaller genus *Callichthys* have a broader, less rounded head. The callused catfish, or hassar, *C. callichthys*, is the species most commonly kept in aquariums. It may attain a length of 7 inches.

Family Loricariidae
loricariid armored catfishes

In this family of South American armored catfishes the entire body is covered with bony plates, which are spineless. The body is flat, much wider than high. The sucking mouth is subterminal, or projected downward, for drawing in organic ooze and plants from the bottom. The strongly developed sucking mouth is used also for anchorage in the swift currents of the streams where these fishes normally live, and the suction is so powerful that it is difficult to pry the fish loose. The armor typically consists of three rows of bony plates that extend the full length of the body.

The twig catfish, *Farlowella acus*, is one of the species commonly imported to the United States. It rarely survives long in captivity, partly because its exclusive plant diet is seldom satisfied.

The whiptail catfish, *Loricaria parva*, noted for its slim, almost threadlike caudal peduncle, is a hardier species then the twig catfish but nevertheless demands special attention to assure its having an adequate supply of algae for food.

The smaller *Otoclinus affinus* and several related species in the same genus, none of them regularly exceeding 2 inches in length, are generally favored by fish hobbyists because their smaller size precludes their being greatly destructive in aquariums. Like other members of the family, however, they are more sensitive than most catfishes and will die quickly if not provided with a suitable quantity and kind of plants.

The largest of the suckermouth catfishes are members of the genus *Plecostomus* and *Ancistrus*, averaging more than 6 inches in length and not uncommonly harvested for food locally. If kept in aquariums, they require a tank of 20 gallons or more. These are aggressive fishes, moving swiftly and attacking others of their kind kept in the same aquarium. Bristlemouth catfishes, *Ancistrus spp.*, are distinguished by their numerous "whiskers," which are sometimes branched.

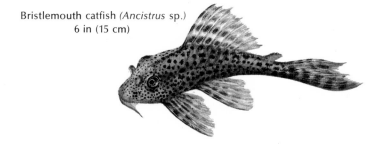

Bristlemouth catfish *(Ancistrus sp.)*
6 in (15 cm)

ORDER PERCOPSIFORMES

Family Amblyopsidae
cavefishes

Amblyopsids, all less than 4 inches long, are related to topminnows and similar surface-dwelling fishes. The swampfish, *Chologaster cornuta*, found along the Atlantic coast from Georgia northward to Virginia, inhabits swamps. It has small but functional eyes and a dark stripe down its sides.

The related spring cavefish, *C. agassizi*, prefers cool spring waters and is found farther west, in the Mississippi River region. Unlike the swampfish, it lacks a dark

streak on its side. It has 12–16 rays in its tail fin, compared to 12 in the swampfish.

The remaining three species comprising this small family are typical cave dwellers. All animals that spend their entire lives in caves share basic features, assuming their cave-dwelling habit has a reasonably long evolutionary history. They are blind, either having lost their eyes totally or having only rudimentary eyes; and their bodies lack pigment. Few cave animals are as large

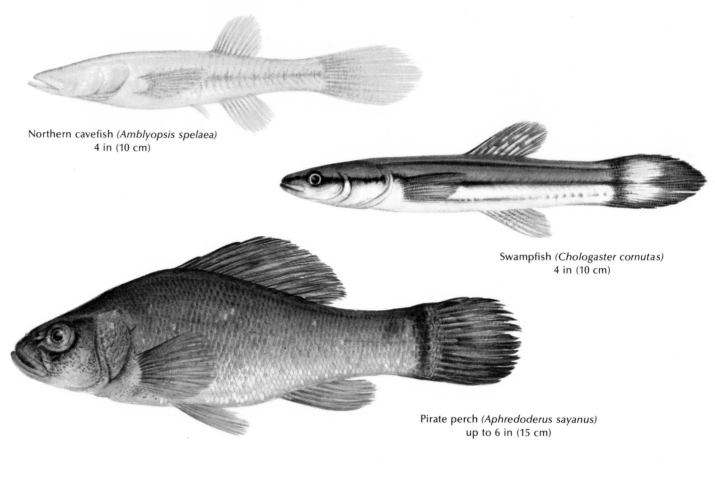

Northern cavefish *(Amblyopsis spelaea)*
4 in (10 cm)

Swampfish *(Chologaster cornutas)*
4 in (10 cm)

Pirate perch *(Aphredoderus sayanus)*
up to 6 in (15 cm)

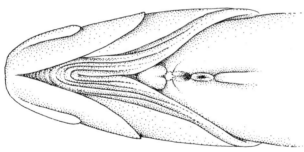

Ventral view of the head of *A. sayanus*,
showing the position of the anal orifice

as their near relatives living at the surface. All cave-dwelling amblyopsids live in limestone caves in the central United States. They include the Ozark cavefish, *Amblyopsis rosae*, and the northern cavefish, *A. spelaea*, which have rows of swellings or bumps of sensory function on the caudal fin. The northern cavefish also has small pelvic fins, not present in any other member of the family. The third species is the southern cavefish *Typhlichthys subterraneus*.

Family Aphredoderidae
pirate perch

The single species in this family is the pirate perch, *Aphredoderus sayanus*, similar to the trout-perch but lacking an adipose fin. Its most unusual feature is the location of its anus. In newly hatched fishes, the anus is in the normal position, but as the fish grows, the anus migrates forward until in adults it is located under the throat. The pirate perch lives in ponds and lakes from Texas and Florida northward to Ontario and Minnesota. Occasionally it may attain a length of 6 inches, but the average length is 3 inches.

Family Percopsidae
trout-perches

Only two species, neither exceeding 6 inches in length, comprise this family of North American fishes. Both have an adipose fin on the caudal peduncle between the

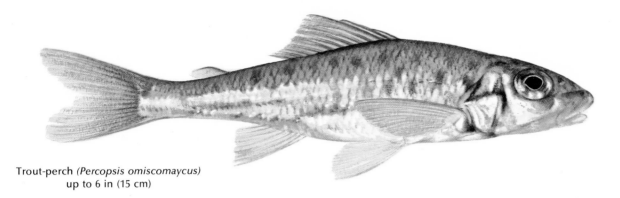

Trout-perch *(Percopsis omiscomaycus)*
up to 6 in (15 cm)

dorsal and caudal fins and spines on the leading edges of the dorsal, anal, and pelvic fins.

The trout-perch, *Percopsis omiscomaycus*, ranges from Hudson Bay to the Yukon and from the Potomac westward to Kansas. Presumably it stays in deep water most of the time, coming into the shallows only at spawning time in spring. The sandroller, *P. transmontana*, is slightly smaller and is found only in the Columbia River Basin of the Pacific Northwest. Trout-perches are important forage fishes for predacious types.

ORDER BATRACHOIDIFORMES

Family Batrachoididae
toadfishes

Bottom-dwellers, toadfishes commonly bury themselves in the sand or mud or hide in seaweeds. They dart from these hiding places to capture their prey. Toadfishes have broad toadlike heads and very large mouths equipped with numerous sharp teeth. The lower jaw projects, and the slime-covered body tapers to a slim tail. The spiny dorsal fin is small, the second dorsal and anal fins long. The pelvic fins are located far forward, under the chin and in front of the pectoral fins.

True to their name, these fishes can make toadlike croaking noises. About three dozen species are recognized, living in temperate and tropical seas with some species inhabiting brackish or fresh water.

The Atlantic midshipman, *Porichthys porosissimus*, to 10 inches long, occurs from the Carolinas to southern Brazil and is also prevalent in the Gulf of Mexico. The body tapers sharply from head to tail, and there are rows of silvery pores on the sides, head, and ventral surface.

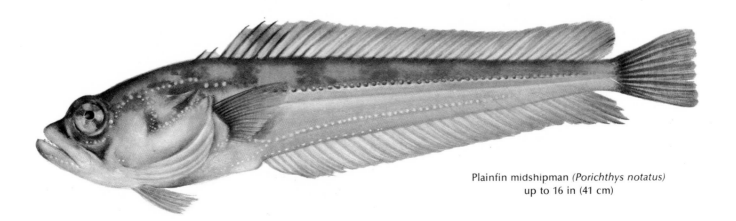

Plainfin midshipman *(Porichthys notatus)*
up to 16 in (41 cm)

The common species along the Pacific coast from Alaska to the Gulf of California is the northern, or plainfin, midshipman, *P. notatus*, to 16 inches long. The photophores under its head form a broad inverted V. Another Pacific species of about the same size is the slim, or specklefin, midshipman, *P. myriaster*. The photophores under its head are in the shape of an inverted U. The slim midshipman is bronze with a bluish cast, usually yellow below. The dorsal fin is speckled with black and also margined with black. The northern midshipman's dorsal fin is dark but has no speckling or black margin.

The oyster toadfish, *Opsanus tau*, averaging less than 10 inches in length but sometimes 18 inches long and weighing two pounds, occurs from Maine southward to the Caribbean. It is most abundant from Massachusetts to the Carolinas. Scaleless and big-headed, with fleshy pendants beneath the chin, the body is brownish mottled with yellow. The toadfish is extremely pugnacious and will snap its jaws shut on anything that comes between them. The male is especially vicious during the breeding season when the females lay their eggs under stones, shells, or other objects, or in cans, and then let the males guard them. Males maintain their vigil for nearly four weeks until the eggs hatch. The oyster toadfish is common in shallow waters as soon as they warm in the spring, remaining there through summer and early fall and then moving into deeper, warmer waters in winter. Toadfishes often take baits intended for other bottom-feeders. The Gulf toadfish, *O. beta*, and the heavily spotted leopard toadfish, *O. pardus*, are found in the Gulf of Mexico and in Caribbean waters.

Species of *Thalassopryne* and *Thalassothia* of tropical American waters can inject venom from the hollow first two spines of their dorsal fin and from a similar spine on the upper edge of each gill cover. The poison makes a stab wound that is extemely painful but not potent enough to cause death.

ORDER GOBIESOCIFORMES

Family Gobiesocidae
clingfishes

These odd, flat-bodied tadpolelike fishes are scaleless and covered with a thick, slippery coat of slime. The head is broad, the tail slim. The ventral fins are united to form a sucking disk with which the fish clings to rocks or other objects to hold its position, even in currents of water. Clingfishes have only one dorsal fin and no spines. Fewer than a hundred species are recognized. They are worldwide in distribution in warm seas. Sev-

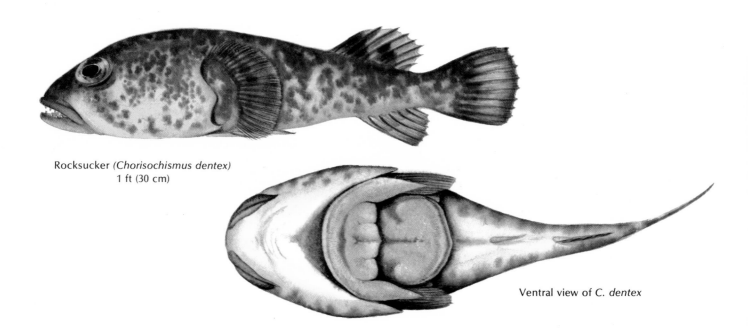

Rocksucker *(Chorisochismus dentex)*
1 ft (30 cm)

Ventral view of *C. dentex*

eral live in fresh water. All are small, most of them 4 inches or less in length.

The common genus in North American waters is *Gobiesox*, and the best known of the half a dozen species in the Atlantic is the skilletfish, *G. strumosus*, which is about 4 inches long and a dull-clay gray in color. It is found close to shore from Virginia southward through the Caribbean. Clingfishes are much more abundant off the Pacific Coast, where the most common of about 20 species is the 6-inch northern clingfish, *G. meandricus*, which occurs from California to Alaska.

Clingfishes are found also off the coasts of Asia, Africa, and Europe. The rocksucker, *Chorisochismus dentex*, grows up to 12 inches long.

Goosefish (*Lophius americanus*)
4 ft (120 cm)

ORDER LOPHIIFORMES

Family Lophiidae
goosefishes

These are giant angler fishes, about a dozen species occurring in tropical and temperate seas. The largest in the family is the goosefish, *Lophius americanus*, to 4 feet long and weighing as much as 70 pounds. It occurs the full length of the Atlantic coast—from the Gulf of St. Lawrence to southern South America. In the tropics, however, it is confined to deep waters.

The goosefish has almost armlike pectoral fins located about midway in its greatly flattened body. Small gill openings are just behind them. The head is very large in proportion to the body, and the mouth is cavernous, filled with sharp, curved teeth and opening upward. Fleshy flaps of skin margin the head and lower jaw, and smaller flaps of flesh run along the sides of the scaleless body. The first three spines of the dorsal fin are thin and sharp, and they are widely separated from one another. On the tip of the first spine is a flap of flesh that serves as a lure for attracting small fishes within grasping range of the mouth. If the prey comes close enough, the goosefish has only to open its big mouth, and the victim is drawn inside by suction, a not uncommon method of catching victims among these fishes and their relatives. The goosefish's body is dark brown with a mottling of black and light spots.

Goosefishes are notoriously rapacious. They can swallow fishes nearly as large as themselves and also have been known to capture diving ducks in fairly deep water. Despite their ugliness, these fishes are good to eat. They have only a few large bones. Those caught in deep water—at depths of half a mile—have firm, white flesh. Those taken from warm shallows tend to be flabby and not flavorful. Goosefishes are not eaten, but an almost identical species, *L. piscatorius*, caught off the coasts of Europe and Africa, is much esteemed and is harvested regularly by commercial fishermen. A similar but smaller species lives in the Pacific.

Family Antenariidae
frogfishes

Most common around coral reefs of subtropical and tropical seas, few frogfishes are as much as 12 inches long. Their bodies are more balloon-shaped than flattened, and most of them do not "angle" for their prey as do other anglers, such as the goosefishes. Rather, they depend on their camouflage and on stealth to make their catches. Though the mouth and teeth are not disproportionately large, as in goosefishes, frogfishes are aggressive and will attack and eat almost any fish or other creature that they can swallow.

The most abundantly represented genus in North American waters is *Antennarius*. One species, the roughjaw frogfish, *A. avalonis*, occurs in warm waters of the Pacific from Point Conception southward. It reaches a length of 14 inches.

Roughjaw frogfish *(Antennarius avalonis)*
14 in (36 cm)

Sargassumfish *(Histrio histrio)*
6 in (15 cm)

Four species are found in the Atlantic. These include the 8-inch splitlure frogfish, *A. scaber*, its fins and much of its body covered with frilly or whiskery filaments that serve both for concealment as a disruptive pattern and also to attract prey. The splitlure frogfish is found from New York southward to Argentina but is abundant only in the warm parts of this range.

There are a number of representatives of *Antennarius* in the western Pacific off the northern coast of Asia and Japan and also in the southern Indo-Pacific, where many are strikingly colored and camouflaged. Some have well-developed "poles and lures" at the front of the head above the snout.

The best-known frogfish is the sargassumfish, *Histrio histrio*, a 6-inch species common along the Florida coast and in the Caribbean, wherever sargassumweed is found. The first ray of its dorsal fin is located on the snout and is split into two or forked at the tip. Rays of the other fins also end in filaments, sometimes with bulbous swellings like those on the sargassumweed. The body is brownish-yellow mottled with darker color. The fish becomes perfectly concealed in the sargassum where it lives, generally climbing about in the floating seaweed by using its pectoral fins as "arms" and rarely swimming. The sargassumfish feeds on small fish or other animals that also live in the sargassumweed. It moves toward its prey slowly and cautiously, and when it opens its large mouth, the sudden current of water drawn into the mouth cavity sweeps the unsuspecting victim in at the same time. The little fish is capable of engulfing a fish half as large as itself and is known also to be cannibalistic. If kept in an aquarium, it must be isolated and provided with a steady supply of fish for food to keep it contented.

Family Ogcocephalidae
batfishes

Sand-bottom dwellers of warm seas throughout the world, batfishes have large pectoral fins that extend out at the sides of the body, their leading edge connected broadly to the head—giving them their "bat wing" appearance. The widely separated pelvic fins are stout and leglike, used for "walking" over the bottom. Batfishes can swim, but they do so poorly. The head is prolonged into a snout that overhangs the small mouth. A modified spine of the dorsal fin hangs down as a tentacle from

Red batfish *(Halieutaea stellata)*
7 to 14 in (18 to 36 cm)

beneath the snout and serves as a lure. The fish settles itself in the sand by burrowing backward, the forepart of its body lifted high and the tentacle waved enticingly. If a small fish swims close enough, the batfish literally explodes from the sand and gulps it down. Fewer than three dozen species are recognized. They often appear close inshore and may be seen waddling along the bottom to find a productive place to pursue their "fishing." Some species, including the common longnosed batfish, have brightly banded pectoral and tail fins that are spread as a warning to frighten intruders or as a distraction when the batfish is approaching potential prey and it is advantageous to keep attention away from its head.

The longnosed batfish, *Ogcocephalus vespertilio*, is a common species of warm Atlantic and Caribbean waters. It rarely exceeds 10 inches in length and is camouflaged in the sand by its brownish, warty body. A similar species with a shorter snout is the shortnose batfish, *O. nasutus*. The spotted batfish, *Zalieutes elater*, lives in warm Pacific waters off the coast of North America. *Halieutaea stellata* is a brick-red species found off the coasts of northern Asia and Japan. Others of the genus occur in warmer Pacific waters to the south.

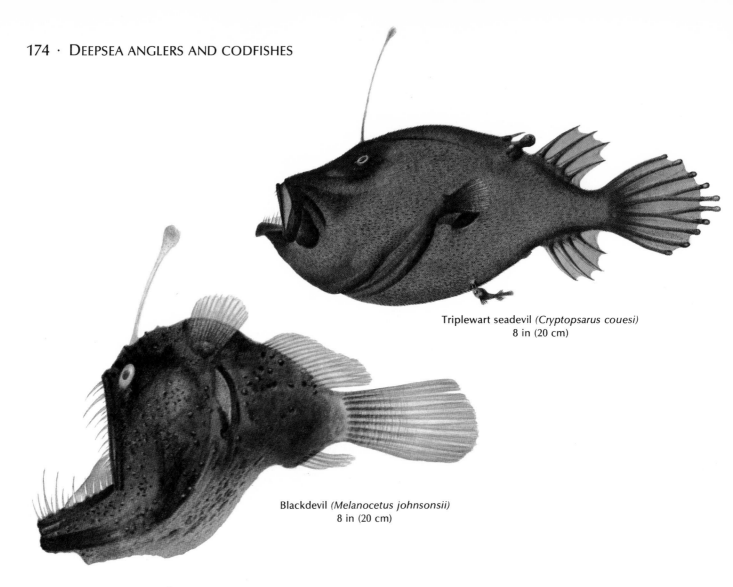

Triplewart seadevil *(Cryptopsarus couesi)*
8 in (20 cm)

Blackdevil *(Melanocetus johnsonsii)*
8 in (20 cm)

Deepsea Anglers

A dozen or more families of fishes that live in the deep sea are "anglers"—they are equipped with "rods and lures" to catch their food. The rods are the modified first spines of their dorsal fin, and many are equipped with fringed or bulbous tips, sometimes luminous. Anglers that live in the dark depths of the sea are generally dull in color—often black—and they have capacious mouths and long, sharp teeth. They are not swift swimmers. The triplewart seadevil of the family Ceratiidae, *Cryptopsarus couesi*, and the blackdevil of the family Melanocetidae, *Melanocetus johnsonii*, are among the kinds of deepsea fish commonly illustrated.

ORDER GADIFORMES

Family Gadidae
codfishes

All members of the cod family live in cold waters of the Northern Hemisphere, some in the Atlantic and some in the Pacific. Most of the species are harvested commercially. Their value to the New England area since colonial times is evidenced by the use of the codfish on the state seal of Massachusetts, where a gilded carving of the "Sacred Cod" hangs in the State House in Boston.

All members of the cod family have spineless fins. The pelvic or ventral fins are located far forward, commonly ahead of the pectorals. The body is elongated, and there is a single barbel on the chin. Most species have two dorsal fins; some have three, others only one.

The Atlantic codfish, *Gadus morhua*, has three dorsal fins and two anal fins. The light lateral line against its dark sides is a distinctive feature. The snout is rounded or cone-shaped on top, the upper jaw projecting slightly beyond the lower jaw. The tail is almost squared or is slightly concave. There are two principal color phases—gray and red; in both, the sides are covered with dark dots.

Years ago, an Atlantic cod that weighed 211¼ pounds and measured 6 feet in length was netted in the North Atlantic. Nowadays a cod weighing more than 100 pounds is extremely rare, and a 50-pound fish is considered large. The largest cod ever taken on rod and reel weighed 98 pounds 12 ounces. Average catches are much smaller—10 pounds or less for those caught close to shore, 20 to 25 pounds for offshore fishes.

The Atlantic cod occurs off both the European and North American coasts in cool waters and from near the surface to depths of a thousand feet or more. Smaller fishes are generally closer to shore, larger ones in deeper water. Cods like cool waters and may sometimes follow cool currents out of their normal range. In winter, for example, they will be found as far south as North Carolina.

Codfishes and other pelagic species in the family produce prodigious numbers of eggs. A 20-pound female may lay 4 or 5 million eggs in a season, and a specimen of 75 pounds may produce over 9 million eggs. Males spread their milt in the sea around the eggs and fertilize them. The eggs float freely, as do also the newly hatched fishes. The young are about an inch long before they are strong enough to swim well. Much remains to be learned about their early life, but the few that survive—an estimated one in a hundred—manage to get into shallow enough water for them to find refuge, feed, and grow. By the time they are three years old, they weigh about 5 pounds. Cods are mainly bottom-dwellers, feeding on small fishes, mollusks, crabs, seaworms, and similar creatures.

Cods are important in both commercial and sport fishing. The harvest off the Atlantic coast of North America is about a billion pounds annually. Some cods are sold fresh, but most of the catch is now processed as frozen fillets. In the early days, cods were preserved mainly by salting. Oil from the cod's liver was the main source of vitamin D.

The Pacific cod, *G. macrocephalus*, is found on both sides of the Pacific. Off the North American coast, it occurs from Oregon northward, only occasionally straying southward. The Pacific cod is almost identical to the Atlantic cod, differing only in having slightly more pointed fins. In size, it averages somewhat smaller. At times, however, the commercial harvest of the Pacific cod has been greater than the Atlantic catch.

Closely related, and sometimes placed in the genus *Gadus*, is the haddock, *Melanogrammus aeglefinus*, found off both the North American and European coasts in the Atlantic. Haddocks, like cods, travel in large schools. In previous years, U.S. commercial fishermen harvested about 100 million pounds annually, but today the catch has declined drastically because of overfishing by Russia and other European nations. Most of the catch is filleted and frozen. Some is smoked, called finnan haddie. The average size of those taken commercially is less than 5 pounds; the biggest ever netted, off Iceland, weighed 36 pounds. The largest haddock fishery is off the Grand Banks of Newfoundland; in Europe, in the North Sea south of Spitsbergen.

Haddocks are bottom-feeders, usually found in greatest numbers in water 100 to 500 feet deep. The two

Atlantic cod *(Gadus morhua)*
1½ to 3 ft (45 to 90 cm)

Haddock (*Melanogrammus aeglefinus*)
1½ to 2 ft (45 to 60 cm)

most common of the several color variations are grayish green with a dark lateral line and golden brown with a yellow lateral line. Like the cod, the haddock has three dorsal and two anal fins, but it lacks spots on its body. The first rays on the leading dorsal fin are exceptionally long. Just above and behind each pectoral fin is a large, dark blotch.

The pollock, *Pollachius virens*, is the most popular of the cod family with rod-and-reel fishermen. Averaging 4 to 10 pounds in weight (but with some catches weighing more than 30 pounds), the pollock is found on both sides of the Atlantic in cool to cold waters, usually close to shore but commonly netted at depths of 400 to 500 feet. The pollock's snout is pointed, the lower jaw projecting beyond the upper; the chin barbel is very small or lacking. The broad caudal fin is forked. Because the back and sides are a greenish brown, another name for the pollock is green cod. There are no spots, however, and the lateral line is white.

Pollocks are active feeders, preying mainly on small fishes but also taking crabs, mollusks, and other small animals. Sport fishermen catch them principally by trolling, using jigs or spoons, but the smaller fishes are known also to take artificial flies along inshore waters.

They are strong fighters, and the number of fishermen setting out specifically for pollocks is a growing, dedicated clan.

The Atlantic tomcod, *Microgadus tomcod*, and its close relative, the Pacific tomcod, *M. proximus*, also have three dorsal and two anal fins, which are rounded as is the long caudal fins. The pelvic fins extend into long filaments that may be sensory in function. The fish is generally olive brown above and lighter below, the sides heavily blotched with black. Tomcods average less than 12 inches long, only occasional individuals weighing more than a pound. The Atlantic tomcod occurs from Virginia northward along the Atlantic coast of North America. The Pacific tomcod, smaller and silvery white, is found from Point Conception northward to Alaska.

Hakes differ from cods in having the second and third dorsal fins joined to make one large fin that typically is indented or notched where the two are joined. Directly below is an indentation on the anal fin. The lower jaw projects beyond the upper, and the chin barbel is either very small or absent. The caudal fin is shallowly forked. Hakes are predators, feeding on smaller fishes and squids. They travel in schools, generally at the edge of

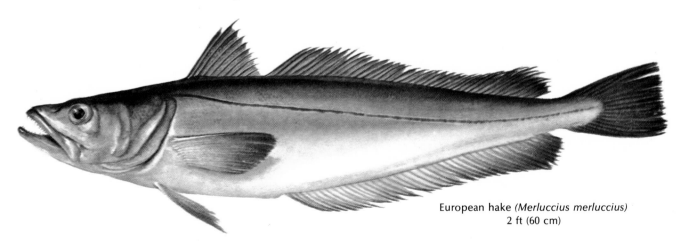

European hake (*Merluccius merluccius*)
2 ft (60 cm)

the continental shelf or below—down to 2,000 feet. Their eggs contain oil droplets so that they rise to the surface and float in the open sea until they hatch. Compared to cods, the flesh of hakes is soft, hence generally less appealing. Hakes are nevertheless harvested commercially in large quantities.

The South African hake, *Merluccius capensis*, is considered the most valuable commercial fish netted off the African coast. It sometimes reaches a length of 4 feet but averages 2 feet or less. The European hake, *M. merluccius*, similar in size, ranges from Norway southward to Africa and occurs also in the Mediterranean.

The common species off the Atlantic coast of North America, from Newfoundland south to the Bahamas, is the silver hake, *M. bilinearis*. On the Pacific, the only representative is the Pacific hake, *M. productus*.

The white hake, *Urophycis tenuis*, ranging from Newfoundland to North Carolina, is a slender fish that may exceed 3 feet in length and weigh more than 30 pounds. The average is about half this size. Like the hakes of the genus *Merluccius*, the second and third dorsal fins are joined. The first ray of the first dorsal is extended into a slim filament, and the caudal fin is rounded. There is a small chin barbel, and the pelvic or ventral fins are reduced to long filaments. The back and sides are reddish, grading into yellowish gray below.

The red hake, *U. chuss*, occurs in the same general range as the white hake. The filament of its first dorsal fin is much longer, and the sides are mottled. The maximum size of the red hake is 8 pounds; the average is about 2 pounds.

Several other species in the genus *Urophycis* are all about the size of the red hake or smaller. These include the southern hake, *U. floridanus*, which averages a pound in weight. It has dark spots above and behind the eyes and also on the gill covers, and the first ray of the dorsal fin is of normal length. There are round white spots at regular intervals along the black lateral line. The southern hake occurs in the Gulf of Mexico and is sometimes caught on hook and line, particularly in winter.

The spotted hake, *U. regius*, also lacks the long filament on the first dorsal fin, and its scales are larger than in other hakes of the genus *Urophycis*. The slim pectoral fin is exceptionally long, extending to the anal fin. The spotted hake is the most common species in the mid-Atlantic region. It is seldom fished for but is caught accidentally on hook and line. Commercial fishermen also catch these hakes from time to time, but the fishery for hakes is not large or well developed.

The common species in European waters is *U. blennoides*, which is much more fat-bodied and blennylike than other species of the genus. About a dozen other rare or commercially unimportant hakes and cods inhabit northern waters.

Only one species of the cod family lives exclusively in fresh water—the burbot, *Lota lota*, found in deep, cold lakes and streams, sometimes in great abundance, from Alaska southward throughout Canada and in the northern portion of the United States. It occurs also in the cold regions of Europe and Asia. Other common names for the burbot are ling, lawyer, eelpout, and freshwater cod. Those seeing the fish for the first time commonly mistake it for some kind of catfish. Its scales are so small that the burbot does appear to be naked, like a catfish, and beneath its chin is a single long barbel, or whisker. The pelvic fins are located far forward, ahead of the pectorals directly under the throat. There are two dorsal fins. The first is short, the second long—nearly matched in length by the anal fin below. The caudal fin is small. The burbot is white or yellowish orange, mottled with black, but the coloration depends greatly on the chemistry of the water where the burbot is living. It is not unusual for the burbot to reach a weight of 5 or 10 pounds and to measure 3 feet in length.

The female burbot may lay as many as a million eggs during a season. She makes no nest, simply broadcasting the eggs in the shallows. The eggs are heavy, sinking to the bottom, where they may be rolled along by the currents until they hatch in three to four weeks.

Burbots are active predators. Given the opportunity, they will stuff their stomachs with other fishes until they are literally stretched out of proportion. There are reports, too, of rocks and other inedibles being taken from a burbot's stomach. In most places they are considered trash fishes that are destructive to the populations of more desirable species, but there is also a growing interest in sport fishing for burbots. Because they continue to feed throughout the winter, burbots also provide fun for ice fishermen. Some fishermen eat their catch and declare that the flavor of the burbot is excellent, as good as the cod. Others say the burbot is either tasteless or has a bad flavor, much too strong and fishy to be desirable. Obviously, whether the burbot is good to eat is strictly a matter of opinion.

Family Ophidiidae
cusk-eels and brotulas

Cusk-eels live in temperate to tropical seas around the world. Fewer than three dozen species are recognized, none of them common. They resemble eelpouts, but their pelvic fins are far forward on the body, directly under the chin, and are used as "feeders" in finding

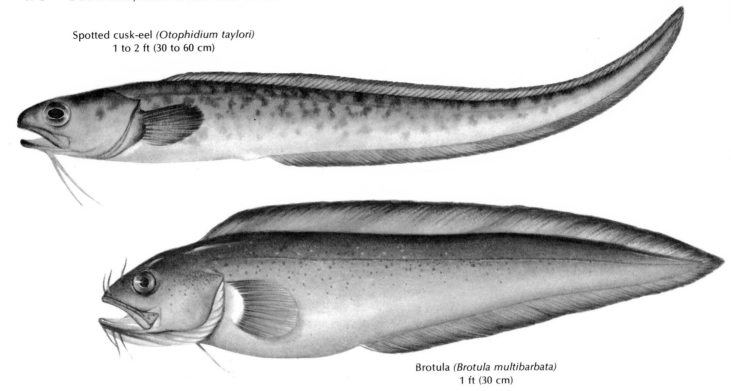

Spotted cusk-eel *(Otophidium taylori)*
1 to 2 ft (30 to 60 cm)

Brotula *(Brotula multibarbata)*
1 ft (30 cm)

food on the bottom. Several species are burrowers, some using their tails to push into sand or soft mud. Most species are small—less than 12 inches long—but several species that live in the Pacific off the coast of South America measure more than 2 feet long. A South African cusk-eel attains a length of 5 feet. Among those found regularly off the coast of North America are the spotted cusk-eel, *Otophidium taylori*, which lives in deep water from central California southward, and the striped cusk-eel, *Rissola marginata*, a 6-inch species found from New York southward to the Gulf of Mexico.

Brotulas number about 150 species. They inhabit the seas at virtually all depths and are commonly found in the deep sea. For example, a brotula was taken from the Sunda Trench at a depth of 23,400 feet. Some species inhabit brackish and fresh waters, and some live in cave waters. Though most are less than 5 inches long, *Acanthus armatus* reaches a length of 3 feet. In the majority of brotulas the pelvic fins are reduced to feelerlike filaments beneath the chin; and the dorsal, caudal, and anal fins are continuous. Brotulas living below 3,000 feet

have small eyes; from 6,000 feet to greater depths the eyes are tiny or lacking. Some lay eggs; others bear their young alive.

Among the largest is the red brotula, *Brosmophycis marginatus*, to 1½ feet long. Found from California to Alaska, it is reddish brown above and white below, as in *Hoplobrotula armata* of Japanese waters. Another common species found off the coasts of Japan and Asia and throughout the Indo-Pacific is *Brotula multibarbata*, which is brown above and white below. Both reach a length of 12 inches but are usually smaller.

Family Carapidae
pearlfishes

These small fishes, found exclusively in tropical seas, have large heads, and the tail tapers to a point. They are unique in their cohabitation with other creatures. The most common genus is *Carapus*, all of which are pearly to semitransparent.

Pearlfish *(Carapus bermudensis)*
up to 5 in (13 cm)

The pearlfish, *C. bermudensis*, usually less than 5 inches long, lives in warm Florida and Caribbean waters, where it inhabits the shells of mollusks or sea cucumbers, emerging at night to feed and then returning to its sanctum during the day. Typical of the family, it moves in reverse, or tail first. A similar species living in the Mediterranean is *C. acus*. Another of the Indo-Pacific region is *C. homei*.

Family Zoarcidae
eelpouts

Similar to wolffishes, eelpouts differ from them in that most species have small pelvic fins, and the caudal fin is not definable; the long dorsal fin that joins the anal fin at the narrowed tail may be bluntly rounded or pointed. The teeth are small, the lips large and fleshy. None of the fins bears spines. Many eelpouts look much like true eels, but they have very large gill openings. Some live in shallow waters close to shore, others at depths as great as a mile. They are worldwide in distribution, occurring in both Arctic and Antarctic seas.

The ocean pout, *Macrozoarces americanus*, is the Atlantic species found from New Jersey northward to the Arctic. It lives at times close to shore and at times at depths of 500 feet or more. The ocean pout is good to eat, as are other species in the family. They are caught mainly in trawl nets by commercial fishermen, but some are taken on hook and line or in lobster traps. This species is an egg layer, and both the male and the female guard the eggs.

In contrast, the viviparous eelpout, *Zoarces viviparus*, a 10-inch European species, gives birth to its young, commonly several dozen at a time. The related shore eelpout, *Z. anguillaris*, a 2-foot species occurring from New Jersey northward, also gives birth to its young. The polar eelpout, *Lycodes turneri*, is circumpolar in Arctic waters. Others species of the genus *Lycodes* are found only in the Atlantic or in the Pacific.

Family Macrouridae
grenadiers

These deepwater fishes have no caudal fin, and the long dorsal and anal fins taper to the slim, pointed, filamentlike tip of the body, which gives these fishes their "rattail" appearance. The head is heavily armored and contains sensory structures that are used for navigation in the dark waters. The eyes are very large, designed for functioning in the dim light of the shadowy mid-depths. Many live where the sea is permanently dark, however, and here their large eyes are useless except to pick up the flashes and flickerings of bioluminescent animals.

As in the closely related cods, the grenadiers' pelvic fins are located farther forward than are the pectoral fins. Some species have a chin barbel, and in some the snout projects far beyond the mouth, useful for rooting in the bottom. Though the family is large, none of the species is well known because they live in the depths. Often their prominent, keeled scales are shed when the fishes are hauled up from the depths.

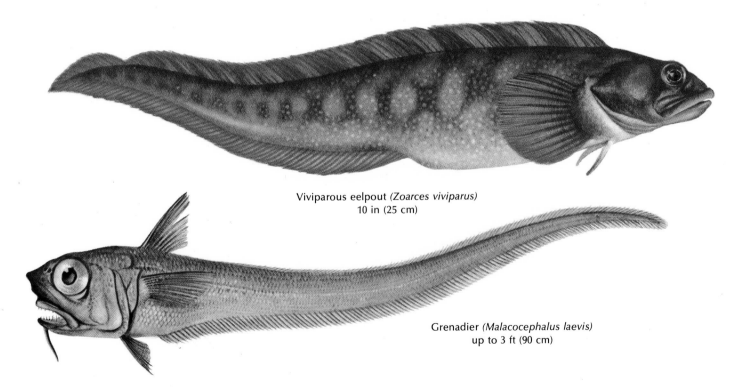

Viviparous eelpout *(Zoarces viviparus)*
10 in (25 cm)

Grenadier *(Malacocephalus laevis)*
up to 3 ft (90 cm)

Grenadiers, or rattails, are known to be abundant, probably more abundant than cods; but they are rarely found in water less than 600 feet deep and often at depths of 2,500 feet or greater. At these depths, they may be the most abundant of the fishes. Their well-developed swim bladders resonate when muscles cause it to vibrate, causing a grunting noise.

Among the common genera are *Coelorhynchus,* *Nezumia, Gadomus, Macrouroides, Malacocephalus,* and *Macrourus*. The species are widely distributed and may be locally abundant. Off the northeastern coast of North America, for example, the marlin-spike, *Nezumia bairdi,* appears to be the most common species. *Macrourus berglax* occurs off both North American and European coasts in the Atlantic, while *Malacocephalus laevis* is worldwide in distribution.

ORDER ATHERINIFORMES

Family Exocoetidae
flying fishes and halfbeaks

Flying fishes, halfbeaks, needlefishes, and sauries are sparkling, silvery fishes that are closely related. All have soft-rayed and spineless fins; the lateral line is extremely low, following the outline of the belly. The dorsal and anal fins are set far back on the body. In the flying fishes, the pectoral fins are greatly expanded, forming winglike structures. Needlefishes have exceptionally long upper and lower jaws, like forceps. Halfbeaks have a normal-size upper jaw but an elongated lower jaw. Sauries and flying fishes have normal jaws. The round eggs are generally equipped with tufts of long filaments that help to anchor the eggs in seaweeds. All four families contain slightly more than a hundred species, most of which travel in schools and are abundant in warm seas.

When a flying fish takes to the air, it comes from below at top speed, estimated at about 40 miles per hour, and bursts into the air. As soon as it is out of the water—not before—it expands its broad spineless pectoral fins and, in some species, its pelvic fins. These are held out stiffly, serving only as gliding membranes. They are not vibrated to help in flying. Last to leave the water is the tail, and the long lower lobe is vibrated rapidly to give additional momentum. As the fish's speed decreases to 20 to 25 miles per hour, it begins to drop back toward the water tail first. As soon as the long lower lobe of the caudal or tail fin enters the water, it is again vibrated rapidly (about 50 times per second), which sometimes gives the fish enough speed to send it airborne again. A succession of these short flights may carry the fish for more than a quarter of a mile.

None of the flights lasts long—usually less than 30 seconds each. Occasionally a flying fish comes out on the crest of high waves so that its glide starts 15 feet or

Atlantic flying fish (*Cypselurus heterurus*)
10 in (25 cm)

Halfbeak *(Hyporhamphus unifasciatus)*
up to 1 ft (30 cm)

more above the trough. As a rule, however, the flying fishes skim just above the surface of the sea. The young of most flying fishes have long filaments—sometimes longer than the body—trailing from the lower jaw. These are lost as the fish matures.

The largest of all the flying fishes is the California flying fish, *Cypselurus californicus*, which may be 1½ feet long. It is found only off the coasts of southern California and Baja California. It is one of several species of flying fishes that are caught commercially for food. They are also used for bait, especially in trolling for big game. It is one of the so-called "four-winged" flying fish, because the pelvic as well as the pectoral fins are large and winglike.

The common Atlantic flying fish, *C. heterurus*, found in warm waters throughout the Atlantic, is two-winged, with a black band extending through the wings. It averages less than 10 inches long, rarely larger.

Other common species of warm Atlantic and Caribbean waters are the margined flying fish, *C. cyanopterus*; the bandwing flying fish, *C. exsiliens*; and the short-winged flying fish, *Parexocoetus mesogaster*, the latter ranging through all warm seas and noted for shorter wings than in most species.

The smallwing flying fish, *Oxyporhamphus micropterus*, which is cosmopolitan in warm seas, also has very short wings, and its glides are never of long duration. Its wings are no longer, in fact, than those of some halfbeaks, and the lower jaw of the young fish is as long as the jaw of halfbeaks.

Another widely distributed genus is *Exocoetus*. About 22 species are found off the Atlantic and Pacific coasts of North America.

A halfbeak's body is elongated, rounded, and flattened from side to side only in the tail region. The dorsal and anal fins are located far to the rear and directly opposite each other. In halfbeaks, only the lower jaw is long; the upper jaw is of normal length. They inhabit warm seas, staying mainly close to shore, commonly leaping or scooting rapidly across the surface with only their tail in the water. The tail is vibrated rapidly to propel them. Typically, halfbeaks travel in schools. Most species lay their eggs in the open sea; a few are ovoviviparous, retaining their eggs in their body until they hatch and then "giving birth" to young.

The wrestling halfbeak, *Dermogenys pusillus*, of southeastern Asia, is one of the few halfbeaks kept in aquariums. An ovoviviparous species, the females carry the eggs for about a month, sometimes longer, before giving birth to the young, usually 20 or more. At birth, the fry are less than half an inch long, and they do not have an extended lower jaw. When mature, about 2½ months later, the females are nearly 3 inches long. The males are slightly shorter, and their anal fin is modified as a sexual organ for internal fertilization of the female. These little halfbeaks feed on insects and other live foods which they capture as they swim along at the surface. Their long lower jaw serves as a sort of scoop, and the open upper jaw is clamped shut to hold the animals.

Male wrestling halfbeaks are pugnacious, circling each other belligerently with their mouths open and their gill covers lifted. Their battles are mainly sparring bluffs, however, and they usually make no physical contact with each other.

The ballyhoo, *Hemiramphus brasiliensis*, is common off the Florida coast and in the Caribbean, traveling northward along the eastern coast occasionally to as far north as Massachusetts in summer. Three black stripes extend the full length of the greenish back. The sides and belly are silvery, and the caudal fin is yellowish orange. Ballyhoos average 6 to 10 inches in length, rarely longer. They are netted, often by attracting them to lights at night, and are used as bait for dolphins, sailfishes, mackerels, and other game fishes. The last ray in the ballyhoo's dorsal fin is elongated—much longer than in most halfbeaks. The closely related longfin halfbeak, *H. saltator*, of the Pacific also has a long ray in its dorsal fin. An Indo-Pacific species, *H. far*, is one of the largest, reaching a length of 2 feet. In Japan, the sayori, *H. sajori*, to 16 inches long, is commonly harvested for food.

The halfbeak, *Hyporhamphus unifasciatus*, to 12 inches long, lives in the same geographical area of the Atlantic as the ballyhoo but occurs also in the Pacific from Point Conception southward to northern South America. It has a single grayish stripe down each side of its body in addition to three dark lines down the middle of the back. The tip of the long lower jaw is red. The halfbeak is used for bait; it makes good eating itself, though it is seldom caught specifically for this purpose. The related California halfbeak, *H. rosae*, is smaller, rarely more than 6 inches long. The Indo-Pacific *H. dussumieri* is sometimes 1½ feet long.

Included among the Pacific halfbeaks off the coast of North America is the ribbon halfbeak, *Euleptorhamphus viridis*, which grows to as much as 1½ feet long. The smaller flying halfbeak, *E. velox*, which lives in the Atlantic, is so named because of its habit of leaping and skittering over the surface and sometimes gliding for short distances, much as the flying fishes do.

Family Belonidae
needlefishes

Most of the more than 50 species of needlefishes live in tropical seas; a few inhabit cooler waters of temperate regions; some stray occasionally into fresh water; and at least one species, *Potomorhopis guianensis*, of the Amazon is found exclusively in fresh water. In most species, both the bones and the flesh are greenish. Nevertheless, needlefishes make good eating.

When disturbed or excited, needlefishes leap from the water and hurtle through the air like spears or arrows. They have a habit of leaping toward lights at night, and so they present a serious hazard to night fishermen. People who have been struck in the neck or head have been badly injured. Often, too, needlefishes will skitter across the surface to escape boats. Only their rapidly vibrating tails are in the water. Beneath the surface, they swim very rapidly.

One of the common species along the Atlantic coast of North America, ranging from New Jersey southward through the Caribbean, is the houndfish, *Tylosurus crocodilus*, which averages 2 feet long or less but occasionally attains a length of 4 or 5 feet. Compared to other, generally smaller members of the family, it has a relatively short, stout beak. Since it also has the habit of leaping from the water with regularity, it can be very dangerous. It readily hits artificial lures and is exciting to take on rod and reel.

Most needlefishes, including the Atlantic needlefish, *Strongylura marina*; the redfin needlefish, *S. notata*; the timucu, *S. timucu*; and the flat needlefish, *Ablennes hians*—all of the warm, shallow Atlantic—are much smaller, as is the California needlefish, *S. exilis*.

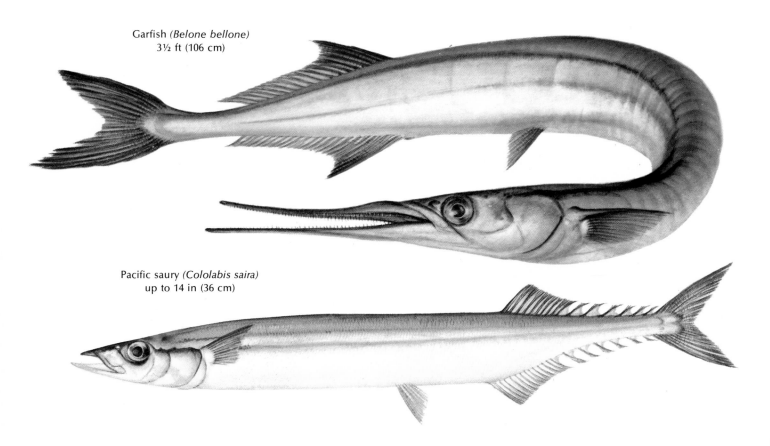

Garfish *(Belone bellone)*
3½ ft (106 cm)

Pacific saury *(Cololabis saira)*
up to 14 in (36 cm)

Family Scomberesocidae
sauries

Sauries are abundant offshore fishes that have only moderately elongated jaws. They are easily distinguished from needlefishes and halfbeaks by the 5–7 finlets behind the dorsal and anal fins, as in mackerels. The family is small, containing fewer than half a dozen species, but some of the species are among the most abundant fishes of the open sea.

The Atlantic saury, *Scomberesox saurus*, found in the Atlantic, travels in schools containing thousands of fishes. They are commonly attacked by a variety of predators that sometimes drive the schools into shallow, near-shore waters. Often a whole school will rise simultaneously from the sea and skitter across the surface. Commercial fishermen refer to them as "skippers." They are sometimes caught commercially when abundant, but they are not fished for regularly. The Pacific saury, *Cololabis saira*, is similar, occurring from Baja California to Japan. Both species may reach a length of about 14 inches but are usually shorter.

Family Cyprinodontidae
killifishes

Also called topminnows and toothed carps, this large family of small fishes is represented most abundantly in warm climates. A few species occur also in temperate regions. The American Fisheries Society recognizes 47 species inhabiting the waters of the United States and Canada.

The fins are soft-rayed, as in cyprinid minnows, but killifishes have scales on their head and have no lateral line. Typical members of the family have a flattened head, and the mouth opens upward, an adapation for feeding at the surface. Many species are valued for mosquito control. Killifishes travel in schools, generally in the shallows. Some species are used as bait, and many tropical species are kept in aquariums. Cyprinodontids are egg layers.

Many killifishes live in brackish water as well as fresh water. The best known of these is the mummichog, *Fundulus heteroclitus*, a robust 3- to 5-inch species found along the Atlantic coast from Florida northward to Labrador. It lives in either fresh water or brackish water. The mummichog is noted for its habit of burrowing into the silt on the bottom, sometimes to depths of 6 inches or more in winter. A rather fat-bodied fish compared to other members of the family, the mummichog varies in color depending on the chemistry of the water from which it is taken. Generally, however, the female is brownish green on the back and sides and light below. The sides are barred with a dark color. Males are brighter, with a much more pronounced contrast between the dark bars and the lighter body color. Mummichogs are popular bait minnows in some regions, often going by the name of hardheads. They are hardy, remaining alive and vigorous on the hook for a long time. They can also be kept successfully in aquariums, adjusting quickly to fresh water and not demanding a constant high temperature, as do many of the more sensitive tropicals.

On the Pacific Coast, the California killifish, *F. parvipinnis*, is similar in size and habits to the mummichog. It occupies the same ecological niche.

The banded killifish, *F. diaphanus*, has many narrow vertical dark bars on its sides. It is a slimmer fish than the mummichog and usually shorter, rarely exceeding 3 inches in length. Also ranging into brackish water, it occurs from South Carolina northward to the St. Lawrence River and westward through the Mississippi Valley. A female may lay as many as 200 eggs, each of which bears a sticky thread by which it is anchored to the bottom or to a plant. This species is sometimes used for bait but is not as hardy as the mummichog.

Another well-known species is the gold topminnow, *F. chrysotus*, inhabiting freshwater and brackish estuaries and streams from Florida northward to South Carolina. Its greenish body is covered with gold or reddish dots that are almost metallic. The female is duller than the male. The gold topminnow adapts well to aquarium life, but as with other topminnows, it has only limited popularity.

The starhead topminnow, *F. notti*, found in fresh water from the Midwest eastward to North Carolina and Florida, is a 2½-inch minnow with a compressed body, distinguished by the bright silvery spot in the middle of its head. Males have bright red dots on their sides.

Other common species of *Fundulus* include the banded topminnow, *F. cingulatus*, which has a red belly, red fins, and red dots on its bluish body; striped killifish, *F. majalis*, a hardy species sometimes as much as 6 inches long, with a metallic-brown body striped with a darker color; plains topminnow, *F. sciadicus*, a strictly freshwater species found in the Mississippi and its tributaries, primarily in headwaters; saltmarsh topminnow, *F. jenkinsi*, a mainly brackish-water species of Florida and adjacent states, where it is valued for mosquito control, as are most killifishes.

Florida has the greatest representation of cyprinodonts in North America. Notable among these is the flagfish, *Jordanella floridae*, a short-bodied, almost sunfishlike species attaining a maximum length of 3 inches. The edges of its scales are bordered with red. In the males, which are brighter than the females, there is a prominent green dot in the middle of each side. This is a hardy, omnivorous species.

Another common Florida species is the pygmy killifish, *Leptolucania ommata*, a slender fish that rarely exceeds 1½ inches in length. Both males and females have a large "eyespot"—a dark dot rimmed with a lighter color—on the caudal peduncle. In aquariums, the pygmy killifish is more sociable than is the flagfish and has the entertaining habit of swimming with short spurts of speed alternated with cruising.

The bluefin killifish, *Lucania goodei*, found in ponds or slow-moving streams of the southeastern United States, is one of the most attractively colored of the killifishes. As in other species, the males in particular are highly colored. The caudal fin is bright red, with a coppery spot at its base. The dorsal and anal fins are striped with varied colors, and a wavy black line runs from the snout to the caudal fin. The bluefin killifish can be kept in an aquarium, but like most species in the family, it may be sensitive to changes in the water temperature, becomes diseased easily, and must be fed only live foods.

Greatest attention has been given to the rare Devil's Hole pupfish, *Cyprinodon diabolis*. Measuring less than half an inch long, the species survives only in the warm, murky waters of Devil's Hole, a cave at the edge of Death Valley. In pumping water from a nearby well, a rancher lowered the water level in Devil's Hole so that more than half of a natural shelf on which the fishes feed and spawn became exposed. With extinction of the Devil's Hole pupfish imminent, the U.S. government brought suit against the rancher to halt pumping.

Related species, not cave dwellers, live in the streams in the West. These include the Amargosa pupfish, *C. nevadensis*; Red River pupfish, *C. rubrofluviatilis*; desert pupfish, *C. macularius*; and several others.

Among their relatives in eastern waters is the sheepshead minnow, *C. variegatus*, a deep-bodied, 3-inch, popular bait minnow that lives in fresh water and also brackish water from Massachusetts southward and westward to Mexico. It is sometimes kept in aquariums but does not adapt well to confinement. The smaller Lake Eustis minnow, *C. hubbsi*, rarely more than an inch long, is restricted to Florida.

Favorite cyprinodonts with aquarium hobbyists among the several hundred tropical species are small, slender fishes of the genus *Aphyosemion*, native to western Africa. The red lyretail, *A. bivittatum*, about 2½ inches long, is typical of the group, often demanding live foods but sometimes shifted successfully to suitably prepared dried food, particularly freeze-dried live

SIZES OF CYPRINODONTIDAE
1¼ in to 4 in (3 to 10 cm)

Golden pheasant
(*Roloffia occidentalis*)

Cuban rivulus
(*Rivulus cylindraceus*)

Blue gularis
(*Aphyosemion coeruleum*)

Medaka
(*Oryzias latipes*)

Peruvian longfin
(*Pterolebias peruensis*)

Banded cynolebias
(*Cynolebias adloffi*)

Cinnamon killie
(*Aphyosemion cinnamomeum*)

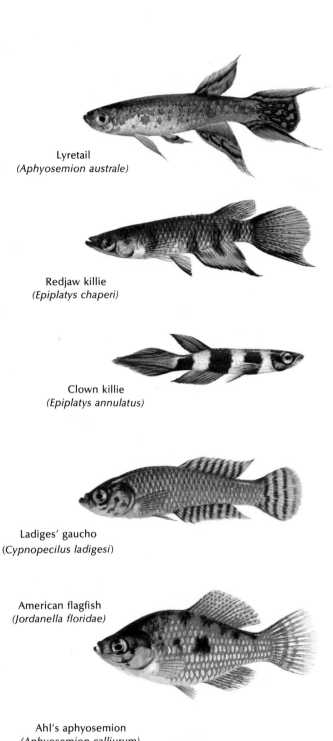

Lyretail
(*Aphyosemion australe*)

Redjaw killie
(*Epiplatys chaperi*)

Clown killie
(*Epiplatys annulatus*)

Ladiges' gaucho
(*Cypnopecilus ladigesi*)

American flagfish
(*Jordanella floridae*)

Ahl's aphyosemion
(*Aphyosemion calliurum*)

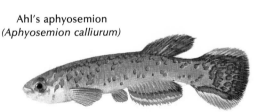

Gery's aphyosemion
(*Aphyosemion geryi*)

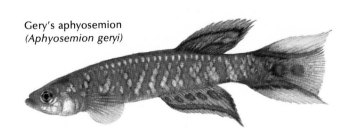

foods. The red lyretail does best in a dimly lit aquarium in which there are plants for hiding places. Like many other species in the genus, the tail is trilobed and the dorsal and anal fins are large—features that are exaggerated by selective breeding. The color varies greatly among the subspecies and also with the chemistry of the water in which the fishes live. A basic feature common to all, however, is a dark band down the sides.

Other species in the genus regularly kept in aquariums are the blue gularis, *A. coeruleum*, the male vividly colored—reddish golden above the steel-blue below; lyretail, *A. australe*, brightly colored but most easily identified by the white tips on the male's fins; and gularis, *A. gulare*, attractively marked with red and yellow. The golden pheasant, *Roloffia occidentalis*, was formerly classified in the genus *Aphyosemion*.

The Argentine pearl fish, *Cynolebias bellotti*, is one of a group of South American cyprinodontids that inhabits grassland ponds that dry up in summer. The adults die, but they leave behind their eggs, buried in the mud. When the rains come again, the eggs hatch, and the cycle is repeated, the young fish reaching maturity in about a month and a half. Argentine pearl fish are kept successfully in aquariums. Spawners are encouraged to lay their eggs in beds of peat moss provided for them in the aquarium. The fish are then removed from the water and placed in another aquarium. Their life-span never exceeds a year. Water is siphoned from the aquarium where the spawners laid their eggs, and the mass of peat moss containing the eggs is stored in a cool, damp place for about four months. Then the peat moss is returned to the water again, and the eggs hatch immediately. This simulates the natural cycle.

The blackfinned cynolebias, *C. nigripinnis*, and the fighting gaucho, *C. melanotaenia*, are among other species in the genus that are kept in aquariums.

The veil carp, *Pterolebias longipinnis*, also from northern South America, is a species that spawns in the same manner as the species of *Cynolebias*. It can also be induced to lay its eggs in peat moss in aquariums.

The medaka, or rice fish, *Oryzias latipes*, is a killifish that lives in paddies in Japan. Several other species of *Oryzias* are found in paddies and ponds in southeastern Asia, where they are especially valued for their control of mosquitoes. They are kept occasionally in aquariums but are not favorites.

The Spanish killifish, *Aphanius iberus*, lives in brackish and fresh water in Spain and Algeria. Other species in the genus are found in Asia Minor. In aquariums, they may require the addition of some salt to keep them comfortable and active. The temperature of the water is not critical. Males are bright blue-green, females duller.

Family Anablepidae
foureye fishes

One of the oddities of the fish world is the foureye fish, *Anableps anableps*, which lives in shallow muddy streams in Mexico and Central America. It has bulbous eyes, like a frog's, on the top of its head. As the fish swims along the surface, the eyes are half in and half out of the water. At the water line, the eye is actually divided by a band of epithelium into upper and lower lobes so that the fish's two eyes actually function as four eyes.

Most remarkable, the lens in a foureye fish's eye is egg-shaped rather than spherical. When the fish looks under the surface of the water, light passes through the full length of the egg-shaped lens. The fish is thus nearsighted under water, as are most fishes. When it looks out into the air, however, the light rays pass through the short width of the lens. This gives the fish good distance vision. At the back of the fish's eye are separate retinas for recording these two different kinds of images.

Foureye fishes are commonly displayed in public aquariums as novelties, but they are difficult for the home hobbyist to keep. They need a large tank to provide them with adequate space for cruising, and the tank must also be covered because the fishes jump. The fishes averages 6 inches long, rarely attaining a length of 12 inches.

Another peculiarity of these fishes is that both males and females have sex organs that are turned either to the right or to the left. A "left" female can mate only with a "right" male, and vice versa. This feature is shared with the few species of *Jenynsia*, comprising the

closely related family Jenysiidae. Found only in South America, several of *Jenynsia* are from time to time imported for tropical-fish hobbyists, but their popularity is limited.

Mosquitofish
(Gambusia affinis)
2 in (5 cm)

Family Poeciliidae
livebearers

These little fishes are closely related to killifishes or cyprinodonts, differing from them mainly in bringing forth their young alive rather than laying eggs. Also, they are limited in their native distribution to the warm regions of the Americas. The American Fisheries Society lists 18 species, 6 of which have been introduced. Livebearers are hardy, and included among them are some of the most popular aquarium fishes. Few livebearers exceed 2 inches in length.

The mosquitofish, *Gambusia affinis*, native to the southeastern United States, has been introduced to suitable warm waters around the world, making it probably the most widely distributed of all freshwater fishes. Females are about 2 inches long, the males only half as large. As in other species of livebearers, the anal fin of the male is modified to form an intromittent organ for introducing sperm into the female. A mature female may produce three or four broods during one season, sometimes giving birth to 200 or more young at a time. When she is carrying young, the female becomes obviously plumper and develops a large black area on each side just in front of the anal fin. Although easily kept in aquariums and not sensitive to temperature variations, the mosquitofish does not rate high in popularity, mostly because of its commonness but also because it does not adjust well to living with other fishes.

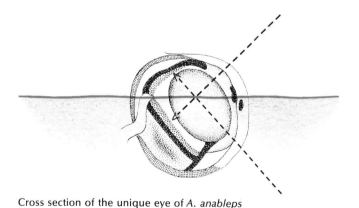

Cross section of the unique eye of *A. anableps*

Foureye fish *(Anableps anableps)*
6 in to 1 ft (15 to 30 cm)

Sunset hi-fin
(platy)

SIZES OF POECILIIDAE
¾ in to 5 in (2 to 13 cm)

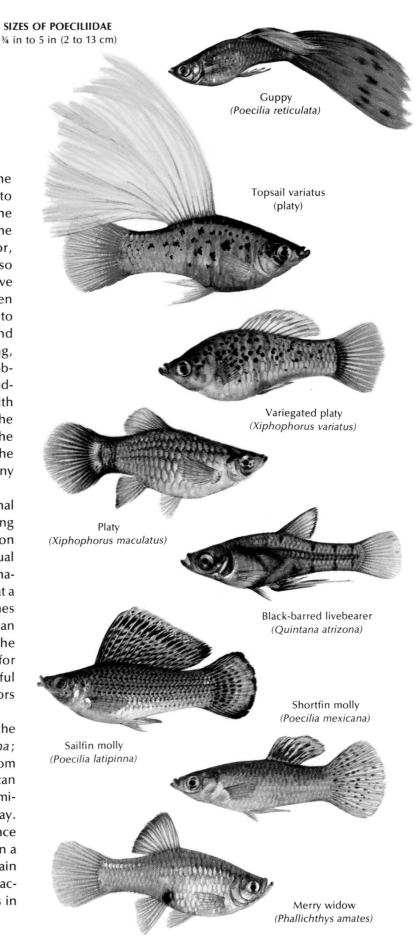

Guppy
(Poecilia reticulata)

Topsail variatus
(platy)

Variegated platy
(Xiphophorus variatus)

Platy
(Xiphophorus maculatus)

Black-barred livebearer
(Quintana atrizona)

Shortfin molly
(Poecilia mexicana)

Sailfin molly
(Poecilia latipinna)

Merry widow
(Phallichthys amates)

Probably the most popular aquarium fish next to the goldfish is the guppy, *Poecilia reticulata*, native to northern South America and the nearby islands of the West Indies. Females are about 2½ inches long, the males shorter. Males are extremely variable in color, particularly on their fins. The dorsal and anal fins also vary greatly in shape and are the prime focus of selective breeders. Like the mosquitofish, the guppy has been widely introduced throughout the world for mosquito control. As an aquarium fish, the guppy is hardy and presents few problems in regard to feeding or breeding, producing young so easily and so rapidly that the hobbyist soon has more than he needs. Guppies are friendly, not quarrelsome either among themselves or with other kinds of fishes. Males are always attentive to the female, and if a female pauses even momentarily, she will probably be fertilized. The sperm is retained in the female's body so that a fertile female may have as many as half a dozen broods even if no male is present.

Pregnant females have a dark area just behind the anal fin, and their sides are noticeably swollen. The young are generally born in about a month, though gestation may require longer if the water is cool. The usual number of young is 30 to 50. Occasionally a large, mature female will give birth to several hundred young at a time and will repeat the process three or more times every year. The newly born fry are about an eighth of an inch long. They need plants and other places in the aquarium for hiding, for they make excellent meals for larger fishes, even their mother. Breeders make careful selections to preserve and perpetuate desired colors and fin types.

Other favorites among the aquarium fishes are the Amazon molly, *P. formosa*; sailfin molly, *P. latipinna*; and shortfin molly, *P. mexicana*. These are found from extreme southern United States into the American tropics. The merry widow, *Phallichthys amates*, is a similar species that was once more popular than it is today. Mollies are not quite as hardy as the guppy, hence beginners sometimes have trouble with them. Given a good basic diet and checked regularly to make certain they have no fungus disease, they do well and are attractive. There are numerous varieties, with differences in color, fin shape, and size.

Green swordtail (*Xiphophorus helleri*)
4 in (10 cm)

Smallest of the livebearers and one of the smallest of all vertebrates is the least killifish, *Heterandria formosa*. The males are only slightly more than half an inch long, the females a little more than an inch long. These tiny fishes live in the southeastern United States, from South Carolina southward. Despite its small size, the least killifish is aggressive and will attack a fish larger than itself to defend or claim territorial space. Females give birth to about two dozen young at a time. The least killifish has a black stripe down each side of the body and another stripe, which is sometimes red, on the dorsal fin.

One of the largest livebearers is the pike killifish, *Belonesox belizanus*, the females sometimes attaining a length of 8 inches. As the name implies, the pike topminnow is slim and pikelike, the head long and flattened and the big mouth studded with teeth. At the base of the tail fin is a black spot bordered with a light or yellowish ring. Pike topminnows are natives of the American subtropics, preferring standing water or sluggish streams. They are aggressive and so are best kept alone. They need a large tank, and some salt should be added to the water.

Platys and swordtails, both members of the genus *Xiphophorus*, are imported from the American subtropics for tropical-fish hobbyists. The green swordtail, *X. helleri*, has a long extension on the lower lobe of its caudal fin, forming the "sword." This is usually present only in males but is found on some females. The southern platyfish, *X. maculatus*, is the other common species in the genus. Of these two, many hybrids and variations have been developed.

Family Atherinidae
silversides

Silversides occur throughout the world. Some are valued as food fishes, and a few are caught for keeping in aquariums. All silversides lack a lateral line and have small, almost useless teeth. Their pelvic fins are located well behind the pectoral fins, and the small, spiny dorsal is well separated from the soft dorsal. The body is typically elongated. Some silversides live in fresh waters; others are marine, found near shore. They are often called shiners but are more commonly referred to as "smelt," though they are not related to the true osmerid smelts.

California grunion, *Leuresthes tenuis*, to 8 inches long, are famous for their moonlight spawning runs. From March through June, and sometimes continuing through August or September, they spawn approximately every two weeks, riding in on the waves of the highest tides during the full moon. Millions of the little fishes swarm over the beaches just as the tide begins to ebb. Their abdomens swollen with eggs, the females squirm their bodies to make depressions in the wet sand and then lay their eggs. The males fertilize them immediately. By the time the next wave breaks over the beach, the fishes are ready to get back into the water. It

Celebes sailfin (*Telmatherina ladigesi*)
2½ to 3 in (6 to 8 cm)

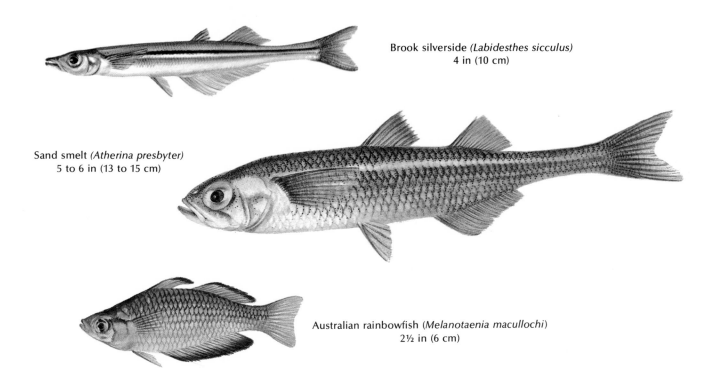

Brook silverside *(Labidesthes sicculus)*
4 in (10 cm)

Sand smelt *(Atherina presbyter)*
5 to 6 in (13 to 15 cm)

Australian rainbowfish *(Melanotaenia macullochi)*
2½ in (6 cm)

is remarkable that the entire egg-laying process takes less than a minute, yet is timed so precisely that it occurs only on the peak wave of the highest tide. In season, large numbers of fishermen gather on the beaches to fill buckets with the fish as they spawn in the sand.

For two weeks the eggs incubate in the warm sand and then hatch at the next peak tide, the waves sweeping the tiny fishes out to sea. Grunion are bluish green above and silvery below, a blue-tinged silvery band bordered with violet running the full length of the body. They have no teeth.

The Gulf grunion, *L. sardina*, is restricted to the Gulf of California. Its spawning habits are similar to the California grunion's, but it differs in that it may also spawn during the day.

Jacksmelt, *Atherinopsis californiensis*, reported to 22 inches long, have small, unforked teeth in bands, differentiating it from the California grunion and also from the topsmelt. It is found from Baja California to Oregon. Greenish gray above and silvery below, it has a silvery stripe bordered with blue extending the full length of the body. A schooling species, the jacksmelt is caught commercially and also by sport fishermen.

Topsmelt, *Atherinops affinis*, to 12 inches long, occurs generally in the same range as the jacksmelt, from which it is most easily distinguished by its forked teeth set in a single row rather than in bands. Its color is similar to the jacksmelt's, and it also constitutes a sizable portion of the Pacific Coast "smelt" catch.

Along the Atlantic Coast, the tidewater silverside, *Menidia beryllina*, to 3 inches long, ranges from Massachuetts southward to the Gulf of Mexico. Although it is predominantly a saltwater species, it is also found in brackish and fresh waters. Other names frequently used for this species are whitebait and spearing. Several similar species occur in the same general range. These include the Atlantic silverside, *M. menidia*, and the Mississippi silverside, *M. audens*, a freshwater species.

The brook silverside, *Labidesthes sicculus*, to 4 inches long but usually smaller, is also found only in fresh water, from the St. Lawrence River southward through the southeastern United States. The schools, often skipping along the surface (which has earned them the name of skipjacks), are common sights. Olive green above and silvery below, it has a prominent silver stripe down each side. The snout is projected into a short beak, and the first dorsal fin is so small that it may go unnoticed. The brook silverside is sometimes used for bait but is not hardy.

The Australian rainbowfish, *Melanotaenia maccullochi*, is a schooling species that may appear reddish or bluish green, depending on how the light strikes its body. About 2½ inches long, this species lives peacefully with others in large aquarium tanks.

The lesser-known goodeid topminnows, Goodeidae, of Mexico and Central America, and the jenynsid topminnows, Jenynsidae, of La Plata, Argentina, are included in the order Atheriniformes.

ORDER BERYCIFORMES

Family Polymyxiidae
beardfishes

These relatives of squirrelfishes live in water 600 to 1,500 feet deep. Their name is derived from their two long chin whiskers, or barbels. The widely distributed beardfish, *Polymixia lowei*, has a black spot at the front of the dorsal fin, the forked caudal fin is margined with black, and the scales are small. The stout beardfish, *P. nobilis*, is similar. Biologists speculate that the half a dozen species in the family may eventually be considered one.

Family Anomalopidae
lantern-eye fishes

These small fishes of the middle depths of the sea are unique among fishes capable of producing light because they can turn them on and off at will. The two common genera, from Indo-Pacific waters, are *Anomalops*, to 12 inches long, and *Photoblepharon*, about 3 inches long. A third genus, *Kryptophanaron*, also small, occurs in the Caribbean.

Beneath each eye is an oval-shaped, cream-colored organ about as long as the eye. Inside each organ is a colony of luminous bacteria that give off light continuously. The fishes have different ways of exposing them. In *Anomalops*, which "flicks" its lights about five times a minute, the whole organ can be rotated downward until the light is shut off by a black tissue. In *Photoblepharon* and *Kryptophanaron*, which keep their lights on most of the time, a black tissue is drawn up over the light organ, like an eyelid working in reverse. The lights presumably help to keep enemies away as well as possibly attracting food.

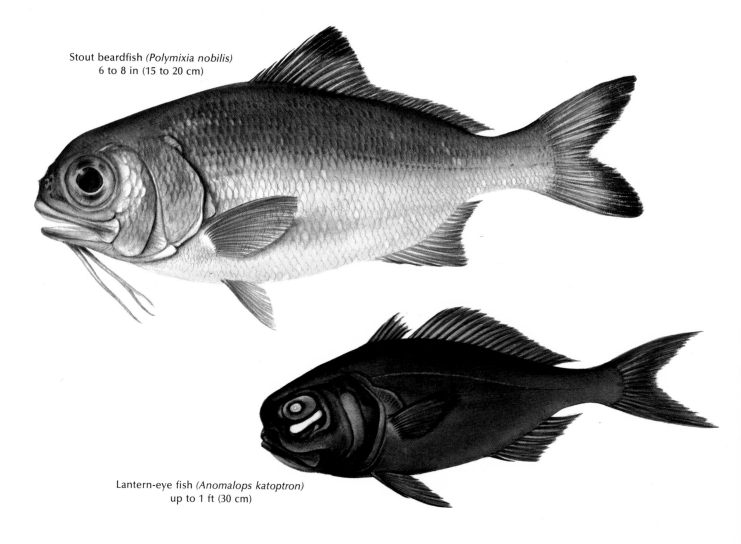

Stout beardfish (*Polymixia nobilis*)
6 to 8 in (15 to 20 cm)

Lantern-eye fish (*Anomalops katoptron*)
up to 1 ft (30 cm)

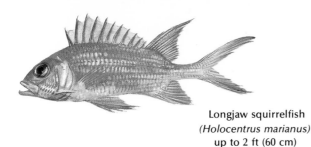

Longjaw squirrelfish
(*Holocentrus marianus*)
up to 2 ft (60 cm)

Family Holocentridae
squirrelfishes

Squirrelfishes, which are wary and difficult to catch but good to eat, are brightly colored fishes that inhabit coral reefs of the subtropics and tropics. All species have very large eyes and one or more sharp spines at the leading edges of the fins. Typically the body is red, the fins yellow. During the day, squirrelfishes stay hidden in cracks and crevices in the coral, coming out at night to feed. The fewer than a hundred species are worldwide in distribution. Adults do not travel long distances and stay close to the bottom. They are distributed more widely when the very young fishes move into open waters and are carried long distances by the currents.

The squirrelfish, *Holocentrus ascensionis*, found in the Caribbean and in warm waters off Florida, is generally less than a foot long and weighs about a pound. Individuals 2 feet in length are reported occasionally, and these larger fishes may weigh as much as 4 pounds. *H. spinifer*, found in the Pacific, regularly attains a length of 2 feet. Other species of Atlantic reefs are the longspine squirrelfish, *H. rufus*; reef squirrelfish, *H. coruscus*; longjaw squirrelfish, *H. marianus*; and dusky squirrelfish, *H. vexillarius*. A common species in Hawaiian waters is the striped squirrelfish, *H. xantherythrus*; in Indo-Pacific waters, *H. caudimaculatus* and *H. diadema*. All members of this genus have a prominent spine on the gill cover.

Members of the genus *Myripristis*, the second largest genus in the family, are similar in body shape to members of the genus *Holocentrus* and *Holotrachys* but do not have spines on the body. They travel in schools, and some species are caught commercially. Species are most abundant in Pacific and Indo-Pacific waters, where one of the most common and widely distributed is *M. murdjan*. An Atlantic representative is the blackbar soldierfish, *M. jacobus*.

ORDER ZEIFORMES

Family Zeidae
dories

Dories live in the middle depths of the sea. They are easily distinguished from other fishes by the large black spot ringed with yellow located in the middle of the body. In older fishes, long filaments develop on the first 8–10 spiny rays of the dorsal fin. There are short spines along the bases of both the dorsal and anal fins and commonly also along the midline of the belly.

Classification of the few species in the family is still in a state of flux. Generally, however, the species caught in the Atlantic off the coast of North America is considered

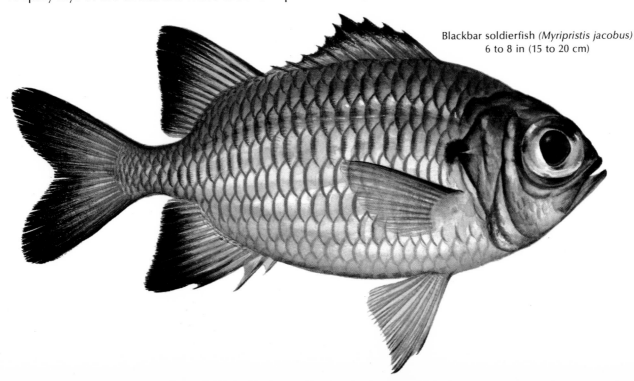

Blackbar soldierfish (*Myripristis jacobus*)
6 to 8 in (15 to 20 cm)

John Dory (*Zeus faber*)
up to 3 ft (90 cm)

to be the American John Dory, *Zenopsis ocellata*, distinct from the very similar European John Dory, *Zeus faber*, that occurs from the British Isles southward to Africa and also in the Mediterranean. Another species, *Zeus japonicus*, is found in Indo-Pacific waters; *Z. nebulosa*, in Japanese waters and occasionally off the Pacific coast of North America. Dories are netted commercially and sold in markets. Some people consider them delicacies; others do not find them edible.

Family Caproidae
boarfishes

These close relatives of dories are slim-bodied, red fishes that also live in relatively deep waters—800 feet or deeper. The body is roughly as deep as it is long, the snout is longer than in dories, and typically these fishes have three anal spines that are completely separated from the soft rays of the anal fin.

ORDER LAMPRIDIFORMES

Family Lamprididae
opahs

The opah, *Lampris regius*, also called moonfish, is the only member of its family. Found worldwide in warm seas, the opah reaches a length of 6 feet and may weigh more than 500 pounds. The average size of those caught is about 50 pounds, however. The opah is toothless; the fins are soft-rayed, with the pelvic fins very long and

Boarfish *(Antigonia rubescens)*
up to 7 in (18 cm)

Opah *(Lampris regius)*
up to 6 ft (180 cm)

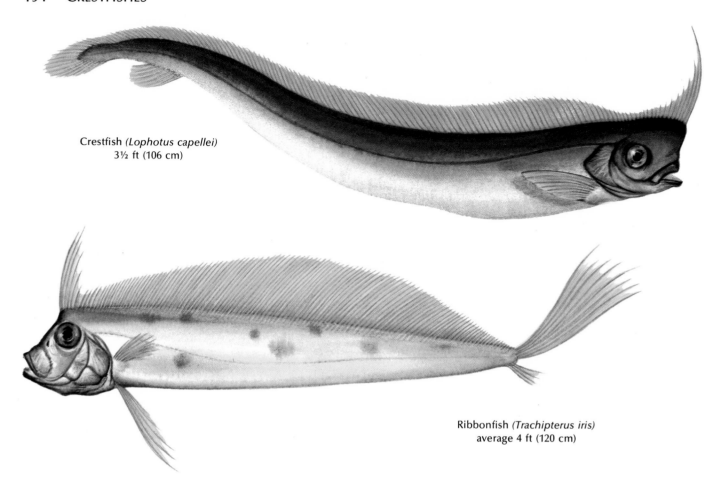

Crestfish *(Lophotus capellei)*
3½ ft (106 cm)

Ribbonfish *(Trachipterus iris)*
average 4 ft (120 cm)

sickle-shaped. The oval-shaped, greatly compressed, scaleless body is steel blue above, grading into green below. The sides are silvery, the belly flushed with rose. Silver spots are scattered over the entire body, and the fins and jaws are red. The flesh is pinkish, like the salmon, and has a tunalike flavor.

Because the opah is so attractive and is not caught commonly, it commands great attention. Biologists speculate that a greater abundance of opahs may be discovered when the habits of the species are better known. Those taken to date have come from relatively near the surface and have been solitary individuals.

Family Lophotidae
crestfishes

Cosmopolitan and resembling ribbonfishes, the crestfish, *Lophotus capellei*, is scaleless and lacks pelvic fins. It has an anal fin. The first rays of the dorsal fin form a crest, as they do in the oarfish. The unicornfish, *Eumecichthys fiski*, occurs regularly off the south-eastern coast of Florida.

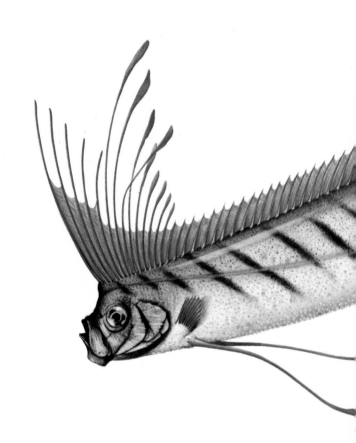

Family Trachipteridae
ribbonfishes

These are deepwater fishes with an incredibly thin body, the dorsal fin starting on top of the head and extending all the way to the vertical lobe of the caudal fin. In young fishes, the pelvic fins may be large and then become increasingly smaller as the fish matures. Members of this family have no anal fin. The most common genus is *Trachipterus*.

The king-of-the-salmon, *T. altivelus*, reaching a length of about 6 feet and found off the northern Pacific coast of North America, was believed by the Indians to possess some mystical power over salmons, controlling their appearance and thus determining whether the fishing would be good or bad.

The most common species in the Atlantic is the deal-fish, *T. arcticus*. The scalloped ribbonfish, *Zu cristatus*, and the polka-dot ribbonfish, *Desmodema polysticta*, are found in both the Atlantic and Pacific. The tapertail ribbonfish, *T. fukuzakii*, of the Pacific grows to about 56 inches in length.

Family Regalecidae
oarfishes

The cosmopolitan oarfish, *Regalecus glesne*, the only representative in the family, resembles ribbonfishes but has extremely long, slender pelvic fins—its "oars." Exceeding 10 feet in length, with unauthenticated reports of individuals 20 feet long, the oarfish is believed to be responsible for some of the mythical tales about sea serpents, as it swims with a rippling wavelike movement. Its flat, ribbonlike body, about a foot broad, is silvery, transparent, and almost jellylike in appearance, generally with a bluish cast and dark longitudinal stripes. The dorsal fin is bright red, and the rays at the front of the fin can be lifted or lowered at will to form a crest. The pectoral and pelvic fins are also red, and there is no anal fin. Oarfish are sometimes found washed ashore after storms, but their thin, watery bodies quickly dry and disintegrate.

Oarfish *(Regalecus glesne)*
10 ft (300 cm)

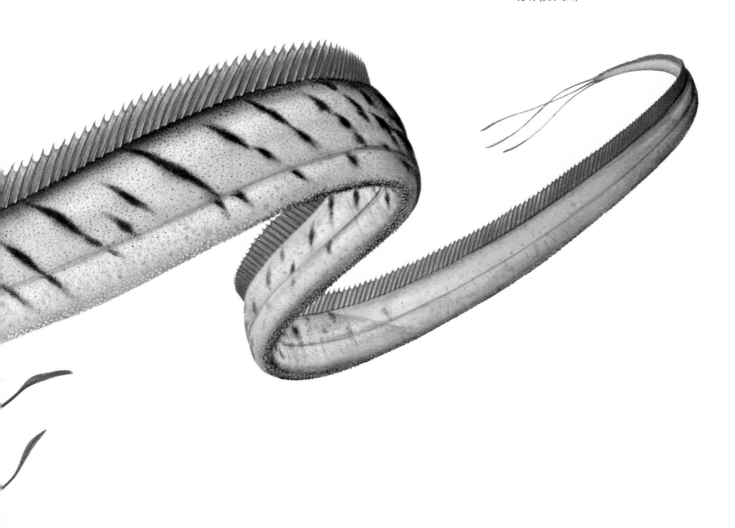

ORDER GASTEROSTEIFORMES

Family Gasterosteidae
sticklebacks

These small, slim fishes, rarely more than 3 inches long, are confined to the Northern Hemisphere, occurring most abundantly in North America. They are primarily freshwater fishes, but some occur also in brackish or shallow inshore waters of seas. The family contains only about a dozen species totally.

Sticklebacks get their name from the short, stout spines in their first dorsal fin, the number of spines generally identifying the species. Most also have a spine at the leading edge of the anal fin and each pelvic fin. The body lacks scales, but in most species it is armored along the sides with bony plates.

Several species of sticklebacks are kept in aquariums. They swim with short spurts of speed, then pause. This makes them interesting to watch. Their greatest appeal, however, is their courtship and spawning behavior. At spawning time, the males are decked in courtship colors—the belly bright red in some, velvety black in others. Among the stems of some aquatic plants, each male builds a nest—hollow inside but completely covered on the top, bottom, and sides, with stems held together with a secretion of sticky threads. When the nest is built, the male then goes searching for a female and begins driving her toward the nest he has built, nipping at her fins and chasing after her if she turns the wrong way.

As soon as the female has laid her eggs, she leaves the nest, sometimes squirming out through the bottom. The male enters the nest immediately and fertilizes the eggs. Often he may go out again and get one or two other females to lay eggs in the nest. Some males build several nests at the same time. The eggs hatch in a week or less. While the eggs are incubating, the male aerates them by fanning currents of water through the nest. The male of one species builds his nest with two holes in the top. He sucks water from one of the holes to cause a circulation over the eggs. After the eggs hatch, the male continues to tend the fry for several days, generally trying to keep them near the nest.

One of the common species in North America is the brook stickleback, *Culaea inconstans*, found in streams from Pennsylvania westward to Kansas and northward throughout southern Canada. It is generally less than 3 inches long. The five or six spines on its back are completely separate from one another rather than joined by a membrane, and the caudal peduncle is very slender. Like most sticklebacks, it is quarrelsome and guards its territory, particularly its nest, from intruders.

The threespine stickleback, *Gasterosteus aculeatus*, ranges over northern Eurasia and North America, living in both brackish and fresh waters. A number of subspecies are recognized. The ninespine stickleback, *Pungitius pungitius*, found both in northern Europe and northern North America, is dark brown, and the male becomes a rich black during the courtship and spawning periods. The fifteenspine stickleback, *Spinachia spinachia*, is a European saltwater species restricted to

Threespine stickleback *(Gasterosteus aculeatus)*
2 to 3 in (5 to 8 cm)

Ninespine stickleback *(Pungitius pungitius)*
2 to 3 in (5 to 8 cm)

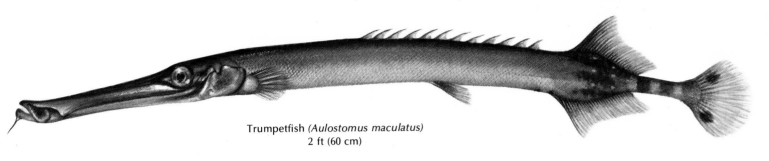

Trumpetfish *(Aulostomus maculatus)*
2 ft (60 cm)

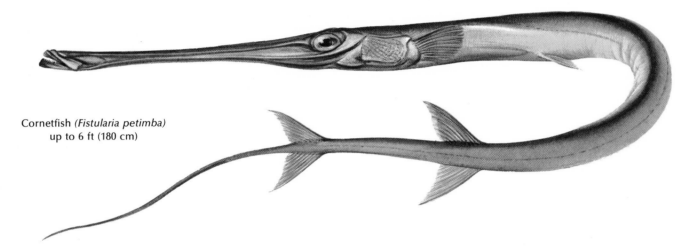

Cornetfish *(Fistularia petimba)*
up to 6 ft (180 cm)

the British Isles and the North Sea region. The fourspine stickleback, *Apeltes quadracus*, is found only along the eastern coast of North America, from Virginia northward. The blackspotted or twospine stickleback, *G. wheatlandi*, is another Atlantic species. The tubesnout, *Anlorhynchus flavidus*, is an uncommon species occurring in the Pacific.

Family Aulostomidae
trumpetfishes

Occurring in the same regions and habitats as the cornetfishes, trumpetfishes have one to several spines in front of the dorsal fin and do not have a caudal filament. They are shorter than cornetfishes, rarely exceeding 2 feet in length. Their colors are generally rather dull, and they have a remarkable ability to camouflage themselves. Trumpetfishes, like cornetfishes, seem to drift along in the water, exerting almost no swimming effort. This is deceptive, however, for their fins are nearly transparent and make their constant, rapid motion difficult to see.

The trumpetfish, *Aulostomus maculatus*, is common in coral reefs throughout the Caribbean, ranging northward to Bermuda. It is generally brown, but some individuals are a very light brown, almost yellow. *A. valentini* is a similar species of the Indo-Pacific region, and *A. chinensis* occurs off the coast of Asia.

Family Fistulariidae
cornetfishes

Found in tropical and subtropical seas, and especially abundant near coral reefs, cornetfishes are distinguished by their long, tubular snout and by a long filament that extends from between the lobes of their caudal fin. Cornetfishes use their long snouts like pipettes to pick up small morsels of food.

The bluespotted cornetfish, *Fistularia tabacaria*, of the Atlantic may attain a length of 6 feet, but because its body is so slim, even a fish this long may weigh only about 5 pounds. Another of the fewer than half a dozen species in the family is the red cornetfish, *F. villosa*, of Indo-Pacific reef waters and occasionally in the warm Atlantic. Also reaching a length of 6 feet, it is distinguished by the rough ridges on its head. The similar-size *F. petimba*, also of the Indo-Pacific, lacks these ridges.

Family Centriscidae
shrimpfishes and snipefishes

Shrimpfishes are long-snouted, deep-bodied fishes that have an extremely flat body from side to side—so much so, in fact, that they go also by the name razorfishes. The body is encased in a transparent armor consisting of numerous separate plates. Stiffened by this armor, the fishes swim by movements of their fins.

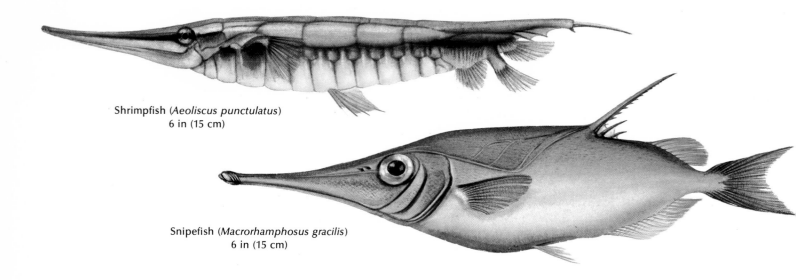

Shrimpfish (*Aeoliscus punctulatus*)
6 in (15 cm)

Snipefish (*Macrorhamphosus gracilis*)
6 in (15 cm)

The shrimpfishes contain two principal genera—*Aeolisius*, in which the long dorsal spine is jointed, and *Centriscus*, in which the spine is solid. Both have the unusual habit of swimming vertically, the head down. They are found from Hawaii westward in the Pacific and throughout the Indian Ocean, and their average length is about 6 inches. One of the common and widely distributed species is *Aeoliscus punctulatus*.

Snipefishes, which are sometimes placed in a separate family, have a deep body, a long dorsal fin, and a long snout. Their body is only half enclosed in an armor of bony plates. The fewer than half a dozen species are found most abundantly in tropical and subtropical seas, though some range into cool, temperate waters. Some are very attractively colored. The banded snipefish, *Centriscops obliquus*, of New Zealand waters is orange with broad black bands. Like shrimpfishes, snipefishes

regularly swim in a head-down position. The slender snipefish, *Macrorhamphosus gracilis*, is worldwide in warm seas and common in the eastern Pacific. A closely related species, the longspine snipefish, *M. scolopax*, is found in the Atlantic.

Family Sygnathidae
pipefishes and seahorses

Seahorses and pipefishes are most abundant in shallow subtropical and tropical seas, but some range into temperate waters. They are identical in anatomical features except for body shape. Pipefishes, as their name implies, are straight. In seahorses the head is bent down, joining the body almost at right angles. Both have

African freshwater pipefish *(Syngnathus pulchellus)*
6 to 8 in (15 to 20 cm)

Japanese pipefish *(Syngnathus schlegeli)*
6 to 8 in (15 to 20 cm)

long, tubular snouts, though not as pronounced as in the previous three families. There are more than a hundred species of pipefishes, some of them even invading fresh water. The two dozen or so species of seahorses are all marine. Both have very small scales that form rings of hard, protective armor around the body. Seahorses do not have a caudal fin. In pipefishes, the caudal fin is greatly reduced. Both swim by a rapid, rippling movement of the dorsal, pelvic, and pectoral fins. Seahorses swim in an upright positon, stiffly but gracefully. Both use their long prehensile tails for holding on to seaweeds or other objects. Like chameleons, both can move their eyes independently.

Their breeding habits are most unusual. The female lays her eggs in a pouch on the male's belly. Often the female may lay several hundred eggs, which are fertilized, incubated, and then hatched inside the pouch. They emerge as miniature adults.

The northern pipefish, *Sygnathus fuscus*, averaging 6 inches in length but occasionally as long as 12 inches, is one of the common species in northern waters. It ranges from North Carolina to Nova Scotia. In mating, the male and female swim vertically in the water, their bodies meeting in S-shaped curves. As their bodies come together, the female lays her eggs in the pouch of the male.

One of the largest pipefishes is the kelp pipefish, *S. californiensis*, which may attain a length of 18 inches. More than a dozen species of *Sygnathus* occur along the Atlantic and Pacific coasts of North America. They are difficult to identify, distinguished mainly by differences in the number or shape of the body rings and in the number of rays in their fins. There are also representatives of the genus along the Atlantic coast of Europe and in the Mediterranean, where the most common species are *S. abaster* and *S. typhle*. Among the species found in the Pacific are *S. schlegeli*, of Japanese waters, and *S. spicifer*, common in shallow, warm waters of the Indo-Pacific. The little sargassum pipefish, *S. pelagicus*, is one of the community of sea creatures adapted for life in sargassumweed, and it is amazingly well camouflaged. All pipefishes and seahorses are able to change their colors to some degree to match their surroundings.

Another widely distributed genus of pipefishes is *Corythoichthys*, which includes the whitenose pipefish, *C. albirostris*, and the crested pipefish, *C. brachycephalus*, both of the warm Atlantic, and *C. fasciatus*, of Indo-Pacific waters. An East Indian species, *Phyllopteryx foliatus*, has leafy filaments over its body, concealing it in the seaweeds where it lives. Species of *Micrognathus* and *Penetopteryx*, also cosmopolitan genera, are burrowers, some of them spending most of

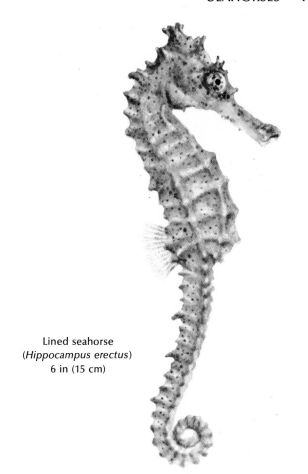

Lined seahorse
(*Hippocampus erectus*)
6 in (15 cm)

their time as much as a foot beneath the rubble of reefs.

Seahorses, *Hippocampus*, are more familiar to most people than are pipefishes. Largest is the Pacific seahorse, *H. ingens*, which reaches a length of 12 inches; it occurs from northern Peru to San Diego, including the Gulf of California.

The lined seahorse, *H. erectus*, which may reach a length of 6 inches but is usually smaller, ranges from South Carolina to Massachusetts and to Nova Scotia as a stray. The smallest seahorse is the dwarf seahorse, *H. zosterae*, only 1½ inches long when full grown; it lives in the warm Atlantic off Florida and also in the Gulf of Mexico. Two other Atlantic species are the offshore seahorse, *H. obtusus*, and the longsnout seahorse, *H. reidi*. A common European species is the Mediterranean seahorse, *H. guttulatus*. *H. Kelloggi*, *H. japonicus*, and *H. coronatus* are found in Japanese waters, and about 10 species of *Hippocampus* live in the Indo-Pacific region.

Seahorses swim very slowly, resting often by holding on to seaweeds with their prehensile tails. The rippling movement of the dorsal fin provides the propulsion for swimming, the pectoral and pelvic fins serving principally as guides. The air bladders of seahorses are exceptionally large, which is important to them in their floating, drifting movements. If the air is released from these bladders, the fishes sink immediately.

Snakehead *(Channa argus)*
6 in to 3 ft (15 to 90 cm)

ORDER CHANNIFORMES

Family Channidae
snakeheads

These round-bodied freshwater fishes of Asia and Africa share with labyrinth fishes the elaborate channels above the gill chambers, enabling them to breathe for long periods out of water. They are sold in local markets while still very much alive and squirming. Though they are eaten and thus have value, they are also considered a pest fish because they destroy other native species in whatever waters they inhabit.

The Asiatic snakehead, *Channa asiatica*, lacks pelvic fins. All other species in the family belong to the genus *Ophicephalus* and have pelvic fins. Many are barred with black along the sides of the body.

ORDER SYNBRANCHIFORMES

Family Synbranchidae
swamp eels

Eel-like in body shape, the swamp eels share with lungfishes the ability to breathe air directly. This enables them to live in swampy areas that are flooded only part of the year. They lack both pectoral and pelvic fins, and their dorsal and anal fins are only ridges along the body. Swamp eels are found in South America, Africa, Asia, and on some islands of Oceania.

The rice eel, *Monopterus albus*, is a 2½-foot species of southeastern Asia and the Philippines, where it is often caught for food. The openings to its gills are located on the throat, but most of the respiration takes place in the highly vascularized throat membrane.

Cuchia, *Amphipnous cuchia*, of India, has lunglike air sacs connected to its gill chambers. A common genus of tropical America is *Synbranchus*, with one species to 5 feet long.

Rice eel *(Monopterus albus)*
2½ ft (75 cm)

ORDER SCORPAENIFORMES

Family Scorpaenidae
scorpionfishes and rockfishes

This is a large family comprised of perhaps 300 species, about 82 of which live in North American waters. All of them have a bony support or stay running beneath the eye from the cheek to the operculum. Included in the family are the most spiny of all fishes and also the most venomous. Most species live in rather deep water but close to shore. They hide in rocks, waiting in ambush for small fishes to swim close. Their typical color is red.

The plumed scorpionfish, *Scorpaena grandicornis*, averaging about 6 inches in length and occasionally as long as 12 inches, lives in the warm Atlantic off Florida and in the Caribbean. It sometimes straggles far up the coast—to Massachusetts or beyond. Spines and fleshy protuberances around its head form a shaggy mane, like a lion's. All the spines in the first dorsal fin are stout and sharp. The first several are hollow and serve as hypodermic needles that inject poison into the stab wound from glands at their base. Brownish or gray, mottled with black, red, yellow, and sometimes other colors, plumed scorpionfishes blend with their surroundings and can also change their color to match the background, as can most members of the family.

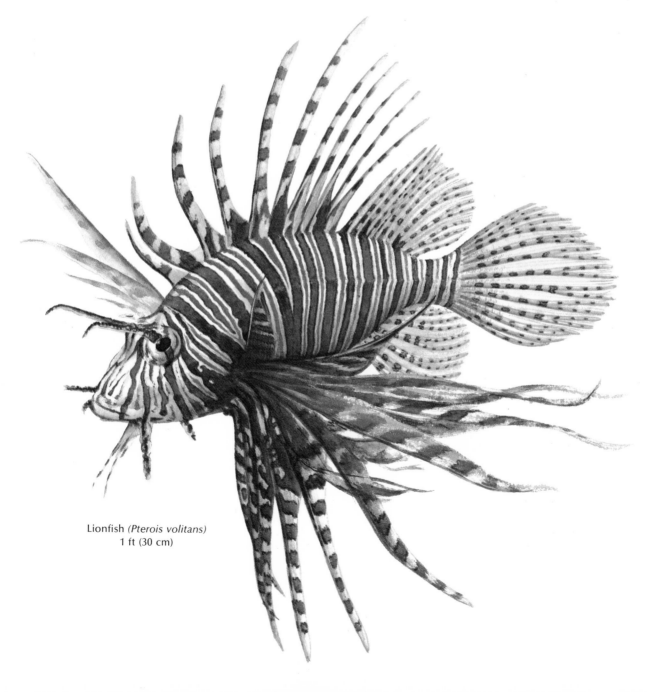

Lionfish *(Pterois volitans)*
1 ft (30 cm)

Redfish or ocean perch *(Sebastes marinus)*
up to 2 ft (60 cm)

The lionfish is one of about a dozen similar species found along the Atlantic coast. These include the barbfish, *S. brasiliensis*, which is most prevalent in warm waters of the Caribbean and southward to South America; spotted scorpionfish, *S. plumieri*, of the same range and with bright yellow on the inner surface of its pectoral fins; and the mushroom scorpionfish, *S. inermis*, only 6 inches long and sometimes called unarmed scorpionfish because it has fewer spines than other species.

Off the Pacific coast of North America the genus is represented by the California scorpionfish, *S. guttata*, known locally as sculpin. Attaining a length of 1½ feet, though usually shorter, it is reddish above, grading to pink below, and mottled with purple, brown, olive, and other colors. The California scorpionfish is a popular catch with anglers, and it must be handled with great care because of the 12 sharp spines in its dorsal fin.

The most dangerous scorpionfishes live in the Indo-Pacific region. Stonefish of the genus *Syanceja* are shallow-water dwellers, their ugly, warty brownish-black bodies providing almost perfect camouflage on the coral and rock bottoms. The pain produced by the venom that flows down their spines into the stab wound is excruciating. It starts immediately and continues for hours. Deaths from puncture wounds are not uncommon.

Zebrafishes, *Pterois spp.*, also of the Indo-Pacific, are extremely handsome fish, their bodies striped vertically with black and white or other colors. The spiny rays of their dorsal fins and also the rays of their pectoral fins are separate and are drawn into filamentlike extensions. Despite their beauty, however, these fishes are poisonous and can kill.

Only one rockfish—the redfish, or ocean perch, *Sebastes marinus*—lives in the Atlantic, in cold, deep waters from New Jersey northward to the Arctic and also abundantly off the coast of northern Europe. Red in color, it reaches a length of about 2 feet and may weigh as much as 12 pounds. Those off the coast of Europe average a third larger than those off the coast of North America. Millions of pounds are netted annually.

About 60 species of rockfishes of the genus *Sebastes* live off the Pacific coast of North America. All have 13 (rarely 14) stout spines in the dorsal fin, and some have spines on top of the head. Many are brightly colored. One of the most valuable species is the bocaccio, *S. paucispinis*, which is brownish on the back grading to reddish on the sides and pink or white on the belly. Some are blotched with black. The lower jaw projects beyond the upper, and there are normally 9 rays in the anal fin. Found from San Diego northward to Alaska, the bocaccio reaches a length of 3 feet and may weigh as much as 20 pounds.

Equally important and occurring in the same range as the bocaccio is the chilipepper, *S. goodei*. It usually has 8 rays in the anal fin. The chilipepper's maximum size is about 2 feet. It is pinkish red—darker above and lighter below—with a light pink stripe down the lateral line.

A species important to sport fishermen is the blue rockfish, *S. mystinus*, which goes also by the name priestfish. Very basslike in general appearance but much more spiny, it is blackish, blotched with gray, and has a white belly. The young are red until they reach a length of about 6 inches. Sometimes exceeding 18 inches in length, the blue rockfish is found mainly in shallow waters, from Baja California to Alaska.

Other important species are the vermilion rockfish, *S.*

miniatus, which is red in color and with a lower jaw rough to the touch; chameleon rockfish, *S. pinniger*, mainly orange and with a lower jaw smooth to the touch; yellowtail rockfish, *S. flavidus*, its caudal fin distinctly yellow; and black rockfish, *S. melanops*, similar to the blue rockfish but with a larger mouth, the rear of the upper jaw extending to the rear of the eye and the membrane between the spines of the dorsal fin spotted with black.

Family Triglidae
sea robins

These unusual fishes have split pectoral fins—the lower portion consisting of several stiff, separate rays and the upper part with soft rays, broad and winglike, though not as large as in the flying gurnards. The upper part is used for swimming; the lower portion is used to probe for food and also for turning rocks and debris to find food. The pectoral fins may also be used in combination with the pelvic fins for "walking" over the bottom. Almost all sea robins are brightly colored, and most species live in subtropical and tropical seas, generally in relatively deep water. All are carnivorous. Nineteen Atlantic species and two Pacific species inhabit the waters of the United States and Canada.

The northern sea robin, *Prionotus carolinus*, averaging 12 inches in length but sometimes as long as 18 inches, ranges from Nova Scotia to northern South America but is not common north of Massachusetts. Its most distinguishing color feature is its black chin. The body is mottled black on an olive-brown or gray background. A bottom-dweller, the northern sea robin comes close to shore in summer but moves back into deeper, warmer water in winter. Like other sea robins, it makes a loud noise by vibrating muscles attached to its air bladder.

Similar Atlantic species include the striped sea robin, *P. evolans*, marked with five dark lines along its sides; and the leopard sea robin, *P. scitulus*, a foot-long species common in the Gulf of Mexico and along the southern Atlantic, its yellowish-brown body marked with dark blotches.

Sea robins occur also off the coasts of Europe and Africa, where the most common genus is *Trigla*, and in the western Pacific from Japan southward. In some areas they are considered a delicacy.

Family Hexagrammidae
greenlings

This is another small family of fishes restricted in distribution to the Pacific, off the coast of North America from Point Conception on the California coast northward to Alaska. Like the lingcod, these fishes have a long, low dorsal fin, the spiny and soft-rayed portions joined but with a deep notch between them. Typically they have several lateral lines. Most species live close to shore in kelp or among rocks.

The kelp greenling, *Hexagrammos decagrammus*, to 1½ feet long and up to 4 pounds in weight, has five lateral lines on its sides and back. The male is bluish, mottled with brown; the female is brownish, mottled with black. This is one of the most popular catches of sport fishermen along the Pacific coast.

Similar and related species of the same general range are the whitespotted greenling, *H. stelleri*; the rock greenling, *H. lagocephalus*; and the masked greenling, *H. octogrammus*.

The painted greenling, *Oxylebius pictus*, also called convict fish, is grayish white with five or six vertical black bars on its sides. An active fish, about 10 inches long, it is commonly seen along rocky shores from southern California northward to Washington.

Northern sea robin (*Prionotus carolinus*)
1 ft (30 cm)

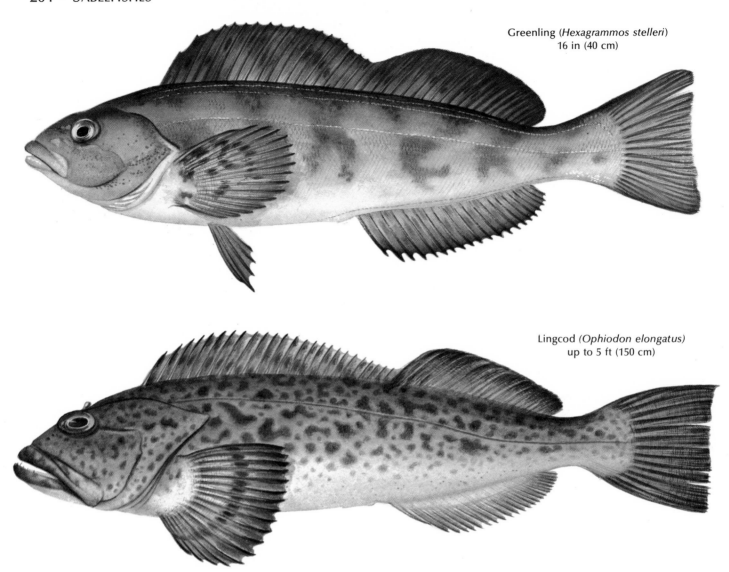

Greenling (*Hexagrammos stelleri*)
16 in (40 cm)

Lingcod *(Ophiodon elongatus)*
up to 5 ft (150 cm)

The lingcod, *Ophiodon elongatus*, is found from Alaska to Baja California—most abundantly north of Point Conception. Also called cultus, it is a popular sport fish and is also caught commercially. The two dorsal fins are joined but are deeply notched between the spiny and the soft-rayed portions. The mouth is large and contains numerous large canine teeth. Over each eye is a fleshy flap of skin. The color varies with where the fish lives but is usually a mottled bluish gray or greenish tan, with dark blotches. The flesh of the lingcod is greenish, but this does not affect its edibility. The maximum size is 5 feet with a weight of about 70 pounds.

The longspine combfish, *Zanionlepis latipinnis*, and the shortspine combfish, *Z. frenata*, are two other greenlings, both less than a foot long, inhabiting cool Pacific waters. They live at moderate depths but have been netted in waters more than 350 feet deep.

Family Anoplopomatidae
sablefishes

The sablefish, *Anoplopoma fimbria*, ranging from southern California to Alaska and Japan, reaches a length of 3 feet and can weigh as much as 50 pounds, the average being less than 20 pounds. It is gray or greenish black on the back, paler below. The two dorsal fins are well separated. A carnivorous fish, it can be caught by bottom-fishing with cut baits but is rarely fished for by anglers. Along the Pacific coast it sometimes is an important part of the commercial catch.

The skilfish, *Erilepis zonifer*, may reach a length of 6 feet and weigh as much as 200 pounds. Ranging from northern California to Alaska, it inhabits much deeper waters than the sablefish (to more than 1,000 feet) and is caught only in the nets of commercial fishermen.

Sablefish *(Anoplopoma fimbria)*
3 ft (90 cm)

Family Cottidae
sculpins

Bottom fishes, living mainly in Arctic waters, sculpins are principally carnivorous, many of them attractive but protectively camouflaged by their mottled patterns. Usually sluggish and waiting in ambush for their prey, they are nevertheless capable of quick, darting escapes. In all sculpins there is a bony support beneath the eye, no spines in the anal fin, and the dorsal fin is deeply notched between the spiny and soft-rayed portions. Some have scales, others lack them. Typically they have broad, flat heads and winglike pectoral fins. Most sculpins live close to shore, some in tidal pools; a few kinds inhabit deep water, and several range into fresh waters or are permanent inhabitants. Most freshwater species are 2 to 4 inches long. The cottids constitute a large family; about 106 species are found off the coasts of the United States and Canada.

The cabezon, *Scorpaenichthys marmoratus*, is the largest of the sculpins, reaching a length of 2½ feet and weighing as much as 25 pounds. It ranges from Baja California to Alaska. Variable in color, it may be reddish brown to gray or greenish, generally mottled with black. Females are usually more greenish, the males more red. The cabezon is a prized catch in California waters, taken on cut baits or with jigs.

Arctic staghorn sculpin *(Gymnocanthus tricuspis)*
up to 1 ft (30 cm)

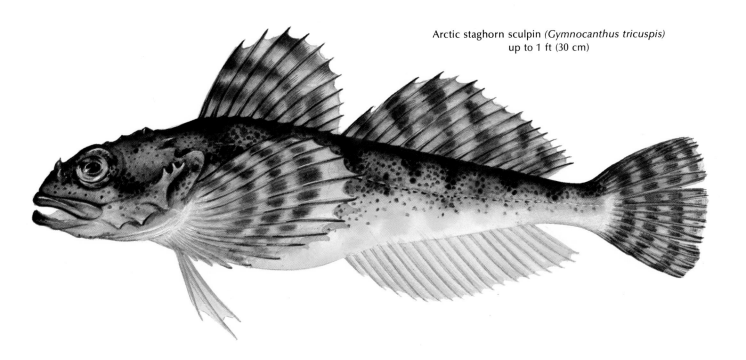

Shorthorn sculpin *(Myoxocephalus scorpius)*
2 ft (60 cm)

The staghorn sculpin, *Leptocottus armatus*, to about a foot long, occurs in the same range as the cabezon but has a greater tendency to go into brackish or fresh waters. The back and sides are olive green to brown, the belly white. The soft dorsal and anal fins are barred with gray or green, the pectoral fins with yellow and black. The staghorn sculpin is caught accidentally by anglers seeking other species and is sometimes used for bait. Another large Pacific Coast species is the red Irish lord, *Hemilepidotus hemilepidotus*, to 1½ feet long. It has white and purplish red spots on its olive-green body.

Numerous smaller sculpins live in the shallows and the tidal pools along the Pacific coast, with an estimated 50 species in Alaskan waters alone. The Arctic staghorn sculpin, *Gymnocanthus tricuspis*, inhabits Atlantic and Pacific polar waters.

Sculpins are not common in the Atlantic. Among them, however, is the unusual sea raven, *Hemitripterus americanus*, to 2 feet long and weighing as much as 5 pounds. This is an uncommon marine species that inflates its stomach when it is taken from the water.

About two dozen species of sculpins occur in fresh waters in North America. The banded sculpin, *Cottus carolinae*, and the mottled sculpin, *C. bairdi*, are two freshwater sculpins common in the cold rapids of streams—the mottled sculpin occurring from Hudson Bay southward through the Great Lakes and in the mountains to Tennessee, the banded sculpin living in the fast warm-water streams south of the mottled sculpin's range. The slimy sculpin, *C. cognatus*, occurs in the same range as the mottled sculpin and can be distinguished most easily by its excessively slimy skin.

The prickly sculpin, *C. asper*, occurring along the coast and in fresh waters from California to Alaska, may be as much as a foot long. In this genus also is the miller's thumb, *C. gobio*, found in freshwater streams throughout Europe except in the extreme southern countries.

Sculpins are found also in northern Asia and Japan. They include *C. pollux* and also the Arctic staghorn sculpin, *Gymnocanthus herzensteini*, which is cosmopolitan in cold seas.

Sturgeon poacher *(Agonus acipenserinus)*
1 ft (30 cm)

Family Agonidae
poachers

Also fishes of cold waters, poachers and alligatorfishes are wholly marine and occur mainly in the Pacific. They are slim fishes, their bodies covered with sawtooth-edged bony plates. Some live at depths as great as 1,500 to 2,000 feet, others in tidal pools. One of the most common and largest species, to a length of 12 inches, is the sturgeon poacher, *Agonus acipenserinus*, of the North Pacific.

Family Cyclopteridae
lumpfishes and snailfishes

Sometimes placed in separate families, lumpfishes and snailfishes have a sucking disk on the underside of their bodies. It is formed from their pelvic fins. Lumpfishes have an almost round or "lumpy" body, often covered with bumps or tubercles. The long, low dorsal fin is deeply notched or divided into two sections. Snailfishes have a long body covered with prickles in some species. The dorsal fin is also long and low but is not divided into two sections. In both lumpfishes and snailfishes the body is flabby and quite unfishlike. Both kinds of fishes are marine and live in cold waters, either deep or polar, some of the snailfishes inhabiting Antarctic waters. About 150 species are recognized, all bottom-dwellers.

The lumpfish, *Cyclopterus lumpus*, is one of the largest members of the family, attaining a length of 2 feet and weighing as much as 18 pounds. It occurs in cold waters on both sides of the Atlantic. The back and sides are bluish gray or olive green, the belly yellowish. In the breeding season, however, the male's belly is red. Females may lay 20,000 or more eggs, which sink and stick to the bottom. They are then guarded and aerated by the male until they hatch.

Most species of lumpfishes are smaller, averaging only about 6 inches in length. Among these are the Atlantic spiny lumpsucker, *Eumicrotremus spinosus*, and the very similar Pacific spiny lumpsucker, *E. orbis*.

Snailfishes are also mostly small; only a few species grow to as much as a foot long. They are generally light brown, some of the deepwater species pinkish to red. They may be blotched, spotted, or striped with numerous lines, as in the striped seasnail, *Liparis liparis*, that occurs off the coast of Europe and also North America. It is the most common of many species in this typical genus, which has representatives on both sides of the Pacific in the Northern Hemisphere.

Striped sea snail *(Liparis liparis)*
6 in (15 cm)

Lumpfish *(Cyclopterus lumpus)*
2 ft (60 cm)

Flying gurnard (*Dactylopterus volitans*)
1 ft. (30 cm)

ORDER DACTYLOPTERIFORMES

Family Dactylopteridae
flying gurnards

In these fishes, the pectoral fins are large and winglike, extending almost to the tail. The stiff-spined pelvic fins are directed downward, enabling the fish to use them as props or to walk along slowly over the bottom. The "wings" become gliding surfaces for brief excursions above the surface, but flying gurnards are not as adept at this as are the flying fishes. There are only a few species in the family, all inhabiting subtropical or tropical seas. The common species of warm Atlantic waters, off Europe and the Mediterranean as well as North America, is *Dactylopterus volitans*, which may attain a length of 12 inches but is usually smaller.

ORDER PEGASIFORMES

Family Pegasidae
sea moths

Fewer than half a dozen species comprise this family of unusual fishes of Indo-Pacific waters, some straying as far north as Japan and east to Hawaii. None exceeds 5 inches in length. The slim body is encased in rings of bony plates, much as in seahorses. The small mouth is located at the base (not tip) of a snout that resembles somewhat the proboscis of a moth. The pectoral fins are large and stick out from the sides of the body like wings; the pelvic fins are reduced to two filamentalike rays. *Pegasus volitans* and *P. papilio* are two species.

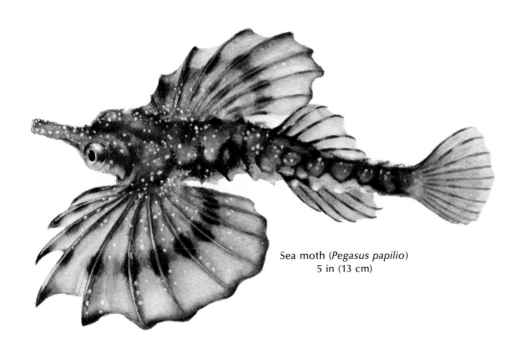

Sea moth (*Pegasus papilio*)
5 in (13 cm)

ORDER PERCIFORMES

Family Centropomidae
snooks

This is a small family of fishes found in warm seas. Robalo is another common name by which they are known. Most familiar of the species is the snook, *Centropomus undecimalis*, found in warm, shallow seas from about central Florida southward to Brazil. Occasionally it strays into brackish waters or may wander far upriver into fresh water. The snook is silvery with a pikelike shape, its lower jaw projecting beyond the upper. The caudal fin is forked. An immediate identification feature is the black lateral line. Like pikes, the snook is a predator, feeding on other fishes and also on shrimps, crabs, and crustaceans. Once considered a commercial species in Florida, it is now listed as a game fish and can be caught only by sport fishermen. The average size is 5 pounds or less, but a 52-pounder was caught on rod and reel off La Paz, Mexico, in 1963. Several weighing more than 40 pounds have been taken in Florida waters.

Snooks can be caught on natural and artificial baits and by trolling or casting. They are moody fish, how-

Snook *(Centropomus undecimalis)*
5 ft (150 cm)

ever. At times, snooks may be so abundant, clearly in view, that it is impossible to move a bait or lure without touching them. If they are not at that moment inclined to feed, however, nothing that is offered will stir them into action. But when a snook does take an offering and the hook is set, it gives a fisherman memorable moments, sometimes erupting from the water and then turning as quickly to bore deep or to dash into the mangrove roots. Despite its rugged appearance, the snook has a soft mouth from which a hook tears easily. A fisherman must use care in handling a snook because of the sharp pre-operculum edge.

Biologists have not resolved the classification of the several species in the genus. The principal distinguishing features are the number of scales in the lateral line and the fish's size. The fat snook, *C. parallelus*, also found in Florida waters, has more than 80 scales in its lateral line and seldom weighs more than 3 pounds. Still smaller is the tarpon snook, *C. pectinatus*, which has more than 67 scales in its lateral line. Because of the dependency of the snooks on shallow inshore waters, estuaries, and even brackish waters—including the miles of mangrove shoreline—as nurseries for their young, these fishes are threatened by coastal developments that are destroying their habitat.

Included in this family, too, are a number of species of small fishes that are popular with aquarium hobbyists. Several species of the genus *Chanda* are imported from African and Indo-Pacific waters.

The Indian glassfish, *C. ranga*, native to brackish and fresh waters of India and Burma, seldom exceeds a length of 2 inches. Typical of the genus, the body is

"glassy" or semitransparent, with some of the internal organs visible. The body has a gold or silvery shine; the fins are yellowish or tinged with red; and in males, the soft rays are edged with bright blue.

Family Serranidae
sea basses

More than 400 species comprise this important, mainly marine family represented most abundantly in subtropical and tropical seas. Included in the family are some of the most valued food fishes. Many are caught on hook and line, and some smaller species are kept in aquariums. They range in size from nearly a thousand pounds to diminutives that measure less than an inch long and are almost weightless. Their features vary greatly, but they generally share a basslike body shape with a strongly spined first dorsal fin and a soft-rayed second dorsal.

Members of the widely distributed genus *Epinephelus* are called groupers. They are nonschooling sea basses that generally congregate in the same area. Dozens of species inhabit all warm seas. They are most abundantly along rocky shores, but some species prefer deepwater reefs. All groupers are good to eat. Many are caught on rod and reel or on hand lines.

The red grouper, *E. morio*, averages less than 10 pounds in weight but may attain a length of 3 feet and weigh as much as 40 pounds. The most common grouper in Caribbean and Florida waters, the red grouper is distinguished from other species by its definitely squared-off tail. The color varies but is usually brownish red, the blotches not in organized pattern.

The Nassau grouper, *E. striatus*, occurs in the same range as the red grouper. It may be slightly larger, and the blotches on the sides are arranged in a distinct pattern, forming vertical bars. One black band extends obliquely through the eye. There is a black spot on top of the caudal peduncle, a diagnostic feature that appears no matter what other color the fish might have.

Other species of *Epinephelus* in Atlantic waters are the red hind, *E. guttatus*, which ranges from North Carolina to Brazil and seldom exceeds 4 pounds in weight. Its body is covered with red spots; the inside of its mouth is red; and the dorsal, anal, and caudal fins are edged with black or dark blue.

The rock hind, *E. adscensionis*, another small species occurring in the same range as the red hind, has orange-red spots on its body, but its fins are not dark-edged. Also, its maxillary lacks scales, while the red hind's is scaled.

The speckled hind, *E. drummondhayi*, is larger than the red or rock hind—sometimes to 30 pounds or more. It has white spots over its body.

Pacific Coast species of *Epinephelus* include the spotted cabrilla, *E. analogus*, which is found from Baja California southward to northern South America. It may reach a weight of 20 pounds but is usually smaller. In color and pattern it resembles the rock hind.

The widespread genus has more than a dozen representatives in Indo-Pacific waters. One of the most widely distributed is the large, somber-hued *E. fuscoguttatus*, which attains a weight of 30 pounds.

Most of the species are spotted or blotched, like those in the warm waters off the coasts of North America and South America. The 8-inch *E. macrospilos* has large round to octagonal spots over its entire body. Each spot is margined with a lighter color. Another heavily spotted species is *E. merra*, which reaches a length of 2 feet.

The jewfish, *E. itajara*, is one of the giants of the clan. Found in the Caribbean and northward to the coasts of Florida and also in the Pacific from Panama to the Gulf of California, this species goes also by the name of spotted jewfish because of the numerous small black spots over its head and the front of its brownish or dusky body. The long first dorsal fin is very low and has short spines. It is not separated from the second dorsal, which has 15 or 16 rays. The pectoral fins are rounded, as is the caudal fin.

The average weight of the jewfish is about 20 pounds. Weights of 100 pounds are not uncommon, however, and there are records of 800 pounds. The present rod-and-reel record is 680 pounds. These larger fishes are caught with shark hooks, chains for leaders, and strong ropes. They are butchered and cut into steaks and fillets. The flavor is strong but not objectionable. Smaller fish are tastier.

Like its giant relatives, the jewfish typically inhabits a deep hole, often surprisingly close to shore. Though it appears to be sluggish because of its bulk, a jewfish can move at great speed for short distances, rushing from its lair to gobble a meal. A jewfish does not ordinarily show an inclination to attack divers and will avoid them, but big jewfishes deserve respect.

Nassau grouper *(Epinephelus striatus)*
up to 3 ft (90 cm)

A South Pacific relative of the jewfish, the Queensland grouper, or brindle bass, *E. lanceolata*, is about a third larger, reaching a length of 12 feet and a weight in excess of half a ton. This behemoth among sea basses has been known to follow divers and to make rushing attacks.

The Warsaw grouper, *E. nigritus*, also lives in warm Atlantic waters. It is fairly common along both coasts of Florida, ranging northward to South Carolina. Compared to the jewfish, the rays of its first dorsal fin are much higher, the pectoral fins are pointed at their tips, and the head is exceptionally large. The body is uniformly dark, with no spots. Only slightly smaller than the jewfish, it attains a length of 6 feet and may weigh 500 pounds. The average size is much smaller—20 pounds or less—but 100-pound catches are not uncommon. This is another giant fished for with heavy tackle, not only because of the size of the fish but also because of its habit of taking the bait into a rocky hideaway. Wire or chain leaders are essential.

A third gargantuan among the sea basses is the giant sea bass, *Stereolepis gigas*, found in the Pacific from the Gulf of California southward to Humboldt Bay and Guadalupe Island. It attains a length of about 7 feet and a weight of over 500 pounds. The rod-and-reel record of 557 pounds 3 ounces was taken off Catalina Island in 1962. Its spiny and soft dorsal fins are separated by only a notch. The first dorsal has 11 spines; the second dorsal, 10 soft rays. The general color is greenish brown or black, with darker fins. The membranes between the rays are generally light, and typically there is a white patch on the throat and beneath the tail. Young fishes are blotched or mottled, these markings sometimes still visible in fishes weighing 25 pounds or more.

The giant perch, or barramundi, *Lates calcarifer*, ranging from Japan through the East Indies in Indo-Pacific waters, is common close to shore, sometimes entering brackish or fresh water. It is rated as one of the best food fishes in Australian waters and is regarded highly as a game fish. Catches weighing 50 pounds are not uncommon. A record catch off the coast of India weighed nearly 600 pounds. Those most preferred for eating weigh 20 pounds or less. Classification of the species has varied. The body is more or less elongated, like a snook's, and some taxonomists place this species in the snook family.

Another member of the same genus is the Nile perch, *L. niloticus*, a strictly freshwater species that may weigh as much as 200 pounds. It is sought by sport fishermen.

Members of the genus *Mycteroperca* are usually considered true groupers. Their head is broad, the forehead high; the upper jaw is short. In most species the anal fin is long and contains more than ten rays. The caudal fin is squared across the tip or only slightly rounded.

The black grouper, *M. bonaci*, occurs in Florida and Caribbean waters. Sometimes it strays northward in summer to as far as Massachusetts. It is one of the largest groupers, occasional individuals attaining a length of 4 feet and weighing as much as 100 pounds. The average weight is less than 20 pounds. Typical of all groupers, the color varies but is usually olive or bluish-black covered with dark blotches. The fins may be bordered with black.

The yellowfin grouper, *M. venenosa*, occurring in the same area as the black grouper, is named for the yellow tips and edges on its pectoral fins. Though variable in color, it generally has large black spots on the head, back, and sides. These black blotches also extend onto the caudal fin, which is barred with black on its tip. In one color phase, the belly is bright red. Like other groupers, however, it can change its color to some degree to match its background. The yellowfin grouper averages about 10 pounds, but a weight of 30 pounds and a length of 3 feet is not uncommon.

Other species in the genus include the gag, *M. microlepis*, common from North Carolina southward along both Florida coasts but not occurring in the Caribbean. It averages less than 3 pounds in weight, but there are records of gags weighing more than 30 pounds. The dark fins are edged with white, the body is pale, and the dark blotches are generally indistinct.

The scamp, *M. phenax*, which may weigh as much as 10 pounds but usually much less, is found in both Florida and Caribbean waters. One color variation is brown or gray with small black spots. Another is pinkish with blotches along the sides. The fins are dark, often bordered with white.

Pacific Coast species include the Gulf grouper, *M. jordani*, and the broomtail grouper, *M. xenarcha*, both occurring from Point Conception southward to Peru. The broomtail grouper, which gets its name from its caudal fin, may reach a weight of 97 pounds.

The Colorado grouper, *M. olfax*, ranges from Panama southward to Peru; it is about the same size as the broomtail grouper. The golden grouper, *M. pardalis*, found in the same area, may be golden-yellow or greenish with small dots over the body. The tiger grouper, *M. tigris*, a 2-foot Caribbean species, is blotched and has yellow tips on its pectoral fins.

Grouper is a name used for species in a number of other genera. One of them is the marbled grouper, *Dermatolepis inermis*, to 1½ feet long, which inhabits warm Atlantic waters off the coast of North America. Its slightly larger relative, *D. striolatus*, reaches a length of 2 feet; it is found off the east coast of Africa.

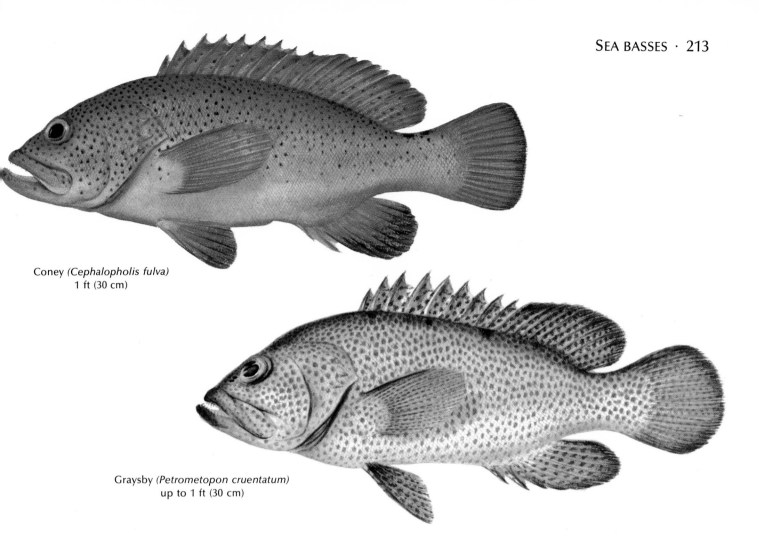

Coney *(Cephalopholis fulva)*
1 ft (30 cm)

Graysby *(Petrometopon cruentatum)*
up to 1 ft (30 cm)

The golden-striped grouper, *Grammistes sexlineatus*, of Indo-Pacific waters, is a rich, velvety black, with four bright yellow stripes down its sides and yellow markings on its head. Despite its attractiveness, this 9-inch fish is slimy and has a bitter flesh.

Among the smaller grouperlike fishes are species of the genus *Cephalopholis*, which have only 9 rays in their spiny first dorsal fin, a rounded caudal fin, and a low-arched forehead. The coney, *C. fulva*, found in the Caribbean and off the Florida coasts, is about a foot long and weighs about a pound. Occasional individuals weigh as much as 3 pounds. There are a number of color phases, but all have a sprinkling of light blue spots over the body, the soft dorsal fin and the tail fin margined with white and the tip of the jaw black. The coney is essentially a reef fish.

Two relatives of the coney found in the Pacific from the Gulf of California southward are the rose coney, *C. popino,* and the Gulf coney, *C. acanthistius*. Both are red and about 2 feet long. Other species occur in the Indo-Pacific—the 6-inch leopard coney, *C. leopardus*, distinguished by a black mark across the upper third of its rounded caudal fin, and the 12-inch blue-spotted argus, *C. argus*, its olive body and darker fins covered with light blue spots.

The graysby, *Petrometopon cruentatum*, of Caribbean and Florida waters, reaches a length of about a foot. It has 14 rays in its soft dorsal fin, compared to 15–17 in the coney, which it resembles. Also a reef fish, it can change its colors from reddish through white to brown with black spots. The graysby is commonly caught on hook and line, as is the coney.

The enjambre, *P. panamaensis*, is a Pacific Coast species similar to the graysby and occurring from Acapulco to Panama.

The sandperch, *Diplectrum formosum*, is small, usually 6 inches or less in length. Both the upper and lower lobes of the caudal fin are extended so that the fin is moderately lunate. The body is usually tan, with five or six vertical blue bars. One bar extends the full length of the body and ends in a dark spot just in front of the caudal fin. There are also blue stripes on the head, and the fins are barred with blue and yellow. This fish commonly rests on the sandy bottom, where it fans a depression in which it takes refuge. It is common off the southern Atlantic and Gulf coasts of North America.

Three abundant serranids on the Pacific coast of North America are the kelp bass, *Paralabrax clathratus*, barred sand bass, *P. nebulifer*, and spotted sand bass, *P. maculatofasciatus*.

Kelp bass *(Paralabrax clathratus)*
1½ ft (45 cm)

The kelp bass, which grows to a length of 1½ feet, is found from central California southward, most commonly around kelp beds. In numbers caught by sport fishermen, it generally tops the list in California. There is a distinct notch between the spiny and soft dorsal fins, and the longest spines in the first dorsal are longer than any of the rays in the soft dorsal.

The sand bass is common in the same general region, in some areas outnumbering the kelp bass. It prefers rocky and sandy bottoms rather than kelp, however. The spiny first dorsal and the soft-rayed second dorsal are not separated by a notch, and the third spine in the first dorsal is distinctly longer than the others. The spotted sand bass is similar to the barred sand bass but is freckled with black spots.

The black sea bass, *Centropristis striata*, lives in relatively cool waters from Massachusetts to North Carolina, sometimes straying southward to Florida. The topmost ray in its caudal fin is elongated as a thin filament. Though the average weight of the black sea bass is only about 2 pounds, it may attain a weight of 8 pounds and measure nearly 2 feet long. A similar but smaller species is the bank sea bass, *C. ocyurus*, found in deep waters of the Gulf of Mexico.

The wreckfish, *Polyprion americanus*, gets its name from its habit of frequenting wrecks or drifting along with floating timbers. Bluish gray, its second dorsal, caudal and anal fins are margined with black, the pectorals with white. It reaches a length of 6 feet and a weight of about 75 pounds. The wreckfish occurs in the

Atlantic from northern Africa northward, occasionally to as far north as England. It makes its meals of other fishes that are attracted to wrecks or similar underwater objects.

One of the smallest sea basses is the belted sandfish, *Serranus subligarius*, 6 inches long at maximum but mature when less than 2 inches long. It is common in warm Atlantic and Caribbean waters down to depths of about 60 feet.

Finally, the sea basses of the genus *Morone* are not only distinctive in shape but also have invaded fresh waters. With the wreckfish and the giant sea bass, they are often placed in a separate family, Percichthyidae. The striped bass, *M. saxatilis*, also commonly known as rock bass, rockfish, or striper, is most abundant along the mid-Atlantic coast of North America but occasionally occurs as far south as northern Florida or northward to the St. Lawrence River. It is also abundant off the coast of California, where it was introudced in 1879 and 1882.

The striped bass is easily identified by the 6–8 bold black stripes down its light olive and silvery sides. It is white below and frequently has yellow on its head, pectoral fins, and caudal fin. The striped bass reaches large size—to more than 100 pounds. The confirmed record taken on rod and reel weighed 72 pounds. The average is about 10 pounds, though 30-pounders are not especially uncommon.

Striped basses move into fresh water to spawn in spring and early summer. A 20-pound female may lay a million eggs that float freely in the water. A 50-pounder may lay as many as 5 million eggs. The young fishes stay in streams until they are two years old. They do not grow fast. Striped basses have become landlocked in some areas. The most famous and successful of these land-locked populations is in the Santee–Cooper Reservoir in South Carolina.

The striped bass is important both as a commercial and a sport fish. In California, it was declared strictly a game fish in the 1930s. Highly accommodating, the striped bass will take artificial and natural baits. Though other kinds of fishes put more flash in their fight, the striped bass is a rugged battler that seldom fails to satisfy the fisherman who has one at the end of his line. Equally important, the catch is good to eat.

Smaller cousins of the striped bass are the white bass, *M. chrysops*, and the yellow bass, *M. mississippiensis*, both of which live in fresh water. Both show their sea bass relationship by their two dorsal fins, the first spiny and the second soft-rayed. Their silvery or yellowish sides are striped with black.

The white bass is a schooling fish found from the St. Lawrence River through the Great Lakes and Mississippi River basin southward to Texas. It has been stocked in many manmade lakes and reservoirs. In the spring the white bass migrates into small streams to spawn. A large female may lay more than half a million eggs, which sink slowly to the bottom, where they adhere. Adults feed on other small fishes, crayfishes, and both immature and adult insects. They reach a length of 1½ feet, and

they may weigh 3 pounds, averaging about a pound. Locally, they may be very abundant.

White basses can be caught on artificial or on natural baits, minnows preferred, when they move in the shallows to feed during the cooler parts of the day. At midday, they retire to deeper water but are still willing to take baits or lures that are trolled deep enough to reach them. They are good to eat.

Yellow basses are not as common as white basses, and their range is restricted mainly to the southern Mississippi region. The background color is typically yellowish, but the two are similar enough in appearance to be confusing where the species overlap in distribution. In the yellow bass, the first and second dorsal fins are joined; in the white bass, separate. In the yellow bass, the second spine in the anal fin is as long or longer than the third spine; in the white bass, distinctly shorter. Also, the upper and lower jaws of the yellow bass are the same length; the lower jaw of the white bass projects slightly. The yellow bass also averages slightly less in weight.

The white perch, *M. americana*, is found in streams along the Atlantic coast and also in tidal waters from Nova Scotia to Florida. With settlement of these coastal regions, the population has moved steadily inland. The white perch averages only about 8 ounces in weight, but there have been reports of individuals weighing as much as 6 pounds. The record on rod and reel weighed 4¾ pounds. White perches are caught for sport and also commercially. Young fishes are barred vertically with

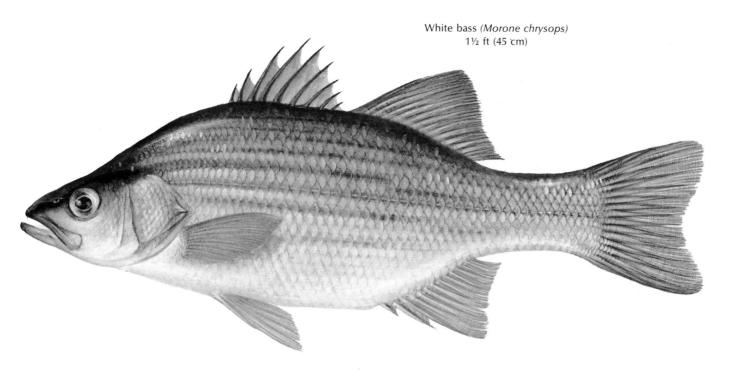

White bass *(Morone chrysops)*
1½ ft (45 cm)

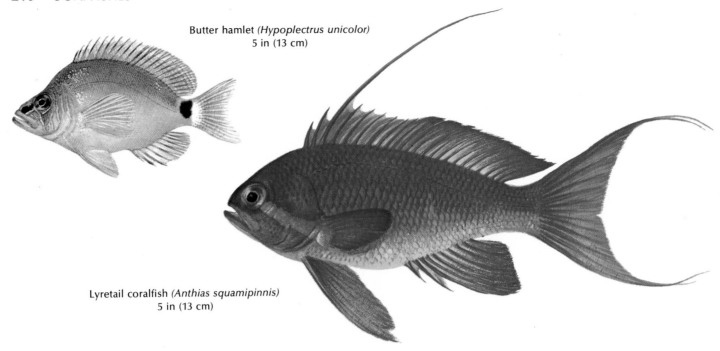

Butter hamlet (*Hypoplectrus unicolor*)
5 in (13 cm)

Lyretail coralfish (*Anthias squamipinnis*)
5 in (13 cm)

black, but these markings disappear as the fish becomes older. Like its relatives, the white perch is carnivorous.

The anthids, previously classified in the family Anthiidae, are beautiful small fishes found in the coral reefs of the Indo-Pacific region. The basic color of most species is red, as in the widely distributed 5-inch *Anthias squamipinnis*. The sexes differ in body shape and coloration. In males, which have a typical basslike body shape, the third spine of the first dorsal fin is extended into a long filament, as are the upper and lower lobes of the caudal fin. Two purplish stripes run obliquely from the eye to the pectoral fin, and the body is covered with yellow spots. The female lacks these features. Her head is domed, and her eyes are twice the size of the male's. The lower jaw projects beyond the upper. A black band bordered with purple runs from the operculum along each side of the caudal fin.

Family Grammistidae
soapfishes

Soapfishes, several species of *Rypticus*, display an unusual defense mechanism when they are attacked or handled—or even if there is an unusual agitation in the water near them. A thick mucus that turns into soapy froth is exuded. It is possible also that the mucus may be mildly poisonous or at least irritating to predators.

The greater soapfish, *R. saponaceus*, is found on both sides of the Atlantic. Its dorsal fin is comprised of three separate spines. Other commonly seen species are the freckled soapfish, *R. bistrispinus*; the whitespotted soapfish, *R. maculatus*; and the spotted soapfish, *R. subbifrenatus*.

Soapfish (*Rypticus saponaceus*)
1 ft (30 cm)

Family Teraponidae
tigerfishes

This is also a small family of Indo-Pacific fishes, mainly marine but with representatives also in brackish and fresh water. Their name is derived from the typically striped body. The three-striped tigerfish, *Terapon jarbua*, which attains a length of about a foot, has three stripes along each side, plus a black tip on the upper lobe of the caudal fin, a black spot on the second dorsal fin, and a large black spot on the first dorsal. The gill covers are spiny. This species is commonly exhibited in aquariums.

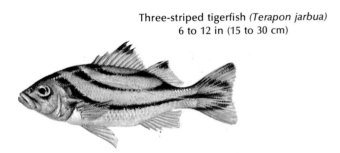

Three-striped tigerfish *(Terapon jarbua)*
6 to 12 in (15 to 30 cm)

Family Kuhliidae
aholeholes

Similar in appearance to centrarchids or freshwater sunfishes, the fewer than a dozen species in this family are all confined to the Indo-Pacific region. Most of them are marine, some straying into brackish water and several living wholly in fresh water. The Hawaiian aholehole, *Kuhlia sandvicensis*, is common in waters around the Hawaiian Islands but does not occur elsewhere. It reaches a length of 12 inches.

The smaller, 8-inch *K. taeniura* occurs widely throughout the Indo-Pacific. Its caudal fin is strikingly marked with five black bars—one median and two oblique.

Another widely distributed species is *K. rupestris*; it has a central black blotch in both the upper and lower lobes of its caudal fin, which is margined with white. Black spots occur also at the tip of the lateral line on each side and on the rays of the caudal fin.

Family Centrarchidae
sunfishes

To most freshwater fishermen in North America, this family has no equal, for included in it are some of the highly popular pan fishes and the black basses that have probably had more words spoken and written about them than even the elite trouts.

Not all of the many members of this family are big, gamy fighters. Most sunfishes, in fact, are less than 6 inches long. But all the centrarchids share features that make them members of the same family. Their scales are rough because of the comblike margins. Their two dorsal fins are united, but the first is heavily spined. The anal fin bears three or more spines. Typically the tail is broad. Males usually make the nest in which the females lay their eggs. The males then guard the nest and also herd the young for a brief time. Adults are carnivorous, eating mainly insects, crayfishes, and other invertebrates; the larger species also prey on smaller fishes. The family is divided into three groups: the black basses, the crappies, and the sunfishes.

The basses, which belong to the genus *Micropterus*, have a more elongated body than either the crappies or the sunfishes. Six species are generally recognized in this genus. Some ichthyologists would make even more divisions; others fewer.

Aholehole *(Kuhlia taeniura)*
8 in (20 cm)

The largemouth bass, *M. salmoides*, is found throughout the United States and southern Canada, having been introduced to states where it was not native. It has also been stocked in fresh waters in Hawaii and in several foreign countries. The largemouth is distinguished from other basses by the size of its mouth. The rear margin of the upper jaw extends beyond the eye. The spiny dorsal is almost separated from the soft dorsal, the notch between them deep. The color varies with the size of the fish and also with the temperature and chemistry of the water in which it lives. Generally, however, the background color is greenish, and there is a dark lateral stripe down each side.

Largemouth bass prefer large lakes and quiet parts of streams, where they seek out the weedy, mud-bottomed areas. They average about 1½ pounds in weight, smaller in the northern limits of the range but larger in the southern regions where the growing season is longer. The largest caught on rod and reel weighed 22 pounds 4 ounces. It was taken from Montgomery Lake in southern Georgia. Because of differences in scale counts along the lateral line and also their consistent large size, these largemouths of the South are sometimes recognized as a distinct subspecies.

With the bluegill, the largemouth is commonly stocked in farm ponds. It serves as the predator to help keep the population of the smaller, faster-breeding fish in better balance.

Spawning occurs in late winter or early spring in the southern parts of the range and in late spring or early summer farther north. The male selects the site, fanning away the silt from the bottom to make a cleaned, circular area. He entices or drives a female into the nest and spreads milt over her eggs as they are laid. A small female will lay only about 2,000 eggs, but a large female can lay 30,000 or more eggs in the nest. The male stays with the eggs—guarding them and driving away intruders and also fanning the eggs constantly. This aerates them and prevents silt from settling on them. When they hatch, the male continues to watch over the fry for two or three weeks, or for as long as they continue to school.

Largemouth basses can be fished for almost the year round. Though they will take natural baits readily, particularly minnows and softshell crayfishes, the favorite way of fishing for them is with artificial bait.

The smallmouth bass, *M. dolomieui*, is basically a more northern fish than the largemouth. It ranges farther north into Canada and does not occur in the Deep South. Another difference, it prefers streams and cold, clear lakes. Compared to the largemouth's, its mouth is smaller—the rear of the upper jaw not extending past the back edge of the eye. The two dorsal fins are joined without a deep notch, and there are dark vertical bars along its sides, which are usually bronze. The average weight of a smallmouth is less than a pound, though it may attain a weight of 10 pounds. What the smallmouth lacks in size is made up for in fight, most fishermen agreeing that it is superior to the largemouth in this category. Perhaps its vigor comes from the nature of its habitat: cooler and more highly oxygenated water. The smallmouth is also an aerialist, which delights fishermen. Comparisons are inconsequential. Much depends on the individual fisherman's experiences. Both species unquestionably provide great sport.

The spotted bass, *M. punctulatus*, has features of both the largemouth and the smallmouth but is generally smaller. It has a dark stripe down each side of its body like the largemouth, but beneath the stripe are numerous dark dots. There is a large black blotch on the rear of each gill cover, and if the fish is in hand, you can feel a small patch of teeth on the tongue. The three species can also be distinguished by counting the rows of scales in a line from the front of the dorsal fin to the lateral line. In the largemouth, there are seven rows of scales; in the spotted bass, nine; and in the smallmouth, eleven.

The spotted bass occurs from Ohio southward to Florida and westward to Kansas and Texas. It grows to about 4 pounds. In northern streams, it seeks out the mud-bottomed areas where the current is sluggish. The smallmouth's choice, by comparison, is the rocky or gravel-bottomed areas where the current is swift; the largemouth is found in the weedy coves. In southern areas the spotted bass prefers the cooler, swifter water, more like the smallmouth. In lakes it tends to go deeper than the other two species—down to 100 feet at times. The smallmouth rarely goes below 50 feet, and the largemouth stays in shallow surface waters.

The three other species of *Micropterus* recognized are the Suwanee bass, *M. notius*, less than a pound in size and restricted to northern Florida; the Guadalupe bass, *M. treculi*, also weighing about a pound at maximum but usually less and restricted to the Guadalupe and adjacent rivers in southern Texas; and the redeye bass, *M. coosae*, to 2 pounds and occurring in the Alabama River and other nearby streams in the southeastern United States. All three differ in only minor ways from the spotted bass.

The second centrarchid group is comprised mainly of the crappies, *Pomoxis*, which are found in ponds and lakes from Canada southward through the Great Lakes and the Mississippi River drainage system. Crappies differ from other sunfishes in having a much longer anal fin, almost equal to the length of the dorsal fin. They are

Bluegill *(Lepomis macrochirus)*
6 to 9 in (15 to 23 cm)

intermediate in size, averaging from half a pound to a pound in weight. Taken from cool waters, they are sweet-fleshed and flavorful; from warm waters, they tend to be soft. They are regarded highly as panfish, however, and in many areas they are the principal catch on rod and reel. They also go by many common names. More than forty names have been recorded for the black crappie, *P. nigromaculatus*, which is the most common of the two species.

The black crappie has seven or eight spines in its first dorsal fin, and the black marks on its sides are not in a regular pattern, which results in a generally darker appearance. The white crappie, *P. annularis*, has only six spines in its first dorsal, and the dark markings on its sides are usually indistinct vertical bars. The distance from the front of the dorsal fin to the eye is equal to the length of the base of the dorsal fin in the black crappie; the distance is much less in the white crappie. Both are silvery white to greenish, variable with the water, and both have large, tender mouths from which a hook tears easily. Black crappies tend to prefer larger lakes and clearer waters, but the two species commonly live together.

Fishermen catch crappies on a variety of natural and artificial baits. Minnows and worms are the favorite baits of most fishermen. The crappies school, and so catching one is a signal that more are ready and waiting

nearby. Favorite places are around fallen snags or other underwater obstructions, which also challenges the fisherman to exercise caution. The record catch for the black crappie is 5 pounds; for the white crappie, 4.

The flier, *Centrarchus macropterus*, limited to the Atlantic coastal plains and the swampy lowlands of the southern Gulf states, is placed with the crappies because of its long anal fin. Another name for the species is round sunfish. The flier, which is not well known except locally, has 11–13 spines in its first dorsal fin, more than either of the crappies. A short, dark bar slants downward from each eye, and younger fish have a black spot midway along the base of the second dorsal fin. Small, squarish black spots occur along the sides. The flier rarely exceeds 6 inches in length.

The sunfishes, most of them less than 6 inches long, seldom get rave notices in sport magazines, but they rank high in the amount of fun they give fishermen. They are surprisingly hard fighters if caught on light tackle. Those large enough also make excellent eating.

The best known of the panfishes and most widely distributed is the bluegill, *Lepomis macrochirus*, which many would list as the most popular of all the hook-and-line-caught fish in North America. It is distinguished by a dark spot on each side of the soft dorsal fin and by another on each ear flap, with no red or white edge as in others that also have a dark extension of the

Green sunfish (*Lepomis cyanellus*)
4 to 6 in (10 to 15 cm)

operculum. The color varies somewhat with the water in which they live but is generally dark on the back. The sides are greenish blue. Usually there is a barred pattern along the sides, particularly in young fishes. Males have a bright red breast during the breeding season. The average size of the bluegill is a quarter of a pound, but a record catch of 4 pounds 12 ounces was made in a Kentucky lake. Pound-size catches are not uncommon.

Where the bluegill did not occur natively in the United States, it has been introduced. It is the species commonly stocked with the largemouth bass in millions of farm ponds, in which it prospers. The bluegill nests in the same manner as the basses, but the females average about 10,000 eggs and may lay more than 50,000. In time, despite the predation of the largemouth bass, the bluegill population in farm ponds builds beyond the carrying capacity of the water. The fish become stunted, their heads large but their bodies small and thin. Then the ponds must be drained and restocked to establish a suitable population level.

Bluegills are hard fighters, and to compensate for their small size, anglers seek them with ultra-light tackle. Then, even the smallest fish provides many thrilling moments. They will take either natural or artificial baits with equal enthusiasm, as do other species of sunfish.

Of the more than a dozen other species of *Lepomis*, all with much more limited ranges than the bluegill, the redear sunfish, *L. microlophus*, is one of the most popular in its native South. It has also been introduced to parts of the Midwest, where, like the bluegill, it is stocked in farm ponds and in small lakes. Another name for the species is shellcracker because its diet includes

snails and small clams. Thick pharyngeal bones armed with blunted molaform teeth make this habit possible. Redears reach a maximum size of about a pound and a half but average only about a quarter of a pound. They resemble bluegills but do not have a black spot on the dorsal fin; the black ear flap is edged with red.

The pumpkinseed, *L. gibbosus*, also called common sunfish, is prevalent in the eastern United States and in southern Canada, occurring as far west as the Dakotas and southward along the Atlantic coastal plain to Georgia. Its dark ear flap has bright red or orange on the rear and lower border. The back and sides are brightly striped with green and blue, and the cheeks and the gill covers are orange. The pumpkinseed is about one-third smaller than the redear.

The longear sunfish, *L. megalotis*, is similar in size and general appearance to the pumpkinseed but has a distinctly long, wide, black ear flap margined with red (or white in some) along the rear. The pectoral fin is short and rounded rather than pointed as in the bluegill, redear, and pumpkinseed. Longears are common in streams.

The green sunfish, *L. cyanellus*, is another widely distributed species, having been introduced to areas where it is not native. Primarily a stream fish, its body is somewhat more elongated than in typical pond and lake sunfishes. The tip of the caudal fin and often the dorsal and anal fins may be edged with white.

The spotted sunfish, *L. punctatus*, goes also by the name of stumpknocker. Primarily a stream fish, it is found also in lakes and ponds. Compared to other sunfishes, it has a large mouth. The pectoral fins are broad, and the short ear flaps bear a small black spot. Along the sides are numerous rows of black spots.

Among the smallest of the sunfishes is the dollar sunfish, *L. marginatus*, so called because of its rounded, dollar-size body. Its maximum length is 3 inches, but it is usually smaller.

Still smaller are species of *Elassoma* and *Enneacanthus*, which average only 2 inches or less in length. These include the banded pygmy sunfish, *Elassoma zonatum*; the Everglades pygmy sunfish, *E. evergladei*; the blackbanded sunfish, *Enneacanthus chaetodon*; and the banded sunfish, *E. obesus*. These attractive little sunfishes and some of their equally small relatives are too small to interest fishermen, but they make excellent aquarium fishes.

One of the largest of the sunfish clan is the rock bass, *Amblopites rupestris*, a stream species identified by its conspicuous red eyes, the dark spots along its sides below the lateral line, and the six spines in its anal fin. The spines set it apart from the warmouth and other sunfishes that have only three spines in the anal fin. The rock bass is found over the entire eastern United States and extreme southern Canada. It averages a quarter of a pound or less in weight, with occasional individuals weighing as much as 2 pounds. The rock bass is an excellent fighter and has a good flavor, making the catches doubly worthwhile.

The warmouth, *Lepomis gulosus*, resembles the rock bass but has only three spines in the anal fin. Warmouths have dark bands on the cheek and a dark spot on each gill cover. There are no spots on the sides and belly, as in the rock bass. The warmouth prefers quiet waters; it occurs in the eastern United States but most abundantly in southern waters. It is good to eat but is not as flavorful as the rock bass.

The Sacramento perch, *Archoplites interruptus*, is native to California, the only member of the sunfish family originally occurring west of the Rockies. It is now rare. Unlike other sunfishes, it does not build a nest or guard its eggs and young. As a result, the eggs are eaten by catfishes, crappies, and other introduced species. The maximum size of the Sacramento perch in days gone by

Family Priacanthidae
bigeyes

These bigeyed red fishes are bottom-dwellers inhabiting subtropical and tropical seas. Most of the two dozen or so species live in deep waters. Catalufa is another name often used for the family.

The bigeye, *Priacanthus arenatus*, about 12 inches long, is common on both sides of the Atlantic, occurring off the coast of North America from Cape Cod southward into the West Indies. Typical of the family, its body is covered with rough scales, and the large mouth is slanted upward. As its name implies, however, the most outstanding features are the eyes—more than an inch in diameter on a fish that is only 10 inches long. The bigeye also has silvery bands (usually 11) on its sides, silver dots below the lateral line, and black dots between the fin rays.

The glasseye snapper, or catalufa, *P. cruentatus*, occurs in the same waters of the Atlantic. It is slightly larger—to 15 inches—and lacks the silvery stripes and black dots. It has indistinct black blotches just above the lateral line. Both the bigeye and the catalufa, as well as other members of the family, can change color, turning almost white or becoming heavily mottled to match more nearly their surroundings.

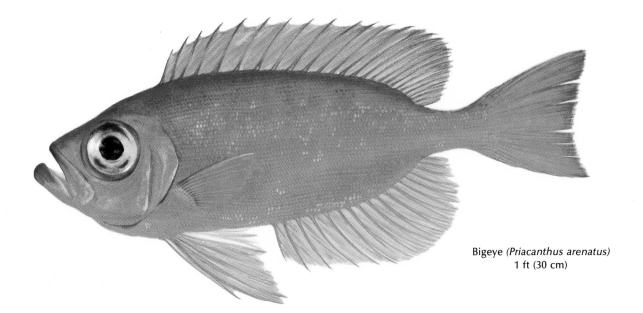

Bigeye *(Priacanthus arenatus)*
1 ft (30 cm)

A common, widely distributed species in Indo-Pacific waters is *P. hamrur*. The popeye catalufa, *Pristigenys serrula*, is a Pacific species ranging from the Gulf of California southward to Peru and the Galápagos Islands.

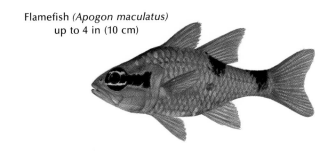

Flamefish *(Apogon maculatus)*
up to 4 in (10 cm)

Family Apogonidae
cardinalfishes

Cardinalfishes are small, averaging less than 4 inches in length (a few grow to 8 inches). They are mainly reef dwellers, but some species live in mountain streams in the Pacific. Most are red, some brownish, and their large eyes mark them as nocturnal. Their two dorsal fins—the first spiny, the second soft-rayed—are widely separated. The anal fin has three prominent spines. Most cardinalfishes carry their eggs in their mouths until they hatch. In some species, only the male performs this duty; in others, the female or both sexes.

A number of cardinalfishes have the unusual habit of associating with mollusks. The conchfish, *Astropogon stellatus*, about 2 inches long, is common in the Caribbean and off the lower Florida coasts. In addition to hiding in conch shells, from which it gets its name, it may frequent the inner cavities of sponges.

Another species prevalent in tropical Atlantic waters is the barred cardinalfish, *Apogon binotatus*, distin-

guished by the black bars on the rear of its body. It reaches a length of 4 inches.

About a dozen species of apogonids are recorded from tropical Atlantic waters. An equal number are known from the Indo-Pacific. One of the most striking of these is *A. semiornatus*, a 2-inch species. Its large eyes are circled with blue, and a black stripe extends from just in front of the first dorsal fin through the base of the second dorsal; another runs from the rear of the eye to the fork of the caudal fin; a third, obliquely from the rear of the eye to the base of the anal fin.

Another common genus of the Indo-Pacific region is *Ostorhinchus*. Most species are striped, the stripes extending onto the fins. Several members of the genus *Apogonichthyoides*, common in weedy waters and tidal pools, are distinguished by the large eyespot behind each gill cover or on their fins. While most species have forked tails, species of *Asperapogon, Neamia, Foa*, and *Fowleria* typically have rounded caudal fins.

Family Percidae
perches

To many people, perches and their larger cousins are the most flavorful freshwater fishes. But by far the largest number of species in the family are much too small to be eaten. These are the literally hundreds of species of darters, few of them more than 4 inches long, that are swift bottom-dwellers inhabiting streams. All members of the family, found in Europe and North America, share basic features, however. Their body is typically long and slender, and the two dorsal fins are distinctly separate. The anal fin has one or two spines, and the pelvic fins are located far forward, near the throat. The gill covers end in sharp, spinelike points; the heavy, ctenoid scales are toothed along their exposed margins.

Yellow perch *(Perca flavescens)*
7 to 16 in (18 to 41 cm)

Walleye *(Stizostedion vitreum)*
15 in (38 cm)

The yellow perch, *Perca flavescens*, is abundant in the eastern and midwestern United States, as far west as Kansas and across central and eastern Canada. It has been introduced to waters in the West. The yellow perch prefers ponds and lakes but may also occur in sluggish, weedy streams, the larger fish staying in deeper water. The yellowish color and the seven vertical black bars are distinctive. The pelvic and anal fins are orange or red. The head is concave just over the eyes, then slopes upward sharply to the dorsal fin. The lack of canine teeth further distinguishes it from the young of others members of the family with which it might be confused. Also, the yellow perch is more deep-bodied than most members of the family. The average size is 8 ounces or less, but a record catch of 4 pounds 3½ ounces was made in New Jersey in 1865.

Yellow perches are caught on both natural and artificial baits, and they feed throughout the year. Many are caught through the ice in winter. They travel in small schools, so that catching one is an indication that more are there for the taking. When abundant in small lakes or ponds, yellow perches may be stunted, with the typical large head and small, thin body. But a fat yellow perch makes a superb panfish meal.

Females lay their eggs in long strings in the weedy shallows in early spring. They do not make nests. A half-pound female may lay as many as 15,000 eggs; larger ones may lay as many as 48,000 eggs. The young travel in schools from the start, but large groups soon break up into smaller ones.

The European perch, *P. fluviatilis*, is similar to the North American yellow perch in appearance and habits. It averages slightly larger in size, however. The European perch occurs throughout central and northern Europe, its range extending also into Siberia.

The walleye, *Stizostedion vitreum*, is the largest member of the perch family, averaging about 2 pounds in weight but with catches up to 10 pounds not uncommon. The record catch on rod and reel weighed nearly 25 pounds and was taken from a lake in Tennessee. Walleyes range from the Mackenzie River, Hudson Bay, and Labrador southward to the Alabama and Tennessee rivers. They prefer cold waters, but the largest come from near the southern limits of their range, where they inhabit the deep waters of lakes.

Walleyes travel in schools, like the yellow perch, and catching one indicates that more are probably nearby. The walleye's eyes are distinctive—large and milky, or opaque. When a light is shone on them at night, they glow like a cat's eyes. The mouth is large and filled with long, sharp teeth, like a pike's, identifying the walleye as a predator. The usual color is olive or yellowish, but color varies considerably depending on where the fish is living. The sides are usually mottled with black or brown, the markings in no definite pattern, and a distinct dark blotch appears on the last rays of the first dorsal fin. The pelvic fins are generally yellowish.

Walleyes feed the year round. In winter, they are caught through the ice, with minnows the favorite bait. At other times of the year trolling is usually most productive, particularly at night when the walleyes move into shallower water to feed. In the big lakes of the South, the giant manmade reservoirs, walleyes generally stay in deep water. They are caught by deep trolling, usually with wire lines to get the bait or lure deep enough and to be able to pull the fish up successfully. Because of their sharp teeth, walleyes can cut through ordinary leaders with ease. They will take either artificial or natural baits.

Spawning occurs in spring, the fishes moving into streams or rocky shallows, where the females scatter their eggs over the bottom. The average number of eggs laid by a female is about 50,000, but a large female can produce as many as half a million eggs.

The blue pike, *S. vitreum glaucum*, is a recognized subspecies found in the Great Lakes. It differs from the walleye mainly in color—bluish rather than yellow—and it is smaller. Three pounds is about maximum.

Sand tilefish *(Malacanthus plumieri)*
1 ft (30 cm)

Saugers, *S. canadense*, are small versions of the walleye. They have small black dots on the first dorsal fin but lack the dark blotch at the rear. The markings on the sides tend to be well organized, forming vertical bars. Saugers average less than a pound in weight. Fish weighing 2 pounds are taken with regularity, however, and the record catch weighed over 8 pounds. The sauger can tolerate more silted waters than can the walleye, which prefers clear lakes. In habits, however, saugers resemble walleyes.

Other large members of the perch family include the pikeperch, *Lucioperca lucioperca*, of cold lakes and ponds in northern Europe and Siberia. It reaches a length of 1½ feet. The ruffe, *Acerina cernua*, of the same region, is smaller, rarely as much as a foot long.

All remaining members of the family, more than 80 species in North America, are referred to collectively as darters. As a group they are easily recognized, but the species are difficult to differentiate. Most species belong to the genus *Etheostoma*, many of which are brightly colored—as is the rainbow darter, *E. caeruleum*.

The logperch, *Percina caprodes*, is a dusky small fish with broad brownish black bars across its body. Widely distributed, it is commonly seen when rocks are picked up in riffles in streams. *Percina* is represented by nearly two dozen species in North America.

Sand darters, *Ammocrypta*, show a preference for sand-bottomed areas of streams.

Family Branchiostegidae
tilefishes

Fewer than a dozen species comprise this family, which is worldwide in distribution. Sometimes referred to as blanquillos, they are found mainly in the tropics, but some species range into temperate waters. Most are less than 2 feet long, their bodies slim. The anal and dorsal fins are long and low; the pelvic fins are located far forward, directly under the pectorals. Tilefishes are closely related to sea basses.

The best-known member of the family is the tilefish,

Lopholatilus chamaeleonticeps, which lives in waters from 300 to 1,200 feet deep where it feeds on crustaceans and small fishes. Beginning with its discovery in 1879, the tilefish supported a sizable fishery from Massachusetts southward to Virginia, the fishermen making their hauls with trawl nets operated at the edge of the continental shelf. In 1882 billions of dead tilefishes floated mysteriously to the surface, presumably killed by some shift in ocean currents bringing in abnormally cold water. Some of the dead fishes weighed as much as 50 pounds. For many years afterward the tilefish could no longer be caught in the traditional fishing grounds. The population has slowly recovered sufficiently to permit commercial harvests.

The tilefish, which regularly attains a length of 3 feet and a weight of 30 pounds, is attractively colored. The back and sides are bluish or greenish gray, sprinkled with yellow spots. The belly and cheeks are rose, grading into white at the midline. The dorsal fin is marked with yellow spots, and a bright yellow tab of skin and flesh rises just in front of the dorsal fin. A similar flap of flesh occurs at the hind margin of the lower jaw. The pectoral fins are dark and margined with black, as is the anal fin.

The sand tilefish, *Malacanthus plumieri*, averaging 12 inches in length and occasionally 24 inches long, is a slim, almost eel-like fish found in reefs and sandy areas of warm Caribbean and Florida waters, rarely deeper than 50 feet. Like the tilefish, it has low, long dorsal and anal fins. The upper and lower lobes of the caudal fin are extended almost into filaments—much more prominently so than in the tilefish. The sand tilefish is light brown above and silvery below, marked with vertical bluish bars, the last of which forms a distinct blotch in front of the caudal fin.

A similar species to the sand tilefish is *M. hoedtii* of the western Pacific. Its tail, squared across the end, is white in the middle and has black upper and lower lobes. Another similar species, *M. latovittatus*, occurs in the Indo-Pacific region.

The ocean whitefish, *Caulolatilus princeps*, found from British Columbia southward to Peru, is the only

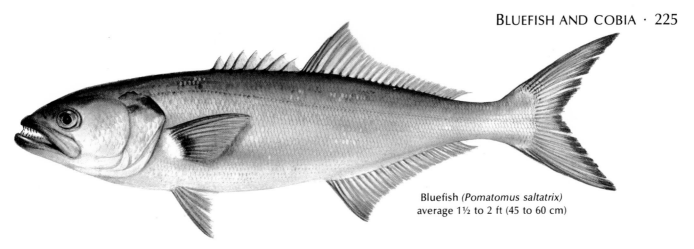

Bluefish *(Pomatomus saltatrix)*
average 1½ to 2 ft (45 to 60 cm)

representative of the family in eastern Pacific waters. Reaching a length of about 3½ feet, it provides considerable sport for fishermen, particularly in winter months. It is also caught commercially and sold in markets. The ocean whitefish has a comparatively small mouth. The back and sides are usually brown, the belly light. The fins are yellowish, tinged or streaked with blue or green.

Family Pomatomidae
bluefish

The only member of its family, the bluefish, *Pomatomus saltatrix*, a schooling, pelagic species, is reputedly the most voracious and cannibalistic fish in the sea. It ranges widely through warm and temperate waters of the world but is not found off the coast of Europe or off the west coasts of North and South America. The bluefish travels in schools, following mehadens, mackerels, herrings, or other fishes on which it feeds. As a result it is at times abundant in an area and at times absent. Off the coast of Florida, for example, bluefishes are generally plentiful in winter. They move northward in summer, and by September schools are as far north as Massachusetts. With cooler weather, schools of bluefishes move southward again. Some years the schools do not appear as usual, and it is presumed that the fishes have simply shifted their migration pattern. In July and August mature fishes travel offshore to spawning areas. Apparently, three separate breeding populations live along the North American coast. The northern group spawn from about two miles offshore to the continental shelf. The eggs drift along with plankton in the upper reaches of the ocean and hatch about forty-eight hours after fertilization. The life history of the bluefish is imperfectly known.

Bluefishes average only about 3 pounds in weight. Specimens weighing 10 pounds are not uncommon, however; in days gone by, fishes weighing as much as 50 pounds were reported. In recent years, the rod-and-reel bluefish record weighed 31 pounds 12 ounces, taken at Hatteras Inlet, North Carolina. Young fishes weighing a pound or less are called snappers; when about a foot long, they are called harbor blues, or tailors.

The bluefish has a fairly long, stout body, and the belly is flat-sided. It is an iridescent greenish blue above with silvery sides and white belly. The fins are dark, except the pelvic fins, which are whitish like the belly. The head and mouth are large, the canine teeth more or less conical. The second dorsal and the anal fins are of nearly equal size and shape, and there is a black blotch at the base of the pectoral fins. The caudal fin is deeply forked.

Large schools of bluefishes keep in constant, swift motion, charging into shoals of small fishes and turning the water turbulent as the prey is chopped into pieces. Generally a bluefish school moves off and then comes back for seconds, giving the smaller fishes enough time to reassemble. Also, they will pick up pieces of their cut prey off the bottom.

Fishermen rate the bluefish highly as a fighter and also as one of the tastiest catches from the sea. When bluefish schools are known to be in an area, they may be lured and held in a fishing location by chumming. They are caught by trolling, still fishing, surf casting, jigging—hungry bluefishes are not particular about how food is presented and will take both artificial and natural baits. Commerical fishermen catch them in nets.

Family Rachycentridae
cobia

The cobia, *Rachycentron canadum*, like the bluefish, is the only representative of its family. A long, slim fish, the cobia has a striking resemblance to the remora but lacks the sucking disk on the top of the body. The cobia's average weight is less than 10 pounds, but a rod-and-reel record weighed 110 pounds 5 ounces and measured 5 feet 3 inches in length.

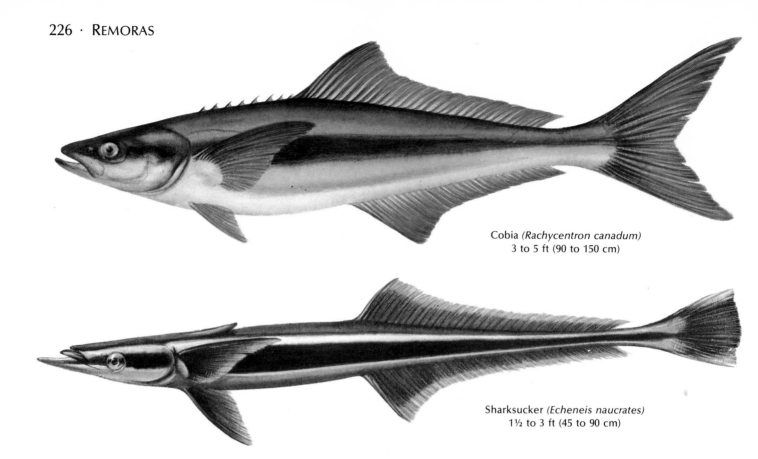

Cobia *(Rachycentron canadum)*
3 to 5 ft (90 to 150 cm)

Sharksucker *(Echeneis naucrates)*
1½ to 3 ft (45 to 90 cm)

The cobia has a very flat head and a big mouth, the lower jaw projecting slightly beyond the upper. A dark stripe extends through the eye and along the side to the tail, tapering at the end. Another, lighter stripe runs from the pectoral fins to the tail, which is broadly forked. The basic color is olive brown on the back and sides down to the lateral line and light to silvery below. The nine or ten spines comprising the first dorsal fin are separated and can be lifted or lowered.

Though not common anywhere, the cobia is almost cosmopolitan in warm seas. Along the Atlantic coast of North America, it may straggle as far north as Massachusetts but is most common in the Gulf of Mexico. It does not occur off the Pacific coast of North America, but it does appear in Indo-Pacific waters.

The cobia feeds on fishes and crustaceans which it finds close to the bottom. A common name for the species is crab-eater, but it goes by various other names in different regions—sergeant fish, cabio, lemon fish, black kingfish, and others. Sometimes it travels in small schools, but it is mostly a solitary fish. Few fishermen set out specifically to catch the cobia, but those who have experienced their express-train strikes and runs may become cobia converts in search of repeat performances. Cobias generally lurk near pilings, wrecks, buoys, or other such objects, stationary or floating. They can be caught with artificials but are generally taken on hooks baited with crabs or fishes.

Family Echeneidae
remoras

These slim fishes are easily recognized by the flat sucking disk on the top of their head. Developed from the first dorsal fin, the sucking disk consists of a series of ridges and spaces that create a vacuum between the remora and the surface to which it attaches—usually sharks or other fishes but sometimes the bottoms of boats or other objects. By sliding backward, the remora can increase the suction, or it can release itself by swimming forward. Remoras usually take an effortless ride with their host; and as the host feeds, the remoras dart out quickly to grab some of the scraps.

On his second voyage into the West Indies, Coumbus saw natives using remoras to catch giant sea turtles. When a big turtle was sighted basking at the surface, a remora with a line tied to its tail was let over the side of the boat. Typically it headed immediately for the turtle and fastened itself tightly to the turtle's shell. Then the turtle was carefully drawn back to the boat, the remora refusing to let loose.

The sharksucker, *Echeneis naucrates*, which averages 1½ feet but may be as much as 3 feet long and weigh up to 2 pounds, is the largest member of the family. Worldwide in distribution in warm seas, it is gray with a broad, white-edged black band down each side, tapering to the tail.

Also cosmopolitan is the remora, *Remora remora*, up to 12 inches long but usually shorter. It is dark with a light stripe down each side. Most species in the family will attach to a variety of fishes or other animals, but some show distinct preferences. The whalesucker, *R. australis*, for example, generally fastens itself to a whale. The spearfish remora, *R. brachyptera*, most commonly attaches to billfishes, such as marlins.

Family Carangidae
jacks and pompanos

This important family, comprised of more than 200 species, has representatives in both temperate and tropical seas throughout the world, a few straying into brackish or even fresh waters. Shape and color vary greatly within the family. Some resemble mackerels and are equally swift; they lack the distinguishing row of finlets, however. Many have extremely small scales, but at the end of the lateral line these are enlarged to form a keel. Usually, too, there are two spines in front of the anal fin. The tail is forked. Jacks are generally most abundant in inshore waters. The young travel in schools, but the adult fishes of most species are solitary.

The leatherjacket, *Oligoplites saurus*, about a foot long, is a mackerel-like member of the jack family found on both the Atlantic and Pacific coasts of North America, most abundantly where the water is warm but straying northward in summer. The spiny dorsal fin consists of five separate spines, and there are two anal spines in front of the soft-rayed portion of the anal fin. Both soft-rayed fins are broken into finlets at the rear. The leatherjacket is bluish green above and silvery below; the fins are yellowish. On light tackle, the leatherjacket is an exciting fish to catch.

The yellowtail, *Seriola dorsalis*, is another jack that resembles a mackerel in body shape. Averaging about 2 feet in length and weighing 10 pounds, but occasionally exceeding 5 feet in length and weighing more than 50 pounds (a record catch weighed 111 pounds), the yellowtail is one of the most highly esteemed game fish off the California coast, ranging from southern Washington southward to Chile. A prominent yellow stripe extends from eye to tail. The back and sides are a metallic blue-green, the belly silvery, and the tail yellowish green. It is caught by trolling or casting and is noted for its powerful runs and deep dives. If allowed to reach the shelter of rocks or kelp, the fish may be lost. Yellowtails are also caught commercially, mainly in Mexican waters. A very similar species (considered by some authorities to be the same species) is *S. grandis*, found abundantly in Australian and New Zealand waters.

About a dozen other species of *Seriola* roam the warm waters of the world. The largest is the greater amberjack, *S. dumerili*, known in some regions as the horse-eye bonito. Averaging about 15 pounds in weight, it commonly exceeds 50 pounds and is reported to attain a weight of 170 pounds. A rod-and-reel record weighed 149 pounds. Ranging from the Carolinas southward to Brazil, the amberjack is abundant off the coasts of Florida and in nearby Caribbean waters.

Live fishes display a conspicuous yellow or coppery band that extends from the upper jaw to the tail. This disappears when the fish dies. Above the lateral line, the sides and the back are blue, almost purple; below, silvery. A black line runs obliquely from the upper jaw through the eye to the top of the head, joining a similar stripe from the opposite side and forming an inverted "V." These bands of black, commonly referred to as fighter stripes, stand out prominently in live fishes, particularly when they are excited. Amberjacks are caught on spoons, bucktails, and other artificials but are most usually fished for with small fishes or squids and by drifting or trolling. Commonly the area is chummed prior to fishing, and sometimes the first fish caught is

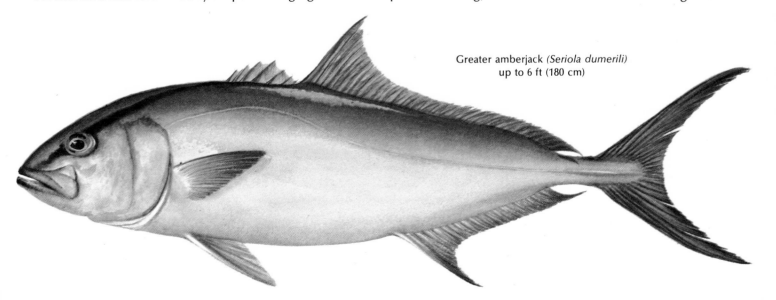

Greater amberjack *(Seriola dumerili)*
up to 6 ft (180 cm)

left in the water to attract others. Like most members of the jack family, the amberjack hits hard and is a strong fighter.

The lesser amberjack, *S. fasciata*, rarely exceeds 10 pounds in weight and averages less. It is the smallest amberjack. It rates high as a sport fish, however, making up for its smallness by vigor. The lesser amberjack lives in warm Atlantic waters.

The similar almaco jack, *S. rivoliana*, is found in the Mediterranean. Some taxonomists consider this fish to be the same species as the lesser amberjack.

The banded rudderfish, *S. zonata*, occurs in the Atlantic from the Caribbean northward to as far as Massachusetts and southward to Brazil. Like the pilotfish, which it resembles, this species is found around floating objects or even in company with sharks. It is typically an inshore fish, however; the pilotfish is found offshore. Older fishes are bluish or brown; the young are generally banded, including a dark, oblique bar through the eye to just in front of the first dorsal fin. The average length is about 12 inches, though occasional individuals may be 2 or even 3 feet long.

The fish most commonly seen following sharks and ships in all warm seas is the pilotfish, *Naucrates ductor*. Its bluish gray body is crossed with 5–7 broad dark bars that continue on to the second dorsal and the anal fins. The first dorsal fin is reduced to 3–5 very short spines. The pilotfish was once believed to lead sharks to their food. To the contrary, the pilotfish follows larger fishes to feed on scraps left over from their meals, or it may pick off infesting parasites. The pilotfish must be fast and agile to keep from being eaten by the shark. On hook and line, the pilotfish puts up a good fight but is not ordinarily fished for. It measures about 12 inches in length—rarely to as much as 2 feet long.

Rainbow runners, *Elagatis bipinnulata*, are swift, slim members of the jack family. They are so streamlined, in fact, that they look unlike other jacks. Behind the second dorsal fin is a single finlet; another is located behind the anal fin. Above the lateral line, the body is bluish; below, yellowish. Two intense, iridescent blue lines extend the full length of the body. Found in all warm seas, the rainbow runner may reach a length of about 4 feet. The rod-and-reel record weighed 30 pounds 15 ounces, but the average specimen is only about 2 feet long and weighs less than 4 pounds. Rainbow runners are not ordinarily fished for, but they are commonly caught on baits or lures trolled for other species.

Still another slim jack is the round scad, *Decapterus punctatus*. Its caudal peduncle bears a dorsal and a ventral finlet, and enlarged scales, or scutes, at the end of the lateral line form a keel along each side of the peduncle. The second or soft dorsal and the anal fins are about the same size and shape. The round scad, so called because its body is nearly round in cross-section, is greenish above and silvery below, with a thin brown line from snout to tail. The sides of the head are yellowish. It is found in the warm Atlantic, sometimes straying as far north as Massachusetts and as far south as southern Brazil.

Occurring in the same waters with the round scad is the toothless mackerel scad, *D. macarellus*. Neither species is more than a foot long. The Mexican scad, *D.*

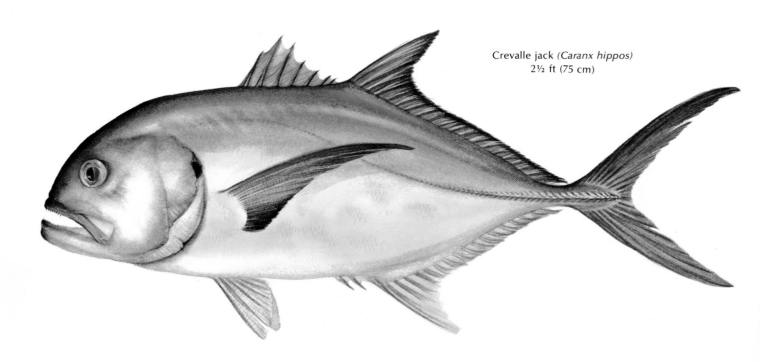

Crevalle jack *(Caranx hippos)*
2½ ft (75 cm)

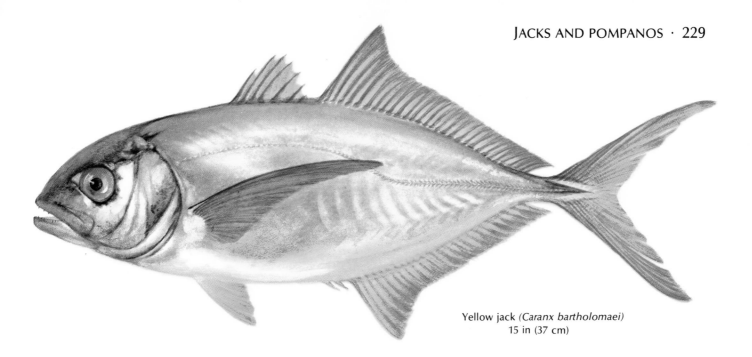

Yellow jack *(Caranx bartholomaei)*
15 in (37 cm)

hypodus, about the same size, is found in the Pacific—from Baja California southward to Panama. In Indo-Pacific waters, *D. lajang* and *D. russellii* are similar.

The slender-bodied jack mackerel, *Trachurus symmetricus*, ranges from British Columbia to Mexico. It is often abundant off the California coast, where it contributes to a sizable commercial fishery. The jack mackerel may weigh as much as 4 pounds and measure 2 feet in length; most are smaller. It is an iridescent bluish green above, often mottled with a darker color; the sides and belly are silvery.

The crevalle jack, *Caranx hippos*, averages 2 pounds or less in weight, but it is not uncommon for individuals to weigh as much as 10 pounds; the record exceeds 50 pounds. A widely distributed species, it is found in the Caribbean and warm waters of the Atlantic, straggling into cooler regions in summer. In the Pacific it occurs from the Gulf of California to Peru and is found also in Hawaiian waters and along the coast of Asia. This species belongs to the group of jacks that have a high, greatly compressed body rather than a slim body like mackerels. The soft dorsal and anal fins are almost identical in size, and the sharply decurved lateral line ends in large scales, or scutes, that form a keel along each side. The pectoral fins are long and curved, and a distinctive black spot appears at the rear margin of each operculum. Another black spot, less pronounced, is located at the base of each pectoral fin. Just in front of the pelvic fins is a triangular patch of scales on the otherwise smooth belly. The forehead is distinctively blunt. The back and sides are bluish green with a bronze cast, the sides silvery or tinged with yellow. In many, the anal fin is yellow.

Crevalle jacks are common in inshore waters and also occur in the open sea. They are caught both by casting and by trolling and on artificial as well as natural baits, usually when fishing for other species. A hooked crevalle jack gives a good account of itself, some fishermen vouching that it is the toughest scrapper of the inshore fishes. When young, it travels in schools, hence one catch can generally be followed by at least several more.

The genus *Caranx* contains dozens of other species, most of them similar in appearance and habits. The yellow jack, *C. bartholomaei*, of the Caribbean and warm Atlantic and sometimes straying into cooler waters, has the typical bluish back of the jacks, but the sides are strongly golden yellow, even more noticeably so in fishes after they die. The fins are also yellow. In contrast to the crevalle jack, it has no black spot on the operculum. The yellow jack averages less than 2 pounds in weight but may occasionally weigh as much as 15 pounds.

The green jack, *C. caballus*, is a Pacific species found from extreme southern California to Peru. It averages less than 16 ounces in weight and never exceeds 5 pounds. It is distinctly greenish, with a black spot at the hind margin of the operculum.

Also averaging less than a pound in weight, the blue runner, *C. crysos*, is found in the Atlantic. Actually more greenish than blue, it is similar to the crevalle jack and has a black spot on the operculum. It is distinguished by being somewhat slimmer and also by having a lower forehead. Some biologists consider the blue runner and the green jack the same species.

The bar jack, *C. ruber*, also sometimes called runner, resembles the blue runner but is generally more south-

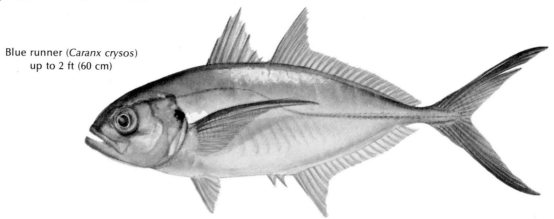

Blue runner (*Caranx crysos*)
up to 2 ft (60 cm)

ern in distribution. It has fewer (less than 40) large scales in the keel along the caudal peduncle, and they are not as prominent as they are in the blue runner. There is a dark bluish band along the base of the dorsal fin and a dark bar on the lower lobe of the caudal fin.

The horse-eye jack, *C. latus*, is distributed widely in the warm Atlantic and also in Indo-Pacific waters. There is considerable confusion regarding this species, some authorities not differentiating it from the crevalle jack.

Those who make the distinction do so mainly on the greater amount of scales on the breast of the horse-eye.

The cavalla, *C. ajax*, also called white ulua, is common in Hawaiian waters. Silvery with a whitish blotch at the base of the pectoral fins, it has a high forehead and a projecting lower jaw. The cavalla averages less than 2 pounds in weight but may occasionally weigh as much as 15 pounds. It is more solitary than most jacks.

The ulua, *C. stellatus*, also called spotted jack, is

Permit *(Trachinotus falcatus)*
up to 3 ft (90 cm)

abundant in Hawaiian waters and throughout the western Pacific; it occurs also off the coast of Mexico. Dark spots are scattered over the body, which is bluish green above and silvery below. This is the giant of the jack family, with reports of individuals weighing as much as 150 pounds. Specimens of 50 pounds are common.

The pauu'u, *C. ignobilis*, is another species prevalent in Hawaiian waters but also occurring throughout the Indo-Pacific region. The cheeks and the upper half of the gill covers are scaled, and there is a patch of scales on the breast. The forehead is steep. The pauu'u may reach a length of 2 feet but is usually smaller.

The trevally, *C. georgianus*, is an Australian species that is placed in the genus *Usacaranx* by some authorities. An abundant and popular fish with sport fishermen, it is silvery and has a subdued keel on each side of the caudal peduncle. The average size is 2 pounds, with occasional individuals weighing as much as 10 pounds.

Of all the jacks—and to many people, of all the fishes in the sea—the Florida pompano, *Trachinotus carolinus*, is by far the most delicately flavored. It is netted commercially, bred in ponds, and sold for high prices in markets and restaurants. It is also caught on hook and line with small artificials (bucktails or jigs) or with sand fleas, clams, or similar natural baits. On light tackle, the pompano makes an exciting catch; some weigh 3 pounds or even as much as 5 or 7 pounds, but most weigh a pound or less. Pompanos are abundant in the warm waters of Florida and the Caribbean and range from Brazil to Massachusetts. They usually travel in schools close to shore and are generally caught in the surf. The body is very deep and flattened; the mouth is small. The back and sides above the lateral line are bluish gray; below, silvery grading into yellow. The head and throat are also yellow, as are the pelvic and anal fins. The tail is deeply forked.

The palometa, *T. goodei*, is found in the same range as the Florida pompano, differing from it in having elongated rays at the front of the dorsal and anal fins. The fins are almost falcate in shape. Also, there are fewer dorsal fin rays—19–20 as opposed to 25 in the pompano. The anal fin has 17–19 rays in contrast to 22 in the Florida pompano. The lateral line bows downward past the midline. The palometa never exceeds 3 pounds in weight.

The paloma pompano, *T. paitensis*, ranging from Peru to Redonda Beach, California, including the Galápagos Islands and the Gulf of California, reaches a length of about 20 inches. It is bluish above and silvery below.

The gafftopsail pompano, *T. rhodopus*, is found from Peru to Zuma Beach, California, including the Galápagos Islands and the Gulf of California. It grows

about 24 inches, has a silvery body and faint yellow bars on its sides.

The largest Atlantic pompano is the permit, *T. falcatus*, sometimes called the great pompano because of its exceptional size. Average weight is about 10 pounds, but it is not uncommon for this species to attain a weight of 25 pounds. Lengths of 3 feet and weights exceeding 50 pounds are reported occasionally. The rod-and-reel record is 50 pounds 8 ounces. Like other pompanos, this giant prefers warm waters and is often found in the deep waters of inlets very close to shore. It may stray northward in summer or move far down the coast of South America in winter. The fins are blackish.

The African pompano, *Alectis crinitus*, is apparently cosmopolitan in warm seas. It averages about 6 pounds in weight but may occasionally exceed 30 pounds. In this silvery species, which is not common, the first dorsal fin is lacking; the head profile is almost vertical.

The strangest Atlantic jack is the lookdown, *Selene vomer*, which has an exceptionally thin, flat body and an unusually high forehead. The mouth is low on the face, the eyes high. The first rays of the second dorsal fin are extended into filaments that go beyond the caudal fin. The first rays of the anal fin are also long and threadlike but not as long as those from the dorsal fin. The sides are silvery iridescent. Lookdowns average less than a pound, but now and then a 3-pounder is reported.

Moonfishes, both the Atlantic, *Vomer setapinnis*, and the Pacific, *V. declivifrons*, are much like the lookdown in general appearance. The head is distinctly concave in profile, however, and there are no extensions on the dorsal and anal fins. Moonfishes average only about a pound in weight.

The Atlantic bumper, *Chloroscombrus chrysurus*, of warm Atlantic and Caribbean waters is a small member of the jack family, rarely weighing more than half a pound. Its back is not high, but its belly bows down, giving the fish a broad profile in the opposite direction. The color is greenish above and yellowish on the sides and belly. There is a black spot on each gill cover. The bumper travels in schools, the fishes making simultaneous turns like a precision flight squadron. A very similar species, the Pacific bumper, *C. orqueta*, is found from Peru to San Pedro, California.

The roosterfish, *Nematistius pectoralis*, is sometimes classified in a separate family, Memastistiidae. An obvious distinguishing feature is the seven long spines on the first dorsal fin. These taper into almost threadlike filaments. Normally, these spines rest in a groove, but they are lifted whenever the fish becomes excited. Unlike most typical jacks of the same general shape, the roosterfish lacks scutes that form a keel along the caudal peduncle.

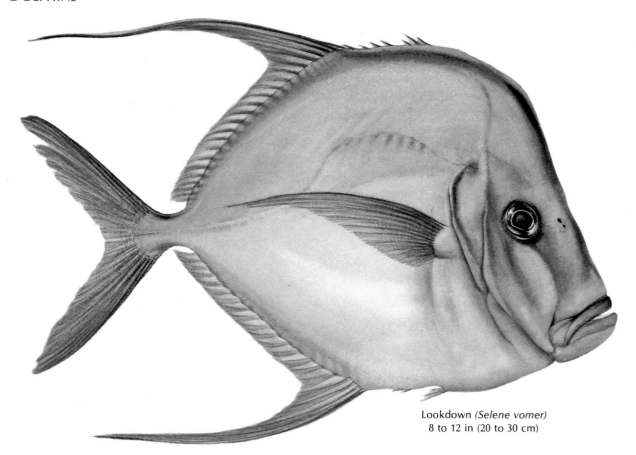

Lookdown *(Selene vomer)*
8 to 12 in (20 to 30 cm)

The silvery blue roosterfish is found only along the Pacific coast of the Americas, from southern California southward to Peru. It averages less than 15 pounds in weight but can reach a much larger size. A rod-and-reel record weighed 114 pounds. It has a prominent black spot on the lower anterior portion of the pectoral fins and vivid, dark bluish bars or bands on its sides when the fish is alive. Among Pacific Coast anglers, the roosterfish is a much-sought-after game fish. A strong fighter, giving long and powerful runs, it is also good to eat. In some coastal areas the roosterfish is caught commercially and sold in markets. It is generally found close to shore.

Family Coryphaenidae
dolphins

In a family of only two very similar species, both of which are cosmopolitan in warm seas, the dolphin, or dorado, *Coryphaena hippurus*, is the larger, averaging about 5 pounds in weight, with 20-pounders not uncommon and occasional catches exceeding 50 pounds. A record dolphin for rod and reel weighed 85 pounds and measured 5 feet 9 inches in length.

The dolphin is so distinctive in body shape and color that it cannot be mistaken for any other fish. The male, or bull, has a high, straight forehead. The female's head is also high but slopes upward to the dorsal fin, which begins far forward—almost directly over the eyes—and extends to the deeply forked caudal fin. The anal fin is also long, stretching over about half the length of the body. The streamlined body, tapering sharply from head to tail, is laterally compressed.

Generally, the dolphin's dorsal fin and back are a deep ocean blue, grading into green on the upper sides and yellow from the lateral line to the silvery belly. The sides are sprinkled with a mixture of dark and light spots. The big caudal fin and the pectoral and pelvic fins are yellow; the anal fin is usually silvery, margined with blue, as are the pelvic fins. But a color description of the dolphin is all but impossible because the fish changes color with rippling suddenness.

In addition to being one of the most beautiful fishes in the seas, the dolphin is also one of the fastest; it is said to make dashes at speeds of up to 50 miles per hour. It can, as many anglers can testify, literally make the line sing as it is ripped from the reel. Dolphins roam the open sea, where they feed on other fishes. Fishermen catch them by trolling, using either flying fishes (the dolphin's favorite food), mullets, or other natural baits, or with spoons, plugs, or jigs. Commonly, the first dolphin hooked is brought close to the boat but is left in the water to attract inquisitive companions close enough so that they can be caught, too, usually by casting.

When small, dolphins travel in schools. Most gratifying to the fisherman, a hooked dolphin leaves the water as though it didn't even belong there—tail-walking over the surface and performing a variety of twisting, turning aerial acrobatics. In the water it charges first in one

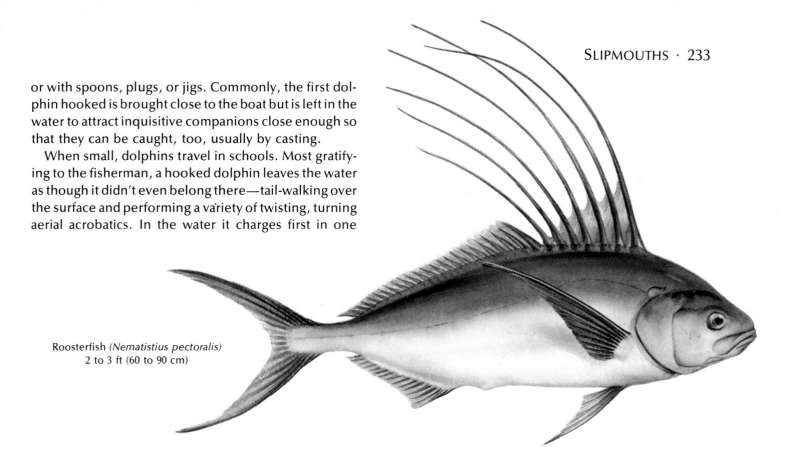

Roosterfish *(Nematistius pectoralis)*
2 to 3 ft (60 to 90 cm)

direction, then another. Keeping a tight line so that the fish cannot throw the hook is truly difficult. It is one of the most delicious of all fishes, whether fried, baked, broiled, or chowdered. Amazingly, not many years ago, the dolphin was considered inedible.

At various times over the years more than a dozen different species of dolphins have been recognized. It is now generally agreed that there are only two. The other is the pompano dolphin, *C. equisetis*, which is rarely more than 2 feet long and which does not have a high forehead. As a further distinction, the pompano dolphin has fewer than 55 rays in its dorsal fin and fewer than 26 in its anal fin. The larger species has more in each—to 65 in the dorsal fin and to 30 in the anal fin.

Family Leiognathidae
slipmouths

This is a family of small, slimy, mostly marine fishes of the Indo-Pacific. They give off a "soapy" mucus when handled. Slipmouths are important primarily as forage fishes because of their abundance. Occasionally, however, they are netted for eating. Their name comes from the exceptionally long, protrusible mouth, which is extended tubelike when the fish feeds. Both the dorsal and anal fins have spines along their bases. Another peculiarity, slipmouths have luminous organs around the esophagus, the light produced by bacteria.

One of the largest species is *Leiognathus equula*, which may attain a length of 12 inches. Most species of *Leiognathus* and also of *Gazza* and *Secutor*, the two other common genera, are less than 6 inches long.

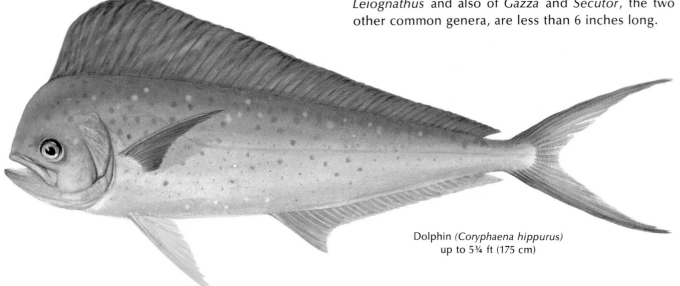

Dolphin *(Coryphaena hippurus)*
up to 5¾ ft (175 cm)

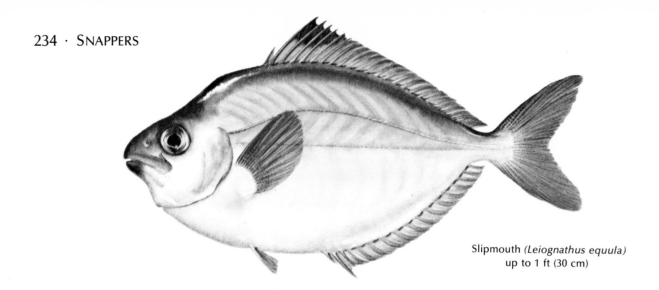

Slipmouth *(Leiognathus equula)*
up to 1 ft (30 cm)

Family Lutjanidae
snappers

More than 250 species comprise this important family of fishes found in warm seas throughout the world. Some are valued as commercial species, others as sport fishes. Snappers are distinguished from sea basses and grunts, often found with them, by their pointed pectoral fins, ten spines in the first dorsal fin, which is joined to the second dorsal, and two or three spines in the anal fin. In most species the tail is forked. The mouth is large, and the eyes are set high on the head. The lateral line is distinct, and the scales are large. Many species resemble one another so closely that identification is difficult.

Of the North American species, the most valuable commercially is the red snapper, *Lutjanus campechanus*, inhabiting water 150 feet deep or deeper from Florida and particularly the Gulf of Mexico southward to Brazil. The red snapper is caught almost totally with hand lines. Many snapper boats from Florida ports sell fishing spaces aboard their boats to fishermen and then buy back their catches at a specified rate per pound. Those who get pleasure from bringing in the fishes all day can have their fun and make money at the same time. The skippers of the boats locate the shoals of fishes by using fathometers, and as long as the boat stays over the snappers, fishes can be hauled in literally as fast as a line can be dropped down to their level and brought out again. Most red snappers weigh about 5 pounds, but 20-pound catches are not uncommon. An occasional fish weighing 30 to 40 pounds is taken.

The red snapper is bright red, even to its eyes and fins. It is sometimes tinged with bluish green on the back, grading into pinkish on the belly. There is a diffuse black spot at the base of each pectoral fin, and the dorsal and caudal fins may be edged with black. The caudal fin is sharply angular at the tips and in the central

V. The similar silk snapper, *L. vivanus*, of the Caribbean is also red but has a yellow tail.

About a dozen other species of *Lutjanus* occur in warm Atlantic, Gulf, and Caribbean waters, and there are as many or more in Indo-Pacific waters. All are schooling fishes, a few attaining a weight of 30 or 40 pounds but most of them weighing 1 to 3 pounds. Many species are caught by fishermen, both for fun and for food.

The mutton snapper, *L. analis*, which averages about 3 pounds but which may weigh as much as 25 pounds, is prevalent in Florida and Caribbean waters, straying as far south as Brazil and as far north as Massachusetts. Like all the essentially reef-dwelling snappers, the mutton snapper can change color. Basically, however, it is olive green, with seven darker vertical bars on its sides. These are usually prominent when the fish is resting on the bottom but disappear when it swims in the open.

Like all snappers (excluding the red snapper), the mutton snapper is caught by bottom fishing. Cut mullets or shrimps are common baits, and the area is frequently chummed to attract fishes. It will also take bucktails, jigs, or similar artificials. These are fished deep or bounced along the bottom with a jerky retrieve. Like snappers, the mutton snapper is good to eat.

The gray snapper, *L. griseus*, is probably best known in Florida as the mangrove snapper. It averages only about a pound in weight, though fishes up to 3 pounds are not uncommon. Though rare, fishes weighing more than 15 pounds have been caught. This is the most common snapper inhabiting Florida's mangrove shores, and it is also caught in deeper waters around reefs. It is found throughout the Caribbean, southward to Brazil and sometimes straggling as far northward as North Carolina. In shallow waters it is bluish or grayish green, with dark vertical bars along the sides. In deeper water it generally becomes reddish. The fins are pinkish or flesh-colored.

The cubera snapper, *L. cyanopterus*, resembles the gray but is larger, with fishes weighing as much as 50 pounds not uncommon and reports of individuals weighing twice as much. The cubera ranges from Florida southward to Brazil, but the greatest concentration is in waters off Cuba.

Among the common *Lutjanus* species of the Indo-Pacific are the 3-foot, reddish Roman, or red, snapper, *L. argentimaculatus*, which is caught both for sport and for food; the yellowish *L. johni*; and the very striking emperor snapper, *L. sebae*, which is mostly white but has three broad oblique stripes across its body. The dorsal and anal fins are margined with red. The upper lobe of the caudal fin is tipped with red, and the lower lobe is the termination of one of the diagonal stripes. A number of the Indo-Pacific species of *Lutjanus* are poisonous when eaten, either in particular areas or only at some times of the year.

The yellowtail snapper, *Ocyurus chrysurus*, to 2 feet long but usually smaller (average 8 ounces but occasionally to 6 pounds or more), is easily identified by its large, deeply forked yellow tail and by the broad yellow stripe that extends from the snout through the eye and along the sides to the tail. Above the lateral line, the back and sides are bluish gray; below the lateral line, the color is light, with fine yellowish horizontal lines. The eye is red. Unlike other snappers, this species is commonly solitary, often swimming 20 feet or more above the bottom rather than hugging it as most snap-

pers do. The yellowtail snapper, ranging from Florida southward to Brazil, is also more slender than are most snappers. It is an excellent sport fish, found in large schools off Bermuda.

The vermillion snapper, *Rhomboplites aurorubens*, is found off the Atlantic coast of Florida and sometimes as far north as South Carolina. It ranges southward to Brazil, occurring throughout most of the Caribbean and also in the Gulf of Mexico. The body is elongated, and the lower jaw projects beyond the upper. The reddish sides are usually faintly lined with yellow. The dorsal, pelvic, and anal fins are red; the caudal and pectoral fins, yellow. The vermillion snapper attains a weight of 3 to 4 pounds.

Family Lobotidae
tripletails

Tripletails are close relatives of sea basses. Their name comes from the position and shape of their second dorsal and anal fin, which extend backward along the caudal peduncle so that the fishes appear to have a three-lobed, or triple, tail. The few species in the family are found only in warm seas.

The tripletail, *Lobotes surinamensis*, occurs in tropical Atlantic waters and in the Gulf of Mexico—off the coast of North America from Florida to Texas and some-

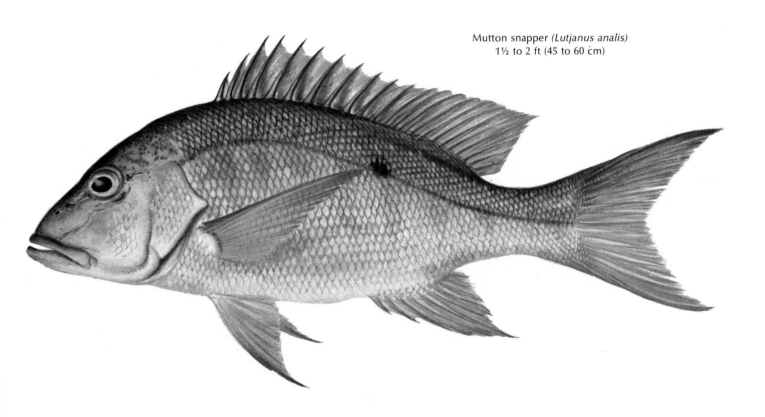

Mutton snapper *(Lutjanus analis)*
1½ to 2 ft (45 to 60 cm)

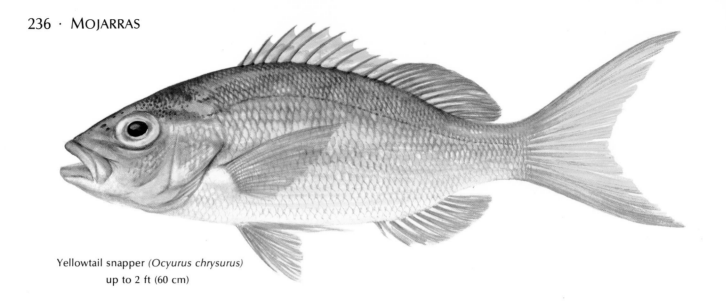

Yellowtail snapper *(Ocyurus chrysurus)*
up to 2 ft (60 cm)

times straying as far north as Massachusetts in summer. It ranges southward to Uruguay and occurs also from Africa northward to the Mediterranean and along the southern coasts of Europe. The usual color is brownish green, commonly with dark mottlings along the side. The eyes are located far forward along the short snout, and immediately behind the eyes the body slopes upward sharply so that the fish appears to have a very high forehead. The tripletail may reach a length of 3 feet and weigh as much as 50 pounds, but any fish that weighs more than 20 pounds is considered large. Most unusual, the tripletail swims on its side or floats with its head down. It is sometimes caught on live baits.

A similar species, *L. pacificus*, is found in the Pacific off Panama, and two other species inhabit Indo-Pacific waters.

Family Gerridae
mojarras

Found in all subtropical and tropical seas but most abundantly in American waters, mojarras are small, silvery fishes that have an extremely protrusible mouth. The upper jaw fits into a clearly discernible slot when the mouth is not extended or "pursed." For feeding, the mouth is protruded and directed downward. The first, or spiny, dorsal fin is high in front, sloping into the second, or soft-rayed, dorsal. The tail is forked and the body greatly compressed. Most mojarras are less than 10 inches long. They are used as bait for other fishes, or in some regions larger specimens are eaten. Mojarras are most common along sandy shores, some moving into brackish or even fresh waters.

Tripletail *(Lobotes surinamensis)*
up to 3 ft (90 cm)

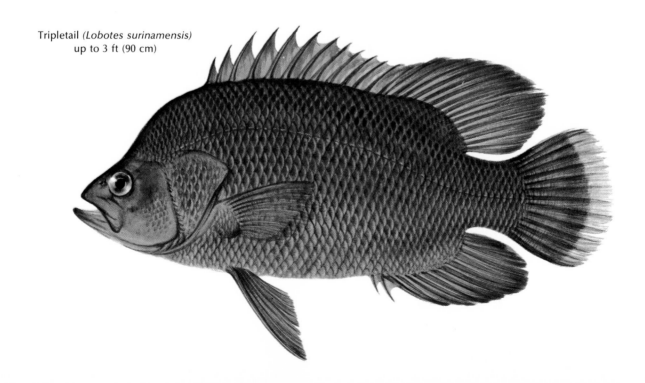

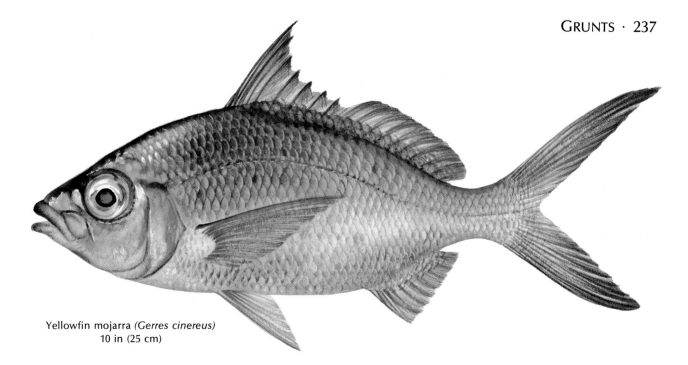

Yellowfin mojarra *(Gerres cinereus)*
10 in (25 cm)

A common species in Florida and Caribbean waters is the yellowfin, *Gerres cinereus*, sometimes but rarely as much as a foot long. Its silvery body is crossed by dark bands, most evident in young fishes. The genus *Gerres* has a number of similar representatives also in the Indo-Pacific, several as much as a foot long and locally prized as food.

The spotfin mojarra, *Eucinostomus argenteus*, is abundant off the Atlantic coast from New Jersey to Brazil and occurs also along the Pacific coast from southern California to Peru. The silver jenny, *E. gula*, is a 6-inch species prevalent in the Atlantic from the Carolinas to Brazil. Neither species, or the several others in the genus, has dark bands on the body, though some individuals may have dusky blotches.

Family Pomadasyidae
grunts

Grunts of several hundred species are abundant in warm seas throughout the world. Their name is derived from the grunting noises thay make by grinding their pharyngeal teeth, the sounds amplified by the taut swim bladder that serves as a resonator. Their pharyngeal teeth are well developed; the jaw teeth are weak. Most grunts are deep-bodied fishes. Typically they travel in schools.

Grunts are bottom-feeders. Fishermen catch them on light tackle, using shrimps, cut fishes, or other natural baits or, occasionally, artificials. Most of them are sensitive to the feel of a line and may also bite lightly, so the rigs generally used have lead weights that carry the bait

or lure to the bottom but permit the line to run freely through the weight. Fishermen typically give the bait or lure a slight motion by jerking it. This is sufficient to attract the attention of the fish. Most grunts are good to eat, but they may be ignored because of their small size. Off the coasts of the United States grunts are predominantly Atlantic species.

The French grunt, *Haemulon flavolineatum*, averages less than half a pound in weight, rarely to a pound. Abundant off the Florida coasts and in the Caribbean, it is striped longitudinally with blue and yellow. The fins are yellowish, and the inside of the mouth is red. Like many grunts, it has the habit of "kissing" others of its kind, the fishes coming face to face, pressing their open mouths together, and then pushing against each other.

Common in the same waters is the white grunt, *H. plumieri*, which is slightly larger—averaging less than a pound but sometimes weighing as much as 3 pounds. It is light bluish gray and has blue and yellow stripes like the French grunt but on the head only. Behind the head, the yellowish spots on the scales form indistinct stripes, parallel above the lateral line but slanting upward below the lateral line. As with the French grunt, the inside of the mouth is red. The fins are grayish, tinged with yellow.

The bluestriped grunt, *H. sciurus*, resembles the French grunt but may be as much as one-third larger. Also, the vertical fins are bordered with black, and the blue stripes are much broader.

The margate, *H. album*, is pearl gray, with two or three black bands running the length of its body. The most prominent of these extends from the snout through the eye to the tail. Though most individuals weigh less than a pound, the margate is known to attain a weight of 8 pounds. It may be found farther offshore than the previously described species. Also grayish is the smaller sailors choice, *H. parrai*, a typical inshore species.

Tomtates, *H. aurolineata*, are small grunts that average less than 6 inches in length but now and then reach 10 inches or more. Slim-bodied and silvery, they have a large oval black spot at the base of the caudal fin. The edges of the scales are margined with light yellow, the spots tending to form horizontal lines below the lateral line and oblique lines above it. A distinct yellow line runs from the snout through the eye to the caudal fin and another from the top of the head along the back to the rear of the soft dorsal fin. The pelvic and anal fins are yellowish. Tomtates travel in large schools and are commonly seen congregated around piers or docks.

Off the west coast of North America, there are several similar small species in the genera *Pomadasys* and *Xenistius*. In Indo-Pacific waters, the common genera are *Gaterin* and *Lethrinus*; these are sometimes classified in separate families but are similar to grunts in habits and appearance.

One of the most striking of all grunts is the black margate, *Anisotremus surinamensis*, which averages only about a pound but grows much larger. A deep-bodied fish with a small mouth and thick lips, it is silvery gray, the fins bordered or edged with black. A broad light band extends obliquely up the body behind the pectoral fins. The inside of the mouth is white.

The closely related porkfish, *A. virginicus*, found also in the warm Atlantic, is a common inshore species that attains a weight of 2 pounds but averages only about 4 ounces. It is distinguished by the two black bars on the front of the body—one from the top of the head through the eye to the rear angle of the upper jaw and the other from the base of the spiny dorsal to the base of the pectoral fin. Behind this bar, the body is striped horizontally with blue and yellow.

The sargo, *A. davidsoni*, occurs in the Pacific from Point Conception southward to Mexico. Silvery with yellow fins, it has a black bar from the spiny dorsal fin to the pectoral fin on each side.

Pigfish, *Orthopristis chrysoptera*, usually less than half a pound in weight but occasionally to as much as 2 pounds, have long anal fins, matching the soft dorsal fin in shape and in size. The head is pointed, the snout almost piglike, and the lips thin. A background color of bluish gray is marked with brassy spots in indistinct lines—horizontal below the lateral line but extending obliquely upward and backward above the lateral line. This species is caught in large numbers both on hook and line and also in nets. It is used mainly as bait for larger fishes.

Family Sparidae
porgies

Porgies are similar to grunts, but the body is even more flattened from side to side, or compressed, and high through the area just in front of the dorsal fin. As in some grunts, the eyes are located high on the head and just behind the hind margin of the mouth. The second, or soft, dorsal fin and the anal fin are both large and are about the same shape. Most of the more than a hundred

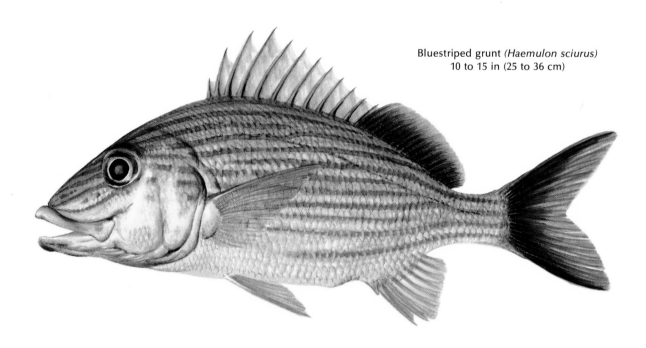

Bluestriped grunt *(Haemulon sciurus)*
10 to 15 in (25 to 36 cm)

Scup *(Stenotomus chrysops)*
average less than 10 in (25 cm)

species live in warm seas, a few ranging into cooler waters. As a group, they are worldwide in distribution.

Porgies are medium-size to small. Some live close to shore, others in offshore waters. They are prevalent around reefs, but some are found only over sandy bottoms; others inhabit rocky bottoms. Most kinds can change their colors from solid to blotched or barred and from dark to light, effecting a better camouflage against the background. They are omnivorous and typically travel in schools. Included in the group are a number of species that are harvested for food. Many also provide sport for fishermen. They are relatively easy to catch and, for their size, put up a strong fight. Porgies, like grunts, are predominantly an Atlantic species off the coast of the United States. Only the Pacific porgy is found off the West Coast.

The scup, *Stenotomus chrysops*, averages less than 10 inches in length and a pound in weight, but occasional individuals are as much as 2 feet long and weigh up to 4 pounds. Scups range from Cape Cod southward to the Carolinas, shifting northward in summer and then southward again in winter. The scup's body is about the same depth all the way to the caudal peduncle, where it narrows abruptly. The caudal fin is crescent-shaped or lunate. The body is a dull silver, with some iridescence and darker above than below. There is usually a blue streak along the base of the dorsal fin. The scup is an important commercial species that is also popular with fishermen. It is caught by bottom-fishing with shrimps, clams, crabs, or cut bait.

The jolthead porgy, *Calamus bajonado*, is one of a large group of porgies found in warm waters of the Caribbean and off southern Florida, occasionally drifting with the Gulf Stream as far north as Bermuda. It is the largest member of the genus *Calamus*, attaining a length of 2 feet and a weight of 8 to 10 pounds. The high, rounded forehead gives the body a distinctive profile, typical of the genus. It eyes are large and are located high on the head. Yellowish brown, with an almost

Porkfish *(Anisotremus virginicus)*
1 ft (30 cm)

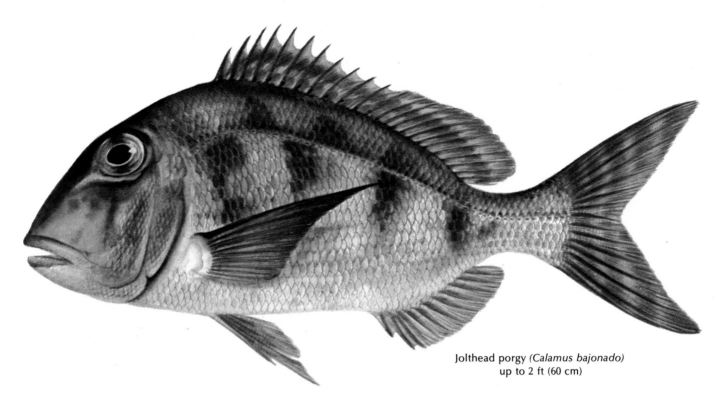

Jolthead porgy *(Calamus bajonado)*
up to 2 ft (60 cm)

metallic luster, it may be blotched with dusky splotches or nearly solid in color, depending on the bottom over which it is swimming. Some individuals are grayish. Over each eye is a blue streak, and sometimes there are faint blue lengthwise stripes on the body. Small schools of this most common of the porgies are often seen feeding near shore. The common name comes presumably from the fish's habit of using its head to bump or jolt clams or other mollusks loose from their attachments. The jolthead porgy is caught in limited numbers commercially and also by sport fishermen.

Several close relatives of the jolthead porgy live in the same region, all having the same distinctive shape. The saucereye porgy, *C. calamus*, averages about half a pound in weight but occasionally reaches a weight of a pound or more. Compared to other members of the genus, it has very small scales. Its body is deep, from top to underside—much more so than the jolthead porgy's. Its silvery sides are tinged with blue, and an intense blue or violet streak appears beneath each yellow eye. Like other porgies, the jolthead can change its color to match its background.

The littlehead porgy, *C. proridens*, to about a foot long, is bright silver. It has bright blue to violet lines on the head and rows of blue or violet spots on the sides, each with an orange spot below.

The grass porgy, *C. arctifrons*, inhabits mainly grassy areas, as its name implies, and is found most abundantly in the Gulf of Mexico. Compared to other members of

the genus, its scales are large, and the grayish body is marked with broad, dusky vertical bars. In most individuals there are yellow spots along the sides, and the fins are blotched with black. The grass porgy is usually only about 6 inches long, rarely attaining a length of 12 inches and a weight of 2 pounds.

The sheepshead porgy, *C. penna*, about the same size as the grass porgy, sometimes goes by the name littlemouth porgy. It looks much like the closely related sheepshead, described below, but the vertical bars are less intense, and the tail is more deeply forked.

The sheepshead, *Archosargus probatocephalus*, averages about a pound in weight but may attain a weight of 25 pounds and measure as much as 3 feet long. Its original range was from Massachusetts to Texas, but it now inhabits mostly southern waters. The basic color is black, including the fins, but the sides and caudal peduncle are striped alternately with broad bands of silver and black. The stripes are most prominent in young fishes. The mouth is small to medium in size, and the teeth are broad and flat for crushing the shells of crustaceans and mollusks. This is the most popular member of the porgy family with sport fishermen. Sheepsheads are usually caught with crabs, shrimps, or cut baits, and it is best to use a rig that allows the line to slip freely through the sinker. The sheepshead is wary and bites gently—so lightly, in fact, that its presence may go undetected. It can steal bait from a hook without the fisherman being aware of it. The hook must be set firmly because of the hard mouth. When hooked, a sheepshead fights gamely; it also makes excellent eating.

The sea bream, *A. rhomboidalis*, is a smaller species, usually less than a foot long, and is found only in Caribbean and in extreme southern Florida waters. Its bluish back is streaked with gold, the belly is silvery, and there is a black spot on each side just above the pectoral fins.

Pinfish, *Lagodon rhomboides*, are small, abundant porgies that rarely reach 10 inches in length. They are sometimes found as far north as Virginia but are common only in warm Florida, the Gulf of Mexico, and Caribbean waters. The sides are striped horizontally with gold, and there are broad, dusky vertical bars. A round black spot at the upper rear margin of each gill cover is distinctive. The name of the species comes from the needle-sharp spines on the first dorsal fin. All fins are yellowish. Pinfish, like many porgies, can strip a hook of bait without making enough commotion to alert the fisherman. This makes them unpopular. They are netted and sold as bait, used either whole or cut, depending on the size of the pinfish and also on the size of the fish being sought.

The spottail pinfish, *Diplodus holbrooki*, is another small porgy, averaging less than 10 inches long but with occasional larger individuals. Found in the Gulf of Mexico and in Florida waters, it is identified by the large black band across the base of the caudal peduncle and by the black margin on the gill covers. Otherwise the body is silvery, with only faint black bars. The spottail pinfish is common over rocky bottoms and around docks and piers. In the Caribbean it is replaced by the almost identical silver porgy, *D. argenteus*.

Porgies are less abundantly represented in the Pacific.

One of the most important food fishes of Japan is a porgy, however—*Chrysophrys major*. Of equal importance in Australia is *C. guttulatus*. Also popular in Australian waters is the pound-size Australian snapper, *Pagrosomus auratus*. Other common species found from Japan southward in the western Pacific are *Taius tumifrons*, *Evynnis japonica*, and *Mylio macrocephalus*. The mu, *Monotaxis grandoculis*, widely distributed in the Pacific, is an important commercial and sport species.

Still fewer species are found off the European coast, most of them occurring in the Mediterranean and southward. The toothed bream, *Dentex vulgaris*, sometimes ranges as far north as England. Usually found in deep water, it may reach a length of 3 feet and is an important commercial species. Other species of the genus *Pagellus* are found only in more southern waters.

Porgies are abundant off the coast of Africa and in Indo-Pacific waters. One of the largest is the steenbras, or musselcracker, *Pagrus nasutus*, which averages about 25 pounds but may weigh as much as 120 pounds. In older fishes, a fleshy snout overhangs the upper lip, and the broad, powerful teeth are used to crush the shells of mollusks and crustaceans. This big porgy is netted commercially and also caught on hook and line.

The red steenbras, *Petrus rupestris*, of the same region, reportedly gets even larger than the steenbras—to as much as 200 pounds. It occurs in two color phases. One is bright red above and yellow below; the other is bright yellow over the entire body.

Still another African species that goes by the name musselcracker is large for a porgy, sometimes exceeding 50 pounds in weight. This is *Sparus durbanensis*, the genus containing a number of other species that are much smaller.

Sheepshead *(Archosargus probatocephalus)*
6 to 12 in (15 to 30 cm)

Family Sciaenidae
drums

Like grunts, drums and croakers are known for the noises they make. Typically, these fishes have a muscle close to the swim bladder, and when that muscle is vibrated, the bladder acts as a resonator and amplifier for the sound. In some species, only the male can make a noise; in others, both sexes can drum or croak. Still others—specifically, members of the genus *Menti-cirrhus*—do not have a swim bladder, hence can make no noise.

Drums and croakers of about 200 species, none colorful, inhabit tropical and temperate seas. Almost all are inshore fishes usually found over sandy bottoms, either in schools or in small groups. Usually the spiny dorsal fin is separated from the soft-rayed dorsal by a deep notch, and the anal fin is short—never as long as the soft dorsal fin. The lateral line is exceptionally long, extending on to the caudal fin. Many members of the family are caught on hook and line for sport or are harvested commercially with nets. All are good to eat.

Weakfishes or sea trouts include about 15 different species in the genus *Cynoscion*. They are found along both the Atlantic and Pacific coasts of North America. These are slim-bodied and troutlike, the name weakfish describing the tender mouths from which hooks tear easily. In bringing these fishes into a boat or landing them on shore, fishermen use landing nets to keep from losing their catches.

The common species along the Atlantic coast is the weakfish, *C. regalis*, known also as sea trout, gray trout,

and squeteague. This is a popular species with sport fishermen because it responds to both natural and artificial baits and can generally be caught in respectable quantities wherever it occurs. It strikes hard and makes one or two strong runs, then usually fights less energetically, if at all, until it is about to be taken from the water. Though it averages only about a pound in weight, 3-pounders are not uncommon. The present rod-and-reel record is 19 pounds 8 ounces. This species ranges from Massachusetts to Florida and may also be found in the Gulf of Mexico. It is most abundant from the Carolinas northward to Long Island, however. Harvested commercially, it brings a high price at the market. Weakfishes—all species in the genus—are delicately flavored when freshly caught but must be eaten soon because their flesh spoils more rapidly than almost any other fish. This limits the commercial harvesting.

The spotted sea trout, *C. nebulosus*, is similar to the weakfish in size and habits but more southern in its distribution. It is the common species caught off the Florida coasts and in the Gulf of Mexico. As its name indicates, it is heavily spotted, the large, black spots occurring not only on its back and sides but also on its dorsal and caudal fins. The weakfish also has spots, but they are smaller and almost indistinct. Both species are olive to grayish above, silvery below; the background of the spotted weakfish is much lighter.

Two smaller species are also taken with regularity by fishermen. The sand sea trout, *C. arenarius*, found only in the Gulf of Mexico, seldom reaches a pound in weight. It lacks spots and has ten rays in its anal fin.

The equally small and unspotted silver sea trout, *C.*

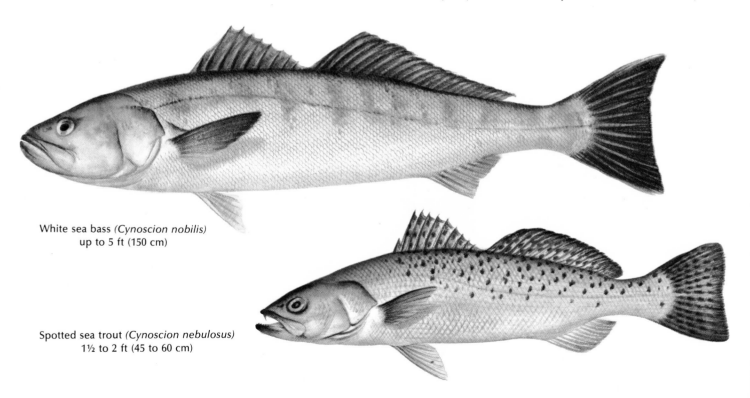

White sea bass *(Cynoscion nobilis)*
up to 5 ft (150 cm)

Spotted sea trout *(Cynoscion nebulosus)*
1½ to 2 ft (45 to 60 cm)

Red drum *(Sciaenops ocellata)*
1½ to 2½ ft (45 to 75 cm)

nothus, occurs not only in the Gulf of Mexico but also up the Atlantic coast to Chesapeake Bay. It has only eight or nine rays in its anal fin.

Off the Pacific coast from southern Alaska to Mexico and most abundantly in kelp beds, the white sea bass, *C. nobilis*, is the largest and most popular of several species in the genus. Its average weight is 10 pounds, with records to 80 pounds and lengths of 5 feet. The largest taken on rod and reel weighed 83 pounds 12 ounces. Bluish gray above and silvery below, the white sea bass typically has a dark spot at the base of each pectoral fin. As in other weakfishes, the lower jaw projects slightly beyond the upper. Like its cousins in the Atlantic, the white sea bass accommodates anglers by taking a wide variety of natural and artificial baits that can be offered by trolling, still-fishing, or casting.

The white sea bass lacks caninelike teeth in its upper jaw. It has a distinct ridge of scales on its belly, from the pelvic fins to the anus. This distinguishes it from the very similar but much larger (to 200 pounds) totuava, *C. macdonaldi*, found in Mexican waters and southward to Panama.

The orangemouth corvina, *C. xanthalus*, and the shortfin corvina, *C. parvipinnis*, are less common Pacific species that lack the ridge of scales on the belly and have distinct canine teeth. The orangemouth, which has an orange lining in its mouth, may attain a length of 2 feet or more. The smaller shortfin corvina's mouth is white inside. Its caudal fin is slightly concave rather than squared off, and it lacks spots on its body.

The silver perch, *Bairdiella chrysura*, sometimes confused with the white perch, is a common inshore species found from New York southward along the Atlantic coast and also in the Gulf of Mexico. It averages half a pound or less in weight and never more than a pound. The silver perch's silvery scales are marked with a black spot on the back and side. The fins are yellowish. Silver perches are generally abundant. Because they are

good to eat, many are harvested by commercial fishermen using nets. Hook-and-line fishermen also catch them, usually with shrimps or cut bait but also on artificials. The closely related bairdiella, *B. icistia*, native to the Gulf of California, is one of a number of marine species that have been introduced successfully into the Salton Sea.

Red drum, *Sciaenops ocellata*, also called channel bass or redfish, is found along the Atlantic coast from New Jersey to Florida and also along the Gulf coasts. It averages about 5 pounds in weight, but fishes weighing more than 10 pounds are not uncommon. A rod-and-reel record weighed 90 pounds. The smaller ones, 15 pounds or less, are sometimes called "puppy drum." The red drum is easily recognized by the large black spot at the base of its tail. The body is coppery, usually changing to a brick red after death. The nose is blunt, and the tail is square across the tip.

When small, red drums feed in rivers, sounds, and inlets. Larger fishes feed in the surf. Surf casting for big red drums is a popular sport, but many are caught also by drifting, casting, or trolling in inshore waters and on both natural and artificial baits. The red drum is not a flashy fighter, but it is stubborn and determined, persistent in heading for the bottom. The red drum has also been reported inhabiting permanent fresh water.

Black drums, *Pogonias cromis*, are the largest members of the family, attaining a weight of 125 pounds or more and a length of 4 feet. The average is less than 10 pounds. The heavy body, deepest through the pectoral fins, is silvery, crossed by five broad black vertical bands. The fins are dark. A number of short whiskers, or barbels, hang from the lower jaw.

Black drums occur in the same range as red drums but tend to be more northern. They are bottom-feeders, with a special liking for oysters that does not make them popular with commercial oystermen. The fishes are harvested commercially and also caught on hook and line. Like most drums, they can make a noise; in fact, they are perhaps the noisiest of the clan, combining their drumming with a sort of purring.

Atlantic croakers, *Micropogon undulatus*, also known in some regions as hardheads, are found from Massachusetts to Texas. They average only about a pound in weight but sometimes weigh as much as 6 to 8 pounds. Like the black drum, this species has numerous small barbels on the lower jaw. These are sensory in function, helping the fish to locate food on the bottom. Compared to the black drum, the Atlantic croaker has more rays in its soft dorsal fin: 28–29 as compared to 20–22. The middle rays of the caudal fins are longer than those above and below, giving the caudal fin a wedge-shaped appearance. The body is silvery below and greenish above, with brownish-black spots on the sides and the dorsal fins. Atlantic croakers are netted commercially and caught on hook and line. They are good to eat, which is a bonus value to a fishing trip.

The spot, *Leiostomus xanthurus*, which occurs in the same range as the Atlantic croaker, lacks chin barbels and has a round black spot above each pectoral fin. The body is somewhat deeper or stouter than the Atlantic croaker's, and the tail is slightly forked. The soft dorsal fin has more than 30 rays, the anal fin more than 12. The spot averages only about half a pound in weight, rarely as much as 2 pounds. It is netted commercially and also caught on hook and line by fishermen. When spots are abundant, it may be possible to bring in a hundred or more of these small, flavorful fishes in a short time— just as fast as a fish can be unhooked and the baited line put back into the hungry, waiting school.

The spotfin croaker, *Roncador stearnsi*, is a Pacific Coast species found from Point Conception to Baja California. As in most croakers that are bottom-feeders, the mouth is inferior—that is, the upper jaw projects beyond the lower. The spotfin croaker's long, pointed pectoral fins have a black spot at their base. The caudal fin is square-tipped. The average size of the spotfin croaker is less than a pound, but a record catch weighed more than 10 pounds. The basic color is steel gray or bluish on the back, grading into silvery white below. Some have indistinct black wavy lines on the back. Spotfins are popular with sport fishermen. They are caught from shore or from boats in inshore waters.

The yellowfin croaker, *Umbrina roncador*, another popular sport fish in California, occurs in the same range as the spotfin croaker. It also averages less than a pound in weight but is known to weigh as much as 5 pounds. Silvery and usually iridescent, it has yellow fins. Wavy olivaceous lines extend upward and backward along the sides. There is a single barbel at the tip of the lower jaw.

Black croakers, *Cheilotrema saturnum*, found in the same range as the above species and about the same size as the yellowfin croaker, have a much deeper body—more humpbacked—and though the spiny and soft-rayed dorsal fins are joined as in other croakers, the notch between them is deep. Black croakers do not have chin whiskers. The edge of the gill cover, or operculum, is black. The body is dusky with a coppery sheen, more silvery below. A faint dark band extends from the second dorsal fin to the pelvic fins on each side. This is not a common species compared to either the spotfin croaker or the yellowfin croaker.

The queenfish, *Seriphus politus*, is sometimes found north of Point Conception but is generally most abundant in the same more southern waters as the previously described croakers. Black above and silvery below, with yellowish fins, the queenfish may reach a length of a foot but is usually smaller. It is a slim, schooling species. The tip of the lower jaw extends beyond the tip of the upper jaw. There is no chin whisker, or barbel, on the lower jaw. The spiny, soft-rayed dorsal fins are widely separated, distinctive for members of the drum and

Jackknife-fish *(Equetus lanceolatus)*
up to 8 in (20 cm)

croaker family, and there is a dusky blotch at the base of each pectoral fin. The queenfish is commonly caught by anglers fishing in shallow waters. Most of the catches are accidental, and the queenfish is disdained except for bait to catch larger fishes.

The white croaker, *Genyonemus lineatus*, is another pound-size croaker of the Pacific Coast—from central California northward to British Columbia. Silvery with a brassy tinge and lighter below, it has a black spot at the base of each pectoral fin and black wavy lines along its sides. The fins are yellowish. The upper jaw projects beyond the lower, and several barbels are on the lower jaw. Like the queenfish, large numbers of white croakers are caught accidentally by sport fishermen.

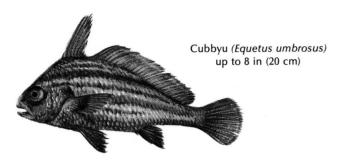

Cubbyu *(Equetus umbrosus)*
up to 8 in (20 cm)

The jackknife-fish, *Equetus lanceolatus*, occurring in Florida and Caribbean waters, is one of the most unusual croakers. Seldom more than 8 inches long, it has three dark stripes through its gray body—a vertical stripe through the eye, a slanted one from the pectoral fin upward to the forehead, and a horizontal stripe from the spiny dorsal to the caudal fin. In living fishes, these stripes are bordered with white. Unlike other croakers, the jackknife-fish is solitary in habit, hiding in holes in coral reefs during the day and coming out at night to feed. It generally lives at depths of 50 feet or greater.

The cubbyu, *E. umbrosus*, is similar in size and shape to the jackknife-fish, sometimes ranging northward to the Carolinas. Seven narrow dark brown stripes line its silvery sides.

The banded drum, *Larimus fasciatus*, is a small species, to 10 inches or sometimes slightly longer. It occurs along the Atlantic coastline from New York to Florida and also along the coasts of the Gulf of Mexico. The banded drum has a deep body, much compressed, and 7–9 black bars along each side. There are no barbels, and the mouth is distinctly oblique—extremely so. This distinguishes it from the silver perch. The inside of the mouth is yellowish, as are the rays of the anal, pelvic, and caudal fins.

A species closely related to the banded drum is the cabezon, *L. breviceps*, found in the Caribbean and southward to Brazil. It has a series of indistinct dark bars along its sides.

The northern kingfish, *Menticirrhus saxatalis*, averages about a pound in weight, sometimes to as much as 3 pounds. It is found close to shore from Maine to Florida. Like other members of this genus, the snout is decidedly rounded, and there is a single stout barbel on the chin. The dorsal fin is high and spiny, and the caudal fin is concave above and convex below, forming an S shape. The olivaceous sides are blotched with black in an irregular pattern. Because it lacks a swim bladder, this species (and others in the genus) cannot make a croaking noise. Also, it cannot float easily and commonly rests on the bottom.

The southern kingfish, *M. americanus*, has seven dark, oblique bands along its sides. The ranges of these two closely related species overlap in the mid-Atlantic region, but the southern kingfish is the dominant species south of the Carolinas and in the Gulf of Mexico. The two can be distinguished by the number of rays in the anal fin: seven in the southern kingfish, eight in the northern kingfish. Also, the southern kingfish does not have as long spines in its dorsal fin.

The Gulf kingfish, *M. littoralis*, also called surf whiting, is most abundant in the Gulf of Mexico. It lacks dark markings and is a solid silvery gray above, white below. The average size is about half a pound, with occasional individuals weighing as much as 2 pounds. The pectoral fins are comparatively shorter than are those of the two species previously described.

The California corbina, *M. undulatus*, found in the Pacific from Point Conception to the Gulf of California, resembles the northern kingfish of the Atlantic in general shape, averaging about a pound in weight and reported at 8½ pounds and 30 inches in length. Metallic blue above, they are often marked with dark spots or wavy lines. One fleshy barbel is attached to the chin, and one (or sometimes two) weak spines are located at the front of the anal fin. In the yellowfin croaker, with which the California corbina might be confused, there are two strong spines at the leading edge of the anal fin. This is one of the most popular of the surf fishes in California waters and is caught on both natural and artificial baits.

The freshwater drum, *Aplodinotus grunniens*, is the only member of the family Sciaenidae inhabiting fresh water. Like most marine species, it can make a loud drumming noise. Its otoliths, or "ear bones," are espe-

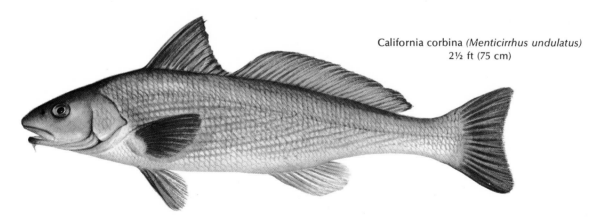

California corbina *(Menticirrhus undulatus)*
2½ ft (75 cm)

cially large and are collected and carried by some people for good luck. The freshwater drum can be distinguished from all other freshwater fishes by its lateral line, which extends to the tip of the caudal fin, as in other members of the family. The caudal fin is bluntly pointed. The spiny and soft-rayed dorsal fins are almost separated, and the large, silvery scales are rough to the touch. Like many other members of the family, the freshwater drum has an inferior mouth, an adaptation for feeding on the bottom. It eats clams and mussels.

Found from the St. Lawrence River through the Great Lakes and the Mississippi River drainage basin, the freshwater drum may be locally abundant, so much so that it is harvested commercially. It is also caught on hook and line but does not generally rate high either as a sport fish or as a fish for eating. The average size is less than 2 pounds, but 10-pounders are not uncommon. Years ago, freshwater drums weighing more than 100 pounds were caught with regularity; and kitchen middens indicate that before the coming of the white man, the Indians may have been eating freshwater drums that weighed as much as 200 pounds.

Family Mullidae
goatfishes

Living in subtropical and tropical seas, particularly near reefs, goatfishes, or surmullets, are easily recognized by their long chin whiskers, or barbels. These are stretched forward and down in front of the fish to probe the bottom for food, mainly crustaceans and other invertebrates. At other times the barbels are held close to the body and may actually be difficult to see.

Most of the nearly 50 species of goatfishes are basically pinkish, but they become flushed with color—even turning bright red—when excited. Some are striped with yellow, and most can change color, at least from a bold mottling or striped pattern to a solid. The first, or spiny, dorsal is widely separated from the second, or soft-rayed, dorsal; this is a distinctive feature. Some goatfishes travel in schools; others are solitary. Few are more than a foot long, usually elongated.

The spotted goatfish, *Pseudupeneus maculatus*, is a common goatfish living off the coasts of Florida and also in the Caribbean. It is rosy, with three dark blotches on its side.

The Mexican goatfish, *P. dentatus*, is similar to the spotted species, occurring in the Pacific from southern California to Panama. It has a red stripe down each side. About a dozen species of this genus are found in the Indo-Pacific, most of them only about 10 inches long.

The red goatfish, *Mullus auratus*, is another species occurring abundantly in the Caribbean and occasionally straying northward. Typical of the group, it is reddish above; but it has yellowish sides, with two rows of blue spots above the lateral line.

The similar red surmullet, *M. surmuletus*, of the Mediterranean and warm waters along the European coast, sometimes straggling even as far north as Norway, is ranked as one of the best-flavored fishes.

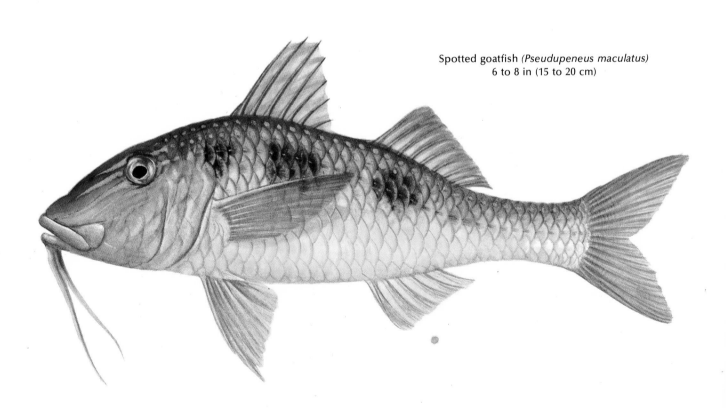

Spotted goatfish *(Pseudupeneus maculatus)*
6 to 8 in (15 to 20 cm)

The yellow goatfish, *Mulloidichthys martinicus*, another goatfish found off the Atlantic coast of North America, differs from most goatfishes in that it travels in dense schools. Its name comes from the bright yellow stripes that run from the snout through the eye and along the full length of the whitish or silvery body. Similar species in this genus occur in the Indo-Pacific.

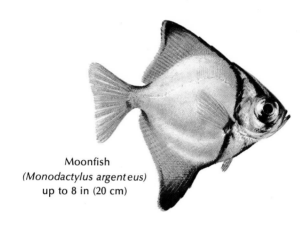

Moonfish
(Monodactylus argenteus)
up to 8 in (20 cm)

Family Monodactylidae
fingerfishes

Only about half a dozen species comprise this family of Indo-Pacific fishes that inhabit both salt and fresh waters. All have a highly compressed body, and the scales typically extend onto the fins. The moonfish, *Monodactylus argenteus*, is commonly imported for aquarium hobbyists. Its silvery body, to 8 inches long, is marked with two black bands—one from the top of the head to and through the eye and the other from the leading edge of the dorsal fin to the gill cover, or operculum. The first rays of the dorsal fin are long, as are those of the anal fin, both sloping downward to the caudal peduncle. The fins are yellow, edged with black in front. The squared caudal fin is yellow.

Deepsea herring *(Bathyclupea argentea)*
6 in (15 cm)

Family Bathyclupeidae
deepsea herrings

These herringlike fishes of the depths possess huge eyes, large mouths, and elongated anal fins. Taxonomists differ widely concerning their classifica-tion; some place these fishes in a separate order. The deepsea herring, *Bathyclupea argentea*, has large eyes, a large mouth, a single dorsal fin, and a long anal fin.

Archerfish *(Toxotes jaculatrix)*
6 in (15 cm)

Family Toxotidae
archerfishes

The archerfish, *Toxotes jaculatrix*, the most common of the four similar species comprising the family, is an excellent example of proof that some fishes have good vision. It actually shoots down at least a portion of its prey by spitting drops of water at them. It can knock spiders from their webs or insects from the air and is accurate at distances up to 4 feet. Archerfishes are na-tive to southeastern Asia, where they live in mangrove swamps and in brackish waters, sometimes straying far up rivers. Their average length is about 6 inches. Be-cause of their peculiar spitting habit, they are regularly exhibited in aquariums.

Family Kyphosidae
sea chubs

These oval-shaped schooling fishes have a habit of fol-lowing ships, which explains why they go by the name of rudderfishes. The family contains only about half a dozen species, which are widely distributed.

The most familiar of the species is the Bermuda chub, or striped rudderfish, *Kyphosus sectatrix*, occurring from Massachusetts southward into the Caribbean and also in the eastern Atlantic from England to the Canary Islands—most abundantly in warm waters. Its com-pressed body is steel gray with yellowish stripes; the scales are usually edged with blue. The fins are dusky. In another color phase, the body is covered with large white spots. The head is short and the mouth small; the tail is forked. Because of its small mouth, the Bermuda chub nibbles its food. It is a superb bait stealer. To catch it, fishermen must use very small hooks, which are baited with shrimps, crabs, or cut bait. Fishermen must be ready to set the hook firmly at the slightest indication that the fish is there. A hooked Bermuda chub puts up an energetic fight. It has good flavor but must be eaten soon after being caught because it spoils quickly. The

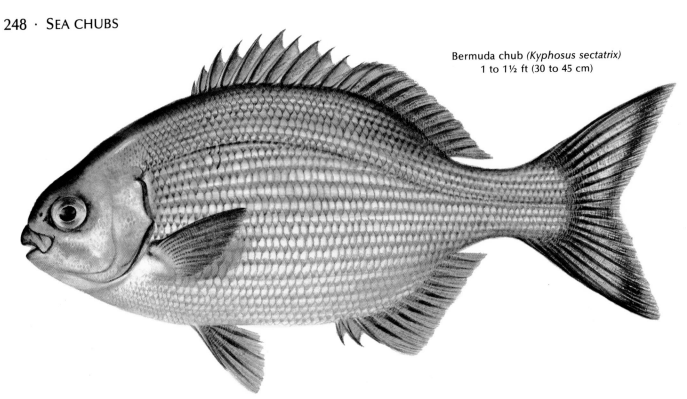

Bermuda chub *(Kyphosus sectatrix)*
1 to 1½ ft (30 to 45 cm)

Bermuda chub may reach a weight of 10 pounds but usually weighs about 2 or 3 pounds.

The less common yellow chub, *K. incisor*, is found in the same range as the Bermuda species and is larger—to as much as 30 pounds. The color pattern is about the same, but the yellow is much brighter. Because of its larger size, the yellow chub makes an even more exciting catch for fishermen than the Bermuda chub.

Similar species in the same genus occur in Indo-Pacific waters. The zebra perch, *Hermosilla azurea*, is a related species that lives in the warm waters of the Pacific from California southward.

Halfmoons constitute a small family of fishes that resemble sea chubs and are sometimes placed in the family Scorpidae. The halfmoon, *Medialuna californiensis*, occurs from the Klamath River southward to the Gulf of California. It is gray with black spots and dusky fins and reaches a weight of about 4 pounds. Often abundant along rocky shores, it sometimes constitutes a major portion of the commercial catch in an area.

Nibblers are active, inshore fishes that live mainly in warm waters. The group is comprised of only a few species. The opaleye, *Girella nigricans*, found from central California to Baja California, is common along rocky shores and in kelp. The young live in tidal pools. The opaleye averages less than 10 inches long, but occasional individuals may be as much as 25 inches and weigh 13 pounds. The color is green over the entire body, darker above and lighter below. The distinctive eye is an opalescent blue. Another diagnostic feature is the white or yellowish spot below the spiny dorsal fin. In some regions, the opaleye is highly popular with sport fishermen.

Other species in the same genus include *G. punctata*, which is harvested commercially in the waters off Japan, and *G. tricuspidata*, an Australian species taken in nets by commercial fishermen and also caught on hook and line by sport fishermen.

Halfmoon *(Medialuna californiensis)*
1 ft (30 cm)

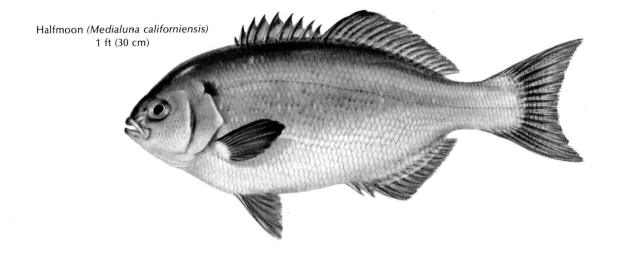

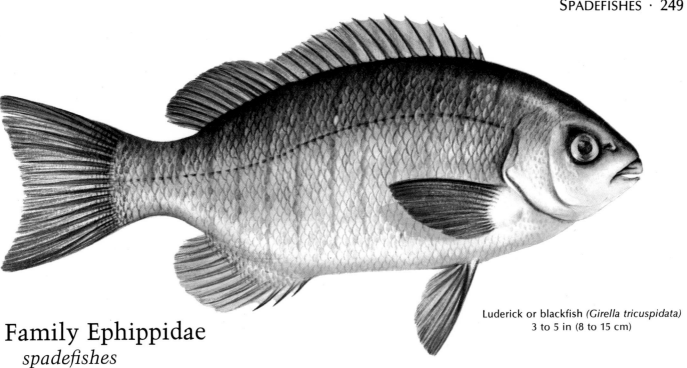

Luderick or blackfish *(Girella tricuspidata)*
3 to 5 in (8 to 15 cm)

Family Ephippidae
spadefishes

Occurring mainly in subtropical and tropical seas but sometimes straying into temperate waters, the several species of spadefishes are distinctively shaped—the body much flattened and nearly as deep as it is long. The first, or spiny, dorsal fin is separate from the second, or soft-rayed, dorsal, which has exceptionally long rays at the front and is matched in size and shape by the anal fin directly beneath it. The body is silvery with black crossbands that may be absent in older fishes. The

Atlantic spadefish *(Chaetodipterus faber)*
up to 3 ft (90 cm)

broad caudal fin has long rays at the tips of the upper and lower lobes so that the fin is concave. The mouth is small.

The Atlantic spadefish, *Chaetodipterus faber*, sometimes ranges as far north as Massachusetts but is essentially a fish of warm Florida and Caribbean waters. It averages about a foot in length and weighs 2 to 3 pounds. Now and then a giant is reported—to as much as 3 feet long and weighing 20 pounds. The Atlantic spadefish eats mainly crabs and shrimps, which can also be used as bait to catch it.

The very similar Pacific spadefish, *C. zonatus*, ranges from extreme southern California southward to Mexico.

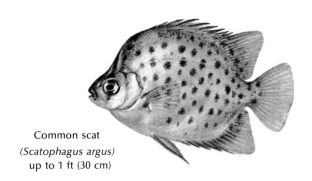

Common scat
(Scatophagus argus)
up to 1 ft (30 cm)

Family Scatophagidae
scats or argus fishes

About half a dozen species comprise this family of fishes found in southeastern Asia, Australia, and eastern Africa. They are primarily marine but range into brackish and fresh waters.

Most common is the common scat, or argus, *Scatophagus argus*, which may reach a length of 12 inches. While young, it makes a handsome aquarium fish—glossy red to greenish brown and covered with large round black spots. Old fishes become dull and less attractive. Typical of the group, the body is high and greatly compressed, or sunfishlike. There are four strong spines at the front of the anal fin.

Family Chaetodontidae
butterflyfishes

Butterflyfishes and angelfishes differ mainly in size. Butterflyfishes are small and swift; angelfishes are larger and swim more slowly but with exceptional grace. Both are most abundantly represented over reefs and are found worldwide in warm waters. The precise number of species is not known but exceeds 150.

Butterflyfishes get their name from their active, flitting movements and also from their bright colors. Most of them are less than 6 inches long. Despite their bright colors, butterflyfishes are surprisingly well patterned so that it is difficult to distinguish the head from the tail. In most, for example, a dark line runs through the eye, hiding this vital part. To add to the confusion, there is often a large "eyespot" near the tail. A predator unfamiliar with these little fishes is likely to grab for the "eyed" end, thinking it is the head, and is amazed when the fish moves off at great speed, seemingly in reverse. A butterflyfish's small mouth is located at the end of a long snout on which the fish feeds. Some butterflyfishes have the habit of plucking the parasites from the bodies of larger fishes, which permit them to do so.

The spotfin butterflyfish, *Chaetodon ocellatus*, which regularly exceeds 6 inches in length, is an abundant species in Florida and Caribbean waters, sometimes straggling northward to as far as Massachusetts in summer. The basic color is yellow. There is a dark line through the eye and usually also a dark spot, not ocellated, at the base of the soft dorsal fin. Sometimes the spot forms a band rather than being rounded.

The foureye butterflyfish, *C. capistratus*, only slightly smaller and occurring in the same range as the spotfin, has a large ocellated spot at the rear of its body, which is covered with spots.

The banded butterflyfish, *C. striatus*, similar in size to the foureye, is found in Caribbean and Florida waters but does not stray into cooler waters. It lacks spots, and its white or light yellow body is crossed with black bands. It has no eyespot.

Three or four other species of *Chaetodon* inhabit the Atlantic reefs, but the genus is much more abundantly represented in South Pacific waters, where there are more than 50 species. A typical example is the redfin butterflyfish, *C. trifasciatus*. All are similar in general shape and habits to those already described, but each is distinctively striped or spotted. Many have yellow as the basic color; others are basically black, blue, or red.

The unusual saddleback butterflyfish, *C. epihippium*, has a high-arched back above the pectoral fins, but it slopes sharply to the caudal fin, forming a "saddle."

The basically white clown butterflyfish, *C. ornatissimus*, has a yellow head with vertical black stripes, yellow pelvic fins, and black bars on the dorsal and caudal fins. The body is striped obliquely with orange.

Other butterflyfishes occurring in Indo-Pacific waters belong to the unusual *Forcipiger* genus, known as forceps fishes because of the extremely long snout that is used like a pair of forceps to reach deep into crevices. Forceps fishes are about 6 inches long.

Angelfishes, which are commonly 12 inches long and

sometimes as long as 24 inches, have grace as well as beauty. Like butterflyfishes, they are surprisingly unafraid and can be approached closely by swimmers and divers. They will turn slowly in front of a diver as if wanting to display themselves. In most angelfishes, the lips are a different color from the body, so that they appear to be painted on. The dorsal and anal fins are generally drawn out at their tips into filamentlike projections. While young butterflyfishes look much like the adults in color and pattern, young angelfishes are usually quite different from their parents. Also, angelfishes have a heavy spine at the base of the gill cover, and the

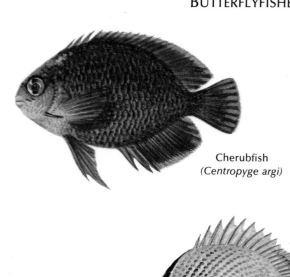

Cherubfish
(*Centropyge argi*)

Banded butterflyfish
(*Chaetodon striatus*)

Foureye butterflyfish
(*Chaetodon capistratus*)

Forceps butterflyfish
(*Forcipiger longirostris*)

Copperband butterflyfish
(*Chelmon rostratus*)

Redfin butterflyfish
(*Chaetodon trifasciatus*)

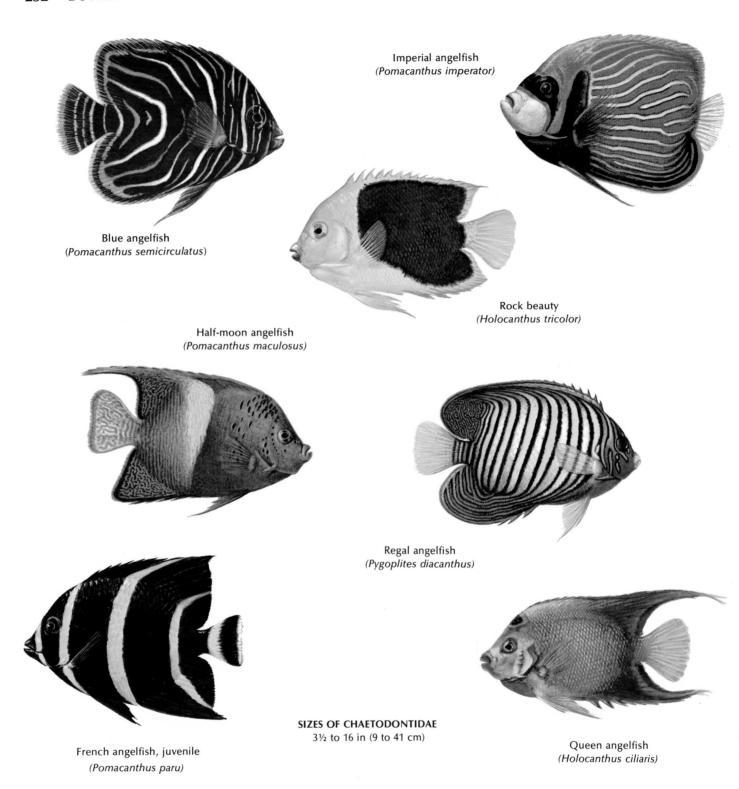

Imperial angelfish
(*Pomacanthus imperator*)

Blue angelfish
(*Pomacanthus semicirculatus*)

Rock beauty
(*Holocanthus tricolor*)

Half-moon angelfish
(*Pomacanthus maculosus*)

Regal angelfish
(*Pygoplites diacanthus*)

SIZES OF CHAETODONTIDAE
3½ to 16 in (9 to 41 cm)

French angelfish, juvenile
(*Pomacanthus paru*)

Queen angelfish
(*Holocanthus ciliaris*)

typical body shape is almost rectangular. Many larger angelfishes are netted, caught on hook and line, or speared for eating.

The queen angelfish, *Holacanthus ciliaris*, to 2 feet long, is common in Florida and Caribbean waters. The body is yellowish with a bluish cast; the dorsal and anal fins are yellow, edged with blue; and the pectoral, pel-vic, and caudal fins are yellow with no blue. A black eyespot ringed with blue is on the forehead. The amount of blue varies with the individual and also differs in intensity. The young have a black bar through the eye and light bluish bars along the body.

The rock beauty, *H. tricolor*, to 12 inches long, is another angelfish of warm Atlantic and Caribbean waters. Its body is mainly black, but the head, belly, and caudal fins are bright yellow—a striking contrasting combination. The spectacular cherubfish, *Centropyge argi*, is from Indo-Pacific waters, as is the copperband butterflyfish, *Chelmon rostratus*.

The French angelfish, *Pomacanthus paru*, found in Florida and Caribbean waters and also in warm waters of the eastern Atlantic, may reach a length of 1½ feet. The young are striped vertically with yellow. The French angelfish was introduced into Bermuda.

The larger gray angelfish, *P. arcuatus*, to 2 feet long and weighing as much as 6 pounds, is grayish, each scale marked with a black spot. The pectoral fins are yellow on the inside, the color "flashed" as the fish swims. The mouth is white. The young are black with vertical bars, almost precisely like the French angelfish. The two species can be distinguished by counting the number of scales in the lateral line: 50–55 in the gray angelfish as opposed to 70–90 in the French angelfish.

The genus *Pomacanthus* also has representatives in the Pacific. *P. zonipectus* is common from southern Mexico southward to Panama. The half-moon angelfish, *P. maculosus*, lives in the Red Sea.

Others occur in the Indo-Pacific. The blue angelfish, *P. semicirculatus*, is deep blue or indigo with swirled, almost semicircular stripes of light blue and white along its sides. Imperial angelfish, *P. imperator*, have a similar semicircular pattern of white stripes on a black or purplish background; the dorsal and caudal fins are white. Both species reach a length of about 1½ feet. The regal angelfish, *Pygoplites diacanthus*, is basically orange, with vertical stripes of white bordered by black.

Family Nandidae
leaffishes

These small freshwater fishes are best known to aquarium hobbyists. There are representatives in South America, Asia, and Africa, one of the indications that these continents were joined in the geologic past. Typical members of the family have a greatly compressed body; in many of the species, the soft-rayed dorsal fin, the caudal fin, and the soft-rayed portion of the anal fin are transparent. Most members of the family hide under rocks or in similar cavelike places from which they dash out to capture their prey. Males guard the eggs and the fry until they are able to swim freely.

The leaffish, *Monocirrhus polyacanthus*, of tropical South American streams, is a 3- to 4-inch species that looks remarkably like a leaf floating in the water, a deception that permits the fish to get close to its meals. A chin barbel has the appearance of a broken leaf stem.

Most individuals are brownish, but some are gray; both are usually mottled with black. The leaffish has an unusually large mouth, enabling it to gobble prey at least half as large as itself. In aquariums this species regularly consumes its own weight in food daily, so the hobbyist must be prepared to provide live food in ample amounts. Guppies are the usual fare.

Another species of the same region is *Polycentrus schomburghi*. Because of the transparent portions of its fins, this fish looks chopped off at the rear. Brownish or bluish black, this species does not mimic a leaf. It catches its prey by rushing at them from ambush.

A West African genus of leaffishes, *Polycentropsis*, is remarkably like the species of *Polycentrus* in South America, some authorities not differentiating them. The most common species is *P. abbreviata*, which is brownish with dark mottling. Another genus of African leaffishes is *Afronondus*, the single known species, *A. sheljuzhkoi*, measuring less than half an inch long.

The leaffishes of southeastern Asia are much more perchlike in body shape, none of them mimicking leaves and the body only slightly compressed. The most common species is *Badis badis*, which lives in streams in India and Indochina. It occurs in numerous color variations. Males are usually basically black or bluish, with reddish bands across the body. During the spawning season, however, these bands are lacking. The dorsal fin is banded with colors, the most outstanding of which is a glowing blue-green. Females are more somberly colored. Both sexes, about 3 inches long, can change color rapidly.

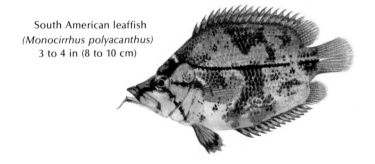

South American leaffish
(Monocirrhus polyacanthus)
3 to 4 in (8 to 10 cm)

Family Embiotocidae
surfperches

The nearly two dozen species comprising this family are all marine with the exception of the small tule perch, *Hysterocarpus traski*, which lives in California's lower Sacramento River. The shiner perch, *Cymatogaster aggregata*, is primarily a marine species but may stray into fresh water from time to time.

None of the species in the family is large—1½ feet is maximum; some are less than 5 inches long. They give birth to their young rather than laying eggs, unusual for a saltwater fish. The parents guard the nest and the young. All are found off the Pacific coast of North America from Alaska to southern California, with the exception of two species occurring off the coasts of Japan and nearby Asia.

Surfperches have compressed bodies, more or less oval in shape and generally silvery. The spiny and soft-rayed dorsal fins are joined. Most species inhabit the surf, along both sandy and rocky coasts, but several species live mainly in bays or in similar shallow inshore waters. One species occurs in relatively deep water (to 300 feet), and two smaller species inhabit only tidepools. The larger species are popular with sport fishermen and are caught the year round. They contribute to the commercial catch but not to a significant extent.

The barred surfperch, *Amphistichus argenteus*, to 16 inches long but usually less than 10 inches, occurs along sandy coasts from central California to Baja California. Its sides are marked with a series of dusky, brassy vertical bars with spots between them. The back and sides are gray to olive, the belly white. This is one of the most important of the surfperches because of its popularity with anglers.

The redtail surfperch, *A. rhodoterus*, is more northern in range than the barred species; it is found from Washington to central California. Its vertical bars and the pelvic and caudal fins are usually reddish.

The calico surfperch, *A. koelzi*, occurs from northern California to Baja California. Its lower jaw projects slightly beyond the upper, whereas in the barred surfperch the lower jaw is shorter than the upper.

The walleye surfperch, *Hyperprosopon argenteum*, occurring from British Columbia to Baja California, is another surfperch that is highly popular with anglers. To about 12 inches long, it is distinguished by its large eyes and by the black tips on its pelvic, anal, and caudal fins. The back and sides are bluish, the belly white or silvery. The last spiny rays of the dorsal fin are higher than any of the rays of the soft dorsal.

Relatives of the walleye surfperch include the spotfin surfperch, *H. anale*, found from central California to Baja California; it has no black tips on its fins but does have a distinctive black spot on its spiny dorsal fin and sometimes a black blotch on the anal fin. The silver surfperch, *H. ellipticum*, ranging from Washington to southern California, has no black markings on its body. All three species are found mostly along sandy shores.

The rainbow surfperch, *Hypsurus caryi*, to 12 inches long, lives principally along rocky shores, from northern California southward to Baja California. Somewhat less oval in shape than other surfperches, its silvery body is striped horizontally with blue, orange, and red. The fins are generally orange, and a large black blotch appears on both the soft dorsal and the anal fins.

The white seaperch, *Phanerodon furcatus*, distinguished by its deeply forked tail, has a rather slim body compared to other surfperches. About 12 inches long, it ranges from British Columbia to southern California, occurring mainly off sandy coasts. There is usually a black spot on the anal fin. This is the species most commonly caught by commercial fishermen.

The sharpnose seaperch, *P. atripes*, very similar to the white seaperch, lives in deeper water just offshore from central California to Baja California. The tips of its pelvic fins are black, and it has red spots along its sides.

Largest in the surfperch family is the rubberlip sea-

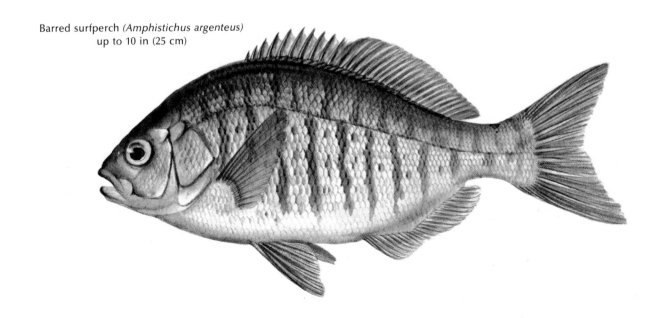

Barred surfperch *(Amphistichus argenteus)*
up to 10 in (25 cm)

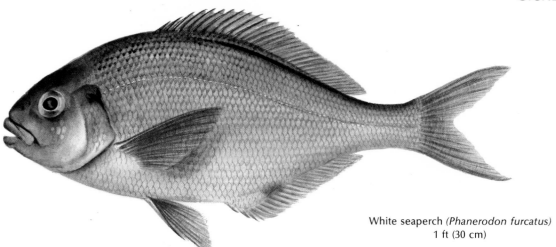

White seaperch *(Phanerodon furcatus)*
1 ft (30 cm)

perch, *Rhacocilus toxotes*, which reaches a length of 1½ feet. Occurring from central to southern California, it is also one of the important catches of both commercial and sport fishermen not only because of its size but also because it is good to eat. Its most distinguishing feature is its thick white to pinkish lips, so large in some individuals that they droop. The whitish background color is usually tinged with smoky or blackish color, and the pectoral fins are yellow.

Closely related to the rubberlip is the pile perch, *R. vacca*, ranging from Alaska to Baja California. It is only slightly smaller—to 16 inches long. It is distinguished by its deeply forked tail and by the very high first rays in the second dorsal fin. The color is silvery, with a blackish or brownish cast on the back. The fins are dark.

The black perch, *Embiotoca jacksoni*, reaches a length of 12 inches. Found from central California midway down Baja California, it is dark brownish black and often tinged with blue or yellow. It has thick reddish lips. A group of scales between the pectoral and pelvic fins are exceptionally large, and the spiny rays of the dorsal fin are all shorter than the soft rays. The tail is slightly forked.

The striped seaperch, *E. lateralis*, ranging from Baja California northward to Alaska and most abundant in the cooler waters north of Point Conception, has a less forked tail than the black perch, and its coppery body is striped horizontally with orange and blue. Above the lateral line, the scales are spotted with black.

The pink seaperch, *Zalembius rosaceous*, lives in deeper water than any other member of the family—from 75 to 300 feet or even deeper. Its body is rosy red, with two large brown spots on the back just under the spiny and soft dorsal fins. In males, the top rays of the caudal and anal fins are commonly drawn into filaments. This surfperch is seldom caught either by commercial or sport fishermen, but the few that are taken always attract much attention because of the bright colors of the fishes. The maximum size is about 8 inches.

Among the other small surfperches is the previously mentioned shiner perch, a 6-inch species that is common along sandy shores and in bays, occasionally straying into fresh water. It is generally greenish or silvery but may be reddish.

The kelp perch, *Brachyistius frenatus*, to 8 inches long, is most common in the kelp off the rocky coasts from British Columbia to Baja California. The dorsal fin is high, the spiny portion higher than the soft. The color is coppery red, including the fins.

The dwarf perch, *Micrometrus minimus*, 3 inches or less in length, is abundant from central California to central Baja California. The reef perch, *M. aurora*, occurs in the same range but may be 6 inches long. The two species are most accurately differentiated by the number of spines in the dorsal fin: 8–11 spiny and 12–16 soft in the dwarf perch; 7–9 spiny and 16–19 soft in the reef perch.

Family Cichlidae
cichlids

One of the largest families of fishes, with more than 600 species, the cichlids are represented most abundantly in subtropical and tropical American waters, mostly in freshwater streams and lakes but some inhabiting brackish water or coastal areas. They are numerous also in Africa, and one species occurs in India. Seven species have been thus far introduced to the United States.

Medium to small in size, cichlids have only one nostril on each side of the head. They are variable in body shape; some are perchlike, others long and slim, and still others deep-bodied. Typically the dorsal fin is long, the spiny and soft-rayed portions united. In the anal fin, three spines precede the soft-rayed portion.

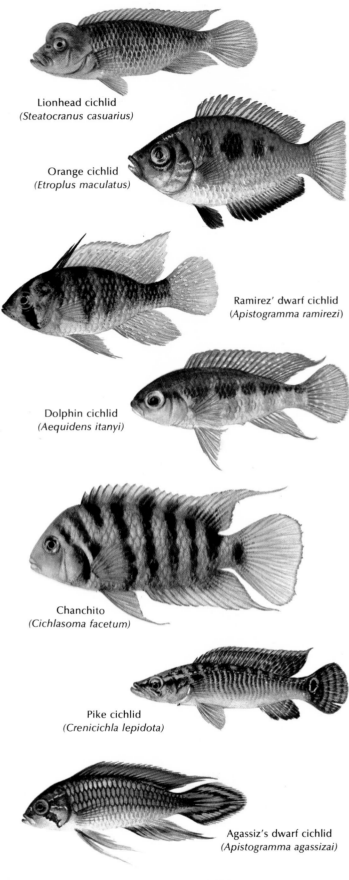

Lionhead cichlid
(*Steatocranus casuarius*)

Orange cichlid
(*Etroplus maculatus*)

Ramirez' dwarf cichlid
(*Apistogramma ramirezi*)

Dolphin cichlid
(*Aequidens itanyi*)

Chanchito
(*Cichlasoma facetum*)

Pike cichlid
(*Crenicichla lepidota*)

Agassiz's dwarf cichlid
(*Apistogramma agassizai*)

SIZES OF CICHLIDAE
2 to 10 in (5 to 25 cm)

Cichlids are carnivorous. If kept in an aquarium, they must be provided with a constant supply of live food. Many species become so aggressive that other fishes cannot be kept with them, and some also root up plants, particularly when they are nesting. In very large tanks, where space is not at a premium, cichlids generally live peacefully with their own kind and with other species. It is best to provide them with the largest possible tank, however. Fifteen gallons is the minimum size advisable.

Both parents usually take care of the eggs and tend the young. While the young are still schooling, the parents insist that they remain with the others in the school. If one begins to stray, a parent will pick it up in its mouth and spit it back into the group. Some cichlids are mouthbrooders, either the male or the female holding the eggs in its mouth until they hatch. The newly hatched fishes may also return to the mouth cavity for protection until they are quite large.

African cichlids include the many species of *Tilapia*, many of which are mouthbrooders and some of which grow to large size—as much as 20 pounds. In their native range these large species have long been harvested for food; and since the days of the Egyptians, some species of *Tilapia* have also been reared in pools. They were once heralded as the fishes that would provide protein for the world's starving millions because they produce prolifically in ponds, tolerate crowding, resist disease, and thrive on a diet of plankton easily produced in quantities in ponds. *Tilapia* were introduced to warm-water ponds throughout the world before serious drawbacks were discovered.

Very quickly they become overcrowded in ponds. The stunted fishes mature and breed before they weigh as much as 3 ounces, aggravating the overpopulation condition. Not uncommonly, yields of as great as 2 tons per acre can be obtained from these ponds, but the fishes are too small to eat. Fishes that escape the ponds will crowd out native species. In the United States, the *Tilapia* has been experimented with in carefully guarded ponds to prevent their escape.

Researchers have successfully bred two different species of *Tilapia* to produce offspring that are almost all males. Trained fish-sorters weed out the few females to provide all-male populations of fishes for stocking and thus prevent population rampages. This portends a bright future for the *Tilapia* as a source of food.

The species commonly used in aquaculture is the 2-pound, sunfish-shaped Mozambique mouthbrooder, *T. mossambica*, but the genus contains more than 50 species that are difficult to differentiate and that hybridize freely. *T. mossambica* normally lives in brackish water. In fresh water, it tends to grow more slowly. A native of Africa, it was introduced to Java about 1940 and

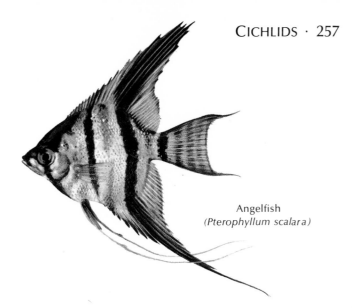

Angelfish
(*Pterophyllum scalara*)

has since become so identified with the Indonesian area that it goes by the name of Javan Tilapia. In the United States, this species is now established in the wild in California, Texas, and Montana. A similar species, the blackchin mouthbrooder, *T. melanotheron*, lives as an escapee in Florida waters near Tampa.

Species of *Tilapia* kept in aquariums are generally those 6 inches or less in length. Omnivorous, they must be given a diet of both plants and animals.

The jewelfish, *Hemichromis bimaculatus*, to 5 inches long, is among the other African cichlids kept in aquariums. A slender fish, it has a long, low dorsal fin. The long pelvic fins end in sharp points. Ordinarily dull in color, both sexes become bright red at mating time, the females often brighter than the males. Except when breeding and rearing their young, they are quarrelsome with each other and also with other species.

Still another African species commonly kept in aquariums is the purple cichlid, *Pelyicachromis pulcher*,

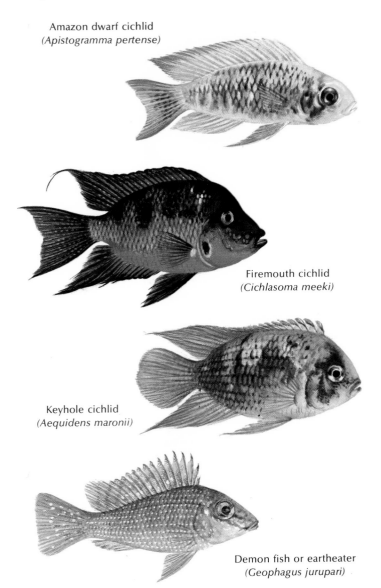

Amazon dwarf cichlid
(*Apistogramma pertense*)

Firemouth cichlid
(*Cichlasoma meeki*)

Keyhole cichlid
(*Aequidens maronii*)

Demon fish or eartheater
(*Geophagus jurupari*)

which averages 3 to 4 inches in length. It has a large purplish spot on each side of its yellowish or brownish body. The dorsal fin has a broad silvery or gold band; and in males there are spots, usually ocellated, on the upper lobe of the caudal fin, which in many species is almost diamond-shaped and in others is rounded.

A number of species of *Cichlasoma* are exported from South America to aquarium hobbyists around the world. They have a perchlike body shape, with a large head and eyes. Most of them are quarrelsome. Among the common species are the firemouth, *C. meeki*, which has the unusual habit of lowering a goiterlike pouch of red skin from its throat when it becomes excited; the Jack Dempsey, *C. octofasciatum*, marked by eight dark bands and named after a famous fighter because of its pugilistic temperament; and festivum, *C. festivum*, peaceful compared to others in the genus.

Only one species of cichlids occurs natively in the United States. This is the Rio Grande perch, *C. cyanoguttatus*, found from extreme southern Texas southward into Mexico. It is bluish or gray with blue dots over its body. The Rio Grande perch is sometimes kept in aquariums but is a quarrelsome species. Any specimen over 10 inches in length is unusual.

The bumphead cichlid, *Steatocranis arius*, is an unusual African species that develops an enlarged forehead. The swelling eventually pushes outward over the eyes so that it looks like a cap on the fish's head.

The most familiar cichlids come from South America. Angelfishes, *Pterophyllum scalara*, are perhaps the best-known freshwater tropicals. From the Amazon region, angelfishes reach a length of six inches and may be nearly twice as tall, their greatly compressed body making them almost circular in body outline. The dorsal and anal fins are extended into points at their tips and are swept back almost the length of the caudal fin. The rays of the pelvic fins are drawn into threadlike filaments, as are the upper and lower rays of the caudal fin.

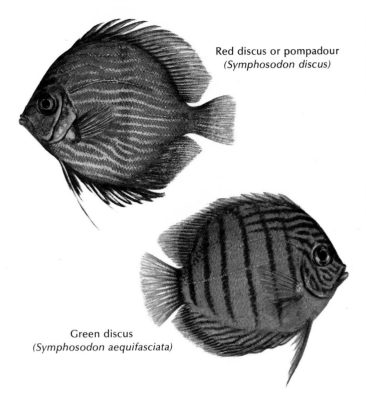

Red discus or pompadour
(Symphosodon discus)

Green discus
(Symphosodon aequifasciata)

Angelfishes are popular because they are peaceful in aquariums, tolerating other species as well as their own kind.

Resembling *Cichlasoma* in shape, the eyespot cichlid, *Cichla ocellatus*, is an attractive species that grows too large— to 2 feet—for the ordinary aquarium. It is grayish green with dark vertical bars that may not extend past the lateral line. The eyespot cichlid has a conspicuous "eyespot" at the base of the caudal fin.

The pike cichlid, *Crenicichla lepidota,* is a slim fish that grows to 8 inches long and has a large pikelike mouth for catching prey. It is variously colored and has been bred to produce a variety of color patterns. At the base of the caudal fin is a black spot ringed with gold.

The discus, *Symphysodon discus*, is one of several species in this genus of fishes from the Amazon region. It is peaceful and also one of the most handsome cichlids, its much-compressed body yellowish or grayish and crossed with dark or bright blue-green bands. The discus is not easy to keep in an aquarium, demanding soft and slightly acid water that is maintained at about 80 degrees F. It also becomes diseased easily. Because of its beauty, however, the discus challenges an increasing number of hobbyists to keep it.

The blue acara, *Aequidens pulcher*, delights in rooting in the bottom, making it difficult to keep an aquarium provided with plants. This is an attractive 6-inch fish, bluish green with red dots and streaks over its body. The dorsal and anal fins are reddish at their

base. The closely related *A. maronii*, slightly smaller, does not have the objectionable rooting habit. It usually has a dark "keyhole"-shaped blotch on each side. The black acara, *A. portalegrensis*, another South American species, was introduced to southeastern Florida.

Dwarf cichlids, *Apistogramma*, of several species, all less than 3 inches long, are generally peaceful and do not disturb plants. These slim little fishes are highly colorful and have a poorly developed lateral line.

The oscar, *Astronotus ocellatus*, to 12 inches long, lives in large streams; because of its size, it requires a large aquarium. It has a big head and large eyes, the color pattern changing with the fish's age. Mature fishes are attractively banded with yellow and have a large dark spot circled with orange on the caudal peduncle. Proposals are sometimes made to release this species in warm-water streams in the southern United States as a sport fish, but unfortunate experiences with other exotics has so far kept wary officials from so doing.

Oscar cichlid
(Astronotus ocellatus)

Family Pomacentridae
damselfishes

Damselfishes are mostly marine species of shallow subtropical and tropical waters. Few are more than 6 inches long, and they are typically highly colored. The damselfish is active, aggressive, and deep-bodied; the mouth is small. In typical species the lateral line stops at the rear of the soft dorsal fin.

Members of the genus *Abudefduf* are exceptions to the rule because their colors are rather dull. The sergeant major, *A. saxatilis*, usually less than 6 inches long, has black vertical bars on a yellowish green background; in another color phase, the basic color is bluish and the vertical bars lacking. Sergeant majors are cosmopolitan in warm seas, particularly in reef areas. The genus is well represented also with species in Indo-Pacific waters.

The beaugregory, *Pomacentrus leucostictus*, represents another genus of many and widely distributed

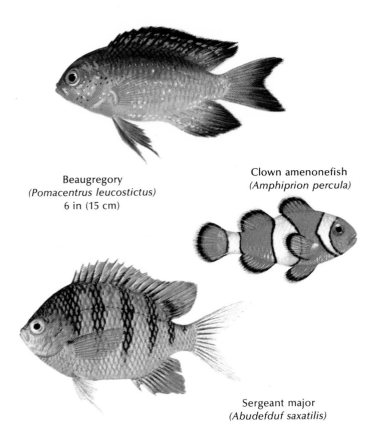

Beaugregory
(Pomacentrus leucostictus)
6 in (15 cm)

Clown amenonefish
(Amphiprion percula)

Sergeant major
(Abudefduf saxatilis)

The yellowtail damselfish, *Microspathodon chrysurus*, is a 6-inch species, common mainly in the reefs of warm Atlantic and Caribbean waters. Mature fishes have yellow tails and yellow underparts. The young are spotted with bright blue.

The genus *Dascyllus* of the Indo-Pacific region contains several attractive species that are becoming increasingly popular with aquarium hobbyists. *D. trimaculatus*, to 5 inches long, is dark with a single light spot on each side at the base of the dorsal fin between the spiny and soft-rayed portions. There is usually another light spot on the forehead.

The smaller *D. aruanus*, to 2 inches long, has three broad, dark vertical stripes. One runs from the base of the dorsal fin down the forehead to and including the lips. Another starts midway in the dorsal fin on each side and extends obliquely to the pelvic fins, and a third extends from the soft-rayed dorsal fin to the anal fin. The black-tailed dascyllus, *D. melanurus*, has an all-black head and a black-barred tail, plus two broad black bands on its sides—one from the front of the dorsal fin to the pelvic fins and the other from the rear of the dorsal fin to the anal fin.

Black-tailed dascyllus
(Dascyllus melanurus)
5 in (13 cm)

species. The beaugregory is abundant in Bermuda, Caribbean, and Florida waters and occurs also in the Pacific off the coast of Mexico. About 6 inches long, it is variously colored—from a dull brown to ocean blue spattered with yellow spots. The caudal fin is typically yellow. About a dozen similar species are found in the Indo-Pacific region.

Also widespread and with nearly a dozen species in the Indo-Pacific are species of *Chromis*. The yellowtail reeffish, *C. enchrysurus*, is the common representative in Florida, Bermuda, Bahamas, and Caribbean waters, often traveling in schools. To 6 inches long, the species is easily recognized by its deeply forked tail fin. The tips of the rays in its fins are usually black, forming a distinctive black margin. One of the two color phases is brown, the other bright blue. The closely related blue chromis, *C. cyaneus*, is also bright blue but generally found only in deeper, offshore waters. In the warm waters off the Pacific coast, the blacksmith, *C. punctipinnis*, is almost identical but darker.

The garibaldi, *Hypsypops rubicunda*, is the largest damselfish. Some exceed 12 inches in length, though the average is less than 8 inches. Found from southern California southward into tropical waters along rocky shores and in kelp beds, the garibaldi is easily recognized by its uniformly reddish gold color. When young, it is green with blue spots.

Among the most famous of the damselfishes are the dozen or so species of anemone fishes of the genus *Amphiprion*, widely distributed in reef areas of the world. Of these, one of the most common is the clown anemonefish, *A. percula*, its body marked with alternating broad bands of orange and white. The fins are rounded, and the dorsal, caudal, pelvic, and anal fins are margined with black. These fishes have a strange relationship with sea anemones, swimming in and out of the anemone's poisonous tentacles without being stung themselves. They clean the anemone's tentacles of debris. One of the most attractive Indo-Pacific species is *A. epihippium*, which is banded with black, orange, and blue-gray.

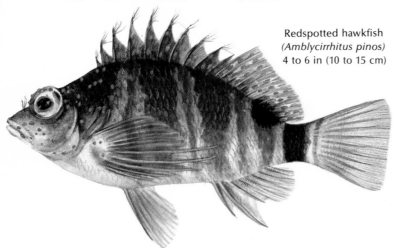

Redspotted hawkfish
(Amblycirrhitus pinos)
4 to 6 in (10 to 15 cm)

Family Cirrhitidae
hawkfishes

Occurring only in Indo-Pacific waters, hawkfishes are small, colorful fishes that inhabit coral reefs where they seem to spend most of their time resting or lying on bits of coral. Only a few species are in the family. In all, the lower rays of the pectoral fins are thickened and extended as feelers. The two common genera are *Cirrhitichthys* and *Paracirrhites*.

Family Mugilidae
mullets

Mullets, like silversides, are schooling fishes. Blunt-nosed and small-mouthed, they pick up mud from the bottom and strain plant and animal material from it through their sievelike gill rakers and pharyngeal teeth. Indigestible materials are spit out. In most species, the stomach is gizzardlike for grinding food. Mullets have the unusual habit of leaping from the water as they race along in their schools. In their jumps, their bodies are stiff, and they fall back into the water with a loud splat. The sound of a leaping mullet stirs most newcomers to mangrove coasts because they think a leaping fish signifies a sporting species. Mullets do not ordinarily take baits or lures, however. Occasionally they are caught on artificial flies or doughballs or even wads of algae; when hooked, they fight gamely. They are caught commercially in nets or in traps. Mullets are worldwide in distribution in shallow, warm seas. A few species live in fresh water, and some are reared in ponds. All are good food fish, though smaller ones may be too bony to eat.

The striped mullet, *Mugil cephalus*, cosmopolitan in warm seas and the only member of the mullet family found off the Pacific coast of North America, may reach a length of 3 feet and weigh as much as 15 pounds. The average is about a pound in weight. The striped mullet, also called black mullet, or fatback, has silvery sides marked with faint black stripes.

Another species common in Florida and Caribbean waters is the smaller white mullet, *M. curema*, which is bluish gray on the back and silvery below, lacking stripes. Small scales extend onto its soft dorsal and anal fins, while the striped mullet has no scales on its fins.

Two other mullets of warm Atlantic and Caribbean waters are the fantail mullet, *M. trichodon*, and the mountain mullet, *Agonostomus monticola*. The fantail mullet may weigh as much as a pound, about the same

Striped mullet *(Mugil cephalus)*
up to 3 ft (90 cm)

White mullet *(Mugil curema)*
5 in (13 cm)

size as the white mullet but with a broad, fan-shaped forked tail. Mountain mullets rarely exceed half a pound in weight. Their lower lip is much thicker and fleshier than the upper. There are no scales on the dorsal and anal fins, and the base of the caudal fin is tinged with yellow.

The Brazilian mullet, *M. brasiliensis*, to 1½ feet long but much slimmer than the American species, is prevalent in the southern Caribbean southward along the South American coast. Common species off the coasts of Europe and Africa and in the Mediterranean are the thick-lipped mullet, *M. chelo*; the thin-lipped gray mullet, *M. capito*; and the golden mullet, *M. auratus*.

Other species occur in Indo-Pacific waters. These include the three-foot *Valamugil buchanani* and the two-foot *Crenimugil crenilabis*. *Agonostomus telfairi* is one of the several species restricted to fresh waters. Other freshwater mullets are found in the West Indies.

The great barracuda, *Sphyraena barracuda*, averages about 3 feet long and weighs from 5 to 10 pounds, but a rod-and-reel record fish weighed 83 pounds. Prevalent in warm Atlantic and Caribbean waters, sometimes straying northward in summer, the great barracuda is sea green with dark bars and oval spots on its back and sides. The belly is white. Like other barracudas, this species is sometimes eaten and is delicious. Among the fishes thought to be toxic or poisonous, the barracuda seems to have the most widespread reputation. The toxic condition apparently is due to an accumulation of toxins from smaller fishes that the barracuda feeds on. Actually, the flesh of the barracuda is rarely poisonous; only a few of the many thousands eaten proved toxic. Sport fishing for barracudas is popular. They are caught by trolling or casting and on both natural and artificial baits. When hooked, a barracuda makes fast runs and often leaps from the water several times. It tires quickly.

Great barracuda *(Sphyraena barracuda)*
average 3 ft (90 cm)

Family Sphyraenidae
barracudas

Barracudas draw unusual interest because of their sharp, fearsome teeth. They have big forked tails, large eyes, and usually dark blotches on a silvery background. The dorsal fins are widely separated, and the lower jaw projects beyond the upper. Slim and cigar-shaped, barracudas of about 20 species occur in warm waters throughout the world. When small, they travel in schools. Large individuals are typically solitary.

Curiosity is a trait of all barracudas. They will follow swimmers, divers, boats, or even people walking along the shore. Most reports of people being attacked by barracudas are false. They seem especially attracted to shiny, flashing objects, feeding by sight rather than by smell.

The Pacific barracuda, *S. argentea*, is shorter than the great barracuda—to 4 feet maximum—and rarely weighs more than 10 pounds. It is the only barracuda found along the Pacific coast of North America; it is rare north of Point Conception in California, although it strays to Alaska.

The Mexican barracuda, *S. ensis*, has dark bars along the sides of its body, distinguishing it from the Pacific barracuda. Its pectoral fins are also larger. Otherwise the species are similar. The Mexican barracuda seldom exceeds 3 pounds in weight.

Other barracudas include the foot-long golden barracuda, *S. flavicauda*, an Indo-Pacific species with a golden stripe from its eye to its tail and with yellowish fins; the striped barracuda, *S. obtustata*, a western Pacific species that may weigh as much as 50 pounds; the shortfin barracuda, *S. novae-hollandiae*, a mainly Australian species that may reach a length of 3 feet but is usually shorter; and the European barracuda, *S. sphyraena*, a foot-long species that may appear on both sides of the Atlantic. The similar-sized northern sennet, *S. borealis*, occurs from the Carolinas to Massachusetts, while the identical southern sennet, *S. picudilla*, is found from the Carolinas to the Caribbean—many authorities considering these two species to be the same. The guaguancho, *S. guachancho*, another small species, is found principally in southern waters.

These species are generally distinguished from one another by the number of scales in the lateral line and also by the length of the pectoral fins. The taxonomy is not clear, however.

Family Polynemidae
threadfins

Threadfins resemble mullets, but the pectoral fin is divided into two parts, the lower portion consisting of half a dozen or more threadlike rays that are used as feelers in finding food on the bottom. The nose is even more blunt than in mullets but is projected into a distinct piglike snout. The eyes are large. Threadfins occur in all warm seas. None occurs off the coast of Europe.

The Atlantic threadfin, *Polydactylus octonemus*, which reaches a length of about 12 inches, lives in the Atlantic from the Carolinas southward and also in the Gulf of Mexico, where it is most abundant. Found in almost the same range but most abundant in the Caribbean is the similar-size barbu, *P. virginicus*.

Related species of about the same size in Pacific waters are the blue bobo, *P. approximans*, and the yellow bobo, *P. opercularis*. A common species in the western Pacific is *P. sexfilis*.

The largest member of the family is the 6-foot *Eleutheronema tetradactylum*, found off the southeastern coast of Asia.

Family Labridae
wrasses

About 500 species comprise the wrasse family, an extremely varied group that is represented most abundantly in warm seas around the world but with some species occurring also in temperate to cool waters. Pro-

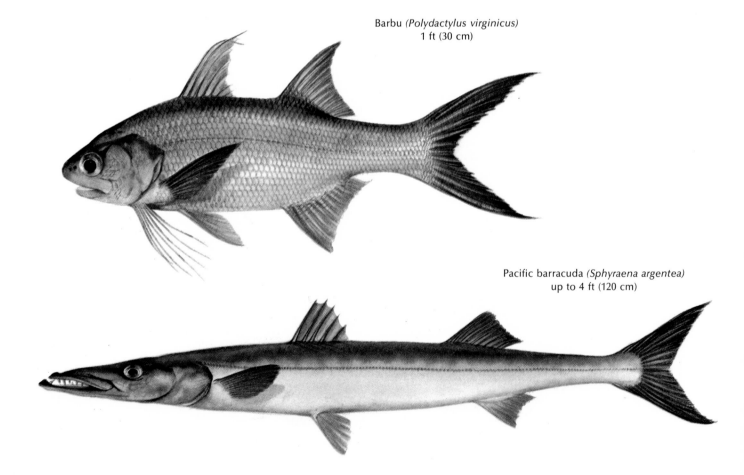

Barbu *(Polydactylus virginicus)*
1 ft (30 cm)

Pacific barracuda *(Sphyraena argentea)*
up to 4 ft (120 cm)

jecting canine teeth and thick, protrusible lips give the face a distinctive profile. Most species are brightly colored, and the body is elongated. The spiny and soft dorsal fins are united as one, and the anal fin is the same size and shape as the soft-rayed portion of the dorsal fin. Typically the pectoral and caudal fins are rounded, and the caudal peduncle is clearly set off from the body. The color of wrasses varies greatly, often differing from young to mature fishes and becoming different during the breeding season as well as changing with the background over which the fishes swim. Most species are greenish, but they may be marked with red, yellow, or blue. The yellow wrasse, *Coris gaimardi*, of tropical Pacific waters, is a hardy, popular aquarium fish, most colorful while still young. Many smaller wrasses of tropical reefs have the unusual habit of cleaning parasites from the bodies of larger fishes.

Among the wrasses living in cool waters is the tautog, *Tautoga onitis*, found from Maine southward to the Carolinas but most abundant in the Massachusetts–New Jersey portion of this range. Known also as blackfish and oysterfish, the tautog averages 3 pounds or less in weight. Specimens weighing 10 pounds are caught with regularity, however, and record fishes have weighed more than 20 pounds. Blunt-nosed and thick-lipped, the tautog has a high forehead and a heavy body. It is brownish on the back and sides, lighter below, with blackish mottling over the entire body. Tautogs are darker over a dark background and lighter over a light background. The caudal fin is rounded on the corners and squared across the tip; the soft-rayed dorsal and the anal fins are rounded.

The tautog prefers rocky-bottomed areas and uses the flat, rounded, stout teeth located in the rear of its mouth to crush the shells of mollusks or crustaceans. The front teeth do the picking. Sometimes the tautog moves in with the incoming tide to feed on mussels that are normally above the low-tide level. Fishermen who

know this habit make a special effort to catch these tide-running individuals. Tautogs are usually fished for on the bottom, the hook baited with seaworms, clams, crabs, or similar natural baits. The experienced fisherman does not fish for tautogs with light tackle, for they can move rapidly into the rocks where a line can be sawed in two quickly. Fishing is best from spring until fall, the fishes moving into deeper, warmer water in winter.

The cunner, *Tautogolabrus adspersus*, occurs even farther north than the tautog, ranging from New Jersey to Labrador. Where their ranges overlap, the two species are often found together. They are similar in general body shape, but the cunner is slimmer and has a much lower head profile. Further, the cunner has scales on its gill covers and only about 40 scales in a count along its lateral line. The tautog does not have scales on

Yellowtail wrasse *(Coris gaimardi)*
up to 1 ft (30 cm)

its gill covers and has about 70 scales in a lateral-line count. Cunners are smaller fishes, averaging only about a quarter of a pound and only rarely exceeding 2 pounds. Fishermen catch cunners more by accident than by choice. The fish is a superb bait stealer, but if one is hooked, its spiny fins make it a formidable creature to take off the hook. On very light tackle and with a cunner-catching attitude, this species can be sporting,

Tautog *(Tautoga onitis)*
3 ft (90 cm)

California sheepshead *(Pimelometopon pulchrum)*
up to 3 ft (90 cm)

however. The cunner is generally considered a good table fish. Some fishermen prefer them in a chowder.

The California sheepshead, *Pimelometopon pulchrum*, is one of the most unusual wrasses in color pattern. Males have a black high-profiled head and are also black from the second dorsal and anal fins to and including the caudal fin. The middle of the body is orange-red, and the chin or lower jaw is white. During the breeding season, males also get a fatty hump on their foreheads. Females are generally uniformly orange-red, though some are all black or are blotched. In both sexes, the large canine teeth are conspicuously slanted forward, and the body appears to have an almost rectangular shape.

California sheepshead reach a length of 3 feet and may weigh as much as 36 pounds, though they average 3 pounds or less. They range from Monterey Bay to the Gulf of California and are found most abundantly in kelp beds or along rocky shores. Fishermen catch this species year round but in greatest numbers in winter, using natural baits that are fished on the bottom as for the tautog.

Hogfishes, *Lachnolaimus maximus*, are large, warm-water wrasses of Florida and Caribbean waters, including Bermuda and the Bahamas. They may weigh as much as 20 pounds and exceed 2 feet in length. The head slopes upward sharply from the piglike pointed snout to the first dorsal fin, the first three spines of which extend into long filaments. The first rays of the soft dorsal and anal fins are long and pointed, as are the rays at the top and bottom of the caudal fin. The teeth are set in the mouth at different angles so that the fish appears to be much in need of orthodontic attention. In most individuals, the basic color is red or pink with yellow mottling; in some the yellow dominates, and the mottling is red. The fins are generally reddish. Often the soft-rayed dorsal, caudal, and anal ribs are barred with blue. A dark blotch at the back of the dorsal fin is characteristic of the species.

The hogfish is generally solitary but sometimes travels in small groups, frequenting reefs, rocks, and wrecks. Like other members of the family, it feeds primarily on mollusks and crustaceans. Though seldom fished for, it fights gamely and makes an exciting catch on light tackle. It is also good to eat.

The brightly colored spotfin hogfish, *Bodianus pulchellus*, goes also by the names scarlet hogfish and Cuban hogfish. Common also in Florida and Caribbean waters, it is slimmer than the common hogfish and lacks extensions on its fins. It is sometimes kept by hobbyists.

Blueheads, *Thalassoma bifasciatum*, of Florida, Bermuda, the Bahamas, and Caribbean waters, are about 6 inches long. Males have a blue head and a collar of two black bands; the body and tail are greenish with a yellowish cast. Females are yellowish with black blotches along their sides. This is probably the most common reef fish of the region.

Razorfishes, *Hemipteronotus*, of a number of species are common in warm waters. They average about 6 inches long; a few are larger. The body is much com-

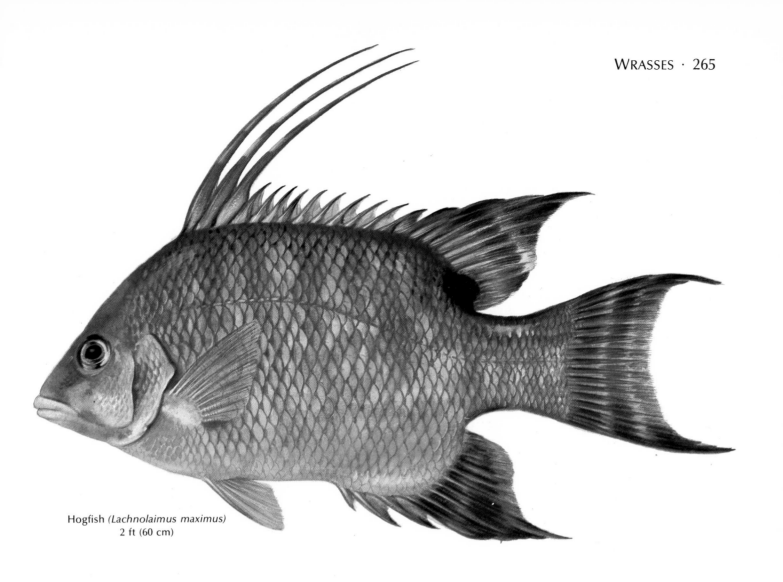

Hogfish *(Lachnolaimus maximus)*
2 ft (60 cm)

Slippery dick *(Halichoeres bivittatus)*
6 in (15 cm)

Spotfin hogfish *(Bodianus pulchellus)*
1 ft (30 cm)

pressed, and the forehead sometimes forms a sharp, razorlike edge. Common species, their names describing their predominant coloration, are rosy razorfish, *H. martinicensis*; green razorfish, *H. splendens*; and pearly razorfish, *H. novacuia*. Like most wrasses, they have the peculiar habit of burying themselves in the sand at night and emerging to feed during the day. In razorfishes, the sharp edge on the head makes it possible for them to burrow under the sand rapidly.

Also common in the warm Atlantic and the Caribbean, particularly around reefs, are small wrasses of the genus *Halichoeres*, most of them pearly or iridescent and with bright bands or blotches on the body. Among these are the yellowhead wrasse, *H. garnoti*; greenband wrasse, *H. bathyphilus*; slippery dick, *H. bivittatus*; clown wrasse, *H. maculipinna*; and others. Largest of the group is the puddingwife, *H. radiatus*, which may attain a length of 1½ feet.

One species, the rock wrasse, *H. semicinctus*, occurs

off the coast of southern California southward into Mexican waters. It has a conspicuous blue bar behind each pectoral fin. Another Pacific Coast species is the senorita, *Oxyalis californica*, a brownish, 6-inch species that is creamy white below and has a large black blotch at the base of its tail.

The largest of all wrasses, *Cheilinus undulatus*, may reach a length of 6 feet and weigh 150 pounds or more. This giant wrasse, identified even when it is small by the two prominent black lines behind each eye, lives in Indo-Pacific waters. Others in its genus in the same general area are less than a foot long.

Also occurring in Indo-Pacific waters are two unusual wrasses of the genus *Gomphosus*, their snouts greatly elongated and curved down slightly at the tip. Similarly, the Indo-Pacific *Epibulus insidiator* can extend its mouth into a long tube for feeding in rocky crevices. All three species are less than 10 inches long.

Older individuals of *Hemigymnus fasciatus*, another Indo-Pacific species, acquire exceptionally thick lips. As elsewhere, the reef wrasses are among the most colorful of all fishes, some of the color combinations and patterns literally defying description.

Wrasses are rare off the coast of Europe, where the water is too cool for most species; but one species, the cuckoo wrasse, *Labrus ossifagus*, occurs from the Mediterranean northward to Norway. Surprisingly, for a fish of northern distribution, it is riotously colored, the head and most of the body purple and a purple bar extending across the caudal fin. The belly and the soft dorsal fin are a bright orange.

Family Scaridae
parrotfishes

Parrotfishes, found in subtropical and tropical seas around the world, are almost as uniquely identifiable with coral reefs as the coral itself. Their name comes from their heavy, parrotlike beak, which is formed of their fused teeth. Sharp and powerful, the beak is used for crushing the hard outer skeletons of the reef-forming corals to get at the soft animals inside or to scrape growths from the outer surface of the reef rocks.

All 75 to perhaps 100 species have large scales and thick bodies that are brighly colored. Parrotfishes are usually seen in groups, but they are not schooling fishes. They are steady but not swift swimmers. Some parrotfishes have the unusual habit of secreting a mucous sac around the body at night and emerging from it in the morning.

The rainbow parrotfish, *Scarus guacamaia*, is the largest North American parrotfish, sometimes attaining a weight of 20 pounds and a length of 3 feet. It averages about a foot in length. The rainbow parrotfish lives in reefs off the Florida coast, Bermuda, the Bahamas, and in the Caribbean. As its name indicates, adults of this species are a combination of many colors, but they have a greenish-blue beak, and the throat and breast are orange or reddish brown. The dorsal and anal fins are bordered with blue-green. Color varies considerably with the individual. The distinctively colored beak is shared with other species that are sometimes grouped in a different genus—*Pseudoscarus*.

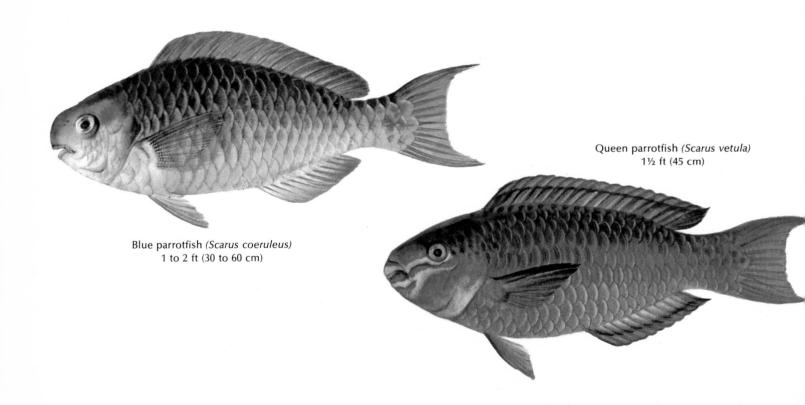

Blue parrotfish *(Scarus coeruleus)*
1 to 2 ft (30 to 60 cm)

Queen parrotfish *(Scarus vetula)*
1½ ft (45 cm)

Sailfin sandfish (*Arctoscopus japonicus*)
up to 1 ft (30 cm)

The midnight parrotfish, *S. coelestinus*, may exceed 2 feet in length, nearly as large as the rainbow parrotfish and occurring in the same range. The basic color is a dark purplish blue; the front of the head, the jaws, and the base of the spiny dorsal fin are a bright greenish blue. The beak is greenish blue.

The blue parrotfish, *S. coeruleus*, is also of Florida, Bermuda, Bahamas, and Caribbean waters but sometimes strays far northward in the Atlantic. Its average length is 12 inches, but not uncommonly it exceeds 2 feet. This species and several others in the genus are unique in that the lower jaw is shorter than the upper; the beak is white or sometimes rosy. Blue parrotfishes are bright blue when mature; the young are brownish. The outer rays of both the upper and lower lobes of the caudal fin are long, especially in older fishes, and older males acquire a characteristic hump on their snout. The lateral line stops about midway on the body, then begins again on the caudal peduncle.

The blue parrotfish is very common, and it has a number of close relatives in Florida and Caribbean waters: the striped parrotfish, *S. croicensis*, a 10-inch brown to bluish gray species with a yellow patch on its nose and two light stripes down each side of its body; queen parrotfish, *S. vetula*, a 1½-foot species with red edges on its jaws and its caudal and pectoral fins; painted parrotfish, *S. punctulatus*, a strictly Caribbean species about 12 inches long and with two bright green stripes on the head—one above and one below the eye; white-banded parrotfish, *S. gnathodus*, another common Caribbean species that is about a foot long and distinguished by a broad white stripe down each side of the body.

The stoplight parrotfish, *Sparisoma viride*, represents another group of parrotfishes that averages about a foot in length. Over most of the body the scales are a dull green, but they are bright green on the tail, which has orange on its base and is margined with blue. A close relative of this species in Caribbean waters is the gray or olive mud parrotfish, *S. flavescens*, to 12 inches long.

The red parrotfish, *S. abildgaardi*, which occurs in the same area, is about the same size and has a pinkish beak, red fins, and white scales outlined with black.

Parrotfishes of different but similar genera occur abundantly in the reefs of the Indo-Pacific. The most common genera are *Callyodon* and *Xanathon*.

Family Trichodontidae
sandfishes

This family is comprised of only two known species. *Arctoscopus japonicus*, the sailfin sandfish, is found in the eastern Pacific and harvested commercially for food in Japan. A slim, silvery fish that attains a maximum length of 12 inches, it spends most of its time in water 300 to 500 feet deep but moves into shallow water to spawn. The young remain there until the following summer. Adults are scaleless, their mouths nearly vertical and their lips fringed.

These features are also characteristic of the other species, the Pacific sandfish, *Trichodon trichodon*, which lives along the Pacific coast from California northward to Alaska. It has 14–15 spines in its first dorsal fin; *Arctoscopus* has 10–11.

Family Opistognathidae
jawfishes

A small family of fishes of subtropical and tropical waters, jawfishes have a very large blennylike mouth and head. In some species, extensions of the jawbones make it possible for the fish to open its mouth so wide that it can engulf fishes larger around than its own head when the jaws are in their normal position. Most of the species are small—6 inches or less in length.

Seven species in the genus *Opistognathus* live in warm Atlantic, Gulf, and Caribbean waters. Included is the 4-inch yellowhead jawfish, *O. aurifrons*, which has been studied in considerable detail and has provided

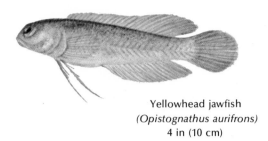

Yellowhead jawfish
(Opistognathus aurifrons)
4 in (10 cm)

most of the information known about these fishes.

The Indo-Pacific *O. muscatensis* is 1½ feet long; its long, low dorsal fin is marked by an ocellated spot at the front margin.

Some species in the genus dig burrows a foot or more deep into an enlarged chamber in which they spend much of their time. They may rest with their heads at the opening and then retreat rapidly in reverse if disturbed.

Family Dactyloscopidae
sand stargazers

This smaller family of stargazers is distinguished from the electric stargazers, or uranoscopids, by their lack of electric organs. They also have a well-developed lateral line, which uranoscopids do not. Otherwise these stargazers are similar in appearance to electric stargazers. The sand stargazer, *Dactyloscopus tridigitatus*, lives in warm Atlantic, Caribbean, and Gulf of Mexico waters. Four other species of sand stargazers are included in the American Fisheries Society's list of fishes of the United States and Canada.

Family Uranoscopidae
stargazers

Widely distributed in warm seas throughout the world, the roughly two dozen chunky-bodied, toadlike species in this family are among the kinds of fishes capable of producing electric shocks with which they stun their prey and discourage intruders. Their electric organs, located behind their eyes and derived from optic nerve tissue, can generate 50 volts or more. Typically the fishes lie buried with only their bulbous eyes and their mouths protruding above the surface of the sand. In some, a wormlike filament in the wide-open mouth dances enticingly and lures small fishes close enough to be stunned by the electrical discharge that can be released at the fish's will.

The electrical shocking equipment is only one weapon used by these fishes. They also have two poisonous spines above each pectoral fin. Grooves in the spines are connected to venom glands; in some species the poison is potent enough to kill a man.

The northern stargazer, *Astroscopus guttatus*, averaging 6 to 8 inches long and to 20 inches maximum, occurs in the Atlantic from New York southward to Cape Hatteras, where it is replaced by the smaller southern stargazer, *A. y-graecum*, which ranges southward to Brazil. The European stargazer, *Uranoscopus scaber*, is similar to the rest of the species.

Northern stargazer *(Astroscopus guttatus)*
6 to 20 in (15 to 51 cm)

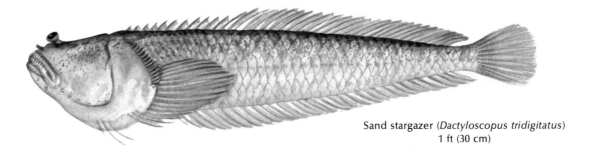

Sand stargazer (*Dactyloscopus tridigitatus*)
1 ft (30 cm)

Family Blenniidae
combtooth blennies

These small, scaleless fishes of tropical waters are similar to gobies in habits and general appearance. They swim more gracefully, however, resting by propping themselves on their pelvic fins. The spiny and soft-rayed dorsal fins are joined rather than separate as in gobies. Similar to gobies, blennies and their relatives can live out of water for long periods of time if they are kept moist. Some spend much time perched out of water along the shore, jumping back in like frogs when they become alarmed. Like frogs, too, they have broad heads and large eyes. Blennies are among the most attractive of all the fishes, their colors commonly providing them with an effective camouflage. As in gobies, the male typically makes a nest to which he lures a female to lay her eggs. He then guards the eggs until they hatch. The approximately 500 species of blennies and their relatives are sometimes placed in one family, or they may be classified in several families, as here.

The molly miller, *Blennius cristatus*, to 4 inches long, is a common species of warm to tropical seas, occurring from Florida to Brazil. A crest or comb of filaments on top of its head is the most identifying feature. Closely related species also of the Atlantic are the fringe blenny,

B. pilicornis, and the highfin blenny, *B. nicholsi*. The freckled blenny, *Hypsoblennius ionthas*, also a small fish of tidal pools or similar shallows, has generic counterparts on the Pacific coast—the bay blenny, *H. gentilis*, and rockpool blenny, *H. gilberti*.

Family Anarhichadidae
wolffishes

Eel-like in body shape, wolffishes are blenny relatives that live in cold to Arctic waters of the Atlantic and Pacific. They lack pelvic fins. The dorsal fin, which begins just behind the head, extends to the caudal fin but is not joined to it. The anal fin extends along about half the length of the ventral surface. Wolffishes have powerful jaws and numerous broad teeth that are used to crush the shells of mollusks and crustaceans. They also have sharp canine teeth, which makes them dangerous to handle.

The Atlantic wolffish, *Anarhichas lupus*, to 5 feet long and weighing as much as 30 pounds, is found from Massachusetts northward and also off the northern coast of Europe. The sides of its brownish gray to purplish body are crossed by as many as a dozen vertical black bars. Though it appears sluggish, it is easily pro-

Atlantic wolffish *(Anarhichas lupus)*
up to 5 ft (150 cm)

voked, can move rapidly for short distances, and gives severe bites. Also in the North Atlantic the slightly larger spotted wolffish, *A. minor*, and the smaller jelly cat, *A. latifrons*, are both caught commercially off the coast of Europe, the latter generally only for bait.

In the Pacific, the very similar Bering wolffish, *A. orientalis*, occurs in the Sea of Japan and from Alaska southward to central California. The wolf-eel, *Anarrichthys ocellatus*, has a similar range; it reaches a length of 6 feet 8 inches. These fishes are caught regularly in trawls by commercial fishermen. They make excellent eating, despite their ugly appearance.

Family Clinidae
clinids

This large family of blennies is distinguished from the previous family principally by the possession of scales. In addition to those described here, there are many species in the Southern Hemisphere. The American Fisheries Society includes 45 species present off the shores of the United States and Canada.

The giant kelpfish, *Heterostichus rostratus*, is the largest of the blennies, reaching a length of 2 feet. Found from Baja California to central California, it has a much longer head than most blennies. It is usually brownish or greenish, mottled with white, but the colors and patterns vary with the environment. It lives mainly in the giant kelps.

The hairy blenny, *Labrisomus nuchipinnis*, to 8 inches long, is common on both sides of the tropical Atlantic. The sarcastic fringehead, *Neoclinus blanchardi*, to 9

inches long, is a California species with a cavernous mouth that gives it a smirking or sarcastic grin.

Half a dozen species in the genus *Paraclinus* are found most abundantly in reef waters. Pikeblennies, *Chaenopsis*, are slim and pikelike in body shape and are known for the fierce defense of their territories.

Family Stichaeidae
pricklebacks

The several dozen blennies in this family are scaled. The rays of the long dorsal fin are all spiny except for a few near the end.

The monkeyface blenny, *Cebidichthys violaceous*, lacks pelvic fins, but its pectoral fins are almost as long as its head. The eel-like body may be up to 2½ feet long and is a mottled green or brownish green above, paler below. Often there are orange or reddish spots on the sides. This species is fished for regularly by people who consider it a delicacy. They use a stout pole, short line, and a hook baited with cut bait, crabs, or small fishes.

The similar rock prickleback, *Xiphister mucosus*, has four branched lateral lines (the monkeyface blenny has only one), and the pectoral fins are small. Reaching a length of 1½ feet, the rock prickleback is blackish green above and paler below, often with patches of yellow. Two greenish brown lines edged with black extend back along the body from each eye. The rock prickleback is another species sometimes caught as a sport fish but never in large numbers.

The decorated warbonnet, *Chirolophis polyactocephalus*, to 1½ feet long, has numerous plumelike filaments on its head. It is found from Washington to

Hairy blenny (*Labrisomus nuchipinnis*)
8 in (20 cm)

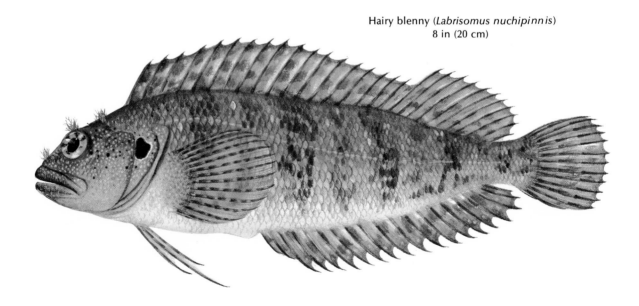

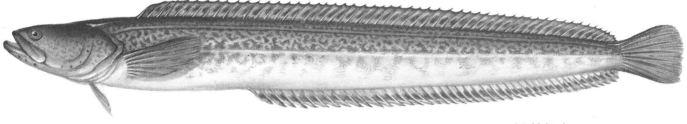

Prickleback
8 in (20 cm)

Alaska. The longsnout prickleback, *Lumpenella lon-girostris*, lives at depths of 1,000 feet or greater in Alaskan waters.

Among the Atlantic species is the wrymouth, *Cryptocanthodes maculatus*, to 3 feet long. It lives along the coast from Massachusetts northward. A bottom-dweller, it inhabits branching burrows that may be 3 inches or more beneath the surface. The burrows are sometimes located above the low-tide level so that they are alternately exposed and submerged. The wrymouth (and its relatives, often placed in a separate family, Cryptacanthodidae) lacks pelvic fins and has no lateral line. The long, low, spiny dorsal fin extends the full length of the fish's back and is joined to the rays of the caudal fin, which in turn is continuous on the underside with the anal fin. The anal fin extends over about half the length of the ventral surface. The brownish sides are flecked with dark dots. The mouth is large, the lower jaw projecting slightly so that the mouth opening is directed upward—in the direction of the prey.

Family Pholidae
gunnels

These eel-like blennies live in shallow waters of the northern Atlantic and Pacific oceans. Their lateral line is incomplete, and the dorsal fin consists only of spines that extend the full length of the back.

The most familiar of the Atlantic species is the rock gunnel, *Pholis gunnellus*, which averages about 8 inches long and is found in cold waters on both sides of the Atlantic. Its basic color is usually yellowish, including the fins, but there are black spots on the sides just under the dorsal fin. The female rolls her mass of eggs into a ball by curling her body around them, and both the male and the female take turns guarding the mass, holding it protectively in a coil of the body until the eggs hatch. The rock gunnel is the largest of several Atlantic species of *Pholis*, a genus with similar representatives in the Pacific.

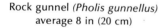

Rock gunnel *(Pholis gunnellus)*
average 8 in (20 cm)

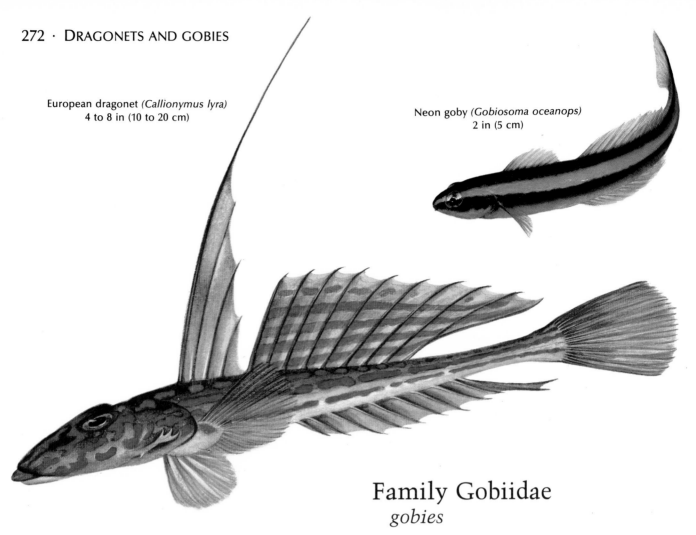

European dragonet *(Callionymus lyra)*
4 to 8 in (10 to 20 cm)

Neon goby *(Gobiosoma oceanops)*
2 in (5 cm)

Family Callionymidae
dragonets

This is a small family of bottom-dwelling fishes found in temperate and tropical seas. The maximum length is 12 inches; most species are smaller. They have small mouths with large lips, and the large eyes are located near the top of the head. The body lacks scales; in most species, a lateral line is distinctly visible but is obscure or lacking in others. At breeding time, the males become brightly colored.

The best-known species is the European dragonet, *Callionymus lyra*, in which the male first courts the female by spreading and displaying his fins and then mates with her. The two press their bodies together and then swim slowly upward from the bottom, the female shedding her eggs and the male discharging milt over them.

The spotfin dragonet, *C. agassizi*, has been netted in waters 300 to 1,500 feet deep off the coast of Florida.

Family Gobiidae
gobies

Gobies are small bottom-dwelling fishes that are usually less than 6 inches long; only a few species grow to as much as 12 inches in length. The bases of their pelvic fins are united, forming a sucking disk with which they hold onto the bottom. In typical members of the family there is no lateral line. The second, or soft-rayed, dorsal fin and the anal fin mirror each other in size and shape. The family consists of about 400 species, most of them marine but some inhabiting brackish or fresh waters.

A stream-dweller of the Philippines, the tiny *Pandaka pygmaea*, only half an inch long when fully grown, is considered the smallest of all vertebrates. It is netted and sold in markets for baking into fish cakes. It requires nearly 15,000 of these tiny fish to weigh a pound. Some of the coral-reef gobies of the Indo-Pacific are nearly as small, several species less than an inch long.

Gobies commonly rest on the bottom, sometimes propped on their pelvic fins, and they dart quickly from place to place. Some live in burrows in the sand or mud. Like blennies, gobies show an inclination to come out of the water, some of the species being able to trap air and water in their gill chambers and thus survive for several hours out of the water. If they are kept damp, they can live literally for weeks without being submerged. Many species of gobies live in tidal pools or close to shore.

Bluebanded goby *(Lythrypnus dalli)*
1 in (2.5 cm)

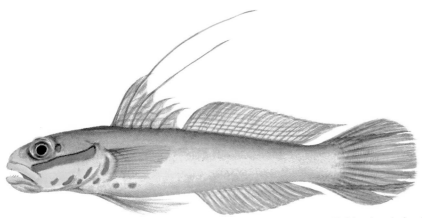

Golden-headed goby *(Eleotroides strigatos)*
4 in (10 cm)

Most gobies go through an elaborate courtship. The male makes a nest, usually in a cavity beneath a rock or in coral, and then spreads his fins and displays himself to attract a female to the nest to lay her eggs. The male fertilizes them immediately and then may entice one or more other females into the nest to lay more eggs. When he is finally satisfied that the nest is well enough provided, he begins his vigilant guard to keep away intruders until the eggs have hatched. The male does not eat during this period.

The frillfin goby, *Bathygobius soporator*, also called mapo or molly miller, sometimes reaches a length of 6 inches but is usually smaller. Occurring along the Atlantic coast from the Carolinas southward throughout the Caribbean and also in the Gulf of Mexico, it is common along shores and also in tidal pools. The habits of this species have been studied in considerable detail, providing much information about gobies as a group.

Among the literally dozens of other species commonly seen along the Atlantic, some occasionally as far north as Massachusetts, are the crested goby, *Lophogobius cyprinoides*, a 2-inch species with a noticeably large head; river goby, *Awaous tajasica*, to 12 inches long though usually shorter, with a conspicuously white belly and dark blotches on its olive to greenish sides; clown goby, *Microgobius gulosus*, a 2- to 3-inch species found also in the Gulf of Mexico, with a large mouth and a projecting lower jaw, filamentlike spine in the first dorsal fin, a pointed tail fin, and a light blue stripe on each side of the head; naked goby, *Gobiosoma bosci*, another species found also in the Gulf of Mexico, a 2½-inch fish with a big mouth, no scales, and seven to nine white crossbars across the muddy-black back and sides; and neon goby, *G. oceanops*, a 2-inch species that is black with a light blue band down each side.

Gobies are also found along the Pacific coast from British Columbia southward, most abundantly in tidal pools and on mudflats in warmer waters.

The longjaw mudsucker, *Gillichthys mirabilis*, ranging from central California to Baja California in bays and straying also into fresh water.(introduced into the Salton Sea), is brownish yellow, speckled with black. It reaches a length of 8 inches. Like other gobies, it is extremely hardy, contributing to its popularity for bait.

Other Pacific species include the blind goby, *Typhlogobius californiensis*, a blind, pink, 2½-inch species that spends its life in holes dug by a ghost shrimp; arrow goby, *Clevelandia ios*, a 2-inch species that shares holes in mudflats with crabs and worms; and blue-banded goby, *Lythrypnus dalli*, an inch-long species with a bright red body crossed with five or six purple bands bordered with black.

Gobies are abundant also in the western Pacific and Indian oceans as well as along the coasts of Europe and Africa in the eastern Atlantic. The golden-headed goby, *Eleotriodes strigatos*, is a western Pacific species. All are similar in general body shape and habits, and only a few species exceed 6 inches in length. Among the smallest are species of *Eviota*, averaging less than an inch long.

Mudskippers, *Periophthalmus spp.* and *Boleophthalmus spp.*, live on mudflats along mangrove shores. When the tide recedes, they stay on the mud, hopping or "skipping" about over the surface like frogs or toads.

Mudskipper *(Periophthalmus barbarus)*
5 in (13 cm)

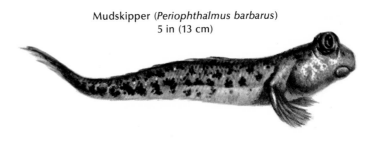

Like them, too, they have large heads and bulbous eyes. Their large pectoral fins are used like legs.

Among the Indo-Pacific species, too, are species that cohabit with other animals. *Obtotiophagus koumansi* and *Cryptocentrus cryptocentrus*, for example, live in burrows with prawns.

Closely related to gobies, and placed in a separate family, Eleotridae, by some scientists, sleepers differ in lacking the sucking disk characteristic of the gobies. The pelvic fins of sleepers are separated. Their name is derived from a common species habit of resting on the bottom as though "sleeping" and rarely moving from this position unless disturbed. Those that do not rest on the bottom remain motionless in the water above, as though suspended there, but they dive down into hiding when frightened or endangered.

The fat sleeper, *Dormitator maculatus*, up to 2 feet in length but usually less than a foot long, lives in Caribbean waters and in the warm Atlantic northward to the Carolinas, commonly invading brackish and fresh waters. The head is bluntly rounded, the mouth large, and the body scaled. There is no visible lateral line, and the caudal fin is rounded. In general body shape, the fat sleeper looks much like a fat mullet, but the second dorsal and the anal fins are large and of equal size. Because it can tolerate a wide range of water conditions, even stagnant water, the fat sleeper makes a good aquarium pet. Its color is variable but usually dark brown and mottled.

The bigmouth sleeper, *Gobiomorus dormitor*, which regularly exceeds 2 feet in length, is found along the Florida coasts and in the Caribbean; it is also found in fresh water. Much slimmer than the fat sleeper, it has a large, pikelike mouth, and its high second dorsal and anal fins are squared off obliquely. The first dorsal is margined with black. The body is olive green.

The blue sleeper, *Isoglossus calliurus*, is a 4-inch species that lives in deep waters of the Gulf of Mexico. The emerald sleeper, *Erotelis smaragdus*, about 6 inches long, is bright green, matching the color of the algae in which it lives off the southern coasts of Florida and in the Caribbean.

The more than two dozen species of sleepers in the Indo-Pacific are mostly less than 6 inches long, and

Fat sleeper *(Dormitator maculatus)*
up to 2 ft (60 cm)

many of the coral-reef inhabitants are colorful. The attractive *Ptereleotris tricolor*, for example, is light greenish blue in front and purplish blue from the second dorsal and anal fins to and including the caudal fin, the center of which is bright yellow. The upper margin of the dorsal fin is also yellow.

The widely distributed *Eleotriodes helsdingenii* has a black stripe bordered on each side by red extending from the snout through the eye and down the side of the body to the upper lobe of the tail fin, which is extended at that point into a filament. A matching stripe runs from the upper jaw to the lower lobe of the tail fin. The fins are yellowish, the spiny dorsal bearing a large black spot and the second dorsal margined with black. The back and sides are yellowish brown to the lateral line; below, whitish to mauve.

Sailfin tang
(Zebrasoma veliferum)

Family Acanthuridae
surgeonfishes

The roughly 100 species of surgeonfishes live in coral reefs around the world. All appear to have a nearly oval body shape because of the identical rounded shapes of the soft dorsal and anal fins. Their name is derived from the sharp, knifelike spine on each side of the caudal peduncle. In most species the spines are folded into a groove normally, but they are lifted when the fish is disturbed or excited. The spines are used as weapons for inflicting slash wounds in victims. Some species have two or more of these spines on each side. Though they are not schooling fishes, surgeonfishes generally travel in small groups, and they use their incisor teeth to scrape growths of plants and animals from rocks.

The ocean surgeon, *Acanthurus bahianus*, about 12 inches long, has a lunate tail, with the upper lobe much longer than the lower. It is bluish to brownish and darker above than below, its sides blotched with a dark brown. There are six to eight dark, parallel horizontal bars on the dorsal fin. The spine on the caudal peduncle is bluish, as are the pelvic and anal fins. The caudal fin is margined with white across its tip. The ocean surgeon

Convict tang
(*Acanthurus triostegus*)
1 ft (30 cm)

Moorish idol
(*Zanclus canescens*)
6 in (15 cm)

Powder blue surgeonfish
(*Acanthurus leucosternon*)
1 ft (30 cm)

lives in warm Atlantic and Caribbean waters, from Brazil to the Carolinas and straying northward in summer.

The blue tang, *A. coeruleus*, about the same size and occurring in the same range as the ocean surgeon, is a rich, deep blue, with 40 or more narrow, longitudinal stripes of light blue or purple. The color varies with the individual and also with the background. The dorsal and anal fins are striped alternately with dark and light blue, and a broad band of brown crosses the blue caudal fin. Also distinctive are the white spines on the caudal peduncle. The young of the blue tang are yellow, so unlike the adults that they were originally classified as a different species.

The doctorfish, *A. chirurgus*, another of the dozen or more species of *Acanthurus* in the Atlantic, is generally dark brown, and the spines on its caudal peduncle are nearly black.

Many more species in this genus occur in Indo-Pacific waters, most of them only about a foot long. One of the smallest and most attractive is the powder-blue surgeonfish, *A. leucosternon*.

The sailfin tang, *Zebrasoma veliferum*, of tropical Pacific, is another species sometimes kept in aquariums. Its exceptionally large dorsal and anal fins are distinctive.

The moorish idol, *Zanclus canescens*, is one of the most spectacular reef fishes. Found only in Indo-Pacific waters, this 6-inch fish has a broad band of black from the leading edge of its dorsal fin to its pelvic fins, extending through the eyes. Another and narrower band runs from the rear of the dorsal fin through the anal fin; a third, through the caudal fin. The spaces between are broad bands of white and creamy yellow. The snout is projected and tubelike, and there are hornlike protuberances over the eyes. The lower jaw is black; the upper jaw and much of the face, white. A narrow black bar that extends down the forehead is winged or broadened at the base of the snout, the center filled with orange. Both the dorsal and anal fins are long and swept back.

Unicorn fish, several species of the genus *Naso*, are Indo-Pacific fishes that typically have an enlarged lump on their heads and two immovable spines on each side of the caudal peduncle.

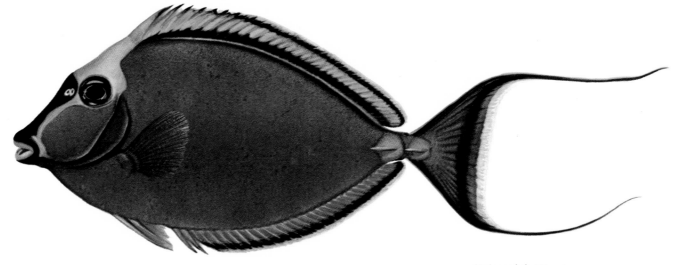

Unicornfish *(Naso)*
6 in (15 cm)

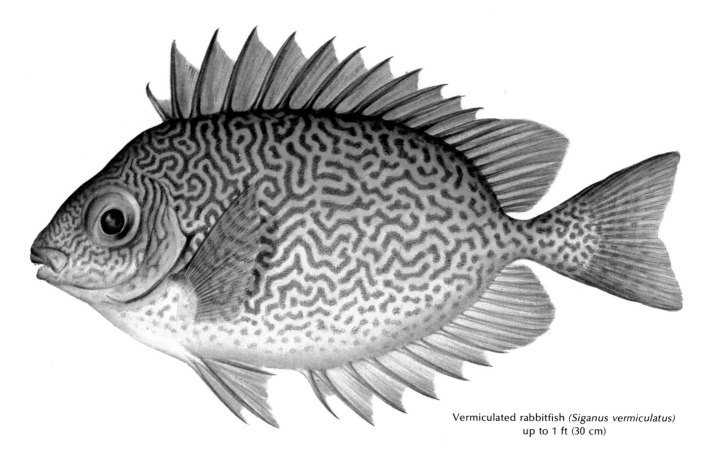

Vermiculated rabbitfish *(Siganus vermiculatus)*
up to 1 ft (30 cm)

Family Siganidae
rabbitfishes

About two dozen species comprise this family of fishes that lives in the tropical Pacific. Their name comes from their rounded head and rabbitlike mouth. Like rabbits, they are grazers, feeding on plants in shallow inshore waters, some species ranging into brackish or even fresh water. The two spines at the leading edge of the pelvic fins, 7 in the anal fin and 13 in the spiny dorsal fin, are all grooved and connected to glands that produce a poison. Stab wounds from these spines are extremely painful. The pain soon passes, but the wounds are slow in healing. The first dorsal spine is directed forward rather than slanting backward as the other spines do.

The most abundantly represented genus is *Siganus*. Only a few of the species exceed 12 inches in length. In many areas, rabbitfishes are considered a delicacy, while in others they are avoided for fear of poisoning. Members of the genus *Lo,* of the western Pacific, have long snouts.

Family Gempylidae
snake mackerels

Found usually in deep waters, to 2,000 feet or more, and mainly in the tropics but ranging into temperate seas, snake mackerels are slim, mackerel-like fishes that do not have keels on the sides of the caudal peduncle as the mackerels do. The spiny and soft-rayed dorsal fins are separate, however, and there are finlets both above and below on the caudal peduncle. All have prominent teeth and a jutting lower jaw.

One of the most common of the roughly 20 species is the oilfish, *Ruvettus prétiosus*, widespread in the Atlantic and occurring also in the Mediterranean. It is most abundant in deep tropical waters but may also appear far north.

Family Trichiuridae
cutlassfishes

Also a family of about 20 species, cutlassfishes are distinguished by their much-flattened or compressed silvery or brownish body, which is almost ribbonlike and tapers to a slim, usually pointed tail. The head is spear-shaped, resembling a barracuda's, and the teeth are prominent. Cutlassfishes are swift swimmers, usually staying close to the bottom.

The Atlantic cutlassfish, *Trichiurus lepturus*, to 5 feet long, is widely distributed and is almost identical with the equally widely distributed *T. nitens* of the Pacific; some authorities consider them the same species.

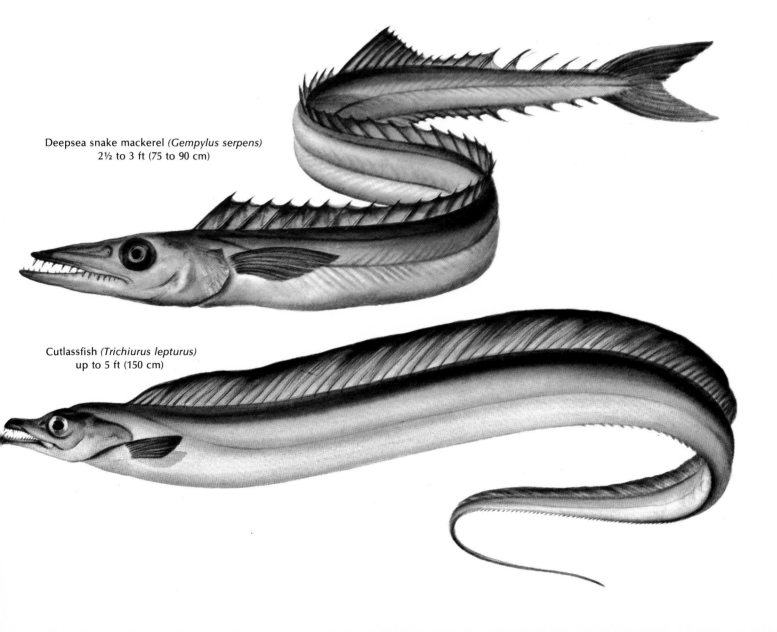

Deepsea snake mackerel *(Gempylus serpens)*
2½ to 3 ft (75 to 90 cm)

Cutlassfish *(Trichiurus lepturus)*
up to 5 ft (150 cm)

Family Scombridae
mackerels and tunas

These mainly schooling fishes of the open sea have probably the most streamlined body shape of all fishes. The body is literally a spindle, with a pointed head and a much-tapered tail. The large caudal fin is lunate or crescent-shaped. Swift swimmers, schools of tunas may cruise at 30 miles per hour, attacking other fishes that cross their path. Mackerels are much smaller but just as speedy. Some of these fishes have slots into which their spinous dorsal fins fit, thus reducing even more their resistance for their great speed. The spiny and soft-rayed dorsal fins are separate, the soft-rayed dorsal matched in size and shape by the anal fin directly beneath it. Following each fin is a series of finlets, the number varying with the species. In all species, the scales are extremely small or lacking.

Most tunas and mackerels are ocean blue or greenish on the back, grading into silvery on the sides and the belly; but some notable exceptions occur in the roughly 75 widely distributed species. Classification is still in a state of flux.

Tunas and mackerels are among the most important fishes, providing sport as well as contributing to a significant commercial fishery. Most of them do not do much of their fighting above the surface, but they can rip line from a reel with almost unequaled speed. All are good to eat.

The Atlantic mackerel, *Scomber scombrus*, one of the most valuable fishes off the New England coast, averages less than a pound in weight, but 2-pounders are caught with regularity. The record catch weighed 7½ pounds. Large schools of this streamlined fish roam the Atlantic, southward to the Carolinas off the coast of North America and to Spain off the coast of Europe. The fish's distinctive feature is the two dozen or more wavy black lines between the midline of the back and the lateral line on each side. There are two keels on each side of the caudal peduncle and no median keel as in other mackerels.

Unlike most mackerels, which are predacious, the Atlantic mackerel feeds mostly on small crustaceans, shrimps, herrings, pilchards, and other small schooling fishes. Each female produces large numbers of eggs—as many as half a million. The eggs contain oil droplets so that they float. Mackerels are caught commercially in nets and are also taken by sport fishermen, generally by trolling with spoons, feathers, or similar artificial baits. After a school is located by trolling, the boat can be stopped and fishes caught by casting directly to them.

The smaller chub mackerel, *S. japonicus* (previously *S. coliss*), is similar in appearance and habits but has fewer and less distinct black markings on its back. It also has black blotches on its sides below the lateral line; in contrast, the Atlantic mackerel is completely silvery below the lateral line.

The chub mackerel in the Pacific is the same fish that is present in Atlantic waters, although it was once considered a separate species and called Pacific mackerel. It is the only mackerel occurring on the west coast of North America, where it ranges from Chile to Alaska. It occurs also off the coasts of Japan and Asia. The largest runs off the California coast are in autumn. Like the Atlantic form in appearance and size, it is caught both commercially and for sport.

The king mackerel, or kingfish, *Scomberomorus cavalla*, averages less than 10 pounds in weight, but 20-pounders are not uncommon. Commercial fishermen sometimes report netting king mackerels that weigh 100 pounds and are more than 5 feet long. The rod-and-reel record is 78 pounds 12 ounces. King mackerels have dark blue-green backs and silvery sides. The lateral line is high at the front of the body but drops sharply beneath the second dorsal fin. The decurved lateral line identifies even the immature king mackerel, which are usually spotted with yellow and can be easily confused with other species. King mackerels are abundant in Caribbean waters in spring, migrating northward into the Gulf of Mexico and along the Atlantic coast of the Carolinas or even farther. They are popular game fishes, caught on trolled feathers or spoons or on ballyhoo or similar live baits. Often an area is chummed to attract the fishes. They make a long, powerful run, rest, and then repeat the performance. Now and then a fish will leap from the water. It is considered one of the Atlantic's prize game fishes and excellent on the table.

The closely related Spanish mackerel, *S. maculatus*, is much smaller, averaging less than 2 pounds and with the maximum size about 12 pounds. It is found in warm areas, in both offshore and inshore waters. Several million pounds are netted and sold commercially every year, and many are also taken on rod and reel. Typical of the group, the Spanish mackerel is ocean blue above and silver below, but its sides are marked with large, round yellow spots. It has no scales on its pectoral fins; the king mackerel and the cero do. Spanish mackerels occur in both eastern and western Atlantic waters.

The cero, *S. regalis*, is less common but occurs in the same waters with the king and Spanish mackerels. It has brown or yellow spots on its sides, but they are more elongated than round and are arranged in distinct rows rather than being scattered as in the Spanish mackerel. The cero is about the same size as the Spanish mackerel, though slightly larger fishes tend to be more common.

The sierra, *S. sierra*, resembles the Spanish mackerel

Frigate mackerel *(Auxis thazard)*
1 to 1½ ft (30 to 45 cm)

and may be the same species. It occurs from Baja California southward into tropical waters.

Two similar-size mackerels occur in Indo-Pacific waters and are very common off Australia: *S. commerson*, a 5-foot species that has numerous dark vertical lines, mostly below the lateral line; and the smaller *S. guttatus*, which has broader but incomplete dark marking on its sides.

The frigate mackerel, *Auxis thazard*, is cosmopolitan in warm seas, sometimes appearing in abundance in a region and then not being seen again in the area for several years. Its tail is more lunate than forked, making it resemble more nearly the tunas than the mackerels. It has dark, oblique markings like typical mackerels but only on the rear of the body. As in other mackerels, the two dorsal fins are widely separated. The general color is dark greenish blue on the back, grading into silvery on the sides and belly. The average weight is about 2 pounds, but specimens probably reach weights of 10 pounds. Accurate records are lacking.

Wahoos, *Acanthocybium solanderi*, rated by anglers as one of the most exciting fishes to catch, are cosmopolitan in warm seas. They average 15–20 pounds in weight but may reach weights of 150 pounds. The present rod-and-reel record is 139 pounds. These handsome fishes are steel blue or greenish and are covered with a silvery or yellowish substance that rubs off easily when the fish is handled. The body is usually crossed by dark bars, more prominent in young fishes but often appearing in older fishes when they are excited. The spiny dorsal is long and low, consisting of about 25 spines and separated from the soft-rayed dorsal, which contains fewer rays. A series of 9 finlets extends along the caudal peduncle, both above and below. The head is pointed and the jaws heavily toothed, much like a barracuda's. The body is fully scaled. A unique feature is the upper jaw, which is movable. Wahoos are usually nonschooling, but at some times of the year they as-

semble in large numbers. At these times they cannot be lured to baits, natural or artificial. When feeding, they strike hard, make unbelievably swift runs, and commonly leap from the water.

The Atlantic bonito, *Sarda sarda*, is one of a group of fishes closely related to tunas. Averaging about 3 pounds in weight but sometimes weighing as much as 15 pounds, the Atlantic bonito commonly strays into cool water, even as far north as Nova Scotia. It occurs also in the eastern Atlantic, from Norway south to the Cape of Good Hope. It is most abundant, however, in warm waters, and it travels in large schools. In this group the spiny and soft-rayed dorsal fin are almost joined. The body is completely scaled, and the lateral line is conspicuous. Unlike tunas, bonitos do not have teeth on the roof of their mouth. The Atlantic bonito is dark blue above and silvery below. Above the lateral line a dozen or more dark lines run obliquely downward and forward. Bonitos are commonly caught by trolling, usually when fishing for other kinds of fishes. The flesh is oily, hence it is not generally liked for food. Some are caught commercially, however.

The Pacific bonito , *S. chiliensis*, is similar in size and coloration to the Atlantic bonito. It ranges from the Gulf of Alaska to Chile, being most common in the warmer portions of this range. Like the Atlantic species, it provides much sport but is not highly thought of as a food fish; those caught commercially are canned. Several other species of *Sarda*, including *S. orientalis* of Japanese waters, are commonly listed, but the taxonomy for the genus is not yet clear.

The little tunny, *Euthynnus alleteratus*, represents another group intermediate between mackerels and tunas. The body lacks scales, except for a corselet near the pectoral fins; the two dorsal fins are only narrowly separated, the first dorsal deeply concave. The teeth are conical. The little tunny has several dark spots below the pectoral fins but has no longitudinal lines. It occurs

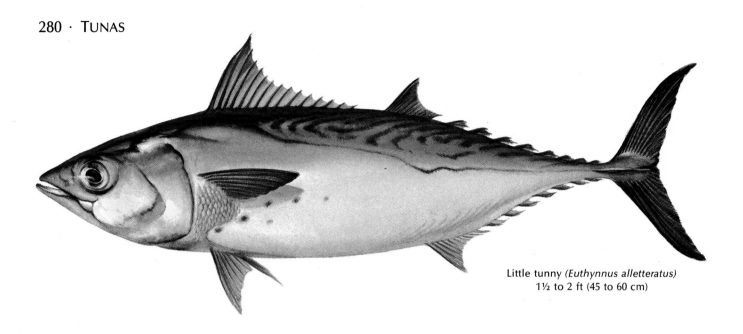

Little tunny *(Euthynnus alletteratus)*
1½ to 2 ft (45 to 60 cm)

from Cape Cod to Brazil and is found also off the coast of Europe, most abundantly in the Mediterranean area. Schools are located by trolling, and then more catches are made by casting. The fish is not one favored for eating. Its average size is about 5 pounds, with records exceeding 30 pounds.

Skipjack tuna, *E. pelamis*, is a cosmopolitan species that gets its name from its habit of seeming to "skip" over the surface as it chases smaller fishes in feeding. Though most abundant in warm waters, it sometimes appears as far north as Massachusetts in the Atlantic. It is also common off Australia and New Zealand, the coasts of South America, the Hawaiian Islands, Japan, and elsewhere. About half a dozen intense black stripes run along the lower half of the body from the pectoral fins to the keeled caudal peduncle. The lateral line dips sharply below the second dorsal fin.

The skipjack tuna averages less than 10 pounds in weight but may reach a weight of 40 pounds. It is a schooling species that commonly comes close to shore, and it is valued both as a commercial and a sport species. Schools are commonly very large, and once located, the fish can be caught by casting. Fast trolling is the usual method of fishing for skipjacks. Off the California coast, the favorite bait is sardines.

Black skipjack, *E. lineatus*, may be the same species as the little tunny. Classification of these widely ranging species has never been resolved. Black skipjacks occur from southern California to Panama.

The kawakawa, *E. affinis*, occurs principally in Hawaiian waters. It is small, usually weighing less than 5 pounds. Again, when more definitive studies are made, several of these species may be grouped as one.

The giants of the family are the tunas, all of which belong to the genus *Thunnus*. They rank among the most important game fishes in the world, most of them valued also as commercial fishes.

The bluefin tuna, *T. thynnus*, is a cosmopolitan species, moving into cool water in summer but retiring to warmer waters in winter. The largest tuna, it averages more than 20 pounds in weight when it is traveling in huge schools. Larger fishes usually travel in small schools, and some are more solitary. They commonly exceed 100 pounds, with the top weight about 1,200 pounds. The length of one of these giants may be greater than 12 feet. Bluefins that weigh over 100 pounds are generally referred to as "giant tuna"; the "school tuna" are in the 10- to 100-pound category.

Dark blue to almost black above and silvery on the sides, the bluefin tuna has a yellowish anal fin and finlets. All the other fins are dark. Living fishes have a bright yellow band from the snout halfway along each side of the body. This fades when a fish dies or is taken from the water. School tunas are commonly caught by trolling or drift fishing, using either natural or artificial baits. The giants are generally first chummed from an anchored boat; trolling, however, is employed exclusively in some areas. The bait used is a sizable mackerel or a comparable fish. To catch these giants requires strong hooks, wire leaders, and big reels filled to capacity, usually with 130-pound test line. A great amount of stamina is necessary, too, for bluefins may fight for hours before tiring. The rod-and-reel record weighed 1,120 pounds.

Along the coast of North America, bluefins begin their northward migration in spring after spawning somewhere in the southern portion of their range. They appear in the Bahamas in late April or May, and by late

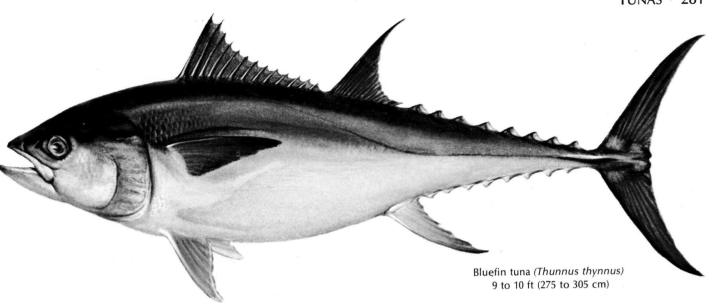

Bluefin tuna *(Thunnus thynnus)*
9 to 10 ft (275 to 305 cm)

summer are off the coast of Nova Scotia. By this time they have gained 200 or 300 pounds in weight. The bluefin provides the action in the greatest sport-fishing events. Nova Scotia is the site of the Annual International Tuna Cup Match in late summer or autumn, attracting anglers from around the world. The Annual Intercollegiate Game Fish Seminar and Fishing Match, directed by Yale University's Department of Outdoor Education and held in Nova Scotia for the past 18 years, is a unique event that introduces giant-tuna fishing to college students. Another example of the economic importance of the bluefin, the annual United States Atlantic tuna tournament, held off the New England coast, includes about 150 sport-fishing craft in three days of exciting fishing.

Inconceivable as it may seem, the bluefin tuna may soon be placed on the endangered species list. This magnificent fish has been exploited by several nations. Unless sound conservation practices are introduced and adhered to by commercial interests, and to a lesser degree by sport fishermen taking the smaller school tuna, the bluefin will become extinct. Bluefins are not common off the Australian or African coasts, but they do occur off the coasts of Europe and Asia, where there are similar seasonal migrations.

The southern bluefin is now considered a separate species, *T. maacoyii*, based on internal differences.

The yellowfin tuna, *T. albacares*, does not attain as large a size as the bluefin, averaging 15 to 25 pounds. Fish weighing over 100 pounds are not common, but the rod-and-reel record is 308 pounds, and fish weighing 400 pounds have been netted. The yellowfin is easily distinguished from other tunas by its unusually long second dorsal and anal fins, which are strikingly bor-

dered with black. Even more distinctive are the long pectoral fins, which are bright yellow. The pelvic fins and the finlets are also yellow. Many of these bright colors, including a yellow stripe that extends from snout to tail, fade soon after the fishes are taken from the water. Yellowfins roam the seas. They often come close to shore. Many are caught commercially.

Albacores, *T. alalunga*, are oceanic tunas that are abundant in the Pacific but not common in the Atlantic. This is the "white meat" tuna or the "chicken of the sea." It is harvested commercially in large quantities. The albacore's extremely long, sickle-shaped, black pectoral fins set it apart from the other tunas. The fins extend past the bases of the soft dorsal and the anal fins. The fish is dark blue above, grading to greenish blue near the tail. In live fishes, there is a metallic bronze cast over the entire body. The dorsal and pelvic fins are dark but not black, and the anal fin is nearly colorless. Albacores average about 10 pounds in weight, but 20-pounders are not uncommon. The present rod-and-reel record is 74 pounds 13 ounces. This is one of the most popular game fishes caught off the California coast, the principal runs occurring in late spring and through the summer. The fishes are caught by trolling with feathers, spoons, and jigs or are taken on sardines and other natural baits. Like most tunas, the albacore strikes hard and makes powerful runs.

The bigeye tuna, *T. obesus*, is a species that resembles the bluefin but has proportionately larger eyes. The finlets are yellowish brown rather than bright yellow, and they are edged with black. Bigeye tunas are less commonly caught than most other tunas, probably because they tend to stay in deeper water. In size this species is about the same as the yellowfin.

Swordfish *(Xiphias gladius)*
13 to 15 ft (396 to 457 cm)

Family Xiphiidae
swordfishes

Famous both as a food and game fish, the swordfish, *Xiphias gladius*, the only species in its family, roams the warm and the temperate seas of the world. It differs from billfishes in its total lack of scales and teeth and in having no ventral fins. In mature fishes, the dorsal fin consists of a single high lobe, concave on its rear margin, plus a very small lobe at the rear of the body. This big fin is soft-rayed and permanently erect. There is only one keel on each side of the caudal peduncle. The broad, flat bill is long, representing 20 to 30 percent of the fish's total length. The back and sides are a dark bronze, the lower sides and belly are grayish, and the fins are dark.

The average weight of a swordfish is greater than 100 pounds. Fishes weighing more than 1,200 pounds have been harpooned, which is the method used to harvest swordfish commercially. Anglers usually make their catches by first sighting a swordfish cruising, its curved dorsal fin exposed above the water's surface. A mackerel, squid (their favorite food), or comparable bait is trolled in front of the fish to encourage a strike. Because of the size of the fish, heavy tackle is essential; even so, the angler must play his catch carefully. Swordfishes have tender mouths from which a hook tears easily. A hooked fish makes powerful runs, and it leaps from the water many times before tiring. Sometimes it sulks, recovers energy, and then begins the battle again. It is not uncommon for an angler to play a swordfish for three or four hours before it is brought to gaff. A rod-and-reel record fish weighed 1,182 pounds.

Family Luvaridae
louvar

The single species in this family is *Luvarus imperialis*, cosmopolitan in tropical seas, a deepsea fish about 6 feet long. Its body is pinkish, the fins bright red, and the head blunt. Most unusual, the anus is located almost directly under the pectoral fins and between the bases of the pelvic fins.

Family Istiophoridae
billfishes

Speed, endurance, and large size are outstanding characteristics of these spectacular fishes, which are cosmopolitan in the open sea. They rate highly with big-game anglers. The identifying feature is the greatly prolonged upper jaw that forms a rounded bill, or spear. All also have a high dorsal fin—unusually high in sailfishes, higher in the front than in the rear in marlins. When the fish is swimming at great speed, the dorsal fin is folded down and fits into a furrow along the back. This reduces body resistance.

Billfishes are predacious, eating mackerels, herrings, and other fishes of similar size. They are toothless. Typically they use their spear to stun prey as they speed through the schools, then turn and pick up any fishes that have been hit by the slashing spear. Billfishes are

generally solitary but may at times travel in pairs. Like most pelagic fishes, their basic colors are ocean blue above and silvery below.

Formerly considered three distinct species, sailfishes from all oceans have been united into a single cosmopolitan species, *Istiophorus platypterus*.

The Atlantic form averages 4 to 6 feet in length and weighs 25 to 50 pounds, but specimens may reach a length of 8 feet and weigh as much as 125 pounds. Ranging from Brazil to Massachusetts but most common in warm waters along the edge of the Gulf Stream, the sailfish is easily recognized by its long, high, sail-like dorsal fin marked with numerous round black spots and also by its comparatively small, slim body. The pelvic fins are notably long, the caudal fin lunate. Two keels are on each side of the caudal peduncle. Sailfishes are usually a purplish or cobalt blue with a bronze cast, lighter on the lower sides and belly.

Like most pelagic species that spawn in the open sea, a female sailfish produces large numbers of eggs—as many as 4 or 5 million. These are fertilized in the open water, where they float with the plankton until they

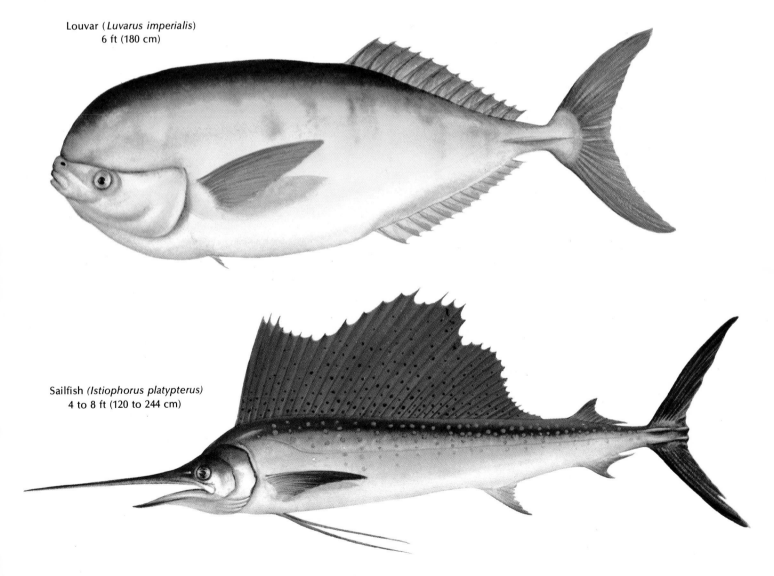

Louvar (*Luvarus imperialis*)
6 ft (180 cm)

Sailfish *(Istiophorus platypterus)*
4 to 8 ft (120 to 244 cm)

hatch. Only a fraction of the young fish survive, but the growth of those that do make it is extremely rapid. They can reach a length of 4 to 6 feet within a year.

Sailfishes are among the most popular game fishes. They are caught by trolling with mullets, ballyhoos, or similar natural baits. The line is typically fastened to an outrigger with a clip. At times, a hungry sailfish will "crash-strike" or grab the bait and thus get hooked immediately. Usually when it strikes, the fish knocks the bait free. If an outrigger is not used, the fisherman must refrain from trying to set the hook on the strike and must allow some line to go slack so that the bait acts like a stunned fish. When the sailfish comes back, picks up the bait, and runs with it, the hook is set, and the battle begins. A sailfish makes runs at speeds as great as 60 miles per hour, combining them with aerial acrobatics that give the angler many moments to be remembered.

The Pacific form is similar in appearance but larger, averaging twice the size of the Atlantic type. It is found from Peru to Baja California, rarely northward. Rod-and-reel record for the Atlantic is 128 pounds 1 ounce; 221 pounds is the record for the Pacific.

Marlins are generally considered the elite of billfishes. As fast or faster than sailfishes, they are well known also as aerialists, often making dozens of jumps before tiring. Like sailfishes, marlins are caught mainly by trolling with mullets, mackerels, ballyhoos, or similar baits, or they will also take artificial imitations of natural baits. Outriggers are usually used. In all marlins, the dorsal fin is high in front, then slopes gradually to the rear. Most species exceed 400 pounds in weight, the exception being the white marlin, *Tetrapturus albidus*.

The white marlin averages about 50 pounds in weight and only rarely attains a weight of 150 pounds; the rod-and-reel record is 159 pounds 8 ounces. The high portion of its dorsal and anal fin is rounded rather than pointed, as in other marlins. The white marlin is found in the warm waters of the western Atlantic, in the Carib-

bean, the Gulf of Mexico, and off the Florida coast, sometimes straggling as far north as Virginia or even farther. Its sides are bluish, grading into silver, and it has no black marks. The lateral line is distinct.

The blue marlin, *Makaira nigricans*, which averages 75 to 100 pounds and may reach a weight of 1,500 pounds, occurs off the coasts of Europe and Africa as well as in the American subtropics and tropics. It is found also in the Pacific and Indo-Pacific. The blue marlin's bluish sides are generally marked with light vertical stripes that disappear when the fish dies. The lateral line is not distinct. Compared to the striped marlin, the bill is shorter and stouter. The rod-and-reel record for blue marlins in the Atlantic is 1,142 pounds; 1,153 pounds in the Pacific.

The striped marlin, *Tetrapturus audax*, is found from California to Japan and southward to Chile and New Zealand, occurring only in the Pacific. Considerably smaller than the blue marlin, its blue-green upper sides and silvery lower sides are striped with about 20 narrow lavender vertical bars. The dorsal fin is dark blue, like the back, and the pelvic fins and caudal fin are black or very dark blue. The bill is long and slim. Many anglers believe this species when hooked is the most active of the group.

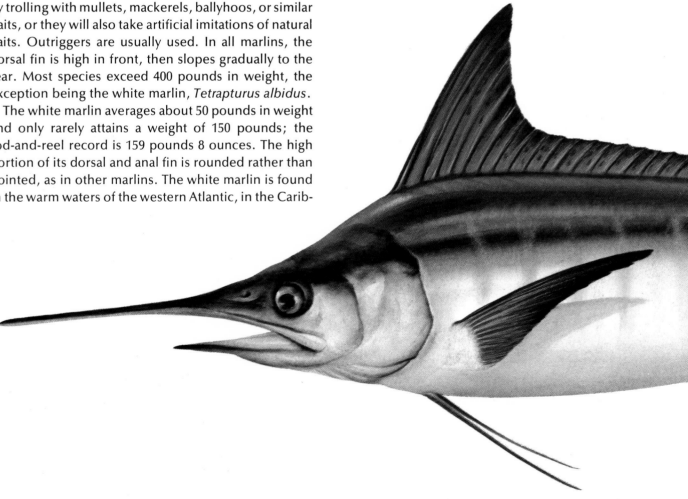

The black marlin, *Makaira indica*, is the largest marlin, with 1,000-pound catches not especially unusual. A 1,560-pound catch off the coast of Cabo Blanco, Peru is the record on rod and reel. It was taken by Alfred Glassell, Jr., and is the largest game fish ever caught in sport fishing. These giants live in warm Pacific waters and also in the Indian Ocean. As the name indicates, they are extremely dark on the back and sides and silvery grayish on the undersurface. The bill is short compared to the bills of other marlins, and the dorsal fin is low. Also, the pectoral fins cannot be folded against the sides of the body, as they can in other marlins, and the body is deeper or thicker.

Spearfishes have features of both marlins and sailfishes. Their dorsal fin is high, though not as high or as long as in sailfishes, and the body is slimmer than a marlin's. Some authorities contend that these fishes are actually an immature stage of the marlins; for the present, however, they are considered a definitive species.

The shortbill spearfish, *Tetrapturus angustirostris*, of the Pacific has a very short bill, not extending far beyond the mouth; the longbill spearfish, *T. pfluegeri*, of the Atlantic has a bill about twice as long as the shortbill's. About 50 pounds appears to be maximum for these species, the average considerably less. Spearfishes are not known abundantly in any region, but they have been caught in Florida waters, the Gulf of Mexico, the Caribbean, and the Pacific.

Family Stromateidae
butterfishes

Schooling fishes, mainly of subtropical and tropical seas, the butterfish has a nearly round body, as deep as it is long, and lacks pelvic fins. The pectoral fins are long and pointed, the snout blunt, and the teeth weak. Large enough individuals are harvested commercially as food fishes. Nineteen species are known to inhabit the waters off the coasts of the United States and Canada.

The most familiar Atlantic species is the butterfish, *Peprilus triacanthus*, which averages about 8 inches in length but may occasionally grow to 12 inches. It lives in cool waters from Nova Scotia to the Carolinas, then in deeper waters south to Florida. It is gray-blue on the back and sides, silvery below.

The harvestfish, *P. alepidotus*, with an even deeper body than the butterfish and with matching long, sickle-shaped dorsal and anal fins, occurs from Massachusetts to the Gulf of Mexico. The closely related *P. paru* occurs from the West Indies to Uruguay. These

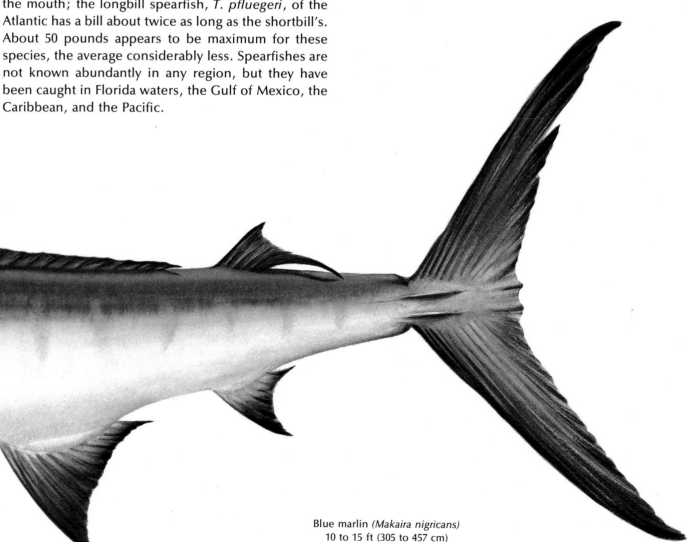

Blue marlin *(Makaira nigricans)*
10 to 15 ft (305 to 457 cm)

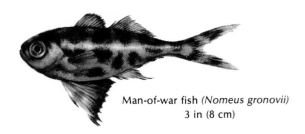

Man-of-war fish *(Nomeus gronovii)*
3 in (8 cm)

fishes have a maximum length of about 8 inches. They are light greenish above and yellow below. They commonly hide under the Portuguese man-of-war's float. The species best known for this habit, however, is the 3-inch man-of-war fish, *Nomeus gronovii*, worldwide in distribution in warm seas.

Off the Pacific coast of North America, the largest representative of the family is the Pacific pompano, *P. simillimus*, about 10 inches long. It ranges from southern California northward to British Columbia. The small medusafish, *Icichthys lockingtoni*, also of the Pacific, regularly inhabits the bells of jellyfishes.

Climbing perch *(Anabas testudineus)*
up to 10 in (25 cm)

Family Anabantidae
climbing perch

The climbing perch, or walking fish, *Anabas testudineus*, to 10 inches long, lives in the ponds, swamps, and paddies of southeastern Asia. It has the remarkable ability to stay out of water for exceptionally long periods of time, often moving over land for considerable distances to find new sources of water when their original home dries up. It walks by using its pectoral fins and the spiny edges of its gill covers as "legs," rocking from side to side as it crawls. Mostly muddy brown and not especially handsome, the climbing perch is occasionally kept in aquariums, which must be kept covered. It attacks other fishes of its own and different species. A number of African species in this family are also capable of "walking."

Family Belontiidae
labyrinthfishes

Some very popular tropical aquarium fishes belong to this family of freshwater fishes that has representatives in Africa and southeastern Asia. Their name is derived from the labyrinthlike accessory breathing organ located in the gill chambers, usually above the gills. The membranes in the labyrinth are richly supplied with blood vessels so that the chambers serve for auxiliary breathing in water that is deficient in oxygen. The fishes take in air by gulping it at the surface.

Most species in this family build a nest of foamy bubbles at the surface. The male generally makes the nest, doing so by taking a bubble of air into his mouth and then releasing it or blowing it into the nest. In his mouth the bubble becomes covered with a sticky mucus that makes the bubbles adhere to one another. After the female lays her eggs, the male fertilizes them. Before the eggs sink to the bottom, the male picks them up and then spits or blows them into the bubbles, where they become imbedded and remain until they hatch. In some species both sexes may participate in taking the eggs to the nest.

Among the labyrinthfishes popular with aquarium hobbyists is the Siamese fighting fish, *Betta splendens*,

Day's paradise fish
(Macropodus cupanus)

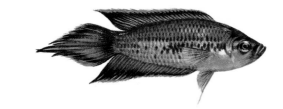

Combtail paradise fish
(Belontia signata)

Paradise fish
(Macropodus opercularis)

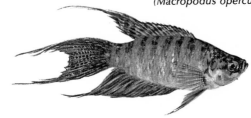

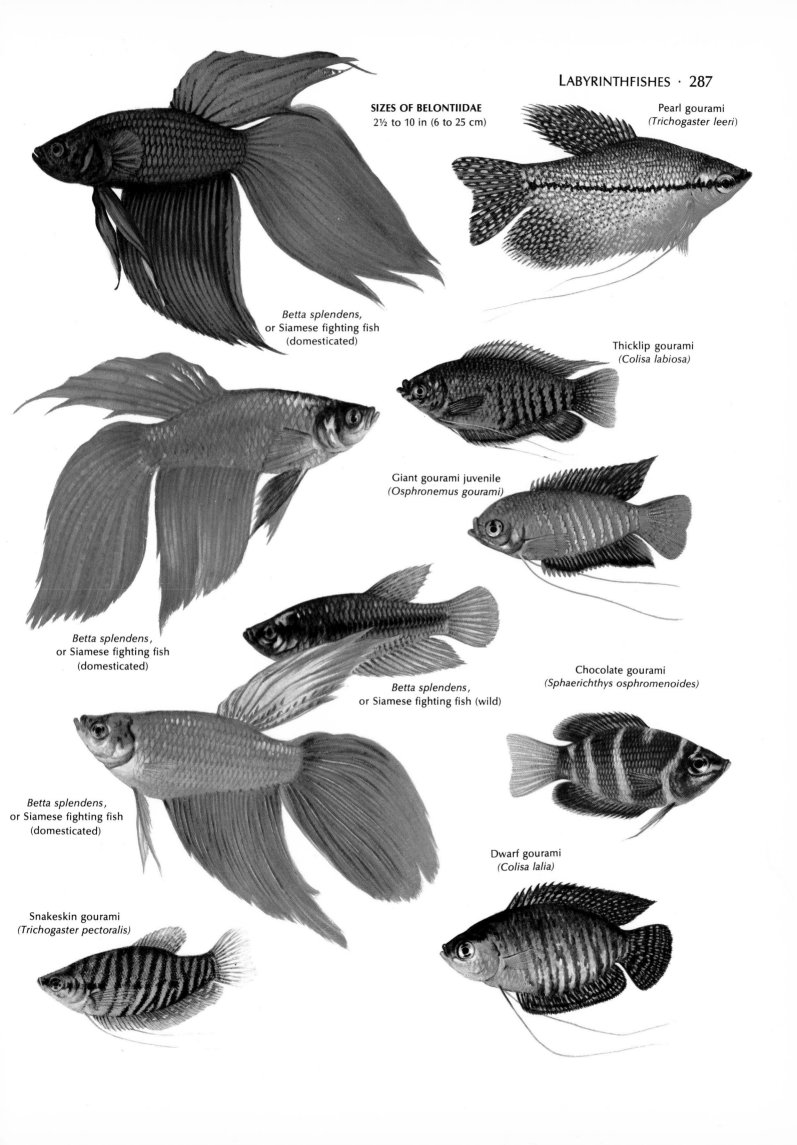

SIZES OF BELONTIIDAE
2½ to 10 in (6 to 25 cm)

Pearl gourami
(Trichogaster leeri)

Betta splendens,
or Siamese fighting fish
(domesticated)

Thicklip gourami
(Colisa labiosa)

Giant gourami juvenile
(Osphronemus gourami)

Betta splendens,
or Siamese fighting fish
(domesticated)

Betta splendens,
or Siamese fighting fish (wild)

Chocolate gourami
(Sphaerichthys osphromenoides)

Betta splendens,
or Siamese fighting fish
(domesticated)

Dwarf gourami
(Colisa lalia)

Snakeskin gourami
(Trichogaster pectoralis)

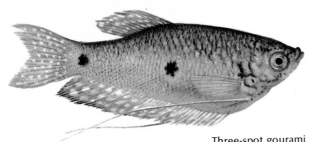

Three-spot gourami
(Trichogaster trichopterus)

Kissing gourami
(Helostomus teminincki)

a native of Thailand, and several other species of *Betta* of southeastern Asia, where they live in ponds, ditches, or quiet stretches of streams. In breeding this species for aquarium hobbyists, it has been varied greatly in color and fin shape from the original form. The fins in particular are emphasized; the most popular varieties are those with very large fins. These are especially handsome in males, typically red with green and blue lines, the pelvic fins red with blue tips. In females, the fins are shorter. In both sexes, the body color is basically brown with bluish-green dots. Males fight during the breeding season. In Thailand large wagers are made on these battles. Siamese fighting fish are about 2½ inches long, the females slightly shorter than the males.

Gouramis are also members of this family. The kissing gourami, *Helostomus teminincki*, a favorite with fish hobbyists, has thick lips that can be extended or pursed. Fishes of this species have the unusual and interesting habit of fitting their lips against another's in a "kiss." The kissing gourami may reach a length of 10 inches.

The thicklip gourami, *Colisa labiosa*, to 4 inches long, has extremely thick lips, their appearance exaggerated by a dark band. This species does not "kiss." It is not nearly as handsome as the closely related dwarf gourami, *C. lalia*, to 2½ inches long, which is a shiny emerald green crossed by bright red bars.

The pearl gourami, *Trichogaster leeri*, and others of its genus are small, averaging 2½ inches long. They are distinguished from the various species of *Colias* by their shorter dorsal fin and by a pelvic fin that is extended into a slim thread used as a "feeler" in finding food on the bottom. Like other gouramis, the lips are thick, but they are not used for "kissing."

Blue gouramis, *T. trichopterus*, may be shiny blue or purplish red, with dark bars across the body showing most prominently when the fish is excited. In males, the dorsal fin is long and pointed; in females, shorter and rounded. The snakeskin gourami, *T. pectoralis*, is a hardy and peaceable fish of the Malay Peninsula.

The croaking gourami, *Trichopsis vitattus*, about 2½ inches long, is named for the rattling or croaking noises made by the male during courtship. The chocolate gourami, *Sphaerichthys osphromenoides*, is a small, handsome species from Malaya and Sumatra. The giant gourami, *Osphronemus gourami*, to 2 feet long, is raised as a food fish in Southeast Asia.

Family Icosteidae
ragfishes

These strange fishes appear to be absolutely boneless—as limp as rags. Their skeleton consists mainly of cartilage, which is flexible. The few known species live in deep waters of the North Pacific. The ragfish, *Icosteus aenigmaticus*, to 1½ feet long, is a scaleless, greatly compressed fish with spines along the lateral line and over the fins. *Acrotus willoughbyi*, to 7 feet long, lacks spines and also has no pelvic fins.

Ragfish (*Icosteus aenigmaticus*)
1½ ft (45 cm)

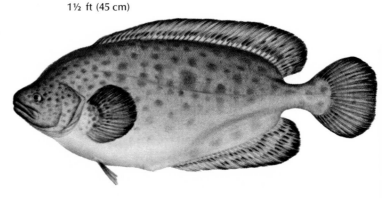

Family Mastacembelidae
spiny eels

About 50 species of these unusual freshwater fishes live in Asia and Africa. Their body is long and eel-like, and the first dorsal fin often consists of numerous (as many as 40 or more in some) separate spines that can be raised or lowered at will. The second, or soft-rayed, dorsal, caudal, and anal fins are joined in African species but

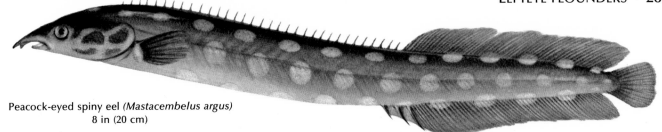

Peacock-eyed spiny eel *(Mastacembelus argus)*
8 in (20 cm)

separate in Asiatic species. As in eels, but more exaggerated, the sensitive snout is pointed, and the two nostrils are tubular extensions. Most spiny eels are nocturnal, hiding in the mud during the day. There are no pelvic fins.

Most species belong to the genus *Mastacembelus*, with the largest species being the 3-foot *M. armatus*. One of the most attractive is the so-called peacock-eyed

spiny eel, *M. argus*, an 8-inch species that has round yellowish dots on its reddish-brown body.

The only other genus in the family is *Macrognathus*, containing a single species, the elephant trunk fish, *M. aculeatus*. In this species the snout is extended into a trunklike prehensile snout; the body is covered with about two dozen horny plates, each having a "tooth" in its center.

ORDER PLEURONECTIFORMES

Family Bothidae
lefteye flounders

When they first hatch from the egg, flounders look like any other fishes. Within a few days, they begin to lean to one side. The eye on the underside starts migrating upward and across the head so that both eyes are on top of the body. In this family, the flounders typically lean to

the right, and the right eye migrates so that both eyes become located on the top or left side of the body. These are the lefteye, or sinistral, flounders. Those in which both eyes are on the right side are the righteye, or dextral, flounders of the family Pleuronectidae. Some

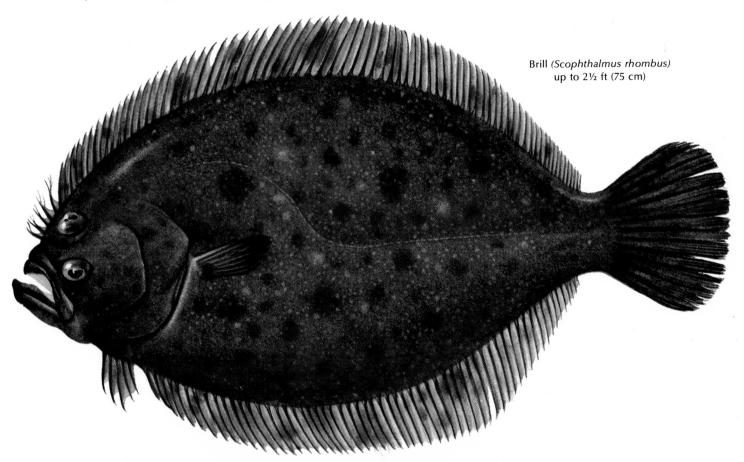

Brill *(Scophthalmus rhombus)*
up to 2½ ft (75 cm)

species may be either lefteyed or righteyed, depending on which way the young fish begins to lean.

As the eye migrates, the baby flounder's skull also twists; and in many species, the mouth also twists upward. The parts turned under lose their pigment and become white. When the fish is finally flat, the transformation completed, it is dark above and white below. In the process, the little fish sinks to the bottom and begins its life as a bottom-hugging species, its blind side pressed against the bottom. Flounders usually lie buried in the sand or mud, but they can swim swiftly to catch prey or to escape if disturbed. Flounders are good to eat. Some are netted, or they may be speared or caught on hook and line.

Many flounders can change color to match their background. Most species are a mottled dark brown or yellowish brown, but a few are strikingly patterned. Among these is the peacock flounder, *Bothus lunatus*, to 1½ feet long, found off the coasts of Florida and southward to Brazil. Its body is covered with large round spots rimmed with blue or purple rings that, in turn, are outlined with black.

The smaller eyed flounder, *B. ocellatus*, to 10 inches long, has similar "eyespots" that provide excellent camouflage. The eyed flounder is common only in warmer waters of the Atlantic and the Caribbean.

Males of *B. pantherinus* of the Indo-Pacific have very long filamentlike pectoral fins that may extend to the tip of the tail. The female's fins are of normal size.

The ocellated flounder, *Ancylopsetta quadrocellata*, found in warm Atlantic and Gulf of Mexico waters, has dark spots ringed with white.

The summer flounder, or northern fluke, *Paralichthys dentatus*, lives off the Atlantic coast of North America from Maine southward to Florida, overlapping from the Carolinas southward the range of the southern flounder, *P. lethostigma*, which is most abundant in the Gulf region. Summer flounders average about 2 pounds in weight, occasionally attaining a length of 3 feet and weighing as much as 25 pounds. Southern flounders are about the same size. Summer flounders generally have a dozen or more distinct eyespots (dark with a white rim), while the southern flounder has either poorly defined or no spots.

The less-than-a-foot-long Gulf flounder, *P. albigutta*, is found in the same range as the southern flounder but is most abundant in the Gulf. It has numerous pale spots on its yellowish brown body. The Gulf flounder has no more than 80 rays in its dorsal fin; both the southern and the summer have more. The southern flounder has 8–11 gill rakers, the summer flounder 13–18.

The fourspot flounder, *P. oblongus*, is a small species occurring from the Carolinas northward to Nova Scotia but most abundantly off New England. It is easily identified by the four oblong black spots edged with pink on the top side of its body. It averages only about 12 inches in length and has fewer than 80 rays in its dorsal fin.

Still another Atlantic species in this genus is the lenguad, *P. brasiliensis*, which averages 5 to 10 pounds but may weigh as much as 50 pounds. It is important both as a sport and commercial species along the coast of South America.

The windowpane, *Scopthalmus aquosus*, is a common small flounder, less than a foot long, that occurs from the Gulf of St. Lawrence southward to the Carolinas. It is often abundant but is generally too small and too thin to be of commercial value, although it has fine table qualities.

In European and Mediterranean waters, the brill, *S. rhombus*, is an important commercial species. Other valuable lefteye flounders of European waters are the large turbot, *S. maxima*, and the smaller scaldfish, *Arnoglossus laterna*, both widely distributed. *Lepidorhombus whiff-iagonis*, *Phrynorhombus norvegicus*, and *Zeugopterus punctatus* live in colder, more northern waters.

Lefteye flounders of the Pacific include the Pacific sanddab, *Citharichthys sordidus*, to 1½ feet long. Found from Baja California to Alaska, it is brown to blackish, generally mottled. Closely related species of the same general region are the speckled sanddab, *C. stigmaeus*, heavily speckled with black, and the longfin sanddab, *C. xanthostigma*, in which the pectoral fins are longer than the head.

The fantail sole, *Xystreurys liolepis*, a foot-long species found from central California southward to Baja California, belongs to the lefteye flounder family but is commonly righteyed. Dark brown mottled with reddish or black, it typically has a large, dark eyelike spot just behind the head, another just in front of the caudal fin. The lateral line arches above the pectoral fin.

The bigmouth sole, *Hippoglossina stomata*, found from Point Conception southward, is another species in which the lateral line is highly arched over the pectoral fin. The brownish body is tinged with blue.

The most important of the lefteye flounders in the Pacific is the California halibut, *Paralichthys californicus*, which may be as much as 5 feet long and weigh up to about 70 pounds. It ranges from Baja California to British Columbia. A similar species, *P. olivaceus*, is found off the coasts of Asia and Japan. As frequently righteyed as it is lefteyed, the California halibut is greenish or grayish brown, sometimes mottled with darker and lighter shades and occasionally with white

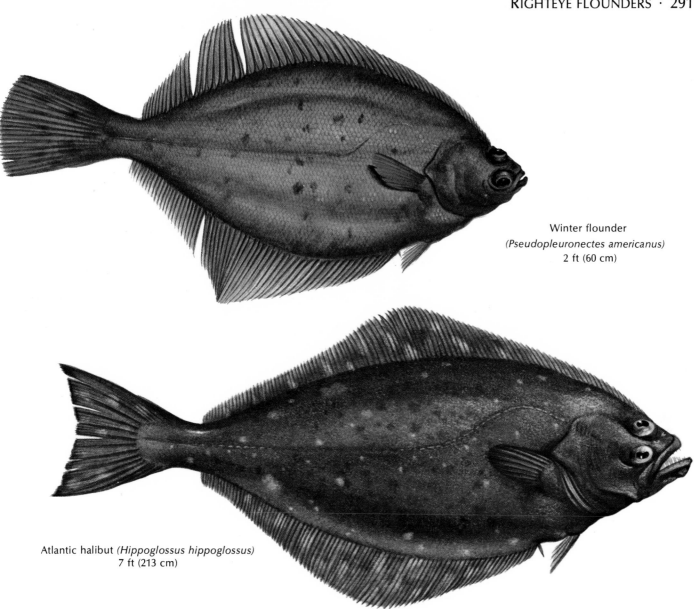

Winter flounder
(Pseudopleuronectes americanus)
2 ft (60 cm)

Atlantic halibut *(Hippoglossus hippoglossus)*
7 ft (213 cm)

spots on its body. This species is caught commercially and also provides sport for fishermen, taking either natural or artificial baits. Like all flatfishes, its fight is slab-sided but powerful.

Family Pleuronectidae
righteye flounders

Righteye flounders generally have both eyes on the right side of the body, though lefteyed individuals are not uncommon in some species. Some of the numerous species occur also in the Southern Hemisphere.

Typical of the family is the Pacific halibut, *Hippoglossus stenolepis*. Females may reach a length of 9 feet and weigh as much as 500 pounds; males weigh up to 125

pounds. Dark brownish black with only occasional mottling or pale blotches, the lateral line arches over the pectoral fin. The caudal fin is broad and lunate. Found from central California northward to Alaska and sometimes off the coasts of northern Asia and Japan, this is an important commercial species, caught mainly on long lines in deep water—to depths of 3,000 feet.

The Atlantic halibut, *H. hippoglossus*, occurs from New York northward to Greenland and also off the northern coast of Europe. It is even larger than the Pacific species, 700-pound catches having been recorded. Most are smaller—about 7 feet long and weighing 300 pounds. Both Atlantic and Pacific species are very prolific, a female weighing 150 pounds producing as many as 2 million eggs. Both are voracious, pursuing their prey in the open water. Their harvests are under regulation by the International Fisheries Commission.

European sole *(Solea solea)*
1½ ft (45 cm)

Zebra sole (Zebrias zebra)
7 in (18 cm)

The arrowtooth flounder, *Atherestes stomias*, found from central California to Alaska, is a smaller species, to 2½ feet long at maximum. The lateral line is not arched. The mouth is very large, developed equally well above and below. The white underside is dotted with black. This species sometimes occurs as deep as 2,000 feet.

Other Pacific Coast species, most of them rare south of Point Conception and ranging as far north as Alaska, include the petrale sole, *Eopsetta jordani*, a 1½-foot species that weighs 6 to 8 pounds; rex sole, *Glyptocephalus zachirus*, which has a small mouth and jaws that are better developed on the blind side; sand sole, *Psettichthys melanostictus*, a 1½-foot species that may weigh 4 pounds, also called fringe sole because the first few rays of the dorsal fin are not attached to each other or lack membranes; and the curlfin sole, *Pleuronichthys decurrens*, a 12-inch species.

At least half a dozen other either smaller or not common species are found along the Pacific coast of North America. Several are caught regularly by sport fishermen. Among these is the attractive starry flounder, *Platichthys stellatus*, an important sport and commercial fish, that may reach a length of 3 feet and weigh as much as 20 pounds but is usually smaller. Its outstanding feature is the black bars on its dorsal and anal fins, with the spaces between either orange or yellow. The mouth and jaws are developed best on the blind side, and there are patches of shiny starlike scales on the body.

Another species taken regularly by sport fishermen is the diamond turbot, *Hypsopsetta guttulata*, about 1½ feet long and weighing 4 pounds. The name comes from its body shape, which is widest about midway and with angular high points on the dorsal and anal fins. These give the fish its roughly diamond shape. It is greenish brown above, mottled with lighter colors.

In the Atlantic, the winter flounder, *Pseudopleuronectes americanus*, is the most common flounder of shallow coastal waters. Averaging less than a foot long and sometimes growing to 2 feet in length and weighing 8 pounds, this oval, flat-bodied fish is highly favored as a commercial species. Many are caught also by sport fishermen. Winter flounders are usually dark brown above, often with a reddish brown cast and with small black spots. Typically they are white below, but some are dark. They occur from Labrador to Georgia.

Asiatic tonguefish (*Rhinoplagusia japonica*)
up to 1 ft (30 cm)

The yellowtail flounder, or rusty dab, *Limanda fer-ruginea*, lives along the Atlantic coast from New York to Newfoundland. Averaging about a foot in length but sometimes as long as 1½ feet, it generally inhabits water 50 to 200 feet deep. In the past few years there has been a serious depletion of this once extremely important commercial species. The yellowtail flounder's most identifying features are its pointed snout and the concave profile of its head. The olive brown body is marked with reddish brown spots, and the underside is white except for the yellowish caudal peduncle. The lemon sole, *L. limanda*, is a much-esteemed food fish caught off the northern coast of Europe.

The witch flounder, *Glyptocephalus cynoglossus*, known also as gray flounder, is found on both sides of the Atlantic, generally in water 200 to 600 feet deep. To 1½ feet long and weighing 4 to 5 pounds but generally smaller, this species is distinguished from other similar brownish flatfishes by its many more fin rays.

The American plaice, *Hippoglossoides platessoides*, is a large righteye flounder—to as much as 2 feet long and weighing 4 pounds. It ranges from Massachusetts northward and is found also off the northern coast of Europe. An important commercial species, it is caught mainly in otter trawls but it is also taken on hook and line. The color is a uniform reddish brown above, whitish below. Unlike the Atlantic halibut, which might be confused with this species when young, the American plaice has a rounded rather than a forked tail.

The European plaice, *Pleuronectes platessa*, is a much larger fish, to 3½ feet long and weighing as much as 20 pounds. Its greenish olive topside is covered with orange dots, and a row of bony protuberances runs from the snout between the eye and back to the pectoral fin. This is a valuable commercial species.

Also valuable commercially is the Greenland halibut, *Reinhardtius hippoglossoides*, which is about the same length and weight as the European plaice. The Greenland halibut is found from Newfoundland northward to Greenland and off the northern coasts of Europe. It occurs also from British Columbia to Alaska and along the northern coasts of Asia.

Family Soleidae
soles

Soles are flatfishes that typically have a very rounded body. Their small eyes are close together. Most are righteyed. They live mainly in warm waters, and several species migrate into fresh waters.

The European sole, *Solea solea*, gave rise to the "filet of sole" expression that is now used for almost any flatfish. It may weigh as much as 3 pounds and reach a length of 1½ feet. It is a favorite food flatfish.

In American waters, the complement of the European sole is the hogchoker, *Trinectes maculatus*, but it is smaller, rarely as much as 10 inches long. The hogchoker is found from Massachusetts southward to the Gulf of Mexico but is not common north of Virginia. It is grayish brown with a hatching of dark lines along the lateral line; the lower surface is spotted. Young fishes often move far up freshwater streams.

The lined sole, *Achirus lineatus*, about 6 inches long, occurs in the same range and is also found over mud and sand bottoms.

Family Cynoglossidae
tonguefishes

These are lefteyed flatfishes in which the tail is pointed and ribs are lacking. The dorsal, caudal, and anal fins are united. There are no pectoral fins. The eyes are tiny and set close together. Most tonguefishes are less than a foot long and are of no commercial importance, but several Asiatic species—*Areliseus joyneri*, *Corysyphaesopia cornuta*, and *Rhinoplagusia japonica*—are caught for food, particularly in Japanese waters.

The blackcheek tonguefish, *Symphurus plagiusa*, about 6 inches long, is one of several species found from the Carolinas through the Caribbean.

The California tonguefish, *S. atricauda*, ranges from Point Conception southward to Baja California. It is a small species that reaches a length of only about 6 inches.

ORDER TETRADONTIFORMES

Family Balistidae
triggerfishes and filefishes

In triggerfishes, the stout first spine of the dorsal fin is locked into place when erect by the much shorter second dorsal spine, which slides forward. The long first spine can be lowered again only by sliding the second spine back. This can be done by depressing the third spine—the "trigger"—which is attached by a bony base to the second spine. In this manner—by erecting the first spine and locking it in place—triggerfishes can lodge themselves immovably in crevices.

The second dorsal and the anal fin are the same size and shape. Pelvic fins are lacking, and the belly has a sharp-edged outline, with its greatest depth just in front of the anal fin. Triggerfishes are covered with an armor of bony plates. The leathery skin lacks the slime or mucus usually found on fishes. Approximately three dozen species inhabit coral reefs around the world.

The queen triggerfish, *Balistes vetula*, about 12 inches long, occurs in warm Atlantic waters northward to the Carolinas and also in the Caribbean. Though its color varies considerably with its background, the queen triggerfish always has an iridescent bluish purple stripe circling the mouth and extending back on each side to beneath the pectoral fin. A second stripe crosses the snout and runs along the cheeks to the base of the pectoral fin. The base of the caudal fin is also bluish purple. The back is generally greenish, the throat and belly orange. The front of the dorsal fin and both lobes of the caudal fin are elongated. The queen triggerfish

Undulate triggerfish
(Balistapus undulatus)
10 to 12 in (25 to 30 cm)

Clown triggerfish *(Balistoides conspicillum)*
1 ft (30 cm)

usually travels alone or in pairs but may occasionally be seen in small groups.

The gray triggerfish, *B. capriscus*, less than a foot long but sometimes exceeding 1½ feet and weighing to 3 pounds, is widely distributed in the warm Atlantic, Gulf of Mexico, and Mediterranean, ranging farther north than most triggerfishes. In the open water it is a dull gray, but when it is swimming near seaweeds or over rocks, it is usually mottled.

Another Atlantic species is the ocean triggerfish, *Canthidermis sufflamen*, which reaches a length of 2 feet and may weigh 10 pounds—one of the largest members of the family. Found off the Florida coasts and also in the Caribbean, this is a dark brown to grayish fish, with black spots at the base of the caudal fin. Like some other triggerfishes, it emits noises, made either by grinding its pharyngeal teeth or by vibrating the muscles attached to the swim bladder. These are connected to the "tympanum" just above the pectoral fin on each side. Like most triggerfishes, this species is fun to catch on hook and line, taking most any bait that is offered. Triggerfishes can be skinned and eaten, but some people avoid them because poisoning has occurred after eating triggerfishes or their near relatives. Several species of *Canthidermis* occur off the coast of Japan.

The redtail triggerfish, *Xanthichthys mento*, is a 10-inch species found off the western coast of Mexico and also in reefs of the western Pacific. It is a bright purplish blue, with blue spots on its sides and black lines across its cheeks. The tail is reddish.

A close relative of the redtail is the sargassum triggerfish, *X. ringens*, found in reef waters around the world. Its caudal fin is pinkish and the bases of the dorsal and anal fins are black. The bony plates of the brownish body are outlined with black, each bearing a white dot in its center. Purplish horizontal lines cross the cheeks, and the head is olive green.

Among the more than a dozen triggerfishes of the Indo-Pacific is *Balistapus undulatus*, a 12-inch species with yellow stripes and dots on a purple background; yellow rays in the dorsal, pectoral, and anal fins; and a bright yellow caudal fin. *Balistoides conspicillum*, also about 12 inches long, has a mouth set off by a broad band of orange "lips," a slash of white over the snout, large round white dots on its sides and belly, and a white band across the caudal peduncle. In *Pseudobalistes flavimarginatus*, a 2-foot species, from the head to the pectoral fins is a rusty orange, as are the pectoral fins; the second dorsal, anal, and caudal fins are striped horizontally with red, white, and blue.

Two other strikingly colored species of the Indo-Pacific are *Rhinecanthus rectangulus*, which has a black triangular patch on each side of the caudal peduncle and a broad black band running obliquely from the eye down and back to the anal fin; and *R. aculeatus*, which has several medium-width purplish and light bands from the lateral line extending obliquely back to the anal fin.

Abalistes stellaris, a triggerfish widespread in the tropical Indo-Pacific, may be at least 24 inches long.

Closely related to true triggerfishes but sometimes placed in a separate family, Monocanthidae, are the filefishes, in which the dorsal fin consists of a single long spine that in most species is saw-toothed on its rear margin. Both soft dorsal and anal fins are longer and positioned lower than in triggerfishes, and the body is narrower and deeper in outline. The small mouth is usually at the end of a medium-length snout used for poking into crevices as the fishes graze in reefs or around rocks or docks. Filefishes are often seen either in a head-down or a head-up position as they feed. The rough skin of some species has been used as a sort of sandpaper, like the shagreen made from shark skin. Like triggerfishes, filefishes are found in warm seas throughout the world. Poor swimmers, they may be carried far north of their usual range by the currents.

The orange filefish, *Aluterus schoepfi*, usually less than 12 inches long but occasionally as long as 2 feet, is found along the coasts of North and South America from Maine to Brazil, sometimes drifting far northward with the currents. It is common off Bermuda and in the Caribbean. Its dorsal spine is smooth. The caudal fin is yellow, and the body is gray-brown with orange mottling and black spots that are generally arranged in a line down the sides. The orange filefish is most common close to shore but is sometimes found in groups several miles from land and at depths of 50 feet or more. The young often drift with seaweeds undetected.

The scrawled filefish, *A. scriptus*, cosmopolitan in warm seas, sometimes exceeds 3 feet in length, making it the largest member of the family. Its tail is long and usually kept folded so that it appears as a pointed or spear-tipped fin. The head is concave in profile, and numerous black spots are on the greenish brown body and light blue head. The dorsal and anal fins are yellow, the caudal red. The skin is smooth, almost chamoislike.

The unicorn filefish, *A. monoceros*, also widespread, may be 2 feet long. Its body is mottled, the head more convex than concave in profile, and the tail is short.

The planehead filefish, *Monacanthus hispidus*, is one of the smaller filefishes of the Atlantic, most abundant in the Caribbean and warm waters of the Atlantic but sometimes drifting as far north as Maine. Its maximum length is 10 inches. The basic color is gray or green, with dark blotches on the sides; but the color changes with the background—brown, for example, over a sandy bottom. The first ray of the dorsal fin is usually extended into a filament. The fringed filefish, *M. ciliatus*, found in the same range as the planehead, does not have a long filament on its dorsal fin and has spines along the sides of the caudal peduncle. *M. setifer*, a species occurring off the coast of Japan, has a long dorsal fin filament.

Among the filefishes of the Indo-Pacific is the widespread and attractive 4-inch *Oxymonacanthus longirostris*, its almost emerald green body covered with orange spots. Another 4-inch species is *Pervagor melanocephalus*, also green but with a bright scarlet tail.

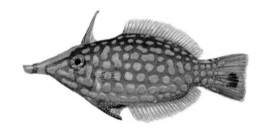

Orange-spotted filefish (*Oxymonacanthus longirostris*)
up to 1 ft (30 cm)

Family Ostraciidae
boxfishes

Boxfishes, or trunkfishes, have a hard outer case that completely encloses the body, like a turtle's shell. It consists of fused six-sided scales or plates. Because of this inflexible coat or armor, trunkfishes are poor swimmers. The body is literally immovable, and they propel themselves with their caudal and pectoral fins. Pelvic fins are lacking. When young, trunkfishes have a round or oval body in cross-section, but it becomes triangular in older fishes. Easily caught in nets, their dried bodies are sold as curios. Sometimes they are eaten, roasted in their shells. Some are called cowfishes because of the hornlike protuberances on their head just above the eyes. In feeding, boxfishes often stand on their head and squirt streams of water into the sand or mud to expose the small plants and animals which they then suck into their small mouths. These unusual fishes are worldwide in distribution in warm and tropical seas.

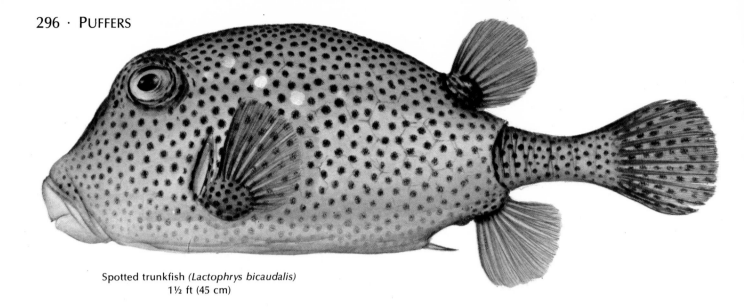

Spotted trunkfish *(Lactophrys bicaudalis)*
1½ ft (45 cm)

The scrawled cowfish, *Lactophrys quadricornis*, lives in warm Atlantic and Caribbean waters, sometimes carried northward by currents. It is occasionally as much as a foot long but usually shorter. Its shell is a blotched green with iridescent blue and yellow spots. There is a single "horn" over each eye and two at the rear of the shell. The trunkfish, *L. trigonus*, has a distinctive black blotch around a white center behind each gill opening and a prominent spine on the lower or ventral surface just in front of the anus. The eyes are bright green.

The spotted trunkfish, *L. bicaudalis*, of the same range as the scrawled cowfish and with a spine in front of the anus, has numerous black spots over the body and on the caudal peduncle and fin. It may be as much as 1½ feet long.

Still another species of the genus is the smooth trunkfish, *L. triqueter*, which lacks spines. Its whitish body bears black spots and narrow black bars.

Common species of trunkfishes in Indo-Pacific waters are *Lactoria, Ostracion, Tetrosomus,* and *Rhynchostracion*. The unusual *R. nasus* has purplish red lips and forehead, a green body, and a blue tail.

Family Tetraodontidae
puffers

Also called swellfishes, puffers have the ability to inflate their bodies with air or water or both, gulping quickly, and then turning upside down so that they float to the surface. They can expel the air or water as rapidly, usually with a loud belch, to return to normal size and position. This sudden bloating of the body is generally sufficient to discourage an attacker.

The teeth of puffers are fused to form a beak, similar to the beak of a parrotfish but not as large. It is divided in the middle both above and below so that the fish are literally "four toothed," as their family name describes. They use their beak to crunch through the shells of mollusks and crustaceans on which they feed. Puffers can make a loud rasping noise by grinding their teeth. They are not swift swimmers, using mainly their fins rather than their bodies. The family is worldwide in distribution, found principally in warm seas with some living in temperate waters. Some are good to eat, but others are poisonous, particularly the internal organs and the roe. Despite this danger, they are considered a delicacy in some places, especially in Japan.

The smooth puffer, *Lagocephalus laevigatus*, attains a length of 2 feet and may weigh as much as 7 pounds, the largest member of the family. Found in the Caribbean and in warm Atlantic waters, sometimes straying northward to New York or beyond and southward to Brazil, it is greenish above and silvery below. Because of the blunt shape of its head and mouth, it goes also by the name rabbitfish. The skin is smooth except for some spiny projections on the ventral surface. This puffer is caught regularly on hook and line.

The smaller southern puffer, *Sphoeroides nephelus*, mostly less than 10 inches long, has 10 or more black spots on its sides and ventral surface and 2 black bands across its caudal fin, one at the base and the other at the tip. It is often seen feeding close to shore; if disturbed, it "puffs" its body to unbelievable size. The southern puffer is found mostly south of the Carolinas and in the Caribbean but may drift northward with the currents.

The common species north of the Carolinas, to as far north as Maine, is the northern puffer, *S. maculatus*, which is identical to the southern species except for its lack of black bars on the tail. In both species, the body is covered with numerous small prickly scales.

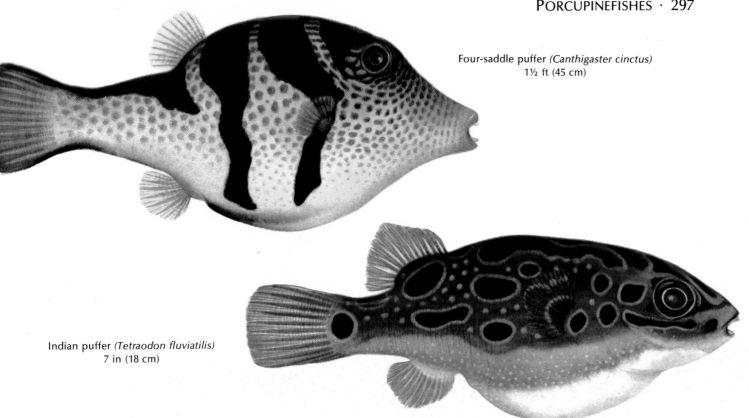

Four-saddle puffer *(Canthigaster cinctus)*
1½ ft (45 cm)

Indian puffer *(Tetraodon fluviatilis)*
7 in (18 cm)

The bullseye puffer, *S. annulatus*, to 1½ feet long, is dark brown with longitudinal cream streaks along its body. There are also dark spots. It is found in the warm Pacific from San Diego southward.

The four-saddle puffer, *Canthigaster cinctus*, is one of about half a dozen species of *Canthigaster* widely distributed in reefs of Indo-Pacific waters. All are brightly colored, and most are less than 6 inches long. In most, the snout is narrow and sharp-pointed, used for probing in the coral. One species, *C. rivulatus*, is found in Japanese waters, where the puffer for eating is *Fugu rubripes*.

Family Diodontidae
porcupinefishes

Porcupinefishes resemble puffers and are also able to inflate their bodies. The beak is not divided in the middle, however, and so they are "two toothed," as their family name describes. They have long, sharp spines over the body, which is generally square in outline. Boxfish is another name often used for the family. When inflated, the body is round and the spines protrude formidably. They can inflict nasty wounds. South Sea Islanders once made helmets of their skins, and in the Orient the inflated skins were hung as lanterns, each with a candle inside. Puffers are found around the world in warm seas.

The porcupinefish, *Diodon hystrix*, averaging 12 inches in length but occasionally as long as 3 feet, is found worldwide in warm seas. It is brownish yellow above and white below, with round black spots over the body and fins. In the Indo-Pacific, *D. hystrix* reaches a length of 1½ feet, while *Lophodiodon calori* may be 2 feet long.

The striped burrfish, *Chilomycterus schoepfi*, to 10 inches long, has short broad spines resembling stout thorns and a yellowish body with dark stripes. It is sometimes found as far north as Massachusetts. Several other species of *Chilomycterus* live in the warm Atlantic and in Caribbean waters; and the Pacific burrfish, *C. affinis*, occurs in the warm Pacific from southern California southward.

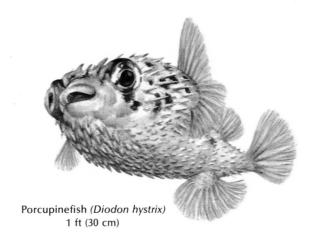

Porcupinefish *(Diodon hystrix)*
1 ft (30 cm)

Family Molidae
molas

These strange relatives of triggerfishes, puffers, and porcupinefishes are giant-size fishes of the open seas. Because they appear to be all head, another name for them is headfish. The caudal fin exists, but it is a narrow band with no caudal peduncle. Pelvic fins are lacking, and both the dorsal and anal fins are long. The skin is leathery and the skeleton poorly developed.

When they are young, molas, or ocean sunfishes, swim with the body in a vertical position like other fishes. Mature fishes spend most of their time on their sides, floating as though dead. They swim feebly and are sometimes carried by currents into waters that are too cold for their survival.

The ocean sunfish, *Mola mola*, is the largest species, growing to 10 feet long and weighing as much as 600 pounds. It is gray-blue above and white below.

The family contains only two other species: the sharptail mola, *M. lanceolata*, which is nearly as large as the ocean sunfish; and the slender mola, *Ranzania laevis*, similar in body shape but only 2½ feet long. The slender mola travels in schools. In Hawaii, it was called "king of the mackerels" and considered sacred.

Ocean sunfish *(Mola mola)*
up to 10 ft (305 cm)

SELECTED BIBLIOGRAPHY

Adler, Helmut E., *Fish Behavior: Why Fishes Do What They Do*. Neptune City, N. J.: T.F.H. Publications, Inc., 1975

American Fisheries Society, *Common and Scientific Names of Fishes from the United States and Canada*. Special Publication No. 6, Washington, D.C., 1970

Beebe, William, and Tee-Van, John, *Field Book of the Shore Fishes of Bermuda and the West Indies*. New York: Dover Publications, 1970

Berg, Leo S., *Classification of Fishes*. Ann Arbor, Michigan: J. W. Edwards, 1947

Breder, Charles M., Jr., *Field Book of Marine Fishes of the Atlantic Coast*. New York: G. P. Putnam's Sons, 1948

Chaplin, Charles C. G., and Scott, Peter, *Fishwatcher's Guide to West Atlantic Coral Reefs*. Valley Forge, Pennsylvania: Harwood Books, 1972

Curtis, Brian, *The Life Story of the Fish*. New York: Dover Publications, 1961

De Graaf, Frank, *Marine Aquarium Guide*. Harrison, New Jersey: Pet Library Ltd., 1973

Faulkner, Douglas, and Atz, James W., *Aquarium Fishes, Their Beauty, History and Care*. New York: The Viking Press, 1971

Gosline, William A., and Brock, Vernon C., *Handbook of Hawaiian Fishes*. Honolulu: University of Hawaii Press, 1960

Hardy, Sir Alister, *The Open Sea: Its Natural History*. Boston: Houghton Mifflin Co., 1965

Hart, J. L., *Pacific Fishes of Canada*. Fisheries Research Board of Canada, 1973

Herald, Earl S., *Fishes of North America*. New York: Doubleday & Co., Inc., 1972

————, *Living Fishes of the World*. New York: Doubleday & Co., Inc., 1961

Idyll, C. P., *Abyss: The Deep Sea and the Creatures that Live in It*. New York: T. Y. Crowell, 1971

Julian, J. W., *Encyclopedia of Tropical Fish*. New York: Dell Publishing Co., 1974

Lagler, Karl F., Bardach, John E., and Miller, Robert R., *Ichthyology*. New York: John Wiley and Sons, Inc., 1962

Lineaweaver, Thomas H. III, and Backus, Richard H., *The Natural History of Sharks*. Philadelphia and New York: J.B. Lippincott Co., 1970

Marshall, Norman B., *The Life of Fishes*. Cleveland and New York: World Publishing Co., 1966

Migdalski, Edward C., *Fresh Water Sport Fishes of North America*. New York: Ronald Press Co., 1958

————, *Salt Water Game Fishes—Atlantic and Pacific*. New York: Ronald Press Co., 1962

Moy-Thomas, J. W., and Miles, R. S., *Palaeozoic Fishes*. Philadelphia: W. B. Saunders Co., 1971

National Geographic Society, *The Wondrous World of Fishes*. Washington, D.C., 1969

Norman, J. R., and Greenwood, P. H., *A History of Fishes*. New York: John Wiley & Sons, 1975

Randall, John E., *Caribbean Reef Fishes*. Neptune City, N.J.: T.F.H. Publications, Inc., 1974

Smith, J. L. B., *The Sea Fishes of Southern Africa*. South Africa: Central News Agency, Ltd., 1949

Spotte, Stephen, *Marine Aquarium Keeping: The Science, the Animals and Art*. New York: John Wiley & Sons, 1973

Sterba, Dr. Gunther, *Freshwater Fishes of the World*, Vols. 1 and 2. Neptune City, N.J.: T.F.H. Publications, Inc., 1973

Veşey-Fitzgerald, Brian, and LaMonte, Francesca, *Game Fishes of the World*. New York: Harper & Brothers, 1949

Zim, Herbert S., and Shoemaker, Hurst H., *Fishes. A Guide to Fresh- and Salt-water Species*. New York: Simon and Schuster, 1956

SALTWATER RECORDS*

Common Name	Scientific Name		Lb.-Oz.	Length	Girth	Where	When	Angler
ALBACORE	Thunnus alalunga		74-13	50"	34¾"	Canary Islands	Oct. 28, 1973	Olof Idegren
AMBERJACK, Greater	Seriola dumerili		149	71"	41¾"	Bermuda	June 21, 1964	Peter Simons
BARRACUDA, Great	Sphyraena barracuda		83	72¼"	29"	Lagos, Nigeria	Jan. 13, 1952	K. J. W. Hackett
BASS, Black Sea	Centropristis striata		8	22"	19"	Nantucket Sound, Mass.	May 13, 1951	H. R. Rider
BASS, Giant Sea	Stereolepis gigas		563-8	89"	72"	Anacapa Island, Calif.	Aug. 20, 1968	James D. McAdam, Jr.
BASS, Striped	Morone saxatilis		72	54½"	31"	Cuttyhunk, Mass.	Oct. 10, 1969	Edward J. Kirker
BLUEFISH	Pomatomus saltatrix		31-12	47"	23"	Hatteras Inlet, N.C.	Jan. 30, 1972	James M. Hussey
BONEFISH	Albula vulpes		19	39⅝"	17"	Zululand, So. Africa	May 26, 1962	Brian W. Batchelor
COBIA	Rachycentron canadum		110-5	63"	34"	Mombasa, Kenya	Sept. 8, 1964	Eric Tinworth
COD	Gadus morhua		98-12	63"	41"	Isle of Shoals, N.H.	June 8, 1969	Alphonse J. Bielevich
DOLPHIN	Coryphaena hippurus		85	69"	37½"	Spanish Wells, Bahamas	May 29, 1968	Richard Seymour
DRUM, Black	Pogonias cromis		113-1	53⅛"	43½"	Lewes, Delaware	May 15, 1975	Gerald M. Townsend
DRUM, Red	Sciaenops ocellata		90	55½"	38¼"	Rodanthe, N.C.	Nov. 7, 1973	Elvin Hooper
FLOUNDER	Paralichthys spp.		30-12	38½"	30½"	Vina del Mar, Chile	Nov. 1, 1971	Agusto Nunez Moreno
JEWFISH	Epinephelus itajara		680	85½"	66"	Fernandina Beach, Fla.	May 20, 1961	Lynn Joyner
MACKEREL, King	Scomberomorus cavalia		78-12	65½"	30"	LaRomana, Dom. Rep.	Nov. 26, 1971	Fernando Viyella
MARLIN, Atlantic Blue	Makaira nigricans		1142	166"	80"	Nags Head, N.C.	July 26, 1974	Jack Herrington
MARLIN, Black	Makaira indica		1560	174"	81"	Cabo Blanco, Peru	Aug. 4, 1953	A. C. Glassell, Jr.
MARLIN, Pacific Blue	Makaira nigricans		1153	176"	73"	Ritidian Point, Guam	Aug. 21, 1969	Greg D. Perez
MARLIN, Striped	Tetrapturus audax		415	132"	52"	Cape Brett, N.Z.	Mar. 31, 1964	B. C. Bain
MARLIN, White	Tetrapturus albidus		159-8	108"	36"	Pompano Beach, Fla.	Apr. 25, 1953	W. E. Johnson
PERMIT	Trachinotus falcatus		50-8	44¾"	33¾"	Key West, Fla.	Mar. 15, 1971	Marshall E. Earnest
POLLOCK	Pollachius virens		46-7	50½"	30"	Brielle, N.J.	May 26, 1975	John Tomes Holton
ROOSTERFISH	Nematistius pectoralis		114	64"	33"	LaPaz, Mexico	June 1, 1960	Abe Sackheim
RUNNER, Rainbow	Elagatis bipinnulata		30-15	47"	22"	Kauai, Hawaii	Apr. 27, 1963	Holbrook Goodale
SAILFISH, Atlantic	Istiophorus platypterus		128-1	106¼"	34¼"	Luanda, Angola	Mar. 27, 1974	Harm Steyn
SAILFISH, Pacific	Istiophorus platypterus		221	129"		Galapagos Islands	Feb. 12, 1947	Carl W. Stewart
SEABASS, White	Cynoscion nobilis		83-12	65½"	34"	San Felipe, Mexico	Mar. 31, 1953	L. C. Baumgardner
SEATROUT, Spotted	Cynoscion nebulosus	TIE{	15-3 15-6	34½" 33"	20½" 23¾"	Fort Pierce, Fla. Jensen Beach, Fla.	Jan. 13, 1949 May 4, 1969	C. W. Hubbard Michael J. Foremny
SHARK, BLUE	Prionace glauca	TIE{	410 410	138" 134"	52" 52½"	Rockport, Mass. Rockport, Mass.	Sept. 1, 1960 Aug. 17, 1967	Richard C. Webster Martha C. Webster
SHARK, Hammerhead	Sphyrnidae		703	172"	63"	Jacksonville, Fla.	July 5, 1975	H. B. "Blackie" Reasor
SHARK, Porbeagle	Lamna nasus		430	96"	63"	Channel Islands, England	June 29, 1969	Desmond Bougourd
SHARK, Shortfin Mako	Isurus oxyrinchus		1061	146"	79½"	Mayor Island, N.Z.	Feb. 17, 1970	James B. Penwarden
SHARK, Thresher	Alopias vulpinus		739	106"	68"	Tutukaka, N.Z.	Feb. 17, 1975	Brian Galvin
SHARK, Tiger	Galeocerdo cuvieri		1780	166½"	103"	Cherry Grove, S.C.	June 14, 1964	Walter Maxwell
SHARK, White	Carcharodon carcharias		2664	202"	114"	Ceduna, So. Australia	Apr. 21, 1959	Alfred Dean
SNOOK (Robalo)	Centropomus undecimalis		52-6	49½"	26"	LaPaz, Mexico	Jan. 9, 1963	Jane Haywood
SWORDFISH	Xiphias gladius		1182	179¼"	78"	Iquique, Chile	May 7, 1953	L. Marron
TANGUIGUE	Scomberomorus commerson		81	71½"	29¼"	Karachi, Pakistan	Aug. 27, 1960	George E. Rusinak
TARPON	Megalops atlantica		283	86³/₅"		Lake Maracaibo, Ven.	Mar. 19, 1956	M. Salazar
TAUTOG	Tautoga onitis		21-6	31½"	23½"	Cape May, N.J.	June 12, 1954	R. N. Sheafer
TUNA, Atlantic Bigeye	Thunnus obesus		335-1	100¾"	60¼"	Canary Islands	July 11, 1975	Wilhelm Rapp
TUNA, Blackfin	Thunnus atlanticus	TIE{	38 38	39¼" 41"	28¾" 28"	Bermuda Islamorada, Fla.	June 26, 1970 May 22, 1973	Archie L. Dickens Elizabeth Jean Wade
TUNA, Bluefin	Thunnus thynnus		1120	122"	85½"	Prince Edward Island	Oct. 19, 1973	Lee Coffin
TUNA, Pacific Bigeye	Thunnus obesus		435	93"	63½"	Cabo Blanco, Peru	Apr. 17, 1957	Dr. Russel V. A. Lee
TUNA, Skipjack	Euthynnus pelamis	TIE{	39-15 40	39" 38¾"	28" 27½"	Walker Cay, Bahamas Mauritius	Jan. 21, 1952 Apr. 19, 1971	F. Drowley J. R. P. Caboche, Jr.
TUNA, Yellowfin	Thunnus albacares		308	84"	57"	San Benedicto Is., Mex.	Jan. 18, 1973	Harold J. Tolson
TUNNY, Little	Euthynnus alletteratus		21-12	33½"	21½"	Key Largo, Fla.	June 29, 1975	Paul F. Leader
WAHOO	Acanthocybium solanderi		149	79¾"	37½"	Cat Cay, Bahamas	June 15, 1962	John Pirovano
WEAKFISH	Cynoscion regalis		19-8	37"	25¾"	Trinidad, West Indies	Apr. 13, 1962	Dennis B. Hall
YELLOWTAIL	Seriola dorsalis		111	62"	38"	Bay of Islands, N.Z.	June 11, 1961	A. F. Plim

The SPECIES columns (Common Name, Scientific Name) and CAUGHT BY ROD AND REEL columns (Lb.-Oz., Length, Girth, Where, When, Angler) are grouped under those two headings.

*Saltwater Records compiled by International Game Fish Association

FRESHWATER RECORDS*

	SPECIES				CAUGHT BY ROD AND REEL		
Common Name	Scientific Name	Lb.-Oz.	Length	Girth	Where	When	Angler
BASS, Largemouth	Micropterus salmoides	22-4	32½"	28½"	Montgomery Lake, Ga.	June 2, 1932	George W. Perry
BASS, Redeye	Micropterus coosae	7-8	23"	18"	Lazer Creek, Ga.	Apr. 9, 1975	Jimmy L. Rogers
BASS, Rock	Ambloplites rupestis	3	13½"	10¾"	York River, Ontario	Aug. 1, 1974	Peter Gulgin
BASS, Smallmouth	Micropterus dolomieui	11-15	27"	21⅔"	Dale Hollow Lake, Ky.	July 9, 1955	David L. Hayes
BASS, Spotted	Micropterus punctulatus spp	8-10½	23½"	19⅞"	Smith Lake, Alabama	Feb. 25, 1972	Billy Henderson
BASS, White	Morone chrysops	5-5	19½"	17"	Ferguson Lake, Calif.	Mar. 8, 1972	Norman W. Mize
BASS, Yellow	Morone mississippiensis	2-2	14"	13"	Lake Monona, Wis.	Jan. 18, 1972	James Thrun
BLUEGILL	Lepomis macrochirus	4-12	15"	18¼"	Ketona Lake, Alabama	Apr. 9, 1950	T. S. Hudson
BOWFIN	Amia calva	19-12	39"		Lake Marion, S.C.	Nov. 5, 1972	M. R. Webster
BUFFALO, Bigmouth	Ictiobus cyprinellus	47-2	43"	30"	Tippecanoe L., Ind.	May 10, 1975	David F. Hulley
BUFFALO, Smallmouth	Ictiobus bubalus	22-11	33½"	24½"	L. Wylie, N.C.	Aug. 25, 1975	Douglas E. Brogden
BULLHEAD, Black	Ictalurus melas	8	24"	17¾"	Lake Waccabuc, N.Y.	Aug. 1, 1951	Kani Evans
CARP	Cyprinus carpio	55-5	42"	31"	Clearwater Lake, Minn.	July 10, 1952	Frank J. Ledwein
CATFISH, Blue	Ictalurus furcatus	97	57"	37"	Missouri River, S.D.	Sept. 16, 1959	Edward B. Elliott
CATFISH, Channel	Ictalurus punctatus	58	47¼"	29⅛"	Santee-Cooper Res., S.C.	July 7, 1964	W. B. Whaley
CATFISH, Flathead	Pylodictis olivaris	79-8	44"	27"	White River, Indiana	Aug. 13, 1966	Glenn T. Simpson
CHAR, Arctic	Salvelinus alpinus	29-11	39¾"	26"	Arctic R., N.W.T.	Aug. 21, 1968	Jeanne P. Branson
CRAPPIE, Black	Pomoxis nigromaculatus	5	19¼"	18⅝"	Santee-Cooper Res., S.C.	Mar. 15, 1957	Paul E. Foust
CRAPPIE, White	Pomoxis annularis	5-3	21"	19"	Enid Dam, Miss.	July 31, 1957	Fred L. Bright
DOLLY VARDEN	Salvelinus malma	32	40½"	29¾"	L. Pend Oreille, Idaho	Oct. 27, 1949	N. L. Higgins
DRUM, Freshwater	Aplodinotus grunniens	54-8	31½"	29"	Nickajack Lake, Tenn.	Apr. 20, 1972	Benny E. Hull
GAR, Alligator	Lepisosteus spatula	279	93"		Rio Grande River, Texas	Dec. 2, 1951	Bill Valverde
GAR, Longnose	Lepisosteus osseus	50-5	72¼"	22¼"	Trinity River, Texas	July 30, 1954	Townsend Miller
GRAYLING, American	Thymallus arcticus	5-15	29⅞"	15⅛"	Katseyedie R., N.W.T.	Aug. 16, 1967	Jeanne P. Branson
KOKANEE	Oncorhynchus nerka	6-9¾	24½"	14½"	Priest L., Idaho	June 9, 1975	Jerry Verge
MUSKELLUNGE	Esox masquinongy	69-15	64½"	31¾"	St. Lawrence River, N.Y.	Sept. 22, 1957	Arthur Lawton
PERCH, White	Morone americanus	4-12	19½"	13"	Messalonskee Lake, Me.	June 4, 1949	Mrs. Earl Small
PERCH, Yellow	Perca flavescens	4-3½			Bordentown, N.J.	May 1865	Dr. C. C. Abbot
PICKEREL, Chain	Esox niger	9-6	31"	14"	Homerville, Georgia	Feb. 17, 1961	Baxley McQuaig, Jr.
PIKE, Northern	Esox lucius	46-2	52½"	25"	Sacandaga Res., N.Y.	Sept. 15, 1940	Peter Dubuc
REDHORSE, Silver	Moxostoma anisurum	4-2	20½"	14"	Gasconade R., Mo.	Oct. 5, 1974	C. Larry McKinney
SALMON, Atlantic	Salmo salar	79-2			Tana River, Norway	1928	Henrik Henriksen
SALMON, Chinook	Oncorhynchus tshawytscha	92	58½"	36"	Skeena River, B.C.	July 19, 1959	Heinz Wichman
SALMON, Chum	Oncorhynchus keta	24-4	40½"	22⅞"	Margarita Bay, Alaska	Aug. 19, 1974	Richard Coleman
SALMON, Landlocked	Salmo salar	22-8	36"		Sebago Lake, Maine	Aug. 1, 1907	Edward Blakely
SALMON, Coho	Oncorhynchus kisutch	31			Cowichan Bay, B.C.	Oct. 11, 1947	Mrs. Lee Hallberg
SAUGER	Stizostedion canadense	8-12	28"	15"	Lake Sakakawea, N.D.	Oct. 6, 1971	Mike Fischer
SHAD, American	Alosa sapidissima	9-2	25"	17½"	Enfield, Connecticut	Apr. 28, 1973	Edward P. Nelson
STURGEON, White	Acipenser transmontanus	360	111"	86"	Snake River, Idaho	Apr. 24, 1956	Willard Cravens
SUNFISH, Green	Lepomis cyanellus	2-2	14¾"	14"	Stockton Lake, Missouri	June 18, 1971	Paul M. Dilley
SUNFISH, Redear	Lepomis microlophus	4-8	16¼"	17¾"	Chase City, Virginia	June 19, 1970	Maurice E. Ball
TROUT, Brook	Salvelinus fontinalis	14-8	31½"		Nipigon River, Ontario	July 1916	Dr. W. J. Cook
TROUT, Brown	Salmo trutta	39-8			Loch Awe, Scotland	1866	W. Muir
TROUT, Cutthroat	Salmo clarki	41	39"		Pyramid Lake, Nevada	Dec. 1925	John Skimmerhorn
TROUT, Golden	Salmo aguabonita	11	28"	16".	Cook's Lake, Wyoming	Aug. 5, 1948	Chas. S. Reed
TROUT, Lake	Salvelinus namaycush	65	52"	38"	Great Bear L., N.W.T.	Aug. 8, 1970	Larry Daunis
TROUT, Rainbow, Stlhd. or Kamloops	Salmo gairdneri	42-2	43"	23½"	Bell Island, Alaska	June 22, 1970	David Robert White
TROUT, Sunapee	Salvelinus aureolus	11-8	33"	17¼"	Lake Sunapee, N.H.	Aug. 1, 1954	Ernest Theoharis
TROUT, Tiger	Brown X Brook	10	27"	16¾"	Deerskin River, Wis.	May 23, 1974	Charles J. Mattek
WALLEYE	Stizostedion vitreum	25	41"	29"	Old Hickory Lake, Tenn.	Aug. 1, 1960	Mabry Harper
WARMOUTH	Lepomis gulosus	2	12"	12½"	Sylvania, Ga.	May 4, 1974	Carlton Robbins
WHITEFISH, Lake	Coregonus clupeaformis	13	32¼"	19"	Great Bear L., N.W.T.	July 14, 1974	Robert L. Stintsman
WHITEFISH, Mountain	Prosopium williamsoni	5	19"	14"	Athabasca R., Alberta	June 3, 1963	Orville Welch

* Freshwater Records compiled by *Field & Stream*

INDEX

Common names of the fishes are in
roman, scientific names are in italics, and
pages on which the illustrations occur are
indicated by bold-face numerals.

Ablennes hians (flat needlefish), 182
Abramis brama (bream), 150, **151**
Abramites (headstanders), 141
Abudefduf, 258
    saxatilis (sergeant major), 258, **259**
Acanthocybium salanderi (wahoo), 279
Acanthodoras spinosissimus (walking
    catfish), 164
Acanthopthalmus (kuhli loaches), 156–57
    kuhli (coolie loach), 156, **158**
    semicinctus (half-banded loach),
    156, **158**
Acanthuridae (surgeonfishes), 274–75
Acanthurus, 274–75
    bahianus (ocean surgeon), 274–75
    chirurgus (doctorfish), 275
    coeruleus (blue tang), 275
    leucosternon (powder-blue
    surgeonfish), 275, **275**
    triostegus (convict tang), **275**
Acanthus armatus, 178
Acerina cernua (ruffe), 224
Acipenser, 91–92
    brevirostrum (shortnose sturgeon),
    92
    fulvescens (lake sturgeon), 92, **92**
    medirostris (green sturgeon),
    91–92, **91**
    oxyrhynchus (Atlantic sturgeon),
    91, 92
    sturio (European sturgeon), 92
    transmontanus (white sturgeon),
    91, **91**
Acipenseridae (sturgeons), 90–93
Acipenseriformes (order), 90–94
Acrotus willoughbyi, 288
Aeneus catfish (*Corydoras aeneus*),
    166, **167**
Aeoliscus punctulatus (shrimpfish),
    198, **198**
Aeolisius, 198
Aequidens
    itanyi (dolphin cichlid), **256**
    maroni (keyhole cichlid), **257,** 258
    portalegrensis (black acara), 258
    pulcher (blue acara), 258
Aetoplatea, 79
African freshwater pipefish (*Syngnathus
    pulchellus*), 198
African knifefish (*Notopterus afer*), 112
African lungfish (*Protopterus annectans*),
    89
African lungfishes (Lepidosirenidae),
    88–89
African pompano (*Alectis crinitus*), 231
African spotted catfish (*Parauchenoglanis
    macrostoma*), 161, **161**
Afronondus sheljuzhkoi, 253
Agassiz's dwarf cichlid (*Apistogramma
    agassizai*), **256**
Age of fishes, 35–36
Agnatha (jawless fishes), 18, 39–42
Agonidae (poachers), 207
Agonostomus
    monticola (mountain mullet),
    260–61
    telfairi, 261
Agonus acipenserinus (sturgeon
    poacher), **206**, 207
Ahl's aphysemion (*Aphyosemion
    calliurum*), **185**
Aholehole (*Kuhlia taeniura*), 217, **217**
Aholeholes (Kuhliidae), 217
Alabama shad (*Alosa alabamae*), 107
Alaskan blackfish (*Dallia pectoralis*),
    131, **131**

Albacore (*Thunnus atalunga*), 281
Albulidae (bonefishes), 98–99
Alectis crinitus (African pompano), 231
Alepisauridae (lancetfishes), 134
Alepisaurus ferox (longnose lancetfish),
    134, **134**
Alepocephalidae (deepsea slickheads),
    133
Alepocephalus tenebrosus (California
    slickhead), **133**
Alewife (*Alosa pseudoharengus*), 106–7,
    107, 108
Alligator gar (*Lepisosteus spatula*), 21,
    95–96
Alligator shark (*Echinorhinus brucus*),
    66–67
Allosmerus elongatus (whitebait smelt),
    126
Almaco jack (*Seriola rivoliana*), 228
Alopias, 52–53
    superciliosus (bigeye thresher shark),
    52
    vulpinus (thresher shark), 52, **53**
Alopiidae (thresher sharks), 52
Alosa, 106–8
    aestivalis (blueback herring), 108
    alabamae (Alabama shad), 107
    crysochloris (skipjack herring), 107–8
    mediocris (hickory shad), 107
    pseudoharengus (alewife), 106–7,
    107, 108
    sapidissima (American shad),
    106–7, **107**
Aluterus
    monoceros (unicorn filefish), 295
    schoepfi (orange filefish), 295
    scriptus (scrawled filefish), 295
Amargosa pupfish (*Cyprinodon
    nevadensis*), 184
Amazon dwarf cichlid (*Apistogramma
    pertense*), 257
Amazon molly (*Poecilia formosa*), 187
Amblopites rupestris (rock bass), 221
Amblycirrhitus pinos (red-spotted
    hawkfish), **260**
Amblydoras hancocki (spiny catfish),
    164, **164**
Amblyopsidae (cavefishes), 167–68
Amblyopsis
    rosae (Ozark cavefish), 168
    spelaea (northern cavefish), **168**
American eel (*Anguilla rostrata*), **24**,
    34–35, 99–100
American John Dory (*Zenopsis ocellata*),
    192
American plaice (*Hippoglossoides
    platessoides*), 293
American shad (*Alosa sapidissima*),
    106–7, **107**
Amia calva (bowfin), 96, 97
Amiidae (bowfins), 96
Amiiformes (order), 96
Ammocrypta (sand darters), 224
Amphipnous cuchia (cuchia), 200
Amphiprion, 259
    epihippium, 259
    percula (clown anemonefish), **259**
Amphisticus
    argenteus (barred surfperch),
    254, **254**
    koelzi (calico surfperch), 254
    rhodoterus (redtail surfperch), 254
Amur River pike (*Esox reicherti*), 128
Anabantidae (climbing perch), 286
Anabas testudineus (climbing perch, or
    walking fish), 286, **286**
Anablepidae (foureye fishes), 186
Anableps anableps (foureye fish),
    186, **186**
Anarchis yoshiae (pygmy moray), 101
Anarhichadidae (wolffishes), 269–70
Anarhichas, 269–70
    latifrons (jelly cat), 270
    lupas (Atlantic wolffish), **269**, 269–70

minor (spotted wolffish), 270
orientalis (Bering wolffish), 270
Anarrichthys ocellatus (wolf-eel), 270
Anchoa
    compressa (deepbody anchovy),
    109
    delicatissima (slough anchovy), 109
    hepsetus (striped anchovy), 109
    mitchili (bay anchovy), 109
Anchoveta (*Cetengraulis mysticetus*), 109
Anchoviella miarcha (slim anchovy), 109
Anchovies (Engraulidae), 109
Ancistrus spp. (bristlemouth catfishes),
    167
Ancylopsetta quadrocellata (ocellated
    flounder), 290
Angelfish (*Pterophyllum scalara*), **257**,
    257–58
Angelfishes, 22, 250–53
Angel shark (*Squatina dumerili*), 67, **67**
Angel sharks (Squatinidae), 67
Anguilla, 99–100
    anguilla (European eel), 99–100, **100**
    japonica (Japanese eel), 99
    rostrata (American eel), 99–100
Anguillidae (freshwater eels), 99–100
Anguilliformes (order), 99–104
Anisotremus
    davidsoni (sargo), 238
    surinamensis (black margate), 238
    virginicus (porkfish), 238, **239**
Anlorhynchus flavidus (tubesnout), 197
Anomalopidae (lantern-eye fishes), 190
Anomalops, 190
    katoptron (lantern-eye fish), **190**
Anoplopoma fimbria (sablefish), 204, **205**
Anoplopomatidae (sablefishes), 204
Anoptichthys jordani (blind cavefish),
    138, **139**
Anostomidae (headstanders), 141
Anostomus anostomus (striped
    headstander), 140
Antennariidae (frogfishes), 172
Antennarius, 172
    avalonis (roughjaw frogfish),
    172, **172**
    scaber (splitlure frogfish), 172
Anthias squamipinnis (lyretail coralfish),
    216, **216**
Antigonia rubescens (boarfish), **193**
Apeltes quadracus (fourspine
    stickleback), 197
Aphanius iberus (Spanish killifish), 185
Aphredoderidae (pirate perches), 168
Aphredoderus savanus (pirate perch),
    168, **168**
Aphyocharax rubripinnis (bloodfin), **140**
Aphyosemion, 184–85
    australe (lyretail), 185, **185**
    bivittatum (red lyretail), 184–85
    calliurum (Ahl's aphyosemion), **185**
    cinnaomoeum (cinnamon killie), **184**
    coeruleum (blue gularis), **184**, 185
    geryi (Gery's aphyosemion), **185**
    gulare (gularis), 185
Apistogramma, 258
    agassizai (Agassiz's dwarf cichlid),
    256
    pertense (Amazon dwarf cichlid),
    257
    ramirezi (Ramirez' dwarf cichlid),
    256
Apisturus
    brunneus (brown cat shark), 55
    kampae (longnose cat shark), 55
Aplocheillichthys katangae (Katanga
    lampeye), 152
Aplodinotus grunniens (freshwater
    drum), 245–46
Apogon
    binotatus (barred cardinalfish), 222
    maculatus (flamefish), **222**
    semiornatus, 222
Apogonichthoides, 222

Apogonidae (cardinalfishes), 222
Aprionodon isodon (finetooth shark), 60
Arapaima (*Arapaima gigas*), 110, **110**
Arapaima gigas (arapaima), 110, **110**
Arapaimas (Osteoglossidae), 21, 110
Arawana (*Osteoglossum bicirrhosum*),
    110, **110**
Arawanas (Osteoglossidae), 110
Archerfish (*Toxotes jaculatrix*), 247, **247**
Archerfishes (Toxotidae), 32, 247
Archirus lineatus (lined sole), 293
Archoplites interruptus (Sacramento
    perch), 221
Archosargus
    probatocephalus (sheepshead),
    240–41, **241**
    rhomboidalis (sea bream), 241
Arctic char (*Salvelinus alpinus*),
    121–22, **122**
Arctic grayling (*Thymallus arcticus*), 122,
    122
Arctic staghorn sculpin (*Gymnocanthus
    tricuspis*), **205**, 206
Arctoscopus japonicus (sailfin sandfish),
    267, **267**
Areliseus joyneri, 293
Argentina
    semifasciatus, 126
    sialis (Pacific argentine), 126
    silus (Atlantic argentine), 126, **127**
    sphyraena, 126
Argentines (Argentinidae), 126
Argus (*Scatophagus argus*), 250, **250**
Argus fishes (Scatophagidae), 250
Argyropelecus, 132
    hemygenus (deepsea hatchetfish),
    132
Ariidae (sea catfishes), 163–64
Arius, 163–64
    dispar (Kanduli catfish), 164
    felis (sea catfish), 163, **164**
Armored catfishes, 164, 166–67
Arnoglossus laterna (scaldfish), 290
Arnoldichthys spilopterus (redeye
    characin), **140**
Arrow goby (*Clevelandia ios*), 273
Arrowtooth flounder (*Atherestes
    stomias*), 292
Asiatic featherback (*Notopterus chitala*),
    112, **112**
Asiatic snakehead (*Channa asiatica*), 200
Asiatic tonguefish (*Rhinoplagusia
    japonica*), 293, **293**
Asperapogon, 222
Aspredinichthys, 165
Aspredinidae (banjo catfishes), 164–65
Astroconger myriaster, 102
Astrodoras asterifrons (helmeted catfish),
    164
Astronotus ocellatus (oscar cichlid),
    258, **258**
Astropogon stellatus (conchfish), 222
Astroscopus
    guttatus (northern stargazer),
    268, **268**
    y-graecum (southern stargazer), 268
Astyanax mexicanus (Mexican tetra), 138
Atherestes stomias (arrowtooth
    flounder), 292
Atherina presbyter (sand smelt), **189**
Atherinidae (silversides), 188–89
Atheriniformes (order), 180–90
Atherinops affinis (topsmelt), 189
Atherinopsis californiensis (jacksmelt),
    189
Atlantic argentine (*Argentina silus*),
    126, **127**
Atlantic bonito (*Sarda sarda*), 279
Atlantic bumper (*Chloroscombrus
    chrysurus*), 231
Atlantic codfish (*Gadus morhua*),
    175, **175**
Atlantic cownose ray (*Rhinoptera
    bonasus*), 80, **80**

Atlantic croaker (Micropogon undulatus), 244

Atlantic cutlassfish (Trichiurus lepturus), 277, **277**

Atlantic flying fish (Cypselurus heterurus), **180**, 181

Atlantic guitarfish (Rhinobatos lentiginosus), 70, **71**

Atlantic hagfish (Myxine glutinosa), **40**, 41

Atlantic halibut (Hippoglossus hippoglossus), 291, **291**

Atlantic herring (Clupea harengus harengus), 104–5, **105**

Atlantic mackerel (Scomber scombrus), 278

Atlantic manta (Manta birostris), **81**, 82, **82**

Atlantic menhaden (Brevoortia tyrannus), **105**, 106

Atlantic midshipman (Porichthys porosissimus), 169

Atlantic moonfish (Vomer setapinnis), 231

Atlantic needlefish (Strongylura marina), 182

Atlantic nurse shark (Ginglymostoma cirratum), 50, **50**

Atlantic salmon (Salmo salar), **114**, 115–16

Atlantic saury (Scomberesox saurus), 183

Atlantic sharpnose shark (Rhizoprionodon terraenovae), 56, 59, **59**

Atlantic silverside (Menidia menidia), 189

Atlantic sleeper shark (Somniosus antarcticus), 66

Atlantic spadefish (Chaetodipterus faber), **249**, 250

Atlantic spiny lumpsucker (Eumicrotremus spinosus), 207

Atlantic stingray (Dasyatis sabina), 75–76, **76**

Atlantic sturgeon (Acipenser oxyrhynchus), **91**, 92

Atlantic threadfin (Polydactylus octonemus), 262

Atlantic thread herring (Opisthonema oglinum), 106

Atlantic tomcod (Microgadus tomcod), 176

Atlantic torpedo ray (Torpedo nobiliana), 72, **73**

Atlantic wolffish (Anarhichas lupas), **269**, 269–70

Auchenoglanis occidentalis, 161

Aulostomidae (trumpetfishes), 197

Aulostomus
    chinensis, 197
    maculatus (trumpetfish), 197, **197**
    valentini, 197

Australian carpet shark (Orectolobus ornatus), 50

Australian crampfish (Hypnos monopterygium), 72

Australian lungfish (Neoceratodus forsteri), 87, **87**

Australian lungfishes (Ceratodontidae), 87

Australian mobula (Mobula diabola), 83

Australian numbfish (Narcine tasmaniensis), 72

Australian rainbowfish (Melanotaenia maccullochi), 189, **189**

Australian smooth stingray (Dasyatis brevirostris), 76

Australian snapper (Pagrosomus auratus), 241

Australian swell shark (Cephaloscyllium laticeps), 55

Auxis thazard (frigate mackerel), 279, **279**

Awaous tajasica (river goby), 273

Ayu (Plecoglossus altivelis), 124, **125**

Backswimmer (Synodontis nigriventris), 163, **163**

Badis badis, 253

Bagre marinus (gafftopsail catfish), 163–64

Bagridae (bagrid catfishes), 161

Bagrid catfishes (Bagridae), 161

Bairdiella chrysura (silver perch), 243

Balistapus undulatus (undulate triggerfish), 294, **294**

Balistes
    capriscus (gray triggerfish), 294
    undulatus (orange-striped triggerfish), 295
    vetula (queen triggerfish), 294

Balistidae (triggerfishes and filefishes), 294–95

Balistoides conspicillum (clown triggerfish), 294, **294**

Ballyhoo (Hemiramphus brasiliensis), 181

Banded butterflyfish (Chaetodon striatus), 250, **251**

Banded copeina (Pyrrhulina vittata), **140**

Banded cynolebias (Cynolebias adloffi), **184**

Banded drum (Larimus fasciatus), 245

Banded guitarfish (Zapteryx exasperata), 70–71

Banded knifefish (Gymnotus carapo), 142, **142**

Banded knifefish (Notopterus chitala), 112

Banded pygmy sunfish (Elassoma zonatum), 221

Banded rudderfish (Seriola zonata), 228

Banded sculpin (Cottus carolinae), 206

Banded snipefish (Centriscops obliquus), 198

Banded sunfish (Enneacanthus obesus), 221

Banded topminnow (Fundulus cingulatus), 183

Banded wobbegong (Orectolobus ornatus), 50

Bandwing flying fish (Cypselurus exsiliens), 181

Banjo catfish (Bunocephalus coracoideus), 164–65, **165**

Banjo catfishes (Aspredinidae), 164–65

Bank sea bass (Centropristis ocyurus), 214

Barbfish (Scorpaena brasiliensis), 202

Barbodes lateristriga (spanner barb), **152**

Barbs (Barbus), 151–52

Barbu (Polydactylus virginicus), 262, **262**

Barbus, 151–52
    schwanenfeldi (tinfoil barb), 151–52, **152**
    tetrazona (tiger or sumatra barb), 152, **152**
    tor (mahseer), 151, **151**

Bar jack (Caranx ruber), 229–30

Barndoor skate (Raja laevis), 75

Barracudas (Sphyraenidae), 28, 261–62

Barramundi (Lates calcarifer), 212

Barred cardinalfish (Apogon binotatus), 222

Barred sand bass (Paralabrax nebulifer), 213–14

Barred surfperch (Amphistichus argenteus), 254, **254**

Basking shark (Cetorhinus maximus), 46, **53**, 54

Basses (Micropterus), 33–34, 217–18

Batfishes (Ogcocephalidae), 172–73

Bathyclupea argentea (deepsea herring), 247, **247**

Bathyclupeidae (deepsea herrings), 247

Bathygobius soporator (frillfin goby), 273

Bathylagidae (deepsea smelts), 127

Bathyleptus lisae (deepsea giganturid), **103**, 135

Batrachoididae (toadfishes), 169–70

Batrachoidiformes (order), 169–70

Bat ray (Myliobatus californica), 80

Bay anchovy (Anchoa mitchili), 109

Bay blenny (Hypsoblennius gentilis), 269

Beardfish (Polymixa lowei), 190, **190**

Beaugregory (Pomacentrus leucosticus), 258–59, **259**

Belone bellone (garfish), **182**

Belonesox belizanus (pike killifish), 188

Belonidae (needlefishes), 180, 182

Belontia signata (combtail paradise fish), **286**

Belontiidae (labyrinthfishes), 286–88

Belted sandfish (Serranus subligarius), 214

Beluga (Huso huso), 93

Benthabella dentata (northern pearleye), 135, **135**

Bering wolffish (Anarhichas orientalis), 270

Bermuda chub (Kyphosus sectatrix), 247–48, **248**

Beryciformes (order), 190–91

Betta splendens (Siamese fighting fish), 286–88, **287**

Bichir (Polypterus weeksi), **90**

Bichirs (Polypteridae), 86, 90

Bigeye (Priacanthus arenatus), 221, **221**

Bigeyes (Priacanthidae), 221–22

Bigeye thresher shark (Alopias superciliosus), 52

Bigeye tuna (Thunnus obesus), 281

Bigmouth buffalo (Ictiobus cyprinellus), **155**, 156

Bigmouth sleeper (Gobiomorus dormitor), 274

Bigmouth sole (Hippoglossina stomata), 290

Bignose shark (Carcharhinus altimus), 56

Big skate (Raja binoculata), 75

Billfishes (Istiophoridae), 26, 282–85

Bitterling (Rhodeus sericeus), 150, **150**

Black acara (Aequidens portalegrensis), 258

Blackbanded sunfish (Enneacanthus chaetodon), 221

Black-barred livebearer (Quintana atrizona), **187**

Blackbar soldierfish (Myripristis jacobus), 191, **191**

Blackbelly dogfish (Etmopterus hillianus), 64–65

Black bullhead catfish (Ictalurus melas), 159

Blackcheek tonguefish (Symphurus plagiusa), 290

Blackchin mouthbrooder (Tilipia melanotheron), 257

Black crappie (Pomoxis nigromaculatus), 219

Black croaker (Cheilotrema saturnum), 244

Blackdevil (Melanocetus johnsonii), 174, **174**

Black dogfish (Centroscymnus fabricii), 65

Black drum (Pogonias cromis), 243–44

Blackedge moray (Gymnothorax nigromarginatus), 101

Blackfinned cynolebias (Cynolebias nigripinnis), 185

Blackfish (Dallia pectoralis), 131, **131**

Blackfish (Girella tricuspidata), 248, **249**

Black grouper (Mycteroperca bonaci), 212

Black hagfish (Eptatretus deani), 41

Black margate (Anisotremus surinamensis), 238

Black marlin (Makaira indica), 285

Black neon tetra (Hyphessobrycon herbertaxelrodi), 138, **139**

Blacknose dace (Rhinichthys atratulus), 149

Blacknose shark (Carcharhinus acronotus), 56

Black perch (Embiotica jacksoni), 255

Black rockfish (Sebastes melanops), 203

Black sea bass (Centropristis striata), 214

Black skipjack (Euthynnus lineatus), 280

Blacksmith (Chromis punctipinnis), 259

Black-spot barb (Puntius filamentosus), 152, **152**

Blackspotted pike (Esox reicherti), 128

Blackspotted stickleback (Gasterosteus wheatlandi), 197

Black swallower (Chiasmodus niger), 103

Black-tailed dascyllus (Dascyllus melanurus), 259, **259**

Blacktip shark (Carcharhinus limbatus), 58

Black whaler (Carcharhinus macrurus), 59

Bleeding heart tetra (Hyphessobrycon rubrostigma), 138, **139**

Blennies, 269–71

Blenniidae (Combtooth blennies), 269

Blennius
    cristatus (molly miller), 269
    nicholsi (highfin blenny), 269
    pilicornis (fringe blenny), 269

Blind cavefish (Anoptichthys jordani), 138, **139**

Blind goby (Typhlogobius californiensis), 273

Blind torpedo ray (Typhlonarke aysoni), 72

Blood circulation of fishes, 30–31

Bloodfin (Aphyocharax rubripinnis), **140**

Blue acara (Aequidens pulcher), 258

Blue angelfish (Pomacanthus semicirculatus), 252

Blueback herring (Alosa aestivalis), 108

Bluebanded goby (Lythrypnus dalli), 273, **273**

Blue bobo (Polydactylus approximans), 262

Blue catfish (Ictalurus furcatus), 160

Blue catfish (Neoarius australis), 164

Blue chromis (Chromis cyaneus), 259

Bluefin killifish (Lucania goodei), 184

Bluefin tuna (Thunnus thynnus), **23**, 36, 280–81, **281**

Bluefish (Pomatomidae), 28, 225

Bluefish (Pomatomus saltatrix), 225, **225**

Bluegill (Lepomis macrochirus), **219**, 219–20

Blue gularis (Aphyosemion coeruleum), **184**, 185

Blueheads (Thalassoma bifasciatum), 264

Blue marlin (Makaira nigricans), 284, **284–85**

Blue (orange-finned) loach (Botia modesta), 158

Blue parrotfish (Scarus coeruleus), **266**, 267

Blue pike (Stizostedion vitreum glacum), 223

Blue rockfish (Sebastes mystinus), 202

Blue runner (Caranx crysos), 229, **230**

Blue shark (Lamna nasus), 47, 53–54, **54**

Blue shark (Prionace glauca), **58**, 59

Blue sleeper (Isoglossus calliurus), 274

Blue-spotted argus (Cephalopholis argus), 213

Bluespotted cornetfish (Fistularia tabacaria), 197

Bluestriped grunt (Haemulon sciurus), 237, **238**

Blue tang (Acanthurus coeruleus), 275

Bluntnose minnow (Pimephales notatus), 149

Bluntnose stingray (Dasyatis sayi), 75

Boarfish (Antigonia rubescens), **193**

Bocaccio (Sebastes paucispinis), 202

Bodianus pulchellus (spotfin hogfish), 264, **265**

Boleophthalmus spp. (mudskippers), 273–74

Bonefish (Albula vulpes), 98, **99**

Bonito shark. See Shortfin mako shark

Bonnet shark (Sphyrna tiburo), **61**, 63

Bony fishes (Osteichthyes), 19–20, 85–298

Bonytail (Gila robusta), 149

Bothidae (lefteye flounders), 289–91

Bothriolepis (placoderm), **20**
Bothus
    lunatus (peacock flounder), 290
    ocellatus (eyed flounder), 290
    pantherinus, 290
Botia, 157–58
    horae (skunk loach), 158, **158**
    hymenophysa (tiger loach), **157**, 158
    macracanthus (clown loach),
      157, 158
    modesta (orange-finned loach), 158
Boulengerella lucius (pike characin), 138
Bowfin (*Amia calva*), 96, **97**
Bowfins (Amiidae), 30, 96
Boxfishes (Ostraciidae), 295–96
Brachydanio
    albolineatus (pearl danio), **153**
    frankei (leopard danio), 153, **153**
    nigrofasciatus (spotted danio),
      153, **152**
Brachyplatystoma jilamentosum (lau-lau),
    161
Bramble shark (*Echinorhinus brucus*),
    66–67, **66**
Branchiostegidae (tilefishes), 224–25
Brazilian guitarfish (*Rhinobatos horkelli*),
    70
Brazilian mullet (*Mugil brasiliensis*), 261
Bream (*Abramis brama*), 150, **151**
Brevoortia
    gunteri (finescale menhaden), 106
    patronus (Gulf menhaden), 106
    smithi (yellowfin menhaden), 106
    tyrannus (Atlantic menhaden, or
      mossbunker), **105**, 106
Brill (*Scophthalmus rhombus*), **289**, 290
Brilliant rasbora (*Rasbora einthoveni*),
    153, **153**
Brindle bass (*Epinephelus lanceolata*), 212
Brisling (*Clupea sprattus*), 105
Bristlemouth catfishes (*Ancistrus spp.*),
    167
Bristol shubunkin, **145**
Bronze catfish (*Corydoras aeneus*),
    166, **167**
Bronze whaler (*Carcharhinus ahenea*), 59
Brook silverside (*Labidestes sicculus*),
    189, **189**
Brook stickleback (*Culaea inconstans*),
    196
Brook trout (*Salvelinus fontinalis*), 26, 34,
    120, 120–21
Broomtail grouper (*Mycteroperca
    xenarcha*), 212
Brosmophycis marginatus (red brotula),
    178
Brotula (*Brotula multibarbata*), 178, **178**
Brotulas (Ophidiidae), 177–78
Brown bullhead catfish (*Ictalurus
    nebulosus*), 159
Brown cat shark (*Apisturus brunneus*), 55
Brown mudfish (*Neochanna apoda*), 127
Brown smoothhound (*Mustelus henlei*),
    60
Brown trout (*Salmo trutta*), 120
Buenos Aires tetra (*Hemigrammus
    caudovittatus*), **140**
Bullnose ray (*Myliobatus freminvillei*), 80
Bulls-eye puffer (*Sphoeroides annulatus*),
    297
Bullhead sharks (Heterodontidae), 49
Bull shark (*Carcharhinus leucas*), 56, **57**
Bumblebee catfish (*Leiocassis siamensis*),
    161
Bumphead cichlid (*Steatocranus arius*),
    257
Bunker (*Brevoortia tyrannus*), **105**, 106
Bunocephalus coracoideus (banjo
    catfish), 164–65, **165**
Burbot (*Lota lota*), 177
Butterfish (*Peprilus triacanthus*), 285
Butterfishes (Stromateidae), 285–86
Butterflyfishes (Chaetodontidae), 250–53
Butterfly rays (Gymnuridae), 77–79

Butter hamlet (*Hypoplectrus unicolor*),
    216

Cabezon (*Larimus breviceps*), 245
Cabezon (*Scorpaenichthys marmoratus*),
    205
Calamoichthys calabaricus (reedfish), 90
Calamus, 239–40
    arctifrons (grass porgy), 240
    bajonado (jolthead porgy),
      239–40, **240**
    calamus (saucereye porgy), 240
    penna (sheepshead porgy), 240
    proridens (littlehead porgy), 240
Calico surfperch (*Amphistichus koelzi*),
    254
California butterfly ray (*Gymnura
    marmorata*), 79
California corbina (*Menticirrhus
    undulatus*), 245, **245**
California flying fish (*Cypselurus
    californicus*), 181
California grunion (*Leuresthes tenuis*), 36,
    188–89
California halfbeak (*Hyporhamphus
    rosae*), 182
California halibut (*Paralichthys
    californicus*), 290
California killifish (*Fundulus parvipinnis*),
    183
California lizardfish (*Synodus lucioceps*),
    134
California moray (*Gymnothorax mordax*),
    101
California needlefish (*Strongylura exilis*),
    182
California scorpionfish (*Scorpaena
    guttata*), 202
California sheepshead (*Pimelometopon
    pulchrum*), 264, **264**
California skate (*Raja inornata*), 75
California slickhead (*Alepocephalus
    tenebrosus*), **133**
California smoothtongue (*Leuroglossus
    stilbius*), 127
California tonguefish (*Symphurus
    atricauda*), 293
Callichthyidae (callichthyid armored
    catfishes), 166–67
Callichthyid armored catfishes
    (Callichthyidae), 166–67
Callichthys, 167
    callichthys (callused catfish, or
      hassar), 167
Callionymidae (dragonets), 272
Callionymus
    agassizi (spotfin dragonet), 272
    lyra (European dragonet), 272, **272**
Callorhinchidae (chimaeras), 84
Callorhinchus (plownosed, or elephant,
    chimaeras), 84
Callused catfish (*Callichthys callichthys*),
    167
Callyodon, 267
Campostoma anomalum (stoneroller),
    149, **149**
Candiru (*Vandellia cirrhosa*), 166, **166**
Canthidermis sufflamen (ocean
    triggerfish), 294
Canthigaster
    cinctus (four-saddle puffer), 297, **297**
    rivulatus, 297
Capelin (*Mallotus villosus*), 125, **126**
Capoeta
    oligolepis (checkerboard barb),
      152, **152**
    semifasciolatus (half-banded barb),
      152, **152**
    titteya (cherry barb), 152, **152**
Caproidae (boarfishes), 192
Carangidae (jacks and pompanos),
    227–32
Caranx, 229–31

    ajax (cavalla), 230
    bartholomaei (yellow jack), 229, **229**
    caballus (green jack), 229
    crysos (blue runner), 229, **230**
    georgianus (trevally), 231
    hippos (crevalle jack), **228**, 229
    ignobilis (pauu'u), 231
    latus (horse-eye jack), 230
    ruber (bar jack), 229–30
    stellatus (ulua), 230–31
Carapidae (pearlfishes), 178–79
Carapus, 178–79
    acus, 179
    bermudensis (pearlfish), **178**, 179
    homei, 179
Carassius auratus (common goldfish),
    144, 146–47
Carcharadon carcharias (white shark, or
    man-eater), 46, 47, 52–53, **54**
Carcharhinidae (requiem sharks), 56–60
Carcharhinus, 56–59
    acronotus (blacknose shark), 56
    ahenea (bronze whaler), 59
    altimus (bignose shark), 56
    falciformis (silky shark), 56, **57**
    grevi (South Australian whaler), 59
    leucas (bull shark), 56, **57**
    limbatus (blacktip shark), 58
    longimanus (whitetip shark), 56
    macrurus (black whaler), 59
    maculipinnis (spinner shark), 58
    milberti (sandbar shark), **56**, 57
    nicaraguensis (Lake Nicaragua
      shark), 56
    obscurus (dusky shark), 58
    porosus (smalltail shark), 56
    remotus (narrowtooth shark), 58–59
    springeri (reef shark), 59
    zambezensis (river shark), 56
Cardinalfishes (Apogonidae), 222
Cardinal tetra (*Cheirodon axelrodi*),
    138, **139**
Carnegiella strigata (marbled hatchetfish),
    141, **141**
Carnero (*Vandellia cirrhosa*), 166, **166**
Carp (*Cyprinus carpio*), 143, **143**
Carpet sharks (Orectolobidae), 49–50
Carps (Cyprinidae), 35, 142–53
Cartilaginous, jawed fishes
    (Chondrichthyes), 18–19, 43–84
Catalufa (*Priacanthus cruentatus*), 221
Catfish eel (*Plotosus anguillaris*), 165, **165**
Catfishes (Siluriformes), 25, 27, 30, 32, 33,
    158–67
Catla (*Catla catla*), 151
Catostomidae (suckers), 154–56
Catostomus, 154–55
    commersoni (white sucker), **154**,
      154–55
Cat shark (*Scyliorhinus boa*), 55, **55**
Cat sharks (Scyliorhinidae), 55–56
Caulolatilus princeps (ocean whitefish),
    224–25
Cavalla (*Caranx ajax*), 230
Cave catfish (*Typhlobagrus kronei*), 166
Cavefishes (Amblyopsidae), 167–68
Cebidichthys violaceous (monkeyface
    blenny), 270
Celebes sailfin (*Telmatherina ladigesi*),
    188
Celestial goldfish, **145**
Central mudminnow (*Umbra limi*), 131
Centrarchidae (sunfishes), 217–21
Centrarchus macropterus (flier), 219
Centriscidae (Shrimpfishes and
    snipefishes), 197–98
Centriscops obliquus (banded snipefish),
    198
Centriscus, 198
Centropomidae (snooks), 209–10
Centropomus, 209–10
    parallelus (fat snook), 210
    pectinatus (tarpon snook), 210
    undecimalis (snook), 209, **210**

Centropristis
    ocyurus (bank sea bass), 214
    striata (black sea bass), 214
Centropyge argi (cherubfish), **251**, 253
Centroscymnus, 64–65
    coelolepis (Portuguese shark),
      64, **65**
    fabricii (black dogfish), 65
Cephalopholis, 213
    acanthistius (Gulf coney), 213
    argus (blue-spotted argus), 213
    fulva (coney), 213, **213**
    leopardus (leopard coney), 213
    popino (rose coney), 213
Cephaloscyllium
    laticeps (Australian swell shark), 55
    ventriosum (swell shark), 55
Ceratiidae, 174
Ceratobatis robertsi (Jamaican ray), 83
Ceratodontidae (Australian lungfishes),
    87
Cero (*Scomberomorus regalis*), 278
Cetengraulis mysticetus (anchoveta), 109
Cetominiformes (order), 135
Cetorhinidae, 54
Cetorhinus maximus (basking shark), 46,
    53, 54
Ceylonese fire barb (*Rasbora vaterifloris*),
    153, **153**
Chaenopsis (pikeblennies), 270
Chaetodipterus
    faber (Atlantic spadefish), **249**, 250
    zonatus (Pacific spadefish), 250
Chaetodon, 250–51
    capistratus (foureye butterflyfish),
      250, **251**
    epihippium (saddleback
      butterflyfish), 250
    ocellatus (spotfin butterflyfish), 250
    ornatissimus (clown butterflyfish),
      250
    striatus (banded butterflyfish),
      250, **251**
    trifasciatus (redfin butterflyfish),
      250, **251**
Chaetodontidae (butterflyfishes), 250–53
Chain dogfish (*Scyliorhinus retifer*), 55, **55**
Chain moray (*Echidna catenata*), 101
Chain pickerel (*Esox niger*), 128, 130, **130**
Chameleon rockfish (*Sebastes pinniger*),
    203
Chancito (*Cichlasoma facetum*), **256**
Chanda, 210
    ranga (Indian glassfish), 210
Chanidae (milkfishes), 136
Channa
    argus (snakehead), **200**
    asiatica (Asiatic snakehead), 200
Channallabes apus (eel catfish), **162**
Channel catfish (*Ictalurus punctatus*),
    160, **160**
Channidae (snakeheads), 200
Channiformes (order), 200
Chanos chanos (milkfish), 136, **136**
Characidae (characins), 137–41
Characins (Characidae), 137–41
Charax gibbosus (humpback characin),
    140, 141
Chars (*Salvelinus*), 28, 120–22
Chauliodontidae (deepsea viperfishes),
    132
Chauliodus, 132
    macouni (Pacific viperfish), **132**
Checkerboard barb (*Capoeta oligolepis*),
    152, **152**
Cheilinus undulatus, 266
Cheilotrema saturnum (black croaker),
    244
Cheirodon axelrodi (cardinal tetra),
    138, **139**
Chelmon rostratus (copperband
    butterflyfish), **251**, 253
Cherry barb (*Capoeta titteya*), 152, **152**
Cherubfish (*Centropyge argi*), **251**, 253

Chiasmodus niger (black swallower), 103
Chilipepper (*Sebastes goodei*), 202
Chilomycterus
   affinis (Pacific burrfish), 297
   schoepfi (striped burrfish), 297
Chilotus (headstanders), 141
Chimaera
   affinis, 84
   montrosa, 84
   phantasma, 84
Chimaeridae (chimaeras), 83–84
Chimaeriformes (order), 83–84
Chinook salmon (*Oncorhynchus tshawytscha*), 36, 116–17, **116**
Chirocentridae (wolf herrings), 109
Chirocentrus dorab (wolf herring), 109, **109**
Chirolophis polyactocephalus (decorated warbonnet), 270–71
Chlamydoselachidae (frill sharks), 47
Chlamydoselachiformes (order), 47
Chlamydoselachus anguineus (frill shark), 47, **47**
Chloroscombrus
   chrysurus (Atlantic bumper), 231
   orqueta (Pacific bumper), 231
Chocolate gourami (*Sphaerichthys osphromenoides*), **287**, 288
Chologaster
   agassizi (spring cavefish), 167
   cornuta (swampfish), 167, **168**
Chondrichthyes (cartilaginous, jawed fished), 18–19, 43–84
Chorisochismus dentex (rocksucker), **170**, 171
Chromis, 259
   cyaneus (blue chromis), 259
   enchrysurus (yellowtail reeffish), 259
   punctipinnis (blacksmith), 259
Chrysophrys
   guttulatus, 241
   major, 241
Chub (*Coregonus zenithicus*), 124
Chub mackerel (*Scomber japonicus*), 278
Chum salmon (*Oncorhynchus keta*), 36, **117**, 118
Cichla ocellatus (eyespot cichlid), 258
Cichlasoma, 257
   cyanoguttatus (Rio Grande perch), 257
   facetum (chancito), **256**
   festivum (festivum), 257
   meeki (firemouth cichlid), 257, **257**
   octofasciatum (Jack Dempsey), 257
Cichlids (Cichlidae), 255–58
Cinnamon killie (*Aphyosemion cinnamoeum*), **184**
Cirrhitichthys, 260
Cirrhitidae (hawkfishes), 260
Cisco (*Coregonus artedii*), 124, **124**
Ciscos (Coregonidae), 122–24
Citharichthys
   sordidus (Pacific sanddab), 290
   stigmaeus (speckled sanddab), 290
   xanthostigma (longfin sanddab), 290
Clarias batrachus (walking catfish), 162
Clariidae (labyrinthic catfishes), 162
Classification
   criteria for, *12°13*
   method of, *17*
   past and present systems of, *13°16*
Clearnose skate (*Raja eglanteria*), 75
Clevelandia ios (arrow goby), 273
Climatius (placoderm), **18**
Climbing perch (Anabantidae), 30, 286
Climbing perch (*Anabas testudineus*), 286, **286**
Clingfishes (Gobiesocidae), 170–71
Clinids (Clinidae), 270
Clown anemonefish (*Amphiprion percula*), 259, **259**
Clown butterflyfish (*Chaetodon ornatissimus*), 250
Clown goby (*Microgobius gulosus*), 273

Clown killie (*Epiplatys annulatus*), **185**
Clown loach (*Botia macracanthus*), **157**, 158
Clown triggerfish (*Balistoides conspicillum*), 294, **294**
Clown wrasse (*Halichoeres maculipinna*), 265
Clupea, 104–6
   harengus harengus (Atlantic herring), 104–5, **105**
   harengus pallasi (Pacific herring), 106
   sprattus (sprat, or brisling), 105
Clupeidae (herrings), 104–9
Clupeiformes (order), 104–9
Clupisudis, 110
Cobia (Rachycentridae), 225–26
Cobia (*Rachycentron canadum*), 225–26, **226**
Cobitidae (loaches), 156–58
Cobitis taenia (spined loach), 157, **157**
Coccosteus (placoderm), **19**
Codfishes (Gadidae), 174–77
Coelacanth (*Latimeria chalumnae*), 86, **86**
Coelacanthidae (coelacanths), 86–87
Coelacanthiformes (order), 86–87
Coelacanths (Coelacanthidae), 86–87
Coelorhynchus, 180
Coho salmon (*Oncorhynchus kisutch*), 117, **117**
Colisa
   labiosa (thicklipped gourami), **287**, 288
   lalia (dwarf gourami), **287**, 288
Cololabis saira (Pacific saury), **182**, 183
Colorado grouper (*Mycteroperca olfax*), 212
Colorado squawfish (*Ptychocheilus lucius*), 147
Coloration of fishes, 25–26
Combtail paradise fish (*Belontia signata*), **286**
Combtooth blennies (Blenniidae), 269
Comet goldfish, **145**
Common goldfish (*Carassius auratus*), **144**, 146–47
Common scat (*Scatophagus argus*), 250, **250**
Common shiner (*Notropis cornutus*), 147, **147**
Common skate (*Raja batis*), **23**, **74**, 75
Conchfish (*Astropogon stellatus*), 222
Coney (*Cephalopholis fulva*), 213, **213**
Conger eel (*Conger oceanicus*), 102, **102**
Conger eels (Congridae), 102
Conger oceanicus (conger eel), 102, **102**
Congo tetra (*Micralestes interruptus*), **140**
Congridae (conger eels), 102
Convict fish. See Painted greenling
Convict tang (*Acanthurus triostegus*), **275**
Coolie loach (*Acanthophthalmus kuhli*), 156, **158**
Copeina arnoldi (splash tetra), 138, **139**
Copperband butterflyfish (*Chelmon rostratus*), 251, 253
Coregonidae (ciscos), 122–24
Coregonus, 123–24
   alpenae (longjaw cisco), 124
   artedii (lake herring, or cisco), 124, **124**
   clupeaformis (lake whitefish), **123**, 123–24
   kiyi (kiyi), 124
   oxyrhynchus (European whitefish), 123
   zenithicus (shortjaw cisco, or chub), 124
Coris gaimardi (yellow wrasse), 263, **263**
Cornetfish (*Fistularia petimba*), **197**
Cornetfishes (Fistulariidae), 197
Corydoras, 166–67
   aeneus (bronze, or aeneus, catfish), 166, **167**
   arctuatus (streamlined, or skunk, cat), 166

   hastatus (dwarf catfish), 166–67
   melanistus (spotted corydoras), 166
   paleatus (peppered catfish), 166
   punctatus (leopard catfish), 166
   rabauti (rabaut's catfish), 167
Corynspoma rüsei (swordtail characin), 140, 141
Coryphaena, 232–33
   equisetis (pompano dolphin), 233
   hippurus (dolphin, or dorado), 232, **233**
Coryphaenidae (dolphins), 232–33
Corysyphaesopia cornuta, 293
Corythoichthys, 199
   albirostris (whitenose pipefish), 199
   brachycephalus (crested pipefish), 199
   fasciatus, 199
Cottidae (sculpins), 205–6
Cottus
   asper (prickly sculpin), 206
   bairdi (mottled sculpin), 206
   carolinae (banded sculpin), 206
   cognatus (slimy sculpin), 206
   gobio (miller's thumb), 206
   pollux, 206
Cownose rays (Rhinopteridae), 80
Cow sharks (Hexanchidae), 48
Crappies (*Pomoxis*), 218–19
Creek chub (*Semotilus atromaculatus*), 147
Crenichichla lepidota (pike cichlid), **256**, 258
Crenimugil crenilabis, 261
Crenuchus epilurus (sailfin characin), **140**, 141
Crested goby (*Lophogobius cyprinoides*), 273
Crested pipefish (*Corythoichthys brachycephalus*), 199
Crestfish (*Lophotus capellei*), 194, **194**
Crestfishes (Lophotidae), 194
Crevalle jack (*Caranx hippos*), **228**, 229
Croakers, 32, 244–45
Croaking gourami (*Trichopsis vittatus*), 288
Croaking tetra (*Mimagoniates inequalis*), 138, **140**
Cryptacanthodidae, 271
Cryptacanthodes maculatus (wrymouth), 271
Cryptocentrus cryptocentrus, 274
Cryptopsarus couesi (triplewart seadevil), 174, **174**
Ctenopharyngodon idellus (white amur, or grass carp), 146
Cuban dogfish (*Squalus cubensis*), 64
Cuban rivulus (*Rivulus cylindraceus*), **184**
Cubbyu (*Equetus umbrosus*), 245, **245**
Cubera snapper (*Lutjanus cyanopterus*), 235
Cuchia (*Amphipnous cuchia*), 200
Cuckoo wrasse (*Labrus ossifagus*), 266
Culaea inconstans (brook stickleback), 196
Cunner (*Tautogolabrus adspersus*), 263–64
Curlfin sole (*Pleuronichthys decurrens*), 292
Cusk-eels (Ophidiidae), 177–78
Cutlassfishes (Trichiuridae), 22, 277
Cutlips minnow (*Exoglossum maxillingua*), 149
Cutthroat trout (*Salmo clarki*), **119**, 119–20
Cyclopteridae (lumpfishes and snailfishes), 207
Cyclopterus lumpus (lumpfish), 207, **207**
Cyclostomes (hagfishes and lampreys), 18
Cyclothone (bristlemouths), 131
Cymatogaster aggregata (shiner perch), 253

Cynoglossidae (tonguefishes), 293
Cynolebias
   adloffi (banded cynolebias), **184**
   melanotaenia (fighting gaucho), 185
   nigripinnis (blackfinned cynolebias), 185
Cynoscion, 242–43
   arenarius (sand sea trout), 242
   macdonaldi (totuava), 243
   nebulosus (spotted sea trout), 242, **242**
   nobilis (white sea bass), **242**, 243
   nothus (silver sea trout), 242–43
   parvipinnis (shortfin corvina), 243
   regalis (weakfish), 242
   xanthulus (orangemouth corvina), 243
Cypnopecilus ladigesi (Ladiges' gaucho), **185**
Cyprinidae (minnows and carps), 137, 142–53
Cypriniformes (order), 137–58
Cyprinodon
   diabolis (Devil's Hole pupfish), 184
   hubbsi (Lake Eustis minnow), 184
   macularius (desert pupfish), 184
   nevadensis (Amargosa pupfish), 184
   rubrofluviatilis (Red River pupfish), 184
   variegatus (sheepshead minnow), 184
Cyprinodontidae (killifishes), 183–85
Cyprinus carpio (carp), 143, **143**
Cypselurus
   californicus (California flying fish), 181
   cyanopterus (margined flying fish), 181
   exsiliens (bandwing flying fish), 181
   heterurus (Atlantic flying fish), **180**, 181

Dace (*Phenacobius*, *Rhinichthys*), 149
Dactylopteridae (flying gurnards), 208
Dactylopteriformes (order), 208
Dactylopterus volitans (flying gurnard), 208, **208**
Dactyloscopidae (sand stargazers), 268
Dactyloscopus tridigitatus (sand stargazer), 268, **269**
Dalatias licha (kitefin shark), 65
Dalatiidae, 65
Dallia pectoralis (Alaskan blackfish), 131, **131**
Damselfishes (Pomacentridae), 258–59
Danio (danios), 153
Danios (*Danio*), 153
Dascyllus, 259
   aruanus, 259
   melanurus (black-tailed dascyllus), 259, **259**
   trimaculatus, 259
Dasyatidae (stingrays), 75–79
Dasyatis, 75–77
   americana (southern stingray), 76, **77**
   bleekeri, 76
   brevirostris (Australian smooth stingray), 76
   centroura (roughtail stingray), 76
   sabina (Atlantic stingray, or stingaree), 75–76, **76**
   sayi (bluntnose stingray), 75
   sephen, 76
   violacea (pelagic stingray), 76
Day's paradise fish (*Macropodus cupanus*), **286**
Dealfish (*Trachipterus arcticus*), 195
Decapterus, 228–29
   hypodus (Mexican scad), 228–29
   lajang, 228
   macarellus (mackerel scad), 228
   punctatus (round scad), 228
   russellii, 229

Decorated warbonnet (Chirolophis polyactocephalus), 270–71
Deepbody anchovy (Anchoa compressa), 109
Deepsea anglers, 24, 174
Deepsea bristlemouth (Cyclothone pallida), 131
Deepsea bristlemouths (Gonostomatidae), 131
Deepsea dragonfish (Grammatostomias flagellibarba), 133
Deepsea giganturid (Bathyleptus lisae), 103, 135
Deepsea giganturids (Giganturidae), 135
Deepsea hatchetfish (Argyropelecus hemygenus), 132
Deepsea herring (Bathyclupea argentea), 247, 247
Deepsea scaly dragonfishes (Stomiatidae), 132–33
Deepsea slickheads (Alepocephalidae), 133
Deepsea smelt (Leuroglossus stilbius), 127
Deepsea smelts (Bathylagidae), 127
Deepsea snake mackerel (Gempylus serpens), 277
Deepsea viperfishes (Chauliodontidae), 132
Delta smelt (Hypomesus transpacificus), 126
Demon fish (Geophagus jurupari), 257
Dentex vulgaris (toothed bream), 241
Dermatolepis
    inermis (marbled grouper), 212
    striolatus, 212
Dermogenys pusillus (wrestling halfbeak), 181
Desert pupfish (Cyprinodon macularius), 184
Desmondema polysticta (polka-dot ribbonfish), 195
Devil ray (Mobula hypostoma), 82, 83
Devil's Hole pupfish (Cyprinodon diabolis), 184
Diamond tetra (Moekhausia pittieri), 139
Diamond turbot (Hypsopsetta guttulata), 292
Diaphus, 135
Digestion, fish, 28–29
Diodon hystrix (porcupinefish), 297, 297
Diodontidae (porcupinefishes), 297
Diplectrum formosum (sandperch), 213
Diplobatus pictus, 72
Diplodus
    argenteus (silver porgy), 241
    holbrooki (spottail pinfish), 241
Dipteriformes (order), 87–89
Doctorfish (Acanthurus chirurgus), 275
Dogfishes (Scyliorhinidae), 55, 55
    smooth (Triakidae), 60
Dogfish sharks (Squalidae), 63–67
Dollar sunfish (Lepomis marginatus), 221
Dolly Varden trout (Salvelinus malma), 122
Dolphin (Coryphaena hippurus), 232, 233
Dolphin cichlid (Aequidens itanyi), 256
Dolphins (Coryphaenidae), 26, 232–33
Doradidae (doradid armored catfishes), 164
Doradid armored catfishes (Doradidae), 164
Dorado (Coryphaena hippurus), 232, 233
Dories (Zeidae), 191–92
Dormitator maculatus (fat sleeper), 274, 274
Dorosoma
    cepedianum (gizzard shad), 108
    petenense (threadfin shad), 108
Dragonets (Callionymidae), 272
Dragon moray (Muraena pardalis), 101

Drums (Sciaenidae), 242–46
Dunkleosteus (placoderm), 19
Durham ranger fly, 38
Dusky piranha (Pygocentrus calmoni), 137
Dusky shark (Carcharhinus obscurus), 58
Dusky squirrelfish (Holocentrus vexillarius), 191
Dwarf Australian rainbowfish (Melanotaenia maccullochi, 189
Dwarf catfish (Corydoras hastatus), 166–67
Dwarf gourami (Colisa lalia), 287, 288
Dwarf seahorse (Hippocampus zosterae), 199

Eagle rays (Myliobatidae), 68–69, 79–80
Eastern mudminnow (Umbra pygmaea), 131, 131
Echeneidae (remoras), 226–27
Echeneis naucrates (sharksucker), 226, 226
Echidna
    catenata (chain moray), 101
    zebra (zebra moray), 101
Echinorhinus, 66–67
    brucus (bramble or alligator shark), 66–67
    cookei (prickly shark), 67
Eel catfish (Channallabes apus), 162
Eelpouts (Zoarcidae), 179
Eels, 22, 33, 99–103
Eggfish, 144
Elagatis bipinnulata (rainbow runner), 228
Elassoma, 221
    evergladei (Everglades pygmy sunfish), 221
    zonatum (banded pygmy sunfish), 221
Electric catfish (Malapterurus electricus), 162, 162–63
Electric catfishes (Malapteruridae), 162–63
Electric eel (Electrophorus electricus), 141–42, 142
Electric eels (Gymnotidae), 33, 141–42
Electric rays (Torpedinidae), 69, 71–72
Electrophidae, 141
Electrophorus electricus (electric eel), 141–42, 142
Eleotridae (sleepers), 274
Eleotriodes
    helsdingenii, 274
    strigatos (golden-headed goby), 273, 273
Elephant chimaeras (Callorhinchus), 84
Elephant-nosed mormyrid (Gnathonemus numenius), 113
Elephant trunk fish (Macrognathus aculeatus), 289
Eleutheronema tetradactylum, 262
Elopidae (tarpons), 97–98
Elopiformes (order), 97–99
Elops
    affinis (machete), 98
    saurus (ladyfish, or ten-pounder), 98, 98
Eluachon (Thaleichthys pacificus), 125, 126
Embiotica
    jacksoni (black perch), 255
    lateralis (striped seaperch), 255
Embiotocidae (surfperches), 253–55
Emerald shiner (Notropis atherinoides), 147–48, 148
Emperor snapper (Lutjanus sebae), 235
Emperor tetra (Nematobrycon palmeri), 139
Engraulidae (anchovies), 109
Engraulis
    encrasicolus (European anchovy), 109, 109
    mordax (northern anchovy), 109

Enjambre (Petrometopon panamaensis), 213
Ennearcanthus, 221
    chaetodon (blackbanded sunfish), 221
    obesus (banded sunfish), 221
Eopsetta jordani (petrale sole), 292
Epalzeorhynchus kallopterus (trunk barb, or flying fox), 153, 153
Ephippidae (spadefishes), 249–50
Epibulus insidiator, 266
Epinephelus (groupers), 210–12
    adscensionis (rock hind), 211
    analogus (spotted cabrilla), 211
    drummondhayi (speckled hind), 211
    fuscoguttatus, 211
    guttatus (red hind), 211
    itajara (jewfish), 211
    lanceolata (Queensland grouper, or brindle bass), 212
    macrospilas, 211
    merra, 211
    morio (red grouper), 210–11
    nigritus (Warsaw grouper), 212
    striatus (Nassau grouper), 211, 211
Epiplatys
    annulatus (clown killie), 185
    chaperi (redjaw killie), 185
Eptatretus
    deani (black hagfish), 41
    stouti (Pacific hagfish), 41
Equetus
    lanceolatis (jackknife-fish), 244, 245
    umbrosus (cubbyu), 245, 245
Erilepis zonifer (skilfish), 204
Esocidae (pikes), 128–31
Esomus danrica (flying barb), 153
Esox, 128–30
    americanus (redfin pickerel), 128, 130
    americanus vermiculatus (grass pickerel), 128, 130, 130
    lucius (northern pike), 128–30, 129
    masquinongy (muskellunge, or musky), 128, 128–30
    niger (chain pickerel), 128, 130, 130
    reicherti (blackspotted, or Amur River, pike), 128
Etheostoma caeruleum (rainbow darter), 224
Etmopterus, 64–65
    hillianus (blackbelly dogfish), 64–65
    spinax, 65
    virens (green dogfish), 65
Etropellius debauwi (three-striped glass catfish), 162, 162
Etroplus maculatus (orange cichlid), 256
Eucinostoma
    argenteus (spotfin majorra), 237
    gula (silver jenny), 237
Euleptorhamphus
    velox (flying halfbeak), 182
    viridis (ribbon halfbeak), 182
Eumecichthys fiski (unicornfish), 194
Eumicrotremus
    orbis (Pacific spiny lumpsucker), 207
    spinosus (Atlantic spiny lumpsucker), 207
Eurasian catfishes (Siluridae), 161
European anchovy (Engraulis encrasicolus), 109, 109
European angel shark (Squatina squatina), 67
European barracuda (Sphyraena sphyraena), 262
European dragonet (Callionymus lyra), 272, 272
European eel (Anguilla anguilla), 99–100, 100
European hake (Merluccius merluccius), 176, 177
European John Dory (Zeus faber),192, 192
European longnosed skate (Raja oxyrinchus), 75

European manta (Mobula mobular), 83
European mudminnow (Umbra krameri), 131
European perch (Perca fluviatilis), 223
European plaice (Pleuronectes platessa), 293
European skate (Raja miraletus), 75
European smelt (Osmerus eperlanus), 125, 126
European sole (Solea solea), 292, 293
European stargazer (Uranoscopus scaber), 268
European sturgeon (Acipenser sturio), 21, 92
European weatherfish (Misgurnus fossilis), 156, 157
European whitefish (Coregonus oxyrhynchus), 123
Eurypharyngidae (gulpers), 104
Eurypharynx pelecanoides (gulper), 104, 104
Euthynnus, 279–80
    affinis (kawakawa), 280
    alleteratus (little tunny), 279–80, 280
    lineatus (black skipjack), 280
    pelamis (skipjack tuna), 280
Eutrumeus teres (round herring), 108–9, 108
Everglades pygmy sunfish (Elassoma evergladei), 221
Eviota, 273
Evynnis japonica, 241
Exclamation-point rasbora (Rasbora urophthalma), 153, 153
Exocoetidae (flying fishes and halfbeaks), 180–82
Exocoetus, 181
Exoglossum maxillingua (cutlips minnow), 149
Eyed flounder (Bothus ocellatus), 290
Eyed skate (Raja ocellata), 75
Eyespot cichlid (Cichla ocellatus), 258

Fallfish (Semotilus corporalis), 146, 147
False cat shark (Pseudotriakis microdon), 55–56
False vineyi (Hyphessobrycon heterohabdus), 138
Fantail mullet (Mugil trichodon), 260–61
Fantail sole (Xystreurys liolepis), 290
Farlowella acus (twig catfish), 167
Farming, fish, 20, 136
Fat sleeper (Dormitator maculatus), 274, 274
Fat snook (Centropomus parallelus), 210
Featherbacks (Notopteridae), 112
Fathead minnow (Pimephales promelas), 149
Fertilizer, fish used as, 20
Festivum (Cichlasoma festivum), 257
Fifteenspine stickleback (Spinachia spinachia), 196–97
Fighting gaucho (Cynolebias melanotaenia), 185
Filefishes (Balistidae), 294–95
Filetail cat shark (Parmaturus xaniurus), 55
Finescale menhaden (Brevoortia gunteri), 106
Finetooth shark (Aprionodon isodon), 60
Fingerfishes (Monodactylidae), 247
Firemouth cichlid (Cichlasoma meeki), 257, 257
Fistularia
    petimba (cornetfish), 197, 197
    tabacaria (bluespotted cornetfish), 197
    villosa (red cornetfish), 197
Fistulariidae (cornetfishes), 197
Flagfish (Jordanella floridae), 183–84, 185
Flamefish (Apogon maculatus), 222
Flame tetra (Hyphessobrycon flammeus), 138, 139
Flathead chub (Hybopsis gracilis), 148

Flat needlefish (*Ablennes hians*), 182
Flier (*Centrarchus macropterus*), 219
Flies, fishing, **37**, **38**
Florida gar (*Lepisosteus platyrhincus*), 95
Florida pompano (*Trachinotus carolinus*), 231
Florida smoothhound (*Mustelus norrisi*), 60
Flounders, 289–93
Flying barb (*Esomus danrica*), 153
Flying fishes (Exocoetidae), 26, 180–82
Flying fox (*Epalzeorhynchus kallopterus*), 153, **153**
Flying gurnard (*Dactylopterus volitans*), 208, **208**
Flying halfbeak (*Euleptorhamphus velox*), 182
Foa, 222
Forceps butterflyfish (*Forcipiger longirostris*), **251**
Forceps butterflyfishes (*Forcipiger*), 250
Forcipiger (forceps butterflyfishes), 250
Forcipiger longirostris (forceps butterflyfish), **251**
Forms of fishes, 21–24
Fossil fishes, 18
Foureye butterflyfish (*Chaetodon capistratus*), 250, **251**
Foureye fish (*Anableps anableps*), 186, **186**
Foureye fishes (Anablepidae), 32, 186
Four-saddle puffer (*Canthigaster cinctus*), 297, **297**
Fourspine stickleback (*Apeltes quadracus*), 197
Fourspot flounder (*Paralichthys oblongus*), 290
Fowleria, 222
Freckled blenny (*Hypsoblennius ionthas*), 269
Freckled madtom (*Noturus nocturnus*), 161
Freckled soapfish (*Rypticus bistrispinus*), 216
French angelfish (*Pomacanthus paru*), **252**, 253
French grunt (*Haemulon flavolineatum*), 237
Freshwater butterflyfish (*Pantodon buchholzi*), 111, **111**
Freshwater cod. *See* Burbot
Freshwater drum (*Aplodinotus grunniens*), 245–46
Freshwater eels (Anguillidae), 99–100
Frigate mackerel (*Auxis thazard*), 279, **279**
Frillfin goby (*Bathygobius soporator*), 273
Frill shark (*Chlamydoselachus anguineus*), 47, **47**
Fringe blenny (*Blennius pilicornis*), 269
Fringed filefish (*Monacanthus ciliatus*), 295
Frogfishes (Antenariidae), 172
Fundulus
    chrysotus (gold topminnow), 183
    cingulatus (banded topminnow), 183
    heteroclitus (mummichog), 183
    jenkinsi (saltmarsh topminnow), 183
    majalis (striped killifish), 183
    notti (starhead topminnow), 183
    parvipinnis (California killifish), 183
    sciadicus (plains topminnow), 183

Gadidae (codfishes), 174–77
Gadiformes (order), 174–80
Gadomus, 180
Gadus
    macrocephalus (Pacific cod), 175
    morhua (Atlantic cod), 175, **175**
Gafftopsail catfish (*Bagre marinus*), 163–64
Gafftopsail pompano (*Trachinotus rhodopus*), 231
Gag (*Mycteroperca microlepis*), 212

Galaxiias
    alepidotus, 127
    attentuatus (galaxiid), **127**
Galaxiid (*Galaxiias attenuatus*), **127**
Galaxiidae (galaxiids), 127
Galaxiids (Galaxiidae), 127
Galeorhinus, 59–60
    australis (school shark), 60
    zyopterus (soupfin shark), 59–60
Gambusia affinis (mosquitofish), 186, **186**
Gardonus (minnows), 150
Garfish (*Belone bellone*), **182**
Garibaldi (*Hypsypops rubicunda*), 259
Gars (Lepisosteidae), 28, 30, 94–96
Gasteropelecidae (hatchetfishes), 141
Gasteropelecus sternicla (silver hatchetfish), 141, **141**
Gasterosteidae (sticklebacks), 196–97
Gasterosteiformes (order), 196–99
Gasterosteus, 196–97
    aculeatus (threespine stickleback), 196, **196**
    wheatlandi (blackspotted or twospine stickleback), 197
Gastromyzon (hillstream fish), **156**
Gaterin, 238
Gazza, 237
Gefilte fish, 146
Gempylidae (snake mackerels), 277
Gempylus serpens (deepsea snake mackerel), **277**
Gemuendina (placoderm), **19**
Genyonemus lineatus (white croaker), 244
Geophagus jurupari (demon fish or eartheater), **257**
Gerres, 237
    cinereus (yellowfin mojarra), 237, **237**
Gerridae (mojarras), 236–37
Gery's aphyosemion (*Aphyosemion geryi*), **185**
Giant gar (*Lepisosteus tristoechius*), 96
Giant guitarfish (*Rhyncobatos djiddensis*), 70
Giant gourami (*Osphronemus gourami*), **287**, 288
Giant kelpfish (*Heterostichus rostratus*), 270
Giant perch (*Lates calcarifer*), 212
Giant sea bass (*Stereolepis gigas*), 212
Gigantura, 135
Giganturidae (deepsea giganturids), 135
Gila
    atraria (Utah chub), 149
    crassicauda (thicktail chub), 149
    nigrescens (Rio Grande chub), 149
    robusta (roundtail chub, or bonytail), 149
Gila trout (*Salmo gilae*), 119
Gillichthys mirabilis (longjaw mudsucker), 273
Gills, fish, 29–30
Ginglymostoma cirratum (Atlantic nurse shark), 50, **50**
Girella
    nigricans (opaleye), 248
    punctata, 248
    tricuspidata (luderick, or blackfish), 248, **249**
Gizzard shad (*Dorosoma cepedianum*), 108, **108**
Glass catfish (*Kryptopterus bichirrhus*), 161, **161**
Glasseye snapper (*Priacanthus cruentatus*), 221
Glowlight tetra (*Hemigrammus erythozonus*), **139**
Glyptocephalus
    cynoglossus (witch flounder), 293
    zachirus (rex sole), 292
Gnathonemus, 113-14
    curvirostris, 113
    macrolepidotus (largescale

gnathonemus), **113**, 114
    niloticus, 114
    numenius (elephant-nosed mormyrid), 113
    petersi (Ubangi mormyrid), **113,** 114
Goatfishes (Mullidae), 246–47
Gobies (Gobiidae), 272–74
Gobiesocidae (clingfishes), 170–71
Gobiesociformes (order), 170–71
Gobiesox, 171
    meandricus (northern clingfish), 171
    strumosus (skilletfish), 171
Gobiidae (gobies), 272–74
Gobiomorus dormitor (bigmouth sleeper), 274
Gobiosoma
    bosci (naked goby), 273
    oceanops (neon goby), **272**, 273
Goblin shark (*Scapanorhynchus owstoni*), 52
Goblin sharks (Scapanorhynchidae), 52
Golden barracuda (*Sphyraena flavicauda*), 261
Golden grouper (*Mycteroperca pardalis*), 212
Golden-headed goby (*Eleotriodes strigatos*), 273
Golden mullet (*Mugil auratus*), 261
Golden pheasant (*Roloffia occidentalis*), **184**, 185
Golden shiner (*Notemigonus crysoleucas*), 148, **148**
Golden-striped grouper (*Grammistes sexlineatus*), 213
Golden trout (*Salmo aguabonita*), 120
Goldeye (*Hiodon alosoides*), 111
Goldfish (*Carassius auratus*), **144**, 146–47
Goldfishes, 144–47
Gold topminnow (*Fundulus chrysotus*), 183
Gomphosus, 266
Gonorynchiformes (order), 136
Gonostomatidae (deepsea bristlemouths), 131
Goodeidae (goodeid topminnows), 189
Goodeid topminnows (Goodeidae), 189
Goosefish (*Lophius americanus*), 171, **171**
Goosefishes (Lophiidae), 28, 171
Grammistes sexlineatus (golden–striped grouper), 213
Grammistidae (soapfishes), 216
Grass carp (*Ctenopharyngodon idellus*), 146
Grass pickerel (*Esox americanus vermiculatus*), 128, 130, **130**
Grass porgy (*Calamus arctifrons*), 240
Gray angelfish (*Pomacanthus arcuatus*), 253
Graylings (Salmonidae), 114, 122–24
Gray nurse shark (*Odontaspis*), 51–52
Graysby (*Petrometopon cruentatum*), 213, **213**
Gray smoothhound (*Mustelus californicus*), 60
Gray snapper (*Lutjanus griseus*), 234
Gray triggerfish (*Balistes capriscus*), 294
Great barracuda (*Sphyraena barracuda*), **23**, 261, **261**
Great blue shark (*Prionace glauca*), **58**, 59
Greater amberjack (*Seriola dumerili*), 227, **227**
Greater soapfish (*Rypticus saponaceus*), 216, **216**
Great hammerhead shark (*Sphyrna mokarran*), 61, **62**
Greenband wrasse (*Halichoeres bathyphilus*), 265
Green discus (*Symphosodon aequifasciata*), **258**
Green dogfish (*Etmopterus virens*), 65
Green jack (*Caranx caballus*), 229
Greenland halibut (*Reinhardtius hippoglossoides*), 293
Greenland shark (*Somniosus*

microcephalus), 44, 65–66, **65**
Greenlings (Hexagrammidae), 203–4
Green moray (*Gymnothorax funebris*), 100–101, **101**
Green razorfish (*Hemipteronotus splendens*), 265
Green sturgeon (*Acipenser medirostris*), 91–92, **91**
Green sunfish (*Lepomis cyanellus*), 220, **220**
Green swordtail (*Xiphophorus herreri*), 188, **188**
Grenadier (*Malacocephalus laevis*), **179**, 180
Groupers, **23**, 210–13
Grunion, 188–89
Grunts (Pomadasyidae), 32, 237–38
Guadalupe bass (*Micropterus treculi*), 218
Guaguancho (*Sphyraena guachancho*), 262
Guitarfishes (Rhinobatidae), 68, 70–71
Gularis (*Aphyosemion gulare*), 185
Gulf coney (*Cephalopholis acanthistius*), 213
Gulf flounder (*Paralichthys albigutta*), 290
Gulf grouper (*Mycteroperca jordani*), 212
Gulf grunion (*Leuresthes sardina*), 189
Gulf kingfish (*Menticirrhus littoralis*), 245
Gulf menhaden (*Brevoortia patronus*), 106
Gulf toadfish (*Opsanus beta*), 170
Gulper (*Eurypharynx pelecanoides*), 104, **104**
Gulpers (Eurypharyngidae), 104
Gunnels (Pholidae), 271
Guppy (*Poecilia reticulata*), **34**, 187, **187**
Gymnallabes, 162
Gymnocanthus
    herzensteini, 206
    tricuspis (Arctic staghorn sculpin), **205**, 206
Gymnothorax, 100–101
    eurostus, 101
    flavimarginatus (puhi-paka), 101
    funebris (green moray), 100–101, **101**
    mordax (California moray), 101
    moringa (spotted moray), 101
    nigromarginatus (blackedge moray), 101
Gymnotidae (electric eels and knifefishes), 33, 141–42
Gymnotus carapo (spotted, striped, or banded knifefish), 142, **142**
Gymnura
    altavela (spiny butterfly ray), **78**, 79
    japonica, 79
    marmorata (California butterfly ray), 79
    micrura (smooth butterfly ray), 79
Gymnuridae (butterfly rays), 77–79
Gyrinocheilids (Gyrinocheilidae), 153
Gyrinocheilus, 153
    aymonieri (sucker loach), 153, **158**

Hackleback sturgeon (*Scaphirhynchus platorynchus*), 92–93, **93**
Haddock (*Melanogrammus aeglefinus*), 175–76, **176**
Haemulon, 237–38
    album (margate), 237–38
    aurolineata (tomtates), 238
    flavolineatum (French grunt), 237
    parrai (sailors choice), 238
    plumeri (white grunt), 237
    sciurus (bluestriped grunt), 237, **238**
Hagfishes (Mixinidae), 18, 24, 40–41, **40**
Hairy blenny (*Labrisomus nuchipinnis*), 270, **270**
Hakes, 176–77
Half-banded barb (*Capoeta semifasciolatus*), 152, **152**
Half-banded loach (*Acanthopthalmus semicinctus*), 156, **158**

Halfbeak (*Hyporhamphus unifasciatus*), 181, 182
Halfbeaks (Exocoetidae), 26, 180–82
Halfmoon (*Medialuna californiensis*), 248, **248**
Half-moon angelfish (*Pomacanthus maculosus*), **252**, 253
Half-striped leporinus (*Leporinus agissiz*), 138, **140**
Halichoeres, 265–66
    bathyphilus (greenband wrasse), 265
    bivittatus (slippery dick), 265, **265**
    gamoti (yellowhead wrasse), 265
    maculipinna (clown wrasse), 265
    radiatus (puddingwife), 265
    semicinctus (rock wrasse), 265–66
Halieutaea stellata (red batfish), 173, **173**
Hammerhead sharks (Sphyrnidae), 46, 47, 60–63
Hardhead (*Mylopharodon conocephalus*), 147
Harlequin rasbora (*Rasbora heteromorpha*), 153, **153**
Harriotta raleighana (longnose chimaera), 84
Harvestfish (*Peprilus alepidotus*), 285
Hassar (*Callichthys callichthys*), 167
Hatchetfishes (Gasteropelecidae), 141; see also Deepsea hatchetfishes
Hawaiian aholehole (*Kuhlia sandvicensis*), 217
Hawkfishes (Cirrhitidae), 260
Headstanders (*Anostomus, Chilotus, Abramites*), 141
Helmeted catfish (*Astrodoras asterifrons*), 164
Helostomus terminincki (kissing gourami), 288, **288**
Hemicephalaspis (placoderm), **18**
Hemichromis bimaculatus (jewelfish), 257
Hemigrammus
    caudovittatus (Buenos Aires tetra), **140**
    erythozonus (glowlight tetra), **139**
Hemigymnus fasciatus, 266
Hemilepidotus hemilepidotus (Irish lord), 206
Hemipteronotus, 264–65
    martinicensis (rosy razorfish), 265
    novacuia (pearly razorfish), 265
    splendens (green razorfish), 265
Hemiramphus
    brasiliensis (ballyhoo), 181
    far, 181
    sajori (sayori), 181
    saltator (longfin halfbeak), 181
Hemitripterus americanus (sea raven), 206
Heptranchias
    dakini, 48
    perlo (sevengill shark), 48
Hermosilla azurea (zebra perch), 248
Herrings (Clupeidae), 104–9
Heterandria formosa (least killifish), 188
Heterobranchus, 162
Heterodontidae (bullhead sharks), 49
Heterodontiformes (order), 49
Heterodontus
    francisci (horned shark), 49
    portusjacksoni (Port Jackson shark), 49, **49**
Heterostichus rostratus (giant kelpfish), 270
Hexagrammidae (greenlings), 203–4
Hexagrammos
    decagrammus (kelp greenling), 203
    lagocephalus (rock greenling), 203
    octogrammus (masked greenling), 203
    stelleri (whitespotted greenling), 203, **204**
Hexanchidae (cow sharks), 48
Hexanchiformes (order), 48

Hexanchus griseus (sixgill shark), 48, **48**
Hickory shad (*Alosa mediocris*), 107
Highfin blenny (*Blennius nicholsi*), 269
Hillstream fish (*Gastromyzon*), **156**
Hillstream fishes (Homalopteridae), 156
Hiodon
    alosoides (goldeye), 111
    tergisus (mooneye), 111, **111**
Hiodontidae (mooneyes), 111
Hippocampus, 199
    coronatus, 199
    erectus (lined seahorse), 199, **199**
    guttulatus (Mediterranean seahorse), 199
    ingens (Pacific seahorse), 199
    japonicus, 199
    kelloggi, 199
    obtusus (offshore seahorse), 199
    reidi (longsnout seahorse), 199
    zosterae (dwarf seahorse), 199
Hippoglossina stomata (bigmouth sole), 290
Hippoglossoides platessoides (American plaice), 293
Hippoglossus
    hippoglossus (Atlantic halibut), 291, **291**
    stenolepis (Pacific halibut), 291
Histrio histrio (sarsassumfish), 172, **172**
Hogchoker (*Trinectes maculatus*), 293
Hogfish (*Lachnolaimus maximus*), 264, **265**
Holocanthus, 252–53
    cilaris (queen angelfish), 252, **252**
    tricolor (rock beauty), **252**, 252–53
Holocentridae (squirrelfishes), 191
Holocentrus, 191
    ascensionis (squirrelfish), 191
    caudimaculatus, 191
    coruscus (reef squirrelfish), 191
    diadema, 191
    marianus (longjaw squirrelfish), 191, **191**
    rufus (longspine squirrelfish), 191
    spinifer, 191
    vexillarius (dusky squirrelfish), 191
    xantherythrus (striped squirrelfish), 191
Holohalaelurus regani (skaamong, or shy eye shark), 56
Holotrachys, 191
Homalopteridae (hillstream fishes), 156
Hoplobrotula armata, 178
Horned shark (*Heterodontus francisci*), 49
Hornyhead chub (*Nocomis biguttatus*), **148**, 149
Horse-eye jack (*Caranx latus*), 230
Houndfish (*Tylosurus crocodilus*), 182
Hubbs, Carl L., 13
Humpback characin (*Charax gibbosus*), **140**, 141
Huso huso (beluga), 93
Hybopsis, 148–49
    gracilis (flathead chub), 148
Hydrocyanus goliath (tigerfish), 138
Hydrolagus colliei (ratfish), **83**, 84
Hypentelium nigricans (northern hog sucker), **154**, 155–56
Hyperprosopon
    anale (spotfin surfperch), 254
    argenteum (walleye surfperch), 254
    ellipticum (silver surfperch), 254
Hyphessobrycon, 138–39
    callistus (jewel tetra), 138
    flammeus (flame tetra), 138, **139**
    herbertaxelrodi (black neon tetra), 138, **139**
    heterohabdus (false vineyi), 138, **139**
    innesi (neon tetra), 138, **139**
    peruvianus (Loreto tetra), **139**
    pulchripinnis (lemon tetra), 138, **140**
    rosaceus (rosy tetra), 138, **139**
    rubrostigma (bleeding heart tetra), 138, **139**

Hypnos monopterygiurn (Australian crampfish), 72
Hypomesus, 125–26
    olidus (pond smelt), 125–26
    pretiosus (surf smelt), 125
    transpacificus (delta smelt), 126
Hypophthalmichthys (silver carp), 151
Hypoplectrus unicolor (butter hamlet), **216**
Hypoprion signatus (night shark), 60
Hyporhamphus
    dussumieri, 182
    rosae (California halfbeak), 182
    unifasciatus (halfbeak), **181**, 182
Hypsoblennius
    gentilis (bay blenny), 269
    gilberti (rockpool blenny), 269
    ionthas (freckled blenny), 269
Hypsopsetta guttulata (diamond turbot), 292
Hypsurus caryi (rainbow surfperch), 254
Hypsypops rubicunda (garibaldi), 259
Hysterocarpus traski (tule perch), 253

Icichthys lockingtoni (medusafish), 286
Icosteidae (ragfishes), 288
Icosteus aenigmaticus (ragfish), 288, **288**
Ictaluridae (North American freshwater catfishes), 158–61
Ictalurus, 159–60
    catus (white catfish), 160
    furcatus (blue catfish), 160
    melas (black bullhead catfish), 159
    natalis (yellow bullhead catfish), 159, **159**
    nebulosus (brown bullhead catfish), 159
    punctatus (channel catfish), 160, **160**
Ictiobus cyprinellus (bigmouth buffalo), **155**, 156
Idiacanthidae, 133
Imperial angelfish (*Pomacanthus imperator*), **252**, 253
Inconnu (*Stenodus leucichthys*), 122, **123**
Indian catfish (*Mystus vittata*), 161
Indian eel (*Phisodnopsis boro*), 99
Indian glassfish (*Chanda ranga*), 210
Indian puffer (*Tetraodon fluviatilis*), **297**
Indomanta, 83
Inshore lizardfish (*Synodus foetens*), 134
Irish lord (*Hemilepidotus hemilepidotus*), 206
Isistius brasiliensis (luminous shark), 66, **66**
Isoglossus calliurus (blue sleeper), 274
Istiophoridae (billfishes), 282–85
Istiophorus platypterus (sailfish), 283, **283**

Jack Dempsey (*Cichlasoma octofasciatum*), 257
Jackknife-fish (*Equetus lanceolatus*), **244**, 245
Jack mackerel (*Trachurus symmetricus*), 229
Jacks (Carangidae), 227–32
Jacksmelt (*Atherinopsis californiensis*), 189
Jamaican ray (*Ceratobatis robertsi*), 83
Japanese eel (*Anguilla japonica*), 99
Japanese pipefish (*Syngnathus schlegeli*), **198**, 199
Jawfishes (Opistognathidae), 267–68
Jawless fishes (Agnatha), 18, 39–42
Jelly cat (*Anarhichas latifrons*), 270
Jenynsia, 186
Jenysid topminnows, 189
Jenysiidae, 186, 188
Jewelfish (*Hemichromis bimaculatus*), 257
Jewel tetra (*Hyphessobrycon callistus*), 138
Jewfish (*Epinephelus itajara*), 211

John Dory, American and European, 192
Jolthead porgy (*Calamus bajonado*), 239–40, **240**
Jordanella floridae (flagfish), 183–84, **185**

Kanduli catfish (*Arius dispar*), 164
Katanga lampeye (*Aplocheillichthys katangae*), 152
Kawakawa (*Euthynnus affinis*), 280
Kelp bass (*Paralabrax clathratus*), 213–14, **214**
Kelp greenling (*Hexagrammos decagrammus*), 203
Kelp pipefish (*Syngnathus californiensis*), 199
Keyhole cichlid (*Aequidens maroni*), **257**, 258
Killifishes (Cyprinodontidae), 183–85
Kingfish (*Scomberomorus cavalla*), 278
King mackerel (*Scomberomorus cavalla*), 278
King-of-the-salmon (*Trachipterus altivelus*), 195
King salmon (*Oncorhynchus tshawytscha*), 116–17
Kissing gourami (*Helostomus teminincki*), 288, **288**
Kitefin shark (*Dalatias licha*), 65
Kiyi (*Coregonus kiyi*), 124
Knifefishes (Gymnotidae), 141–42
Knifefishes (Notopteridae), 112
Koi, **144**
Kryptophanaron, 190
Kryptopterus
    bichirrhus (glass catfish), 161, **161**
    macrocephalus, 161
Kuhlia
    rupestris, 217
    sandvicensis (Hawaiian aholehole), 217
    taeniura (aholehole), 217, **217**
Kuhliidae (Aholeholes), 217
Kuhli loaches (*Acanthopthalmus*), 156–57
Kyphosidae (sea chubs), 247–48
Kyphosus, 247–48
    incisor (yellow chub), 248
    sectatrix (Bermuda chub, or striped rudderfish), 247–48, **248**

Labeo
    bicolor (red-tailed shark), **152**, 153
    rohita (rohu), 151, 153
Labidestes sicculus (brook silverside), 189, **189**
Lab-lab, 136
Labridae (wrasses), 262–66
Labrisomus nuchipinnis (hairy blenny), 270, **270**
Labrus ossifagus (cuckoo wrasse), 266
Labyrinthfishes (Belontiidae), 286–88
Labyrinthic catfishes (Clariidae), 162
Lachnolaimus maximus (hogfish), 264, **265**
Lactophrys
    bicaudalis (spotted trunkfish), 296, **296**
    quadricornis (scrawled cowfish), 296
    trigonis (trunkfish), 296
    triqueter (smooth trunkfish), 296
Ladiges' gaucho (*Cypnopecilus ladigesi*), **185**
Ladyfish (*Elops saurus*), 98, **98**
Lagocephalus laevigatus (smooth puffer), 296
Lagodon rhomboides (pinfish), 241
Lake Eustis minnow (*Cyprinodon hubbsi*), 184
Lake herring (*Coregonus artedii*), 124, **124**
Lake Nicaragua shark (*Carcharhinus nicaraguensis*), 56
Lake sturgeon (*Acipenser fulvescens*), 92, **92**

Lake trout (*Salvelinus namaycush*), 36, 121, **121**
Lake whitefish (*Coregonus clupeaformis*), **123**, 123–24
Lamna, 53–54
 ditropis (salmon shark), 53–54
 nasus (porbeagle, blue, or mackerel shark), 53–54, **54**
Lamnidae (mackerel sharks), 44, 52–54, **54**
Lampreys (Petromyzontidae), 18, 24, 29, 41–42
Lamprididae (opahs), 192–94
Lampridiformes (order), 192–94
Lampris regius (opah), 192, **73**
Lancetfishes (Alepisauridae), 134
Lantern-eye fish (*Anomalops katoptron*), **190**
Lantern-eye fishes (Anomalopidae), 190
Lanternfishes (Myctophidae), 135
Largemouth bass (*Micropterus salmonides*), 28, 31, 33, 34, 36, 218
Largescale gnathonemus (*Gnathonemus macrolepidotus*), **113**, 114
Largescale lizardfish (*Saurida brasiliensis*), 134
Large spotted dogfish (*Scyliorhinus stellarius*), 55
Largetooth sawfish (*Pristis perotteti*), 69
Larimus
 breviceps (cabezon), 245
 fasciatus (banded drum), 245
Lates
 calcarifer (giant perch, or barramundi), 212
 niloticus (Nile perch), 212
Latimeria chalumnae (coelacanth), 86, **86**
Lau-lau (*Brachyplatystoma jilamentosum*), 161
Leaffish (*Monocirrhus polyacanthus*), 253, **253**
Leaffishes (Nandidae), 253
Least killifish (*Heterandria formosa*), 188
Leatherjacket (*Oligoplites saurus*), 227
Lefteye flounders (Bothidae), 289–91
Leiocassis siamensis (bumblebee catfish), 161
Leiognathidae (slipmouths), 233
Leiognathus equula (slipmouth), 233, **234**
Leiostomus xanthurus (spot), 244
Lemon shark (*Negaprion brevirostris*), 46, 59
Lemon sole (*Limanda limanda*), 293
Lemon tetra (*Hyphessobrycon pulchripinnis*), 138, **140**
Lenquad (*Paralichthys brasiliensis*), 290
Leopard catfish (*Corydoras punctatus*), 166
Leopard coney (*Cephalopholis leopardus*), 213
Leopard danio (*Brachydanio frankei*), 153, **153**
Leopard sea robin (*Prionotus scitulus*), 203
Leopard shark (*Triakis semifasciatus*), 60
Leopard toadfish (*Opsanus pardus*), 170
Lepidorhombus whiff-iagonis, 290
Lepidosirenidae (South American and African lungfishes), 88–89
Lepisosteidae (gars), 94–96
Lepisosteus
 oculatus (spotted gar), 95, **95**
 osseus (longnose gar), 95, **95**
 platostomus (shortnose gar), 95, **95**
 platyrhincus (Florida gar), 95
 spatula (alligator gar), 95–96
 tristoechius (giant gar), 96
Lepomis, 219–21
 cyanellus (green sunfish), 220, **220**
 gibbosus (pumpkinseed), 220
 gulosus (warmouth), 221
 macrochirus (bluegill), **219**, 219–20
 marginatus (dollar sunfish), 221

 megalotis (longear sunfish), 220
 microlophus (redear sunfish), 220
 punctatus (spotted sunfish), 220–21
Leporinus
 agissiz (half-striped leporinus), 138, **140**
 maculatus (spotted leporinus), 138, **139**
Leptocottus armatus (staghorn sculpin), 206
Leptolucania ommata (pygmy killifish), 184
Lesser amberjack (*Seriola fasciata*), 228
Lesser electric ray (*Narcine brasiliensis*), 72, **73**
Lesser spotted dogfish (*Scyliorhinus caniculus*), 55
Lethrinus, 238
Leucisus (minnows), 150
Leuresthes
 sardina (Gulf grunion), 189
 tenuis (California grunion), 188–89
Leuroglossus stilbius (deepsea smelt), **127**
Limanda
 ferruginea (yellowtail flounder, or rusty dab), 293
 limanda (lemon sole), 293
Lined seahorse (*Hippocampus erectus*), 199, **199**
Lined sole (*Archirus lineatus*), 293
Lingcod (*Ophiodon elongatus*), 204, **204**
Lionfish (*Pterois volitans*), **201**
Lionhead, **145**
Lionhead cichlid (*Steatocaranus casuarius*), **256**
Liparis liparis (striped sea snail), 207, **207**
Lirocaria parva (whiptail catfish), 167
Loricariid armored catfishes (Loricariidae), 167
Lota lota (burbot), 177
Louvar (Luvaridae), 282
Louvar (*Luvarus imperialis*), 282, **283**
Lucania goodei (bluefin killifish), 184
Lucioperca lucioperca (pikeperch), 224
Luderick (*Girella tricuspidata*), 248, **249**
Luminous shark (*Isistius brasiliensis*), 66, **66**
Lumpenella longirostris (longsnout prickleback), 271
Lumpfish (*Cyclopterus lumpus*), 207, **207**
Lumpfishes (Cyclopteridae), 207
Lungfishes, 30, 86, 87–89
Lutjanidae (snappers), 234–35
Lutjanus, 234–35
 analis (mutton snapper), **234**, 235
 argentimaculatus (Roman snapper), 235
 campechanus (red snapper), 234
 cyanopterus (cubera snapper), 235
 grisens (gray snapper), 234
 johni, 235
 sebae (emperor snapper), 235
 vivanus (silk snapper), 234
Luvarus imperialis, 282, **283**
Lycodes, 179
 turneri (polar eelpout), 179
Lycodontis petelli, 101
Lyretail (*Aphyosemion australe*), 185, **185**
Lyretail coralfish (*Anthias squamipinnis*), 216, **216**
Lythrypnus dalli (bluebanded goby), 273, **273**

Machete (*Elops affinis*), 98
Mackerels (Scombridae), 33, 278–81
Mackerel scad (*Decapterus macarellus*), 228
Mackerel shark (*Lamna nasus*), 53–54, **54**
Mackerel sharks (Lamnidae), 44, 52–54, **54**
Macrognathus aculeatus (elephant trunk fish), 289
Macrohamphosus
 gracilis (snipefish), 198, **198**
 scolopax (longspine snipefish), 198
Macropinna microstoma (Pacific barreleye), 127, **127**
Macropodus
 cupanus (Day's paradise fish), **286**
 operculans (paradise fish), **286**
Macrouridae (grenadiers), 179–80
Macrouroides, 180
Macrourus, 180
 berglax, 180
Macrozoarces americanus (ocean pout), 179
Madtoms (*Noturus*), 160–61
Mahseer (*Barbus tor*), 151, **151**
Makaira, 284–85

 indica (black marlin), 285
 nigricans (blue marlin), 284, **284–85**
Malacanthus
 hoedtii, 224
 latovittatus, 224
 plumieri (sand tilefish), 224, **224**
Malacocephalus, 180
 laevis (grenadier), **179**, 180
Malapterudae (electric catfishes), 162–63
Malapterurus electricus (electric catfish), **162**, 162–63
Mallotus villosus (capelin), 125, **126**
Mandi (*Pimelodella gracillis*), 166
Man-eater shark (*Carcharodon carcharias*), 52–53, **54**
Man-of-war fish (*Nomeus gronovii*), 286, **286**
Manta
 birostris (Atlantic manta), **81**, 82, **82**
 hamiltoni (Pacific manta), 82
Mantas (Mobulidae), 68, 81–83
Marbled grouper (*Dermatolepis inermis*), 212
Marbled hatchetfish (*Carnegiella strigata*), 141, **141**
Marcusenius, 114
 longianalis (shortnose mormyrid), **113**
Margate (*Haemulon album*), 237–38
Margined flying fish (*Cypselurus cyanopterus*), 181
Marlins, 22, 284–85
Marlin-spike (*Nezumia bairdi*), 180
Masked greenling (*Hexagrammos octogrammus*), 203
Mastacembelidae (spiny eels), 288–89
Mastacembelus argus (peacock-eyed spiny eel), 289, **289**
Mayfly, **123**
Medaka (*Oryzias latipes*), **184**, 185
Medialuna californiensis (halfmoon), 248, **248**
Mediterranean guitarfish (*Rhinobatos rhinobatos*), 70
Mediterranean seahorse (*Hippocampus guttulatus*), 199
Mediterranean sleeper shark (*Somniosus rostratus*), 66
Medusafish (*Icichthys lockingtoni*), 286
Megalops atlantica (tarpon), 97–98, **97**
Melanocetidae, 174
Melanocetus johnsonii (blackdevil), 174, **174**
Melanogrammus aeglefinus (haddock), 175–76, **176**
Melanotaenia maccullochi (Australian rainbowfish), 189, **189**
Melastomiatidae, 133
Memastistiidae, 231
Menhadens, 28, 106
Menidia
 audens (Mississippi silverside), 189
 beryllina (tidewater silverside), 189
 menidia (Atlantic silverside), 189
Menticirrhus, 242
 americanus (southern kingfish), 245
 littoralis (Gulf kingfish), 245
 saxatalis (northern kingfish), 245
 undulatus (California corbina), 245, **245**
Merluccius
 bilinearis (silver hake), 177
 capensis (South African hake), 177
 merluccius (European hake), **176**, 177
 productus (Pacific hake), 177
Merry widow (*Phallichthys amates*), 187, **187**
Metynnis, 141
Metynnis maculatus (spotted metynnis), 141
Mexican barracuda (*Sphyraena ensis*), 261

Mexican goatfish (Psuedupeneus dentatus), 246
Mexican scad (Decapterus hypodus), 228–29
Mexican tetra (Astyanax mexicanus), 138
Micralestes interruptus (Congo tetra), **140**
Microgadus
    proximus (Pacific tomcod), 176
    tomcod (Atlantic tomcod), 176
Micrognathus, 199
Microgobius gulosus (clown goby), 273
Micropogon undulatus (Atlantic croaker), 244
Micropterus (basses), 217–18
    coosae (redeye bass), 218
    dolomieui (smallmouth bass), 218
    notius (Suwanee bass), 218
    punctulatus (spotted bass), 218
    salmoides (largemouth bass), 218
    treculi (Guadalupe bass), 218
Microspathodon chrysurus (yellowtail damselfish), 259
Middling thread herring (Opisthonema medirastre), 106
Midnight parrotfish (Scarus coelestinus), 267
Migration, fish, 36
Miles, R. A., 18
Milkfish (Chanos chanos), 136, **136**
Milkfishes (Chanidae), 136
Miller's thumb (Cottus gobio), 206
Mimagoniates inequalis (croaking tetra), 138, **140**
Minnow, **123**
Minnows (Cyprinidae), 35, 137, 142–53
Minytrema melanops (spotted sucker), **154**, 155
Mirror carp, 144
Misgurnus
    anguillicaudatus (oriental weatherfish), 156
    fossilis (European weatherfish), 156, **157**
Mississippi silverside (Menidia audens), 189
Mixine circifrons (whiteface hagfish), 41
Mixinidae (hagfishes), 40–41
Mixiniformes (order), 40–41
Mobula
    diabola (Australian mobula), 83
    hypostoma (devil ray, or little devilfish), **82**, 83
    japonica (spinetail mobula), 83
    lucasana (smoothtail mobula), 83
    mobular (European manta), 83
Mobulidae (mantas), 81–83
Mochokidae (upside-down catfishes), 163
Moekhausia pittiere (diamond tetra), **139**
Mojarras (Gerridae), 236–37
Mola
    lanceolata (sharptail mola), 298
    mola (ocean sunfish), 298, **298**
Molas (Molidae), 21, 298
Mollies, 187
Molly miller (Blennius cristatus), 269
Monacanthus
    ciliatus (fringed filefish), 295
    hispidus (planehead filefish), 295
    setifer, 295
Monkeyface blenny (Cepidichthys violaceous), 270
Monocirrhus polyacanthus (leaffish), 253, **253**
Monodactylidae (fingerfishes), 247
Monodactylus argenteus (moonfish), 247, **247**
Monopterus albus (rice eel), 200, **200**
Monotaxis grandoculis (mu), 241
Mooneye (Hiodon tergisus), 111, **111**
Mooneyes (Hiodontidae), 111
Moonfish (Monodactylus argenteus), 247, **247**
Moor goldfish, **144**

Moorish idol (Zanclus canescens), 275, **275**
Morays (Muraenidae), 100–101
Mormyridae (mormyrids), 113–14
Mormyrids (Mormyridae), 33, 113–14
Mormyriformes (order), 113–14
Mormyrus kanumae (tapir fish), 113
Morone, 215–16
    americana (white perch), 215–16
    chrysops (white bass), 215, **215**
    mississippiensis (yellow bass), 215
    saxatilis (striped bass), 214–15
Mosquitofish (Gambusia affinis), 186, **186**
Mossbunker (Brevoortia tyrannus), **105**, 106
Mottled sculpin (Cottus bairdi), 206
Mountain mullet (Agonostomus monticola), 260–61
Moxostoma, 155
    macrolepidotum (northern redhorse), 155
Mozambique mouthbrooder (Tilapia mossambica), 256–57
Mu (Monotaxis grandoculis), 241
Mudminnows (Umbridae), 131
Mud parrotfish (Sparisoma flavescens), 267
Mudskipper (Periophthalmus barbarus), **273**
Mudskippers (Periophthalmus and Boleophthalmus spp.), 273–74
Mugil, 260–61
    auratus (golden mullet), 261
    brasiliensis (Brazilian mullet), 261
    capito (thin-lipped mullet), 261
    cephalus (striped mullet), 260, **260**
    chelo (thick-lipped mullet), 261
    curema (white mullet), **260**, 260–61
    trichodon (fantail mullet), 260–61
Mugilidae (mullets), 260–61
Muilets (Mugilidae), 260–61
Mullidae (goatfishes), 246–47
Mulloidichthys martinicus (yellow goatfish), 247
Mullus
    auratus (red goatfish), 246
    surmuletus (red surmullet), 246
Mummichog (Fundulus heteroclitus), 183
Muraena pardalis (dragon moray), 101
Muraenidae (morays), 100–101
Mushroom scorpionfish (Scorpaena inermis), 202
Muskellunge (Esox masquinongy), **128**, 128–130
Musselcracker (Sparus durbanensis), 241
Mustelus
    californicus (gray smoothhound), 60
    canis (smooth dogfish), 60, **60**
    henlei (brown smoothhound), 60
    lunulatus (sicklefin smoothhound), 60
    norrisi (Florida smoothhound), 60
    punctulatus (spotted shark), 60
Mutton snapper (Lutjanus analis), 234, **235**
Mycteroperca, 212
    bonaci (black grouper), 212
    jordani (Gulf grouper), 212
    microlepis (gag), 212
    olfax (Colorado grouper), 212
    pardalis (golden grouper), 212
    phenax (scamp), 212
    tigris (tiger grouper), 212
    venenosa (yellowfin grouper), 212
    xenarcha (broomtail grouper), 212
Myctophidae (lanternfishes), 135
Myctophiformes (order), 134–35
Myctophum, 135
    affine (lanternfish), 135
Myliobatidae (eagle rays), 79–80
Myliobatus
    californica (bat ray), 80
    freminvillei (bullnose ray), 80
Mylio macrocephalus, 241

Mylopharodon conocephalus (hardhead), 147
Myoxocephalus scorpius (shorthorn sculpin), **206**
Myrichthys
    acuminatus (sharptail eel), 103
    maculosus, 103
    tigrinus (tiger snake eel), 103
Myripristis, 191
    jacobus (blackbar soldierfish), 191, **191**
    murdjan, 191
Mystus vittata (Indian catfish), 161
Myxine glutinosa (Atlantic hagfish), **40**, 41

Naked goby (Gobiosoma bosci), 273
Namazu (Parasilurus asotus), 161
Nandidae (leaffishes), 253
Nanostomus (pencilfish), 141
Narcine
    brasiliensis (lesser electric ray), 72, **73**
    tasmaniensis (Australian numbfish), 72
Narrowtooth shark (Carcharhinus remotus), 58–59
Naso (Unicornfish), 275, **276**
Nassau grouper (Epinephelus striatus), 211, **211**
Naucrates ductor (pilotfish), 228
Neamia, 222
Needlefishes (Belonidae), 180, 182
Negaprion brevirostris (lemon shark), 46, 59
Nematobrycon palmeri (emperor tetra), **139**
Neoarius australis (blue catfish), 164
Neoceratodus forsteri (Australian lungfish), 87, **87**
Neochanna apoda (brown mudfish), 127
Neoclinus blanchardi (sarcastic fringehead), 270
Neon goby (Gobiosoma oceanops), **272**, 273
Neon tetra (Hyphessobrycon innesi), 138, **139**
Neoscopelus, 135
Netuma thalassima (salmon catfish), 164
Nezumia, 180
    bairdi (marlin-spike), 180
Nicomis biguttatus (hornyhead chub), **148**, 149
Night shark (Hypoprion signatus), 60
Night smelt (Spirinchus starksi), 126
Nile perch (Lates niloticus), 212
Ninespine stickleback (Pungitius pungitius), 196, **196**
Nomatistius pectoralis (roosterfish), 231-32, **233**
Nomeus gronovii (man-of-war fish), 286
North American freshwater catfishes (Ictaluridae), 158–61
Northern anchovy (Engraulis mordax), 109
Northern cavefish (Amblyopsis spelaea), **168**
Northern clingfish (Gobiesox meandricus), 171
Northern fluke (Paralichthys dentatus), 290
Northern hogsucker (Hypentelium nigricans), **154**, 155–56
Northern kingfish (Menticirrhus saxatalis), 245
Northern midshipman (Porichthys notatus), **169**, 170
Northern pearleye (Benthabella dentata), 135
Northern pike (Esox lucius), 128-30, **129**
Northern pipefish (Syngnathus fuscus), 199
Northern puffer (Sphoeroides maculatus), 296

Northern redbelly dace (Phoxinus eos), 149
Northern redhorse (Moxostoma macrolepidotum), 155
Northern sea robin (Prionotus carolinus), 203, **203**
Northern sennet (Sphyraena borealis), 262
Northern squawfish (Ptychocheilus oregonensis), **146**, 147
Northern stargazer (Astroscopus guttatus), 268, **268**
Notemigonous crysoleucas (golden shiner), 148, **148**
Notopteridae (featherbacks), 112
Notopterus
    afer (African knifefish), 112
    chitala (Asiatic featherback, or banded knifefish), 112, **112**
Noturus, 160–61
    flavus (stonecat), 161
    gyrinus (tadpole madtom), 161
    nocturnus (freckled madtom), 161
Notorynchus maculatus (sevengill shark), 48
Notropis, 147–48
    atherinoides (emerald shiner), 147–48, **148**
    cornutus (common shiner), 147, **147**
    hypselopterus (sailfin shiner), 148
Novumbra hubbsi (Olympic mudminnow), 131
Numbfish. See Electric rays

Oarfish (Regalecus glesne), 195, **195**
Oarfishes (Regalecidae), 195
Obtotiophagus koumansi, 274
Oceanic whitetip shark (Carcharhinus longimanus), 56
Ocean perch (Sebastes marinus), 202, **202**
Ocean pout (Macrozoarces americanus), 179
Ocean sunfish (Mola mola), 298, **298**
Ocean surgeon (Acanthurus bahianus), 274–75
Ocean triggerfish (Canthidermis sufflamen), 294
Ocean whitefish (Caulolatilus princeps), 224–25
Ocellated flounder (Ancylopsetta quadrocellata), 290
Ocyurus chrysurus (yellowtail snapper), 235, **236**
Odontaspididae (sand sharks, or sand tigers), 51–52
Odontaspis, 51–52
    arenarius (gray nurse shark), 51–52
    ferox (rugged-tooth shark), 52
    taurus (sand tiger), 51–52, **52**
Offshore seahorse (Hippocampus obtusus), 199
Ogcocephalidae (batfishes), 172–73
Ogcocephalus
    nasutus (shortnosed batfish), 173
    vespertilio (longnosed batfish), 173
Ohio shad. See Alabama shad
Offshore lizardfish (Synodus poeyi), 134
Oilfish (Ruvettus pretiosus), 277
Oligoplites saurus (leatherjacket), 227
Olympic mudminnow (Novumbra hubbsi), 131
Ompok, 161
Oncorhynchus (Pacific salmons), 116–18
    gornuscha (pink salmon), 118, **118**
    keta (chum salmon), **117**, 118
    kisutch (coho or silver salmon), 117, **117**
    nerka (sockeye salmon), 117–18, **118**
    tshawytscha (Chinook or king salmon), 116–17
Opah (Lampris regius), 192, **193**
Opahs (Lamprididae), 192–94

Opaleye (Girella nigricans), 248
Ophicephalus, 200
Ophichthidae (snake eels), 102–3
Ophichthus
    macrorhynchus (snake eel), **102**
    ophis (spotted snake eel), 103
    zophochir (yellow snake eel), 103
Ophidiidae (cusk-eels and brotulas),
    177–78
Ophiodon elongatus (lingcod), 204, **204**
Opisthonema
    medirastre (middling thread herring),
      106
    oglinum (Atlantic thread herring),
      106
Opisthoproctidae (spookfishes), 127
Opistognathidae (jawfishes), 267–68
Opistognathus, 267–68
    aurifrons (yellowhead jawfish),
      267–68, **268**
    muscatensis, 268
Opsanus
    beta (Gulf toadfish), 170
    pardus (leopard toadfish), 170
    tau (oyster toadfish), 170
Orange angel shark (Squatina
    tergocellata), 67
Orange cichlid (Etroplus maculatus), 256
Orange filefish (Aluterus schoepfi), 295
Orangemouth corvina (Cynoscion
    xanthalus), 243
Orange-striped filefish (Oxymonacanthus
    longirostris), 295, **295**
Orange-striped triggerfish (Balistes
    undulatus), 295
Orectolobidae (carpet sharks), 49–50
Orectolobus
    maculatus (spotted wobbegong), 50
    ornatus (banded wobbegong, or
      Australian carpet shark), 50
Oriental weatherfish (Misgurnus
    anguillicaudatus), 156
Orthopristis chrysoptera (pigfish), 238
Oryzias latipes (medaka, or rice fish),
    184, 185
Oscar cichlid (Astronotus ocellatus),
    258, **258**
Osmeridae (smelts), 125–26
Osmerus
    eperlanus (European smelt), 125, **126**
    mordax rainbow smelt), 125
Osphronemus gourami (giant gourami),
    287, 288
Osteichthyes (bony fishes),
    19–20, 85–298
Osteoglossidae (arapaimas and
    arawanas), 110
Osteoglossiformes (order), 110–12
Osteoglossum bicirrhosum (arawana),
    110, **110**
Ostorhinchus, 222
Ostraciidae (boxfishes), 295–96
Ostracoderms, 18, **18**
Otoclinus affinis, 67
Otophidium taylori (spotted cusk-eel),
    178, **178**
Oxyalis californica (senorita), 266
Oxylebius pictus (painted greenling), 203
Oxymonacanthus longirostris (orange-
    striped filefish), 295, **295**
Oxynotus bruniensis (prickly dogfish), 65
Oxyporhamphus micropterus (smallwing
    flying fish), 181
Oyster toadfish (Opsanus tau), 170
Ozark cavefish (Amblyopsis rosae), 168

Pacific abyssal skate (Raja bathyphila), 75
Pacific angel shark (Squatina californica),
    67
Pacific argentine (Argentina sialis), 126
Pacific barracuda (Sphyraena argentea),
    261, **262**

Pacific barreleye (Macropinna
    microstoma), 127, **127**
Pacific bonito (Sarda chiliensis), 279
Pacific bumper (Chloroscombrus
    orqueta), 231
Pacific burrfish (Chilomycterus affinis), 297
Pacific codfish (Gadus macrocephalus),
    175
Pacific electric ray (Torpedo californica),
    72
Pacific hagfish (Eptatretus stouti), 41
Pacific hake (Merluccius productus), 177
Pacific halibut (Hippoglossus stenolepis),
    291
Pacific herring (Clupea harengus pallasi),
    106
Pacific manta (Manta hamiltoni), 82
Pacific moonfish (Vomer declivifrons), 231
Pacific pompano (Peprilus simillimus), 286
Pacific salmons (Oncorhynchus), 116–18
Pacific sanddab (Citharichthys sordidus),
    290
Pacific sandfish (Trichodon trichodon),
    267
Pacific sardine (Sardinops sagax), **105**, 106
Pacific saury (Cololabis saira), **182**, 183
Pacific seahorse (Hippocampus ingens),
    199
Pacific Sharpnose shark (Rhizoprionodon
    longurio), 56, 59
Pacific sleeper shark (Somniosus
    pacificus), 66
Pacific spadefish (Chaetodipterus
    zonatus), 250
Pacific spiny lumpsucker (Eumicrotremus
    orbis), 207
Pacific tarpon (T. cyprinoides), 98
Pacific tomcod (Microgadus proximus),
    176
Pacific viperfish (Chauliodus macouni),
    132
Paddlefish (Polyodon spathula), **93**, 94
Paddlefishes (Polyodontidae), 93–94
Pagellus, 241
Pagrosomus auratus (Australian snapper),
    241
Pagrus nasutus (steenbras), 241
Painted greenling (Oxylebius pictus), 203
Painted parrotfish (Scarus punctulatus),
    267
Pallid sturgeon (Scarus punctulatus), 231
Paloma pompano (Trachinotus paitensis),
    231
Palometa (Trachinotus goodei), 231
Pandaka pygmaea, 272
Pangasianodon gigas, 162
Pantodon buchholzi (freshwater
    butterflyfish), 111, **111**
Paracirrhies, 260
Paraclinus, 270
Paradise fish (Macropodus operculans),
    286
Paralabrax
    clathratus (kelp bass), 213-14, **214**
    maculatofasciatus (spotted sand
      bass), 213–14
    nebulifer (barred sand bass), 213–14
Paralichthys
    albigutta (Gulf flounder), 290
    brasiliensis (lenquad), 290
    californicus (California halibut), 290
    dentatus (summer flounder), 290
    lethostigma (southern flounder), 290
    oblongus (fourspot flounder), 290
    olivaceus, 290
Parasilurus asotus (namazu), 161
Parasitic catfishes (Trichomycteridae), 166
Parauchenoglanis macrostoma (African
    spotted catfish), 161, **161**
Parexocoetus mesogaster (short-winged
    flying fish), 181
Parmaturus xaniurus (filetail cat shark), 55
Parrotfishes (Scaridae), 28, 31, 266–67
Parrs, 116

Pauu'u (Caranx ignobilis), 231
Peacock-eyed spiny eel (Mastacembelus
    argus), 289, **289**
Peacock flounder (Bothus lunatus), 290
Pearl dace (Semotilus margarita), 147
Pearl danio (Brachydanio albolineatus),
    153
Pearleyes (Scopelarchidae), 135
Pearlfish (Carapus bermudensis), **178**, 179
Pearl gourami (Trichogaster leeri),
    287, 288
Pearlscale goldfish, **145**
Pearly razorfish (Hemipteronotus
    novacuia), 265
Pegasidae (sea moths), 209
Pegasiformes (order), 209
Pegasus
    papilio (sea moth), 209, **209**
    volitans, 209
Pelagic stingray (Dasyatis violacea), 76
Pelyicachromis pulcher (purple cichlid),
    257
Pencilfish (Nanostomus), 141
Penetopteryx, 199
Penguinfish (Thayeria spp.), **140**, 141
Peppered catfish (Corydoras paleatus),
    166
Peprilus, 285–86
    alepidotus (harvestfish), 285
    paru, 285
    simillimus (Pacific pompano), 286
    triacanthus (butterfish), 285
Perca
    flavescens (yellow perch), **222**, 223
    fluviatilis (European perch), 223
Perches (Persidae), 222–24
Percichthyidae, 214
Percidae (perches), 222–24
Perciformes (order), 209–89
Percina caprodes (logperch), 224
Percopsidae (trout-perches), 168–69
Percopsiformes (order), 167–69
Percopsis
    omiscomaycus (trout-perch),
      169, **169**
    transmontana (sandroller), 169
Periophthalmus barbarus (mudskipper),
    273
Permit (Trachinotus falcatus), **230**, 231
Peruvian longfin (Pterolebias peruensis),
    184
Petrale sole (Eopsetta jordani), 292
Petrometopon
    cruentatum (graysby), 213, **213**
    panamaensis (enjambre), 213
Petromizontiformes (order), 41–42
Petromyzontidae (lampreys), 41–42
Petronyzon, 41–42
    marinus (sea lamprey), **41**
Petrus rupestris (red steenbras), 241
Phallichthys amates (merrow widow),
    187, **187**
Phanerodon
    atripes (sharpnose seaperch), 254
    furcatus (white seaperch), 254, **255**
Phenacobius (dace), 149
Phisodnopsis boro (Indian eel), 99
Pholidae (gunnels), 271
Pholis, 271
    gunnellus (rock gunnel), 271, **271**
Photoblepharon, 190
Photophores, 131
Phoxinius (minnows), 150
Phoxinus
    eos (northern redbelly dace), 149
    erythrogaster (southern redbelly
      dace), 149, **149**
Phrynorhombus norvegicus, 290
Phyllopteryx foliatus, 199
Phylsailia pellucida, 162
Pickerels (Esocidae), 128–31
Pigfish (Orthopristis chrysoptera), 238
Pikeblennies (Chaenopsis), 270
Pike characin (Boulengerella lucius), 138

Pike cichlid (Crenicichla lepidota),
    256, 258
Piked dogfish (Squalus megalops), 64
Pike killifish (Belonesox belizanus), 188
Pikeperch (Lucioperca lucioperca), 224
Pikes (Esocidae), 128–31
Pile perch (Rhacocilus vacca), 255
Pilotfish (Naucrates ductor), 228
Pimelodella gracillis (mandi, or slender
    catfish), 166
Pimelodidae (pimelodid catfishes),
    165–66
Pimelodid catfishes (Pimelodidae),
    165–66
Pimelodus clarias (pintado, or polka-dot
    catfish), 165
Pimelometopon pulchrum (California
    sheepshead), 264, **264**
Pimephales
    notatus (bluntnose minnow), 149
    promelas (fathead minnow), 149
Pinfish (Lagodon rhomboides), 241
Pink salmon (Oncorhynchus gornuscha),
    36, 118, **118**
Pink seaperch (Zalembius rosaceous), 255
Pintado (Pimelodus clarias), 165
Pipefishes (Syngnathidae), 198–99
Piranhas (Serrasalmus), 137–38
Pirate perch (Aphredoderus savanus),
    168, **168**
Placoderms, 18, **18**, **19**, **20**
Plainfin midshipman (Porichthys notatus),
    169, 170
Plains topminnow (Fundulus sciadicus),
    183
Planehead filefish (Monacanthus
    hispidus), 295
Platichthys stellatus (starry flounder), 292
Platyrhinoidis triseriata (thornback), 71
Platys, 188
Plecoglossidae (sweetfishes), 124
Plecoglossus altivelis (sweetfish, or ayu),
    124, **125**
Plecostomus (suckermouth catfishes), 167
Pleuronectes platessa (European plaice),
    293
Pleuronectidae (righteye flounders),
    291–93
Pleuronectiformes (order), 289–93
Pleuronichthys decurrens (curlfin sole),
    292
Plotosid sea catfishes (Plotosidae), 165
Plotosus
    anguillaris (catfish eel), 165, **165**
    arab, 165
Plownosed chimaeras (Callorhinchus), 84
Plumed scorpionfish (Scorpaena
    grandicornis), 201
Poachers (Agonidae), 207
Poecilia
    formosa (Amazon molly), 187
    latipinna (sailfin molly), 187, **187**
    mexicana (shortfin molly), 187, **187**
    reticulata (guppy), 187, **187**
Poeciliidae (livebearers), 186–88
Pogonias cromis (black drum), 243–44
Pogonichthys macrolepidotus (splittail),
    147
Polar eelpout (Lycodes turneri), 179
Polka-dot catfish (Pimelodus clarias), 165
Polka-dot catfish (Synodontis angelicus),
    163
Polka-dot ribbonfish (Desmondema
    polysticta), 195
Pollachius virens (pollock), 176
Pollock (Pollachius virens), 176
Polycentropsis abbreviata, 253
Polycentrus schomburghi, 253
Polydactylus
    approximans (blue bobo), 262
    octonemus (Atlantic threadfin), 262
    opercularis (yellow bobo), 262
    sexfilis, 262
    virginicus (barbu), 262, **262**

Polymixia
    lowei (beardfish), 190, **190**
    nobilis (stout beardfish), 190
Polymyxiidae (beardfishes), 190
Polynemidae (threadfins), 262
Polyodon spathula (paddlefish), **93**, 94
Polyodontidae (paddlefishes), 93–94
Polyprion americanus (wreckfish), 214
Polypteridae (bichirs), 90
Polypteriformes (order), 90
Polypterus, 90
Polypterus weeksi (bichir), **90**
Pomacanthus, 253
    arcuatus (gray angelfish), 253
    imperator (imperial angelfish), **252**, 253
    maculosus (half-moon angelfish), **252**, 253
    paru (French angelfish), **252**, 253
    semicirculatus (blue angelfish), **252**, 253
    zonipectus, 253
Pomacentridae (damselfishes), 258–59
Pomacentrus leucosticus (beaugregory), 258–59, **259**
Pomadasyidae (grunts), 237–38
Pomadasys, 238
Pomatomidae (bluefish), 225
Pomatomus saltatrix (bluefish), 225, **225**
Pompadour (*Symphosodon discus*), 258, **258**
Pompano dolphin (*Coryphaena equisetis*), 233
Pompanos (Carangidae), 227–32
Pond smelt (*Hypomesus olidus*), 125–26
Popeye catalufa (*Pristigenys serrula*), 222
Porbeagle shark (*Lamna nasus*), 47, 53–54, **54**
Porcupinefish (*Diodon hystrix*), 22, **23**, 297, **297**
Porcupinefishes (Diodontidae), **22**, 297
Porgies (Sparidae), 238–41
Porichthys, 169–70
    myriaster (slim, or specklefin, midshipman), 170
    notatus (plainfin, or northern, midshipman), **169**, 170
    porosissimus (Atlantic midshipman), 169
Porkfish (*Anisotremus virginicus*), 238, **239**
Port Jackson shark (*Heterodontus portusjacksoni*), 49, **49**
Portuguese shark (*Centroscymnus coelolepis*), 44, 64, **65**
Potamotrygonidae, 76
Potomorhopis guianensis, 182
Powder-blue surgeonfish (*Acanthurus leucosternon*), 275, **275**
Poxomis (crappies), 218–19
    annularis (white crappie), 219
    nigromaculatus (black crappie), 219
Priacanthidae (bigeyes), 221–22
Priacanthus, 221–22
    arenatus (bigeye), 221, **221**
    cruentatus (glasseye snapper, or catalufa), 221
    hamrur, 222
Pricklebacks (Stichaeidae), 270–71
Prickly dogfish (*Oxynotus bruniensis*), 65
Prickly sculpin (*Cottus asper*), 206
Prickly shark (*Echinorhinus cookei*), 67
Priestfish. *See* Blue rockfish
Prionace glauca (blue shark), **58**, 59
Prionotus
    carolinus (northern sea robin), 203, **203**
    evolans (striped sea robin), 203
    scitulus (leopard sea robin), 203
Pristidae (sawfishes), 69–70
Pristigenys serrula (popeye catalufa), 222
Pristiophoridae (saw sharks), 63

Pristiophorus cirratus, 63, **63**
Pristis, 69–70
    cuspidatus, 69
    leichhardti, 69–70
    microdon, 69
    pectinata (smalltooth sawfish), 69, **70**
    perotteti (largetooth sawfish), 69
    pristis, 69
Protopterus, **88–89**, 89
Protopterus annectans (African lungfish), **89**
Psephurus gladius, 94
Psettichthys melanosticus (sand sole), 292
Pseudoplatystoma (tiger catfishes), 166
Pseudopleuronectes americanus (winter flounder), **291**, 292
Pseudoscarus, 266
Pseudotriakidae (false cat sharks), 55–56
Pseudotriakis, 55–56
    acrages, 56
    microdon (false cat shark), 55–56
Pseudupeneus
    dentatus (Mexican goatfish), 246
    maculatus (spotted goatfish), 246, **246**
Pteraspis (ostracoderm), **18**
Ptereleotris tricolor, 274
Pterichthyoides (placoderm), **19**
Pterichthys (placoderm), **20**
Pterodiscus levis (winged disc), 141
Pterois, 201–2
    spp. (zebrafishes), 202
    volitans (lionfish), **201**
Pterolebias
    longipinnis (veil carp), 185
    peruensis (Peruvian longfin), **184**
Pterophyllum scalara (angelfish), **257**, 257–58
Ptychocheilus
    grandis (Sacramento squawfish), 147
    lucius (Colorado squawfish), 147
    oregonensis (northern squawfish), **146**, 147
    umpouae (Umpqua squawfish), 147
Puddingwife (*Halichoeres radiatus*), 265
Puffers (Tetraodontidae), 296–97
Puhi-paka (*Gymnothorax flavimarginatus*), 101
Pumpkinseed (*Lepomis gibbosus*), 220
Pungitius pungitius (ninespine stickleback), 196, **196**
Puntius
    filamentosus (black-spot barb), 152, **152**
    saschi (golden barb), **152**
    ticto (two-spot barb), 152, **152**
Puppy drum, 243
Purple cichlid (*Pelyicachromis pulcher*), 257
Pygmy killifish (*Leptolucania ommata*), 184
Pygmy moray (*Anarchis yoshiae*), 101
Pygocentrus calmoni (dusky piranha), **137**
Pygolites diacanthus (regal angelfish), **252**, 253
Pyrrhulina vittata (banded copeina), 140

Queen angelfish (*Holocanthus cilaris*), 252, **252**
Queenfish (*Seriphus politus*), 244
Queensland grouper (*Epinephelus lanceolata*), 212
Queen parrotfish (*Scarus vetula*), **266**, 267
Queen triggerfish (*Balistes vetula*), 294
Quillback (*Carpiodies cyprinus*), **155**, 156
Quintana atrizona (black-barred livebearer), **187**

Rabaut's catfish (*Corydoras rabauti*), 167
Rabbitfishes (Siganidae), 276–77
Rachycentridae (cobia), 225–26

Rachycentron canadum (cobia), 225–26, **226**
Ragfish (*Icosteus aenigmaticus*), 288, **288**
Ragfishes (Icosteidae), 288
Rainbow darter (*Etheostoma caeruleum*), 224
Rainbow parrotfish (*Scarus guacamaia*), 266
Rainbow runner (*Elagatis bipinnulata*), 228
Rainbow smelt (*Osmerus mordax*), 125
Rainbow surfperch (*Hypsurus caryi*), 254
Rainbow trout (*Salmo gairdneri*), 26, 118–19, **119**
Raja
    bathyphila (Pacific abyssal skate), 75
    batis (common skate), **74**, 75
    binoculata (big skate), 75
    clavata (thornback skate), 75
    eglanteria (clearnose skate), 75
    erinacea (little skate), **74**, 75
    inornata (California skate), 75
    laevis (barndoor skate), 75
    miraletus (European skate), 75
    ocellata (winter, or eyed, skate), 75
    oxyrinchus (European longnosed skate), 75
    rhina (longnose skate), 75
    texana (roundel skate), 75
Rajidae (skates), 72, 74–75
Rajiformes (order), 68–83
Ramirez' dwarf cichlid (*Apistogramma ramirezi*), **256**
Ranzania laevis (slender mola), 298
Rasbora, 152–53
    einthoveni (brilliant rasbora), 153, **153**
    heteromorpha (harlequin rasbora), 153, **153**
    trillineata (scissor-tailed rasbora), 153, **153**
    urophthalma (exclamation-point rasbora), 153, **153**
    vaterifloris (Ceylonese fire barb), 153, **153**
Rasboras (*Rasbora*), 152–53
Ratfish (*Hydrolagus colliei*), **83**, 84
Rayfinned fishes, 86
Razorfishes (*Hemipteronotus*), 264–65
Record catches, 21, 300–301
Red batfish (*Halieutaea stellata*), 173, **173**
Red-bellied piranha (*Serrasalmus nattereri*), **137**
Red brotula (*Brosmophycis marginatus*), 178
Redcap veiltail, **144**
Red cornetfish (*Fistularia villosa*), 197
Red discus (*Symphosodon discus*), 258, **258**
Red drum (*Sciaenops ocellata*), 243, **243**
Redear sunfish (*Lepomis microlophus*), 220
Redeye bass (*Micropterus coosae*), 218
Redeye characin (*Arnoldichthys spilopterus*), **140**
Redfin butterflyfish (*Chaetodon trifasciatus*), 250, **251**
Redfin needlefish (*Strongylura notata*), 182
Redfin pickerel (*Esox americanus*), 128, 130
Redfish (*Sebastes marinus*), 202, **202**
Red goatfish (*Mullus auratus*), 246
Red grouper (*Epinephelus morio*), 210–11
Red hake (*Urophycis chuss*), 177
Red hind (*Epinephelus guttatus*), 211
Redhorses (*Moxostoma*), 155
Redjaw killie (*Epiplatys chaperi*), **185**
Red lyretail (*Aphyosemion bivittatum*), 184–85
Red lizardfish (*Synodus synodus*), 134
Red parrotfish (*Sparisoma abildgaardi*), 267
Red River pupfish (*Cyprinodon rubrofluviatilis*), 184

Red snapper (*Lutjanus campechanus*), 234
Red-spotted hawkfish (*Amblycirrhitus pinos*), **260**
Red steenbras (*Petrus rupestris*), 241
Red sturgeon. *See* Lake sturgeon
Red surmullet (*Mullus surmuletus*), 246
Red-tailed shark (*Labeo bicolor*), **152**
Redtail surfperch (*Amphistichus rhodoterus*), 254
Redtail triggerfish (*Xanthichthys mento*), 294
Reedfish (*Calamoichthys calabaricus*), 90
Reedfishes (Polypteridae), 90
Reef shark (*Carcharhinus springeri*), 59
Reef squirrelfish (*Holocentrus coruscus*), 191
Regal angelfish (*Pygolites diacanthus*), **252**, 253
Regalecidae (oarfishes), 195
Regalecus glesne (oarfish), 195, **195**
Reinhardtius hippoglossoides (Greenland halibut), 293
Remora (*Remora remora*), 227
Remora remora (remora), 227
Remoras (Echeneidae), 226–27
Requiem sharks (Carcharhinidae), 56–60
Rex sole (*Glyptocephalus zachirus*), 292
Rhacocilus
    toxotes (rubberlip seaperch), 254–55
    vacca (pile perch), 255
Rhamphichthys rostratus, 142
Rhinecanthus
    aculeatus, 295
    rectangulus, 295
Rhinichthys
    atratulus (blacknose dace), 149
    cataractae (longnose dace), 149
Rhinobatidae (guitarfishes), 70–71
Rhinobatos
    horkelli (Brazilian guitarfish), 70
    lentiginosus (Atlantic guitarfish), 70, **71**
    productus (shovelnose guitarfish), 70
    rhinobatos (Mediterranean guitarfish), 70
Rhinochimaeridae (chimaeras), 84
Rhinoplagusia japonica (Asiatic tonguefish), 293, **293**
Rhinoptera
    bonasus (Atlantic cownose ray), 80, **80**
    brasiliensis, 80
    javanica, 80
    marginata, 80
Rhinopteridae (cownose rays), 80
Rhizoprionodon, 56, 59
    longurio (Pacific sharpnose shark), 56, 59
    terraenovae (Atlantic sharpnose shark), 56, 59, **59**
    walbeehmi, 56, 59
Rhodeus sericeus (bitterling), 150, **150**
Rhomboplites aurorubens (vermillion snapper), 235
Rhyncobatos djiddensis (giant guitarfish), 70
Ribbonfish (*Trachipterus iris*), **194**
Ribbonfishes (Trachipteridae), 195
Ribbon halfbeak (*Euleptorhamphus viridis*), 182
Rice eel (*Monopterus albus*), 200, **200**
Rice fish (*Oryzias latipes*), **184**, 185
Righteye flounders (Pleuronectidae), 291–93
Rio Grande chub (*Gila nigrescens*), 149
Rio Grande perch (*Cichlasoma cyanoguttatus*), 257
Rissola marginata (striped cusk-eel), 178
River goby (*Awaous tajasica*), 273
River herring. *See* Skipjack herring
River shark (*Carcharhinus zambezensis*), 56
Rivulus cylindraceus (Cuban rivulus), **184**
Roach (*Rutilus rutilus*), 150, **150**

Rock bass (*Amblopites rupestris*), 221
Rock beauty (*Holocanthus tricolor*), **252**, 252–53
Rockfishes (Scorpaenidae), 201–3
Rock greenling (*Hexagrammos lagocephalus*), 203
Rock gunnel (*Pholis gunnellus*), 271, **271**
Rock hind (*Epinephelus adscensionis*), 211
Rockpool blenny (*Hypsoblennius gilberti*), 269
Rock prickleback (*Xiphister mucosus*), 270, **271**
Rock sturgeon. *See* Lake sturgeon
Rocksucker (*Chorisochismus dentex*), **170**, 171
Rock wrasse (*Halichoeres semicinctus*), 265–66
Roe shad, 106
Rohu (*Labeo rohita*), 151
Roloffia occidentalis (golden pheasant), **184**, 185
Roman snapper (*Lutjanus argentimaculatus*), 235
Roncador stearnsi (spotfin croaker), 244
Roosterfish (*Nomatistius pectoralis*), 231–32, **233**
Rose coney (*Cephalopholis popino*), 213
Rosy razorfish (*Hemipteronotus martinicensis*), 265
Rosy tetra (*Hyphessobrycon rosaceus*), 138, **139**
Roughjaw frogfish (*Antennarius avalonis*), 172, **172**
Roughtail stingray (*Dasyatis centroura*), 76
Roundel skate (*Raja texana*), 75
Round herring (*Eutrumeus teres*), 108–9, **108**
Round scad (*Decapterus punctatus*), 228
Round stingray (*Urolophus halleri*), 77
Round sunfish. *See* Flier
Roundtail chub (*Gila robusta*), 149
Rubberlip seaperch (*Rhacocilus toxotes*), 254–55
Rudd (*Scardinius erythrophthalmus*), 150, **151**
Rudderfishes. *See* Sea chubs
Ruffe (*Acerina cernua*), 224
Rugged-tooth shark (*Odontaspis ferox*), 52
Rusty dab (*Limanda ferruginea*), 293
Rutilus rutilus (roach), 150, 150
Ruvettus pretiosus (oilfish), 277
Rypticus, 216
    bistrispinus (freckled soapfish), 216
    maculatus (whitespotted soapfish), 216
    saponaceus (greater soapfish), 216, **216**
    subbifrenatus (spotted soapfish), 216

Sablefish (*Anoplopoma fimbria*), 204, **205**
Sablefishes (Anoplopomatidae), 204
Saccopharyngidae (swallowers), 103
Saccopharynx
    ampullaceus (swallowers), 103, **103**
    harrisoni, 103
Sacramento perch (*Archoplites interruptus*), 221
Sacramento squawfish (*Ptychocheilus grandis*), 147
Saddleback butterflyfish (*Chaetodon epihippium*), 250
Sailfish (*Istiophorus platypterus*), 22, 283, **283**
Sailfin characin (*Crenuchus epilurus*), **140**, 141
Sailfin molly (*Poecilia latipinna*), 187, **187**
Sailfin sandfish (*Arctoscopus japonicus*), 267, **267**
Sailfin shiner (*Notropis hypselopterus*), 148

Sailfin tang (*Zebrasoma veliferum*), **274**, 275
Sailors choice (*Haemulon parrai*), 238
Salmo, 115–16, 119–20
    aguabonita (golden trout), 120
    carpio, 120
    clarki (cutthroat trout), **119**, 119–20
    gairdneri (rainbow trout), 118–19, **119**
    gilae (gila trout), 119
    salar (Atlantic salmon), **114**, 115–16
    trutta (brown trout), 120
Salmon catfish (*Netuma thalassima*), 164
Salmonidae (trouts, salmons, whitefishes, and graylings), 114–24
Salmoniformes (order), 114–35
Salmons (Salmonidae), 26, 30, 33, 35, 36, 114–18
Salmon shark (*Lamna ditropis*), 53–54
Saltmarsh top minnow (*Fundulus jenkinsi*), 183
Salvelinus (chars), 120–22
    alpinus (Arctic char), 121–22, **122**
    aureolus (Sunapee trout), 121–22
    fontinalis (brook trout), **120**, 120–21
    malma (Dolly Varden trout), 122
    namaycush (lake trout), 121, **121**
Sandbar shark (*Carcharhinus milberti*), **56**, 57
Sand darters (*Ammocrypta*), 224
Sand diver (*Synodus intermedius*), 134
Sandfishes (Trichodontidae), 267
Sandperch (*Diplectrum formosum*), 213
Sandroller (*Percopsis transmontana*), 169
Sand sea trout (*Cynoscion arenarius*), 242
Sand smelt (*Atherina presbyter*), **189**
Sand sharks (Odontaspididae), 51–52
Sand sole (*Psettichthys melanosticus*), 292
Sand stargazer (*Dactyloscopus tridigitatus*), 268, **269**
Sand stargazers (Dactyloscopidae), 268
Sand tiger (*Odontaspis taurus*), 51–52, **52**
Sand tigers (Odontaspididae), 51–52
Sand tilefish (*Malacanthus plumieri*), 224, **224**
Sarcastic fringehead (*Neoclinus blanchardi*), 270
Sarda, 279
    chiliensis (Pacific bonito), 279
    orientalis, 279
    sarda (Atlantic bonito), 279
Sardines, 105–6
Sardinops sagax (Pacific sardine), **105**, 106
Sargassumfish (*Histrio histrio*), 172, **172**
Sargassum pipefish (*Syngnathus pelagicus*), 199
Sargassum triggerfish (*Xanthichthys ringens*), 294
Sargo (*Anisotremus davidsoni*), 238
Saucereye porgy (*Calamus calamus*), 240
Sauger (*Stizostedion canadense*), 224
Saurida
    brasiliensis (largescale lizardfish), 134
    caribbaea (smallscale lizardfish), 134
    normani (shortjaw lizardfish), 134
    undosquamis (lizardfish), 134, **134**
Sauries (Scomberesocidae), 180, 183
Sawfishes (Pristidae), **23**, 68–70
Saw sharks (Pristiophoridae), 63
Saxilaga anguilliformis, 127
Sayori (*Hemiramphus sajori*), 181
Scaldfish (*Arnoglossus laterna*), 290
Scalloped hammerhead shark (*Sphyrna lewini*), 61, **62**
Scalloped ribbonfish (*Zu cristatus*), 195
Scaly dragonfishes. *See* Deepsea scaly dragonfishes
Scamp (*Mycteroperca phenax*), 212
Scapanorhynchidae (goblin sharks), 52
Scapanorhynchus owstoni (goblin shark), 52
Scaphirhynchus, 92–93
    albus (pallid sturgeon), 93

platorynchus (shovelnose, or hackleback sturgeon), 92–93, **93**
Scardinius erythrophthalmus (rudd), 150, **151**
Scaridae (parrotfishes), 266–67
Scarlet hogfish. *See* Spotfin hogfish
Scarus, 266–67
    coelestinus (midnight parrotfish), 267
    coeruleus (blue parrotfish), **266**, 267
    croicensis (striped parrotfish), 267
    gnathodus (white-banded parrotfish), 267
    guacamaia (rainbow parrotfish), 226
    punctulatus (painted parrotfish), 267
    vetula (queen parrotfish), **266**, 267
Scatophagidae (scats or argus fishes), 250
Scats (Scatophagidae), 250
Schilbeidae (shilbeid catfishes), 162
School shark (*Galeorhinus australis*), 60
Sciaenidae (drums), 242–46
Sciaenops ocellata (red drum), 243, **243**
Scissor-tailed rasbora (*Rasbora trillineata*), 153, **153**
Scomber
    japonicus (chub mackerel), 278
    scombrus (Atlantic mackerel), 278
Scomberesocidae (sauries), 180, 183
Scomberesox saurus (Atlantic saury), 183
Scomberomorus, 278–79
    cavalla (king mackerel, or kingfish), 278
    commerson, 279
    guttatus, 279
    maculatus (Spanish mackerel), 278
    regalis (cero), 278
    sierra (sierra), 278
Scombridae (mackerels and tunas), 278–81
Scopelarchidae (pearleyes), 135
Scophthalmus
    aquosus (windowpane), 290
    maxima (turbot), 290
    rhombus (brill), 290
Scorpaena
    brasiliensis (barbfish), 202
    grandicornis (plumed scorpionfish), 201
    guttata (California scorpionfish), 202
    inermis (mushroom scorpionfish), 202
Scorpaenichthys marmoratus (cabezon), 205
Scorpaenidae (scorpions and rockfishes), 201–7
Scorpaeniformes (order), 201–7
Scorpions (Scorpaenidae), 201–3
Scrawled cowfish (*Lactophrys quadricornis*), 296
Scrawled filefish (*Aluterus scriptus*), 295
Sculpins (Cottidae), 205–6
Scup (*Stenotomus chrysops*), 239, **239**
Scyliorhinidae (cat sharks), 55–56
Scyliorhinus
    boa (cat shark), 55, **55**
    caniculus (lesser spotted dogfish), 55
    retifer (chain dogfish), 55, **55**
    stellarius (large spotted dogfish), 55
Sea basses (Serranidae), 210–16
Sea bream (*Archosargus rhomboidalis*), 241
Sea catfish (*Arius felis*), 163, **164**
Sea chubs (Kyphosidae), 247–48
Seahorses (Sygnathidae), 22, **22**, 35, 198–99
Sea lamprey (*Petronyzon marinus*), 28, **41**, 41–42
Sea moth (*Pegasus papilio*), 209, **209**
Sea moths (Pegasidae), 209
Sea raven (*Hemitripterus americanus*), 206
Sea robins (Triglidae), 203
Sebago salmon. *See* Atlantic salmon

Sebastes, 202–3
    flavidus (yellowtail rockfish), 203
    goodei (chilipepper), 202
    marinus (redfish, or ocean perch), 202, **202**
    melanops (black rockfish), 203
    miniatus (vermilion rockfish), 202–3
    mystinus (blue rockfish), 202
    paucispinis (bocaccio), 202
    pinniger (chameleon rockfish), 203
Secutor, 233
Selene vomer (lookdown), 231, **232**
Semionotiformes (order), 94–96
Semotilus
    atromaculatus (creek chub), 147
    corporalis (fallfish), **146**, 147
    margarita (pearl dace), 147
Senorita (*Oxyalis californica*), 266
Sergeant major (*Abudefduf saxatilis*), 258, **259**
Seriola, 227–28
    dorsalis (yellowtail), 227
    dumerili (greater amberjack), 227, **227**
    fasciata (lesser amberjack), 228
    grandis, 227
    rivoliana (almaco jack), 228
    zonata (banded rudderfish), 228
Seriphus politus (queenfish), 244
Serranidae (sea basses), 210–16
Serranus subligarius (belted sandfish), 214
Serrasalmus
    nattereri (red-bellied piranha), 137, **137**
    piraya, 137
    rhombeus (white piranha), **137**
Sevengill shark (*Heptranchias perlo*), 48
Sevengill shark (*Notorynchus maculatus*), 48
Shad, 36, 106–8
Shark, internal organs of, **44–45**
Sharks (Selachii), 24–25, 26, 29, 35, 44–67.
Sharksucker (*Echeneis naucrates*), 226, **226**
Sharpnose mackerel shark. *See* Shortfin mako shark
Sharpnose seaperch (*Phanerodon atripes*), 254
Sharptail eel (*Myrichthys acuminatus*), 103
Sharptail mola (*Mola lanceolata*), 298
Sheefish (*Stenodus leucichthys*), 122, **123**
Sheepshead (*Archosargus probatocephalus*), 240–41, **241**
Sheepshead minnow (*Cyprinodon variegatus*), 183
Sheepshead porgy (*Calamus penna*), 240
Shellcracker. *See* Redear sunfish
Shilbeid catfishes (Shilbeidae), 162
Shiner perch (*Cymatogaster aggregata*), 253
Shiners, 147–48
Shore eelpout (*Zoarces anguillaris*), 179
Shortbill spearfish (*Tetrapterus angustirostris*), 285
Shortfin barracuda (*Sphyraena novae-hollandiae*), 261–62
Shortfin corvina (*Cynoscion parvipinnis*), 243
Shortfin mako shark (*Isurus oxyrhinchus*), **22**, 45, 46, 47, 53, **54**
Shortfin molly (*Poecilia mexicana*), 187, **187**
Shorthorn sculpin (*Myoxocephalus scorpius*), **206**
Shortjaw cisco (*Coregonus zenithicus*), 124
Shortjaw lizardfish (*Saurida normani*), 134
Shortnose batfish (*Ogcocephalus nasutus*), 173
Shortnose gar (*Lepisosteus platostomus*), 95, **95**
Shortnose mormyrid (*Marcusenius longianalis*), **113**

Shortnose sturgeon (Acipenser brevirostrum), 92
Shortspine combfish (Zanionlepis frenata), 204
Short-winged flying fish (Parexocoetus mesogaster), 181
Shovelnose catfish (Sorubium lima), 166
Shovelnose guitarfish (Rhinobatos productus), 70
Shovelnose sturgeon (Scaphirhynchus platorynchus), 92–93, **93**
Shrimpfish (Aeoliscus punctulatus), 198, **198**
Shrimpfishes (Centriscidae), 197–98
Shubunkin, **145**
Shy eye shark (Holohalaelurus regani), 56
Siamese fighting fish (Betta splendens), 286–88, **287**
Sicklefin smoothhound (Mustelus lunulatus), 60
Sierra (Scomberomorus sierra), 278–79
Siganidae (rabbitfishes), 276–77
Siganus, 277
    vermiculatus (vermiculated rabbitfish), **276**
Silk snapper (Lutjanus vivanus), 234
Silky shark (Carcharhinus falciformis), 56, **57**
Siluridae (Eurasian catfishes), 161
Siluriformes (order), 158–67
Siluris glanis (wels), 161
Silver carp (Hypophthalmichthys), 151
Silver hake (Merluccius bilinearis), 177
Silver hatchetfish (Gasteropelecus sternicla), 141, **141**
Silver jenny (Eucinostomus gula), 237
Silver king. See Tarpon
Silver perch (Bairdiella chrysura), 243
Silver porgy (Diplodus argenteus), 241
Silver salmon (Oncorhynchus kisutch), 117, **117**
Silver sea trout (Cynoscion nothus), 242–43
Silversides (Atherinidae), 188–89
Silver surfperch (Hyperprosopon ellipticum), 254
Sixgill shark (Hexanchus griseus), 48, **48**
Skaamong (Holohalaelurus regani), 56
Skates (Rajidae), 33, 35, 68–69, 72, 74–75
Skilfish (Erilepis zonifer), 204
Skilletfish (Gobiesox strumosus), 171
Skipjack herring (Alosa crysochloris), 107–8
Skipjack tuna (Euthynnus pelamis), 280
Skippers. See Atlantic saury
Skunk cat (Corydoras arcuatus), 166
Skunk loach (Botia horae), 158, **158**
Sleeper sharks, 65–66
Sleepers (Eleotridae), 274
Slender catfish (Pimelodella gracillis), 166
Slender mola (Ranzania laevis), 298
Slickheads. See Deepsea slickheads
Slim anchovy (Anchoviella miarcha), 109
Slim midshipman (Porichthys myriaster), 170
Slimy sculpin (Cottus cognatus), 206
Slipmouth (Leiognathus equula), 233, **234**
Slipmouths (Leiognathidae), 233
Slippery dick (Halichoeres bivittatus), 265, **265**
Slough anchovy (Anchoa delicatissima), 109
Smaller hammerhead shark (Sphyrna tudes), **62**, 63
Smallmouth bass (Micropterus dolomieui), 218
Smallscale lizardfish (Saurida caribbaea), 134
Smalltail shark (Carcharhinus porosus), 56
Smalltooth sawfish (Pristis pectinata), 69, **70**
Smallwing flying fish (Oxyporhamphus micropterus), 181
Smelts (Osmeridae), 35, 125–26

Smolts, 115
Smooth butterfly ray (Gymnura micrura), 79
Smooth dogfish (Mustelus canis), 60, **60**
Smooth dogfishes (Triakidae), 60
Smooth hammerhead shark (Sphyrna zygaena), 61, **61**
Smooth puffer (Lagocephalus laevigatus), 296
Smoothtail mobula (Mobula lucasana), 83
Smooth trunkfish (Lactophrys triqueter), 296
Snailfishes (Cyclopteridae), 207
Snake eel (Ophichthus macrorhynchus), **102**
Snake eels (Ophichthidae), 102–3
Snakefish (Trachinocephalus myops), 134
Snakehead (Channa argus), **200**
Snake mackerels (Gempylidae), 277
Snakeskin gourami (Trichogaster pectoralis), **287**, 288
Snappers (Lutjanidae), 234–35
Snipefish (Macrorhamphosus gracilis), 198, **198**
Snook (Centropomus undecimalis), 209, **210**
Soapfishes (Grammistidae), 216
Sockeye salmon (Oncorhynchus nerka), 117–18, **118**
Solea solea (European sole), **292**, 293
Soles (Soleidae), 293
Somniosus, 65–66
    antarcticus (Atlantic sleeper shark), 66
    microcephalus (Greenland shark), 65–66, **65**
    pacificus (Pacific sleeper shark), 66
    rostratus (Mediterranean sleeper shark), 66
Sorubium lima (shovelnose catfish), 166
Soupfin shark (Galeorhinus zyopterus), 59–60
South African cusk-eel, 178
South African hake (Merluccius capensis), 177
South American leaffish (Monocirrhus polyacanthus), 253, **253**
South American lungfishes (Lepidosirenidae), 88–89
South Australian whaler (Carcharhinus grevi), 59
Southern bluefin tuna (Thunnus maacoyii), 281
Southern cavefish (Typhlichthys subterraneus), 168
Southern flounder (Paralichthys lethostigma), 290
Southern hake (Urophycis floridanus), 177
Southern kingfish (Menticirrhus americanus), 245
Southern platy (Xiphophorus maculatus), **187**, 188
Southern puffer (Sphoeroides nephelus), 296
Southern redbelly dace (Phoxinus erythrogaster), 149, **149**
Southern sennet (Sphyraena picudilla), 262
Southern stargazer (Astroscopus y-graecum), 268
Southern stingray (Dasyatis americana), 76, **77**
Spadefishes (Ephippidae), 249–50
Spanish killifish (Aphanius iberus), 185
Spanish mackerel (Scomberomorus maculatus), 278
Spanish sardine (Sardinella anchovia), 106
Spanner barb (Barbodes lateristriga), **152**
Sparidae (porgies), 238–41
Sparisoma
    abildgaardi (red parrotfish), 267
    flavescens (mud parrotfish), 267
    viride (stoplight parrotfish), 267
Sparus durbanensis (musselcracker), 241

Spearfishes, 285
Speckled hind (Epinephelus drummondhayi), 211
Speckled sanddab (Citharichthys stigmaeus), 290
Specklefin midshipman (Porichthys myriaster), 170
Sphaerichthys osphromenoides (chocolate gourami), **287**, 288
Sphoeroides
    annulatus (bulls-eye puffer), 297
    maculatus (northern puffer), 296
    nephelus (southern puffer), 296
Sphyraena, 261–62
    argentea (Pacific barracuda), 261, **262**
    barracuda (great barracuda), 261, **261**
    borealis (northern sennet), 262
    ensis (Mexican barracuda), 261
    flavicauda (golden barracuda), 261
    guachancho (guaguancho), 262
    novae-hollandiae (shortfin barracuda), 261–62
    obtustata (striped barracuda), 261
    picudilla (southern sennet), 262
    sphyraena (European barracuda), 262
Sphyraenidae (barracudas), 261–62
Sphyrna, 61–63
    bigelowi, **62**
    blochii, **62**
    conardi, **62**
    corona, **62**
    diplana, **62**
    lewini (scalloped hammerhead shark), 61, **62**
    media, **62**
    mokarran (great hammerhead shark), 61, **62**
    tiburo (bonnet shark), **61**, 63
    tudes (smaller hammerhead shark), **62**, 63
    zygaena (smooth hammerhead shark), 61, **61**
Sphyrnidae (hammerhead sharks), 46, 47, 60–63
Spinachia spinachia (fifteenspine stickleback), 196–97
Spined loach (Cobitis taenia), 157, **157**
Spineless dogfishes, 65–66
Spinetail mobula (Mobula japonica), 83
Spinner shark (Carcharhinus maculipinnis), 58
Spiny butterfly ray (Gymnura altavela), **78**, 79
Spiny catfish (Amblydoras hancocki), 164, **164**
Spiny dogfish (Squalus acanthias), 63–64, **64**
Spiny eels (Mastacembelidae), 288–89
Spirinchus
    starksi (night smelt), 126
    thaleichthys (longfin smelt), 126
Splakes, 121
Splash tetra (Copeina arnoldi), 138, **139**
Splitlure frogfish (Antennarius scaber), 172
Splittail (Pogonichthys macrolepidotus), 147
Spookfishes (Opisthoproctidae), 127
Sport fishing, 20, 21, 37–38
Spot (Leiostomus xanthurus), 244
Spotfin butterflyfish (Chaetodon ocellatus), 250
Spotfin croaker (Roncador stearnsi), 244
Spotfin dragonet (Callionymus agassizi), 272
Spotfin hogfish (Bodianus pulchellus), 264, **265**
Spotfin mojarra (Eucinostoma argenteus), 237
Spotfin surfperch (Hyperprosopon anale), 254

Spottail grindle. See Bowfin
Spottail pinfish (Diplodus holbrooki), 241
Spotted bass (Micropterus punctulatus), 218
Spotted batfish (Zalieutes elater), 173
Spotted cabrilla (Epinephelus analogus), 211
Spotted corydoras (Corydoras melanistus), 166
Spotted cusk-eel (Otophidium taylori), 178, **178**
Spotted danio (Brachydanio nigrofasciatus), 153, **153**
Spotted dogfishes (Scyliorhinidae), 55
Spotted duckbilled ray. See Spotted eagle ray
Spotted eagle ray (Aetobatus narinari), **79**, 80
Spotted gar (Lepisosteus oculatus), 95, **95**
Spotted goatfish (Pseudupeneus maculatus), 246, **246**
Spotted hake (Urophycis regius), 177
Spotted jack. See Ulua
Spotted knifefish (Gymnotus carapo), 142, **142**
Spotted leporinus (Leporinus maculatus), 138, **139**
Spotted metynnis (Metynnis maculatus), 141
Spotted moray (Gymnothorax moringa), 101
Spotted sand bass (Paralabrax maculatofasciatus), 213–14
Spotted sea trout (Cynoscion nebulosus), 242, **242**
Spotted shark (Mustelus punctulatus), 60
Spotted snake eel (Ophichthus ophis), 103
Spotted soapfish (Rypticus subbifrenatus), 216
Spotted sucker (Minytrema melanops), **154**, 155
Spotted sunfish (Lepomis punctatus), 220–21
Spotted trunkfish (Lactophrys bicaudalis), 296, **296**
Spotted wobbegong (Orectolobus maculata), 50
Spotted wolffish (Anarhichas minor), 270
Sprat (Clupea sprattus), 105
Spring cavefish (Chologaster agassizi), 167
Springer's shark. See Reef shark
Squalidae (dogfish sharks), 63–67
Squaliformes (order), 49–67
Squalus, 63–64
    acanthias (spiny dogfish), 63–64, **64**
    cubensis (Cuban dogfish), 64
    megalops (piked dogfish), 64
Squatina
    californica (Pacific angel shark), 67
    dumerili (angel shark), 67, **67**
    squatina (European angel shark), 67
    tergocellata (orange angel shark), 67
Squatinidae (angel sharks), 67
Squawfishes, 147
Squirrelfish (Holocentrus ascensionis), 191
Squirrelfishes (Holocentridae), 191
Staghorn sculpin (Leptocottus armatus), 206
Stargazers (Uranoscopidae), 268
Starhead topminnow (Fundulus notti), 183
Starry flounder (Platichthys stellatus), 292
Steatocranus
    arius (bumphead cichlid), 257
    casuarius (lionhead cichlid), **256**
Steelheads. See Rainbow trout
Steenbras (Pagrus nasutus), 241
Stegophilus, 166
Stegostoma fasciatum (zebra shark), 50
Stenodus leucichthys (inconnu, or sheefish), 122, **123**

Stenotomus chrysops (scup), 239, **239**
Stereolepis- gigas (giant sea bass), 212
Sternoptychidae (deepsea hatchetfishes), 131–32
Stichaeidae (pricklebacks), 270–71
Sticklebacks (Gasterosteidae), 196–97
Stingaree *(Dasyatis sabina)*, 75–76, **76**
Stingrays *(Dasyatidae)*, 68, 75–79
Stizostedion, 223–24
　　canadense (sauger), 224
　　vitreum (walleye), 223, **223**
　　vitreum glacum (blue pike), 223
Stomias (dragonfishes), 132
Stomiatidae (deepsea scaly dragonfishes), 132–33
Stonecat *(Noturus flavus)*, 161
Stoneroller *(Campostoma anomalum)*, 149, **149**
Stoplight parrotfish *(Sparisoma viride)*, 267
Stout beardfish *(Polymixia nobilis)*, 190
Streamlined cat *(Corydoras arctuatus)*, 166
Striped anchovy *(Anchoa hepsetus)*, 109
Striped barracuda *(Sphyraena obtustata)*, 261
Striped bass *(Morone saxatilis)*, 33, 36, 214–15
Striped burrfish *(Chilomycterus schoepfi)*, 297
Striped cusk-eel *(Rissola marginata)*, 178
Striped headstander *(Anostomus anostomus)*, **140**
Striped killifish *(Fundulus majalis)*, 183
Striped knifefish *(Gymnotus carapo)*, 142, **142**
Striped marlin *(Tetrapturus audax)*, 284
Striped mullet *(Mugil cephalus)*, 260, **260**
Striped parrotfish *(Scarus croicensis)*, 267
Striped rudderfish *(Kyphosus sectatrix)*, 247–48, **248**
Striped seaperch *(Embiotica lateralis)*, 255
Striped sea robin *(Prionotus evolans)*, 203
Striped sea snail *(Liparis liparis)*, 207, **207**
Striped squirrelfish *(Holocentrus xantherythrus)*, 191
Stromateidae (butterfishes), 285–86
Strongylura
　　exilis (California needlefish), 182
　　marina (Atlantic needlefish), 182
　　notata (redfin needlefish), 182
　　timucu (timucu), 182
Stumpknocker. See Spotted sunfish
Sturgeon poacher *(Agonus acipenserinus)*, **206**, 207
Sturgeons (Acipenseridae), 24, 32, 35, 90–93
Subrostral fin, 80
Sucker catfish *(Ancistrus spp.)*, **167**
Sucker loach *(Gyrinocheilus aymonieri)*, 153, **158**
Suckermouth catfishes (Plecostomus), 167
Suckers (Catostomidae), 35, 154–56
Summer flounder *(Paralichthys dentatus)*, 290
Sunapee trout *(Salvelinus aureolus)*, 121–22
Sunfishes (Centrarchidae), 217–21
Sunset hi-fin (platy), **187**
Surfperches (Embiotocidae), 253–55
Surf smelt *(Hypomesus pretiosus)*, 125
Surgeonfishes (Acanthuridae), 274–75
Suwanee bass *(Micropterus notius)*, 218
Swallower *(Saccopharynx ampullaceus)*, 103, **103**
Swallowers (Saccopharyngidae), 103
Swamp eels (Synbranchidae), 200
Swampfish *(Chologaster cornuta)*, 167, **168**
Sweetfish *(Plecoglossus altivelis)*, 124, **125**
Swell shark *(Cephaloscyllium ventriosum)*, 55

Swordfish *(Xiphias gladius)*, 282, **282**
Swordtail characin *(Corynopoma riisei)*, **140**, 141
Swordtails, 188
Syanceja, 202
Sygnathidae (pipefishes and seahorses), 198–99
Symphosodon
　　aequifasciata (green discus), **258**
　　discus (red discus, or pompadour), 258, **258**
Symphurus
　　atricayda (California tonguefish), 293
　　plagiusa (blackcheek tonguefish), 293
Synbranchidae (swamp eels), 200
Synbranchiformes (order), 200
Synbranchus, 200
Syngnathus, 198–99
　　abaster, 199
　　californiensis (kelp pipefish), 199
　　fuscus (northern pipefish), 199
　　pelagicus (sargassum pipefish), 199
　　pulchellus (African freshwater pipefish), **198**
　　schlegili (Japanese pipefish), **198**, 199
　　spicifer, 199
　　typhle, 199
Synodontidae (lizardfishes), 134
Synodontis, 163
　　angelicus (polka-dot catfish), 163
　　nigriventris (backswimmer, or upside-down catfish), 163, **163**
Synodus
　　foetens (inshore lizardfish), 134
　　intermedius (sand diver), 134
　　lucioceps (California lizardfish), 134
　　poeyi (offshore lizardfish), 134
　　synodus (red lizardfish), 134

Tadpole madtom *(Noturus gyrinus)*, 161
Taius tumifrons, 241
Talking catfish *(Acanthodoras spinosissimus)*, 164
Tapertail ribbonfish *(Trachipterus fukuzakii)*, 195
Tapir fish *(Mormyrus kanumae)*, 113
Tarpon *(Megalops atlantica)*, 97–98, **97**
Tarpons (Elopidae), 97–98
Tarpon snook *(Centropomus pectinatus)*, 210
Tautog *(Tautoga onitis)*, 263, **263**
Tautoga onitis (tautog), 263, **263**
Tautogolabrus adspersus (cunner), 263–64
T. cyprinoides (Pacific tarpon), 98
Teeth, shark, **45**, 48, **51**, 54, **55**, 57–59, 61, **64–67**
Telmatherina ladigesi (Celebes sailfin), **188**
Tench *(Tinca tinca)*, 149, **150**
Ten-pounder *(Elops saurus)*, 98, **98**
Teraponidae (tigerfishes), 217
Terapon jarbua (three-striped tigerfish), 217, **217**
Tetraodon fluviatilis (Indian puffer), **297**
Tetraodontidae (puffers), 296–97
Tetradontiformes (order), 294–98
Tetrapturus
　　albidus (white marlin), 284
　　angustirostris (shortbill spearfish), 285
　　audax (striped marlin), 284
　　pfluegeri (longbill spearfish), 285
Tetras, 138–39
Thalassoma bifasciatum (blueheads), 264
Thalassoprynea, 170
Thalassothia, 170
Thaleichthys pacificus (eluachon), 125, **126**
Thayeria spp. (penguinfish), 140, 141
Thicklip gourami *(Colisa labiosa)*, **287**, 288

Thick-lipped mullet *(Mugil chelo)*, 261
Thicktail chub *(Gila crassicauda)*, 149
Thin-lipped gray mullet *(Mugil capito)*, 261
Thornback *(Platyrhinoidis triseriata)*, 71
Thornback skate *(Raja clavata)*, 75
Threadfin shad *(Dorosoma petenense)*, 108
Threadfins (Polynemidae), 262
Threespine stickleback *(Gasterosteus aculeatus)*, 196, **196**
Three-spot gourami *(Trichogaster trichopterus)*, 288
Three-striped glass catfish *(Etropiellus debauwi)*, 162, **162**
Three-striped tigerfish *(Terapon jarbua)*, 217, **217**
Thresher shark *(Alopias vulpinus)*, 47, 52, **53**
Thresher sharks (Alopiidae), 52
Thunnus, 280–81
　　albacares (yellowfin tuna), 281
　　atalunga (albacore), 281
　　maacoyii (southern bluefin tuna), 281
　　obesus (bigeye tuna), 281
　　thynnus (bluefin tuna), 280–81, **281**
Thymallidae (graylings), 122
Thymallus arcticus (Arctic grayling), 122, **122**
Tidewater silverside *(Menidia beryllina)*, 189
Tiger barb *(Barbus tetrazona)*, 152, **152**
Tiger catfishes *(Pseudoplatystoma)*, 166
Tigerfish *(Hydrocyanus goliath)*, 138
Tigerfishes (Teraponidae), 217
Tiger grouper *(Mycteroperca tigris)*, 212
Tiger loach *(Botia hymenophysa)*, **157**, 158
Tiger snake eel *(Myrichthys tigrinus)*, 103
Tiger shark *(Galeocerdo cuvieri)*, 45, 46, **58**, 59
Tilapia, 256–57
　　melantheron (blackchin mouthbrooder), 257
　　mossambica (Mozambique mouthbrooder), 256–57
Tilefish *(Lopholatilus chamaeleonticeps)*, 224
Tilefishes (Branchiostegidae), 224–25
Timucu *(Strongylura timucu)*, 182
Tinca tinca (tench), 149, **150**
Tinfoil barb *(Barbus schwanenfeldi)*, 151–52, **152**
Toadfishes (Batrachoididae), 169–70
Tomcods, 176
Tomtates *(Haemulon aurolineata)*, 238
Tonguefishes (Cynoglossidae), 293
Toothed bream *(Dentex vulgaris)*, 241
Toothed carps. See Killifishes
Topminnows. See Killifishes
Topsail variatus (platy), **187**
Topsmelt *(Atherinops affinis)*, 189
Torpedinidae (electric rays), 71–72
Torpedo
　　californica (Pacific electric ray), 72
　　marmorata, 72
　　nobiliana (Atlantic torpedo ray), 72, **73**
Totuava *(Cynoscion macdonaldi)*, 243
Toxotes jaculatrix (archerfish), 247, **247**
Toxotidae (archerfishes), 247
Trachinocephalus myops (snakefish, or offshore lizardfish), 134
Trachinotus
　　carolinus (Florida pompano), 231
　　falcatus (permit), **230**, 231
　　goodei (palometa), 231
　　paitensis (paloma pompano), 231
　　rhodopus (gafftopsail pompano), 231
Trachipteridae (ribbonfishes), 195

Trachipterus, 195
　　altivelus (king-of-the-salmon), 195
　　arcticus (dealfish), 195
　　fukuzakii (tapertail ribbonfish), 195
　　iris (ribbonfish), **194**
Trachurus symmetricus (jack mackerel), 229
Trevally *(Caranx georgianus)*, 231
Triaenodon obseus (whitetip shark), 60
Triakidae (smooth dogfishes), 60
Triakis
　　scyllia, 60
　　semifasciatus (leopard shark), 60
Trichiuridae (cutlassfishes), 277
Trichiurus
　　lepturus (Atlantic cutlassfish), 277, **277**
　　nitens, 277
Trichodontidae (sandfishes), 267
Trichodon trichodon (Pacific sandfish), 267
Trichogaster
　　leeri (pearl gourami), **287**, 288
　　pectoralis (snakeskin gourami), **287**, 288
　　trichopterus (three-spot gourami), **288**
Trichomycteridae (parasitic catfishes), · 166
Trichopsis vittatus (croaking gourami), 288
Triggerfishes (Balistidae), 294–95
Triglidae (sea robins), 203
Trinectes maculatus (hogchoker), 293
Tripletail *(Lobotes surinamensis)*, 235, **236**
Tripletails (Lobotidae), 235–36
Triplewart seadevil *(Cryptopsarus couesi)*, 174, **174**
Trout hybrids (splakes), 121
Trout-perch *(Percopsis omiscomaycus)*, 169, **169**
Trout-perches (Percopsidae), 168–69
Trouts (Salmonidae), 26, 30, 33, 35, 114, 118–22
Trumpetfish *(Aulostomus maculatus)*, 197, **197**
Trumpetfishes (Aulostomidae), 197
Trunk barb *(Epalzeorhynchus kallopterus)*, 153, **153**
Trunkfish *(Lactophrys trigonus)*, 22, 296
Tubesnout *(Anlorhynchus flavidus)*, 197
Tule perch *(Hysterocarpus traski)*, 253
Tunas (Scombridae), 278–81
Turbot *(Scophthalmus maxima)*, 290
Twig catfish *(Farlowella acus)*, 167
Twospine stickleback *(Gasterosteus wheatlandi)*, 197
Two-spot barb *(Puntius ticto)*, 152, **152**
Tylosurus crocodilus (houndfish), 182
Typhlichthys subterraneus (southern cavefish), 168
Typhlobagrus kronei (cave catfish), 166
Typhlogobius californiensis (blind goby), 273
Typhlonarke aysoni (blind torpedo ray), 72

Ubangi mormyrid *(Gnathonemus petersi)*, **113**, 114
Ulua *(Caranx stellatus)*, 230–31
Umbra
　　krameri (European mudminnow), 131
　　limi (central mudminnow), 131
　　pygmaea (eastern mudminnow), 131, **131**
Umbridae (mudminnows), 131
Umbrina roncador (yellowfin croaker), 244
Umpqua squawfish *(Ptychocheilus umpouae)*, 147
Undulate triggerfish *(Balistapus undulatus)*, 294, **294**

Unicorn filefish (Aluterus monoceros), 295
Unicornfish (Eumecichthys fiski), 194
Unicornfish (Naso), 275, **276**
Upside-down catfish (Synodontis nigriventris), 163, **163**
Upside-down catfishes (Mochokidae), 163
Uranoscopidae (stargazers), 268
Uranoscopus scaber (European stargazer), 268
Urolophus
 halleri (round stingray), 77
 jamaicensis (yellow stingray), 77, **77**
 testacens, 77
Urophycis
 blennoides, 177
 chuss (red hake), 177
 floridanus (southern hake), 177
 regius (spotted hake), 177
 tenuis (white hake), 177
Usacaranx, 231
Utah chub (Gila atraria), 149

Valamugil buchanani, 261
Vandellia cirrhosa (candiru, or carnero), 166, **166**
Variegated platy (Xiphophorus variatus), **187**
Veil carp (Pterolebias longipinnis), 185
Vermiculated rabbitfish (Siganus vermiculatus), **276**, 277
Vermilion rockfish (Sebastes miniatus), 202-3
Vermillion snapper (Rhomboplites aurorubens), 235
Viviparous eelpout (Zoarces viviparus), 179, **179**
Vomer
 declivifrons (Pacific moonfish), 231
 setapinnis (Atlantic moonfish), 231

Wahoo (Acanthocybium solanderi), 279
Walking catfish (Clarias batrachus), 30, 162
Walking fish (Anabas testudineus), 286, **286**
Walleye (Stizostedion vitreum), 36, 223, **223**
Walleye surfperch (Hyperprosopon argenteum), 254
Warmouth (Lepomis gulosus), 221

Warsaw grouper (Epinephelus nigritus), 212
Water beetle, **123**
Weakfish (Cynoscion regalis), 242
Wels (Siluris glanis), 161
Whale shark (Rhincodon typus), 21, 44, 45, 46, 50-51, **50-51**
Whiptail catfish (Loricaria parva), 167
White amur (Ctenopharyngodon idellus), 146
Whitebait smelt (Allosmerus elongatus), 126
White-banded parrotfish (Scarus gnathodus), 267
White bass (Morone chrysops), 215, **215**
White catfish (Ictalurus catus), 160
White crappie (Pomoxis annularis), 219
White croaker (Genyonemus lineatus), 244
Whiteface hagfish (Mixine circifrons), 41
Whitefishes (Salmonidae), 114, 122-24
White grunt (Haemulon plumeri), 237
White hake (Urophycis tenuis), 177
White marlin (Tetrapturus albidus), **23**, 284
White mullet (Mugil curema), **260**, 260-61
Whitenose pipefish (Corythoichthys albirostris), 199
White perch (Morone americana), 215-16
White piranha (Serrasalmus rhombeus), **137**
White sea bass (Cynoscion nobilis), **242**, 243
White seaperch (Phanerodon furcatus), 254, **255**
White shark (Carcharodon carcharias), 46, 47, 52-53, **54**
Whitespotted greenling (Hexagrammos stelleri), 203, **204**
Whitespotted soapfish (Rypticus maculatus), 216
White sturgeon (Acipenser transmontanus), 21, 91, **91**
White sucker (Catostomus commersoni), **154**, 154-55
Whitetip shark (Triaenodon obseus), 60
Windowpane (Scophthalmus aquosus), 290
Winged disc (Pterodiscus levis), 141
Winter flounder (Pseudopleuronectes americanus), **291**, 292

Winter skate (Raja ocellata), 75
Witch flounder (Glyptocephalus cynoglossus), 293
Wobbegongs, 50
Wolf-eel (Anarrichthys ocellatus), 270
Wolffishes (Anarhichadidae), 269-70
Wolf herring (Chirocentrus dorab), 109, **109**
Wolf herrings (Chirocentridae), 109
Wrasses (Labridae), 262-66
Wreckfish (Polyprion americanus), 214
Wrestling halfbeak (Dermogenys pusillus), 181
Wrymouth (Cryptocanthodes maculatus), 271

Xanathon, 267
Xanthichthys
 mento (redtail triggerfish), 294
 ringens (sargassum triggerfish), 294
Xenistius, 238
Xiphias gladius (swordfish), 282, **282**
Xiphiidae (swordfishes), 282
Xiphister mucosus (rock prickleback), 270, **271**
Xiphophorus
 herreri (green swordtail), 188, **188**
 maculatus (southern platy), **187**, 188
 variatus (variegated platy), **187**
Xystreurys liolepis (fantail sole), 290

Yellow bass (Morone mississippiensis), 215
Yellow bobo (Polydactylus opercularis), 262
Yellow bullhead catfish (Ictalurus natalis), 159, **159**
Yellow chub (Kyphosus incisor), 248
Yellowfin croaker (Umbrina roncador), 244
Yellowfin grouper (Mycteroperca venenosa), 212
Yellowfin menhaden (Brevoortia smithi), 106
Yellowfin mojarra (Gerres cinereus), 237, **237**
Yellowfin tuna (Thunnus albacares), 281
Yellow goatfish (Mulloidichthys martinicus), 247
Yellowhead jawfish (Opisthognathus aurifrons), 267-68, **268**

Yellowhead wrasse (Halichoeres gamoti), 265
Yellow jack (Caranx bartholomaei), 229, **229**
Yellow perch (Perca flavescens), 36, **222**, 223
Yellow snake eel (Ophichthus zophochir), 103
Yellow stingray (Urolophus jamaicensis), 77, **77**
Yellowtail (Seriola dorsalis), 227
Yellowtail damselfish (Microspathodon chrysurus), 259
Yellowtail flounder (Limanda ferruginea), 293
Yellowtail reeffish (Chromis enchrysurus), 259
Yellowtail rockfish (Sebastes flavidus), 203
Yellowtail snapper (Ocyurus chrysurus), 235, **236**
Yellow wrasse (Coris gaimardi), 263, **263**

Zalembius rosaceous (pink seaperch), 255
Zalieutes elater (spotted batfish), 173
Zanclus canescens (Moorish idol), 275, **275**
Zanionlepis
 frenata (shortspine combfish), 204
 latipinnis (longspine combfish), 204
Zapteryx exasperata (banded guitarfish), 70-71
Zebrafishes (Pterois spp.), 202
Zebra moray (Echidna zebra), 101
Zebra perch (Hermosilla azurea), 248
Zebra shark (Stegostoma fasciatum), 50
Zebra sole (Zebrias zebra), **292**
Zebrasoma veliferum (sailfin tang), **274**, 275
Zeidae (dories), 191-92
Zeiformes (order), 191-92
Zenopsis ocellata (American John Dory), 192
Zeugopterus punctatus, 290
Zeus
 faber (European John Dory), 192, **192**
 japonicus, 192
Zoarces
 anguillaris (shore eelpout), 179
 viviparus (viviparous eelpout), 179, **179**
Zoarcidae (eelpouts), 179
Zomniosus, 44
Zu cristatus (scalloped ribbonfish), 195